FISCAL INCENTIVES

FOR INVESTMENT

AND INNOVATION

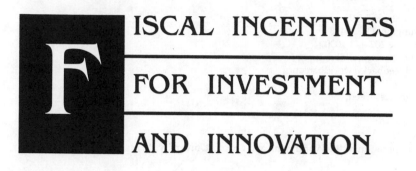

FISCAL INCENTIVES FOR INVESTMENT AND INNOVATION

Anwar Shah, editor

PUBLISHED FOR THE WORLD BANK
Oxford University Press

1818 H Street, NW
Washington, DC 20433
Telephone 202-473-1000
Internet www.worldbank.org
E-mail feedback@worldbank.org

2 3 4 06 05 04

A co-publication of the World Bank and Oxford University Press.

Oxford University Press
198 Madison Avenue
New York, NY 10016

Hard cover: ISBN 0-19-520997-4
Soft cover: ISBN 0-8213-5902-9

Library of Congress Cataloging-in-Publication Data (for hard cover edition)

Shah, Anwar.
    Fiscal incentives for investment and innovation / Anwar Shah.
       p. cm.
    Includes bibliographical references and index.
    ISBN 0-19-520997-4
       1. Investments, Foreign—Developing countries. 2. Investment tax credit—Developing countries. 3. Tax incentives—Developing countries. I. Title
HG5993.S6 1995
332.6'7322—dc20   94-35218
                                                              CIP

CONTENTS

EMPIRICAL EVIDENCE ON THE EFFECTIVENESS OF TAX INCENTIVES

Tax Burden Analysis

9   Indirect Taxes and Investment Incentives
in Malaysia   *375*
    Robin W. Boadway, Dale Chua, and Frank Flatters

10   Fiscal Incentives for Investment in Thailand   *399*
    Robert Halvorsen

11   Patterns in Investment Tax Incentives among
Developing Countries   *437*
    Ngee Choon Chia and John Whalley

**THE EFFECTS OF TAXATION ON PRODUCTION
AND INVESTMENT DECISIONS**

ECONOMYWIDE IMPLICATIONS OF INVESTMENT INCENTIVES

FOREWORD

STIMULATION OF PRIVATE capital formation is a long-established and important objective of tax policy in most countries. Recent theoretical and empirical results suggesting that investment in machinery and equipment generates externalities for growth have only increased interest in tax policies that lower the cost of capital for such investments. Preferential tax rates for certain activities or organizations; tax holidays; investment tax credits for physical stock, research and development, and employment; and accelerated writeoffs are among the instruments commonly used to bolster growth-generating investment.

Until now, policymakers in developing countries have seen little empirical evidence on how well these various instruments actually work in stimulating investment and how the gains compare with the losses in tax revenue. This volume makes an important contribution toward filling that void. Its authors examine existing fiscal incentive regimes in selected developing countries and evaluate the effects of those measures on investment and government revenues. They then use the results to rank tax policy instruments in terms of their usefulness in promoting investment cost-effectively. The principal conclusion is that tax incentives that are selective and are targeted to new investment in machinery, equipment, and research and development—such as investment tax allowances, investment tax credits, and accelerated capital consumption allowances—are better and more cost-effective in stimulating long-term investment than are general tax incentives such as corporate tax rate reductions and tax holidays.

This book deserves to be on the must-read list of policymakers and those interested in public policies for promoting private capital formation in developing countries.

Lawrence H. Summers
Deputy Secretary
U.S. Department of the Treasury
Washington, D.C.

# PREFACE

INVESTMENT PROMOTION IS an important objective of tax policy in developing and industrial countries alike. Governments are active in using tax policy instruments to promote investment, but little information is available to policymakers in developing countries on how effective these measures are in achieving their stated objectives. A careful assessment of past practices can provide data essential for a redesign of public policy measures.

This volume presents the outcome of a research project undertaken by the World Bank's Policy Research Department under the general direction of Johannes Linn and myself, in my former capacity as director of the Policy Research Department, World Bank. The purpose of the project was to examine the effects of fiscal incentives on investment in developing and emerging market economies. This research was part of a larger effort by the department to develop policy guidance for reform of fiscal systems, using rigorous conceptual and empirical analysis.

The conceptual work described in this volume reflects on design issues that influence the effectiveness of incentive policies. The empirical work explores the stimulative impact that fiscal measures may have on investment and compares that effect with forgone revenues. Taken together, this analysis provides a sound basis for identifying the types of incentives that may work and the situations in which their use is justified.

It is my hope that public officials and students of public finance in developing and emerging market economies will find this volume useful.

Nancy Birdsall
Executive Vice-President
Inter-American Development Bank

ACKNOWLEDGMENTS

THIS BOOK REPRESENTS the final output of a small project funded by the World Bank Research Committee in 1990. I am grateful to the authors and collaborators who contributed to this project, which was carried out under the general direction of Lawrence Summers, Stanley Fischer, Johannes Linn, Nancy Birdsall, and Javad Khalilzadeh-Shirazi. In addition, I wish to thank Richard Bird, Robin Boadway, Michael Bruno, Shahid Amjad Chaudhry, S. Shahid Husain, Gregory Ingram, Mieko Nishimizu, Saleh Nsouli, Jeffrey Owens, Manuel Penalver, Vito Tanzi, and Teresa Ter-Minassian for their guidance and support. Thanks are also due to Joel Bergsman and Dale Wiegel for permission to publish the Mintz and Tsiopoulos paper and to the Malaysian Institute for Economic Research for permission to publish the papers by Boadway, Chua, and Flatters. John Baffes, Hamid Davoodi, Björn Larsen, Valerie Mercer, and Francesca Recanatini provided valuable research assistance and Peggy Pender provided excellent secretarial support.

CONTRIBUTORS

Alan Auerbach

Professor, Department of Economics
University of California, Berkeley

John Baffes

Consultant
World Bank, Washington, D.C.

Jeffrey I. Bernstein

Professor, Department of Economics
Carleton University
Ottawa, Ontario, Canada

Nancy Birdsall

Executive Vice President
Inter-American Development Bank
Washington, D.C.

Robin W. Boadway

Professor, Department of Economics
Queen's University
Kingston, Ontario, Canada

Ngee Choon Chia

Professor, Department of Economics
University of Singapore

Dale Chua

Economist, International Monetary Fund
Washington, D.C.

Ramon L. Clarete

Professor, School of Economics
University of the Philippines
Diliman, Quezon City

Antonio Estache

Senior Economist, World Bank
Washington, D.C.

Andrew Feltenstein

Professor, Department of Economics
Virginia Polytechnic Institute
Blacksburg, Virginia

Frank Flatters

Professor, Department of Economics
Queen's University
Kingston, Ontario, Canada

Vitor Gaspar

Professor, Department of Economics
Universidade Nova de Lisboa, Portugal

Robert Halvorsen

Professor, Department of Economics
University of Washington
Seattle, Washington

Andrew Lyon

Professor, Department of Economics
University of Maryland
College Park, Maryland

Jack M. Mintz

Professor, Department of Economics
University of Toronto
Toronto, Ontario, Canada

Dagmar Rajagopal

Professor, Department of Economics
Ryerson Polytechnic University
Toronto, Ontario, Canada

Anwar Shah

Principal Economist, World Bank
Washington, D.C.

Joel Slemrod

Professor, School of Business
University of Michigan
Ann Arbor, Michigan

Lawrence H. Summers

Deputy Secretary
U.S. Department of the Treasury
Washington, D.C.

Thomas Tsiopoulos

Faculty of Management
University of Toronto
Toronto, Ontario, Canada

John Whalley

Professor, Department of Economics
University of Western Ontario
London, Ontario, Canada

OVERVIEW

Anwar Shah

DEVELOPING COUNTRIES CONTINUE to make widespread use of tax policy instruments to promote industrial and technological development. The actual effect of these instruments on business activity and government revenues, however, remains an open question. The studies presented in this volume take an important first step in quantifying the effect of investment incentives on business decisions related to production and investment. In addition, they suggest the consequences of such incentives for government revenues. The analyses presented in subsequent chapters attempt to answer a narrow set of questions. The most fundamental of these questions is:

- Do taxes matter for investment?

Related questions include:

- What have been the investment stimulation (direct and induced) effects of tax policy measures per dollar of forgone revenues?
- Do taxes matter for foreign direct investment (FDI) in developing countries? Do they influence foreign business decisions about location? What are the implications of the home (industrial) country tax regime for the host (developing) country tax system?
- How do taxes interact with other institutional features of a developing country, and what are the implications for the effectiveness of tax incentives? Are corporate taxes largely ineffective (nonmarginal) instruments because of the influence of other policy instruments?
- Do taxes matter for domestic investment? What is their effect on the structure of industrial production?
- What has been the effect of tax instruments on the employment of labor, physical capital, and research and development (R&D) capital?

1

- What has been the effect of business taxes and tax expenditures (forgone revenues) on technological change, expansion of private output, and after-tax profits?
- Are there tax-induced distortions that prevent firms from holding optimal levels of fixed factors?
- How does market power affect tax incentives?
- What is the role of expectations in investment decisions?
- Given empirical estimates on factor substitution, the nature of technical change, and economies of scale, what revenue-neutral alternative tax policy environment would best encourage investment and enhance productivity and growth?

The papers presented in this volume reflect on the above questions at both conceptual and empirical levels and in doing so pay close attention to the tax and nontax policy elements and the existing institutions (market imperfections) in developing and emerging market economies. In the next section the case for tax policy interventions in the marketplace is examined briefly.

Tax Incentives: Basic Concepts

Tax incentives are those provisions in the tax code that afford preferential treatment to some activities over others (say, tax holidays and credits for investment in manufacturing industries), some assets over others (accelerated depreciation provisions for specified assets), some form of organization over others (for example, lower tax rates for small rather than for large businesses), or some forms of financing over others (debt versus equity). Tax incentives also include those provisions in the tax code that attempt to change the time distribution of use of assets (for example, tax holidays, accelerated capital consumption allowances, time-variant statutory tax rates, and depletion allowances for resource industries). The primary intent of all these provisions is to encourage capital accumulation in specific activities. Other provisions in the tax code encourage capital formation without specific intent to do so. Examples include nontaxation of imputed benefits from home ownership and full, immediate expensing of intangible investments. Besides corporate income taxes, other taxes that can influence business investment decisions include property taxes, capital levies, sales taxes on capital inputs, and royalties and charges. Although the focus of this volume is on tax provisions clearly intended to promote capital formation, the authors of several chapters make a special effort to capture the most salient features of the tax code in the service prices of physical and R&D capital.

Tax Policy Interventions: A Summary of the Debate

Robin W. Boadway and Anwar Shah (chapter 1) provide a comprehensive survey of the conceptual and empirical issues concerning the role of investment incentives in developing countries. A few selected arguments for tax policy interventions in the marketplace are summarized here.

Tax Incentives and Allocative Efficiency: The Level-Playing-Field Argument

In a standard externality-free competitive world with constant returns to scale and costless instantaneous adjustment, tax incentives lead to unequal before-tax rates of return on different assets and sectors and therefore to an inefficient allocation of resources. One notion of a "level playing field" with equal marginal effective tax rates across all assets and sectors, in contrast, would direct capital to its most productive use and induce optimal allocation of resources. A level playing field requires that the base of the income tax be consumption plus changes in net worth (the Haig-Simon concept of income). Under this concept, income is taxed on an accrual basis (inclusive of accrued capital gains and imputed benefits of owner-occupied housing) and on real income flows. If the Haig-Simon pure income tax is imposed, all capital income will be subject to the same positive marginal effective tax rate, which will also be equal to the statutory tax rate. Note that under a pure income tax, although intersectoral allocation of capital will be optimal, intertemporal optimality is not guaranteed, and the size of the capital stock is likely to diverge from its optimal value as the tax reduces the return to capital.

An alternative vehicle by which to achieve a level playing field, but one that yields a zero marginal effective tax rate on all capital income, is a pure consumption or cash flow tax. Under such a tax, savings are exempted, and immediate full expensing for all capital expenditures is permitted.

Thus under these two ideal tax systems, hardly any positive role exists for tax incentives. Unfortunately, because of obvious administrative difficulties, neither system has been adopted anywhere in the world, nor is there much hope for their adoption in a theoretically pure form. Existing income taxes are known to generate varying levels of tax incentives across assets, across sectors, and over time. Thus in theory one can devise incentives that would attempt to equalize tax rates across assets and across sectors, but in practice capturing the myriad complexities of existing tax structures in one measure that would implement just the right level of distortion at the margin to achieve tax neutrality is likely to be a difficult task (see Hulten and Klayman 1988).

Tax Incentives, Allocative Efficiency, and Revenue Needs: Is Leveling the Playing Field Desirable?

The literature on optimal commodity taxes recognizes that in practice, all feasible tax systems are distortionary, and it derives rules to achieve a set of revenue objectives with the least possible efficiency costs. A general rule emerging from this large body of literature is that tax rates on commodities should vary inversely with their elasticities of demand. This literature established fairly restrictive conditions under which either a comprehensive income tax or a pure consumption tax would be optimal. For example, a pure consumption tax is optimal only when working period and retirement consumption (both of which can be taxed) are equally good substitutes for retirement leisure (which cannot be taxed). In the real world such restrictive assumptions are unlikely to be obtained and, furthermore, income and consumption taxes in their pure form are not administratively feasible. In such a world optimality requires that different types of capital goods should be subject to different rates of taxation (see Auerbach 1979, 1983; Hulten and Klayman 1988). Tax incentives in the form of varying tax rates, accelerated depreciations, credits, and the like could potentially be used to achieve this effect.

Tax Incentives and Market Imperfections

The case for tax policy interventions is much more transparent in the presence of market imperfections. It is commonly argued that—in the presence of externalities, information asymmetries, unemployment, inadequate growth, imperfect competition, and economies of scale—social rates of return from marginal investment may be higher than the private rate of return. Therefore if the initiative is left to the private sector, resources will be underallocated to activities subject to these conditions. These arguments are briefly discussed here.

EXTERNALITIES. Consider the case of R&D investment. Because of the presence of spillovers, the R&D performer may not be able fully to appropriate benefits associated with R&D activity. In the presence of large numbers either on the side that generates an externality or on the side of those affected by it, a privately negotiated settlement is almost never reached. The situation can be alleviated only by government action. The same argument for public intervention is sometimes couched in terms of the public goods nature of R&D capital. Once knowledge has been created, it is almost freely appropriable, producing strong incentives for free ridership. These arguments are considerably weakened by patents and the requirement for internal R&D capability to benefit from external R&D knowledge.

DeLong and Summers (1991) have put forward a related argument for investment in equipment. They argue that social returns from equipment investment in well-functioning market economies exceed private returns because of the positive externalities for growth that are generated by such an investment. Thus special incentives to promote investment in equipment could be justified (see also Scott 1989).

RISK AND UNCERTAINTY. It is frequently argued that risk-averse individuals discount returns from certain investments more heavily than may be warranted by proper calculation of riskiness of investment and that therefore activities in which investment is risky but which have high social returns receive too little investment. This argument may be of minor importance because returns from risky investments are often larger than can be explained by the risk premium alone. Furthermore, most firms undertake a diversified portfolio of projects, and as a result, although the risk associated with the failure of any particular project may be quite large, the average risk of failure of the whole portfolio is low.

INFORMATION ASYMMETRIES. A powerful argument for public support of some special investments such as R&D can be made on the basis of information asymmetries. The presence of asymmetric information between an R&D performer and a financier limits the financing of R&D projects. The success of the project warrants secrecy, but its financing requires release of vital information. As a result many projects lapse for lack of financing. The asymmetric information in the R&D output market also limits the R&D firm's ability to achieve the licensing gains from trade. It should be noted that investment incentives designed to correct for information asymmetries do involve tradeoffs because such incentives encourage some low-quality firms to enter the market, thereby leading to underinvestment by high-quality firms.

UNEMPLOYMENT AND INADEQUATE GROWTH. One of the Keynesian remedies for unemployment of factors is to provide incentives for new investment through the tax system. It is questionable whether tax incentives would have any effect in an environment characterized by high unemployment, low profitability, and low corporate taxable income. Furthermore, if excess capacity exists, such incentives may not even be desirable. If, however, growth is being stymied because of inadequate investment capital, tax incentives may have a role in fostering economic growth.

IMPERFECT COMPETITION AND ECONOMIES OF SCALE. In the presence of imperfect competition and economies of scale, selective tax incentives—say, for example, for export industries—could enable these industries to reduce costs and capture a somewhat larger market share.

Tax Incentives and the Equity of the Tax System

Tax incentives have serious implications for equity that are often over-looked. They violate the criteria both for horizontal equity (equal treatment of equals) and for vertical equity (consistency of tax burdens with the ability to pay). Capital income is treated more favorably than labor income. Nevertheless, at a conceptual level, it is possible to design tax incentives that embody equity considerations. Note that the vertical and horizontal equity criteria referred to here assume that comprehensive income is the standard. If, on the other hand, consumption is used as the equity criterion, capital income ought to be excluded from the tax base for the sake of equity.

Political Economy of Tax Incentives

Tax incentives often generate powerful clientele. Politicians in democratic nations sometimes depend on the financial support of these special-interest groups for their re-election. Bureaucrats often find tax incentives a convenient base on which to build their dream empires and hand out special favors to powerful individuals and groups. Since the costs of these measures remain largely unknown to the uninitiated general electorate, the incentives take on a life of their own. Only when there is strong pressure for deficit reduction does their existence become more generally noticeable.

Principal Research Findings and Policy Implications

The above discussion suggests that tax incentives are advocated for many different reasons in both industrial and developing countries. This volume deals with the extent to which the prevalent tax measures achieve the objectives sought and what conceptual and design issues are relevant to make the measures more effective. This section distills the principal findings of the studies reported in the book.

This distillation is organized into two parts, conceptual and empirical. The empirical studies in turn are grouped into three sections based on the broad contours of the methods they implement.

Research Guidance on Conceptual and Incentives Design Issues

Many of the studies in this volume contribute to a better understanding of various tax measures. They do so by analyzing how various tax incentives interact with the broader system; suggesting ways to measure the cost of capital under alternate institutional regimes; adapting the marginal effective tax rate methodology to the institutional setting of developing countries; applying the implications of information asymmetries and other capital market imperfections to the design of tax incentives; highlighting the special nature of R&D investment, its effect on production and market structures, and the effectiveness of tax policies in promoting such investment; and developing guidelines for tax policies relating to foreign direct investment (FDI).

CONCEPTUAL ISSUES IN THE MEASUREMENT OF THE EFFECT OF TAXATION ON INVESTMENT. The marginal effective tax rate measures the rate of tax that, if applied to a true economic income measure, would be consistent with the observed differences in after-tax and before-tax rates of return. Such calculations have been carried out for a large number of countries. Alan Auerbach (chapter 2) argues that such calculations may be in error for many reasons. First, they consider only the wedge between the required rate of return and the corporate return before tax and ignore the wedge between required rate of return and the return to investors after *all* taxes. Furthermore, such calculations can be in error to the extent that taxes are borne by imperfectly mobile factors such as land and labor and to the extent that they are shifted to foreign treasuries through the provision of foreign tax credits by home countries. Thus the separation of saving and investment decisions and international capital flows is ignored. Several marginal effective tax rate studies surveyed by Robin W. Boadway and Anwar Shah (chapter 1) use an open economy framework and therefore do not suffer from this limitation. Second, they consider only explicit corporate taxes and ignore credit policies, such as credit rationing, and other tax and nontax policies, such as tariffs and quotas, that have an indirect bearing on the incentive to invest through their effect on the prices of outputs and other inputs. Third, as Auerbach notes, marginal effective tax rate calculations emphasize the tax wedge between gross and net return rather than the amount of the gross return and that therefore a given effective tax rate can correspond to several different levels of the desired capital stock, depending on the incidence of the taxes in question. Also, a given tax wedge can have dramatically different consequences for investment, depending on whether the price is internationally given or determined domestically. The presence of complex tax incentives (for example, tax holidays and varying tax rates) and less developed equity markets further limits the accuracy of the standard marginal effective tax rate methodology. Whereas these models primarily calculate effective tax rates on equity investment, most of the investment in developing countries comes from retained earnings and debt finance.

Auerbach provides a more general cost-of-capital framework to overcome the above limitations of the standard analyses of the marginal effective tax rate. The framework provides a more comprehensive accounting of the tax wedge as well as nontax elements that have a bearing on the cost of capital. In addition to the wedge between the required rate of return and the corporate return before tax, it also considers the wedge between the required rate of return and the return to investors after *all* taxes. Other than corporate income taxes, it incorporates indirect taxes, tariffs, dual exchange rates, quantity controls, and imperfect competition. Finally, Auerbach incorporates such dynamic considerations as changes in tax regime, changes in tax status of a firm, adjustment costs, and tax law asymmetries into the more general cost-of-capital framework developed for this purpose.

CHANGES IN TAX STRUCTURE. A graduated reduction of the corporate tax rate has three effects on the user cost of capital. Its direct effect is to lower the cost of capital. Indirectly, it reduces the present value of capital consumption allowances, thereby increasing the cost of capital, but at the same time, because of phased reduction, the present value of capital consumption allowances declines further over time, thereby creating an incentive for present investment. The overall effect is to make present investment a more attractive alternative. Note that a one-shot reduction would be less stimulative than a phased reduction because only the first two effects mentioned above would operate. Note also that for a given level of investment stimulation, reductions in the tax rate would result in higher forgone revenues than investment tax credits (tax liabilities reduced by a fraction of expenditure on new additions to physical and R&D capital stock or employment); and allowances because they would lower tax payments on existing capital and economic rents in addition to those on new investments.

TAX HOLIDAYS. Tax holidays (tax-free status for an initial specified period) represent one of the most frequently used tax incentives in developing countries. Firms face a zero tax rate during the holiday period and a positive tax rate at the end of the holiday period. Just like the changes in tax structure, tax holidays have three effects on user cost of capital—one positive and two negative. A zero tax rate during the holiday period has a positive effect on investment. The reduction in the present value of depreciation allowances and the rising value of these allowances toward the end of the holiday period, however, would discourage current investment. The overall effect of tax holidays on investment would depend on the extent to which capital consumption allowances and tax losses could be carried forward to the period after the holiday. With no carryforward provisions, some firms would benefit by being taxable in the formative years when they are in a loss position. If a full carryforward is allowed, an effective subsidy in certain instances would be too generous. Jack M. Mintz (chapter 3) notes that a tax holiday would be generous to firms that use nondepreciable factors of production. In any event tax holidays open tax arbitrage opportunities for investors to shift taxable income into activities enjoying tax holidays. Tax holidays thus may encourage fly-by-night or short-term investment at the expense of long-term investment. A tax credit or an investment allowance can encourage long-term investment at a lower revenue cost than under a tax holiday.

TAX LAW ASYMMETRIES AND NONREFUNDABLE TAX LOSSES. Net operating losses for tax purposes are treated differently from unused capital consumption allowances. Both of these are usually allowed to be carried forward but not refunded. These provisions complicate an analysis of incentives to invest. For example, investment incentives are not of much value to firms that have accumulated a large amount of tax loss carryforwards.

CREDIBILITY OF TAX REGIME. Frequent changes in the tax regime also complicate the analyses of tax incentives. A policy that is seen as temporary may have less of an effect. Thus incentives that are more difficult to reverse, such as investment tax credits and accelerated capital consumption allowances, may have a greater stimulative effect than tax rate reductions. If the tax regime is not credible, investors seek expected rates of returns considerably higher than risk-free discount rates. Auerbach reflects on how the measurement of cost of capital could incorporate such considerations.

DEVELOPING COUNTRY INSTITUTIONAL FEATURES AND INVESTMENT INCENTIVES. Many institutional features of developing countries cloud the effectiveness of fiscal incentives for investment. For example, if firms enjoy full market power and have the potential of shifting the tax burden fully forward, taxes will not enter into the expression for the user cost of capital and hence will be ineffective. Previous literature on the subject without exception has ignored this element in examining the effectiveness of investment incentives. After developing appropriate methodologies, contributors to this volume empirically examined this hypothesis for several industries in Pakistan and Turkey. Credit rationing is another feature in developing countries that complicates the analysis of investment incentives. In many developing countries, credits are allocated by the central bank to qualifying firms, and prioritization of credits tends to determine both the pattern and the size of investment. Explicit investment incentives do not for the most part affect the investment activities of credit-constrained firms. Similar arguments apply to the effects of other forms of intervention, including protection and the allocation of scarce foreign exchange. In such circumstances, investment incentives largely result in a reallocation of rents rather than being instruments that have a marginal effect on investment behavior. Finally, foreign tax regimes can have an important influence on inward FDI (see chapters 1, 2, and 6 for a discussion of these issues).

TAX INCENTIVES UNDER INFORMATION ASYMMETRIES AND OUTSIDE FINANCING CHOICES. In chapter 4, Andrew Lyon presents a survey of the effects of taxation and asymmetric information on the financing of investment. In the absence of these two factors, traditional economic models predict that funds for investment will flow to projects with the highest expected return. The particular form in which the investment occurs (for example, by equity, bank loan, or other form of debt finance) is irrelevant. In the presence of either taxation or information asymmetries, however, neither of these predictions necessarily holds. Financing may not go to those projects with the highest expected return, and the form in which the financing is conveyed can affect the profitability of the project to both the provider of funds and the recipient.

Under a classical corporate income tax, dividends, retained earnings, and debt are all treated differently. Firms are expected to adopt the form of finance with the lowest tax costs. If not all firms have equal access to the lowest cost source of funds, however, investment may fail to go to those projects with the highest returns. Firms may find certain projects that would have been profitable to undertake using one source of funds are unprofitable when other sources of funds are used because of the higher tax costs. These tax costs become barriers to the efficient allocation of capital across firms.

Asymmetric information presents a different type of barrier to the efficient allocation of capital. Ultimately, providers of funds for investment projects can never know as much about the projects as the entrepreneurs undertaking the activities. Entrepreneurs have some scope to change the riskiness of a project's returns in unobservable ways and have the ability to pursue other activities that benefit only themselves (for example, leisure). Since the actions of entrepreneurs are not fully observable (or could be observed only at high cost), contracts that dictate under all possible contingencies how the entrepreneurs are to perform cannot be enforced. Instead, as in other principal-agent problems, providers of funds must find indirect means of influencing the behavior of entrepreneurs. The method of financing is an important instrument in guiding such behavior in situations of asymmetric information.

The effects of these factors on the financing of investment have numerous policy implications:

- Depending on technological characteristics, information asymmetries can lead to either overinvestment or underinvestment in an economy. Clearly, policy recommendations to correct the inefficiency will differ, depending on which outcome occurs. Although persistent overinvestment is unlikely to characterize most developing economies, there are certainly many occasions when funds are applied to projects with low expected returns. The possibility that increased availability of funds will result in misdirected investment cannot be ignored.

- Increases in the level of wealth and collateral in an economy can greatly reduce the costs of asymmetric information. Increases in collateral reduce the risks faced by lenders. Entrepreneurs with poor projects are less likely to undertake them when they must risk more of their own wealth. Government policies that increase the ability of individuals to collateralize wealth—for example, by promoting property rights and the establishment of a legal system that allows the transfer of collateral at low cost—can increase the ability of potentially successful projects to receive financing. Policies that facilitate the ability of individuals to accumulate savings play a related role. The ability of entrepreneurs to earn high rates of return increases both their collateral and their opportunity cost of undertaking projects with low expected returns.

- The creation of decentralized securities markets is likely to be less advantageous in situations in which information asymmetries are large. Individual providers of funds have an incentive to free ride on the information about and monitoring of entrepreneurs provided by others. Only firms with established reputations may be able to obtain funds in these markets.

- Similarly, although competition among lenders is generally promoted, such competition can also reduce the incentive of individual lenders to lend to entrepreneurs if information and monitoring costs are large. Competitors would attempt to steal these borrowers away after they were certified as creditworthy. Furthermore, limited competition allows a lender to use the sanction of denying credit as an instrument to influence borrowers to act responsibly in order to obtain future financing.

- As a result of information asymmetries, certain types of projects are more likely to obtain financing at a lower cost by using equity finance rather than debt. If the tax costs of equity are higher than those of debt, however, these projects may be relatively underfinanced. Those making tax policy might wish to reconsider whether the tax treatment of equity and debt should be equalized or whether the tax costs of the projects can be reduced in other ways.

- Although a government may feel an obligation to intervene directly in credit allocation, any such intervention should occur only if the government's ability to identify creditworthy recipients is greater than that of other lenders. In the absence of any comparative advantage, government attention to the basic infrastructure that reduces the costs of obtaining information and enforcing contracts is likely better to assist the efficient allocation of credit.

In sum, outside debt and equity finance creates information asymmetries between shareholders and managers and between lenders and borrowers (see chapter 4). Although many solutions to this problem lie outside the tax policy domain, the issue has some implications for the design of tax incentives for investment. For example, because of the difficulty of monitoring intangible investment, such investment may not be able to secure debt finance. Thus R&D tax credits may be called for to overcome this problem. Another example arises from taxation of capital gains on a realization basis rather than an accrual basis. Under such a tax regime a financial institution would have an incentive to sell a loan portfolio on which it suffers a loss. This problem could be overcome by allowing a mark-to-market rule, that is, the bank values all its portfolios according to their market value and therefore would not have to sell its loan portfolio to receive the tax loss. In the presence of poorly functioning equity markets, allowing full expensing of the investment under the tax system would permit the government to become an equity partner and would promote investments.

R&D Capital, Industrial Performance, and Tax Policies

In chapter 5, Anwar Shah analyzes R&D and the production structure, R&D and the product market structure, the rationale for public intervention in R&D investment, and the effectiveness of tax policies in R&D promoting investment. Conclusions arrived at in the major sections are briefly reported here.

R&D CAPITAL AND THE STRUCTURE OF PRODUCTION. R&D capital serves as an input in a joint production of multiple outputs that include product and process development. Such capital facilitates the mapping of technological possibilities into economic opportunities. Although it takes time to accumulate and uses up scarce resources, R&D widens production opportunities for the economy by enabling it to obtain greater outputs with given inputs or to substitute relatively cheaper inputs for relatively more expensive ones.

A special feature of R&D capital is the imperfect appropriability of returns as a result of intra- as well as interindustry capital spillovers. Spillovers diffuse knowledge through such channels as patents, cross-licensing agreements, mobility of R&D personnel, and input purchases. The overall effect of R&D capital spillovers on the incentive to undertake additional R&D investment is unclear in view of two opposing influences. First, the imperfect appropriability of returns from a firm's own R&D has a disincentive effect. Second, a firm's desire to tap into the external knowledge and associated benefits promotes its incentive to undertake its own R&D so that it can benefit from externally generated knowledge. The net effect of these influences varies by industry and explains the paradox posed by some R&D-intensive industries, such as electronics and chemicals, in which the high levels of spillovers do not seem to have any detrimental effects on the incentive to undertake additional R&D investment.

Available empirical evidence suggests that the overall adjustment process from the initiation of research to product and process development takes three to five years. The marginal adjustment costs for R&D are higher than those for plant and equipment. The own-price elasticity of demand for R&D capital is less than unity regardless of the time period considered. In the long run R&D capital is a complement to physical capital but a substitute for labor. The long-run output elasticity of demand for R&D capital is close to unity; short-run elasticities are much smaller than those for the long run. Output changes exert a much stronger influence on R&D capital than vice versa. R&D capital spillovers are large and significant, and as a result the social rate of return on R&D projects exceeds the private returns by at least two-thirds.

R&D CAPITAL AND PRODUCT MARKET STRUCTURE. The value of cost-reducing R&D is determined by its profitability. Because private returns from R&D understate the true social returns from such investments, R&D will be underprovided. Furthermore, because R&D investments often represent large fixed costs, market structure in R&D-intensive industries is going to be concentrated. The above situation is, however, not unique to R&D. What is unique about R&D is the nature of spillovers. These spillovers reduce industry costs, but they result in inappropriability of returns for the R&D performer and so incentives to perform R&D are reduced. Restoring appropriability does not help matters either because it leads to industrial concentration, incorrect pricing of R&D, and social costs. Perfect appropriability may also result in excessive R&D because too many firms may be fishing for the same information.

The information asymmetry between an R&D performer and a financier distinguishes R&D investment from traditional risky investment. It is in the interest of the R&D performer to keep vital project information secret, but in the absence of detailed information, project financing may not be forthcoming. Asymmetric information also limits the R&D firm's ability to profit from its output.

The following broad conclusions emerge from a survey of empirical evidence on the relation between R&D capital and market structure.

- Success breeds success. Because learning involves costs, successful firms possess an advantage over their rivals in having greater possibilities for further success. Thus monopoly persists in the R&D capital market. Past successes of R&D investments lead to greater current R&D efforts on the part of the successful firms. These firms then tend to produce further innovations and thus widen the gap between themselves and their rivals.

- The relation between R&D and firm size is much looser and more obscure than is implied by the usual statements of the Schumpeterian hypothesis. Although much of the R&D capital is concentrated in large firms, it is more likely that they have become large because of their R&D successes than that they do more and more fruitful R&D because they are large.
- R&D capital and industrial concentration are positively correlated up to moderate levels of industrial concentration.
- Intraindustry spillovers drive a wedge between social and private returns in an industry, as well as between the social rates across industries. Social rates of return diverge from the private rates by 50 to 150 percent, depending on the R&D intensiveness of the industry.
- In the presence of spillovers, society's demand for R&D capital at the existing market rates of return significantly exceeds the private demand.

PUBLIC POLICY AND R&D INVESTMENT. It has been argued that the social rate of return from R&D is higher than the private rate of return because of either spillovers or information asymmetries. In the presence of spillovers, r&D performers are not able fully to appropriate benefits associated with their R&D activities. The existence of asymmetric information between R&D performers and financiers limits financing of R&D projects. Project success warrants secrecy, but project financing requires release of vital information. As a result many projects lapse, lacking financing. The asymmetric information in the R&D output market also limits the R&D firm's ability to achieve licensing gains from trade.

Most industrial nations see the need to intervene through the tax code to encourage R&D activities. Empirical evidence on the effectiveness of such initiatives is quite limited. In chapter 5, Shah examines the effect of the Canadian R&D tax credit on R&D investment using a production structure framework. This framework makes it possible to trace the effect of tax policies on the production and investment decisions of an industry. The framework was implemented by using detailed data on inputs, outputs, factor and output prices, and the tax regimes for eighteen Canadian industries for the period 1963 to 1983. Provisions in the tax code were used to develop estimates for the user cost of capital. A system of simultaneous equations incorporating the cost function and derived input demand functions was estimated by nonlinear interactive methods in translog form. The estimated cost function fitted the data well and was also "well-behaved." An analysis of parameter estimates for this cost function suggests that R&D tax credits had a significant positive effect on R&D investment in Canada and that for every 1983 Canadian dollar of revenue forgone by the national treasury, $1.80 worth of additional R&D investment was undertaken. These results indicate that a properly designed tax incentive can further public policy objectives cost-effectively.

Tax Incentives and FDI

Perceptions regarding foreign investment in developing countries have undergone rapid change in recent years. Previously, such investments were seen as instruments of foreign domination and control. Perceptions are now changing, and developing countries have come to recognize that positive economic gains can be associated with foreign capital, particularly technology transfers and access to world markets. This realization has led to fierce competition among developing countries in the provision of tax incentives to attract foreign capital. It is little recognized, however, that in many instances such incentives simply result in a transfer of resources from the host developing country to foreign treasuries without any special benefit being provided to foreign investors. Thus the taxation of multinational companies by a developing country cannot be examined in isolation from the tax regime of the home country, from tax haven–conduit countries, and from transfer-pricing practices. These factors have a bearing on the tax sensitivity of FDI. We next briefly review the basic principles enunciated by Joel Slemrod (chapter 6) and Anwar Shah and Joel Slemrod (chapter 13) that should guide the tax policies of developing countries toward FDI under different home country tax regimes.

NO HOME COUNTRY TAXATION. Some countries (for example, France) follow a territorial system of taxation and do not tax the foreign earnings of residents. Developing countries that wish to encourage investment from countries following this system of taxation should avoid imposing any taxes on foreign capital, for such taxes will inevitably lead to capital flight until the after-tax rate of return is made equal to the alternative return available elsewhere.

HOME COUNTRY TAXATION WITH FOREIGN TAX CREDITS AND NO TAX SPARING. Several countries (for example, the United States, the United Kingdom, and Japan) tax their residents on their worldwide income but allow tax credits against domestic liability for foreign taxes deemed to have been paid by home country residents. These foreign tax credits are usually limited to a maximum obtained by applying the home country statutory tax rate to net income earned abroad. The credits are usually available in the year that foreign earnings are repatriated. The host country can, without incurring any disincentives to investment, tax a marginal investor from such a country by applying a withholding tax at the home country tax rate. Note that, because such credits are available only on repatriation of earnings, host country taxation of reinvestments at the home country statutory rate would discourage some investments, as the postponement would mean a lower present value of such credits. If only withholding taxes on repatriations are used instead and are levied at rates that do not exceed home country rates, the taxes are immediately creditable and therefore carry no disincentive effects.

A further complication is introduced if a marginal investor is in a position of long-term excess credit, as some U.S. multinational companies currently appear to be. Then the host country taxation would discourage FDI, and host country tax relief would matter. In general, if the credit status of multinationals is ignored to encourage inward investment, the host country's average effective tax rate on corporate income must not exceed the home country tax rate. Note that a tax holiday for new investment would not be a cost-effective instrument because the home country taxes still matter and most investments may not be profitable in the initial years. Positive incentives to reinvestment include immediate full expensing of investment, accelerated capital consumption allowances, and investment tax credits.

HOME COUNTRY TAXATION WITH FOREIGN TAX CREDITS AND TAX SPARING. All the capital-exporting countries with worldwide systems of taxation mentioned earlier, with the exception of the United States, have entered into tax-sparing agreements with developing countries. A standard feature of such agreements is that the home country allows credit at the home country tax rate for foreign taxes that may or may not be assessed. Thus if the host country taxes corporate income at a rate lower than the home rate, the result is a direct subsidy from the capital-exporting country to its outward investment. To encourage FDI from tax-sparing countries, host countries must use such tax incentives as tax reductions, expensing, accelerated depreciations, investment tax credits, and tax holidays. If corporate tax revenue from FDI is not a consideration, then an effective host country tax rate of zero on FDI would have the maximum positive effect on such investments. At the other extreme, when FDI promotion is not actively pursued, the home country average effective tax rate can equal the host country tax rate without having any disincentive effect.

FURTHER COMPLICATIONS INTRODUCED BY TRANSFER PRICING. The ability of multinational companies to attribute income to various locations creates a further complication for home country taxation with foreign tax credits, both with and without tax sparing. It is usually difficult for a high-tax host country to adopt rules of income attribution that will fully circumvent the shifting of income to low-tax countries or to tax havens through transfer pricing. Differences in statutory tax rates among countries are considered to be important determinants for such shifting of income across borders. In view of this, an environment of low statutory taxes and fewer incentives would be more attractive to multinationals than a high-tax, high-subsidy environment.

SOME CONCLUSIONS REGARDING TAXATION OF FDI. The earlier discussion emphasized that optimal taxation of FDI requires host country taxation to discriminate among various foreign investors according to the tax regime for outward investment available in their home countries. But differential statutory corporate income tax rates based on ownership, even if feasible, would not be desirable on neutrality grounds. In contrast, differential withholding taxes on repatriations but no taxation of reinvested earnings could be a feasible alternative. This alternative, however, unless extended to domestic capital as well, will tend to discriminate against reinvestment by domestic corporations and may well encourage reincorporation of domestic corporations as subsidiaries of foreign dummy corporations. These complications lead to the conclusion that perhaps a stable low-tax, low-subsidy environment which is also free of nontax disincentives, such as regulations, exchange controls, credit rationing, and price and quantity controls, offers the best climate for encouraging FDI.

Empirical Evidence on the Effectiveness of Tax Incentives

The empirical analyses presented in this volume can be loosely classified into three broad categories: marginal effective tax rate models, production structure models, and computable general-equilibrium (CGE) analyses. The authors of several chapters have developed cost-of-capital frameworks that take into account market imperfections, foreign tax credit regimes, asymmetric information, financing constraints, and other institutional features of developing countries. They then incorporate the user cost of capital into production structure and CGE models to estimate the effect of investment incentives in selected developing countries. The regions and countries covered by these analyses include Latin America (Brazil and Mexico), East Asia (Indonesia, Malaysia, the Philippines, Singapore, and Thailand), South Asia (Pakistan), and Eastern Europe (Bulgaria, the former Czechoslovakia, Hungary, Poland, Romania, and Turkey). The tax incentives analyzed include tax credits for physical and R&D investment and employment, investment allowances, tax holidays, and accelerated depreciation provisions. In addition, incentive effects of the indirect tax system are analyzed. Country-specific evidence on the effectiveness of various incentives is briefly reviewed below.

Tax Burden Analysis

This broad analysis is an attempt to capture the provisions of the tax code that affect marginal investment. Tax incentives lower the marginal effective tax rate and thereby encourage additional investment in the tax-preferred activity until after-tax rates of return are equalized. Industry- and sector-specific marginal effective tax rates are often used to stimulate investment on an ex ante basis. The six chapters summarized in this section use varying types of tax burden analysis in examining tax policies toward domestic investment and FDI.

Antonio Estache and Vitor Gaspar (chapter 7) apply the King-Fullerton type of marginal effective tax rate analysis to an evaluation of tax incentives in Brazil. They demonstrate that many tax incentives fail to lower significantly the marginal effective rate of tax but instead, because of tax arbitrage and tax evasion, bring about a lower average effective rate. They show that the extensive use of tax incentives leads to a highly distorted system of taxation. The tax system discriminates between investments by sources of financing; by type of assets, sector, or region; and by market orientation and the origin of capital goods. Overall, the authors conclude that fiscal incentives in Brazil lead to high losses of revenue compared with the amount of investment that is generated.

Robin W. Boadway, Dale Chua, and Frank Flatters (chapter 8) use a marginal effective tax rate model to evaluate tax holidays granted to firms that apply successfully for pioneer status, under which the firms incur no tax liability for up to five years. Such firms are not allowed to carry forward initial and annual depreciation allowances to the postholiday period. This tax incentive is intended to promote investment in desirable activities and to assist infant industries and disadvantaged economic and social groups. The authors find that in Malaysia such a tax status imposes a penalty on firms that are not profitable during the holiday period. Profitable firms receive a small net subsidy on all investments, but even for them, tax subsidies on debt-financed investments are lower for pioneer firms than for nonpioneer firms. This is because loss or even postponement of the use of the depreciation allowances costs firms more than they gain from reduction of taxes during the holiday period. The authors conclude that tax holidays are "highly unlikely to be of value to the weak or infant investors or to industries that are claimed to be the intended beneficiaries of the measures."

In a companion chapter (chapter 9) the same authors extend the marginal effective tax rate methodology to determine the effect on investment incentives and disincentives of the indirect tax system in Malaysia. They find that although the contribution of indirect taxes roughly equals that of direct taxes, the distortionary effects of such taxes on investment are disproportionately large. Such taxes create greater intersectoral variations in investment distortions. For example, they penalize the export sector but provide a net subsidy to competing import industries, thereby undermining Malaysia's international competitiveness. Trade taxes are responsible for more than two-thirds of the investment distortions created by the indirect tax system. The authors recommend that the number and levels of import tariffs be reduced and that a broad-based value added tax be introduced.

Thailand, through its Board of Investment, offers a variety of incentives for investment. These include tax holidays or reduction of corporate income taxes, import duties, and business taxes on machinery and raw materials. In addition, the board also grants nonfiscal incentives in the form of restrictions on business activities and employment by foreigners. Robert Halvorsen (chapter 10) examines the cost-effectiveness of these incentives by analyzing survey data on responses by investors and by comparing private and social rates of return on promoted projects. It is interesting to learn that investors ranked exemption or reduction of import duties and business taxes as the most important incentive, followed by reduction of import duties and business taxes on raw materials. Provision of corporate tax holidays was ranked third, and the granting of permission to bring in foreign technicians was ranked fourth. An analysis of private and social rates of return for the supported projects suggests that the private rate of return from these projects ranged from 13 to 61 percent and that therefore these projects would have been undertaken by the private sector even in the absence of any fiscal incentives. Several of these projects had negative social rates of return, and thus public subsidies for them could not be justified. The author concludes that the tax holiday was a particularly poor instrument for stimulating FDI because until recently no tax-sparing agreement with dominant sources of foreign capital had been concluded. The author recommends that Thailand tighten the existing fiscal incentive regime but strengthen existing nonfiscal incentives by, for example, easing restrictions on the employment of foreigners and augmenting the capacity of the One-Stop Service Centre to inform investors and facilitate investment.

Whereas the use of tax incentives for investment is declining in industrial countries and in the developing countries of Latin America, it is growing in the countries of the Association of Southeast Asian Nations (ASEAN) with the exception of Indonesia. In recent years these countries have offered more generous tax holidays, investment tax credits, and import duty exemptions. Ngee Choon Chia and John Whalley (chapter 11) note that the tax competition among ASEAN countries is the driving force behind these generous but conceptually ineffective incentives. A large part of FDI in these countries comes from the United States and Japan, which allow investors foreign tax credits against domestic tax liabilities. Tax incentives in ASEAN countries lead to tax levels lower than the level of home taxation for foreign investors and lead to transfer of revenues from ASEAN to investing countries that do not allow tax sparing. (Note that Japan has tax-sparing treaties with ASEAN countries.) Chia and Whalley observe a Stackleberg-type situation, in which Singapore always takes the lead in accelerating incentives, followed by Malaysia, the Philippines, and Thailand. They suggest that it is in the interest of individual countries to take unilateral action to withdraw incentives, but they are not hopeful that these countries will do so. Therefore they suggest bringing negotiations on investment incentives into the wider trade and integration negotiations currently under way in ASEAN.

Jack M. Mintz and Thomas Tsiopoulos (chapter 12) examine the implications of corporate tax regimes in Bulgaria, the former Czechoslovakia, Hungary, Poland, and Romania for inward FDI. Overall, they find that the corporate income tax regimes in these countries as of mid-1991 were attractive compared with those of other countries competing for FDI from the United States or Germany, two important sources of FDI for Central and Eastern Europe (CEE). Czechoslovakia's effective tax rate was a bit higher, but in all five countries the tax burdens were well below levels that might deter interested investors. The authors pay particular attention to the effects of tax holidays, which are offered as temporary tax relief by all five countries to foreign investors. They show that tax holidays benefit companies if inflation rates are low or if companies finance investment largely with equity. If, however, inflation is high and investments are financed in part by local borrowing, and if the nominal interest costs are fully deductible for tax purposes, the tax holidays become redundant. Without tax holidays, and under the assumption of debt-equity ratio with debt borrowed locally, Czechoslovakia, Bulgaria (manufacturing only), and Romania would not be tax competitive. The authors also examine alternative tax incentives. They find that if tax holidays are eliminated, reducing the corporate tax rate to about 20 percent or instituting an investment tax allowance of about 20 percent would preserve the tax competitiveness of regimes in the CEE countries. Furthermore, tax allowances and credits would probably be more cost-effective than tax holidays in attracting FDI, without undue revenue losses by the treasuries of the CEE countries. The authors also observe that if inflation rates are eventually brought down to the level commonly found in most countries of the Organization for Economic Cooperation and Development (OECD)— that is, less than 5 percent—indexation for inflation will be unnecessary. At the current high inflation rates, however, the CEE countries should consider indexation to provide an improved tax policy environment for business.

A related question is the tax sensitivity of FDI in Mexico. If FDI is not responsive to taxation, it may be an appropriate target for taxation by the host country. Anwar Shah and Joel Slemrod (chapter 13) examine this question for Mexico and find that FDI in that country is sensitive to the tax regimes in Mexico and the United States, the credit status of multinational companies, country credit ratings, and the Mexican regulatory environment. Thus Mexico's current policies of dismantling regulations and employing a tax system competitive with the United States are expected to have a salutary effect on FDI. The conclusions reached here imply that the first priority of other developing countries, especially those in which the degree of FDI penetration is large, should be to ensure that their tax systems are competitive with the home tax regimes of a marginal investor having access to foreign tax credits against domestic liabilities. Special tax incentives will matter only to investors from tax-sparing countries or those with a long-term excess credit position in their worldwide portfolio.

The Effect of Taxation on Production and Investment Decisions

The studies summarized in this section implement several versions of a dynamic production structure approach "to serve as a useful reminder of the limits of our knowledge" (Feldstein 1982, p. 831). The essence of this approach is that taxes influence factor utilization, adjustment, and output expansion through changes in factor prices and through their effect on technological change. A dynamic version of this approach (variable profit function) recognizes that capital is a quasi-fixed factor in the short run and that adjustment can take place only at a cost and with significant lags. Thus the short-run effect of tax policy would be significantly different from its long-run effect. The approach provides estimates as to the stimulative (direct and induced) effects of public policy measures per dollar of forgone revenues. It also yields, as by-products, shadow prices of quasi-fixed inputs, estimates of elasticities of factor substitution, output elasticities of factor demand, and own-price elasticities of product demand. These elasticity parameters are useful for studies dealing with tax analysis, trade liberalization, cost of capital, and general-equilibrium modeling of public policy changes. Much of production structure modeling is of recent origin (see Bernstein and Nadiri 1987), and its applications to the evaluation of tax incentives in both industrial and nonindustrial countries have just begun to be explored.

In order to estimate the effect of taxes on factor substitution, technological change, and output expansion, it is necessary to use cost or profit functions that embody flexible functional forms with fewer a priori restrictions. Typically, the production structure of the economy is unknown to a policy analyst, and often the Cobb-Douglas and constant elasticity of substitution (CES) production functions are assumed, as is common in most CGE work. By these assumptions, one runs the risk of choosing a specification that places inaccurate restrictions on output and factor price elasticities and hence arrives at misleading policy conclusions. Fortunately, in recent years significant advances have taken place in modeling production structures, but empirical work on the tax policy implications of this new technology is significantly lacking both in industrial and developing countries. To estimate the cost structure, one is faced with several modeling strategies, including, broadly, static and dynamic formulations. A static equilibrium framework is easier to implement but is useful only under a special set of circumstances, when there are no indivisibilities and rigidities in the system and adjustment is costless and instantaneous. These conditions are unlikely to be fulfilled in any practical economic environment, let alone in a developing country. This framework would lead to misleading policy prescriptions if quasi-fixed factors indeed diverged from their static equilibrium levels in the short run. Thus it is essential that appropriate tests of static equilibrium precede actual estimation in this framework. This framework in any case does not distinguish between short-run and long-run behavioral responses. In an explicitly dynamic framework, by contrast, factor disequilibrium is recognized, adjustment costs are explicitly modeled, and an expectation hypothesis is specified. The adjustment costs are usually treated as internal to the firm and are measured by the reduction in output supply brought about when variable factors are pulled away from producing output to adjust a firm's capital stock. Thus a firm increases its stock of a given quasi-fixed factor as long as the present value of future additions to output is at least as great as the cost of bringing in new capital as measured by the sum of the after-tax user cost of capital and the reductions in current output attributable to capital adjustment. This framework, used in several chapters in this volume, enables the researcher to trace the dynamic adjustment path under specified conditions.

Jeffrey Bernstein and Anwar Shah (chapter 14) have developed a dynamic model of production (variable profits function) to analyze the influence of tax policies on output supply and input demands for selected industries in Mexico, Pakistan, and Turkey. Tax instruments considered include corporate income tax rates, investment tax credit rates, investment allowances, capital cost allowance rates, payroll tax rates, and sales tax rates on intermediate inputs. The dynamics of production in their model arise from internal adjustment costs associated with the installation of capital stock into the production process. Capital inputs differ from other factors of production because costs arise from capital adjustment. The model formulation allows the speed of capital adjustment to be estimated internally. In addition to the dynamic nature of the model, there are other interesting features. Output supply is endogenous and is not solely a function of factor demand or of investment. Product markets are not assumed to be purely competitive: the nature of firm interdependence governs their structure. Finally, financial capital markets imperfections emerge as firms are constrained by the rate of return that can be earned on their financial capital. The authors applied this model to detergent and other chemical industries in Mexico, using data for the period 1970 to 1983; to apparel and leather products industries in Pakistan for the period 1966 to 1984; and to electrical machinery, nonelectrical machinery, and transport equipment industries in Turkey for the period 1973 to 1985. Tax incentives evaluated for these industries included investment tax credits, investment allowances, accelerated capital consumption allowances, and reductions in corporate income tax rates. For each of these incentive measures, estimates of revenue losses per dollar of investment were derived in the short, intermediate, and long runs. When the last period evaluations for four Mexican and Pakistani industries were used, the incremental benefit-cost ratio for investment tax credits exceeded one in the short and intermediate runs only for the Mexican detergent industry, whereas in the long run it exceeded one for both the Mexican detergent and Pakistani apparel industries. The results are therefore quite mixed on the performance of investment tax credits.

Investment allowances given to Turkish industries did significantly better. In the short run, revenue losses exceeded more than a dollar per dollar of investment in two of the three industries analyzed, but in the long run investment in all three industries exceeded revenue losses to the national treasury. Accelerated capital consumption allowances were cost-effective in the short, medium, and long runs for Mexican industries but only in the long run for the three Turkish industries. These allowances were ineffective in stimulating investment in Pakistan. Note that the first two countries had experienced significant inflation, and in a nonindexed tax system, immediate expensing of investment has important benefits. Corporate tax rate reductions, by contrast, appeared to be an ineffective tax incentive in the short, medium, and long runs for the seven industries examined in the three countries. Investment stimulation was small compared with revenue losses.

Dagmar Rajagopal and Anwar Shah (chapter 15) argue that analyses of the effectiveness of tax incentives can be considerably enriched if they incorporate the industrial market structure of the industry at hand. The authors propose an empirical procedure to test the market power hypothesis. Such a test has important implications for the effectiveness of fiscal incentives for investment. If the producers in an industry have market power, they may be able to shift taxes forward completely so that any tax incentive would simply lead to windfall gains for those firms. In a competitive industry, however, producers are not able to shift taxes forward completely, so tax incentives stimulate investment. Rajagopal and Shah test the market power hypothesis empirically, using data for selected industries: in Turkey, chemical and petroleum derivatives, and in Pakistan, textiles, as well as chemicals and pharmaceuticals. The authors also examine the effect of investment tax credits (credits against tax liability), investment allowances (deductions against taxable income), and R&D expensing on production and investment decisions and on government revenues. They introduce three empirical innovations. First, they specify an expression for the rental price of capital consistent with rational rather than static expectations. Second, instead of assuming perfect competition, they implement an empirical test of market power. Third, they empirically derive an incremental cost-benefit ratio for each of the incentives evaluated. They conclude that firms in those industries had limited market power and were therefore able to shift taxes forward only partially. Thus tax incentives did influence production and investment decisions of firms in the industries studied. The effects, however, varied greatly among different industries, and in three of eleven cases, tax incentive measures led to revenue losses that were higher than the amount invested in physical or knowledge capital. The performance of investment tax credits was mixed. It was cost-effective for Pakistani chemical and pharmaceutical industries but was ineffective for the textile industries. Investment allowances also had little effect on investment in Turkish chemical and petroleum-derivative industries. R&D expensing stimulated Pakistani chemical industries but did little to stimulate investment in Pakistani pharmaceutical and Turkish chemical and petroleum-derivative industries.

Anwar Shah and John Baffes (chapter 16) employ a flexible accelerator-type dynamic factor demand model with endogenous capacity utilization to examine the effectiveness of tax incentives available to large private manufacturing industries in Pakistan. Their data are for the period 1956 to 1985. The tax incentive measures evaluated include investment tax credits, full expensing of R&D investment, and reductions in corporate income tax rates. The authors find that although investment in physical and knowledge capital was sensitive to tax measures, the elasticity values were without exception quite small. Further incremental benefit-cost ratios associated with changes in investment tax credits and the corporate tax rate were smaller than one in the short run. A full-expensing option for R&D was found to be cost-effective.

Economywide Implications of Investment Incentives

Most complex interactions in an economy are assumed away by partial-equilibrium analysis. An applied general-equilibrium model, however, can provide a disaggregated view of the economy and thereby yield quantitative estimates of all important interactions. It is therefore a valuable tool for assessing the relative merits of alternate tax policy changes. Two chapters in this volume employ this tool in evaluating investment incentives in Mexico and in the Philippines.

Mexico has experimented with many tax instruments designed to promote private capital formation. Among such initiatives were general and industry-specific tax credits, employment tax credits, and reductions in corporate taxes. Using a dynamic computable general-equilibrium model, Andrew Feltenstein and Anwar Shah (chapter 17) examine the relative efficacy of such instruments. They carry out model simulations using three scenarios involving equal-yield investment incentives: increases in investment tax credits, increases in employment tax credits, and reductions in the corporate tax rate. They find that reductions in corporate taxes have the most stimulative effect on investment, followed by increases in investment tax credits. Increases in employment tax credits had the least positive effect on investment.

Several plausible explanations can be given for the superiority of tax rate reductions over increased investment tax credits in Mexico. Mexico had high inflation, high nominal interest rates, and a negative real interest rate for certain years, and firms faced severe financing constraints. In such a macroeconomic climate, tax rate reductions increase cash flows, as well as signal an improved public policy climate. Furthermore, in a period of economic uncertainty and decline, nonrefundable unindexed tax credits on new investment would be less valuable than immediate reduction in tax liability from both old and new capital.

Ramon Clarete (chapter 18) develops a general-equilibrium model of the Philippine economy to analyze the effects of investment incentives in the Philippines. The incentives considered are tax rebates and drawbacks on imports of machinery and equipment by priority industries. Three policy simulations are carried out. The first entails withdrawal of all tax incentives but retention of existing subsidies on investments. The second simulation involves retention of tax incentives and provision of investment subsidies on a uniform-rate basis to all sectors while real government spending is held at a constant level. The third simulation includes withdrawal of the entire package of tax and duty rebates on imported capital equipment as well as discontinuation of investment subsidies. The authors find that in the first and third policy scenarios private investment falls (restricting the use of available incentives) but that in the second scenario (liberal incentives) it increases. Thus the authors conclude that tax incentives do matter for investment in the Philippines.

Some Conclusions

Tax policy instruments are widely used by developing and industrial countries alike to foster industrial and technological development. Commonly used tax incentives include preferential tax rates by type of activity or organization, either on a temporary or on a permanent basis, tax holidays being an extreme but prevalent form of this type of incentive; investment tax credits; and fast writeoffs (accelerated capital consumption allowances and expensing of investment). Only investment tax credits, accelerated depreciations, lower tax rates, and tax rebates are frequently automatically granted; all others are subject to varying degrees of administrative discretion. Administrative discretion often results in discouragement of potential investors, especially nonresidents. For example, the fairly generous tax holidays provided by Brazil, Lesotho, Morocco, Pakistan, and Thailand have failed to provide sufficient stimulus to new investment. Several countries (for example, Brazil, Indonesia, and Mexico), having observed that revenue forgone as a result of various fiscal incentives for investment exceeds the investment stimulation offered by various incentives, have moved to curtail these measures significantly. Although properly designed and executed investment incentives could play an important role in stimulating investments, institutional features in developing countries significantly limit the realization of this potential. Developing countries would be well advised to limit the use of such tax preferences and instead concentrate on eliminating disincentives to invest that arise from infrastructural deficiencies, the regulatory regime, and lack of a legal framework, institutions, and enforcement.

Various studies presented in this volume examine both conceptually and empirically the effectiveness of different tax policy regimes in promoting private capital formation in developing countries. In view of the sharp differences in the methodologies adopted and the country economic situations studied, a worry at the outset is that the results might be contradictory and inconclusive and therefore may not offer any useful lessons for other countries. Surprisingly, the empirical findings present the following quite coherent themes regarding such policies.

Tax incentives that are not properly targeted and that do not take into account limitations in tax administration capabilities more often than not bring in less than a dollar of investment for each dollar lost in government revenues. Thus broad tax incentives, such as tax holidays and general corporate tax rate reductions, that are below comparable levels in industrial countries, prove cost-ineffective in promoting investment.

The experiences of industrial and developing countries alike suggest that broad tax incentives such as tax holidays and corporate rate reductions are a costly way to promote investment. Empirical results presented in this volume for general corporate tax rate reductions in Mexico, Pakistan, and Turkey indicate that more often than not such broad incentives bring about revenue losses for the government that exceed the value of the new investment they generate. The forgone revenues are financed by increased taxes on other economic activities, which are thereby adversely affected. Tax incentives are difficult to target in practice, and they can provide a windfall gain on investments that would have been undertaken anyway in the absence of these measures. Past experience suggests that incentives given to a selected few priority industries lead to pressures from other industries for similar treatment. Over time these incentives proliferate, as happened in Brazil, Indonesia, and Mexico in the early 1980s. As a result the tax system becomes complex, and its ability to raise revenues in an equitable and a less distorting manner becomes impaired. This outcome induces tax avoidance and tax evasion activities.

Tax holidays, as currently instituted in a large number of developing countries, are poor instruments for promoting new investment by domestic investors or by investors from capital-exporting countries that allow foreign tax credits against domestic liabilities.

Tax holidays are among the most frequently used tax incentives in developing countries. Just like the changes in tax structure, the effects of such a policy on the user cost of capital have three possible effects—one positive and two negative. A zero tax rate during the holiday period has a positive effect on investment. Reduction in the present value of depreciation allowances and the rising value of these allowances toward the end of the holiday period, by contrast, discourage current investment. The overall effect of tax holidays on investment depends on the extent to which capital consumption allowances and tax losses can be carried forward to the postholiday period. If there are no carryforward provisions, some firms benefit by being taxable in the formative years, when they are in a loss position. If a full carryforward is allowed, effective subsidies in certain instances would be too generous. In general, a tax holiday is generous to firms that use nondepreciable factors of production. In any event, tax holidays open tax arbitrage opportunities for investors to shift taxable income into activities in which they can take advantage of the tax holiday. Tax holidays may thus encourage fly-by-night or short-term operations at the expense of long-term investment. A tax credit or an investment allowance can encourage long-term investment at lower revenue cost than a tax holiday.

Corporate tax rate reductions beyond the level found in capital-exporting countries (say, below 30 percent) often bring about greater revenue losses than increases in investment. In fact, such rate reductions could generate expectations regarding future tax hikes and may well discourage investment.

Reductions in corporate income tax rates benefit both old and new capital alike. They thus have little influence on investment but cause large revenue losses to the treasury. For a given level of investment stimulation, tax rate reductions would bring about higher forgone revenues than investment tax credits and allowances because they reduce tax payments on existing capital and economic rents, in addition to reducing new investments. Furthermore, corporate tax rate reductions may be seen as temporary in an uncertain economic policy climate and could even discourage further investments in anticipation of future tax increases. Recent attempts at tax reform in developing countries have included broadening the tax base and lowering the tax rate to create a level playing field and so sustain investments guided by economic considerations alone. Tax rate reductions can also be justified if such rates in the capital-importing country are higher than those in the relevant capital-exporting countries with worldwide income taxation. Such a strategy, to be sure, will pay rich dividends if it is seen as credible and permanent. But in a world of mistrust between government and investor, it could be viewed as a "money grab" from the corporate sector by raising the effective rate of business taxation and could therefore discourage investments by raising expectations regarding future tax increases or reversal of current policies. The empirical evidence presented in this volume casts doubt on the effectiveness of such a broad tax reform strategy in promoting investments. A country that is seen to have an unstable political and economic climate and frequent tax changes would have to consider front-loaded incentives, such as full expensing (without interest deductions) or refundable investment tax credits, to promote investments. Of course, such incentives must be designed carefully to take into account their interaction with other institutional features; the country's administration capabilities, and their effect on marginal effective tax rates, loss firms, cash flows, foreign firms, and interasset and intersectoral choices. Furthermore, they must be monitored carefully for their effect on investments and government revenues.

Selective tax incentives that are targeted to new investment in machinery and equipment and R&D and that provide up-front incentives are cost-effective in stimulating investment.

Tax incentives that apply only to new capital (preferably to incremental investment over and above the investment usually undertaken anyway) and are up front (payable when investment is undertaken) are likely to be more effective than others. Thus full expensing of investment (without interest deductibility) would be most effective, followed by (refundable) investment tax credits and accelerated capital consumption allowances. Tax holidays and tax rate reductions, for reasons outlined earlier, are likely to be less effective. Some tax preferences, such as expensing and (refundable) investment tax credits for R&D and machinery and equipment that embody advanced technology, have some theoretical and empirical support. Their conceptual support is based on the externalities of investment for economic growth and the overcoming of information asymmetries between agents that finance such activities and those that undertake them. In the presence of poorly functioning equity markets, allowing full expensing of the investment under the tax system makes the government an equity partner and promotes investments. In 1991 Mexico took an important step in this direction by allowing the present value of capital consumption allowances to be deducted in the initial year of investment.

Special features of developing countries (such as market power vested in few firms, a large number of firms with large accumulated tax losses, ownership and control by foreign investors with access to foreign tax credits against home tax liability, credit rationing, and exchange controls) severely constrain the effect of tax incentives in stimulating investment.

Many institutional features of developing countries cloud the effectiveness of fiscal incentives for investment. For example, if firms enjoy full market power and have the potential to shift the tax burden fully forward, taxes will not affect the rental rate of capital and hence will be ineffective. Investment incentives are also likely to discourage investment by firms with large accumulated losses because the income against which these losses can be written off will be reduced. Credit rationing represents another feature of developing countries that limits the usefulness of investment incentives. In many developing countries credits are allocated by the central bank to qualifying firms, and prioritization of credits tends to determine both the pattern and the size of investment. For credit-constrained firms, investment activities will be largely unaffected by explicit investment incentives. Similar arguments also apply to the effects of other forms of intervention, including the protection and allocation of scarce foreign exchange. In such circumstances, investment incentives largely lead to a reallocation of rents rather than being instruments that have a marginal effect on investment behavior. Finally, as discussed earlier, foreign tax regimes can have important influences on inward FDI.

The credibility of the tax regime is of fundamental importance to the effectiveness of tax incentives.

If the tax regime is inconsistent, a policy may have less effect because it is seen as temporary. Thus incentives that are more difficult to reverse, such as investment tax credits or accelerated capital consumption allowances, may stimulate more investment than would reductions in tax rates. Investors working under a noncredible tax regime seek expected rates of return considerably higher than the risk-free discount rate.

Tax incentives matter for domestic and foreign investment, but elimination of tax and nontax disincentives (lack of infrastructure, legal framework, and institutions) matters even more.

This theme is repeatedly stressed by multinational corporations. For example, infrastructure deficiencies and regulatory regimes in Mexico and Pakistan and the tariff regime in Malaysia were seen as serious barriers to capital formation. Legal institutions also matter. Increases in the level of wealth and collateral in an economy can greatly reduce the costs of asymmetric information. Increases in collateral reduce the risks faced by lenders. Entrepreneurs are less likely to undertake poor projects when they must risk more of their own wealth. Government policies that increase the ability of individuals to collateralize wealth—for example, by promoting property rights and establishing a legal system that allows the transfer of collateral at low cost—can increase the chances that potentially successful projects will receive financing. In addition to increasing the collateral of an entrepreneur, the ability to earn high rates of return increases the opportunity cost of undertaking projects with low expected returns. In the absence of any comparative advantage in allocating credit, government attention to the basic infrastructure that reduces the costs of obtaining information and enforcing contracts is likely to better assist the efficient allocation of credit.

Special measures may be needed to attract FDI.

Tax policies to encourage FDI require that taxation in the host country discriminate among various foreign investors on the basis of the tax regime for outward investment available in the home countries. But different corporate income tax rates based on the nationality of the company, even if feasible, would not be desirable because they would place an uneven tax burden on similar economic activities. Different withholding taxes on repatriations (with no taxation of reinvested earnings) could be a feasible alternative. But unless such a policy were extended to domestic capital as well, it would discriminate against reinvestment by domestic corporations and perhaps even encourage reincorporation of domestic corporations as subsidiaries of foreign dummy corporations.

Thus for most developing countries, a desirable first step of an effective investment promotion strategy is to develop a climate of business confidence by instituting sustainable economic policies and eliminating tax and nontax disincentives to invest. Avoiding frequent tax changes is an element of this strategy. Once business confidence is restored and the credibility of the regime is no longer in question, consideration can be given to well-targeted tax policy interventions.

References

Auerbach, Alan. 1979. "The Optional Taxation of Heterogeneous Capital." *Quarterly Journal of Economics* 93 (November): 589–612.

———. 1983. "Taxation, Corporate Financial Policy and the Cost of Capital." *Journal of Economic Literature* 21 (September): 905–40.

Bernstein, Jeffrey, and Ishaq Nadiri. 1987. "Corporate Taxes and Incentives and the Structure of Production: A Selected Survey." In Jack M. Mintz and Douglas Purvis, eds., *The Impact of Taxation on Business Activity.* Kingston, Ont., Can.: Queen's University, John Deutsch Institute for the Study of Economic Policy.

DeLong, J. Bradford, and Lawrence H. Summers. 1991. "Equipment Investment and Economic Growth." *Quarterly Journal of Economics* 106 (2): 445–502.

Feldstein, Martin. 1982. "Inflation, Tax Rules, and Investment: Some Econometric Evidence." *Econometrica* 50 (4): 825–62.

Hulten, Charles R., and Robert A. Klayman. 1988. "Investment Incentives in Theory and Practice." In Henry J. Aaron, Harvey Galper, and Joseph A. Pechman, eds., *Uneasy Compromise: Problems of a Hybrid Income-Consumption Tax.* Washington, D.C.: Brookings Institution.

Scott, Maurice FitzGerald. 1989. *A New View of Economic Growth.* Oxford, U.K.: Clarendon Press.

PERSPECTIVES ON THE ROLE OF INVESTMENT INCENTIVES IN DEVELOPING COUNTRIES

Robin W. Boadway and Anwar Shah

THE PURPOSE OF this chapter is to survey the role of investment incentives in developing countries. By no means unique to developing countries, such incentives are also widely used in industrial countries, and they take a wide variety of forms. Yet, some forms of incentives are especially common in developing countries, as are some unique institutional features. It is therefore worthwhile to address their role in developing countries separately. Given the number and types of developing countries, and their special economic features, we cannot do justice in a single chapter to the detailed problems of each. Thus we choose a more general perspective and focus on what we take to be a few key characteristics and effects of investment incentives used in developing countries.

We begin with a broad survey of some of the general design issues in applying investment incentives in developing countries. The more common instruments used for encouraging investment in these countries are presented. We then spend some time discussing the economic rationale for providing special investment incentives rather than simply letting the unfettered market determine the allocation of resources to investment. The issue is one of examining the possible sources of capital market failure in developing countries and asking whether these can form a basis for encouraging investment. Some of these reasons reflect special features of developing countries, including problems of information and uncertainty, the important role investment plays in the growth process, and the heavy reliance on foreign-owned capital. Particular attention is paid to outlining the role of the corporate tax, because many incentives are delivered through that tax system.

We then turn to a discussion of how to measure the effect of investment incentives. This involves adapting the methodology of marginal effective tax rates to the institutional setting of developing countries. Some of the problems encountered in providing investment incentives there become clear in this discussion. These include particularly the problems of providing investment incentives in economies in which a good deal of investment takes place in risky activities and in firms that are in a loss position, and in economies in which foreign capital is important. We illustrate some of these problems with a case study involving the Malaysian tax system.

Finally, we provide a summary of the recent empirical work that has been done to estimate the effectiveness of investment incentives in developing countries.

Investment Incentives in Developing Countries: Types of Instruments and Frequency of Use

As outlined below, a wide variety of types of investment incentives are used in developing countries, and they might be expected to have different effects. Yet, a number of common issues affect many of these incentives and we repeatedly refer to them in the analysis to follow. The purpose of this section is to highlight at the beginning some of the more important of these issues and to discuss their relevance for the evaluation of investment incentives.

Some Issues of General Relevance

The first of these issues concerns whether or not the incentives are "discretionary" or "automatic" policy instruments. Discretionary investment incentives are those that are implemented on a case-by-case basis by administrative decision. There may, of course, be general rules that the administrators follow. The decision as to whether to award an incentive, however, is contingent on administrative approval. Automatic incentives, in contrast, are those that are available to any firms meeting certain stated objective criteria. Examples include type and size of investment, location of firm, ownership of firm, and profitability of firm.

Economists stress the advantages of using automatic policy instruments whenever possible. Such instruments reduce the uncertainty attached to incentives, reduce the planning time for investments, and reduce the possibility that noneconomic considerations or favoritism will enter the decision. Presumably they also reduce the costs of administering the incentives. It could be argued, however, that discretion allows the administrators to be more selective in awarding grants and thereby increases the cost-effectiveness of the grants by screening out inframarginal projects.

In practice, the line between discretionary and automatic incentives may not be clear-cut. The criteria for eligibility may themselves require administrative decisions, the more so the more selective the incentives are intended to be. Furthermore, administrators will rarely be completely informed about whether the firms using incentives are fully entitled to use them. Enforcement and compliance will necessarily require some administrative participation. Therefore incentives will differ only in the degree to which they are nondiscretionary. We take the general view that less administrative discretion is a good thing.

Another general issue concerns the treatment of tax loss firms, that is, firms that have negative taxes owing. Many incentives operate through the tax system and ultimately influence the firm by affecting its tax liabilities. Furthermore, many of the firms eligible for incentives are in a nontaxpaying position, if only temporarily. In fact, these may be precisely the types of firms for which incentives would be most socially beneficial. For firms that are in a nontaxpaying position, the incentives will increase the size of "negative tax liabilities" held by the firm. It is important to know whether these negative tax liabilities are treated symmetrically to positive ones, that is, whether they actually give rise to tax refunds or their equivalent.

Fully symmetric treatment of positive and negative tax liabilities would require refundability of all negative tax liabilities. Failing that, unlimited carryforward (and backward) with full interest would be equivalent in present-value terms, although it would give rise to a different cash flow for the firm. The appropriate interest cost to ensure present-value equivalence would be problematic, however, for firms that faced credit constraints on capital markets. Partial loss-offsetting measures might involve the carrying forward and backward of losses but probably only for a limited time period and without interest. Compared with full loss offsetting, this would be similar to the firm's giving an interest-free loan to the government. Loss-offsetting provisions may differ from one component of the firm's tax base to another. For example, depreciation allowances may be taken at the discretion of the firm, which is equivalent to extending the carryforward of losses arising from this type of capital cost. Also, some types of investment incentives, such as investment tax credits, might be refundable even though other components of tax liabilities are not.

Loss offsetting is important for ensuring that the tax system applies uniformly across different types of firms. The sorts of firms that are in a negative tax liability position would generally include small, growing firms; firms engaged in large, risky projects; and perhaps declining firms. Furthermore, the small, growing ones might be in a cash-constrained position, given their relatively large investments and given the fact that they may not have established a reputation for themselves on the capital market. The absence of full loss offsetting would tend to discriminate against risky investments, precisely those that might have a high expected return. It would discriminate against small, growing firms that might already have a high cost of capital because of imperfections in the capital market. Anything short of full refundability would serve to worsen their already tight cash flow position. The absence of refundability might also postpone the exit from the market of firms that are declining. They have an incentive to stay in business to write off as many of their capital costs as they can. Finally, refundability will be important in cases in which the credibility of the government is questionable. In this situation, uncertainty about future government actions will cause firms to discount future funds from the government in relation to those received up front. Thus refundable investment tax credits will be more valuable to the firm than the equivalent present value of funds received, say, through future tax reductions.

A third important issue is the distinction between temporary and permanent incentives. Some incentives may be introduced for a limited length of time, or they may be available to the firm for only a fixed period. In these cases, the incentive may have as its primary effect a change in the timing of the firm's investment rather than a change in the level of its capital stock in the long run. In some circumstances, however, a temporary incentive to invest may have a permanent effect on the fortunes of the firm. This will be the case if there are capital market imperfections that discriminate against young firms starting up (for example, infant industry arguments for protection).

Incentives may differ in the degree to which they are selective rather than general. Selectivity may be according to various criteria, such as type of asset, type of sector, ownership, and location. In the absence of market inefficiencies, selectivity of incentives will introduce distortions in the allocation of capital across sectors.

One final consideration that is important in evaluating investment incentives is the extent to which capital markets are open to the rest of the world so capital can flow freely into and out of the country. Typically, developing economies are capital importers and rely heavily on foreign investment. The tax treatment of foreign investment will influence the incentive for foreign firms to invest in the host (developing) country. Furthermore, foreign investors typically are faced with tax liabilities in their home country and have opportunities to invest in alternative locations. This means that the interaction of the host country tax system with that of the home country one will be important in determining the effectiveness of investment incentives. For example, under a system of foreign tax crediting (in which the foreign investor receives a credit in the home country for taxes paid abroad), investment incentives could simply reduce foreign tax credits of firms operating in the host country and have little or no effect on the actual incentive to invest.

Types of Instruments to Encourage Investment

Developing countries have traditionally given a wide variety of special preferences to encourage investment broadly or in specific sectors and regions. The most typical of these incentives include tax rates differentiated over time, size, location, ownership, and activity of firm; accelerated capital consumption allowances; and investment and employment tax credits and allowances. These and other incentives are briefly discussed in the following paragraphs. Further details are provided in the appendix to this chapter.

PREFERENTIAL TAX RATES. Certain types of firms may receive lower tax rates than others, either on a temporary or on a permanent basis. The use of preferential tax rates is a blunt instrument for providing investment incentives, because the incentive does not vary with the amount of investment undertaken. Furthermore, the absence of full loss-offsetting provisions often renders the incentive relatively ineffective. Also, if marginal tax rates are already low, the incentive effect is minimal.

An extreme case of this is a tax holiday, whereby a firm is tax free for a given period of time. Tax holidays may be awarded on a discretionary basis to firms in designated industries or areas. Firms awarded tax holidays are typically those just starting up, and are referred to as "pioneer firms." The tax holiday is a widely used incentive in developing countries and is currently practiced in Bangladesh, Brazil, Côte d'Ivoire, Lesotho, Malaysia, Morocco, Pakistan, and Thailand. Of these, Morocco and Lesotho have extended tax holiday provisions to foreign investors as well.

INVESTMENT TAX CREDITS AND ALLOWANCES. Under an investment tax credit, companies in a specific industry, or more generally, are allowed as a deduction against their tax liabilities a fraction of expenditure on new additions to physical or research and development (R&D) capital stock or employment. Tax credits can be granted for specific activities and, by providing a direct subsidy, can be more effective than rate reductions. (An investment allowance is similar in effect to a tax credit except that it is a deduction from the taxable income for corporate tax purposes.) Their effectiveness depends on whether they are refundable and therefore provide cash up front to the firm, and, if not, the extent to which they can be carried forward. The less generous the loss-offsetting provisions, the less effective the incentive effect will be for firms in a loss position in relation to others. These include firms that are small and growing and firms that are engaged in risky activities. Tax credits may be targeted to specific types of investments, both tangible and intangible, and they may be discretionary or automatic. They may reduce future depreciation allowances. In the case of foreign subsidiaries, a relevant consideration is whether or not the credits are offset by the system of foreign tax crediting. To the extent that they are, they may represent at least partly a transfer of tax revenues to foreign treasuries. An investment allowance is a deduction from the taxable income for corporate tax purposes. Greece, Malaysia, Mexico, and Pakistan permit investment tax credits. Turkey provides 100 percent investment allowance for priority industries and scientific research and development.

FAST WRITE-OFFS. Certain types of costs may obtain a fast write-off. Most commonly these are depreciation (capital consumption) allowances that can be accelerated (initial allowance) or can even be expensed. Intangible investments are also commonly expensed (R&D, exploration, advertising, and so on.) In principle, any type of cost could be accelerated, including financing (interest) costs. Loss-offsetting provisions are also relevant here. Certain types of write-offs may be "elective" in the sense that the firm has some discretion as to when to claim them. This is particularly attractive to firms in a loss position when carryforward is limited. Some countries combine elective depreciation allowances with tax holidays. Countries with accelerated depreciation schemes include, among others, Brazil, which allows 50 or 100 percent depreciation in the first year for approved investment projects, and Malaysia, which allows qualified expenditure to be fully expensed in the first two years.

FINANCING INCENTIVES. The government may provide incentives that reduce the cost of financing investments. A cash grant would be analogous to a tax credit in this regard. The cash granted may come with various strings attached. The government may provide financial assistance through an investment fund. It may provide cheap loans, or it may provide public sector equity funds with the associated equity participation of the government. Financing assistance may also be provided through the tax system. The flow-through of tax write-offs to shareholders will be beneficial to firms in a loss position. Various methods of imputation of corporate taxes to the shareholders will reduce their cost of finance. Still, this is not so much the giving of an incentive as a removal of a source of double taxation.

EMPLOYMENT INCENTIVES. Although most incentives are directed toward investment, there can be incentives for employment of labor as well. These could be employment or wage subsidies or tax credits. Manpower training programs could also be used. Mexico is an example of a country that allows an employment tax credit.

GENERAL POLICY INSTRUMENTS. In addition to policy instruments directed specifically at certain types of activities, more general policies will affect aggregate investment and its allocation among various uses. Examples include indirect taxes, tariffs, and the establishment of free-trade zones. Investments will also be influenced by infrastructure provided by the public sector, such as industrial parks, roads, and education.

TECHNOLOGY TRANSFER. Governments may have certain provisions that affect the transfer of technology from foreign firms. These include equity participation requirements and the tax treatment of royalties and licenses. As well, the threat of expropriation and uncertainty about future tax policies will influence the incentive for foreign investment. More generally, the existence of uncertainty makes cash up front more valuable than incentives providing benefits in the future.

The Economic Rationale for Investment Incentives

As we have seen, investment incentives typically operate through the tax system either directly or indirectly. That is, they ultimately reduce the tax liabilities faced by the firm, especially those accruing under the corporation income tax. A proper evaluation of incentives requires first an understanding of the role of corporate taxes. We begin this section by discussing the rationale for corporate taxes and, given that rationale, their optimal design. This discussion is followed by one on the efficiency of capital markets and possible sources of market failure. We go on to discuss, in light of the latter, the case for further intervention in the form of investment incentives.

The Role of Corporation Income Taxes

Virtually all countries levy direct taxes on corporations. Ultimately, these taxes will be borne by households, so one might think that it would be ideal to tax households directly rather than indirectly through their ownership of corporations. The essential question to address is why corporate taxes are needed at all, given the alternative of taxing households directly by personal taxes (or indirectly by sales taxes on their consumption purchases). Posing the question this way makes it clear that the corporate income tax is essentially supplementary to the personal income tax. It owes its existence to the fact that for various reasons an ideal tax system cannot be achieved by personal taxation alone. It is useful to distinguish three main reasons for having a corporate tax alongside personal and commodity taxes. We refer to these as the withholding function, the rent-collecting function, and the revenue-raising function. We discuss each in turn.

THE WITHHOLDING FUNCTION. One way to view the corporate income tax is as a device for withholding at source the equity capital income generated in the corporate sector. This is the conventional function of the corporate tax, at least in industrial countries. The need for withholding arises because corporate source income would not otherwise be fully taxed on accrual by the system of personal taxes. There are two distinct types of reasons for this, each of which might call for a different type of corporate tax when considered in isolation. The corporate tax is called on to satisfy both types of withholding functions simultaneously, however, and that makes its design more problematic and judgmental. The two types of withholding are withholding against resident shareholders and withholding against foreign shareholders.

Withholding against resident shareholders. Most personal tax systems are designed with the intention of taxing income on as comprehensive a basis as possible. Among other things, this would require taxing capital gains as they accrue. It seems difficult to do so, however; capital gains are typically taxed on realization, if at all. This implies that asset owners can postpone tax liabilities by not realizing capital gains as they accrue. One of the main ways they can do this is by retaining and reinvesting income within a corporation rather than paying it out. A corporation income tax provides a way for taxing at source equity income earned within the corporation.

If this were the only role for the corporate tax, the design would be straightforward. It would need only to be applied to retained earnings. Its rate might be the top personal rate of shareholders, and the corporate tax payments might be viewed as taxes collected on behalf of the shareholders. This means that the corporate and personal tax systems ought to be integrated so that shareholders are credited with the taxes that have been collected on their behalf. One way to do this might be simply to credit the corporation with the corporate taxes that had previously been paid on funds that are paid out to shareholders. This is referred to as the dividend-paid deduction system, and it would seem to represent perfect imputation. Unfortunately, as we shall see below, this system is not likely to be suitable in an open economy. A system of imputation, such as a dividend tax credit operating at the shareholder level, is required.

The imputation method becomes somewhat imperfect if the corporate tax itself is not applied uniformly. For example, if loss offsetting is imperfect, the effective tax rate paid by the firm will differ from the statutory rate. Suppose the imputation is achieved by a dividend tax credit system applied at a constant rate to all shareholders. If the rate is appropriate for firms that pay full taxes, it will be imperfect for shareholders of tax-loss firms. Different firms, however, may face different tax liabilities as a matter of government policy. In this case, if the imputation system were to reflect the differences in tax treatment of firms, it would essentially undo the preferential treatment intended for the firm by the corporate tax. This would argue in favor of a uniform dividend tax credit system.

A fully integrated system would apply a dividend tax credit at a rate equal to the corporate tax rate, which in turn is set equal to the top personal rate. Let the corporate tax rate be u and the top personal rate be t. If the dividend tax credit rate is d, the effective personal tax rate on dividends received by shareholders in the top bracket is given by $r = (t - d)/(1 - d)$. This is because the dividend tax credit system works as follows: When a dollar of dividends is paid out, taxable income is grossed up by the dividend tax credit rate and so becomes $1/(1 - d)$. This is taxed at the shareholder tax rate t, and a dividend tax credit at the rate d is allowed. A fully integrated system sets $u = t = d$ (so $r = 0$). If capital gains are not taxed, even on realization, this ensures that corporate equity income is taxed once and only once in the hands of the shareholders for those in the top bracket.[1] For those in the lower tax brackets, the system withholds more than required but eventually gives credit when profits are paid out. These shareholders will effectively be giving a small interest-free loan to the government. Thus the imputation system will not be perfect. Because most shareholders are close to the top marginal bracket, however, this should not be a great problem.

In practice, the system may not be fully integrated as described above for two reasons. First, because the corporate tax must fulfill more functions than this one of withholding against resident shareholders, the corporate tax rate may not be set equal to the top personal rate. The dividend tax credit should then be equal to the corporate tax rate. If the latter is set below the personal tax rate, there will still be some small incentive to retain funds within the corporation and vice versa. Second, a capital gains tax may be imposed on realized capital gains. If it is, some personal taxation will implicitly be applied to retained earnings, although at a lower effective rate. This means that the dividend tax credit can be set at less than the fully integrated rate.

Some domestic saving in corporations will be done in a form that is sheltered from the personal tax altogether. The most common example is saving in pension funds. There would be no need to withhold taxes against income accruing to pension funds, but in practice it is impossible for the corporate tax to treat such shareholders differently from taxable ones. This implies that full imputation should apply to these funds, although that is not often done in practice.

Finally, recall that the rationale for withholding against domestic shareholders was to tax capital income on accrual that would otherwise escape full taxation at the personal level. This presumes that comprehensive income is the chosen personal tax base. Many economists would argue that personal consumption has advantages over income as a direct tax base.[2] In fact, many tax systems that purport to tax income come closer to taxing consumption, given the number of assets that are sheltered, such as pension funds, housing and other consumer durables, human capital accumulation, insurance, and cash balances. If countries were to adopt a full consumption tax system, this withholding rationale would disappear. Even so, a corporate tax may still be needed to fulfill some of the other roles discussed below. If that role were the withholding role discussed next, a system of imputation would still be desired.

Withholding against foreign shareholders. Income accruing to foreign shareholders would also escape domestic personal taxation because the latter applies only to residents. If it is desired to tax foreign shareholders, a corporate tax could be used for this purpose (perhaps alongside withholding taxes). The ability to extract tax revenues from foreigners depends on the tax systems facing foreigners in their home countries. Specifically, if the host country into which the foreign capital is imported is small in relation to world capital markets, which is typically the case, taxes can be obtained from foreigners only to the extent that the taxes are creditable against tax liabilities in the home country. Otherwise, any attempt to tax foreigners will result in capital leaving the country until the rate of return before taxes rises to cover tax liabilities. Effectively, the tax is being shifted back to domestic factors of production. If host country taxes can be credited against home country tax liabilities, a pure tax transfer can be made from the home country treasury to that of the host country. Because this transfer is costless it should be fully exploited.

Typically, two sorts of capital income taxes are creditable. Pure withholding taxes are creditable to the extent specified by tax treaties. Many corporate tax systems also provide credits on taxes paid abroad. The credits are limited by the amount of home country tax liabilities, are calculated using the home country tax system, and are available when dividends are repatriated. In addition, full credit is usually available only on shares held in foreign-controlled affiliates, which accounts for most foreign direct investment. To exploit this tax transfer fully requires that the host tax system conform with the foreign one. If host country tax rates are too high, some foreign investment will be discouraged. If they are too low, the host country is forgoing costless tax transfer. Because most countries tax corporations on the basis of some notion of equity income, this is also the sensible tax base for host countries to adopt, despite the fact that for domestic withholding purposes only retained earnings need be taxed. It would not be possible for the corporate tax to apply differently to domestic and foreign firms because that type of discrimination, designed to exploit the tax transfer from foreigners selectively, would presumably result in the denial by host countries of full credit for taxes.

Note that this withholding role is conditional on the tax system of the host country offering full credits for taxes paid by its resident corporations abroad. This is equivalent to implementing the corporate tax on a full origin basis. If foreign tax systems offered only deductions for taxes paid abroad rather than credits, no tax transfer would be possible.[3] Any tax levied on capital income by the home country would be shifted back to domestic residents by induced flows of capital abroad. One of the great mysteries of corporate tax policy, and one that is the subject of current research, is why do creditor nations choose to use the origin principle for their corporate tax systems when by doing so they are simply inviting a tax transfer to debtor nations.

Given this second reason for withholding by use of the corporate tax, the question of integration with the personal tax becomes more contentious. Certainly one would not like to impute corporate taxes paid to foreign shareholders when dividends are paid out. To do so would simply undo the tax transfer that is the reason for taxing foreign firms in the first place. This essentially rules out the dividend-paid deduction mentioned above. Any integration would have to be done at the personal level, say, by a dividend tax credit, so that only domestic shareholders are affected. This mixing of the use of the origin basis for the corporate tax with the residence basis for the imputation makes the integration an imperfect policy device. In an open economy, the saving side of the domestic capital market is effectively segmented from the domestic investment side. In the aggregate, the two need not be equal; the rate of return is exogenously given and does not serve as a domestic market clearing price. This means that tax measures that apply at the personal level influence the saving side of the market, whereas measures applying to corporations influence the investment side. Given that imputation applies at the personal level and the corporate tax applies at the corporate level, integration effectively removes the tax on equity income at the personal level while leaving the corporate tax distortion intact. At the same time, interest income remains taxable at the personal level but deductible for the corporation. Thus households would prefer to hold equity, whereas firms would prefer debt financing. Integration cannot remove this distortion on capital markets. As argued in Boadway and Bruce (1992), where this analysis is developed in more detail, this makes the case stronger for taxing consumption rather than income at the personal level.

These problems would be avoided under a corporate tax system that allows deductions rather than credits for foreign taxes paid. In this case, the only withholding role for the corporate tax would be against domestic shareholders because it would no longer be possible to transfer taxes from the foreign treasury. Integration could be achieved at the corporate level by use of a dividend-paid deduction. In this way, foreign shareholders would be exempt from tax, and domestic shareholders would be taxed once on equity income. Interest and equity income would be treated on a par.

THE RENT-COLLECTING FUNCTION. The theoretical literature on taxation has stressed the desirability of taxing corporations in a nondistorting manner. The purpose of a nondistorting tax is to tax pure profits or rents. To do so, the tax base must correspond with rents or economic profits. Measuring pure profits is extremely difficult to do because it involves measuring all real imputed costs on an accrual basis, including true depreciation, asset depletion, costs of risk and finance, and so on. As is well known, however, the equivalent can be achieved in a feasible way by using a cash flow tax. Should a cash flow tax not be palatable because of the way it postpones the tax liabilities of the firm, any tax base that is equivalent in present-value terms will do. Boadway and Bruce (1984a) present an example of such a scheme that is flexible and easy to implement. If such a tax were to be used, no imputation would be desired because it would undo the purpose of the tax.

Although it is easy to see why economists would find a tax of the cash flow type attractive, it is not clear that it makes much sense as a base for a corporate tax. For one thing, a cash flow tax is not compatible with the withholding function, which is a main role of the corporate tax. For another, one should not confuse the rent-generating sector with the corporate sector. One would expect that a good portion of the latter would earn only a market rate of return. It might be better to target a rent tax to those sectors most susceptible to earning rents. A prime candidate would be the resource industries. Most countries already impose special taxes on them at least partly for the purpose of giving the public sector a share of the rents. It might be better to direct cash flow taxation specifically to those sectors rather than to the corporate sector as a whole. This would mean revising inefficient resource taxes such as severance taxes (royalties) and other levies that do not properly account for costs.

One interesting phenomenon frequently observed in industrial countries is that corporate tax systems often favor precisely these industries. Special tax measures such as depletion allowances and the rapid write-off of exploration and development expenses imply that effective tax rates on resource industries (both marginal and average) are less than for other industries.

THE REVENUE-RAISING FUNCTION. In developing countries many taxes are costly to use in the administrative sense of compliance and enforcement, especially direct taxes. A good part of what should be included in income escapes taxation because of difficulties in detection and measurement. In these circumstances a tax on corporations may be a relatively efficient way to raise revenues because there are fewer taxpayers and evasion may be more difficult. The use of a corporate tax simply as a revenue-raising device alongside personal and indirect taxes might be reinforced if capital incomes are otherwise difficult to detect at the personal level. A corporate tax used for revenue-raising purposes presumably need not be integrated with the personal tax, although this means double taxation of capital income and the discouragement of saving and investment.

In an open economy the extent to which the corporate tax can be effective at raising revenue from capital owners is limited. As mentioned above, except to the extent that tax payments are credited abroad, a tax on foreign-owned capital imposed by a small economy will end up being shifted back to other, less mobile factors of production, such as labor, and will leave the economy with less capital. It may be more efficient to tax the immobile factors directly, if possible. Even if the economy is large enough to have some effect on its return to capital, say, because of country-specific risk, a corporate tax would not be useful in exploiting it. What the country wants to do in this case is to increase the amount of capital imported; this goal would be achieved by subsidizing capital, not taxing it. We return to this issue below in our discussion of investment incentives.

To summarize this discussion, the main reason for a corporate tax is withholding, both against domestic shareholders and against foreign-owned firms. A subsidiary reason might be simply to raise revenue in an economy in which no tax is perfect. Because the corporate tax cannot treat foreign firms differently from domestic ones, a common tax must satisfy all objectives. The withholding functions can best be satisfied by a tax on corporate equity income defined in a similar way to that of capital-exporting countries. Also, to take full advantage of foreign tax-crediting systems, the tax rate should be comparable to that used in creditor countries. An imputation system could be established, but it must be done through the personal tax (that is, on a residence basis). If there is full imputation, capital gains taxes are not necessary. Whether or not there is an imputation of corporate taxes at the personal level, the corporate tax will distort the investment side of the capital market and will leave firms with an incentive to finance by debt rather than by equity. This could be avoided only if all countries were to move from a system of foreign tax crediting to one of deductibility of foreign taxes. In this case, imputation would be better done by a dividend-paid deduction, and corporate taxes would effectively be levied on a residence basis. This system could be achieved if creditor nations moved unilaterally (and independently) to a system of deductions. What is unclear is why they have not done so already.

The Efficiency of Capital Markets

Investment incentives involve interfering with capital markets to encourage particular types of investment. The justification for this would seem to imply some sort of inefficiency in the way capital markets allocate investment. In this section we summarize the various sources of market failure on capital markets. This will serve as a basis for considering the rationale for investment incentives in the following section.

CAPITAL INCOME TAXES. We have already seen that in an open economy a corporate tax will impose an unavoidable distortion on investment, even if it is imposed optimally. This is part of the consequence of using the corporate tax as a withholding device both against foreigners and against domestic residents on their accrued capital income earned in corporations. In a closed economy this distortion could be avoided by reducing capital income tax rates. The extent of the distortion on capital markets would be determined by trading off the equity gains of taxing capital income with the efficiency costs of distorting investment. In an open economy the distortion arises partly because the corporate tax is being used to transfer funds from foreign treasuries to the domestic one. Because of tax-crediting arrangements, this does not affect the allocation of foreign-owned capital, but domestic capital accumulation is discouraged.

Investment incentives could represent an effective policy instrument only to the extent that they could be made to apply to domestically owned capital rather than foreign-owned capital. If they applied to the latter, they would serve only to reduce the tax transfer from foreign treasuries by reducing creditable tax liabilities. Also, tax measures operating on the personal tax side, such as imputation and tax sheltering, would have no effect on the investment distortion, although they would encourage saving.

DYNAMIC INEFFICIENCY. Inefficiency exists when it is possible to make some persons better off without making anyone worse off. The so-called fundamental theorems of welfare economics state that, under a set of conventional assumptions, (a) all competitive equilibriums will be efficient and (b) all efficient allocations can be supported by a competitive equilibrium. In a dynamic setting, this principle is applied to an economy evolving over an indefinite period of time. Dynamic inefficiency exists if it is possible to make one cohort better off without making any cohort worse off. The basic result stated in the literature is that a competitive allocation that is efficient in the static setting will be dynamically efficient unless the rate of return on capital is below the rate of growth of the economy into the indefinite future—that is, unless the economy is "overcapitalized." In a finite-horizon economy, or in an infinite-horizon one in which the rate of return on capital is at least as great as the rate of growth (or becomes so in the future), the two fundamental theorems of welfare economics apply.

Empirically, it would be virtually impossible to make the case that actual economies are dynamically inefficient, especially developing ones. Rates of return on capital (before taxes) seem to be well above rates of growth of modern economies. Furthermore, in principle, to know whether an economy is dynamically inefficient would require knowing the relation between the rate of growth and the rate of return on capital into the indefinite future, and that is clearly not possible. Thus it is difficult to base arguments for capital market failure on dynamic inefficiency. Moreover, even if dynamic inefficiency did exist, investment incentives would not be called for. On the contrary, dynamic inefficiency is associated with too much capital accumulation, so measures would have to be taken to reduce investment.

INTERGENERATIONAL EXTERNALITIES. A common form of market failure is externalities or public goods. Some economists have argued that saving for bequest purposes may have a positive externality associated with it.[4] They contend that part of saving is for bequests and this is motivated by altruism toward future generations. If each saver gets utility from the well-being of all members of future generations and not just their own heirs, saving will yield external benefits that are not taken into account by individuals. This will lead to too little saving or, equivalently, a market discount rate that is higher than the social discount rate. Government intervention to increase saving will be required.

Valid though this argument may be, it is not clear that it could be used to make a case for investment incentives, especially in an open economy. If the root of the problem is undersaving, the appropriate remedy would be to provide incentives for saving rather than for investment. In an open economy, in which the saving and investment sides of the markets are segmented, investment incentives will do little to increase saving, except through general equilibrium effects. They would primarily encourage investment financed by foreign capital inflows. A further difficulty is that if altruism does exist, measures to facilitate intergenerational transfers may be fairly ineffectual. As Barro (1974) has argued, attempts to make pure redistributive transfers among generations will be undone by rational households that have an intergenerational altruistic motive. Thus saving for future generations can be increased only by providing relative price incentives.

Related to the possibility of intergenerational externalities are intergenerational equity arguments. Some generations will be better off than others simply because of their date of birth. If one applied some intergenerational social welfare function, equity arguments may well call for a set of intergenerational redistributive transfers from better-off to less-well-off generations. Ramsey (1928) recognized this possibility long ago, and Eckstein (1957) made it operational. The simple idea is as follows: suppose that the growth rate of consumption (lifetime wealth) across generations is g, and the elasticity of lifetime utility with respect to wealth is ε. Suppose also that r is the rate of return on capital, n is the rate of growth of population, and α is the rate at which the social welfare function discounts per capita utilities across generations.[5] Then the optimal rate of growth of wealth across generations would be that for which $g\varepsilon = r - n - \alpha$. In the long run the economy should approach a steady state in which $r - n = \alpha$. Per capita consumption should be rising over time as long as $r - n > \alpha$, that is, as long as the economy is out of the steady state. The rate of approach to the steady state depends on the elasticity of the marginal utility of income, ε. The policy instrument for implementing the optimal policy in this case should be intergenerational transfers, not investment incentives.

Of course, the whole notion of optimal policy in this context is fraught with difficulties because it depends on social values that are not objectively given. Two dimensions of social value enter the determination of optimal policy. One is the degree of social discounting, α, which affects the steady state to which the economy should move in the long run. The other is the degree of intergenerational inequality aversion, ε, which affects the path to the long-run steady state. There is unlikely to be general agreement on what these should be, especially because some of the persons involved are not yet born.

EXTERNALITIES OF GROWTH. The above type of capital market failure involves externalities on the saving side of the market. Externalities may also occur on the supply side. Several economists have stressed the possible importance of externalities in the process of economic growth. For example, Romer (1986) has argued that capital accumulation generates external benefits (for example, technological improvements) to firms other than those undertaking the investment.[6] The results hark back to those of the growth theories of the 1960s, in which the rate of technological change was made endogenous and dependent on the rate of investment. They also bear some resemblance to the infant industry arguments of trade theory. In the context of growth theory, they are interesting because they can account for differences in the rate of growth of economies as well as differences in the levels of income achieved. To the extent that they are true, we would expect to see a correlation between rates of investment and rates of growth in per capita incomes.

Scott (1989) examined the causes of the rate of growth of output in pooled data on twenty-six period averages for ten developed countries (with nineteen of twenty-six observations for the United Kingdom, the United States, and Japan). He used an ordinary least-squares regression with the only explanatory variables the share of investment in output, the rate of growth of quality-adjusted employed labor force, and the ratio of output per quality-adjusted labor in nonresidential output—excluding agriculture—in the country to that in the United States in a base year (considered as a "catch-up" factor). He found that, for the sample as a whole, nearly half of the growth in nonresidential business output can be explained by changes in the share of investment. Scott further estimates that marginal social rates of return to investment in the United Kingdom (1951–73) and the United States (1948–73) exceeded the marginal private return by about seven percentage points, the former averaging 12.6 percent and the latter 5.3 percent. Taxation accounts for a third of this gap. Three other factors explain the rest of the gap: the "learning externality" (firms other than the firm undertaking the investment benefit disproportionately from increased opportunities), the "demand externality" (firms selling in imperfect markets receive lower marginal than average returns because of higher marginal selling costs), and "animal spirits" (a positive externality based on a tendency of firms to value increases in output by more than their value to shareholders); see Scott (1989: xlvi).

Because it is the act of investment per se that yields an externality, the appropriate course of action would be to implement measures that influence investment directly. Policies operating on the saving side will not be effective. This may be the strongest argument for investment incentives. Indeed, it might also be the argument for incentives for investment in human capital and R&D. For example, Lucas (1988) has argued that precisely the same sorts of externalities may be involved with human capital investment as others, such as Romer (1986), have analyzed for physical investment.

INCOMPLETE OR IMPERFECT CAPITAL MARKETS. Capital markets may not be perfectly functioning or complete for institutional reasons. Two examples of these reasons follow:

Liquidity constraints. Households or firms may be liquidity-constrained. If households are prevented from borrowing early in life against their future labor income, they will be forced to consume less than the desired amount, and aggregate saving will be higher.[7] Again, policies operating on the saving side of the market would be appropriate here rather than investment incentives.

Firms may be liquidity-constrained as well, especially, as noted above, young, growing firms. Corporate tax policies can be of some help here to the extent that they make cash available to firms that are strapped for funds. Because many such firms are in a negative tax liability position, full refundability of tax losses would be helpful. Refundable investment incentives would also offset the effects of liquidity constraints.

Incomplete markets for risk. Complete markets for the trading of risk require that the number of assets be at least as great as the number of possible states of nature (outcomes per asset). Given that the latter can be large, it is quite likely that such markets are incomplete. Furthermore, because government policy itself contributes to the risky environment in ways that cannot be foreseen, it would be difficult to insure against future government policies. By offering less than full loss offsetting, tax policy itself may contribute to the inefficiency in trading in risk. There is no particular reason why the government should be any better informed than the private sector, so it is not clear that the government can improve the efficiency of allocating risk except by making sure that tax policies do not distort it further.

One particular form of risk trading that the government may have a role in influencing is the sharing of risks across generations. Strictly speaking, this is not an efficiency argument but an equity argument. It may be analyzed precisely as an insurance problem, however, when cohorts are put behind the "veil of ignorance."[8] The argument goes as follows: some cohorts are luckier than others because of their date of birth. The larger the cohort of a person, the less well off will that person be because the group has lower wages in working periods, when labor is more plentiful, and lower capital incomes in retirement, when labor is scarcer. In addition to this demographic effect will be productivity differences and other shocks; business cycles, too, will have a different effect on some cohorts than others. Although risk is associated with when a particular person is born, it is "insurable" to society because the risks of being born at different times largely cancel out across different generations. There will be no market for insurance against time of birth, however, because such insurance would have to be acquired before the date of birth was known! Still, the possibility exists for the government to provide "social insurance" by a set of intergenerational transfers from those who are less lucky to those who are more lucky. The existence of such intergenerational transfers will naturally influence saving and investment behavior. Investment incentives per se, however, are not involved.

INFORMATION ASYMMETRIES. Different participants in the capital market may be differently informed. The most common case is that in which the profitability of an investment or a firm is better known to one agent than to others. For example, persons in the firm may know more about the prospects of the firm than outside investors. Or managers may know more than shareholders. These asymmetries in information will cause persons to behave differently from the way they would behave if they were perfectly informed. We are particularly interested in how investment is affected by asymmetries in information. The literature describes two sorts of asymmetries of information that affect investment: adverse selection and moral hazard. We discuss each in turn.

Adverse selection models. Adverse selection occurs when some characteristic of the firm, such as its quality, is known to the firm but not to outsiders. In this case it will be to the advantage of the high-quality firms to signal their quality by engaging in some activity that the lower-quality firms find costly to mimic. Originally, signaling models were used to explain why firms might prefer one financial structure over another, given that with full information the theorem of Modigliani and Miller (1958) implied that the financial structure was irrelevant. For example, Ross (1977) argued that if managers face a loss in welfare when their firms go bankrupt, managers of firms with low probabilities of bankruptcy can signal their quality by taking on more debt. Signaling models of the financial structure of firms typically take the level of investment as fixed. Their implication for investment can readily be inferred, however. Because signaling entails a cost if financial instruments are used, it will raise the cost of financing and thereby reduce the level of investment.

Investment per se may be used as a signal. For example, Miller and Rock (1985) consider a model in which higher-quality firms have higher cash flows; they argue that firms will signal their quality (cash flow) by the size of their net dividend, defined as the payout of dividends less the use of external funds. To prevent lower-quality firms from mimicking their behavior, they underinvest. Lower-quality firms can only mimic higher cash flows by taking funds away from investment. Williams (1988) obtains a similar underinvestment equilibrium by considering a model in which the firms solve for an optimal mix of costly signals. Myers and Majluf (1984) also obtain a signaling equilibrium in which profitable investments may be forgone to avoid taking on external financiers who can benefit from the existing (known) wealth of firms.

In all these cases of adverse selection, the fact that signaling is costly raises the cost of undertaking new investments and results in an equilibrium in which investment is below the full information level. This might be expected to give a prima facie rationale for encouraging investment, although the literature has not really addressed the issue. One problem is that the government is not likely to have any better information than the private sector. Any investment incentives will have to apply uniformly to all firms, both those of high quality and those of low quality.

There have, however, been some models in which overinvestment can result from adverse selection. For example, Heinkel and Zechner (1990) suggest that overinvestment can occur in the presence of adverse selection when securities are priced at the average, or expected, value. In such cases a firm with a project with a negative expected present value may be able to sell overvalued securities that more than compensate its equity holders for taking such a project. John and Senbet (1988) consider the case in which limited liability of equity holders induces overinvestment. Overinvestment is perhaps less plausible than underinvestment if only because firms always have investment options with nonnegative (zero) net present value available to them outside the firm. It is not clear how it could be in the interest of shareholders to undertake negative net present-value investments in the firm (that is, to overinvest) when zero present-value assets could always be obtained on the capital market.

Moral hazard models. The effects of moral hazard (or agency problems) for investment have been analyzed in two main contexts—conflicts of interest between equity holders and debt holders and between inside (sometimes owner-managers) and outside (sometimes new) equity holders. Several papers in the literature argue that agency problems are likely to lead to underinvestment. The classic papers are those by Myers (1977) and Jensen and Meckling (1976). Myers shows that a potential moral hazard problem exists between the firm (whose management is assumed to operate in the best interest of shareholders) and debt holders that can lead to underinvestment. The problem arises because the firm will raise capital for investment only if there is positive net present value to the existing shareholders. If the capital structure includes debt whose owners must be reimbursed before shareholders, new capital will be raised only if the returns are great enough to cover both the required repayment of debt and the required outlay for investment. This will lead to underinvestment because it would be efficient to undertake any investment with returns great enough to cover the outlay alone. The Jensen and Meckling paper is somewhat more general because it includes, in addition to the conflict between equity holders and debt holders, a conflict between insiders and outsiders. Managers who are fractional owners of the firm will want to consume too many perquisites because they receive all the benefits but bear only part of the cost. This possibility leads equity capital suppliers to pursue methods, such as monitoring and covenants, that induce optimal behavior from managers. These additional costs lead to lower levels of investment. Other papers in the literature have come to the same conclusion of underinvestment, including Jensen (1986) and Shleifer and Vishny (1986).

Darrough and Stoughton (1986) have included both adverse selection and moral hazard in the same model. The adverse selection involves an unknown quality of manager, whereas the moral hazard is the manager's unobservable effort. The equilibrium involves an optimal tradeoff by the owner-manager among excess risk incurred, effort provided, and communication of information. In making such a tradeoff, the owner-manager uses an optimal mix of debt and equity financing to shed risk, which leads to real agency costs that again reduce investment.

INTERNATIONAL TAX COMPETITION. From a national perspective, there may be gains from attracting capital from the rest of the world. In the literature, policies for attracting capital from other countries are often treated as being purely strategic in the sense that inflows of foreign investment will reduce the domestic rate of return and cause part of the burden of the taxes on the investment to be exported.[9] Alternatively, if there are rents associated with investments, governments will have a private incentive to reduce the tax on rents to attract more capital and thus generate more domestic rents.[10] Finally, terms-of-trade effects may be associated with capital inflows, as has been stressed in the trade literature.[11] In each of these cases, wasteful (beggar-thy-neighbor) tax competition will be the result. Investment incentives are obviously the prime policy instrument for attracting foreign investment into a country. As mentioned, their effectiveness is contingent on foreign tax-crediting systems that do not merely cause them to transfer tax revenues abroad.

Information asymmetries may also characterize international capital flows. Thus foreign investors may not have full information about which countries are high-profit countries and which are not. This is especially true if there is some uncertainty about future government policies. In this case, countries with high returns may want to "signal" their quality by offering special incentives to potential investors. Bond and Samuelson (1986) have used this as an argument for tax holidays in developing countries, a phenomenon that appears to be quite widespread. Because much of the uncertainty about investment returns in developing countries might come from uncertainty about future government policies and their effect on after-tax cash flows, incentives that improve cash flows up front would probably be the most effective signals. It is not clear that tax holidays fall into this category, especially when marginal effective tax rates are low to begin with, as discussed below. Refundable investment incentives, such as investment tax credits, would be more effective.

DISTORTIONS ON OTHER MARKETS. So far our discussion has been entirely about market failure on capital markets. In developing economies, however, other markets may be significantly distorted; such distortions may be relevant in evaluating the effects of investment incentives. Two markets in particular are liable to be distorted: labor markets and foreign exchange markets. The literature on project evaluation in developing countries deals largely with the issue of investment criteria when there are distortions in these markets.[12] On the basis of first principles (that is, when demanders and suppliers face different prices because of taxes on imperfectly functioning markets), we know that distortions should be dealt with directly in the markets involved. Where this is not possible, however, their implications for investment decisions should be dealt with on a case-by-case basis. Some general results that may be relevant to investment incentives are given below for labor market distortions.

The efficiency implications of labor market distortions depend on the nature of the distortion. Labor market distortions, most of which show up as unemployment, can take several forms. Unemployment may be frictional and a result of the costly search process observed in labor markets. In this case inefficiencies may result from search externalities (Diamond 1981), and a case can be made for subsidizing search—say, through unemployment insurance schemes. Unemployment may be structural, resulting from the adjustment of the economy to shocks of productivity, terms of trade, shifting tastes, and so on. In this case, as shown by Mussa (1978), it is not obvious that the public sector can do any better than the private sector in adjusting to change. Unemployment may be temporary, as modeled in the implicit contract literature (Azariadis 1975; Baily 1974; Feldstein 1976). Temporary unemployment may be exacerbated by government schemes, such as unemployment insurance. Finally, there are efficiency wage types of arguments for unemployment, in which wages are set above the market clearing level to deter shirking or voluntary turnover, both of which involve costs to firms. As Shapiro and Stiglitz (1984) have shown, efficiency wages cause unemployment inefficiencies that can be addressed by wage subsidies, at least to those sectors subject to the problem.

In the context of developing countries, unemployment has often been modeled as a dual economy phenomenon arising from an exogenously given high wage in the urban sector with unemployment as a migration equilibrium device. Harberger (1971) has argued convincingly in the context of this model that the market wage and the shadow wage are identical in the urban sector and that therefore no special employment incentives are called for.[13] Once the wage rate is made endogenous, however—say, by an efficiency wage argument—the case for employment subsidies reappears.[14] Countering this are the theoretical arguments against efficiency wages as a source of unemployment. For example, Carmichael (1985) has argued that efficiency wages would not be necessary as a worker discipline device if workers could be required to post bonds (explicitly or implicitly) when hired.

In an efficiency wage context in which employment subsidies are not available for whatever reason, investment subsidies may prove to be a useful second-best instrument for increasing employment. For example, efficiency wages may be relatively more important in capital-intensive industries. If so, investment incentives may be a more selective instrument for dealing with the problem than employment incentives. If this is the rationale for investment incentives, it would call for permanent incentives rather than short-run ones so as to raise the level of employment permanently. Of course, investment incentives would not be fully efficient because they would cause firms to substitute capital for labor.

TIME INCONSISTENCY IN GOVERNMENT POLICY. A key feature of investment is its intertemporal nature. Capital invested at one period of time yields returns into the future. To the extent that investment is irreversible, capital, once acquired, becomes a quasi-fixed factor. This gives rise to a well-known problem of time inconsistency in government policy. A far-sighted government that is planning its future tax policies would naturally want to take into consideration the effect that future taxes would have on current investment decisions and design them accordingly. If current governments cannot commit future ones to a predetermined set of tax policies, however, the quasi-fixed nature of accumulated capital stocks will provide an incentive for future governments to renege on those tax policies. In particular, there will be an incentive to try to tax "old capital," whose return now takes the form of a quasi rent.

If the government is unable to commit future governments to a tax policy, and if decisionmakers correctly anticipate that this is the case, the result will be a rational expectations equilibrium in which the inability to commit is taken into account by all persons. This result has been analyzed in the literature in various guises (for example, Bond and Samuelson 1989a; Chamley 1986; Fischer 1980). The general result is the no-commitment equilibrium, in which capital tax rates are higher and investment is lower than in the full-commitment (optimal tax) equilibrium.

Such a result has been thought to be a particular problem for government policy in the case of foreign firms operating in developing countries, presumably both because foreign investment is especially important in developing countries and because foreign investors in these countries might have less direct influence on government policy than domestic firms. The phenomenon is more widespread than tax policy. Expropriation is another way in which future governments can capture the quasi rents of foreign investors. This has been analyzed by Eaton and Gersovitz (1981). More generally, the incentive to renege on foreign debt is another example of time inconsistency in developing countries. In all cases, the result is likely to be underinvestment, perhaps of a significant amount.

The Role of Investment Incentives

We are now in a position to summarize the arguments for using investment incentives as policy instruments. The various arguments will also suggest some principles of design for investment incentives.

OFFSETTING THE CORPORATE TAX DISTORTION. We have mentioned that in an open economy the corporate tax will impose a distortion on domestic investment if it is used as a withholding device. This will be the case regardless of whether an imputation system is in effect for domestic residents. The distortion will apply only on domestic-owned capital as long as the corporate tax rate does not exceed that which can be credited abroad. This suggests that investment incentives that apply at source to domestically owned capital will offset the corporate tax distortion.

The difficulty with using investment incentives for this purpose is that either they should be applied to domestic investment alone or, if applied on foreign investment, they should be such as not to reduce the foreign tax credit. Otherwise, much of the force of the incentive as it applies to foreign investment will be dissipated as a tax transfer to foreign treasuries. It is likely that foreign countries would view a country's selective imposition of an incentive on domestically owned firms as discriminatory and would disallow the normal foreign tax credit. It is not clear, however, how investment incentives that would not reduce the foreign tax credit could be applied on foreign firms. Thus it is not clear that investment incentives could do much to eliminate the unavoidable distortion of the corporate tax without undoing the withholding purpose of the tax in the first place.

One imperfect way in which a country might eliminate this distortion would be to target investment incentives to specific sectors—in particular, those that are domestically owned to a relatively high degree. Such targeting would minimize the tax transfer abroad without at the same time appearing discriminatory. At the same time it would be distortionary because it would make the tax distortion different in different industries. Furthermore, if preferential treatment were desired in the first place, it would be more sensible simply to have differential corporate tax rates across sectors, with higher rates in those sectors in which foreign ownership is the highest. In other words, the investment incentive should take the form of reduced tax rates.

ATTRACTING FOREIGN INVESTMENT. Related to the elimination of the tax distortion is the desire to attract foreign investment because of its net benefits, such as the increase in tax base, the generation of employment, the transfer of technology, and, where possible, the strategic exploitation of terms of trade and rates of return on capital. Again, the ability to do this is limited by the extent to which investment incentives applying on foreign investment can actually affect the behavior of foreign firms rather than simply transferring tax revenues abroad. If the investment incentives can be applied in a way that does not affect the foreign tax credit, then foreign investment can be attracted and all of its benefits (including the exploitation of foreign treasuries) can be achieved. It is unlikely, however, that this can be done.

It may still be possible for a country to attract foreign investment using investment incentives even though they reduce the foreign tax credit. Because foreign tax crediting is not instantaneous but occurs only when dividends are repatriated, the exploitation of foreign treasuries cannot be perfect. The existence of tax deferral implies that the domestic tax system will have a marginal effect on investment financed by the retained earnings of the firm even if foreign firms have not fully exploited their foreign tax credits.[15] Thus investment incentives will have some effect in attracting foreign investment, although it will be at the expense of some tax transfer forgone when the earnings are repatriated. Once again, the way to deal with the offsetting effect of investment incentives on the transfer of revenues from foreign treasuries is to set the corporate tax rate in the first place so as to achieve the appropriate tradeoffs among the distorting effect of the corporate tax, the induced inflow of foreign investment, and the tax transfer from foreign treasuries. The setting of the tax rate will vary from country to country. Presumably it will not necessarily be optimal to mimic the foreign tax system. Instead there will be an incentive to set the domestic tax rate lower than that of the home countries of investing firms.

Because the imperfection of the foreign tax transfer is a result of the deferral of foreign tax liabilities until the repatriation of dividends, tax incentives might well be based on retained earnings specifically. In other words, the corporate tax system might apply differentially to dividends. Unfortunately, this strategy conflicts with the domestic withholding role that involves taxing retained earnings to prevent shareholders from postponing taxes by keeping their funds within the corporation. To the extent that capital income is taxed at the personal level, it will not be desirable to treat retained earnings preferentially in order to improve the withholding properties against foreigners.

INFANT INDUSTRY ARGUMENTS. To the extent that infant industry arguments are valid, temporary investment incentives may be an effective device for assisting firms just starting up. From the point of view of instrument design, investment incentives will be superior to, say, tariff protection. To be effective such investment incentives must be designed to be of specific use to small, growing firms. Many of these firms are in a nontaxpaying position and may be involved in risky projects. They may also be strapped for funds because capital markets are characterized by asymmetric information such that creditors cannot tell good prospects from bad ones. These considerations would seem to imply that investment incentives should provide funds up front to young firms and that refundability is a necessary feature. As we discuss later, reduced tax rates or temporary tax holidays may not have the required preferential effect. If marginal tax rates are low to begin with, reductions in the tax rate will not provide much incentive at the margin. If there is not full loss offsetting, it may provide no incentive. The benefit of tax rate reductions may also occur too far into the future to be of much help to liquidity-constrained firms. Measures that provide funds up front, such as investment tax credits, would be much more effective, although only if one of their features is refundability. To the extent that infant industry arguments are the rationale, the incentives need only be temporary.

Again, it is worth stressing that in an open economy the use of tax incentives, temporary or otherwise, will be partly dissipated as tax transfers to foreign treasuries. This will be the case to the extent that foreign firms can take advantage of such incentives. If it is possible to aim temporary tax reductions to domestic firms without jeopardizing the tax credit status of foreign firms, the tax transfer can be avoided. This may be possible in practice. Some countries apply temporary tax incentives (for example, tax holidays) on a discretionary basis.

If, in so doing, they can apply them discriminately to domestic firms rather than foreign firms, there will not be any reduced tax transfer from foreign treasuries. Of course, even for foreign firms, temporary tax incentives are likely to have some stimulative effect on investment. Because these firms may not be in a profitable position when the incentives apply, any tax loss to foreign treasuries will be deferred. Thus it may be still worth applying temporary incentives to them. Indeed, temporary incentives may be preferable to permanent ones. We return below to another reason why it might be desirable to apply temporary tax incentives to foreign firms.

EXTERNALITIES OF INVESTMENT. One of the most convincing arguments for encouraging investment is that investment generates benefits for the economy over and above those that are captured privately by investors. These benefits may take the form of innovation, learning by doing, or labor training and can affect both the level and rate of growth of the economy. To the extent that this argument is true, there is a case for encouraging investment to be higher than it would otherwise be. Implementing policies to encourage investment involves taking into account the consequences of investment incentives in an open economy. In such an economy, incentives for investment applied at source can be undertaken with little regard for the way in which capital income is treated at the personal level. The main constraint is the conflict between investment incentives and the role of the corporate tax as a withholding device against foreign firms. A reduction in corporate tax liabilities will encourage investment, especially for domestic corporations. To the extent that they must be applied in a nondiscriminatory way to domestic and foreign firms alike, however, they will involve a relatively large revenue loss on foreign firms compared with the extra investment they generate. This is the tradeoff that must be judged when the corporate tax system is designed. The more important the externality arguments for investment incentives, the more a country would be willing to forgo the tax transfer of revenues from foreign governments and the lower tax rates would be in relation to those in the home countries of foreign investors.

CREATION OF EMPLOYMENT. We have argued above that some forms of unemployment may reflect distortions on labor markets that can be offset by government policies. For example, if unemployment is caused by efficiency wages, employment subsidies would be appropriate. Also, frictional unemployment may be treated with subsidies to job search. Typically these sorts of labor market distortions are best corrected by labor market policies. The use of investment incentives would generally be a second-best policy. For some reason, however, whether political or administrative, labor market policies may not be available. Also, as mentioned, efficiency wage sectors may also be capital-intensive ones. There may, therefore, be an argument for using investment incentives as a way of creating employment.

If this is the case, exactly the same issues are relevant as discussed in the section on externalities of investment. The employment-generating benefits of investment along with externality benefits will have to be set against the possible loss of tax revenues to foreign treasuries, assuming countries cannot discriminate against foreign firms.

RISK-SHARING AND FINANCING PROBLEMS. To the extent that capital markets are imperfect, some firms may be liquidity-constrained or may find it costly to undertake risky projects. This may be especially true for small, growing firms that are short of internal finance and that cannot self-insure. These firms may be sensible targets for investment incentives, especially because the corporate tax itself may discriminate against them. As with the infant industry arguments above, incentives that provide funds up front and in a refundable way are particularly attractive in relation to, say, tax reductions. The incentives could be limited to smaller, younger firms and could be temporary. The same conflict with the foreign withholding role as before also exists here.

TAX INCENTIVES AS SIGNALS. As Bond and Samuelson (1986) have argued, temporary tax incentives may be used by countries as signals of their "quality" as locations for foreign investment.[16] To the extent that this is a valid argument, such tax incentives would presumably be more effective if they were designed like other temporary tax incentives; that is, if they provided funds up front in a refundable way. The tradeoff with the foreign withholding function, which was not part of the Bond-Samuelson analysis, would have to be addressed. Tax incentives to foreign firms that involve lost tax revenues to the foreign treasury are a costly, and therefore more effective, signal.

TAX INCENTIVES TO OVERCOME TIME-INCONSISTENCY PROBLEMS. Finally, as mentioned above, underinvestment can occur as a result of the inherent inability of governments to commit to future tax policies, especially those that effectively expropriate the future returns on quasi-fixed capital stocks. Because it is unlikely that mechanisms can be found that commit future governments to predetermined tax policies, one is left with measures that work to offset the disincentive effects of time inconsistency. An obvious example of this involves investment incentives applied up front. Tax holidays and investment tax credits are good examples of such instruments. Again, their effectiveness would be contingent on their not being offset by foreign tax-crediting regimes.

In summary, there are arguments for permanent investment encouragement and for temporary incentives. The effect of temporary incentives on cash flow is often important. Foreign tax-crediting arrangements considerably temper the effectiveness and cost of investment incentives. Investment incentives will typically involve an unavoidable loss in tax revenues to foreign treasuries, unless discriminatory provisions can be applied or the incentives can be applied selectively to sectors that rely less heavily on foreign capital.

The Conceptual Effect of Investment Incentives

Investment incentives are intended to induce firms to invest more by increasing the rate of return from holding assets. They can do so in a wide variety of ways. Firms make a large number of capital decisions, and investment incentives can affect each of them differently. Firms decide how much capital of various types to hold, when to acquire the capital, how durable the capital should be, and how long to hold it. There are many different types of physical capital, including depreciable capital of various sorts (machinery, buildings), inventory, depletable assets (minerals, oil, and gas), renewable resources (forest), and real estate. In addition, firms invest in various forms of intangible assets, such as R&D, advertising, human capital, and goodwill. The tax system can affect all these decisions. It can also affect the financial structure of firms, that is, their decision to use debt or equity instruments of various sorts as a means of financing. The choice of financial instrument, by affecting the cost of funds, will also affect decisions on real investment. Finally, the tax system will affect in different ways capital decisions taken by different types of industries or firms. Thus the effect of investment incentives can vary greatly for different types of investment decisions in the economy. In fact, the same investment incentive can have quite different effects on different decisions. Any attempt to measure the overall effect is bound to be imprecise.

One useful summary device for measuring the effect of investment incentives is the marginal effective tax rate (METR). The METR measures the tax wedge at the margin for a given type of capital demand, that is, the extent to which the tax system affects the marginal rate of return from holding the asset. The effect of investment incentives can be inferred by computing how the METR is affected by the incentive. In this section we outline the computation of METRs, emphasizing some of the problems encountered with investment incentives in developing economies.

Before presenting some sample calculations, we review some of the limitations of METRs. First, the METR measures only the size of the effect of taxes on the rate of return. It does not measure the responsiveness of investment. This means that its usefulness will ultimately be limited to making qualitative judgments and to comparing alternative incentives. This drawback arises essentially because there is currently no acceptable and reliable technique for estimating investment demand empirically. It would therefore be futile to try to extend the use of METRs to determine the effect of investment incentives on actual investment. Our state of knowledge does not permit that. At the same time, the METR does have the advantage that it isolates tax considerations completely from other considerations.

Another limitation is that potentially there are an almost indefinite number of METRs in the economy, each one associated with a different type of investment decision. This means that there must necessarily be some selectivity or aggregation involved in presenting METR calculations. In the end, METR calculations are essentially illustrative.

The METR measures also presuppose a great deal about the structure of the economy and the process by which production and investment decisions are taken. For example, they typically assume competitive conditions and use some variant of the neoclassical theory of investment without adjustment costs as in Jorgenson (1963). They can, however, be extended to include adjustment costs with some additional assumptions. METRs are often computed for a risk-free environment, or at least one in which firms maximize only expected returns. When the costs of risk taking are considered, it is in a fairly rudimentary way. The financial structure of firms is usually taken as given, although it is possible to measure the incentive effect of the tax structure on the financial structure of the firm. In the absence of an accepted financial theory, it is typically necessary to adopt some arbitrage assumption for the firm. That is, because the tax structure treats different types of financing differently, there will be a different tax wedge for different types of financial instruments. One must specify which side of the market bears the differential tax. (We return to the arbitrage assumption below.) The behavior of the firm is modeled quite simply as that of maximizing the present value of dividends to shareholders. Problems of management and labor, such as incentive problems of the principal-agent sort that have figured so prominently in both labor economics and the theory of finance, are essentially assumed away. Finally, the theory typically treats capital decisions as being perfectly divisible. In actual fact, many types of capital decisions are lumpy, and the usual problems of nonconvexities arise. These can best be dealt with on a case-by-case basis.

Despite these limitations, the METR is probably the best available indicator of the incentive effects of the tax structure. There are two other alternatives. The first is to measure average effective tax rates. The other is to do rate-of-return calculations on a project-specific basis. Consider the latter first. Calculating the pre- and posttax rates of return for specific projects is feasible and certainly indicates the proportion of a project's return that accrues to the government. It also might indicate whether tax considerations are critical in determining the viability of the project—that is, whether taxes turn the project from having a positive present value to having a negative one, or vice versa. Unfortunately, the results are not likely to be of more general applicability. The general incentive effects of a tax system depend on how it affects marginal decisions. Marginal investment projects are difficult to identify, and it is not likely that the specific projects analyzed are marginal. This means that at least a portion of the rate of return accruing to the government comes from inframarginal profits. One of the great advantages of METRs is that they are designed to measure the tax rate on the marginal project.

The other alternative is to measure average effective tax rates, by which is meant the ratio of tax liabilities to capital income, where capital income is typically adjusted for inflation and true depreciation and may include both equity and interest income before taxes.[17] Average effective tax rates will differ from METRs for a variety of reasons. Because they are average rates they will include both the tax collected on marginal projects and that collected on inframarginal projects. They also measure taxes collected ex post on past investments, whereas the METR is that applicable on currently undertaken marginal projects. Thus average tax rates include windfall gains and losses resulting from unexpected changes in parameters and statutory tax rates. Average tax rates also fail to account for deferred tax liabilities resulting from temporary losses or favorable tax treatment. For these reasons, the average tax rate is not a useful measure of the incentive effects of the tax system. Typically, average effective tax rates are calculated to be higher than METRs.[18]

We proceed now to summarize the basic theory of METRs and then to consider its application to the measurement of the effect of investment incentives in developing countries.

Measuring Incentive Effects Using METRs

The METR is the amount of taxes collected on the marginal investment, sometimes expressed as a proportion of the rate of return on capital. In absolute terms it is defined as the difference between the before-tax rate of return on capital (r_g) and the after-tax rate of return on savings (r_n). The task of the investigator is to compute r_g and r_n. The measurement of r_n is conceptually straightforward because one can, in principle, observe market rates of return on savings and deduct from them the relevant taxes on savers. The measurement of r_g is more difficult, however. To observe it directly one would have to identify the marginal project and measure its rate of return, which would be impossible to do. Instead, one must deduce it indirectly. Using a theoretical model of investment, one derives an expression showing what the marginal product of capital would have to be in order to cover all costs (the user cost of capital). This is converted to a rate-of-return expression containing the components of cost, including taxes, that must be covered by the marginal project. This rate of return is then calculated through use of the various tax, depreciation, and financial cost parameters facing the firm. As can be seen, this procedure is contingent on the behavioral model used to derive the user-cost-of-capital expression of the firm. We present a simple version of that next for the case of depreciable capital incorporating a simple system of capital income taxes.

DERIVING r_g AND r_n—THE DEPRECIABLE CAPITAL CASE. Much of the theory of taxation and investment has been developed in the context of depreciable capital, so we begin with that case. The marginal tax rate represents the difference between the pretax rate of return on the marginal investment and the after-tax return to those who finance it. To derive an expression for the pretax rate of return, we use the conventional dynamic neoclassical theory of the firm.

Consider a firm that produces output according to the strictly concave production function $F(K_t)$, where K_t is the capital stock at time t. All other arguments are suppressed for simplicity. In the absence of new share issues, the dividend stream D_t of the firm may be written:

$$(1\text{-}1) \qquad D_t = (1 - u)\, P_t F(K_t) - (1 - \phi)\, Q_t\, (\dot{K}_t + \delta K_t)$$

$$+ u\alpha A_t + \dot{B}_t - i\,(1 - u)\, B_t$$

where P_t is the price of output; Q_t is the price of investment goods; u is the corporate tax rate; ϕ is the investment tax credit rate; δ is the depreciation rate on capital; α is the tax depreciation rate; i is the nominal interest rate; A_t is the undepreciated value of capital for tax purposes; and B_t is the debt of the firm.

This formulation makes particular assumptions about the tax structure that could easily be revised.[19] A dot over a variable indicates its time rate of change. Thus $\dot{B}_t = dB/dt$. We work in continuous time purely for convenience, although in practice both the tax system and capital markets operate on a discrete time basis. All rates of return and tax rates are treated as constant for simplicity.

It is convenient to write equation 1-1 in the following form:

$$(1\text{-}2) \qquad D_t = X_t + \dot{B}_t - i\,(1 - u)\,B_t$$

where X_t is called the cash flow of the firm. The latter two terms capture the financial flows of the firm with nonshareholders.

Assuming competitive capital markets, capital market equilibrium requires

$$(1\text{-}3) \qquad \rho E_t = (1 - c)\dot{E}_t + (1 - \theta)\,D_t$$

where ρ is the nominal after-tax rate of return on equity to existing shareholders, E_t is the value of equity in the firm, c is the shareholders' personal tax rate on capital gains (converted to an effective rate on accruals), and θ is the shareholders' tax rate on dividends. Solving equation 1-3 for E_t gives

$$(1\text{-}4) \qquad E_t + \int_t^\infty e^{-\frac{\rho}{1-c}(s-t)}\, D_s \frac{(1-\theta)}{(1-c)}\, ds.$$

Thus the equity value of the firm is the tax-adjusted dividend stream discounted by $\rho/(1 - c)$, which is the pretax return on equity (retained earnings) held in the firm.

The equity value defined by equation 1-4 would be a suitable objective function for the firm. As it stands, however, it will not yield an internal solution. Both an investment policy $(\dot{K})$ and a financial policy $(\dot{B})$ must be determined. As is obvious from inspection, however, the objective function is monotonic in B_t.[20] To avoid this problem, we treat the financial structure as exogenously given, a procedure that is common in this literature. In particular, we assume that the debt-equity ratio is given as $b = B_t/E_t$.[21] Using this definition of b in equation 1-2, substituting the result in equation 1-3, and again solving for equation 1-4 yields

$$(1\text{-}5) \qquad E_t = \left[b + \frac{(1-c)}{(1-\theta)} \right]^{-1} \int_t^\infty e^{-r(s-t)} X_s \, ds$$

where

$$(1\text{-}6) \qquad r = \frac{\dfrac{\rho}{(1-c)} + i\,(1 - u)\,b\,\dfrac{(1-\theta)}{(1-c)}}{1 + b\,\dfrac{(1-\theta)}{(1-c)}}$$

We can think of r as the nominal cost of financial capital to the firm. It is a weighted average of the cost of equity finance, $\rho/(1-c)$, and the cost of debt finance, $i(1-u)$.

Furthermore, the weights can be shown to be the proportions in which additional investment is financed by new debt and retained earnings.[22]

New issues can readily be incorporated as a source of equity finance. The nominal cost of new equity finance can be shown to equal

$$\frac{\sigma}{(1-\theta)} + \pi\left[1 - \frac{(1-c)}{(1-\theta)}\right]$$

where σ is the required return to new shareholders.[23] If a proportion a of equity finance is from retained earnings, the cost of capital can be written as

(1-7) $r = \beta i(1-u) + (1-\beta)\left(a\frac{\rho}{(1-c)} + (1-a)\left\{\frac{\sigma}{(1-\theta)} + \pi\left[1 - \frac{(1-c)}{(1-\theta)}\right]\right\}\right)$

where

$$\beta = \frac{b(1-\theta)/(1-c)}{1 + b(1-\theta)/(1-c)}$$

is the proportion of new investment that is financed by debt.

By equation 1-5, the equity value of the firm is proportional to the present value of the cash flow discounted by the cost of capital r. If we take this latter to be the objective function of the firm, the first-order condition on the real investment decision of the firm can be shown to equal[24]

(1-8) $$\frac{PF'(K)}{Q} = \frac{r + \delta - \dot{Q}/Q}{1-u}(1-\phi)\left(1 - \frac{u\alpha}{r+\alpha}\right)$$

where time subscripts have been suppressed for simplicity. Next, if p and q are denoted as real prices obtained by deflating P and Q by $e^{-\pi t}$, where π is the inflation rate, equation 1-8 becomes

(1-9) $$\frac{pF'(K)}{q} = \frac{r - \pi + \delta - \dot{q}/q}{1-u}(1-\theta)\left(1 - \frac{u\alpha}{r+\alpha}\right).$$

This is a standard expression of the user cost of capital, incorporating taxes. It represents the marginal product of capital gross of tax. To convert it to a rate of return, we subtract the economic depreciation rate. The expression for the gross rate of return r_g is given by

(1-10) $r_g = \dfrac{r - \pi + \delta - \dot{q}/q}{1 - u} (1 - \phi) \left(1 - \dfrac{u\alpha}{r + \alpha}\right) - (\delta - \dot{q}/q).$

The measurement of r_g (that is, the components of its right-hand side) is an essential ingredient of the marginal effective tax calculation. The definition of the METR is simply $t = r_g - r_n$, where r_n is the real after-tax rate of return to savers. In the context of this model, r_n is given by

(1-11) $r_n = \beta i (1 - m) + (1 - \beta) [a\rho + (1 - a)\sigma] - \pi$

where m is the personal tax rate on interest income. Equations 1-10 and 1-11 form the basis for measuring marginal tax rates, the details of which we return to below.

THE IMPLICATIONS OF RELAXING SOME ASSUMPTIONS. The basic formulation above makes several rather restrictive assumptions. Before turning to other sorts of capital decisions, it is worth considering the implications of relaxing some of them.

Nonexponential depreciation. Neither the rate of real depreciation nor the rate of tax depreciation need be exponential. We could define a depreciation function $\Delta(K)$, for example, such that $I = \dot{K} + \Delta(K)$. In this case, the term δ in equations 1-9 and 1-10 would be replaced by $\Delta'(K)$. Similarly, vintage capital could also be incorporated. The tax depreciation rate could take on any arbitrary pattern as well. The term $u\alpha/(r + \alpha)$ is the present value of the tax savings from future depreciation deductions when an exponential depreciation schedule is used. For other depreciation schemes, this would simply be replaced with the appropriate present-value expression.[25]

More generally, it is convenient to write r_g in a slightly more concise way. Define Z as the present value of the future tax savings from depreciation allowances per dollar of gross investment. Then, r_g may be written:

$$r_g = \frac{r + \delta - \dot{q}/q - \pi}{1 - u} (1 - \phi)(1 - Z) - (\delta - \dot{q}/q)$$

Note that this equation could be obtained from the following simplified maximization problem for the firm:

$$\underset{\dot{K}}{\text{Max}} \int_0^\infty e^{-rt} \left[P_t F(K_t)(1 - u) - (1 - \phi)(1 - Z) Q_t (\dot{K}_t + \delta K_t) \right] dt.$$

The term $(1 - \phi)(1 - Z)$ can be interpreted as the effective purchase price of capital goods if one takes into account the tax saving resulting from the investment tax credit and future depreciation deductions.

Time-varying tax parameters. Under some of the tax incentives we are interested in the firm will face a set of tax provisions that vary over time. The simplest case of this is the tax holiday, but other temporary tax provisions are similar in that regard. Tax parameters may vary also because the status of the firm changes over time. For example, the firm may change from having negative to positive taxable income. For illustrative purposes we consider the tax holiday. Define the effective statutory corporate tax rate of the firm as u_t at time t. This may also be the actual statutory tax rate and will be elaborated on further below. The firm's after-tax net revenue at time t is then $P_t F(K_t)(1 - u_t)$. The after-tax net cost of investment to the firm is $Q_t I_t (1 - Z_t)$, where Z_t is the present value at time t of future tax depreciation allowances per dollar of gross investment. For simplicity, we exclude the investment tax credit, although it could easily be added.

The representative firm maximizes the present value of its after-tax cash flow. Following the above simplification, its problem can be formulated as follows:

$$\operatorname*{Max}_{\dot{K}} \int_0^{\infty} R_t \left[P_t F(K_t)(1 - u_t) - (1 - Z_t) Q_t (\dot{K}_t + \delta K_t) \right] dt$$

where R_t is the nominal discount factor in period t and satisfies $\dot{R}_t / R_t = -r_t$. Here r_t is the nominal after-tax cost of finance to the firm at time t, defined as above to be a weighted average of the cost of debt and the rate of return on equity.

The solution to this problem yields a set of conditions characterizing the long-run profit-maximizing choice of K_t at each point of time:

(1-12) $$\frac{P_t F'(K_t)}{Q_t} = \frac{r_t + \delta - \dot{Q}_t/Q_t}{1 - u_t}(1 - Z_t) + \frac{\dot{Z}_t}{1 - u_t}.$$

The last term, involving the change in Z_t, reflects the fact that an additional cost of holding an incremental dollar of capital is the postponing of the purchase of capital that will increase future tax savings by Z_t (which could be positive or negative). Using this expression, r_g becomes

(1-13) $$r_g = \frac{r_t - \pi + \delta - \dot{q}_t / q_t}{1 - u_t}(1 - Z_t) + \frac{\dot{Z}_t}{1 - u_t} - \delta + \frac{\dot{q}_t}{q_t}.$$

To apply this expression to particular cases, we need to specify the paths of u_t, r_t, and Z_t. Consider the case in which the firm operates under a tax holiday for the time period $O \ldots H$. No taxes are paid by the firm during the tax holiday period. Also, suppose that, as in some countries (for example, Malaysia until 1988), depreciation allowances can be delayed until the end of the tax holiday. At that time, all accumulated tax savings from annual depreciation allowances could be set off against revenues earned by the firm in the first tax year following the tax holiday period. Assume that the profits of the firm immediately following the tax holiday are sufficiently large to absorb all depreciation allowances that have accumulated during the tax holiday period. If the firm decides to distribute its profit during the holiday period, the dividends received by its shareholders are also exempted from personal income taxes.

These features of the treatment of tax holiday firms make the computation of the before-tax rate of return on investment complicated. The tax holiday provisions make Z_t, r_t, and u_t all vary over time. Consider the computation of u_t, r_t, and Z_t in turn.[26] The effective statutory corporate tax u_t to the firm during the tax holiday period is zero because the firm is completely exempt from paying any tax on its income. The corporate tax rate will revert to the standard rate u after the tax holiday, however. Therefore

$$(1\text{-}14) \qquad\qquad u_t = \begin{cases} 0 \text{ for } 0 \le t \le H. \\ u \text{ for } t > H \end{cases}$$

The cost of finance to the firm is given by

$$(1\text{-}15) \qquad\qquad r_t = \beta i\,(1 - u_t) + (1 - \beta)\,\rho$$

where we have neglected new equity issues and we treat the parameters β, i, and ρ as fixed. The cost of funds to the firm will differ between the taxable and tax holiday firms because of the differences in u_t.

The calculation of the present value of tax savings resulting from depreciation Z_t must take into account the carryforward from the tax holiday to the taxpaying period of accumulated depreciation expenses as well as the variable discount rate. The value of Z_t will vary, depending on when the investment is undertaken. For investments made during the tax holiday period, Z_t will be given by

$$(1\text{-}16) \qquad Z_t = (R_H - R_t)\left(\int_t^H u\alpha e^{-\alpha(s - t)}\,ds + \int_H^\infty u\alpha e^{-(r + \alpha)(s - H)}\,ds\right).$$

For $t > H$, the expression for Z_t is the same as in equation 1-9. Note that Z_t is a monotonically increasing function with respect to time t within the pioneer period. The time profile of the before-tax rate of return on capital $r_g(t)$ for a pioneer firm can be easily calculated through use of equations 1-14, 1-15, and 1-16 along with 1-13. It will vary throughout the tax holiday period and will become constant after the transition to full taxpaying status. Below we provide some sample calculations for this tax holiday case.

Monopoly behavior. If the firm is a monopolist, the left-hand side of equation 1-8 becomes the marginal revenue product per unit of capital,

$[P + P'F(K)]F'/Q$, or $(1 - 1/\eta)\, PF'/Q$, where η is the elasticity of demand. The use of equation 1-10 to calculate the marginal distortion would capture only the tax distortion, the difference between the private gross rate of return and the net return to savings. The social gross rate of return would have to include the monopoly distortion and would be given by

$$(1\text{-}17) \quad r_g = \frac{r + \delta - \dot{q}/q - \pi}{(1 - 1/\eta)(1 - u)}(1 - \phi)\left(1 - \frac{u\alpha}{r + \alpha}\right) - (\delta - \dot{q}/q).$$

Monopsony power in the purchase of capital inputs is a special case of adjustment costs to which we turn next.

Adjustment costs. The implications of adjustment costs in measuring the marginal tax rate depend on the form of the adjustment costs and on the extent to which they are tax deductible. Consider as an example the case in which adjustment costs are separable and are given by the function $\gamma(K, \dot{K})$. We denote by γi the derivative of the adjustment cost function with respect to its *i*th argument. If a proportion x of adjustment costs is tax deductible, the objective function of the firm must include as part of the cash flow the term $-(1 - xu)\,\gamma(\dot{K}, K)$. The first-order conditions then simplify to

$$(1\text{-}18) \quad \frac{PF'(K)}{Q} - \frac{1 - xu}{1 - u}\frac{(\gamma_2 + r\dot\gamma_1 - \dot\gamma_1)}{Q} = \frac{r + \delta - \dot{Q}/Q}{1 - u}(1 - \phi)\left(1 - \frac{u\alpha}{r + \alpha}\right).$$

The left-hand side represents the gross marginal product of capital after adjustment costs. If adjustment costs were independent of tax, the procedure suggested above for measuring r_g would appropriately capture the social rate of return after adjustment costs. A sufficient condition for this would be that $x = 1$ (so adjustment costs are tax deductible) and r is independent of taxes. Failing this, the proper measurement of r_g would require terms involving the adjustment cost function that is not observable. In practice, we are typically able only to measure r_g without accounting specifically for adjustment costs. To that extent, the METR will inaccurately neglect the interaction of the tax system with adjustment costs and will give only an approximate measure of the full distortion resulting from the tax.

Auerbach (chapter 2, this volume) argues that the usual assumption of instantaneous capital stock adjustment is quite restrictive as the firms attempt to dampen the swings in capital stock due to changes in the rental price of capital. Thus a forward-looking investment behavior would depend on the weighted average of current and future costs of capital, taking into account the adjustment costs of additional investment. He suggests that the introduction of time-variant tax parameters and convex adjustment costs would be consistent with such behavior. This can be accomplished by introducing an adjustment cost parameter in the marginal cost of capital goods to capture increases in effective capital goods prices to the firm per unit of additional investment.

METRS FOR OTHER INVESTMENT DECISIONS. In principle an effective tax rate could be derived and measured for any sort of decision for which taxes impinge at the margin. We present below the derivation of r_g for three different cases—nondepreciable capital, inventory capital, and depletable resource properties. Other interesting cases that could be worked out include research and development, investment and harvesting of renewable resources, labor training, advertising and marketing, and so on. In each case, a derivation of r_g would be involved, which, in turn, would require a theory about the way the capital decision in question is determined. The computation of an effective tax rate as $t = r_g - r_n$ is as before.

Nondepreciable capital. The rate of return on nondepreciable capital (for example, land) is simply the special case of depreciable capital where $\delta = \alpha = 0$. Thus equation 1-10 reduces to

$$(1-19) \qquad r_g = \frac{r - \dot{q}/q - \pi}{1 - u} (1 - \phi) + \dot{q}/q .$$

Recall that taxes generally influence r as in equation 1-7. In general, taxes will have an ambiguous effect on r_g. In the absence of inflation and the investment tax credit ($\pi, \phi = 0$), r_g would be higher than in the absence of taxation because only part of the cost of holding the land would be tax deductible (the interest cost). The ability to deduct nominal interest costs when inflation is present and the ability to claim an investment tax credit would both reduce the effective tax rate.

Inventory capital. A completely general theory of the holding of inventories can be complicated, indeed, because of the dynamic nature of the problem. We make some reasonable simplifications to render the problem both manageable and intuitive. In particular, we model the firm in the steady state.[27] The firm produces an output X, using as an input some raw material. An amount r of the raw material is held as inventory (or work in progress). The average holding period of a unit of inventory is $T = R/X$, chosen by the firm. The firm produces a unit of output containing a unit of raw material drawn from inventory and incurs costs of $C(X, R)$, where $C_1 > 0$, $C_2 < 0$. The price of the output is Q, and the purchase price of raw material is P.

The corporate tax base includes total revenues (QX) less current costs (C) less interest costs less the first in, first out (FIFO) value of raw materials taken out of inventory.[28] We denote P_{-T} as the FIFO value of goods taken out of inventory after being held there a length of time T. The problem of the firm at time zero is

$$(1\text{-}20) \quad \underset{X,\,\dot{R}}{\text{Max}} \int_0^\infty e^{-rt} \left\{ (1-u)\,[QX - C(X,R)] - P(X + \dot{R}) + uP_{-T}\,X \right\} dt$$

where $T = R/X$ and $P(X + \dot{R})$ represents the new acquisition of raw materials. The first-order conditions for this problem reduce to

$$(1\text{-}21) \qquad\qquad \frac{-C_2(X,R)}{P} = \frac{r - (1 - ue^{-\gamma T})\,\gamma}{1 - u}$$

where $\gamma = \dot{P}/P$, the rate of change in the nominal price of the good held as inventory. This expression gives the marginal benefit of a unit of inventory holdings. To convert it to a rate of return, we subtract the real capital loss on holding a unit of inventory (which is the analog of true depreciation here), so

$$(1\text{-}22) \qquad\qquad r_g = \frac{r - (1 - ue^{-\gamma T})\,\gamma}{1 - u} + \frac{\dot{P}}{P}$$

where $\dot{p}/p = \dot{P}/P - \pi$, the rate of change in the price of inventory relative to that of other goods in the economy.

Depletable resources. As with inventories, we must make some simplifying assumption to render the problem of exploiting nonrenewable resources manageable. We consider a firm that is simultaneously involved in exploration, investment in mining facilities, and extraction. Inventories are excluded so that sales equal extraction; the addition of inventories would be a relatively straightforward task. The taxation of resources is notoriously complex in practice. For illustrative purposes we consider a simple scheme that incorporates most of the key issues.[29]

In the exploration stage the firm hires current inputs L at a price W and produces a depletable asset according to the strictly concave production function $S(L)$. It then invests in mining capital K at a price Q to make the asset ready for extraction. The production function is $Z(K,F)$, where F is the current use of the previously discovered asset. This is the only stage at which depreciable capital is used, although it would be straightforward to allow for it at either of the other two stages. Finally, the firm extracts an amount Y of the resource according to the strictly convex nominal cost function $C(Y)$ and sells it at a price P. The dividend flow resulting from this three-stage process is

$$(1\text{-}23) \qquad D = PY - C(Y) - WL - Q(\dot{K} + \delta K) + \dot{B} - iB - T$$

where T is the tax liability.

The expression for tax liabilities can vary widely from jurisdiction to jurisdiction and from one resource to another. Typically, firms will be liable both for a special resource tax and for a corporate income tax. We assume the resource tax is in the form of a severance tax (or royalty) based on the output produced. The corporate tax generally involves generous write-off provisions as well as some deduction for the use of the asset itself (a depletion allowance). We assume a severance tax rate of g based on total revenues. The corporate tax liability will be written:

$$(1\text{-}24)\ T_c = u(PY - C(Y) - WL - \alpha A - R - iB) + \phi Q\ (\dot{K} + \delta K).$$

Here, R is the depletion allowance and is defined as $R = t[PY - C(Y) - \alpha A]$, although most tax systems are more complicated than that. All other variables in equation 1-24 are the same as defined earlier.

Proceeding as before, using the expression for taxes and the severance rate, we define the cash flow of the firm to be

$$(1\text{-}25)\, X = PY[1 - u(1 - t) - g] - C(Y)[1 - u(1 - t)] - WL(1 - u)$$

$$- Q(1 - \phi)\,(\dot{K} + \delta K) + \alpha\, Au\,(1 - t).$$

The firm maximizes the present value of its cash flow, discounted by r as in equation 1-7 and subject to the equation of motion on A and the following two resource constraints:

$$(1\text{-}26) \qquad\qquad \int_0^\infty [Y - Z(F, K)]\, dt \leq 0$$

$$\int_0^\infty [F - S(L)]\, dt \leq 0.$$

The first constraint states that the total resource extracted cannot exceed the total developed, whereas the second states that the total resource developed cannot exceed the total found. In a more general version of this problem, this constraint would have to hold at each point in time.

The first-order conditions for this problem on K, L, and Y, respectively, reduce to

$$(1\text{-}27)\ \frac{(p - c')}{q}\ \frac{\partial Z}{\partial K} = \frac{(r - \pi + \delta - \dot{q}/q)}{[1 - u(1 - t)] - gp/(p - c')}\ (1 - \phi)\left[1 - \frac{\alpha u (1 - t)}{r + \alpha}\right]$$

$$(1\text{-}28)\qquad \frac{(p - c')}{w}\ \frac{\partial Z}{\partial F}\ \frac{\partial S}{\partial L} = \frac{1 - u}{[1 - u(1 - t)] - gp/(p - c')}$$

$$(1\text{-}29)\qquad \frac{\dot{p} - \dot{c}'}{p - c'} = r - \pi + \frac{\dot{p}}{p} - \frac{(r - \pi)g}{[1 - u(1 - t)][1 - (c'/p)]}.$$

The first of these is simply the before-tax gross marginal product of capital. To convert it to r_g, subtract $\delta - \dot{q}/q$, as before. The second equation is the social value of marginal product per unit of input L. An effective tax rate can be obtained directly by subtracting unity from equation 1-28. The final equation is a form of Hotelling's rule. It gives the gross rate of return to society from not extracting the resource. It can be converted to an effective tax wedge by subtracting r_n.

SOME ISSUES IN APPLYING METRS. Effective tax rate computations are based on calculating values for r_n, as given by equation 1-11, and r_g, as given by equation 1-10 or by its analog for other sorts of capital. The procedure typically followed is to attempt to evaluate all the parameters in, say, equations 1-10 and 1-11 for some level of aggregation and for some assumed values for the various parameters. Before outlining the method used to obtain parameter values, we believe it is worth mentioning some of the important conceptual issues and assumptions used as well as their limitations.

The level of aggregation. Given the specificity of most tax structures, there are in principle a large number of marginal distortions on investment in the economy. Some aggregation is inevitable. On the asset side, the minimum amount of disaggregation often used is by type of asset (machinery, building, land, inventory, and depletable assets). Beyond that, METRs may be variously disaggregated by industry, by size of firm, by location (for example, province or region), and by year. On the financing side, some disaggregation may be done by type of asset holder, for example, income class, tax status, and type of financial institution. Two different procedures exist for obtaining aggregate effective tax rates from data that are available at varying degrees of disaggregation. One procedure, followed by King and Fullerton (1984), is to calculate effective tax rates at the lower levels of aggregation and aggregate the METRs up by some weighting procedure. The other is to aggregate the underlying parameters up first and then calculate the aggregate METR at the higher level of aggregation. This is the procedure followed by Boadway, Bruce, and Mintz (1984).

The arbitrage assumption. A key distinguishing feature of alternative effective tax calculations concerns which arbitrage assumption is chosen and consequently which rates of return are taken as given. The need for an arbitrage assumption arises because tax systems impose varying burdens on different sources of finance—debt, retained earnings, and new issues. This implies that differential burdens must be imposed on some agents in capital markets. The arbitrage assumption stipulates which agents in the market are able to compete away differential tax burdens. We outline four arbitrage assumptions that have been used in the literature.

King and Fullerton (1984) adopt two alternative arbitrage assumptions and present the results of each in their intercountry comparisons. They are the so-called fixed-p and fixed-s cases. Their fixed-p assumption involves comparing projects with the same before-tax rate of return. This is analogous to assuming r_g is the same on all projects (10 percent in their calculations). Given the characteristics of the tax system, one can then work backward and compute for each firm the cost of funds r and also the after-tax return to savers i, ρ, and σ. Notice that this implies that different firms face different interest rates and rates of return on equity. Thus the fixed-p assumption cannot correspond to market equilibrium. Therefore it cannot succeed in picking out those investments that are truly marginal in a given economy. It does measure the effective tax rate across similar projects in different circumstances. Those different circumstances, however, involve both different tax systems and different costs of finance.

In their fixed-s case, all arbitrage occurs at the household level so that, in our notation, $i(1 - m) = \rho = \sigma$. Households in different tax brackets can still face different after-tax returns, but for any asset the return is the same to a given household. Starting with given values of the after-tax return to households (King and Fullerton assume 5 percent), one can calculate the cost of funds to firms. Under the fixed-s assumption, firms will face different costs for all three sources of finance.

The fixed-p assumption probably should not be described as an arbitrage assumption because all agents are receiving different returns from the same assets. Nor does the fixed-p assumption represent a market equilibrium, as mentioned above. A variant of the fixed-p case was used by Bradford and Fullerton (1981), who assumed that arbitrage occurred at the firm level. This is the third arbitrage assumption. Arbitrage at this level implies that the firm faces the same cost of finance from all sources, so

$$i(1 - u) = \frac{\rho}{1 - c} = \frac{\sigma}{(1 - \theta)} + \pi \left[1 - \frac{(1 - c)}{(1 - \theta)} \right].$$

Given the cost of funds to the firm, one can calculate the rates of return received by savers in various assets, and thus r_n.

The fourth arbitrage assumption is that used by Boadway, Bruce, and Mintz (1984). It is referred to as the open economy assumption and seems particularly appropriate in developing countries. The basic assumption is that the costs of debt and equity finance facing a country are determined by international capital markets. More particularly, in regard to debt the after-tax return to foreign debt holders is given exogenously. If starred values refer to foreign ones, the following international arbitrage condition must hold:

(1-30) $(i + \pi)(1 - m^*) - (1 - c^*)(\pi - \pi^*) = (i^* + \pi^*)(1 - m^*).$

This arbitrage equation, which determines i, assumes that exchange rate movements reflect differences in expected inflation (and are taxed as capital gains).

In regard to equity financing, a further assumption is made for data reasons. Stock market data do not allow the rate of return on retained earnings to be distinguished from that on new share issues. The rate of return on equity (ρ_g) paid by firms is therefore assumed to be the same for both. It is given by

$$(1\text{-}31) \qquad \rho_g = \frac{\rho}{1-c} = \frac{\sigma}{1-\theta} + \pi \left(1 - \frac{1-c}{1-\theta} \right).$$

The value of ρ_g must satisfy an international arbitrage condition analogous to equation 1-30 with ρ_g replacing i. The net return received by household savers, ρ and σ, can then be computed from equation 1-31 and used to obtain r_n. The value of r paid by firms is simply

$$(1\text{-}32) \qquad r = \beta i \, (1 - u) + (1 - \beta) \, \rho_g \, .$$

Thus given observed measures of i and ρg, all variables of the financial rate of return can be computed. Also, comparative static or counterfactual computations can be done by considering changes in tax or inflation rates domestically, given that the right-hand side of equation 1-30 is exogenous.

One advantage of the open economy arbitrage assumption is that it allows us to disaggregate METR calculations into that attributable to the corporate tax and that attributable to the personal tax. In an open economy facing fixed world rates of return, corporate taxation affects mainly the investment decision, whereas personal taxes affect savings. The magnitudes of the relevant distortions can be obtained by taking the difference between the world cost of funds r^* and either r_g or r_n as appropriate, where $r^* = \beta i + (1 - \beta) \rho - \pi$.

Loss offsetting and risk. The above formulations were based on two implicit assumptions. The first is that negative tax liabilities are treated symmetrically with positive ones. The other is that the analysis is based on a deterministic model of household choice.

The absence of full loss offsetting can, in principle, be incorporated into the above theory. In theory, its effect can either increase or decrease marginal tax rates, although the former seems the most likely to occur. In the context of depreciable assets, the absence of full loss offsetting reduces the present value of depreciation write-offs and the investment tax credit $u\alpha/(r + \alpha)$, ϕ and reduces the value of interest write-offs ui (thereby increasing the effective cost of debt finance). Both these increase r_g to the extent that depreciation or interest write-offs are postponed. To the extent that revenues are earned while the firm is in a nontaxpaying position, however, r_g will fall—because the grossing up of the user cost on the right side of equation 1-10 will be at a rate greater than $(1 - u)$. The methodology for taking these differences into account is similar to that presented above for the tax holiday firm.

The incorporation of risk is somewhat more difficult. One simple way to think of the way risk affects r_g is through its effect on the rate of return to equity, ρ (or σ). One can think of the return to equity ρ as comprising a safe return i^* plus a risk premium h that can be estimated under certain circumstances. It has been established in the literature (for example, Gordon 1985; Mintz 1982) that full loss offsetting is equivalent to allowing a deduction for the cost of risk taking. To the extent that loss offsetting of risks does occur, the risk premium itself ought to be reduced by the tax, $h(1 - u)$. Since our methodology does not reduce the risk premium by the tax, it will yield an overestimate of r_g to the extent that loss offsetting of risk occurs.

Whether or not loss offsetting occurs depends on the source of the risk. If the risk takes the form of capital risk, as discussed in Bulow and Summers (1984), loss offsetting does not occur. In contrast, risks reflected in varying revenues will almost certainly be partly offset.

Risk can also take the form of uncertainty about future government policy—that is, policy risk. Auerbach (chapter 2, this volume) emphasizes the importance of the credibility of the tax regime in the effectiveness of tax policies. If an announced tax policy change is seen as temporary and likely to be reversed, it will not have the same effect as a possibly less stimulative alternative but one that is seen as permanent. Also, in an uncertain tax climate investors are likely to demand a higher expected return from investments.

The data. We briefly outline here the manner in which numbers can be attached to the variables r_g and r_n. The exact manner in which data are obtained depends on the level for aggregation at which effective tax rates are being computed. Nonetheless the same general approach can be followed in all cases. The principles followed in constructing the various types of data are summarized below.

- *Financing ratios* (β , a). King and Fullerton (1984) calculate effective tax rates separately for different sources of finance, so they do not really need to use financing ratios. Some studies, however, have incorporated financial ratios for different types of firms as an element of their calculations, thus picking up the way in which the interest deductibility provision benefits some types of firms more than others. These can be constructed by using the structure of liabilities from published balance sheets. Depending on the application, either differences between end-of-year values of liabilities of debt, retained earnings and new issues, or the stock values themselves can be used to estimate β and a.

- *Rates of return* (i, ρ, σ). As mentioned, King and Fullerton simply present their effective tax rates for arbitrary financial rates of return. Alternatively, one can try to measure the actual effective tax rates for a given year by using observed financial data. The bond rate i can be obtained by using long-term nominal corporate bond yields. The required return on equity before personal taxes can be calculated from the inverse of price-earnings ratios, where book earnings are corrected to account for the effect of inflation on the capital stock, inventories, and debt liabilities. The arbitrage assumption requires that this also equal the before-tax return on new issues. For calculations at the industry level, an industry-specific risk premium can be calculated from capital-asset pricing model studies and adjusted for leverage.
- *Inflation rate* (π). Again, King and Fullerton simply assume a given rate of inflation. Alternatively, the expected inflation rate can be estimated using an ARIMA forecast based on the consumer price index, as in Boadway, Bruce, and Mintz (1984).
- *Real capital gains* $(\dot{q}/q, \dot{p}/p)$. Expected capital gains on capital goods and resources can, in principle, be estimated by the same procedure as that used to estimate inflation if one uses the appropriate capital goods series or resource price index. For resources subject to royalties, it is also necessary to know the profit margin $(p - c')/p$. These can be calculated by using estimates of the short-run cost function. In most applications, real capital gains have simply been ignored because their estimates are regarded as not being reliable.
- *Depreciation rate* (δ). Calculations of the depreciation rate are typically based on length-of-life data for various types of capital. Where necessary, service lives can be aggregated, the proportions of gross investment being used as weights. Service lives L can be converted to equivalent exponential depreciation rates by the formula $\delta = 2/L$. See Hulten and Wykoff (1981).
- *Holding period for inventories* (T). These can be calculated from the ratio of average monthly inventories to average monthly shipments.
- *Corporate tax parameters* (α, u, ϕ). In most countries the corporate tax rate and the investment tax credit rates depend on the type and size of industry and the type of investment. For each type of capital good, statutory tax rates can be aggregated appropriately according to the share of income taxable at various rates. A similar procedure can be used for the investment tax credit. For depreciation rates, when the tax system allows declining balance write-offs, α can be calculated as an average of the rates applicable to various types of capital, the amounts of gross investment being used as weights. When straight-line depreciation is allowed, the expression for r_g has to be amended as indicated earlier.
- *Personal tax rates* (m, θ, c). Typically, very little disaggregation occurs on the saving side. The personal tax rate on interest income is calcu-

lated as an average of the marginal tax rates on capital income across all income classes. In the case of dividends, the tax rate on interest income must be corrected for any dividend tax credit that exists. The capital gains tax rate is somewhat more difficult to calculate because c is an accrued tax rate, whereas capital gains are actually taxed on realization. The accrued tax rate c is calculated such that the present value of the capital gains tax payment based on realized taxation is equal to the present value of taxes levied on accrued gains discounted by the shareholders' after-tax cost of equity finance. The average holding period of shares can be taken as the ratio of shares floated to volume of shares traded. The realized capital gains tax rate itself may differ from the personal tax rate on other forms of capital income.

Using METRs to Evaluate Investment Incentives

In principle it should be relatively straightforward to use the METR methodology to determine the size of incentive offered by various types of measure designed to encourage investment. One can calculate the METR in the presence and the absence of incentives and see explicitly by how much the incentive changes the marginal tax rate on investment decisions of various sorts. As mentioned earlier, there are limitations to using METRs; they apply equally well here. For one thing, a large number of potential METRs will correspond to the many types of capital decisions undertaken by the many different agents in the economy. Most METR studies show considerable dispersion of rates across the economy. The same incentive can have different effects on different types of investment decisions. Thus it is difficult to characterize the effects of investment incentives in a simple and general way. Instead, one may be left with presenting a series of essentially illustrative calculations of the effects of investment incentives in different circumstances. It is naturally quite important for evaluative purposes to select the appropriate sample calculations in illustrating the effects of incentives.

For another thing, the information obtained from an METR is limited. Although it shows the size of the incentive imposed at the margin on a particular sort of investment decision, it does not show the magnitude of response of investment to the incentive. Nor does it show the effects on government tax revenue. This means that, although METR calculations are useful in analyzing tax reform issues, they are less so in the positive analysis of the effect of incentives on economic activity.

The use of the METR methodology in illustrating the effect of investment incentives can be illustrated by some sample calculations. Below we report on a selection of effective tax rate calculations designed to illustrate several different effects. Before doing so, we believe it is worth discussing some of the key dimensions of the effect of investment incentives that are likely to be of interest in evaluating them. These will reveal the sorts of METR calculations that are most worth doing.

COMPARATIVE EFFECTS OF ALTERNATIVE INSTRUMENTS. Different ways of encouraging investment can have very different effects on the incentive to invest, depending on the circumstances. Indeed, some measures that on the surface might appear to provide incentives to invest may actually do the opposite. This can be illustrated by some examples. Consider first the measures involving reductions in tax rates, either permanently or temporarily. The effect of these on investment incentives depends to a great extent on the sign of the METR. This effect can be either positive or negative, depending on the generosity of deductions and credits for capital costs. A result that has been established in the literature is that, in the absence of investment tax credits, a corporate income tax will be neutral if the present value of deductions for capital costs (interest and depreciation) just equal the initial cost of capital.[30] If the present value of deductions exceeds the initial capital cost, the METR is negative, and vice versa. In these circumstances, a reduction in the statutory tax rate typically reduces the absolute value of the METR but does not change its sign.[31] Thus if the effective tax rate is negative to start with, reductions in the tax rate will make it less negative, thereby reducing the incentive that already exists for investment.

This ambiguous effect of reductions in the tax rate arises because the tax rate applies both to deductions and to revenues. Measures that apply only to deductions would be expected to have unambiguous effects on the direction of change in incentive to invest. These would include investment tax credits, accelerated depreciation, enhanced deductions for the cost of finance, and the like.

THE ABSENCE OF FULL LOSS OFFSETTING. Most tax systems allow only partial offsetting of losses. Losses can usually be carried forward for a specified period of time and perhaps backward also. In these circumstances, the effect of various investment incentives will depend on the tax status of the firm and on the nature of the tax incentive. A distinction might be drawn here between three different types of investment incentives. One is a tax rate reduction, as already discussed. Another is an incentive that changes the timing but not the magnitude of deductions, such as accelerated depreciation. The third is an incentive that increases the amount of a deduction, such as an investment tax credit. These three types of incentives can have quite different relative effects on taxpaying and nontaxpaying firms.

For example, temporary tax reductions, such as tax holidays, will have very little, if any, effect on a firm's incentive to invest if the firm is in a tax loss position. Because the firm is not paying taxes when the tax reduction is in effect, the tax rate is essentially irrelevant. The exception to this is if the tax holiday is accompanied by some measures that allow for the selective carryforward of some capital costs. For example, if depreciation deductions are elective, as they are in some tax systems, the firm can choose not to take them until the end of the tax holiday period. In this way they can have an incentive effect on investment.

Similarly, measures that essentially accelerate the timing of a given stream of deductions will have minimal effect if they accelerate them into periods in which the firm is nontaxable. In this case, the firm cannot take advantage of the acceleration and at best simply carries forward the deduction into taxable periods later on. Incentives that increase the total amount of write-off will continue to benefit the investing firm, although not at the same level as it would if there were full loss offsetting. If incentives like the investment tax credit were refundable, this discrimination against tax loss firms would be eliminated.

The implications of tax losses for investment incentives vary, depending on the pattern of taxable income for the firm. An indefinite number of time paths of tax losses are possible, governed by the nature and history of the firm. For example, young, growing firms might be expected to face a period of negative taxable income while they are undertaking investments and establishing themselves in the market. For them, the absence of loss-offsetting provisions is particularly damaging. Large, established firms are more likely to be in a taxpaying position, although older, declining firms may well be in a phase of tax losses. For the latter, carryforward provisions are unlikely to be of much use. The best that can be done to capture these effects is to base illustrative calculations on typical patterns of tax losses, although some attempt has been made in the literature to use information on the actual histories of firms as a basis for effective tax calculations.[32]

THE TREATMENT OF RISK. The treatment of risky firms is related to the issue of loss offsetting because risky ventures can give rise to negative taxable income in some periods. As mentioned, two types of risk have been distinguished in the literature—income risk and capital risk. Income risk involves uncertainty about the future stream of net revenues because of such things as output price, wage rate, and uncertainty of demand. It is reflected in fluctuations in taxable income. As mentioned earlier, full loss offsetting is equivalent to allowing income risk to be deducted. In the absence of full loss offsetting, however, firms faced with income risk would be put at a disadvantage in relation to nonrisky firms. For the same reason, investment incentives will apply differentially to the greater advantage of less risky firms in the absence of full loss offsetting.

Full loss offsetting is not sufficient to guarantee neutrality with respect to capital risk. Capital risk is defined as uncertainty in regard to the rate of economic depreciation of capital after the capital has been installed.[33] Depreciation schedules for tax purposes are predetermined at the time of the investment and are not adjusted for changes in subsequent actual depreciation rates. Indeed, given the fact that depreciation rates are not observable as market prices, it is not obvious how they could be adjusted to account for capital risk. In practice, the only way the deductibility of capital risk could be achieved would be by allowing depreciation write-offs to occur up front.[34] By the same token, incentive measures that accelerate the writing off of capital depreciation, such as accelerated depreciation, would simultaneously reduce the discrimination against risky investments and provide an incentive to investment. By contrast, measures that do not accelerate the pattern of depreciation would not remove the discrimination against capital risky investments.

THE EFFECT OF VARIOUS INCENTIVES ON CASH FLOW. According to the neoclassical investment theory on which effective tax calculations are based, firms can obtain financing for investment at the going costs of finance for various sorts of finance. In practice some firms, particularly small, young ones, may find it relatively difficult to raise capital from external sources and may be viewed as being liquidity-constrained. Presumably, they can obtain outside finance at some price, but that price will be different from the going market price and may be difficult for investigators to determine. Under these circumstances, METRs may not be fully informative about the effects of investment incentives on firms. It might be equally important to know the effects of the incentives on the cash flow position of the firms.

Given this consideration, the earlier investment incentives get funds in the hands of the firms, the more effective the incentives will be. A comparison of the time profile of the tax savings of various incentives is important. From this perspective, investment tax credits are the most beneficial but, for nontaxpaying firms, only to the extent that they are refundable. Accelerated depreciation is less so, and reduced tax rates even less so (because their benefit is greatest when revenues are highest, which is later than when the capital costs are incurred). The scheme of Auerbach and Jorgenson (1980) mentioned earlier would also be beneficial to the cash flow of firms if tax losses were refundable, even though refundability is not an investment incentive as such.

THE EFFECT OF INVESTMENT INCENTIVES ON THE COSTS OF FINANCING AND FINANCIAL STRUCTURE. In the METR methodology, the determination of the financial structure is suppressed from the analysis because of the lack of a widely accepted theory. Two alternative approaches to accounting for the differential tax treatment of different forms of financing follow. First, some studies (for example, King and Fullerton 1984) calculate separate METRs for different sources of finance. In this way the magnitude of the differential treatment of the different types of finance can be observed directly. Second, some studies use observed financial structures to calculate costs of capital for different types of firms. Because different types of firms systematically use different proportions of debt finance, the use of different weights for debt and equity finance in the cost of capital enables one to capture the effect of the differential tax treatment of debt and equity finance in METR calculations across industries.

In a sense, this is not an entirely satisfactory state of affairs. Measuring the differential effect of taxes by source of finance is not sufficient to indicate how firms will change their financial structures in response. In that sense METRs measured by source of finance cannot form the basis for a positive analysis of the effects of taxes on the financial structure of firms. At best, the direction of tax incentives and prescriptions for tax reform can be deduced. Some studies take the extreme view that only taxes matter in determining financial structures.[35] This leads one to the so-called cash flow or pecking order theory of finance, whereby firms use up the least-cost source of finance first. Again, by concentrating solely on tax explanations as determinants of the financial structure, one can most readily understand tax policy arguments about how to avoid distortions of the financing decision.

Perhaps more important, by taking the financial structure and the costs of various sources of finance (i, ρ, and σ) as given to the firm, one may not be capturing important differences between the marginal and average costs of various sources of finance. If firms are optimizing their financial structures, one might expect that the marginal cost of various sorts of finance will be the same. In this case, it might seem inappropriate to attribute different costs of finance to debt and equity in METR studies.[36] As Boadway, Bruce, and Mintz (1987) have argued, however, if financial decisions are separable from investment decisions, the optimizing choice of financial structure will give rise to different equilibrium values of the costs of various sources of finance that are appropriately used in METR calculations.

Consider, for example, the cost of funds given by equation 1-32. In it, $i(1 - u)$ and ρ_g represent the average costs of debt and equity finance to the firm, but not the marginal costs. The calculation of the marginal cost of funds will take into account the effect of an extra dollar of financing of either sort on the amount the firm must pay its creditors as a result of a marginal change in the firm's financial structure. Suppose that the rate of interest the firm must pay increases with the debt-equity ratio. The marginal cost of raising a dollar of debt exceeds $i(1 - u)$ because an extra dollar of debt raises the debt-equity ratio and the interest rate the firm must pay on all its debt. Similarly, the marginal cost of an increment in equity financing is less than rg because this extra equity financing lowers the debt-equity ratio and reduces the cost of debt. Thus the firm will hold a diversified stock of financial liabilities even though the average costs of the two sorts of finance differ. It can be shown that when the cost of finance depends only on the debt-equity ratio, the firm's financial structure will be determined independently of investment, and the marginal cost of funds will exactly equal the weighted average of $i(1 - u)$ and

ρ_g.[37] This would, therefore, justify the procedure used in the METR analysis of treating the cost of finance as a weighted average of the average costs of debt and equity finance.

The relevance of this discussion of financing for investment incentives is rather limited because most investment incentives do not apply to the financing costs. At the same time, investment incentives may well play an important role in providing finance to the firm, as we have already pointed out. Probably the effects of investment incentives on cash flow are the most important ones.

THE INTERACTION OF INFLATION AND INVESTMENT INCENTIVES. Most corporate taxes have few provisions for inflation built into them. Interest deductions tend to be based on nominal interest rates, and depreciation is calculated in historic rather than replacement terms. This implies that inflation affects the real value of the tax base. The effect of inflation on the METR is, however, ambiguous a priori. The lack of replacement cost depreciation implies that increases in inflation will reduce the value of the depreciation write-off, thereby tending to increase the METR. Similar arguments apply to the deduction for inventory usage. At the same time, the ability to deduct nominal interest means that in times of inflation firms are effectively able to write off part of the principal of their debt. This reduces the cost of finance and tends to reduce the METR. Depending on the relative magnitude of these two effects, inflation could increase or decrease the METR. It is more likely to increase it the more important debt is as a source of finance and the slower the write-off for depreciation. This ambiguity has been borne out in various studies of METRs. The absence of full loss offsetting will also be important in determining the effect of inflation on the METR.

Naturally, the effects of investment incentives will differ according to the rate of inflation. Tax rate reductions tend to reduce the absolute size of the METR and so preserve whatever inflation bias already exists. Because accelerated depreciation reduces the disadvantage of historical cost depreciation, it should be especially beneficial in times of inflation. Investment tax credits provide an additional advantage. Because they occur up front and do not affect the existing interest and depreciation deductions, their effect will be relatively independent of the rate of inflation, at least as long as the benefit of the tax credit is not postponed because of imperfect loss offsetting.

THE INTERACTION OF CORPORATE TAX INCENTIVES WITH OTHER POLICIES. The corporate tax system is not the only source of policy influence on the incentive to invest. Other taxes also have an effect, such as indirect taxes. In addition, tariffs have an obvious effect on protected activities. Few researchers have attempted to incorporate other taxes into METR calculations, although, in principle, it should be straightforward to do.[38] In developing countries, it might be particularly useful to include other distortions in the computation of METRs when evaluating investment incentives.

EFFECTS ON THE TIMING AND DURABILITY OF INVESTMENT. Taxes can affect investment in ways other than simply the size of the demand for capital. They can affect the accumulation of capital as well as the durability of capital. Part of the effect of temporary investment incentives may simply be to advance the holding of a given amount of capital. This might be true in a tax holiday, for example. Effective calculations of tax rates can be done on an annual basis during the period of the tax holiday to see how the incentive to invest changes. We present some sample calculations later.

Permanent incentives will affect the long-run demand for capital. They may, however, influence the chosen durability of capital. It is known from the literature that accelerated depreciation schemes are neutral with respect to the durability of capital, whereas investment tax credits induce firms to employ shorter-lived capital. The reason for the latter is that investment tax credits apply on gross investment and thus reduce the cost of replacement capital. The subsidy to replacement capital means that firms will have an incentive to choose capital that depreciates more quickly. This may be viewed as a disadvantage of investment tax credit schemes.[39]

Firms may make other types of decisions involving capital expenditure. One important decision may be technique of production, especially capital intensity. Incentives that apply to capital purchases but not to other inputs will give firms an incentive to substitute capital for the other inputs, including labor. To the extent that the creation of employment is an objective, this is a disadvantage. The ability to make the substitution depends on the elasticity of substitution, which may vary from sector to sector.

SPECIAL PROBLEMS ARISING IN OPEN ECONOMIES. Some additional considerations arise in economies whose capital markets are exposed to international capital markets. In these cases, capital may move across international borders in response to tax measures affecting investment. If there are no impediments to capital moving in and out of the country and if the country is small in relation to the rest of the world, the required rate of return on capital will effectively be predetermined for the country by international capital markets. This means that the saving and investment sides of the domestic capital market will effectively be segmented. That is, in any given year there will be no need for domestic saving to equal domestic investment. Tax measures applying to firms, such as investment incentives, will affect the investment side of the market but not the saving side. Similarly, tax measures applying on households will affect saving alone. Thus imputation measures that are implemented through the personal tax system will have no effect on domestic investment. Any induced changes in the capital account balance will be met by net inflows or outflows of capital from foreigners.

One of the implications of this is that the METR on a capital decision can be disaggregated into that applying on the investment side and that applying on the saving side. Let r^* be the international cost of finance in real terms. It can be defined as follows:

$$(1\text{-}33) \qquad\qquad r^* = \beta i^* + (1 - \beta)\, \rho^* - \pi \,.$$

This represents the opportunity cost of funds to the country as determined in world capital markets. The METR applying on investment decisions can then be defined as follows:

$$(1\text{-}34) \qquad\qquad t_I = r_g - r^*,$$

where r_g is defined as before. Similarly, the METR applying on saving decisions is defined as

$$(1\text{-}35) \qquad\qquad t_s = r^* - r_n.$$

By construction, the METR equals the sum of r_g and r_n.

The open economy assumption makes matters simpler for us in investigating investment incentives. If the incentives operate on firms, we can capture their full effect by looking solely at t_I. In other words, personal taxes become irrelevant. Incentives operating through personal taxes (such as dividend tax credits to domestic shareholders) do not affect investment decisions.[40]

Although that simplification is possible, the ability of capital to flow across borders introduces another issue to be considered. Foreign firms typically are liable for taxes both in the host country and the home country. Some credit may be given in the latter, however, for taxes paid in the host country. Most countries operate a foreign tax-crediting system under which taxes paid abroad are credited against domestic tax liabilities up to the amount of the latter.[41] This means that to the extent that host country tax liabilities are within the limit set by home country taxes, revenues are transferred from foreign treasuries to that of the host country. This provides an incentive for host countries to design their tax systems so as to exploit to the fullest the transfer of tax revenues from foreign treasuries to domestic ones. In these circumstances, the host country tax system may have limited effect on the investment behavior of foreign firms unless host taxes are high enough to exceed home country tax liabilities. If they do not, any effect that host country taxes have on the incentive to invest will be limited to that arising from the deferral nature of home country taxes and tax crediting.[42]

Given these tax-crediting arrangements, investment incentives that reduce the tax liabilities of foreign firms may have limited effect on the incentive of foreign firms to invest and may serve largely to transfer funds to home country treasuries. This transfer could only be avoided if, for some reason, the foreign tax-crediting provision did not apply to the investment incentive.

THE IMPLICATIONS OF ALTERNATIVE CREDITING ARRANGEMENTS. One of the reasons developing countries levy corporate taxes is to effect a tax transfer from treasuries in home countries of foreign corporations. This is a consequence of offering a foreign tax credit for taxes paid in the host country as is done, for example, by the United States. Host countries can raise revenue almost costlessly by setting their tax rates close to those of host countries.[43]

This ability to transfer revenues from foreign treasuries is contingent on the foreign countries' operating a credit system. As has long been recognized, if foreign treasuries allowed firms only to deduct foreign tax liabilities from taxable income rather than crediting them, a tax transfer would no longer be possible. Under these circumstances, the corporate tax would be fully absorbed by a higher required rate of return on capital, and the tax would effectively be borne by other domestic factors of production (such as labor). The corporate tax would then discourage foreign investment, and investment incentives would encourage it.

At the moment, tax credits are the norm. That situation may not persist, however. From the point of view of creditor nations, deduction systems make much more sense than credit systems, as Feldstein and Hartman (1979) have pointed out. Deduction systems avoid the turning over of tax revenues to capital-importing countries. One of the mysteries in the literature on the international taxation of capital income is how credit systems ever came into being, given that it seems not to be in the interest of exporters of capital to have such systems. As countries such as the United States review their arrangements, it will not be surprising to see some changes from crediting to deductions. If such changes do occur, the role of the corporate tax and the efficacy of investment incentives will change significantly.

TAX HAVEN AND CONDUIT COUNTRIES. The ability of firms to siphon profits through tax haven countries also influences the effectiveness of investment incentives. Tax havens are low-tax countries that have some other special features, such as rules governing confidentiality and secrecy, a lack of currency controls, and highly developed banking and financial activities. Tax havens can be used to reduce tax liabilities to the extent that firms can set up in the tax haven and arrange to shift earnings to it via one of a variety of arbitrage mechanisms (financial transactions, transfer pricing, and the like). A disproportionate share of holding and investment companies and shipping companies have been set up in tax haven countries. Many countries have enacted provisions to attempt to limit the extent of tax avoidance through tax havens.[44]

Some Illustrative Calculations of METRs: The Case of Malaysia

In this section we present some sample calculations of the effect of investment incentives on METRs in Malaysia. The Malaysian case is instructive because the types of incentives, as well as the basic tax structure itself, are typical of what one finds in many developing countries. In addition, the tax system underwent a reform in 1989 whose effects we can calculate. We begin with a brief description of the tax system as it affects capital income at the personal and corporation levels.[45]

Most forms of capital income (for example, interest and dividends) are fully taxed at the personal level at ordinary rates. The rate structure is progressive, with rates rising from 5 to 40 percent. The main exceptions to this are dividends received from pioneer firms—that is, those operating under a tax holiday—and capital gains. Both are tax exempt. There are also, as in most countries, various forms of sheltered savings, such as pension savings and housing. For dividends from nonpioneer firms, the personal and corporate tax systems are fully integrated. That is, a dividend tax credit is given to resident corporations for taxes paid at the corporate level. The dividend tax credit rate is 40 percent. Dividends paid to foreigners are subject to a 40 percent withholding tax. The tax reform of 1989 did not affect these provisions.

Before 1989 the company tax rate was 40 percent plus an additional 5 percent development tax. Companies with income in excess of M$2 million paid a 3 percent excess profits tax. In the 1989 tax reform, the income tax rate was reduced to 35 percent, and the development tax was to be phased out over five years. Firms do not pay taxes on capital gains or on intercorporate dividends, so corporate income is taxed only once. Corporation taxable income is defined the way it is in most tax systems to include business income less current and capital costs, where the latter include nominal interest costs and depreciation. Depreciation rates vary by type of asset and by type of industry. Typically, an initial allowance is given, followed by straight-line depreciation of the remainder of the original cost. Although taxpaying firms incur tax liabilities immediately, tax loss firms are not treated symmetrically. Tax losses may be carried forward indefinitely without interest.

Investment incentives take a variety of forms. As mentioned, different industries face different rates of depreciation. In addition, there are two special types of incentives. First, an investment tax credit is available to nonpioneer firms. The investment tax credit is given on a discretionary basis and is awarded at varying rates ranging all the way up to 100 percent. Second, tax holidays are granted to firms that apply successfully for pioneer status. Firms granted pioneer status are free of corporate income taxes for a period of time (usually five years) after the investment in question. Pioneer status may be extended for up to five more years when the first period expires. Before 1989, pioneer firms were permitted to carry forward without interest their depreciation allowances cumulated from the pioneer period to the year following this period. No other component of taxable income could be carried forward in this way. The 1989 tax reform eliminated this carryforward provision.

As can be seen, the tax treatment of firms depends on the industry in which they operate, whether they are taxpaying or tax loss firms and how long they have been so, and whether they are pioneer firms. In evaluating the effects of the 1989 reforms, a separate calculation should be done for each type of firm. In what follows, we distinguish only between taxpaying and tax loss status and between pioneer and nonpioneer status. For simplicity, interindustry differentials are ignored. The calculations are based on rather crude data. Our purpose here, however, is to provide illustrative calculations, not definitive results.

We begin by adapting our earlier theory to the institutional setting at hand. First, we invoke the open economy arbitrage assumption discussed earlier. This involves assuming that the rate of return on capital is determined on international capital markets and allows us to disaggregate the METR into a corporate tax distortion, t_c, and a personal tax distortion, t_p. Consider the derivation of t_c first.

To calculate t_c we need an expression for the pretax rate of return on investment r_g. Our procedure is to adapt equation 1-13 to a discrete-time setting that corresponds with the Malaysian tax system. The firm's problem can be written as

$$\underset{K_t}{\text{Max}} \sum_{t=0}^{\infty} R_t \left[P_t F(K_t)(1 - u_t) - Q_t (K_{t+1} - (1 - \delta) K_t)(1 - Z_t) \right]$$

where the discount factor R_t can be written:

$$R_t = \prod_{s=0}^{t} \frac{1}{1 + r_s}$$

where r_s is the nominal after-tax cost of finance to the firm in period s. It is a weighted average of the one-period interest cost (cost of debt) and the rate of return on equity, where the weights are the proportions of debt and equity used in the financing of cash flows.

Solving this problem as discussed earlier, we find that the analogy to equation 1-13 is

$$(1\text{-}36) \quad r_g(t) = \frac{\left[(r_t - \pi_t + \delta) - (\Delta q/q)_t (1 - Z_t) + 1 + r_t - \pi_t - (\Delta q/q)_t (Z_t - Z_{t-1}) \right]}{1 - u_t}$$

$$-\delta+\left(\frac{\Delta q}{q}\right)_t.$$

Here, $(\Delta q/q)_t = \Delta Q_t / Q_t - \pi_t$ and the rest of the variables are defined as before, except that now they are defined for a discrete period rather than for a point in time. It will simplify matters if we assume that $(\Delta q/q)_t = 0$ and if we ignore $(r_t - \pi_t)(Z_t - Z_{t-1})$ because it will be very small. Then the expression for r_g simplifies to

$$(1\text{-}37)\qquad r_g(t) = \frac{(r_t - \pi_t + \delta)(1 - Z_t)(Z_t - Z_{t-1})}{1 - u_t} - \delta.$$

To implement equation 1-37, we need to compute for each type of investment each of the parameters on the right-hand side, distinguishing especially how they vary with the tax status of the firm. The expected inflation rate π and the depreciation rate δ are independent of the tax status of the firm and are computed as already discussed. We need only discuss how the nominal cost of finance r_t, the present value of future depreciation write-offs Z_t, and the effective statutory corporate tax rate u_t vary with tax status. We do so for firms with three types of tax status—fully taxpaying nonpioneer firms, profit-making pioneer firms, and tax loss nonpioneer firms.[46]

TAXPAYING NONPIONEER FIRMS. A taxpaying nonpioneer firm is simply one that earns positive taxable income in present and future periods. It is taxed at the full rate in each period. Therefore the effective statutory corporate tax rate facing the firm is simply the statutory rate u, which we assume is not expected to change.

The nominal cost of funds r_t faced by the firm is the weighted combination of its after-tax borrowing costs and the cost of raising equity from the financial market. Again, assuming these are expected to be constant over time, the cost of funds for all periods will be given by

$$r = \beta i(1 - u) + (1 - \beta)\rho$$

where these variables are defined as before. Note that with capital gains untaxed and the full imputation of corporate taxes essentially ensuring that dividends are not taxed at the personal level, the cost of equity ρ is the same whether it comes from new issues or retained earnings. At the same time, because interest is tax deductible, the cost of debt financing is $i(1 - u)$. This reflects the tax preference given to financing by debt over financing by equity at the corporate level.[47]

Finally, consider the present value of tax savings due to depreciation, Z_t. As mentioned earlier, firms are given an initial allowance and then permitted to depreciate the remainder under straight-line depreciation. If

τ is the rate of initial allowance and T is the length of time over which the asset can be depreciated (so $1/T$ is the annual rate of depreciation), Z_t will be given by

$$(1\text{-}38) \qquad Z = u\gamma + \frac{(1-\gamma)\,u}{rT}\left[1-\left(\frac{1}{1+r}\right)^{T}\right].$$

We have dropped the time subscripts because here Z_t and Z_{t-1} will be the same under the assumptions we are making. The first term is the tax benefit from the initial allowance, and the second is the present value of the tax savings from the straight-line write-off of the remaining $1-\gamma$ of the investment.

PROFIT-MAKING PIONEER FIRMS. Next, consider the case in which a firm is granted a five-year tax holiday. No taxes are paid by the firm during the tax holiday period. We begin with the pre-1989 tax system, under which initial and depreciation allowances could be delayed until the end of the tax holiday. All accumulated tax savings from the initial and annual depreciation allowances could be set off against revenues earned by the firm in the first tax year following the tax holiday period. We assume that the profits in the period immediately after the tax holiday are sufficiently large to absorb all depreciation allowances that have accumulated during the tax holiday period.

These features of the tax treatment of pioneer firms make the computation of the before-tax rate of return on investment considerably more complicated than in the case of taxpaying nonpioneer firms because u_t, r_t, and Z_t will all vary over time. Consider the computation of the three in turn.

The effective statutory corporate tax to the firm during the tax holiday period is zero because the firm is completely exempt from paying any tax on its income. The corporate tax rate will revert to its full statutory rate u after the tax holiday, however. Therefore,

$$u_t = \begin{cases} 0 \text{ for } 0 \le t \le 4 \\ u \text{ for } t > 4 \end{cases}$$

where $t = 0 \ldots 4$ represent the tax holiday periods. Given these values for u_t, the cost of finance to the firm is given by

$$r_t = \beta i\,(1-u_t) + (1-\beta)\,\rho.$$

Finally, given u_t and r_t, the value of Z_t will be given by

$$Z_t = \left(\frac{1}{1+r_t}\right)^{5-t}\left\{u\gamma + \frac{(5-t)\,u\,(1-\gamma)}{T} + \frac{u\,(1-\gamma)}{rT}\left[1-\left(\frac{1}{1+r}\right)^{T-5+t}\right]\right\}$$

(1-39) $$0 \leq t \leq 4.$$

This equation takes into account the fact that Z_t will vary according to time within the tax holiday period the investment is undertaken. Note that in the tax holiday Z_t is a monotonically increasing function of t. This implies that r_g will vary over the pioneer period, becoming constant with the return of the firm to full taxpaying status.

We have mentioned that firms may also obtain an investment tax credit. Typically, this will be in lieu of the initial allowance and the tax holiday. Like the latter, it is granted on a discretionary basis. How the investment allowance enters into METR calculations was discussed earlier and will not be repeated here.

Subsequent to the 1989 tax reform, firms were no longer allowed to carry depreciation allowances forward from the pioneer period to the fully taxpaying period. This causes the expression for Z_t (equation 1-39) to change to

$$(1\text{-}40) \qquad Z_t = \left(\frac{1}{1+r_t}\right)^{5-t} \left\{ \frac{u\,(1-\gamma)}{rT} \left[1 - \left(\frac{1}{1+r}\right)^{T-5+t}\right] \right\} \qquad 0 \leq t \leq 4.$$

The depreciation and initial allowances from the pioneer period are lost now. The expressions for u_t and r_t remain the same as before. The statutory tax rate u was also reduced by the reform, and this must be taken into account in the calculations.

NONPIONEER FIRMS IN TEMPORARY LOSS POSITIONS. Consider now the case of a firm that is taking a temporary loss over the first few periods of its operation and making a profit thereafter. For illustrative purposes, assume the firm that is incurring tax losses is in years 0 to 4 of its operations. These losses are carried forward into year 5 and set off against income in that year before taxes are paid. Suppose taxable income is large enough in year 5 to absorb all cumulated losses.

Consider first the cost of finance to the firm. Because the firm is in a loss position, it cannot obtain the full instantaneous benefits of the interest deduction. Instead, the benefit is deferred until future periods, when the loss carryforward is offset by taxable income. This deferral reduces the value of the tax saving of the interest deduction and therefore increases the after-tax cost of finance to the firm. The exact amount by which the tax advantage is reduced is rather complicated to calculate. It is useful first to consider a firm that finances new investment entirely with debt. In this case, the effective tax rate that applies to the interest deduction will be less than u because of the deferral of the interest write-off. The cost of interest finance in a period in which the firm is making losses is given by

(1-41) $$r_t = i\left[1 - \frac{u}{\Pi_{s=t}^{4}(1+r_s)}\right] \qquad t = 0, \ldots, 4.$$

This expression reflects the postponement until year 5 of the tax savings from interest costs incurred in an early time period. These tax savings must be discounted back to period t to yield their present value as of the time that the interest cost is incurred. The tax savings in year 5 are evaluated at the full corporate tax rate u applying to the firm at that time.

Equation 1-41 gives relations among the r_t for each of the five loss periods. It must be solved simultaneously for the values of r_t. To do so, we proceed recursively backward. First, solve for the cost of funds in the last period, $t = 4$. In this period, equation 1-41 is quadratic in r_4 alone. Then, substituting this solution for the positive root of r_4 back into equation 1-41, we obtain a quadratic equation in r_3, which can also be solved for its positive root. The entire set of r_t's over the loss period can be obtained by substituting the positive roots recursively into equation 1-41 one at a time. At year 5, once the firm is profit making, the usual expression for r_t applies.

The same principle can be extended to the situation in which the firm uses some equity finance. In this case, r_t is given by

$$r_t = \beta i_t + (1 - \beta)\rho \qquad t = 0, \ldots, 4$$

where

(1-42) $$i_t = i\left[1 - \frac{u}{\Pi_{s=t}^{4}(1+r_s)}\right] \qquad t = 0, \ldots, 4.$$

As above, this equation can be solved recursively for r_t during each loss period. This is the set of r_t's we use in our computations.

A similar derivation applies to u_t. Because tax liabilities are carried forward without interest from the loss years to year 5, the effective tax rate that the firm faces during the period of losses is less than the statutory rate. Using the cost of finance as derived from equation 1-41, we find that the effective corporate tax rate that applies to the revenues of the firm is

$$u_t = \frac{u}{\Pi_{s=t}^{4}(1+r_s)} \qquad t = 0, \ldots, 4.$$

Given r_t, this is straightforward to compute.

Finally, the present value of tax depreciation allowances Z_t will also be modified slightly to account for the fact that unabsorbed depreciation allowance may also be carried forward to year 5. It will be given by

$$Z_t = \prod_{s-t}^{4-t} \left(\frac{1}{1+r_s} \right) \left\{ u\gamma + \frac{(5-t)\, u\, (1-\gamma)}{T} + \frac{u\,(1-\gamma)}{rT} \left[1 - \left(\frac{1}{1+r} \right)^{T-5+t} \right] \right\}$$

(1-43) $t = 0, \ldots ,4.$

For $t \geq 5$ the expression for Z_t is again given by equation 1-38. As before, Z_t increases during the loss period.

Using these expressions for r_p, u_p and Z_p, one can calculate the time profile for $r_g(t)$ for each of the three cases. For $t \geq 5$, the values of $r_g(t)$ will all be the same as they were for taxpaying nonpioneer firms. The marginal effective corporate tax rate will then be given by $t_c = t_g - r^*$, where r^* is the cost of funds determined on international capital markets and is given by $r^* = \beta i + (1 - \beta)\, \rho - \pi$, as discussed before.

We could also calculate the marginal effective personal tax rate t_p as discussed earlier. Given our open economy arbitrage assumption, however, it would be irrelevant in evaluating investment incentives. Its effect is felt entirely on the saving side of the domestic capital market. As mentioned, given the absence of taxation of capital gains and the imputation of corporate taxes to domestic savers, the effective personal tax rate would be near zero for equity funds. Indeed, saving through purchases of new equity could be subsidized, given that the corporate tax rate can exceed the personal tax rate, so the imputation more than offsets any personal taxes owing on dividends. The marginal effective personal tax rate could be substantially larger for interest, however, because interest is not only fully taxed, it is taxed in nominal terms. Therefore the tax system gives a sizable incentive to domestic residents to hold equity rather than bonds. Because the corporate tax system does precisely the opposite, there is a net incentive to import debt capital and export equity capital. The reduction in the corporate tax rate by 10 percentage points by the tax reform of 1989 reduces the magnitude of this relative financing incentive for equity but not its direction.

Some calculations of marginal effective corporate tax rates are presented for the three cases in tables 1-1, 1-2, and 1-3. Each table reports t_c for machinery for five consecutive years under the pre-1989 and post-1989 tax systems. The main differences in the tax systems are that the rate is reduced from 45 percent to 35 percent and the deferral of depreciation allowances for pioneer firms is eliminated by the tax reform. The data used in the tables also differ from one to another. For the fully taxpaying firm, actual data for the years 1983–87 are used for financial variables, whereas for the tax loss and pioneer firms, 1983 data are used. For all examples, t_c is calculated separately for investments financed by debt and those financed by retained earnings as well as for a weighted combination of the two, in which the weights were computed from unpublished data from the Kuala Lumpur Stock Exchange.[48] Rates of return on equity were also calculated from the same source, on the basis of the return to shareholders' fund. Corporate lending rates were not available, so a base case of 12 percent was used for illustrative purposes. Actual inflation rates were used as expected ones and therefore perfectly anticipated. It should be stressed that the calculations in the tables are intended to be illustrative only. A summary of results for each of the cases follows.

Taxpaying nonpioneer firms. As the first column of table 1-1 indicates, t_c is consistently negative for debt-financed investments as a result of the deductibility of nominal interest payments. Fluctuations from year to year are due to changes in the rate of inflation. Apparently, the benefit of nominal interest deductibility in times of inflation more than offsets the disadvantage of historic cost depreciation, which tends to reduce the value of Z_r. Conversely, t_c for retained earnings is positive, as shown in the second column. The cost of equity financing is not tax deductible. In these cases, years of lower inflation (1985 and 1986) tend to lower t_c. The last column uses observed weights of debt and equity financing to calculate t_c when both sources are used at the margin. Naturally, t_c falls between the pure debt-financed and equity-financed cases, but is negative in all years. Thus the corporate tax system actually subsidizes investment at the margin.

The second part of the table reports what t_c would have been had the post-1989 tax structure been in effect. Essentially, u would be reduced from 0.45 to 0.35. The qualitative comparisons among the various cases

Table 1-1. *Marginal Effective Corporate Tax Rates for Machinery in a Profit-Making Nonpioneer Firm, 1983–87*

Year	Debt financing	Retained earnings	Debt and retained earnings
Pre-1989 budget reform			
1983	−0.0436	0.0112	−0.0223
1984	−0.0433	0.0098	−0.0231
1985	−0.0272	0.0066	−0.0155
1986	−0.0277	0.0054	−0.0158
1987	−0.0308	0.0091	−0.0118
Post-1989 budget reform			
1983	−0.0331	0.0073	−0.0173
1984	−0.0329	0.0064	0.0179
1985	0.0207	−0.0043	−0.0121
1986	−0.0211	0.0035	−0.0123
1987	−0.0235	0.0060	−0.0095

Source: Boadway, Chua, and Flatters (1989).

Table 1-2. *Marginal Effective Corporate Tax Rates for Machinery in a Profit-Making Pioneer Firm, 1983*

Profile	Debt financing	Retained earnings	Debt and retained earnings
Pre-1989 budget reform			
Year 1	−0.0118	−0.0135	−0.0124
Year 2	−0.0158	−0.0176	−0.0165
Year 3	−0.0204	−0.0219	−0.0209
Year 4	−0.0255	−0.0263	−0.0258
Steady state	−0.0436	−0.0112	−0.0223
Post-1989 budget reform			
Year 1	0.0302	0.0365	0.0325
Year 2	0.0301	0.0353	0.0320
Year 3	0.0300	0.0339	0.0315
Year 4	0.0296	0.0324	0.0307
Steady state	−0.0331	0.0073	−0.0173

Source: Boadway, Chua, and Flatters (1989).

remain exactly as before, but the absolute magnitudes are all reduced. Positive values of t_c become smaller and so do negative values.

Profit-making pioneer firms. Table 1-2 shows t_c's for a firm granted pioneer status in 1983. Ideally we would show the rates applying to marginal investments undertaken in each of the five years of the tax holiday period; but absence of pertinent data for 1982 precluded this, and so we report rates for only the final four years of the tax holiday. The last entry in each column shows t_c in the absence of pioneer status using 1983 data. It is taken from table 1-1.

Note that pioneer firm investments financed from all sources are subsidized by the tax system. The size of the subsidy is quite small. For debt-financed investments, the tax-induced subsidy is actually less than it is for nonpioneer firms. Pioneer status penalizes such investments. Basically, the advantages of interest deductibility during the tax holiday no longer exist. This is not true for equity financing. Pioneer status converts t_c from positive to negative. There is no loss in forgoing interest deductions. At the same time, firms benefit from being able to carry forward their initial and depreciation allowances until after pioneer status is finished. Thus, in principle it seems that pioneer status might serve either to increase or decrease investment incentives. Which way it works in practice will depend on which of these two effects is most important for the firm in question. If the tax burden on current revenues less interest deduction is larger (in a present value sense) than the tax savings from depreciation allowances, the first effect would be expected to dominate, and pioneer status would increase investment incentives, and vice versa. More generally, the granting of pioneer status tends to reduce the effect of the tax system on marginal investment decisions. If investment is penalized under the general tax laws, then pioneer status will reduce this disincentive. But if investments are subsidized, pioneer status will reduce the size of the subsidy. For Malaysian firms it turns out that pioneer status eliminates the bias of the tax system in favor of marginal investments financed by debt rather than equity, and it provides a net additional subsidy only to investments with sufficiently low debt-equity ratios.

Table 1-2 also reports effective corporate tax rates under the post-1989 tax structure. In addition to the reduction in u, the ability of pioneer firms to defer initial and annual depreciation allowances until the end of the tax holiday period was removed. As can be seen from table 1-2, pioneer firms now face a large positive t_c as compared with the net subsidy received under the previous system. Not only has the sign of the distortion been changed in this case, but its absolute size has been increased considerably.

The tax reform has continued to treat debt-financed marginal investments more favorably in nonpioneer than pioneer firms. For equity-financed investment, machinery is now dealt with slightly better in nonpioneer firms. It is also treated better for the reason mentioned above, that the loss of depreciation tax savings during the pioneer period is more important for machinery. The tax reforms also have the effect of reducing the differences in distortions between pioneer and nonpioneer firms.

TAX LOSS NONPIONEER FIRMS. Table 1-3 presents estimates of t_c for firms in a temporary loss position for five years. We take 1983 as the presumed initial year of the firm's operations. As in the case of a pioneer firm, we calculate t_c during the final four years of the loss period and the steady state for both the pre-1989 and post-1989 tax regimes.

Under the pre-1989 tax rules, debt-financed investments receive a small subsidy during the tax loss period, but it is considerably less than that received for a fully taxpaying firm. The size of the subsidy increases during the tax loss period. In equity-financed investments, t_c is positive. It declines over time but remains more than double that facing taxpaying firms on the same investments. For firms financing investments through a combination of debt and equity, the tax system discourages investment for loss firms while subsidizing investment for taxpaying firms.

The 1989 tax reforms do not change any of the qualitative patterns of investment distortions facing tax loss firms, but they have the uniform effect of reducing the magnitude of all the positive and negative tax incentives. This result is the same as that observed earlier for taxpaying firms.

To summarize, the corporate tax system plays an important role in determining the relative profitability of different types of investments. For some investments, it provides a considerable net subsidy. But many other

Table 1-3. Marginal Effective Corporate Tax Rates for Machinery in a Tax Loss Firm, 1983

Year	Debt financing	Retained earnings	Debt and retained earnings
Pre-1989 budget reform			
Year 1	−0.0022	0.0294	0.0101
Year 2	−0.0041	0.0277	0.0083
Year 3	−0.0064	0.0259	0.0061
Year 4	−0.0092	0.0240	0.0037
Steady state	−0.0436	0.0112	−0.0002
Post-1989 budget reform			
Year 1	−0.0018	0.0205	0.0069
Year 2	−0.0030	0.0191	0.0056
Year 3	−0.0045	0.0176	0.0041
Year 4	−0.0062	0.0160	0.0024
Steady state	−0.0331	0.0073	−0.0173

Source: Boadway, Chua, and Flatters (1989).

investments are faced with sizable tax penalties. The overall pattern of incentives and disincentives bears no obvious relation to social economic goals that might in principle guide the construction of an incentive system. The unintended consequences of these distortions, therefore, almost certainly include significant waste of investment resources. In addition, some incentives can have the opposite effect of that intended. The example of tax holidays is instructive because many developing countries resort to their use. Our calculations show that tax holidays can actually impose a net penalty on investors in some cases. They are of possible value only to firms whose taxable profits are high enough to make use of the benefits of the tax holiday; they are highly unlikely to be of value to the weak or infant investors or to the industries that are usually the intended beneficiaries of the measures. Similarly, tax rate reductions can reduce the incentive to invest, especially for firms that already have negative METRs. Finally, the effects of many measures differ according to the type of firm and investment under consideration. This can be seen especially in comparisons between tax loss and taxpaying firms.

The Effect of Tax Incentives on Investment: A Brief Survey of the Empirical Approaches and Applications in Developing Countries

The empirical analysis of tax incentives for developing countries is of recent origin, and only a few published studies are available as of this date (see, for example, Agell 1986; Ebrill 1987). In industrial nations, empirical approaches to the evaluation of tax incentives have varied from opinion surveys to rigorously derived testable models; from partial equilibrium to general equilibrium; and from macro- to microeconomic analysis. In this section we provide an overview of the principal approaches, note their key assumptions and caveats, and discuss the findings of recent developing country applications.

Surveys of Firms

Opinion surveys of company executives have frequently been used to evaluate the effectiveness of tax incentives (see Guisinger and others 1985). An objective assessment of the effect of tax measures is not possible through opinion surveys, which do not provide data on observed behavior both before and after a policy change. Hence, the validity of their results is doubtful. In spite of these limitations, opinion surveys can serve as a useful complement to more rigorous empirical analyses of these issues.

Two recent opinion surveys have explored the effectiveness of investment incentives in developing countries. Guisinger and others (1985) sought to examine the policies of governments and companies toward foreign direct investment in both industrial and developing countries. In an attempt to be comprehensive, they examined incentives ranging from tariffs to free trade zones. The study, however, failed to provide any hard evidence on the effectiveness of one or more such incentives. It relied on a survey of opinions of company executives selected arbitrarily to measure the effect of incentives on business location decisions. The executives were simply asked whether they would have still located in a particular country if no incentives had been offered to them by the country in question but competitor countries had maintained their incentive packages at their traditional levels. The responses in general were, as expected, negative. The respondents indicated that "in this hypothetical case, the absence of incentives would have affected their decision, even though, in the real instance, the presence of incentive was not a major factor in their decision" (see Guisinger and others 1985: 166). In brief, the Guisinger study suffered from a poor choice of questions for the opinion survey and purely arbitrary sampling design (that is, stratified random sampling procedures were not followed), and it failed to shed any new light on the effectiveness of tax measures to stimulate foreign direct investment.

Halvorsen (chapter 10, this volume) has analyzed the investors' responses to the survey undertaken by the Thailand Board of Investment. It is interesting to learn that investors ranked exemption or reduction of import duties on machinery and equipment and of business taxes as the most important incentive; the second most important incentive named was reduction of import duties and business taxes on raw materials. The corporate tax holiday was ranked third. Permission to bring in foreign technicians was ranked fourth.

Estimation of Ad Hoc and Eclectic Equations

This approach usually specifies private investment to be a function of a host of independent variables, including tax-related variables. Variables selection and model specification are most often based on fishing expeditions for high coefficients of multiple determination, R^2. Ebrill (1987) uses cross-section data on thirty-one developing countries for 1980 to examine the effect of cost of capital on investment. The dependent variable was the share of gross domestic investment in gross domestic product (GDP) for 1980. Other than the cost of capital, independent regressors included average annual growth rate of exports; share of minerals in exports; average annual growth rate of GDP; current account balance; inflation rate; and per capita GDP. He found that the coefficient of the cost of capital was negative and significant for the sample as a whole, but when Argentina and Chile—two high-inflation countries—were excluded, the cost of capital had the negative sign, although it was statistically insignificant. Thus, Ebrill's results confirmed only a weak relation between the cost of capital and the level of investment.

Investment Models

Investment models can be broadly classified into the following five categories:

1. The flexible capital stock adjustment model, or the accelerator theory of investment
2. The Q-theory
3. General, forward-looking models
4. Effective tax rate and return-over-cost models
5. Marginal-effective-tax-rate models

The above list of investment models is not exhaustive. For example, the corporate finance literature suggests that cash flow and the payback period could be important considerations in business investment decisions. These ideas have not yet found application in the empirical work on tax incentives. A brief description of the approaches listed above follows.

THE FLEXIBLE CAPITAL STOCK ADJUSTMENT MODEL. The simple, or naive, form of the acceleration principle postulates a certain fixed relation between the desired capital stock and output. It is argued that tax incentives affect investment through changes in desired capital stock by reducing the relative price of capital. Changes in the desired capital stock then lead to changes in net investment (or disinvestment). Shah and

Baffes (chapter 16, this volume) use this principle in a production structure approach to examine the effectiveness of tax incentives in Pakistan.

THE Q-THEORY. The essence of James Tobin's Q-theory model is that a firm will invest as long as a dollar spent buying capital raises the market value of the firm by more than a dollar. Because *q* is defined as the ratio of the market value of existing capital to its replacement, then investment will take place as long as *q* is greater than unity. Q-theory has not yet been used to analyze the effectiveness of investment incentives in developing countries.

GENERAL FORWARD-LOOKING MODELS. The decision rule governing investment in general forward-looking models is identical to that in the *Q*-theory, but the two theories differ in how the unobservable expectations are related to observable variables. Unobservable expectations have been defined in either one- or two-step transformation procedures. The two-step procedure is based on a decomposition of the investment problem into expectation formation and, given these expectations, the decision to acquire investment goods. Expectations are based on lagged variables, and the parameters derived from expectations equations are used to forecast future variables that replace unobservable expectations. These variables are then used to estimate production and adjustment parameters. Rajagopal and Shah (chapter 15, this volume) incorporate aspects of these models into a production structure framework to evaluate investment incentives in Mexico, Pakistan, and Turkey.

EFFECTIVE TAX RATE AND RETURN-OVER-COST MODELS. Feldstein (1987) is the proponent of an average effective tax rate approach to incentive evaluation. Feldstein posits that net investment is dependent on the net-of-tax real return to capital. The net-of-tax real rate of return depends on the effective tax rate, which is defined as the ratio of a comprehensive measure of all taxes assessed on capital income to operating income less depreciation. Shah and Slemrod (1991) explored the relation between average effective tax rate and inward foreign direct investment and found it to be negatively correlated.

The return-over-cost model (also presented by Feldstein) quantifies investment incentives by contrasting the maximum potential net return on a standard investment project with the cost of funds. The maximum potential net return is influenced by tax incentives. Whenever the maximum potential net return exceeds the cost of funds, firms have an incentive to acquire more capital.

THE METR MODEL. This broad strategy attempts to capture the provisions of the tax code that affect a marginal investment. Tax incentives lower the METR and thereby encourage additional investment in the tax-preferred activity until after-tax rates of return are equalized. Industry and sector-specific METRs are often used to stimulate investment behavior on an ex ante basis.

The methodology of METRs has been used to examine the incentives in the corporate tax systems in many countries. Economies for which the methodology has recently been applied include the Association of Southeast Asian Nations (Manasan 1988), Brazil (chapter 7, this volume), Colombia (McLure and Zodzow 1991), Korea (Kwack 1988), Malaysia (chapter 8, this volume), Mexico (Shah and Slemrod 1991), the Philippines (Manasan 1988), Sri Lanka (Shah 1988), Thailand (Leechor and Mintz 1991). These studies conclude that tax incentives as currently structured in these economies generally lead to windfall gains to investment activities that would have taken place anyway and generate little new investment. Instead, the prevailing incentives often accentuate intersectoral and interasset distortionary effects of taxation. Boadway, Chua, and Flatters find that tax holidays in Malaysia impose a penalty on the firms that are going to be unprofitable during the holiday period and therefore are highly unlikely to be of value to weak or infant investors. Thus, although tax incentives matter, they must be properly designed and targeted to be effective instruments in furthering public policy objectives.

The application of METR methodology to determine the incentive or disincentive effect of an indirect tax system has recently been pioneered by Boadway, Chua, and Flatters (chapter 9, this volume) They develop and apply such a methodology to an examination of the effects of the indirect tax system in Malaysia and find that the distortionary effects of such taxes on investment far exceed the distortionary effect of the direct tax system. Such taxes were seen to penalize the export sector but provide a net subsidy to import substitution industries and thereby undermine Malaysia's competitiveness. The authors' conclusions highlight an important aspect of tax policy for investment that is often overlooked in policy debates. Their work strongly emphasizes the importance of eliminating tax disincentives through the indirect tax system as a first priority for investment and export promotion in most developing nations.

Shah and Slemrod (1991) examine the tax sensitivity of foreign direct investment in Mexico by incorporating METRs on transfers and retained earnings in investment equations. They conclude that foreign direct investment in Mexico is sensitive to tax regimes in Mexico and the United States, to the credit status of multinationals, to country credit ratings, and to the regulatory environment.

A major limitation in analyzing the METR is that it tells us nothing about the actual behavioral responses to various incentives per dollar of forgone revenues. To answer this question, one needs to use METRs in further analysis as done, for example, by Shah and Slemrod (1991). Analyses of METRs also usually ignore tax capitalization and foreign tax credit provisions. These calculations can also be in error for ignoring other taxes and nontax policies. A cost-of-capital framework embodied in the production structure models overcomes the standard limitations of an effective tax rate analysis.

The Production Structure Approach

This approach examines the influence of taxation on business production and investment decisions. Only a handful of studies have yet implemented this approach for developing countries (see, for example, chapters 14, 15, and 16, this volume).

Bernstein and Shah (chapter 14) provide an empirical framework for assessing the effects of tax policy on an array of producer decisions about output supplies and input demands in Mexico, Pakistan, and Turkey. They specify and estimate a dynamic production structure model with imperfect competition for selected industries in these countries. The results from the model suggest that tax policy affects production and investment and that selective tax incentives such as investment tax credits, investment allowances, and accelerated capital consumption (depreciation) allowances are more cost-effective at promoting investment than more general tax incentives, such as corporate tax rate reductions. The long-run cost-effectiveness of these incentives, except corporate tax rate reductions, which proved cost-ineffective in all cases, varies by country. In Turkey, investment allowances and capital consumption allowances were cost-effective. In Mexico, neither the investment tax credit nor accelerated capital consumption allowances were cost-effective. In contrast, in Pakistan, both the investment tax credit and accelerated capital consumption allowances were cost-effective (see also Bernstein and Shah 1994). In the intermediate run (defined as the effect of the tax policy after one year), only the investment allowances and accelerated capital consumption allowances available to Turkish industries proved cost-effective. In order to make selective tax incentives more effective, the country must make investment tax credits refundable and permit investment and depreciation allowances to be carried forward. If stimulation of investment expenditure is the sole objective of tax policy, the reduction of the corporate tax rate is not a cost-effective instrument by which to achieve this objective.

Shah and Baffes (chapter 15) specify a dynamic factor demand model and estimate the effect of tax incentives available to Pakistani manufacturing industries. They conclude that investment tax credits and reductions in corporate tax rates were not cost-effective, whereas a full expensing option for R&D was cost-effective.

Rajagopal and Shah (chapter 16) explicitly incorporate industrial market structure in examining the effectiveness of investment incentives available to Turkish and Pakistani industries. They conclude that sample industries had limited market power and were able to shift taxes forward to consumers only partially. The effect of tax incentives varied greatly across different industries, and in only three of eleven cases did tax incentives prove cost-effective in the short run. Overall, investment tax credits fared better than other tax incentives.

Computable General Equilibrium Models

Most complex interactions in an economy are assumed away by partial equilibrium analysis. An applied general equilibrium model, however, can provide a disaggregated view of the economy and thereby yield quantitative estimates of all important interactions. It is, therefore, a valuable tool in assessing the relative merits of alternative tax policy changes.

Applied general equilibrium analysis entails several sequential steps. First, basic data are collected from a variety of sources. These data are then adjusted for microconsistency. Next, the choice of model, functional forms, and elasticity parameters are specified. Parameter values for model functions are then determined through calibration. A replication test is carried out to check that the calibration parameter values are consistent with the original data on quantities and prices and with the assumed model structure. Once this replication test is passed, a policy change is specified and a new (counterfactual) equilibrium is computed. Policy evaluation is then based on pairwise comparison between the benchmark and the new equilibrium.

Four recent studies have employed computable general equilibrium analysis to evaluate the effects of tax incentives. Clarete (chapter 18, this volume) uses a static general equilibrium model to examine the effects of tax rebates and duty drawbacks on imported machinery and equipment by priority industries. The author observes that these incentives have a strongly stimulative effect on investment. These conclusions, however, must be considered tentative because the author employed a static model. The use of a dynamic model might well lead to different qualitative and quantitative conclusions.

Trela and Whalley (1991) also use an applied general equilibrium model to examine the effect of rebates of direct and indirect taxes on exports, investment tax credits, and tax holidays on growth performance in Korea. They conclude that tax policy accounted for less than one-tenth of the growth of the Korean economy during 1962–82. These results are, however, tentative, because the model developed for this purpose did not explicitly take into account savings, investment, and the accumulation of human capital. The authors, nevertheless, expect these results to stand in a more complete analysis of Korean growth performance.

Feltenstein and Shah examine the relative efficacy of tax incentives by using disaggregated dynamic computable general equilibrium models for Mexico (chapter 17, this volume, and 1995) and Pakistan (1993). In both applications, the authors find that although the investment tax credit was more stimulative in its effect on private capital formation, corporate tax rate reductions appeared to have a superior effect on aggregate output and consumer welfare.

Concluding Remarks

This chapter has been a rather wide-ranging survey of some of the effects of tax incentives on the decision to invest in developing countries. Much of the discussion has been of a conceptual nature because the investment decision is inherently a complicated one and is not completely understood. Obviously, many factors affect the decision to invest. Only some of these factors are the conventional ones of effects on price and income, which economists are used to analyzing. Our analysis has concentrated heavily on these effects.

At the same time, there are many more intangible influences on the decision to invest, many of them specific to a given country. These include the political climate, the reliability of fiscal commitments, capital markets and the availability of cash, and both economic and political uncertainty. It is difficult to capture all these factors in an analytical framework, although some advances have been made on a piecemeal basis. It will ultimately be up to empirical analysis to indicate how successful investment incentives are likely to be in a given setting. To date, such empirical analysis has been rather limited, although that which exists is quite suggestive. We have provided a brief survey of some of the more recent work. Obviously, much remains to be done.

Even in the absence of convincing empirical analysis, there is much to be learned from theoretical reasoning about the design of investment incentives. In particular, the following factors are important considerations to be addressed in evaluating and designing investment incentives in developing economies:

- *The Effect on the* METR. Even simple tax incentives can have perverse effects on the marginal incentive to invest. Many schemes have relatively generous write-offs to begin with, so generous that a negative METR is not uncommon. In these circumstances, tax rate reductions (including tax holidays) can discourage investment. Investment tax credits are more likely to be effective.
- *The Effect on Loss Firms.* Many of the firms that investment incentives are intended to assist are those that are more likely to be in a loss position. These include small, growing firms and firms in risky environments. Incentives that do not have generous loss-offsetting or refundability provisions will be of limited use in these circumstances.

- *The Effect on Cash Flows.* Firms in need of assistance may also be those that are relatively strapped financially. Imperfections in capital markets may make it difficult to obtain outside financing. Again, incentives that improve the cash flows of firms may be much more effective than those that do not. The presence of refundability may be especially important here. Simply adopting costing principles of the cash flow type with refundability may be much more effective than reducing tax rates.
- *The Effect on Foreign Firms.* A significant amount of investment in developing countries is done by foreign-owned firms. Because these firms are typically liable for taxation in their home countries, the manner in which foreign tax-crediting arrangements apply is important in designing tax incentives. If the value of the incentive is fully offset by reduced foreign tax crediting, the incentive effect will be minimal.
- *Inter-Asset Effects.* Many tax incentives affect different types of investment decisions in different ways. Thus some measures may favor short-over long-lived capital, others may affect machinery as opposed to inventory, whereas others may favor some industries over others. In all these cases, although the incentive may encourage investment selectively, it will also cause inefficiencies from distortions in the way in which capital is allocated.

More generally, a variety of other factors must be considered in designing tax incentives. For one, inflation is typically quite high in developing countries, and it can affect investment adversely. The system of incentives should offset the effects of inflation. Another problem common in developing countries is that of tax evasion. Relatively little work has been done on the implications of tax evasion for investment activity, but presumably it is important. Also, one of the more important roles of investment in developing countries, especially foreign investment, is to facilitate the transfer of technology. Investment incentives should be designed with that in mind. Other noneconomic objectives may also be fulfilled by investment, such as social, environmental, and regional goals. Finally, taxes can affect the organization of firms and can encourage takeovers, mergers, and bankruptcies. These possible outcomes should also be borne in mind in designing tax incentives. Unfortunately, the analysis of investment incentives has not itself been developed far enough to take these considerations into account.

Appendix. Characteristics of Corporate Tax Systems in Selected Economies

Table 1A-1. Statutory Corporate Income Tax Rates
(percent)

Economy	Standard	Special		Surcharge
Industrial economies				
Australia	33.0	Fringe benefits	48.4	
Austria	34.0			
Belgium	39.0	Crisis tax	3.0	18.0
Canada	43.5	Manufacturing	35.5	
Denmark	34.0			
Finland	25.0			
France	33.3	Distribution tax	25.0	
Germany	30.0–45.0			7.5
Greece	35.0	Productive investment under 1892 law	40.0	
Ireland	40.0	Manufacturing	10.0	20.0
Italy	36.0			
Japan	37.5			
Netherlands	35.0			
New Zealand	33.0			
Norway	28.0	Oil tax	50.0	
Portugal	36.0			10.0
Spain	35.0			
Sweden	28.0			
Switzerland	21.7–46.7			
United Kingdom	33.0			
United States	35.0			
Developing economies				
Africa				
Botswana	30.0			10.0
Cameroon, Rep. of	38.5			
Congo	49.0	Public and agricultural business	36.4	
Côte d'Ivoire	35.0			
Gabon, Rep. of	40.0			5.0
Ghana	45.0	Real estate development and farming	35.0	
Kenya	35.0			
Liberia	50.0			
Malawi	35.0			
Mauritius	35.0	Medical and agriculture	15.0	
Morocco	36.0			

(Table continues on the following page.)

Table 1A-1 (continued)

Economy	Standard	Special		Surcharge
Africa (*continued*)				
Nigeria	35.0	Manufacturing, agri- culture, and mining	20.0	
Senegal	35.0			
South Africa	40.0		15.0	9.0
Swaziland	37.5	Mining	27.0	
Tanzania	35.0	Mining	17.5	
Uganda	30.0			
Zaire	50.0			
Zambia	35.0	Farming, nontradi- tional exports	15.0	
		Banking	45.0	
Zimbabwe	42.5			
Asia				
China	30.0			3.0
Fiji	35.0	Insurance	30.0	
Hong Kong	17.5			
India	40.0	Private corporations	50.0	15.0
Indonesia	30.0			
Korea, Rep. of	32.0			7.5
Malaysia	32.0	Petroleum	40.0	
Pakistan	43.0	Banking	58.0	
		Public company	33.0	
Papua New Guinea	48.0	Mining	35.0	
		Petroleum	50.0	
Philippines	35.0	Education	10.0–35.0	
		Mutual life	10.0	
Singapore	27.0			
Taiwan (China)	25.0			
Thailand	30.0			
Western Samoa	35.0			
Europe				
Cyprus	25.0			
Czech Republic	41.0			
Hungary	18.0		−38.0	23.00[a]
Malta	35.0			
Russian Federation	35.0			
Turkey	45.0			
Middle East				
Egypt	42.0	Industrial and export	34.0	
		Oil production	42.6	
Iran, Islamic Rep. of	12.0–75.0			
Kuwait	55.0			

Economy	Standard	Special		Surcharge
Middle East (*continued*)				
Oman	75.0	Agriculture	15.0[b]	
Saudi Arabia	45.0			
Latin America and the Caribbean				
Antigua	40.0			
Argentina	30.0			
Barbados	40.0			
Belize	35.0	Oil production companies	50.0	
Bolivia	30.0	Petroleum	40.0	
Brazil	25.0			10.0
Chile	15.0			
Colombia	30.0			
Costa Rica	30.0			
Dominican Republic	26.0			
Ecuador	25.0	Oil companies (distributed profits)	44.4	
		Oil companies (undistributed profits)	25.0	
El Salvador	25.0			
Guatemala	34.0			
Guyana	35.0	Commercial companies	45.0	
Honduras	35.0			15.0
Jamaica	33.3	Life insurance, agriculture, fishing, and book publishing	7.5	
Mexico	34.0		17.0	
Netherlands Antilles	43.0			15.0
Panama	34.0			
Paraguay	30.0	Agriculture	25.0	
Peru	30.0			
St. Lucia	33.3			
Trinidad and Tobago	45.0	Life insurance	15.0	
		Petroleum companies	50.0	
Uruguay	30.0			
Venezuela	30.0	Mining	60.0	
		Oil companies	67.7	

a. Surtax (over the 18 percent) for distributed profits.
b. Foreign corporation taxed up to 50 percent.
Source: Price Waterhouse (1995).

Table 1A-2. *Nonresident Corporation Withholding Tax Rates in Selected Countries*
(percent)

Economy	Nontreaty country			Treaty country		
	Dividends	Interest	Royalties	Dividends	Interest	Royalties
Industrial economies						
Australia	30.00	10.00	30.00	15.00–25.00	10.00–15.00	10.00–25.00
Austria	22.00	0.00	20.00	5.00–25.00	0.00	0.00–20.00
Belgium	25.75	13.39	13.39	5.00–20.00	0.00–13.39	0.00–13.39
Canada	25.00	25.00	25.00	5.00–25.00	10.00–25.00	5.00–25.00
Denmark	30.00	n.a.	30.00	0.00–30.00	n.a.	0.00–20.00
Finland	25.00	30.00	30.00	0.00–25.00	0.00–20.00	0.00–25.00
France	25.00	15.00–50.00	33.33	0.00–25.00	0.00–50.00	0.00–33.33
Germany	25.00	25.00	25.00	5.00–25.00	0.00–25.00	0.00–25.00
Greece	0.00	15.00, 40.00	10.00–20.00	0.00	0.00–40.00	0.00–10.00
Ireland	0.00	27.00	27.00	0.00	0.00–27.00	0.00–27.00
Italy	32.40	12.50–30.00	30.00	0.00–32.40	0.00–25.00	0.00–25.00
Japan	20.00	0.00–20.00	20.00	10.00–20.00	5.00–20.00	0.00–20.00
Netherlands	25.00	0.00	0.00	0.00–25.00	n.a.	n.a.
New Zealand	30.00	15.00	15.00	15.00–20.00	10.00–15.00	10.00–30.00
Norway	25.00	n.a.	n.a.	10.00–25.00	n.a.	n.a.
Portugal	25.00–30.00	20.00	15.00	15.00–20.00	15.00–25.00	5.00–15.00
Spain	25.00	25.00	25.00	5.00–18.00	0.00–15.00	5.00–15.00
Sweden	30.00	0.00	n.a.	0.00–30.00	0.00	5.00–25.00
Switzerland	35.00	35.00	0.00	5.00–35.00	0.00–35.00	n.a.
United Kingdom	0.00	25.00	25.00	15.00	0.00–25.00	0.00–25.00
United States	30.00	30.00	30.00	n.a.[a]	n.a.	n.a.

Developing economies

Africa

Botswana	15.00	15.00	15.00	15.00	15.00	15.00
Cameroon, Rep. of	25.00	0.00	15.00	16.50	16.50	15.00
Congo	20.00–22.00	15.00–30.00	20.00	15.00	n.a.	15.00
Côte d'Ivoire	12.00–18.00	9.00–18.00	20.00	n.a.	n.a.	10.00
Gabon, Rep. of	20.00	10.00	10.00	n.a.	n.a.	n.a.
Ghana	10.00	30.00	n.a.	10.00	30.00	n.a.
Kenya	10.00	12.50	20.00	10.00	12.50	12.50–20.00
Liberia	15.00	15.00	30.00	n.a.	n.a.	n.a.
Malawi	5.00–15.00	5.00–15.00	5.00–15.00	n.a.	n.a.	n.a.
Morocco	15.00	10.00	10.00	5.00–15.00	10.00	10.00
Nigeria	10.00	10.00	15.00	10.00	10.00	15.00
Senegal	16.00	n.a.	35.00	n.a.	n.a.	n.a.
South Africa	15.00	0.00	12.00	5.00–15.00	0.00	0.00–12.00
Swaziland	15.00	10.00	10.00	n.a.	n.a.	n.a.
Tanzania	20.00	15.00	30.00	10.00–20.00	12.50–20.00	15.00–30.00
Zaire	20.00	20.00	30.00	n.a.	n.a.	n.a.
Zambia	10.00	10.00	10.00	0.00–20.00	0.00–30.00	0.00–10.00
Zimbabwe	20.00	10.00	20.00	20.00	10.00	7.50–20.00

Asia

China	20.00	20.00	20.00	5.00–15.00	5.00–10.00	6.00–15.00
Fiji	30.00	15.00	25.00	15.00–20.00	10.00	10.00–15.00
India	20.00	20.00	30.00	15.00–25.00	5.00–25.00	10.00–30.00
Indonesia	20.00	20.00	20.00	15.00–20.00	0.00–20.00	10.00–20.00
Korea, Rep. of	25.00	25.00	25.00	5.00–20.00	5.00–15.00	0.00–15.00

(Table continues on the following page.)

Table 1A-2 (continued)

Economy	Nontreaty country			Treaty country		
	Dividends	*Interest*	*Royalties*	*Dividends*	*Interest*	*Royalties*
Malaysia	0.00	0.00–15.00	10.00	0.00	0.00–15.00	0.00–10.00
Pakistan	15.00	43.00	43.00	5.00–15.00	0.00–30.00	0.00–30.00
Papua New Guinea	17.00	48.00	10.00–30.00	n.a.	n.a.	n.a.
Philippines	30.00–35.00	30.00–35.00	30.00–35.00	15.00–25.00	0.00–25.00	10.00–25.00
Singapore	n.a.	27.00	27.00	0.00	0.00–25.00	0.00–27.00
Taiwan (China)	15.00, 35.00	20.00	20.00	n.a.	n.a.	n.a.
Thailand	10.00	15.00	15.00	10.00	3.00–15.00	5.00–15.00
Western Samoa	15.00	15.00	15.00	n.a.	n.a.	n.a.
Europe						
Cyprus	30.00	25.00	10.00	25.00	15.00	0.00–10.00
Czechoslovakia	25.00	15.00, 25.00	10.00, 25.00	0.00–25.00	0.00–15.00	0.00–25.00
Hungary	23.00	18.00	18.00	5.00–20.00	0.00–25.00	0.00–40.00
Malta	35.00	25.00, 35.00	25.00, 35.00	30.00–35.00	5.00–15.00	0.00–12.50
Turkey	0.00	10.00	25.00	12.00–25.00	10.00–15.00	10.00–12.00
Middle East						
Egypt	n.a.	32.00	25.00	n.a.	n.a.	n.a.
Iran, Islamic Rep. of	12.00–54.00	12.00–54.00	12.00–54.00	15.00, 20.00	15.00	10.00
Latin America and the Caribbean						
Antigua and Barbuda	0.00	0.00–40.00	0.00–25.00	n.a.	n.a.	n.a.
Argentina	0.00	12.00	18.00–24.00	0.00	10.00–12.00	5.00–24.00
Barbados	12.50, 15.00	12.50–15.00	0.00, 15.00	0.00–15.00	5.00–15.00	0.00–15.00
Belize	0.00	25.00	25.00	0.00	25.00	25.00

Bolivia	12.50	12.50	12.50	12.50	12.80
Brazil	15.00	25.00	15.00–25.00	10.00–25.00	10.00–25.00
Chile	35.00	35.00	n.a.	n.a.	n.a.
Colombia	10.00	30.00	n.a.	n.a.	n.a.
Costa Rica	15.00	25.00	n.a.	n.a.	n.a.
Dominican Republic	26.00	27.00	18.00	18.00	18.00
Ecuador	25.00	33.00	n.a.	n.a.	n.a.
El Salvador	0.00	0.00, 20.00	n.a.	n.a.	n.a.
Guatemala	12.50	25.00	n.a.	n.a.	n.a.
Guyana	15.00	0.00, 10.00	n.a.	n.a.	n.a.
Honduras	10.00, 15.00	35.00	n.a.	n.a.	n.a.
Jamaica	33.33	33.33	15.00–22.50	12.50–15.00	0.00
Mexico	0.00	4.90–35.00, 15.00, 35.00	5.00–15.00	10.00–15.00	10.00
Panama	10.00	15.00–17.00	n.a.	n.a.	n.a.
Paraguay	0.00, 5.00	0.00, 35.00	0.00, 35.00	n.a.	n.a.
Peru	0.00	10.00–30.00	0.00–30.00	n.a.	n.a.
St. Lucia	0.00	25.00	n.a.	n.a.	n.a.
Trinidad and Tobago	25.00	20.00	15.00–20.00	0.00–30.00	0.00–30.00
Uruguay	n.a.	30.00	n.a.	n.a.	n.a.
Venezuela	0.00	3.00–20.00	0.00	5.00–10.00	5.00–10.00

n.a. Not applicable.

a. Not subject to U.S. tax, except dividends repatriated in the United States, which get credit for taxes paid abroad.

Source: Price Waterhouse (1995).

Table 1A-3. Depreciation Rules in Selected Economies

Economy	Depreciation methods	Asset price	Initial allowance	Basis of inventory valuation	Acceler- ated CCA
Industrial economies					
Australia	SL, DB			C, M, R	Yes
Austria	SL		15 percent	FIFO, MA, LIFO	No
Belgium	SL, DDB			C, M, LIFO	No
Canada	DB			C, M, LIFO	No
Denmark	DB		30 percent	C, M	No
Finland	DB			FIFO, R	Yes
France	SL, DB			C, M, FIFO, AC	No
Germany	SL, DB			C, FIFO, LIFO	No
Greece	SL			C, M, LIFO	No
Ireland	SL	Current		C, M, LIFO, FIFO	Yes
Italy	SL	Current		FIFO, LIFO, AC	
Japan	SL, DB	Current		All methods	Yes
Netherlands	SL, DB			C, M, FIFO, LIFO, AC	No
New Zealand	DB, SL			C, M, R	No
Norway	DB			C, FIFO	No
Portugal	SL, DB			C, AC, FIFO	Yes
Spain	SL			C, AC	Yes
Sweden	Book			C, M, FIFO	No
Switzerland	SL, DB			AC, FIFO	No
United Kingdom	DB			C, M, FIFO	No
United States	ACRS			FIFO, LIFO	No
Developing economies					
Africa					
Botswana	SL		25 percent building industry	C	No
Cameroon, Rep. of	SL			C, M	No
Congo	SL			C, M, LIFO	Yes
Côte d'Ivoire	SL	Historic		C, M, LIFO	Yes
Gabon, Rep. of	SL			C, M, FIFO, C	Yes
Ghana	DB		3 percent building industry 5 percent mining	C	No
Kenya	SL, DB	Current, historic		C, M	No
Liberia	SL	Historic		LIFO	No
Malawi	SL			C, NRV	No

Economy	Depreciation methods	Asset price	Initial allowance	Basis of inventory valuation	Accelerated CCA
Africa (*continued*)					
Mauritius	SL	Historic	25 percent industry, 50 percent hotels	C, M	No
Morocco	SL			FIFO, AC	No
Nigeria	SL		25 percent manufacturing, construction	FIFO	No
Senegal	SL			C, M	Yes
South Africa	DB,SL			C, M	No
Swaziland	DB		50 percent manufacturing	FIFO, AC	No
Tanzania	SL, DB			C, NRV	No
Uganda	DB			C, M, FIFO	No
Zaire	SL			WA, C, M, LIFO	No
Zambia	SL, DB			C, M, FIFO	No
Zimbabwe	SL, DB			FIFO, C, M	Yes
Asia					
China	SL			SA, C, FIFO, WA	Yes
Fiji	SL		30 percent machinery, 10 percent building	C, FIFO, NR	Yes
Hong Kong	SL		2–20 percent building industry 60 percent machinery and equipment	C, M, LIFO, FIFO	
India	WDV	Historic		LIFO, FIFO, C, M, AC	No
Indonesia	WDV, SL			AC, FIFO	No
Korea, Rep. of	DDB, SL	Current		C, M, LIFO	No
Malaysia	SL			FIFO, AC, C, NRV	No

(Table continues on the following page.)

Table 1A-3 (continued)

Economy	Depreciation methods	Asset price	Initial allowance	Basis of inventory valuation	Accelerated CCA
Asia (*continued*)					
Pakistan	DB, SL			FIFO, C, M	No
Papua New Guinea	SL, DB			C, M, R	No
Philippines	SL			C, M	No
Singapore	SL				No
Taiwan (China)	SL, DB			WA, MA, C, FIFO, LIFO	Yes
Thailand	SL			C, M, LIFO	No
Western Samoa	DB				No
Europe					
Cyprus	SL	Historic		NRV, C, FIFO	Yes
Czech Republic	SL			C, NR	
Hungary	SL			AC, C, FIFO, LIFO	Yes
Malta	DB, SL			C, M	No
Turkey	DB, SL			MA, AC	No
Russian Federation	SL	Historic		LIFO, FIFO	No
Middle East					
Egypt	DB, SL	Historic		LIFO, FIFO	No
Iran, Islamic Rep. of	DB, SL			C, M	No
Kuwait	SL			FIFO, LIFO	No
Oman	SL			FIFO, LIFO	Yes
Saudi Arabia	SL			AC, FIFO	No
Latin America and the Caribbean					
Antigua and Barbuda	DB		2 percent building	NRV, C, FIFO, AC	No
Argentina	SL	Current	2 percent building	FIFO	No
Barbados	SL		4 percent industry, building	C, FIFO, AC, NRV	No
			10–20 percent oil production		No
					No
Belize	WDV			All methods	No
Bolivia	SL			R, NRV	No

Economy	Depreciation methods	Asset price	Initial allowance	Basis of inventory valuation	Accelerated CCA
Latin America and the Caribbean (*continued*)					
Brazil	SL			C, M	No
Chile	SL	Current		Replacement cost	Yes
Colombia	SL	Historic		LIFO, FIFO	No
Costa Rica	SL, SD			C, FIFO, LIFO, AC	No
Dominican Republic	DB			LIFO	No
Ecuador	SL			FIFO, AC, LIFO	No
El Salvador	SL			FIFO, AC, LIFO	No
Guatemala	SL			AC, FIFO	No
Guyana	SL, DB			AC, NRV, C, M, FIFO	Yes
Honduras	SL			C, M, LIFO	No
Jamaica	DB	Historic		C, M	No
Mexico	SL	Current		FIFO, LIFO	No
Netherlands Antilles	AD			LIFO	Yes
Panama	SL, DB, SD			FIFO, LIFO, AC	No
Paraguay	SL			All methods	No
Peru	SL	Current		AC, FIFO	No
St. Lucia	DB		20 percent industry, building, and machinery	C, M	No
Trinidad and Tobago	AD			AC, FIFO, C, M	Yes
Uruguay	SL			FIFO, LIFO	No
Venezuela	SL	Historic		C, M	No

ACRS = accelerated cost recovery system; AD = accelerated depreciation; CCA = capital consumption (depreciation) allowances; C = cost; DB = declining balance; DDB = double-declining balance; FIFO = first in first out; IME = immediate expensing; LIFO = last in first out; M = market selling value; MA = moving average; NRV = net realized value; PC = prime cost; R = replacement price; SA = shifting average; SD = sum of year's digits; SL = straight line; WA = weighted average; WDV = written-down value.

Source: Price Waterhouse (1995).

Table LA-4. Corporate Tax Holidays in Selected Economies

Economy	Period (years)	Exemption (percent)	Treatment of depreciation	Treatment of losses	Other features
Bangladesh	4–12	100	Unused mandatory deductions carried forward	Not carried forward after holiday	5–30 percent of income invested in government bonds exempt from personal income tax
Belgium	5	100	n.a.	n.a.	Investments relating to real estate land, plant, and equipment
Bolivia	3–10	100	n.a.	n.a.	As of 1994, only for companies registered with the Instituto Nacional de Inversiones
China	2	100	n.a.	n.a.	Manufacturing enterprises are eligible for income tax exemption for two years, beginning with the first profit-making year and a 50 percent tax reduction in the following three years
	3 or more years	50	Accelerated	n.a.	
Côte d'Ivoire	7–11	100 percent for up to 8 years and 75, 50, and 25 percent in the last 3 years	Carried forward indefinitely	Carried forward 3 years	Tax holiday granting depends on the nature of the business and the geographical locations
Ecuador	1–20	100	n.a.	n.a.	Companies involved in offshore operations
France	10	100	n.a.	n.a.	Investment in underdeveloped areas
India	5	100	n.a.	n.a.	Export industries and all industries in designated "backward areas"

Korea, Rep. of	5	100	n.a.	n.a.	Applies to foreign investment in high-technology businesses
Malaysia	5–10	70–100	Depreciation delayed until end of holiday	Pioneer firms can carry forward indefinitely	Applies to companies that participate in a promoted activity, or one of strategic importance
Malta	10	100	n.a.	Carried forward indefinitely	Export-oriented industries
Morocco	5–14	100	Carried forward in loss years only	Carried forward 4 years	
Pakistan	5–8	100	n.a.	n.a.	Applies to high technology companies, dairy and poultry farms, fishing industry, and industrial undertakings in specified backward areas
Panama	10–20	100	n.a.	Carried forward three years	Manufacturing and high-tech export firms established in a province other than Panama and Colon
Papua New Guinea	5–10	100	n.a.	n.a.	10 years for investment in a rural development area and 5 years for pioneer industries
Philippines	4–6	100	n.a.	n.a.	Pioneer firms have 6 years; nonpioneer firms have 4 years
Thailand	3–8	100	n.a.	n.a.	For specified sectors and for enterprises located in investment promotion zones
	plus 5–10	50	n.a.		

n.a. Not applicable.
Source: Price Waterhouse (1995).

Table 1A-5. Other Tax Incentives in Selected Economies

Economy	Investment tax credits	Investment allowances	Export incentives	Other incentives
Industrial economies				
Australia	n.a.	150 percent deductions for research and development	Cash grant for export market development expenditure	Accelerated deductions for capital expenditures on exploration and extraction of petroleum
Belgium	3–18.5 percent for qualifying investments	n.a.	n.a.	n.a.
Canada	20–35 percent tax credit for research expenditures in Canada; 15 or 30 of eligible investments	Resource allowance—30 percent of resource profits; mining and oil and gas activities; 100 percent deduction of intangible exploration costs	n.a.	n.a.
Denmark	n.a.	n.a.	n.a.	Long-term loans at a low interest rate on Danish ships
Finland	n.a.	n.a.	n.a.	Depreciation increased by 50 percent for investments in production facilities and tourism
France	50 percent over excess expenses for qualifying research expenditures (after three years)	n.a.	n.a.	n.a.
Greece	n.a.	Yes	1–3 percent of total exports sales deductible from taxable income	n.a.

Ireland	n.a.	n.a.	n.a.	10 percent reduced-rate corporate tax for manufacturing operations; cash grants for research and development
Italy	n.a.	n.a.	n.a.	Loans at low interest rates and grants for depressed regions
Japan	20 percent tax credit for research and experimental expenses; 3.5 percent or 7 percent of acquisition cost for machinery and equipment	n.a.	n.a.	n.a.
Netherlands	18 percent on investment up to Dfl56,000	n.a.	n.a.	n.a.
New Zealand	n.a.	n.a.	n.a.	n.a.
Norway	n.a.	20 percent deduction of pretax annual profit to consolidation fund	n.a.	n.a.
Portugal	n.a.	n.a.	n.a.	Only 60 percent of dividends and 80 percent of interest on bonds subject to tax
Spain	General 5 percent tax credit on new fixed assets; 15–30 percent tax credit on intangibles for R&D; and 30–45 percent for fixed assets	n.a.	n.a.	n.a.
United Kingdom	n.a.	n.a.	n.a.	Regional Selective Assistance grants for projects in designated assisted areas available in cash

(Table continues on the following page.)

Table 1A-5 (continued)

Economy	Investment tax credits	Investment allowances	Export incentives	Other incentives
United States	Energy investment credit allowed for 10 percent of investment in qualified energy property; 10–20 percent credit also available for expenditure related to rehabilitation of older business real estate	n.a.	Preferential tax treatment for export-related earnings of certain corporations	n.a.
Developing economies				
Africa				
Botswana	n.a.	Extra tax reliefs on revenue or capital account for specific building developments	n.a.	n.a.
Cameroon, Rep. of	n.a.	n.a.	n.a.	15 percent reduction of customs duties on imported assets and raw materials
Côte d'Ivoire	n.a.	40–60 percent deductible on expenditures	Export subsidies	n.a.
Gabon, Rep. of	n.a.	n.a.	No turnover tax is levied on export sales	New companies exempt from the minimum corporate tax for 2 years
Kenya	n.a.	85 percent new building and hotels outside Nairobi and Mombasa	n.a.	n.a.
Liberia	n.a.	n.a.	Yes	n.a.
Malawi	n.a.	40 percent on long-term on new and qualifying assets	n.a.	n.a.
Mauritius	n.a.	25 percent hotels and industrial building	n.a.	15 percent reduced corporate tax

Country				
Morocco	n.a.	100 percent exemption of income tax on exports for 5 years	n.a.	n.a.
Nigeria	n.a.	Refund on import duty for export manufacturers	n.a.	Tax reductions for enterprises located in rural areas
Asia				
China	n.a.	n.a.	n.a.	15–30 percent reduction of tax on investment in special economic zones
Fiji	n.a.	55 percent on hotels	Yes	n.a.
Hong Kong	n.a.	n.a.	n.a.	Special tax provision for insurance and shipping companies
India	n.a.	50 percent on new ships, aircraft, and machinery	n.a.	n.a.
Malaysia	n.a.	Up to 60 percent of capital expenditure on factories; research allowance of 50 percent for in-house research and development	5 percent free on board value for exports	Abatement of 70 percent of profits for corporations in the industrial and commercial sector
Pakistan	15 percent for plant and equipment investment	n.a.	Exempt from income tax for 3 years and 100 percent above a certain amount thereafter	n.a.
Papua New Guinea	n.a.	n.a.	n.a.	Quota protection
Philippines	50 percent deduction of incremental labor expenses in special areas	100 percent exemption from taxes and duties on imported capital equipment	n.a.	n.a.

(Table continues on the following page.)

Economy	Investment tax credits	Investment allowances	Export incentives	Other incentives
Europe				
Cyprus	n.a.	Up to 45 percent for fixed assets	90 percent of profits or dividends	Available for offshore entities and ship-owning companies
Hungary	n.a.	Up to 100 percent investment rebates in manufacturing industries; available for joint venture	n.a.	Interests on investment projects financed by banks are tax deductible
Malta	30 percent on plant and machinery; 15 percent on buildings	Tax-free profits distributed to share holders; 120 percent tax-deductible training costs	Yes	n.a.
Turkey	n.a.	20–70 percent of cost of assets acquired in connection with specific projects	n.a.	n.a.
Middle East				
Kuwait	n.a.	n.a.	n.a.	Soft and long-term loans
Oman	15 percent of actual cost of machinery	n.a.	n.a.	Tax free status for companies engaged in economic development
Latin America and the Caribbean				
Antigua and Barbuda	n.a.	n.a.	n.a.	International business company exempt from local taxation for 50 years provided it does not trade in Antigua

Country				
Argentina	n.a.	n.a.	Exports are exempt from value added and excise taxes	n.a.
Barbados	n.a.	n.a.	Depreciation allowance of 120 percent or 140 percent of actual cost for exporters outside CARICOM; export allowance of 93 percent when eligible sales exceed 81 percent of total sales	n.a.
Bolivia	n.a.	n.a.	Exportable goods receive tax reimbursements for value-added, gross income, and excise taxes	Exemption from national, state, and municipal taxes for construction
Brazil	n.a.	n.a.	Excise and sales service tax exemptions for exporters of manufactured goods	Sale of some capital equipment exempt from state sales and service taxes; tax holidays for investments in specified areas
Chile	n.a.	n.a.	Reimbursement of taxes paid to import goods required for export activities	Guaranteed income tax of 42 percent for 10 years
Colombia	n.a.	n.a.	Selected products receive income tax certificates of 5–9 percent; export of nontraditional products	n.a.
Costa Rica	n.a.	50 percent of reinvested profits deductible from taxable income	n.a.	n.a.
Dominican Republic	n.a.	n.a.	n.a.	n.a.

(Table continues on the following page.)

Table 1A-5 (continued)

Economy	Investment tax credits	Investment allowances	Export incentives	Other incentives
Ecuador	n.a.	n.a.	Yes	Special tax treatment for mining and tourism
El Salvador	n.a.	n.a.	Full tax exemption and un-restricted remission of profits	n.a.
Guatemala	n.a.	n.a.	Exemption of import and duties on machinery and equipment	n.a.
Guyana	n.a.	70 percent on equipment	50 percent of export profits	n.a.
Honduras	n.a.	n.a.	10–20 percent rebate on exports	n.a.
Jamaica	n.a.	n.a.	n.a.	Write-off of 120 percent of market equipment cost over time
Mexico	10–40 percent for priority industries and for regional development	n.a.	Duty-free imports for equip-ment and merchandise for production of exports	Present value of CCAs im-mediately deductible
Netherlands Antilles	n.a.	8–12 percent on buildings	Yes	n.a.
Panama	n.a.	n.a.	Yes	Exemption of taxes to encourage expansion of local industries
Paraguay	Yes	n.a.	n.a.	95 percent income tax exemp-tion for investment inome
Peru	n.a.	n.a.	n.a.	Exemption from income tax in frontier zones

n.a. Not applicable.
Source: Price Waterhouse (1995).

Table 1A-6. *Tax Treatment of Losses in Selected Economies*

Economy	Loss carry forward (years)	Loss carry backward (years)
Industrial economies		
Australia	Indefinitely	0
Austria	7	0
Belgium	Indefinitely	0
Canada	7	3
Denmark	5	0
Finland	10	0
France	5	3
Germany	Indefinitely	2
Greece	5	0
Ireland	Indefinitely	3
Italy	5	0
Japan	5	1
Netherlands	8	3
New Zealand	Indefinitely	0
Norway	10	2
Portugal	5	0
Spain	5	0
Sweden	Indefinitely	0
Switzerland	2	0
United Kingdom	Indefinitely	3
United States	15	3
Africa		
Botswana	5	0
Cameroon, Rep. of	3	0
Congo	3	0
Côte d'Ivoire	3	0
Gabon, Rep. of	3	0
Ghana	2	0
Kenya	Indefinitely	0
Liberia	5	0
Malawi	Indefinitely	0
Mauritius	Indefinitely	0
Morocco	4	0
Nigeria	4	0
Senegal	3	0
South Africa	Indefinitely	0
Swaziland	Indefinitely	0
Tanzania	Indefinitely	0
Uganda	Indefinitely	0

(Table continues on the following page.)

Table 1A-6 (continued)

Economy	Loss carry forward (years)	Loss carry backward (years)
Africa (*continued*)		
Zaire	2	0
Zambia	Indefinitely	1
Zimbabwe	6	0
Asia		
China	5	0
Fiji	6	0
Hong Kong	Indefinitely	0
India	8	0
Indonesia	5 or 8	0
Korea, Rep. of	5	0
Malaysia	Indefinitely	0
Pakistan	6–10	0
Papua New Guinea	7 or indefinite for primary production	0
Philippines	Indefinitely	0
Singapore	Indefinitely	0
Taiwan (China)	5	0
Thailand	5	0
Western Samoa	Indefinitely	0
Europe		
Cyprus	Until December 1995	0
Hungary	Indefinitely	0
Malta	Indefinitely	0
Turkey	5	0
Middle East		
Egypt	5	0
Iran, Islamic Rep. of	Indefinitely	0
Kuwait	Indefinitely	0
Oman	5	0
Latin America and the Caribbean		
Antigua and Barbuda	6	0
Argentina	5	0
Barbados	9	0
Belize	Indefinitely	0
Brazil	4	0
Chile	Indefinitely	0
Colombia	5	0
Costa Rica	3-5	0

Economy	Loss carry forward (years)	Loss carry backward (years)
Latin America and the Caribbean (*continued*)		
Dominican Republic	3	0
Ecuador	5	0
El Salvador	0	0
Guatemala	4	0
Guyana	Indefinitely	0
Honduras	3 for some sectors	0
Jamaica	Indefinitely	0
Mexico	5	0
Netherlands Antilles	5	0
Peru	4	0
St. Lucia	6	0
Trinidad and Tobago	Indefinitely	0
Uruguay	3	0
Venezuela	3	0

Source: Price Waterhouse (1995).

Table 1A-7. Source Rules for Corporations in Selected Economies

Economy	Rule	Treatment
Industrial economies		
Australia	Residence	Credit
Austria	Residence	n.a.
Belgium	Residence	Credit, treaty
Canada	Residence	Credit
Denmark	Residence	Credit
France	Source	n.a.
Germany	Residence	Credit, treaty
Italy	Residence	Credit, treaty
Japan	Residence	Credit, treaty
Netherlands	Residence	Credit, treaty
Norway	Residence	Credit, treaty
Sweden	Residence	Credit, treaty
Switzerland	Residence	Treaty
United Kingdom	Residence	Credit
United States	Residence	Credit
Developing economies		
Africa		
Kenya	Residence	Credit, treaty
Liberia	Source	n.a.
Morocco	Source	n.a.
Nigeria	Residence, source	Treaty
Zambia	Residence	Credit
Zimbabwe	Source	Credit
Asia		
China	Residence	Credit
Hong Kong	Source	n.a.
India	Residence, Source	Treaty
Indonesia	Residence	Credit
Korea, Rep. of	Residence, source	Credit
Malaysia	Residence	Credit
Pakistan	Residence	Credit
Philippines	Residence, source	Credit
Singapore	Residence	Credit
Taiwan (China)	Residence	Credit
Thailand	Residence, source	Credit, treaty
Europe		
Hungary	Residence, except foreign dividends	Credit
Turkey	Residence	n.a.

Economy	Rule	Treatment
Middle East		
Iran, Islamic Rep. of	Source	n.a.
Saudi Arabia	Source	n.a.
Latin America and		
the Caribbean		
Ecuador	Residence	Credit
El Salvador	Source	n.a.
Guatemala	Source	n.a.
Honduras	Residence	None
Jamaica	Residence	Treaty, deduction
Mexico	Residence	Credit
Netherlands Antilles	Residence	Treaty
Panama	Source	n.a.
Peru	Residence	Credit
Trinidad and Tobago	Residence	Credit
Uruguay	Source	n.a.
Venezuela	Source, with exceptions	n.a.

n.a. Not applicable.
Source: Price Waterhouse (1995).

Notes

The authors are grateful for the assistance provided by Alan Douglas and Marianne Vigneault in the preparation of this chapter.

1. This is discussed more formally in Boadway and Bruce (1992).

2. The arguments are well known and are presented in Meade (1978) and U.S. Treasury (1977), among other places.

3. This point has been long recognized in the literature. See, for example, Feldstein and Hartman (1979); Gersovitz (1987); and Musgrave (1969).

4. This argument is from Marglin (1963) and Sen (1967), who made the point in the context of the literature on social discount rates.

5. α could be defined so that cohorts with larger populations have proportionately higher weights. For example, α could equal $\hat{\alpha} - n$, where $\hat{\alpha}$ is the rate of discount of the future. Thus the social welfare function would be

$$W = \sum_{t=1}^{\infty} \frac{u_t}{(1 + \hat{\alpha})^t} (1 + n)^t.$$

6. Some key references are Arrow (1962); Kaldor and Mirrlees (1962); and Kennedy (1961). This literature is surveyed in Hahn and Matthews (1965).

7. The consequences of this have been analyzed by Hubbard and Judd (1987).

8. For examples of such an analysis see Smith (1982) and Gordon and Varian (1988).

9. See, for example, Bond and Samuelson (1989b).

10. The classic paper in this area is MacDougall (1960).

11. See the survey in Harris (1989).

12. For a general treatment, see Boadway and Bruce (1984b) and Drèze and Stern (1987). See also the various manuals for project evaluation in developing countries.

13. Boadway and Flatters (1981), however, make a case for regional employment subsidies in a more general version of the Harris-Todaro model, in which labor migrates from a low-wage sector to a high-wage sector with unemployment.

14. In fact, Stiglitz (1974) developed one of the earliest models of efficiency wages, using it to explain dual economy features of a developing economy.

15. This is analyzed in Leechor and Mintz (1991).

16. Bond and Samuelson (1986) used tax holidays as the government's choice of instrument, but others would do as well.

17. Examples of these calculations may be found in Feldstein, Dicks-Mireaux, and Poterba (1983) and Fullerton and others (1981).

18. For example, see King and Fullerton (1984).

19. The tax base is revenue less nominal interest (iB_t) less tax depreciation (αA_t), where

$$A_t = e^{-\alpha t} A_0 + \int_t^{\infty} e^{\alpha(t-s)} (1 - \theta) Q_s I_s \, ds$$

and $I_s = \dot{K}_t + \delta K_t$ is gross investment. The base for tax depreciation is reduced by the investment tax credit, which is commonly the case. Other variants could be readily incorporated.

20. The financial part of the objective function may be written:

$$\int_t^\infty e^{-\frac{\rho}{1-c}(s-t)} \left(\dot{B}_s - i\,(1 - u)\, B_s \right) \frac{(1 - \theta)}{(1 - c)}\, ds \,.$$

21. This procedure of assuming that a firm's optimization can be treated as a two-stage problem with the first stage representing the choice of a financial structure and the second stage a real capital structure can be justified under certain restrictive assumptions. For example, if the firm's costs of debt and equity capital are increasing functions of the debt-equity ratio, that will be the case. (This is demonstrated analytically in Boadway 1987.) It will also be true if the firm is quantity-constrained in debt or if the financial structure of the firm is determined by its cash flow according to the pecking order of costs of various sorts of finance.

22. From the capital market equilibrium condition in equation 1-3, for a given value of E_t, reducing current dividends by \$1 causes share values to rise by $(1 - \theta)/(1 - c)$ dollars. Therefore increasing retained earnings by $(1 - \beta)$ will cause the value of equity to rise by

$$(1 - \beta)\frac{(1 - \theta)}{(1 - c)}\,.$$

The fixed debt-equity ratio requires that $B = bE$. Therefore to keep b fixed, the debt increase β accompanying the increase in retained earnings is given by

$$\beta = b\,(1 - \beta)\,\frac{(1 - \theta)}{(1 - c)}.$$

Solving this expression for β gives

$$\beta = \frac{b\,(1 - \theta)/(1 - c)}{1 + b\,(1 - \theta)/(1 - c)}$$

as in the text.

23. The logic behind this is as follows: treat equation 1-4 as though it referred to value per share. Let $d = De^{-\pi t}$ be the flow of real dividends per share. If d were constant over time, integration of equation 1-4 would yield

$$E = d\,\frac{(1 - \theta)/(1 - c)}{(\rho/(1 - c) - \pi)}.$$

For generality we allow the required rate of return to new equity owners σ to differ from existing shareholders ρ. From the point of view of new equity owners the analogous expression for the value per share would be

$$E = d\,\frac{(1 - \theta)/(1 - c)}{(\sigma/(1 - c) - \pi)}.$$

Consider now a new share issue of \$1. In itself, this will cause the value of existing equity to fall by \$1. Using the above expression for E, we find that a change in E of \$1 is equivalent to a change in the perpetual flow of dividends of

$$d = \frac{\sigma}{(1 - \theta)} - \pi\,\frac{(1 - c)}{(1 - \theta)}.$$

This is the flow cost to existing shareholders of raising \$1 of new equity. See also Auerbach (1979).

24. The actual problem of the firm is

$$\max_{\dot{K},\dot{A}} \int_0^\infty e^{-rt} \left[P_t F(K_t)(1-u) - (1-\phi) Q_t (\dot{K}_t + \delta K_t) + u\alpha A_t \right] dt.$$

$$\text{s.t. } \dot{A}_t + \alpha A_t = (1-\phi) Q_t (\dot{K}_t + \delta K_t)$$

25. For example, indexing the book value of capital for depreciation would change the present-value expression to $u\alpha/(r + \alpha - \pi)$. Alternatively, straight-line depreciation over a length of life T would give a present value of tax savings of $u(1 - e^{-rT})/rT$.

26. This computation is adapted from Boadway, Chua, and Flatters (1989).

27. The following analysis is adopted from Boadway, Bruce, and Mintz (1982). It might be noted that from an analytical point of view, the treatment of renewable resources would be similar to that of inventories.

28. We analyze the case of FIFO tax accounting for illustrative purposes. Some countries (for example, the United States) allow firms to use last in, first out (LIFO) accounting for taxes.

29. The following analysis is adapted from Boadway, Bruce, McKenzie, and Mintz (1987).

30. This result is originally from Smith (1963) but is discussed more fully in Stiglitz (1973) and Boadway and Bruce (1984a). It can easily be generalized to include investment tax credits.

31. We say "typically" because r_g is nonlinear in the tax rate u, and in some circumstances the effect can go the other way. A reduction in u will increase the cost of funds r and reduce the present value of tax savings from depreciation Z but will also reduce the taxation of revenues. The outcome of these opposing tendencies might usually be expected to reduce METR but need not always do so.

32. See, for example, Auerbach and Poterba (1987).

33. Capital risk was first analyzed by Bulow and Summers (1984).

34. One such scheme that would accomplish this would be the proposal by Auerbach and Jorgenson (1980) for capital write-offs. Under this scheme firms would be allowed to deduct the present value of their future depreciation allowances up front. The scheme would also substitute for the indexation of depreciation allowances in inflationary periods.

35. Examples include Auerbach (1983); Boadway and Bruce (1992); Poterba and Summers (1983); and Stiglitz (1976).

36. This point has been made by Hansson and Stuart (1985).

37. This is demonstrated formally in Boadway (1987) and is discussed in more detail in Boadway, Bruce, and Mintz (1987).

38. One exception is Chua (1991), who has incorporated the system of indirect taxes into calculations of METRs in Malaysia using input-output data.

39. Bradford (1980) analyzes the design of investment tax credits that are neutral in relation to the durability of capital. He shows that no simple rule is possible. In general, a credit that varies with the durability of the investment is required.

40. That is not altogether true. They will have some general equilibrium effect on investment, but that will presumably be of second-order importance.

41. Often, the domestic tax liabilities are not calculated until funds are repatriated, and crediting does not occur until then. Other complicating features of these systems involve the averaging of credits over time and countries as well. For a full discussion see Alworth (1988).

42. See Leechor and Mintz (1991) and Hines (1992) for formal analyses of this.

43. Given the advantages of deferral, host country taxes will impose some distortion, as mentioned earlier.

44. Some discussion of the problems arising with tax haven countries may be found in Alworth (1988).

45. A more detailed description can be found in Boadway, Chua, and Flatters (1989), from which these illustrative calculations are drawn.

46. Tax loss pioneer firms are not explicitly considered because they are similar to taxpaying pioneer firms if they become profitable before pioneer status is finished, and otherwise they are similar to tax loss nonpioneer firms.

47. Note that, given the taxability of interest but not equity income at the personal level, households have an incentive to hold equity.

48. From the point of view of the corporation, the tax system affects new equity and retained earnings in the same way.

References

The word "processed" describes informally reproduced works that may not be commonly available through libraries.

Agell, J. N. 1986. "Subsidy to Capital through Tax Incentives." In P. Shome, ed. *Fiscal Issues in South-East Asia.* New York: Oxford University Press.

Alworth, Julian. 1988. *The Finance, Investment, and Taxation Decisions of Multinationals.* Oxford, U.K.: Basil Blackwell.

Arrow, K. J. 1962. "The Economic Implications of Learning by Doing." *Review of Economic Studies* 29 (2): 155–73.

Auerbach, Alan J. 1979. "Wealth Maximization and the Cost of Capital." *Quarterly Journal of Economics* 93 (3): 433–46.

_____. 1983. "Taxation, Corporate Financial Policy, and the Cost of Capital." *Journal of Economic Literature* 21 (3):905–40.

Auerbach, Alan J., and D. Jorgenson. 1980. "Inflation-Proof Depreciation of Assets." *Harvard Business Review* 58 (5):113–18.

Auerbach, Alan J., and J. M. Poterba. 1987. "Tax Loss Carryforwards and Corporate Tax Incentives." In M. S. Feldstein, ed. *Effect of Taxation on Capital Accumulation.* Chicago, Ill.: University of Chicago Press.

Azariadis, Costas. 1975. "Implicit Contracts and Unemployment Equilibria." *Journal of Political Economy* 83 (6): 1183–1202.

Baily, M. N. 1974. "Wages and Employment under Uncertain Demand." *Review of Economic Studies* 41 (1): 37–50.

Barro, R. J. 1974. "Are Government Bonds Net Wealth?" *Journal of Political Economy* 82 (6): 1095–1117.

Bernstein, Jeffrey I., and M. Ishaq Nadiri. 1987. "Corporate Taxes and Incentives and the Structure of Production: A Selected Survey." In Jack M. Mintz and Douglas Purvis, eds., *The Impact of Taxation on Business Activity.* Kingston, Ont., Can.: Queen's University, John Deutsch Institute for the Study of Economic Policy.

Bernstein, Jeffrey I., and Anwar Shah. 1994. "Taxes and Production: The Case of Pakistan." *International Tax and Public Finance* 1: 227–245.

Boadway, Robin W. 1987. "The Theory and Measurement of Effective Tax Rates." In Jack M. Mintz and Douglas Purvis, eds., *The Impact of Taxation on Business Activity.* Kingston, Ont., Can.: Queen's University: John Deutsch Institute for the Study of Economic Policy.

Boadway, Robin W., and Neil Bruce. 1984a. "A General Proposition on the Design of a Neutral Business Tax." *Journal of Public Economics* 24 (2): 231–39.

———. 1984b. *Welfare Economics.* Oxford, U.K.: Basil Blackwell.

———. 1992. "Problems with Integrating Corporate and Personal Income Taxes in an Open Economy." *Journal of Public Economics* 48 (1): 39–66.

Boadway, Robin W., Neil Bruce, K. McKenzie, and Jack M. Mintz. 1987. "Marginal Effective Tax Rates on Capital for the Canadian Mining Industry." *Canadian Journal of Economics* 20 (1): 1–17.

Boadway, Robin W., Neil Bruce, and Jack M. Mintz. 1982. "Corporate Taxation and the Cost of Holding Inventories." *Canadian Journal of Economics* 15 (2): 278–93.

———. 1984. "Taxation, Inflation, and the Marginal Tax Rate on Capital in Canada." *Canadian Journal of Economics* 17 (1): 62–79.

Bernstein, Jeffrey I., and Anwar Shah. 1994. "Taxes and Production: The Case of Pakistan." *International Tax and Public Finance* 1: 227–245.

———. 1987. *The Taxation of Capital Income in Canada: Theory and Policy.* Toronto: Canadian Tax Foundation.

Boadway, Robin W., Dale Chua, and Frank Flatters. 1989. "Fiscally-Induced Investment Distortions in Malaysia: The Direct Tax System." Malaysian Institute for Economic Research, Kuala Lumpur.

Boadway, Robin W., and Frank Flatters. 1981. "The Efficiency Basis for Regional Employment Policy." *Canadian Journal of Economics* 14 (1): 58–77.

Bond, E. W., and L. Samuelson. 1986. "Tax Holidays as Signals." *American Economic Review* 76 (4): 820–26.

———. 1989a. "Bargaining with Commitment, Choice of Techniques, and Direct Foreign Investment." *Journal of International Economics* 26 (1): 77–97.

———. 1989b. "Strategic Behaviour and the Rules for International Taxation of Capital." *Economic Journal* 99 (398): 1099–1111.

Bradford, D. F. 1980. "Tax Neutrality and the Investment Tax Credit." In H. J. Aaron and M. J. Boskin, eds., *The Economics of Taxation.* Washington, D.C.: Brookings Institution.

Bradford, D. F., and Don Fullerton. 1981. "Pitfalls in the Construction and Use of Effective Tax Rates." In C. R. Hulten, ed., *Depreciation, Inflation, and the Taxation of Income from Capital.* Washington, D.C.: Urban Institute Press.

Bulow, J. I., and L. H. Summers. 1984. "The Taxation of Risky Assets." *Journal of Political Economy* 92 (1): 20–39.

Carmichael, Lorne. 1985. "Can Unemployment Be Involuntary? Comment." *American Economic Review* 75 (5): 1213–14.

Chamley, C. P. 1986. "Optimal Taxation of Capital Income in General Equilibrium with Infinite Lives." *Econometrica* 54 (3): 607–22.

Chirinko, R. S. 1988. "Business Investment and Tax Policy: A Perspective on Existing Models and Empirical Results." *National Tax Journal* 39(1): 137–55.

Chua, D. H. H. 1991. *Essays on Public Finance in Developing Countries.* Ph.D. diss., Queen's University, Department of Economics, Kingston, Ont., Can.

Darrough, Masako N., and Neal M. Stoughton. 1986. "Moral Hazard and Adverse Selection: The Question of Financial Structure." *Journal of Finance* 41 (2): 501–13.

Diamond, P. A. 1981. "Mobility Costs, Frictional Unemployment, and Efficiency." *Journal of Political Economy* 89: 798–812.

Drèze, Jean, and N. Stern. 1987. "The Theory of Cost-Benefit Analysis." In Alan J. Auerbach and Martin S. Feldstein, eds., *Handbook of Public Economics.* Vol. 2. Amsterdam: North-Holland.

Eaton, Jonathan, and Mark Gersovitz. 1981. "Debt and Potential Repudiation: Theoretical and Empirical Analysis." *Review of Economic Studies* 48 (2):289–309.

Ebrill, L. P. 1987. "Income Taxes and Investment: Some Empirical Relationships for Developing Countries." In V. P. Gandhi, ed., *Supply-Side Tax Policy: Its Relevance to Developing Countries.* Washington, D.C.: International Monetary Fund.

Eckstein, Otto. 1957. "Investment Criteria for Economic Development and the Theory of Intertemporal Welfare Economics." *Quarterly Journal of Economics* 71 (1): 58–85.

Feldstein, Martin S. 1976. "Temporary Layoffs in the Theory of Unemployment." *Journal of Political Economy* 84 (5): 937–57.

_____, ed. 1987. *The Effects of Taxation on Capital Accumulation.* Chicago, Ill.: University of Chicago Press.

Feldstein, Martin S., and D. Hartman. 1979. "The Optimal Taxation of Foreign Source Investment Income." *Quarterly Journal of Economics* 93 (4): 613–24.

Feldstein, Martin S., Louis Dicks-Mireaux, and James Poterba. 1983. "The Effective Tax Rate and the Pretax Rate of Return." *Journal of Public Economics* 21 (1): 129–58.

Feltenstein, Andrew, and Anwar Shah. 1993. "General Equilibrium Effects of Taxation in Investment in a Developing Country: The Case of Pakistan." *Public Finance* 48 (3): 366–86.

_____. 1995. "General Equilibrium Effects of Investment Incentives in Mexico." *Journal of Development Economics* 46: 253–69.

Fischer, S. 1980. "Dynamic Consistency, Cooperation, and the Benevolent Dissembling Government." *Journal of Economic Dynamics and Control* 2 (1): 93–107.

Fullerton, Don, A. T. King, J. B. Shoven, and J. Whalley. 1981. "Corporate Tax Integration in the United States: A General Equilibrium Approach." *American Economic Review* 71 (4): 677–91.

Gersovitz, Mark. 1987. "The Effects of Domestic Taxes on Foreign Private Investment." In David Newbery and Nicholas Stern, eds., *The Theory of Taxation for Developing Countries.* New York: Oxford University Press.

Gordon, R. H. 1985. "Taxation of Corporate Capital Income: Tax Revenues versus Tax Distortions." *Quarterly Journal of Economics* 100 (1): 1–27.

Gordon, R. H., and H. R. Varian. 1988. "Intergenerational Risk Sharing." *Journal of Public Economics* 37 (2): 185.

Guisinger, Stephen E., and Associates. 1985. *Investment Incentives and Performance Requirements: Patterns of International Trade, Production, and Investment.* New York: Praeger.

Hahn, F. H., and R. C. O. Matthews. 1965. "The Theory of Economic Growth: A Survey." In *Surveys of Economic Theory.* Vol. 2. London: Macmillan.

Hansson, Ingemar, and Charles Stuart. 1985. Review of Mervyn A. King and Don Fullerton, "The Taxation of Income from Capital: A Comparative Study of the United States, the United Kingdom, Sweden, and West Germany." *Journal of Political Economy* 93 (4): 826–31.

Harberger, A. C. 1971. "On Measuring the Social Opportunity Cost of Labor." *International Labour Review* 103 (3): 559–79.

Harris, R. G. 1989. "The New Protectionism Revisited." *Canadian Journal of Economics* 22 (4): 751–78.

Heinkel, Robert, and Joseph Zechner. 1990. "The Role of Debt and Preferred Stock as a Solution to Adverse Selection Investment Incentives." *Journal of Financial and Quantitative Analysis* 25 (1): 1–24.

Hines, James R., Jr. 1992. "Credit and Deferral as International Investment Incentives." Discussion Paper 4192. National Bureau of Economic Research, Cambridge, Mass.

Hubbard, R. G., and K. L. Judd. 1987. "Social Security and Individual Welfare: Precautionary Saving, Liquidity Constraints, and the Payroll Tax." *American Economic Review* 77 (4): 630–46.

Hulten, C. R., and F. C. Wykoff. 1981. "The Measurement of Economic Depreciation." In C. R. Hulten, ed., *Depreciation, Inflation, and the Taxation of Income from Capital.* Washington, D.C.: Urban Institute Press.

Jensen, M. C. 1986. "Agency Costs of Free Cash Flow, Dividends, Corporate Finance, and Takeovers." *American Economic Review* 76 (2): 323–39.

Jensen, Michael G., and William H. Meckling. 1976. "Theory of the Firm: Managerial Behavior, Agency Costs, and Ownership Structure." *Journal of Financial Economics* 3 (3): 305–60.

John, Kose, and Lemma Senbet. 1988. "Limited Liability, Corporate Leverage, and Public Policy." New York University and University of Wisconsin-Madison.

Jorgenson, D. W. 1963. "Capital Theory and Investment Behavior." *American Economic Review* 53 (1): 247–59.

Kaldor, Nicholas, and James A. Mirrlees. 1962. "A New Model of Economic Growth." *Review of Economic Studies* 29 (2): 174–92.

Kennedy, Charles. 1961. "Technical Progress and Investment." *Economic Journal* 71 (282): 292–99.

King, Mervyn A., and Don Fullerton. 1984. *The Taxation of Income from Capital: A Comparative Study of the United States, the United Kingdom, Sweden, and West Germany.* Chicago, Ill.: University of Chicago Press.

Kwack, Taewon. 1988. "Public Finance, Trade, and Economic Development: The Role of Fiscal Incentives in Korea's Export-Led Economic Growth." Paper presented at the Forty-fourth Congress of the International Institute of Public Finance, Istanbul, Turkey, August.

Leechor, Chad, and Jack M. Mintz. 1991. "On the Taxation of Multinational Corporate Investment When the Deferral Method Is Used by the Capital Exporting Country." In Javad Khalilzadeh-Shirazi and Anwar Shah, eds., *Tax Policy in Developing Countries.* Washington, D.C.: World Bank.

Lucas, R. E., Jr. 1988. "On the Mechanics of Economic Development." *Journal of Monetary Economics* 22 (1): 3–42.

MacDougall, G. D. A. 1960. "The Benefits and Costs of Private Investment from Abroad: A Theoretical Approach." *Economic Record* 36 (1): 13–35.

McLure, Charles, Jr., and George Zodzow. 1991. "Tax Reform in Colombia: Process and Results." In Javad Khalilzadeh-Shirazi and Anwar Shah, eds., *Tax Policy in Developing Countries*. Washington, D.C.: World Bank.

Manasan, R. G. 1988. "A Review of Investment Incentives in ASEAN countries." Working Paper Series 88-27. Philippine Institute of Development Studies, Manila, Philippines.

Marglin, S. A. 1963. "The Social Rate of Discount and the Optimal Rate of Investment." *Quarterly Journal of Economics* 77 (1): 95–112.

Meade, J. A. 1978. *The Structure and Reform of Direct Taxation: Report of a Committee Chaired by Professor James A. Meade*. London: Allen and Unwin.

Miller, Merton H., and Kevin Rock. 1985. "Dividend Policy under Asymmetric Information." *Journal of Finance* 40 (4): 1031–51.

Mintz, Jack M. 1982. "Neutral Corporate Taxation, Risk-Taking, and Optimal Profit Taxation." *Recherches Economiques de Louvain* 48 (1): 107–32.

Modigliani, Franco, and Merton Miller. 1958. "The Cost of Capital, Corporation Finance, and the Theory of Investment." *American Economic Review* 48 (2): 261–97.

Musgrave, P. B. 1969. *United States Taxation of Foreign Investment Income: Issues and Arguments*. Cambridge, Mass.: Harvard Law School International Tax Program.

Mussa, Michael. 1978. "Dynamic Adjustment in the Heckscher-Ohlin-Samuelson Model." *Journal of Political Economy* 86 (5): 775–91.

Myers, Stewart C. 1977. "Determinants of Corporate Borrowing." *Journal of Financial Economics* 5 (2):147–75.

Myers, Stewart C., and Nicholas S. Majluf. 1984. "Corporate Financing and Investment Decisions When Firms Have Information That Investors Do Not Have." *Journal of Financial Economics* 13 (2): 187–221.

Poterba, J. M., and L. H. Summers. 1983. "Dividend Taxes, Corporate Investment, and 'Q.'" *Journal of Public Economics* 22 (2): 136–67.

Price Waterhouse. 1995. *Corporate Taxes: A Worldwide Summary*. New York.

Rajagopal, Dagmar, and Anwar Shah. 1995. "A Rational Expectations Model for Tax Policy Analysis: An Evaluation of Tax Incentives for the Textile, Chemical, and Pharmaceutical Industries of Pakistan." *Journal of Public Economics* 57: 249–76.

Ramsey, F. P. 1928. "A Mathematical Theory of Savings." *Economic Journal* 38 (152): 543–59.

Romer, P. M. 1986. "Increasing Returns and Long-Run Growth." *Journal of Political Economy* 94 (5): 1002–37.

Ross, S. A. 1977. "The Determination of Financial Structure: The Incentive-Signalling Approach." *Bell Journal of Economics* 8 (1): 23–40.

Scott, M. F. 1989. *A New View of Economic Growth*. Oxford, U.K.: Clarendon Press.

Sen, A. K. 1967. "Isolation, Assurance, and the Social Rate of Discount." *Quarterly Journal of Economics* 81 (1): 112–24.

Shah, Anwar. 1988. "Tax Restructuring Options for Sri Lanka." World Bank, Country Economics Department, Washington, D.C. Processed.

Shah, Anwar, and Joel Slemrod. 1991. "Taxation and Foreign Direct Investment." In Javad Khalilzadeh-Shirazi and Anwar Shah, eds., *Tax Policy in Developing Countries*. Washington, D.C.: World Bank.

Shapiro, Carl, and Joseph E. Stiglitz. 1984. "Unemployment Equilibrium as a Worker Discipline Device." *American Economic Review* 74 (3): 433–44.

Shleifer, Andrei, and Robert W. Vishny. 1986. "Large Shareholders and Corporate Control." *Journal of Political Economy* 94 (3): 461–88.

Smith, Alisdair. 1982. "Intergenerational Transfers as Social Insurance." *Journal of Public Economics* 19 (1): 97–106.

Smith, V. L. 1963. "Tax Depreciation Policy and Investment Theory." *International Economic Review* 4 (1): 80–91.

Stiglitz, J. E. 1973. "Taxation, Corporate Financial Policy, and the Cost of Capital." *Journal of Public Economics* 2 (1): 1–34.

_____. 1974. "Wage Determination and Unemployment in L.D.C.s: The Labor Turnover Model." *Quarterly Journal of Economics* 88 (2): 194–227.

_____. 1976. "The Corporation Tax." *Journal of Public Economics* 5 (3): 303–11.

Trela, Irene, and John Whalley. 1991. "Taxes, Outward Orientation, and Growth Performance in the Republic of Korea." In Javad Khalilzadeh-Shirazi and Anwar Shah, eds., *Tax Policy in Developing Countries*. Washington, D.C.: World Bank.

U.S. Treasury. 1977. *Blueprints for Basic Tax Reform*. Washington, D.C.: U.S. Government Printing Office.

Williams, Joseph. 1988. "Efficient Signalling with Dividends, Investment, and Stock Repurchases." *Journal of Finance* 43 (3): 737–47.

THE COST OF CAPITAL AND INVESTMENT IN DEVELOPING COUNTRIES

Alan Auerbach

FOR GOVERNMENTS IN developing countries, an important policy objective is the creation of an environment that attracts capital to high-return fixed investment projects. Like more advanced countries, these economies seek the increases in labor productivity and living standards that capital deepening brings. For many reasons, however, the design of government policy toward investment in developing countries is both more critical and more complex.

First, such countries may lack fully functioning internal capital markets, making it difficult to measure the cost of capital for new projects. Second, the inadequacy of domestic capital may force a significant dependence on foreign direct investment, which requires a more complete involvement on the part of the investor than simply supplying funds. Third, such countries typically impose more significant trade and production distortions in the form of excise taxes, tariffs, quotas, and restrictions, which must be taken into account in estimating the incentives facing a potential investment. Fourth, certain types of investment incentives require an administrative infrastructure that may be absent in all but the most developed countries. Finally, the governments in developing countries may lack the credibility needed to persuade investors to respond to an announced change in policy.

Although the problems of policy design are considerable, so are the potential social returns from an appropriate investment climate. This chapter develops measures of the incentive to invest that can be used to evaluate existing policies and guide the design of new ones, taking account of the complications just mentioned. The next section introduces the basic notation and modeling assumptions; subsequent sections develop the model and its implications more fully.

The Model

To evaluate the incentive to invest, let us consider the decisions of a firm that uses a single capital input—labor—and intermediate inputs in the production process. The simplifying assumptions that capital and labor are homogeneous are not critical for most purposes of analysis. Initially, let us also assume that the firm's investments are riskless and that the firm faces a constant tax system with full loss offset, has perfect certainty about the future, may adjust capital instantaneously, and is perfectly competitive (that is, takes all prices as given). Although these restrictions are often made in analyzing investment incentives, they influence the results considerably and are particularly inappropriate in the present context. They are imposed initially for purposes of exposition and to permit a comparison of the approach used in this chapter with those found elsewhere.

The model's notation is summarized in table 2-1. The firm to be examined produces gross output X using capital K, labor L, and inputs M, according to the following relationship:

$$(2\text{-}1) \qquad\qquad X = X(K, L, M)$$

where $X(\cdot)$ is a general production function with nonincreasing returns to scale.

Let r be the real discount rate that the firm uses in valuing future cash flows from the investment project. As discussed in Auerbach (1983b), this may be constructed as a weighted average of the real costs of debt and equity finance. For example, in a closed economy without an indexed tax system, the formula for r would be

$$(2\text{-}2) \qquad\qquad r = b[i(1-\tau) - \pi] + \frac{(1-b)\mu}{1-\Phi}$$

where i is the nominal interest rate, τ is the corporate tax rate against which interest payments are normally tax deductible, μ is the real discount rate of equity-holders, Φ is the household tax rate effectively applied to real equity returns, π is the inflation rate, and b is the fraction of the project financed with debt. The construction of this measure depends on a number of institutional factors, such as the source of marginal equity funds, for this determines the extent to which the tax rate on dividends actually exerts a marginal influence. In developing countries, calculation of the relevant interest rate, as well as the importance of foreign investors, may be more significant. These issues are discussed further below. For the moment, the analysis simply takes the determination of r as given. Let the prices of output, materials, and capital goods that the company faces be p, v, and g, respectively, and let w be the wage rate. Because of taxes and other distortions in product and factor markets, these will not necessarily be

Table 2-1. Notation

$X(\cdot)$	General production function, with capital, labor, and materials as arguments
$F(\cdot)$	Residual production function, with capital as an argument, obtained by subtracting labor and materials costs from $X(\cdot)$ and solving for labor and materials as functions of K (defined in equation 2-10)
$G(\cdot)$	Residual production function normalized for fluctuations in the profitability of capital (defined in equation 2-13)
θ	Term representing the fluctuation in the profitability of capital due to variation in input prices (defined in equation 2-13)
δ	Capital depreciation rate (geometric)
i	Nominal interest rate
b	Debt-value ratio
π	Inflation rate
μ	Required real after-tax return to equity holders
υ	$= \mu/(1 - \Phi)$ real required return to equity, before personal taxes
n	Real return to bondholders after tax (defined in equation 2-16)
r	Weighted average cost of capital (defined in equation 2-2)
p	Output goods price
p_w	World output goods price
v	Material goods price
v_w	World material goods price
g	Capital goods price
q	Capital goods price, including marginal adjustment costs
ϕ	Adjustment cost parameter
w	Nominal wage rate
Φ	Effective household tax rate on equity income
k	Investment tax credit
$D(a)$	Depreciation deduction for a capital good of age a
Γ	Present value of investment credits and depreciation deductions (defined in equation 2-3)
τ	Corporate tax rate
e_c	Effective corporate tax rate (defined in equation 2-15)
e_T	Effective total tax rate (defined in equation 2-17)
t_p	Personal tax rate of bondholders
T_m	Tariff rate on material good
T_p	Tariff rate on output good
t'_m	Excise tax on material good

observed "market" prices. They should simply be interpreted as the effective marginal prices that firms face for the associated commodities.

Let Γ be the present value of the after-tax cash flow attributable to depreciation allowances, investment grants, and investment tax credits received by the firm per dollar of new investment. That is, if grants and credits, k, are received immediately and depreciation deductions, $D(t - s)$, are received at each date t after the initial investment at date s, then

$$(2\text{-}3) \qquad \Gamma = k + \tau z = k + \int_{s}^{\infty} \tau e^{-(r+\pi)(t-s)} D(t-s) \, dt.$$

There are many types of investment incentives used in practice. Although some are more complicated, most can be expressed using this framework, as is discussed below.

The corporation's problem of maximizing the wealth of its shareholders at date s may then be shown (Auerbach 1983b) to be equivalent to maximizing

$$(2\text{-}4) \quad V_s = \int_{s}^{\infty} e^{-(r+\pi)(t-s)} \left\{ (1-\tau) \left[p_t X(K_t, L_t, M_t) - w_t L_t - v_t M_t \right] \right.$$
$$\left. - g_t (1-\Gamma) I_t \right\} dt$$

where I is the firm's investment at date t. Under the familiar assumption that capital decays exponentially at rate δ, the evolution of the capital stock obeys the equation

$$(2\text{-}5) \qquad\qquad K_t = I_t - \delta K_t.$$

The firm chooses I, L, and M at each date after t in order to maximize the function V_s. In order to focus on the investment decision, it will sometimes be useful to consider this decision conditional on the optimal decisions with respect to labor and material inputs. Since each is a variable factor of production, the optimization produced for each yields the standard rule of setting equal contemporaneous marginal revenues and costs at each date $t > s$

$$(2\text{-}6) \qquad\qquad X_{Lt} = w_t / p_t$$

$$(2\text{-}7) \qquad\qquad X_{Mt} = v_t / p_t.$$

The decision rules 2-6 and 2-7 provide two equations in the variables L, M, and K. Hence they may be used to define L and M implicitly in terms of K. That is, from equations 2-6 and 2-7 we may obtain the equations

$$(2\text{-}8) \qquad\qquad L^* = L(K, w/p, v/p)$$

$$(2\text{-}9) \qquad\qquad M^* = M(K, w/p, v/p)$$

which may be used to obtain a production function of K alone:

$$(2\text{-}10) \qquad F_t(K) = X\ (K, L^*, M^*) - (w/p)_t\, L_t^* - (v/p)_t\, M_t^* .$$

A time subscript must be attached to the new function $F(\cdot)$ because of its dependence on the real wage, w/p, and the real price of materials, v/p.

Using the function $F(\cdot)$, we may rewrite the firm's optimization problem at date s as

$$(2\text{-}11) \qquad \max\ V_s = \int_s^{\infty} e^{-(r+\pi)\,(t-s)} \Big[(1-\tau)\, p_t\, F_t(K_t)$$

$$- g_t\,(1-\Gamma)\,(\dot{K}_t + \delta K_t)\Big]\, dt$$

which yields the Euler equation familiar from the literature:

$$(2\text{-}12) \qquad F_t'\,(K_t) = \frac{g_t\,(r+\delta)\,(1-\Gamma)}{P_t\,(1-\tau)}.$$

The right-hand side of equation 2-12 has traditionally been called the *user cost of capital* (for example, Jorgenson 1963), for it defines the shadow price to which the marginal product of capital should be set equal. With other factors of production, however, the desired capital stock is a function of all input prices, not just the direct input price of capital. Thus if one is interested in knowing the capital stock itself, rather than its marginal product, an alternative formulation of the user cost will prove more useful.

For purposes of exposition, let us assume that $F(\cdot)$ has the separable form[1]

$$(2\text{-}13) \qquad F_t(K) = \theta\ (w_t\,/\,p_t',\ v_t\,/\,p_t)\ G(K) = \theta_t\, G(K).$$

Then, the first-order condition (equation 2-12) may be rewritten:

$$(2\text{-}14) \qquad G'\,(K_t) = c_t = \frac{g_t\,(r+\delta)\,(1-\Gamma)\,/\,(1-\tau)}{\theta_t\, p_t}.$$

Because of the assumption that the firm can adjust its capital stock instantaneously, equation 2-14 is a solution for the capital stock at date t and, given the initial capital stock, the rate of investment as well.[2] Therefore, since the function $G(\cdot)$ is time-invariant, the right-hand side of equation 2-14 represents a sufficient statistic for the incentive to use capital in production. We may think of this as the "full" user cost of capital. It incorporates effects on investment working directly through the effective rental price of capital as well as indirectly through the costs of other factors of production.

The Effective Tax Rate

Many researchers (for example, Auerbach 1983a; King and Fullerton 1984) have found it useful to summarize the effects of the tax system on investment through an "effective tax rate" calculation. Although most of the literature has focused on industrial countries, the method has also been carefully applied to developing countries (Pellechio 1987). The thought experiment giving rise to this measure is to ask what rate of tax applied to a broadly based income measure would lead to the same wedge between after-tax and before-tax returns as is actually observed. Put differently, for a given user cost of capital, what rate of tax on broadly based or "true" economic income would lead to the observed after-tax return?

Despite its apparent simplicity, the concept does not give rise to a unique definition, with the measure depending on which taxes are included in the calculation and what level of after-tax or before-tax rate of return is used as a benchmark. Moreover, the calculation of an effective tax rate alone does not provide enough information to infer the effects of tax policy on investment. Since the user cost of capital will result from adding the tax wedge to the after-tax rate of return, it is important to know not only how big the tax wedge is but to what extent it leads to a higher before-tax return rather than a lower after-tax return. Even in small, open economies that must take world prices and rates of return as given, not all taxes will necessarily be fully reflected in a higher cost of capital. Some will be borne by imperfectly mobile factors (such as land and labor). Even with perfect capital mobility, some capital income taxes may be shifted abroad if they are credited by foreign governments.

In spite of these limitations, the effective tax rate concept is a popular one that can be useful for certain purposes, particularly in comparing the *relative* incentive to invest in different assets. Therefore I will describe in somewhat more detail how it fits into the current framework.

One may think of the total tax wedge affecting the return to capital as being divided into two parts. The first is the wedge between the required rate of return, r, and the corporation's return before tax. The second is the wedge between r and the return to investors after *all* taxes. The first wedge is the effective rate of corporate tax, which indicates how provisions that directly affect investment affect the corporate tax base. One may also think of this as the effective rate of tax at the corporate level for an equity-financed investment, ignoring any provisions permitting a deduction for dividends paid.

To calculate the effective corporate tax rate, one would estimate how the tax rate τ in equation 2-14 would need to change to offset the repeal of investment incentives and the imposition of a system of economic depreciation allowances. This would involve varying τ to offset the replacement of

Γ with the present value of economic depreciation deductions, $\tau\delta/(r + \delta)$, holding all other terms in the equation fixed. The resulting effective tax rate equation is

(2-15) $$e_c = \frac{[(r+\delta)(1-\Gamma)/(1-\tau)-\delta]-r}{(r+\delta)(1-\Gamma)/(1-\tau)-\delta}$$

where the denominator is the before-tax return to capital (equal to the before-tax rate of return, net of actual depreciation) and the numerator is the "tax wedge" between this return and the corporate costs of funds r (see Auerbach 1983a). This equation provides the standard results that immediate write-off of assets ($\Gamma = \tau$) leads to a zero effective tax rate and that with economic depreciation allowances—for which $\Gamma = r\delta/(r + \delta)$—$e_c = \tau$.

A more comprehensive effective tax rate measure (see King and Fullerton 1984) is one that accounts not only for investment-oriented provisions at the corporate level but also for the second wedge discussed above, that between the rate of return to firms after corporate taxes and the rate of return to savers. This second wedge would account for interest deductibility at the corporate level and taxes paid by individuals or other entities receiving the corporate-source income. To get a total wedge equal to the sum of the two wedges, one would add to the gap between the before-tax corporate return and the corporate costs of funds, r, the gap between r and the rate of return to suppliers of funds, say, s.

To calculate this total effective tax rate, one must express r in relation to the net return to savers. This is achieved by substituting into equation 2-2 the net real return to bondholders (say, n) and the income tax rate on interest received (say, t_p)

(2-16) $$i = (n + \pi)/(1 - t_p).$$

The result is an expression for r in terms of the underlying real returns, after all taxes, to equity, μ, and debt, n, that can be substituted into equation 2-15 to determine the total effective tax rate that the tax encompasses, the tax provisions embodied in Γ, the corporate tax rate τ, and the individual tax rates Φ and t_p. Contrary to the previous case, one would measure the tax wedge in relation to μ and n rather than r. Here the calculation depends on which of a variety of assumptions one makes concerning the relationship of the two net rates of return, μ and n. The choice depends on which concept of financial equilibrium one chooses (King and Fullerton 1984). For the "fixed s" case, in which these net returns are assumed to be equal (that is, $\mu = n = s$),[3] this broader effective tax rate equals

$$(2\text{-}17) \qquad e_T = \frac{[\,(r+\delta)\,(1-\Gamma)\,/(1-\tau)-\delta\,]-s}{(r+\delta)\,(1-\Gamma)\,/(1-\tau)-\delta} \,.$$

The numerator of equation 2-17 is the "total" tax wedge, incorporating the effects of interest deductibility and personal taxes that manifest themselves through the relationship of the corporation's cost of funds, r, and the net return to asset owners, s.

The effective tax rate, e_T, describes the total tax burden on domestic investment, domestically financed. In a closed economy, in which there is no distinction between taxes on saving and on investment, it would therefore be informative about the effect of the tax system on investment. In a world with open economies, however, saving and investment may occur in different places. Policies aimed at encouraging saving in a country need not encourage investment there but may simply cause more capital to flow abroad. To the extent that the marginal investor supplies funds from abroad, a different calculation that distinguishes taxes on saving and investment may be necessary.

One approach would be to consider the tax treatment of equity and debt owned by foreigners and include these in the calculation as well. For example, Anderson and others (1991) calculate the effective tax rates, e_T, for investment in the United States financed not only by domestic debt and equity funds but also by debt and equity supplied via portfolio investment from Japan. They likewise calculate the effective tax rates on Japanese investment financed in Japan and from the United States.

The basic question to be addressed is how the firm's cost of funds, r, relates to the required returns to equity and debt μ and n when such funds come from abroad. (For a small developing economy the returns μ and n may be taken as fixed, so that the associated gap between the net returns μ and n and the gross return r translates directly into a higher cost of capital.)

The answer to this question depends on the host country's tax treatment of such capital flows, as well as the home country's mechanism for crediting foreign taxes paid. This, in turn, depends on the type of entity that is supplying the capital, for foreign direct investment by corporations is treated differently from portfolio investment by individuals. Although Anderson and others treat the case of portfolio investment, foreign direct investment and investment via financial intermediaries represent a more significant portion of the flows between the United States and Japan. This must be even more true of capital flows into most developing countries.

It therefore seems most appropriate to consider the case in which the investment is by a foreign corporation. I will discuss the implications of this assumption further below.

The Effective Tax Rate and the User Cost of Capital, More Broadly Defined

For industrial economies such as Japan and the United States, the major effects of policy on the incentive to invest may well come through the tax system. Hence the use of the various effective tax rate measures already discussed may suffice. In developing countries the most important effects of policy may not work through the tax system at all or may do so indirectly.

By the equation on the right-hand side of equation 2-14, the user cost of capital, we may distinguish between policies that affect the price of capital goods, g; the required rate of return, r; the output price, p; and the productivity term, θ, through the effective real wage, w/p, or the effective cost of material inputs, v/p.

Policies affecting g and r may be seen as the equivalent of capital income taxes, since they influence the gap between the gross and net returns to capital. Put another way, they appear only in the first-order condition for capital, equation 2-12, and not in the conditions for labor and materials, equations 2-6 and 2-7. For purposes of measuring relative costs of capital and other inputs, one would add only such policies to those previously considered, and the way of doing so is straightforward. If one wishes to measure the incentive to invest, however, effects on p, w/p, and v/p matter, too, since each of these variables appears on the right-hand side of equation 2-14. For example, a subsidy to labor or a protective tariff on an industry's output may well increase investment. Although it is misleading to equate such policies with a reduction in capital income taxes, it is important to consider them along with policies directed at capital specifically.

Some examples of how such policies affect the cost of capital defined in equation 2-14 follow.

INDIRECT TAXES. If material goods face an ad valorem tax rate, t_m, then the real materials cost, v, appearing as an argument of $\theta(\cdot)$—see equation 2-13—would equal $(1 + t_m)v_w$, if v_w is the price net of tax (the term includes the subscript w to indicate that this will be the world price if other price distortions are absent). Assuming that indirect taxes are not applied to exports, they will have no effect on the expression for the output price, p, which will equal the world price, p_w.

TARIFFS. A tariff on materials inputs at rate T_m affects the cost of materials to the firm just as an indirect tax would $[v = (1 + T_m)v_w]$. A tariff at rate T_p per output would raise the output price in relation to the world price to $p = (1 + T_p)p_w$. As is well known, this output price effect is equivalent to a *general* production subsidy to the firm.

DUAL EXCHANGE RATES. If there is a controlled and an uncontrolled sector in the exchange market, we may treat the difference between the two exchange rates as a general trade intervention. Importers forced to buy foreign currency at the (presumably higher) controlled rate are essentially facing a tariff.

QUANTITY CONTROLS. In general, each type of quantity control has an analogous price distortion. A well-known example is tariffs and quotas, the equivalence of which requires some assumption about the price-elasticity of demand of the commodity in question.

Other examples of quantity controls occur in the capital market. Here, one can estimate the subsidy inherent in targeted funds by comparing the stated interest rate with the market interest rate, as long as the latter rate is available. To the extent that such funds are used *at the margin*, the implied subsidy rate should be used to adjust the interest rate appearing in r (see equation 2-2).

IMPERFECT COMPETITION. If firms are not price takers, this introduces the possibility of a markup of the sales price, p, over marginal cost. The extent of the markup will, of course, depend on the nature and degree of imperfection in the product market.

One type of imperfection that is relatively easy to analyze is monopolistic competition, under which each firm faces a downward-sloping demand curve with price elasticity η, where η depends on the overall elasticity of demand, the number of firms, and the degree to which import substitution is possible. In this case, the firm behaves as if it faces an output price $p(1 - 1/\eta)$ rather than p in each of its factor utilization decisions. The case is analogous to that of production tax at rate $1/\eta$.

In summary, policies affecting the numerator of the right-hand side of equation 2-14 are capital related; whether or not they are capital income taxes as typically included in effective tax rate measures or policies with similar effects, they have marginal effects equivalent to a change in the rate of capital income taxation. In this sense, they are appropriate for inclusion in an accurate calculation of the "effective tax rate" on capital income.

Tax and nontax policies that affect the denominator of the right-hand side of equation 2-14 also affect investment and should therefore be considered in any analysis that seeks to measure the full effects of policy on investment. Although significant, their marginal effects differ from those of capital income tax changes, for they also influence the real cost of labor and materials. Moreover, because these policies affect the attractiveness of capital indirectly through the price of output or other inputs, their effect on investment cannot be measured without additional information about the production process. That is, policies that affect p, w/p, or v/p all work through the term θ in equation 2-14, and the form of θ depends on the exact specification of the production function, particularly the degree to which other inputs are substitutes or complements for capital.

For example, suppose the production process requires a fixed ratio of materials to output and that value added by capital and labor is described by a Cobb-Douglas function. Then $X(\cdot)$ has the form

$$(2\text{-}18) \qquad X(K, L, M) = \min(AK^{\alpha} L^{\beta}, M/m)$$

for constants α, β, and m, and $\theta(\cdot)$ has the form (dropping time subscripts)[4]

$$(2\text{-}19) \qquad \theta(w/p, v/p) = (w/p)^{-1/(1-\beta)} [1 - m(v/p)]^{1/(1-\beta)}.$$

In this case, both labor and materials are complementary to capital in the production process: an increase in either the real price of materials or the real price of labor reduces the desired capital stock. The elasticity of the user cost of capital, defined by the right-hand side of equation 2-14, with respect to the real wage is $1/(1 - \beta)$; the elasticity with respect to the real cost of materials is $m(v/p)/[1 - m(v/p)]$. By comparison, the elasticity with respect to the corporate tax rate τ (holding Γ constant), is $\tau/(1 - \tau)$.[5] For more general specifications of production, it will not be possible to express $F(\cdot)$ even in the separable form given in equation 2-13 and the term θ can only be locally approximated.

Up to this point, all policies discussed have worked in markets with fixed world prices. Policies driving a wedge between such world prices and the prices facing the firm translate directly into changes in the user cost of capital. One must add the marginal burden of capital income taxes to the net returns required by suppliers of funds. Likewise, the domestic prices for output and inputs, p and v, equal the world prices plus any tariff or tariff-equivalent quantity restriction, such as an import quota, that is imposed domestically. Unlike in a closed economy, no general equilibrium calculations are necessary to estimate how much the gross return or price rises with the tax. This makes the resulting effective tax rate more directly informative about the user cost itself.

This simplicity is absent for labor market interventions, since (for most countries) labor is not nearly as mobile as capital. Thus one cannot immediately compute the effect on the real wage rate and hence the user cost of capital of tax and nontax policies that drive a wedge between the real wage received by workers and the cost of labor facing firms. Incorporating the gap between gross and net wages in a grand "effective tax rate" computation may, as a result, be extremely misleading if the incidence of labor income taxes falls largely on workers rather than firms.

Summary

If one wishes to estimate the effects of tax policy on the incentive to invest, the augmented user cost equation given in equation 2-14 provides a sufficient statistic, given the modeling assumptions adopted in this section. Traditional measures of the "effective tax rate" on capital fail in several respects to provide an equally useful measure.

First, they typically ignore the separation of saving and investment decisions and the importance of international capital flows. Second, they consider only explicit taxes on capital and capital income, ignoring both nontax capital policies (such as targeted lending) and tax and nontax policies (such as tariffs and quotas) that indirectly influence the incentive to invest through their effects on the prices of outputs and other inputs. Finally, in emphasizing the magnitude of the tax wedge between gross and net returns to capital, rather than the level of the gross return, a given effective tax rate can correspond to several different levels of the desired capital stock, depending on the incidence of the taxes in question. A given tax wedge added to a price that is fixed in world markets may reduce investment more than if the price were determined domestically.

Although the analysis to this point represents a useful summary of much of the literature to date, it is static in nature. It therefore ignores the dynamics of the investment process, a specification of which is necessary for empirical work on investment. The characterization of the investment process itself can be particularly important in cases in which changes in the tax system are being considered.

Changes in Tax Regime

Over time, the economic conditions affecting investment may change quite markedly. Among these economic changes are shifts in tax regime, caused not only by policy shifts affecting all firms but also by shifts in an individual firm's tax status. For example, a firm may face a zero marginal tax rate on its taxable income for a period of years because it is carrying a large stock of losses and depreciation allowances forward and then become taxable once again as these deductions expire or are used up. Both types of change in tax regime, economy-wide and firm- or sector-specific, can exert a powerful, if temporary, effect on investment incentives. Indeed, in an unstable economic environment, such "temporary" effects may nearly always be present. Thus one should go beyond examination of tax systems applicable only in a "long run" that is unlikely ever to occur.

Once one admits the importance of changes in economic conditions, the assumption of instantaneous capital stock adjustment made above becomes even more restrictive. It is clear that firms will not cause their capital stocks to swing wildly in response to each instantaneous change in the user cost of capital. To model investment behavior realistically, therefore, it is necessary to replace this assumption. The introduction of convex adjustment costs for the capital stock provides such a smoothing incentive.[6] The following analysis follows closely that first presented in Auerbach (1989). For the interested reader, the full derivation is provided in the appendix to this chapter. An empirical application for the United States can be found in Auerbach and Hines (1988).

Let us begin again with a firm seeking to maximize its value as in equation 2-11, but with two changes. First, the tax parameters may vary over time, so that, in particular, τ, k, and hence Γ require time subscripts. For the moment, we continue to assume perfect certainty about these tax changes and the absence of any risk. Second, we replace the exogenous price of capital goods, g, with a total cost $g(1 - \delta\phi K + \frac{1}{2}\phi\dot{K})$, chosen to give rise to a simple equation for the marginal cost of capital goods:

$$(2\text{-}20) \quad q = d\left\{g[1 - \delta\phi K + \frac{1}{2}\phi(I - \delta K)]\,I\right\}/dI = g(1 + \phi\dot{K}).$$

The term ϕ is an adjustment cost parameter, equal to the percentage increase in effective capital goods prices to the firm per unit of additional investment.

Replacing g in equation 2-11 with q as defined in equation 2-20, and adding subscripts to the tax parameters, we obtain the following Euler equation for the firm, replacing equation 2-12:

$$(2\text{-}21) \quad F_t'(K_t) = \frac{q_t(r + \delta)(1 - \Gamma_t)/p_t - [\dot{q_t}(1 - \Gamma_t)/p_t]}{(1 - \tau)}$$

where the after-tax present value of investment incentives is

$$(2\text{-}22) \quad \Gamma_s = k + \int_s^{\infty} \tau_t\, e^{-(r+\pi)(t-s)}\, D_t(t-s)\, dt.$$

Equation 2-21 is no more than a user cost of capital that takes explicit account of expected changes in the real, after-tax relative price of capital goods $q(1 - \Gamma)/p$ (Auerbach 1983b). Because q is a function of investment itself, however, equation 2-21 is a first-order condition only, rather than a direct solution for K. To obtain the latter, one must substitute the expression for q given in equation 2-20 into equation 2-21, obtaining a second-order differential equation in K that must then be solved. Because this equation is nonlinear, a closed-form solution will not generally be available. Such a closed-form solution may be derived, however, if one linearizes the differential equation around its steady-state solution.[7] The solution for investment may be expressed as a model of partial adjustment toward a "desired" capital stock:[8]

$$(2\text{-}23) \quad I_t = (-\sigma_1)(\hat{K}_t - K_t) + \delta K_t$$

where the desired capital stock satisfies

(2-24) $$G'(\hat{K}_t) = C_t = \int_t^\infty \sigma_2\, e^{-\sigma_2\,(s-t)}\, c_s\, ds,$$

the instantaneous cost of capital term c_t equals

(2-25) $$c_t = \frac{g_t\,[(r+\delta)\,(1-\Gamma_t) - (1-\dot{\Gamma}_t)]}{\theta_t\, p_t\,(1-\tau_t)},$$

and the terms σ_1 (≤ 0) and σ_2 $[\ge (r + \delta)]$ are the roots of the second-order differential equation.[9] As before, the function $G(\cdot)$ is defined in equation 2-13 as the production function divided by the term θ.

Because the weights $\sigma_2\, e^{-\sigma_2\,(s-t)}$ sum to one, we can view equation 2-24 as indicating that the desired capital stock that influences investment at date t depends on a weighted average, C_t, of present and future user costs of capital. Only if adjustment costs are zero and hence adjustment is instantaneous (in which case $\sigma_2 = \infty$), or if the cost of capital is constant over time, will the current cost of capital be sufficient to describe the effects of the tax system on investment. In general, forward-looking investment behavior that depends on the weighted average of current and future costs of capital may be quite different from that implied by assuming a constant cost of capital without changing tax rates. The use of this new methodology is straightforward. It differs from traditional specifications primarily in its dependence on predicted *future* capital costs rather than lagged ones. To apply it, one first calculates the instantaneous user cost of capital at each date t, c_t, and then aggregates these user costs over all future dates. The weights to use in this aggregation depend on a number of parameters (see note 9), not all of which are precisely known (such as ϕ). Hence experimentation with different weighting schemes seems called for. In the first step, one must allow for potential changes in the tax rate τ when calculating Γ and must also allow for potential changes in Γ itself.

The following examples illustrate this approach. It is helpful in making these examples realistic to draw them from the policies and experiences of particular countries. The examples, however, should not be interpreted as an overall evaluation of the tax policies of the countries in question.

Changes in Tax Structure

Many countries have recently enacted tax reforms aimed at broadening the tax base while at the same time lowering tax rates. The effects on investment of the 1986 U.S. reform are discussed in Auerbach (1989).

Among developing countries, Mexico has recently moved to an indexed corporate tax system, with a phased reduction in the corporate tax rate from 42 to 35 percent. During the transition period, the tax rate reduction itself has three effects on the instantaneous user cost of capital given in equation 2-25. First, it reduces the tax rate term appearing in the denominator, lowering the cost of capital. Second, it reduces the after-tax present value of depreciation deductions, Γ (calculated using equation 2-22), increasing the cost of capital. Third, it makes $\dot{\Gamma}$, the time derivative of Γ, negative: the present value of depreciation deductions declines over the period as the tax cut is phased in. This last effect reduces the user cost: there is an incentive to invest while depreciation allowances may still be deducted at the higher tax rate. On balance, the instantaneous user cost, as well as the weighted average of current and future user costs relevant to current investment, will likely fall, stimulating investment.[10] It is even possible that investment will be stimulated more by a phased reduction in the tax rate than by an immediate one, since the anticipated decline in the value of Γ, by itself, stimulates investment.[11] This possibility emphasizes the distinction between average and marginal tax rates— between the level of taxes paid by a company and its incentive to invest. A delayed reduction in the tax rate τ will certainly cause the firm to pay more taxes in the short run, even if it faces a lower cost of capital and hence invests more.

A similar distinction may be made between the effects of investment-oriented incentives, such as investment tax credits and allowances, and cuts in the tax rate τ. While both will spur investment, rate reductions will reduce tax payments by more, given the level of investment stimulus, because they will also reduce the taxes the firm pays from sources of income other than new investment, including existing capital and economic rents.

Tax Holidays

Many countries provide tax holidays to attract new investment. Tax holidays provide the investing firm with an exemption from tax on its normally taxable income during some time period after the firm's initial investment is made. As discussed by Mintz in chapter 3 in this volume, such a holiday does not necessarily imply that the firm's user cost of capital is the same as it would be in the absence of taxation, since the holiday is not permanent. In considering whether to invest, the firm must calculate the taxes it will pay on today's asset purchase once the holiday is over, as well as the tax incentives to invest at a later date. Neither factor would apply if the holiday were permanent for all present and prospective investments.

The problem of tax holidays can be analyzed in exactly the same manner as the "global" tax rate change just considered. The situation is the same as it would be if the firm faced a zero tax rate for a predetermined length of time, followed by the normal rate of tax τ thereafter.

Once again, there are three effects on the instantaneous user cost of capital during the holiday period. The tax rate at the current date is zero. To the extent that the depreciation allowances on the firm's current investment extend beyond the holiday period, the present value of after-tax depreciation allowances, Γ, would be reduced but not eliminated.[12] Finally, the time derivative of this present value, $\dot{\Gamma}$, would be positive, since the fraction of allowances deductible from tax would rise as the end of the holiday period approached. The first effect would be positive; the second and third, negative. The effect on investment during the holiday period would depend on the generosity of the investment incentives themselves. It is entirely possible that some types of investment would be discouraged. This would be most likely in cases where the initial investment allowances were larger than the concurrent cash flow. In such cases, new investments would generate a negative tax base in the years immediately after an investment, so firms would actually benefit (with respect to the *new* investment) by being taxable (see Auerbach 1983a).

The revenue cost of a tax holiday depends on whether or not it applies to assets already in place. If it does, then, like a permanent tax rate reduction, the tax holiday reduces the taxes that firms pay during the holiday period on preexisting sources of income other than the new investment that the policies aim to encourage. This makes the tax holiday more costly than more targeted investment incentives, such as investment tax credits or grants.

Tax Law Asymmetries

Most countries allow firms with net operating losses to carry these losses forward, to be used to offset subsequent taxable income. Some countries also allow losses to be carried back, providing refunds against taxes previously paid. Firms that are currently not paying taxes but probably will be doing so in the future can be treated as if they are facing a tax regime with marginal tax rates that change over time. In this sense, the case is similar to the previous one of tax holidays. In this case, however, one cannot simply assume a current marginal tax rate of zero for a firm that is not currently paying taxes. In present value, additional income earned today may well lead to a significant tax liability, even if no taxes are paid immediately.

For example, suppose a firm has a tax loss this year, which it will carry forward and, with certainty, use up next year, when it will be paying taxes once again. If the firm generates another dollar of income this year, this income will reduce the tax loss carried forward by one dollar. This reduction, in turn, will increase by one dollar the firm's taxable income the following year, since the size of the deductible tax loss will be smaller. Hence the firm will pay taxes on an additional dollar of income with a delay of one year. The true marginal tax rate for the current period, which one may think of as a "shadow" tax rate, is therefore the statutory rate, τ, discounted for one period at the nominal interest rate.

Of course, one cannot be certain of the date at which a firm not currently paying taxes will begin doing so, but this does not pose a conceptual problem for the application of the preceding methodology. If one can estimate a probability distribution of when a firm will begin paying taxes again, one can simply multiply the tax rate for each date by the associated probability and add the discounted values of these products together to obtain today's shadow tax rates for a given firm, which can then be used to calculate the user cost of capital.

Illustrations of this strategy are presented in Auerbach (1983a), Auerbach and Poterba (1987), and Altshuler and Auerbach (1990). It can be applied even in cases in which firms are permitted to carry losses back and in which different rules for carrying forward apply to different components of taxable income. In the United States, for example, the rules for carrying forward unused investment tax credits have differed from those applying to ordinary losses. In other countries, such as Pakistan, net operating losses exclusive of depreciation allowances can be carried forward for only six years, whereas unused depreciation allowances themselves can be carried forward indefinitely. Hence the shadow tax rate applicable to depreciation deductions should be closer than the shadow tax rate applicable to ordinary income to the statutory tax rate. In Mexico, the value of losses carried forward is indexed for inflation. Therefore the deferral of tax payments should be discounted by a real rather than a nominal interest rate when shadow tax rates are computed.

The importance of allowing for tax losses and related asymmetries depends on the empirical significance of such phenomena. In the United States, for example, Altshuler and Auerbach (1990) estimated that firms faced an average marginal shadow tax rate of 32 percent in the early 1980s even though the statutory marginal tax rate during the period was 46 percent. The importance of tax losses has been demonstrated for Canada as well (Mintz 1988).

As with tax holidays, a temporary respite from taxes induced by tax loss carryforwards can have complicated effects on the incentive to invest. If a program of generous investment incentives is in place, investment by firms that are not paying taxes may actually be discouraged. In such situations, alternative forms of investment incentives may be desired, such as direct grants that do not work through the tax system.

Uncertainty and Risk

As the discussion of tax law asymmetries illustrates, uncertainty about the tax regime a firm will face in the future may have a significant effect on its current investment. A realistic treatment of the effects of tax policy must also account for the uncertainty that firms will attach to government policy itself. Countries without an established reputation for following through on announced policies may face difficulties making investment incentives effective. The possibility of dynamic inconsistency on the part of governments has played a role in past discussions of the design of tax policy, suggesting why generous tax holidays might be necessary to attract foreign investment (Doyle and van Wijnbergen 1984).

This issue has several implications for the cost-of-capital specification. First, anticipated tax rates that appear in the cost-of-capital equation should not necessarily be those listed in government documents. One must allow past behavior to inform the determination of such tax rates. Second, the efficacy of a tax policy should be judged with respect not to its announced changes but rather to the changes it induces in the policy anticipations of investors. One policy may appear more stimulative than another but may be found to be less plausible or permanent. For example, a promised reduction in the tax rate, τ, may be reversed or postponed more easily than an investment tax credit already given can be taken back from the taxpayer in the future (Hansson and Stuart 1989). Finally, the uncertainty with respect to tax policy may cause risk-averse investors to demand a risk premium, a higher rate of expected return. Hence a climate of uncertainty about tax policy may, in itself, discourage investment. More generally, risk is a central aspect of the investment process. Even with a riskless tax environment, investors may be subject to considerable uncertainty about the future profitability of their prospective investments and may as a result demand an expected rate of return considerably in excess of the risk-free interest rate. The required rate of return, r, that appears in the user-cost-of-capital equation derived above (equation 2-25) must reflect this risk premium. Likewise, the rate of discount applied to future depreciation allowances must account for any risk associated with such tax benefits. Indeed, there is nothing requiring that the discount rates appropriate for tax benefits and other after-tax flows be the same. Although such differences may be easily accommodated in the cost-of-capital calculation, they make standard effective tax rate calculations based on a uniform rate of return inappropriate and potentially quite misleading (Auerbach 1983a). The discount rates applicable to future tax benefits are especially important in the design of tax incentives.

Institutional Factors: Calculating Γ and r

To implement the model of investment behavior derived in the previous section, one must incorporate the relevant tax and nontax provisions affecting the firm's required rate of return, r, and the present value of its investment incentives, Γ.

Measuring Investment Incentives

Most countries provide schedules of straight-line or declining-balance depreciation allowances. Such schedules may be extremely accelerated in relation to actual economic depreciation. Turkey, for example, provides a 50 percent declining-balance depreciation rate for equipment. These allowances, however, are typically not indexed for inflation and so must be discounted using a nominal discount rate. Mexico has recently introduced the choice of a one-time, first-year deduction in lieu of all subsequent depreciation allowances, which is meant to provide roughly the present value of such depreciation allowances and protect them from inflation.[13]

In addition, many developing countries provide initial relief for investors above normal depreciation deductions. In Turkey, for example, there are investment allowances of 30 to 60 percent for certain types of investment. In Pakistan, the initial allowance for machinery and equipment is 40 percent, and the allowance is deducted from the basis used for subsequent depreciation.

Other investment incentives do not fit as directly into the equation for Γ given above but may be expressed in equivalent terms. For example, the value of a subsidized loan associated with a particular investment may be computed by estimating the present after-tax value of the interest and principal payments made on the loan and subtracting this from the face value of the obligation, that is, the amount of money initially provided to the investor.

A somewhat more complicated investment scheme is the "investment fund" or (as it is referred to in Turkey) "financing fund" system. Such a scheme provides firms with a tax deduction for setting funds aside in the investment fund. The funds may subsequently be drawn down for the purpose of making investments. Their use in Sweden has been the subject of previous discussion in the literature (for example, Taylor 1982; Södersten 1989).

In Turkey, firms may contribute up to 25 percent of their taxable profits to the fund in a given year and receive a deduction for doing so. The funds are deposited in a government bond account at the central bank and may be drawn down to the extent of new investment in the future. The firm must add the contributed funds back into taxable income one year hence, however, so that it receives a one-year tax deferral on the contribution regardless of how long the funds remain in the account. Balancing the benefit associated with this tax deferral may be the cost of keeping funds in an account yielding what may be a below-market interest rate. Even if a net tax benefit remains, a serious question is posed about the efficacy of such a program in stimulating investment.

The problem with investment fund schemes is that the tax benefit may well be unrelated to the *marginal* investment decision. If firms are investing at least a quarter of their earnings anyway (this is not an especially high rate of reinvestment), the scheme in practice is equivalent to one that simply gives firms a one-year tax deferral on a quarter of their earnings in exchange for placing these earnings in a government account for a year. Although this scheme may benefit the firm, it does not provide any subsidy to new investment. It encourages investment only in the sense that it reduces the effective tax burden on 25 percent of the future earnings that such investment generates, in precisely the way that a very small reduction in the rate of income tax τ would.

Measuring the Required Rate of Return

There are several issues that relate to the measurement of the required rate of return, r. Already discussed above is the need to use realistic rates of return that reflect the risk premiums required by the market. In an economy with well-developed financial markets in which most investment is undertaken by public corporations, the required nominal return to debt i in equation 2-2 would be well approximated by the observed nominal interest rate, and the required return to equity before personal taxes, $\mu/(1 - \Phi)$, could be based on observed returns to equity. One could use either an after-corporate-tax earnings-price ratio or a market return (dividend yield plus capital gain) for this purpose. A benefit of this method is that specification of the tax treatment of those who supply the funds to corporations may not be necessary.[14]

In a developing country, such returns to debt and equity may not be as easily observable. In this case, one may need to use information on world interest rates, combined with the tax rules that apply to foreign source capital income. For example, suppose the U.S. interest rate is i^*. An American investing in foreign debt must pay whatever taxes are withheld abroad on the repatriated interest income, plus U.S. taxes net of any allowable foreign tax credit. (If the foreign taxes are fully creditable, the U.S. investor bears only the U.S. tax rate on the interest received.) Let t_p be this U.S. tax rate. Then the investor's net return in the United States will be $i^*(1 - t_p) - \pi^*$, where π^* is the U.S. inflation rate. Assuming that exchange rate gains and losses are not taxable, the dollar rate of return available abroad will be $i(1 - t_{max}) - \pi - d$, where i is the foreign nominal interest rate, t_{max} is the higher of t_p and the rate of withholding tax, π is the foreign inflation rate, and d is the rate of foreign currency depreciation against the dollar.

Equating these two net rates of return yields

$$(2\text{-}26) \qquad i = \frac{i^*(1 - t_p) - (\pi^* - \pi - d)}{(1 - t_{max})}.$$

In cases where the liability is denominated in dollars, the term $(\pi^* - \pi - d)$ vanishes because all transactions are in the same currency. (The term will also vanish if purchasing power parity is satisfied.) If, in addition, taxes withheld are fully creditable, then $t_{max} = t_p$ and $i = i^*$. More generally, however, both of these sources of difference between i and i^* will be present. The low rates of income tax now in effect in many industrial countries (including the United States), may in some cases be exceeded by foreign rates of withholding tax on interest. For example, whereas the top tax rates in the United States are 35 percent for corporations and 39.6 percent for individuals, Mexico withholds 42 percent of interest payments. Further, some countries follow the territorial approach to taxation and offer no credit at all for foreign taxes withheld. Even after one allows for the effects of these tax provisions, it is still necessary to account for differences in risk among countries that would be reflected in required rates of return after taxes. However uncertain one is about the size of such risk premiums, equation 2-26 is still useful because it shows how changes in the domestic withholding tax rate affect the cost of capital, given the level of risk.

Computing the required return to equity by using rates of return observed abroad is even more problematic than in the case of debt. First of all, since equity normally bears a considerably greater fraction of investment risk than debt, the problem of measuring risk premiums is more significant in this case. Second, the tax treatment of equity investment from abroad is more complicated than the treatment of debt. The effective rate of a tax depends not only on the rates at which taxes are withheld and credited but also on whether the funds come from another corporation via foreign direct investment or from the household or banking sector, and whether the equity funds for investment abroad come from earnings retained from existing projects abroad or from new equity contributions by the investing country (see Gordon 1986; Hartman 1985). A comprehensive discussion of this problem is beyond the scope of this chapter. Still, one may cite some basic results that are helpful in guiding the specification of the required return to equity.

Consider the case of foreign direct investment in the "host" country. Let $v = \mu/(1 - \Phi)$ be the required return to equity in the country from which the funds come, the "home" country, and ignore for the moment differences in risk. If such funds are sent abroad and all their earnings repatriated, the rate of return after taxes in the host country must equal v plus any additional taxes imposed in the home country upon repatriation, net of foreign tax credits. If t_f^* is the foreign tax rate imputed by the home country for such receipts from abroad, and t_c^* is the home country's corporate tax rate on repatriated earnings, the required return to equity abroad after foreign taxes will be $v \ (1 - t^*_{min})/(1 - t_c^*)$, where t^*_{min} is the smaller of t_f^* and t_c^*. If the foreign tax rate used when imputing the credit (typically not the statutory tax rate τ but some estimate of the presumably lower effective corporate tax rate in the host country) is at least as high as the home country's tax rate on foreign earnings, t_c^*, then this required rate is just the rate of return required at home, v: no further corporate taxes will be owed in the home country. If additional taxes are due on repatriated earnings, however (this will never be the case for home countries following the territorial approach, where $t_c^* = 0$), the required return to equity will exceed v.

When foreign direct investment is funded by retained earnings already in the host country, however, the calculation of the required return to equity v is simpler. In this case, the tax treatment of repatriated funds is irrelevant because repatriated funds will bear the same rate of tax and, in present value, the same tax burden regardless of when they are repatriated (Hartman 1985). Thus the required rate of return will always be v. Therefore for countries with tax rates sufficiently high to provide enough foreign tax credits to offset further corporate tax liability on repatriation, the required rate of return to equity after corporate taxes (except for differences in risk) will be the required rate of return to equity in the countries supplying the investment funds.

Thus for both debt and equity, the major difficulty involved in estimating the firm's required return is the estimation of the domestic risk premium.

Conclusion

This review of the literature on investment and the cost of capital shows how the effects of tax and nontax government policies should be incorporated in the analysis of investment behavior. The methodology is in several respects more general than calculations of tax wedges and effective tax rates. Its application in a developing country context should throw light on the ability of policy to influence investment, the efficacy of the policies currently being pursued, and the appropriate directions for reform.

Appendix. Derivation of Firm Decision Rule

This appendix shows how the decision rule given in equations 2-24 and 2-25 can be derived as a solution of the linearized version of the Euler equation, equation 2-21.

For simplicity, we normalize the output price, p, to one. First, letting $F_t(K) = \theta_t G(K)$, express equation 2-21 as a differential equation in q:

(A-1) $\dot{q} = - G'(K)\,\theta\left(\dfrac{1-\tau}{1-\Gamma}\right) + q\,(r+\delta) - q\left(\dfrac{1\div\Gamma}{1-\Gamma}\right).$

Linearizing around the steady state (where $q = g$ and $\dot{\Gamma} = 0$), we obtain (letting * denote steady-state values):

(A-2) $\dot{q} \approx - G''(K^*)\,\dfrac{1-\tau^*}{1-\Gamma^*}\,(K-K^*) + (r+\delta)\,(q-g)$

$\qquad - \dfrac{G'(K^*)}{1-\Gamma^*}\,\theta^*\,[(1-\tau)-(1-\tau^*)] - \dfrac{G'(K^*)\,(1-\tau^*)}{(1-\Gamma^*)}\,(\theta - \theta^*)$

$\qquad + \dfrac{G'(K^*)}{(1-\Gamma^*)^2}\left[(1-\Gamma)-(1-\Gamma^*)\right] - g\,\dfrac{\delta\,(1\div\Gamma)}{1-\Gamma^*}.$

Using equation 2-20 for q and using the following:

$$G'(K) = c* = \dfrac{g*\,(r+\delta)\,(1-\Gamma^*)}{\theta^*\,(1-\tau^*)}$$

we obtain:

(A-3) $\ddot{K}_t - (r+\delta)\,\dot{K}_t - [\alpha\,(r+\delta)]/\Phi = -(x_t/\Phi)$

where

$$\alpha = - G''/G',\ x_t = \alpha(r+\delta)/\Phi\ K^*\,[1 - 1/\alpha K^*\,a_t\,]$$

(A-4) $a_t = -\dfrac{(1-\tau)-(1-\tau^*)}{1-\tau^*} + \dfrac{(1-\Gamma^*)-(1-\Gamma^*)}{1-\Gamma^*}$

$\qquad - \dfrac{\theta_t - \theta^*}{\theta^*} - \dfrac{1}{r+\delta}\,\dfrac{(1\div\Gamma)}{1-\Gamma^*}.$

Equation A-3 has roots:

(A-5) $\sigma_i = \dfrac{1}{2}\left[r+\delta \pm \sqrt{(r+\delta)^2 + \dfrac{4\alpha\,(r+\delta)}{\phi}}\ \right]\qquad i=1,2.$

Solving the unstable root, $\sigma_2 > 0$, forward, one obtains the first-order equation:

(A-6)
$$\dot{K}_t - \sigma_1 K_t = \int_t^\infty e^{-\sigma_2 (s-t)} x_s \, ds$$

which may be rewritten as the partial adjustment model given in equation 2-23 in the text, where

$$\hat{K}_t = K^* - (\Omega_t / \alpha)$$

and

(A-7)
$$\Omega_t = \int_t^\infty \sigma_2 \, e^{-\sigma_2 (s-t)} \, a_s \, ds.$$

By another first-order approximation,

(A-8)
$$G'(\hat{K}_t) \approx G'(K^*) + G''(K^*)(\hat{K}_t - K^*)$$

$$= G'(K^*)[1 - \alpha(\hat{K}_t - K^*)]$$

$$= G'(K^*)(1 + \Omega_t).$$

Substitution of equation A-7 and the value of $G'(K^*)$ into equation A-8 yields:

(A-9) $$G'(\hat{K}_t) \approx \int_t^\infty \sigma_2 \, e^{-\sigma_2 (s-t)} \left\{ \frac{g(r+\delta)(1-\Gamma^*)}{\theta^*(1-\tau^*)} (1 + a_s) \right\} ds.$$

However, from inspection of equation A-4, we observe that a_s is simply the first-order deviation of c_s (as defined in equation 2-25) from c^*.

(A-10)
$$c_s \approx \frac{g(r+\delta)(1-\Gamma^*)}{\theta^*(1-\tau^*)} (1 + a_s).$$

Substitution of equation A-10 into A-9 yields equation 2-24 in the text.

When there are constant returns to scale in production, $\sigma_1 = \alpha = 0$. Hence the solution based on equation A-6 is:

(A-11)
$$\dot{K}_t = -\int_t^\infty e^{-\sigma_2 (s-t)} \frac{r+\delta}{\phi} \, a_s \, ds$$

$$= -\int_t^\infty \frac{\sigma_2}{\phi} e^{-\sigma_2 (s-t)} \, a_s \, ds$$

$$= -\frac{1}{c^* \phi} - \int_t^\infty \sigma_2 \, e^{-\sigma_2 (s-t)} \, c^* \, (1 + a_s) \, ds + \frac{1}{\phi}$$

$$\approx \frac{1}{\phi} - \frac{1}{c^* \phi} - \int_t^\infty \sigma_2 \, e^{-\sigma_2 (s-t)} \, c_s \, ds.$$

Once again, investment depends on current and future values of the instantaneous user cost of capital, c.

Notes

1. A particular example of a production structure giving rise to $F(\cdot)$ having this separable form is given below.

2. As has long been recognized, a problem arises if the underlying production function $X(\cdot)$ satisfies constant returns to scale. In that case, the derivative of the production function $F(\cdot)$ is not a function of K, so that equation 2-14 is overdetermined. In this case, the optimal capital stock is zero, infinite, or indeterminate, depending on whether or not equation 2-14 is satisfied. It is therefore necessary to assume decreasing returns to scale in K, L, and M, a lag in adjusting capital stock, or a nonhorizontal marginal revenue curve for the firm. The latter two assumptions also make the characterization of the firm's decision more realistic. This is discussed further below.

3. One could also assume equal before-tax returns (the "fixed-p" case) or equal intermediate returns (the "fixed-r" case). The problem of choosing among these assumptions arises from the fact that debt and equity coexist even though the tax wedges imposed on debt and equity returns differ. This highlights a limitation of the procedure: its ignorance of risk and other considerations that might help explain observed patterns of financial structure and asset ownership.

4. The whole function $F(\cdot)$ has the form $G(\cdot) \, \theta \, (w/p, v/p)$, where

$$G(K) = A^{1/(1-\beta)} \, \beta^{\beta/(1-\beta)} \, (1 - \beta) \, K^{\alpha/(1-\beta)}.$$

5. Given this formulation, one can readily see the relation of this discussion to the concept of effective protection. Given fixed world prices p_w for the output good and v_w for the input good, the institution of tariffs T_p on the output good and T_m on the input good causes the term $p\theta$ in the denominator of equation 2-14 to equal

$$P(1 + T_p) \, w^{-1/(1-\beta)} \, \frac{1 - m \, (v_w/p_w) \, (1 + T_m)}{(1 + T_p)^{1/(1-\beta)}}.$$

If we define T_e to be the uniform tariff that provides the same protection for the industry and hence the same desired capital stock, we obtain

$$T_e = (1 + T_p) \left[\frac{1 - m \, (v/p) \, [(1 + T_m) / (1 + T_p)]}{1 - m \, (v/p)} \right]$$

which is less than T_p if and only if $T_m > T_p$. The relation of effective protection to effective tax rates is discussed by Guisinger (1989).

6. Although the result will not be used here, the convex adjustment cost model can also be used to provide a rigorous underpinning for the "q" theory of investment first envisioned by Tobin (1969), under which the firm's investment behavior is related to its market value (Hayashi 1982). Given the market value of the firm, one can then regress investment on the tax-adjusted q ratio of market value to asset replacement cost to obtain estimates of the adjustment cost function (Summers 1981). Unfortunately, this method does not permit one to measure directly the effect of future costs of capital on investment.

7. An alternative strategy, found in Pindyck and Rotemberg (1983), is to estimate the production function and adjustment cost parameters directly from the Euler equation, without solving for the underlying investment rule. That is, instead of solving for an equation for K that is not a function of K, they estimate the Euler equation obtained by substituting equation 2-20 into equation 2-21 with instrumental variables, treating K as an endogenous regressor. Like the method of estimating the Euler equation based on equation 2-21 alone, that is, regressing investment on q, this technique does not provide any insight into the effects of future costs of capital on investment.

8. When there are constant returns to scale in production, K is infinite, zero, or indeterminate. Even in the former two cases, however, the rate of *investment* will still depend on the costs of capital as defined in equation 2-24.

9. Given the formulation of the problem, these roots have the form

$$\sigma_1 = \frac{1}{2} (r + \delta) - \sqrt{(r + \delta)^2 + 4\varepsilon (r + \delta)/\phi} \qquad i = 1, 2$$

where $\varepsilon = - G''/G'$ at the point of linearization. When there are constant returns to scale, $\varepsilon = 0$. If, however, the firm faces a downward-sloping demand curve, the relevant elasticity ε would be based on pG rather than G. The negative relationship between price and output would impart more curvature to the marginal revenue product $d(pG)/dK$. Even with $G'' = 0$, there would still be curvature in the revenue resulting from additions to the capital stock.

10. A full analysis of the Mexican reform would be considerably more complicated, for it would require inclusion of the program's other changes, notably the effects of indexation of depreciation allowances and interest payments. The former effects would be incorporated via the allowances D(•) in the calculation of $\bar{\Gamma}$ and Γ using equation 2-22, and the latter would be treated through induced changes in the corporate cost of funds r.

11. For further discussion, see Auerbach (1989).

12. This assumes that the firm cannot defer depreciation allowances occurring during the holiday period. If they can, there would be a much smaller decline in Γ, due only to the discounting of these delayed deductions. In such a case, the incentive to invest during the holiday period would be much greater because Γ would be larger and $\bar{r}$ smaller. See chapter 3 in this volume for further discussion.

13. Such a scheme and its advantages are discussed in Auerbach and Jorgenson (1980).

14. This simplicity is based on the "$q = 1$" assumption that a dollar invested by the firm costs shareholders a dollar and that a dollar of earnings is worth a dollar to shareholders whether distributed or not. Under the "tax capitalization hypothesis," the ratio of shareholders' value to firm value, q, may be less than one, equal to the ratio of the after-tax proceeds of a dollar distributed to those of a dollar retained by the firm. In this case, an appropriate measure of equity cost based on observed earnings would multiply these earnings by q (see Auerbach

1983b) to offset the multiplication by q already implicit in the firm's value. To make this correction, however, one would have to know the tax rates of the "representative" shareholder.

Whether the "$q = 1$" or "tax capitalization" view is valid depends on the firm's marginal source of funds. If the firm finances its marginal investments using retained earnings, it faces a lower cost of capital because a dollar of funds retained does not cost taxable investors one dollar. There may be other reasons why firms face a lower cost of capital when using internal funds, for example, because of information asymmetries. One way of identifying which equity regime a firm is in is by the level of its internal funds. Within the cost-of-capital framework, one could posit that some function of cash flow determines the appropriate adjustment to observed earnings-price ratios (that is, whether earnings should be multiplied by some value of $q < 1$). An alternative, more ad hoc, approach has been to put cash flow separately into the investment equation. Doing so has recently been found to be quite significant in explaining the investment behavior of smaller U.S. firms (Fazzari, Hubbard, and Petersen 1988).

References

Altshuler, Rosanne, and Alan J. Auerbach. 1990. "The Importance of Tax Law Asymmetries: An Empirical Investigation." *Quarterly Journal of Economics* 105 (February): 63–86.

Anderson, Krister, Kenji Aramaki, A. Lans Bovenberg, and Sheetal K. Chand. 1991. "Tax Incentives and International Capital Flows: The Case of the United States and Japan." In Assaf Razin and Joel Slemrod, eds., *International Aspects of Taxation*. Chicago, Ill.: University of Chicago Press.

Auerbach, Alan J. 1983a. "Corporate Taxation in the United States." *Brookings Papers on Economic Activity* 2:451–505.

_____. 1983b. "Taxation, Corporate Financial Policy, and the Cost of Capital." *Journal of Economic Literature* 21 (September): 905–40.

_____. 1989. "Tax Reform and Adjustment Costs: The Impact on Investment and Market Value." *International Economic Review* 30 (November): 939–62.

Auerbach, Alan J., and James R. Hines. 1988. "Investment Tax Incentives and Frequent Tax Reforms." *American Economic Review* 78 (May): 211–16.

Auerbach, Alan J., and Dale W. Jorgenson. 1980. "Inflation-Proof Depreciation of Assets." *Harvard Business Review* (September–October): 113–18.

Auerbach, Alan J., and James M. Poterba. 1987. "Tax Loss Carryforwards and Corporate Tax Incentives." In M. Feldstein, ed., *The Effects of Taxation on Capital Accumulation*. Chicago, Ill.: University of Chicago Press.

Doyle, Chris, and Sweder van Wijnbergen. 1984. "Taxation of Foreign Multinationals: A Sequential Bargaining Approach to Tax Holidays." Seminar paper 284. Institute for International Economic Studies.

Fazzari, Steven M., R. Glenn Hubbard, and Bruce Petersen. 1988. "Financing Constraints and Corporate Investment." *Brookings Papers on Economic Activity* 1:141–95.

Gordon, Roger. 1986. "Taxation and Investment in a World Economy." *American Economic Review* 76 (December): 549–59.

Guisinger, Stephen. 1989. "Total Protection: A New Measure of the Impact of Government Interventions on Investment Profitability." *Journal of International Business Studies* 20 (Summer): 280–95.

Hansson, Ingemar, and Charles Stuart. 1989. "Why Is Investment Subsidized?" *International Economic Review* 30 (August): 549–59.

Hartman, David. 1985. "Tax Policy and Foreign Direct Investment." *Journal of Public Economics* 26 (February): 107–21.

Hayashi, Fumio. 1982. "Tobin's Marginal *q* and Average *q*: A Neoclassical Interpretation." *Econometrica* 50 (January): 213–24.

Jorgenson, Dale. 1963. "Capital Theory and Investment Behavior." *American Economic Review* 53 (May): 247–59.

King, Mervyn, and Don Fullerton, eds. 1984. *The Taxation of Income from Capital.* Chicago, Ill.: University of Chicago Press.

Mintz, Jack M. 1988. "An Empirical Estimate of Corporate Tax Refundability and Effective Rates." *Quarterly Journal of Economics* 103 (February): 225–31.

Pellechio, Anthony. 1987. "A Model for Analysis of Taxation of Capital Investment in Developing Countries." DRD Discussion Paper 263. World Bank, Development Research Department, Washington, D.C.

Pindyck, Robert, and Julio Rotemberg. 1983. "Dynamic Factor Demands, Energy Use, and the Effects of Energy Price Shocks." *American Economic Review* 73 (December): 1066–79.

Södersten, Jan. 1989. "The Investment Funds System Reconsidered." *Scandinavian Journal of Economics* 91:671–87.

Summers, Lawrence. 1981. "Taxation and Investment: A Q-Theory Approach." *Brookings Papers on Economic Activity* 1:67–127.

Taylor, John. 1982. "The Swedish Investment Funds System as a Stabilization Rule." *Brookings Papers on Economic Activity* 1:57–99.

Tobin, James. 1969. "A General Equilibrium Approach to Monetary Theory." *Journal of Money, Credit, and Banking* 1 (February): 15–29.

3 TAX HOLIDAYS AND INVESTMENT

Jack M. Mintz

THE CORPORATE INCOME tax holiday is a tax incentive frequently used by developing countries to promote capital investment. In the usual form of the holiday a country allows a new ("pioneer") firm operating in a designated industry to be fully or partly exempt from corporate taxation during its formative years and then applies full taxation after the holiday period. Of the fifty-four tax systems used by developing countries that are described in a Price Waterhouse survey (1986), twenty-seven include tax holidays of one form or another. Although tax holidays are prevalent in developing countries, it is not difficult to find examples of holidays in industrial countries, such as Canada, France, and Belgium.

Much of the current literature on capital formation and effective tax rates has concentrated on investment tax credits, accelerated depreciation, and statutory tax rate abatements as tax incentives (see, for example, Boadway, Bruce, and Mintz 1984; King and Fullerton 1984).[1] These tax incentives are not particularly difficult to analyze because it can be assumed that the firm anticipates that the tax system will not change over time. With additional assumptions, time-invariant effective tax rates are derived that are useful for describing the effect of the tax system on capital in the long run. For example, the usual assumptions include the following: prices of real capital goods increase at a constant rate over time, capital depreciates exponentially at a constant rate, and the real net-of-tax discount rate of the firm is time invariant. The steady-state condition in a dynamic perfect foresight model without adjustment costs implies that the firm's capital decision is determined at the point at which the value of marginal product per dollar of capital is equal to the tax-adjusted annual cost of depreciation and financing (see Boadway and Bruce 1979). With this type of model, the cost of capital and effective tax rate faced by the firm is independent of time.

With tax holidays, the firm anticipates that the tax system will change over time. In particular, the corporate income tax rate rises after the holiday is finished. This implies that the cost of capital is no longer time invariant, making the tax holiday problem more difficult to analyze compared with other tax incentives that have been treated in the literature. The scant literature on this subject has concentrated on issues related to the reasons why countries use tax holidays as an incentive without trying to derive the effective tax rate on capital during a holiday (Bond and Samuelson 1986; Doyle and van Wijnbergen forthcoming).[2] The task of this chapter is quite different. The user cost of capital, which varies over time, is derived for a firm that correctly anticipates the length of the holiday and the tax regime that exists after the holiday. The time consistency of tax policy is not an issue here.

If the firm is fully exempt from corporate income taxation during the holiday, what is its effective tax rate? A first response would be that capital bears no tax at all. This would be correct for short-term capital that fully depreciates before the end of the holiday. As shown later, however, the effective tax rate on long-lived holiday assets depends on the relation between tax depreciation and true economic depreciation. Even though the firm is tax exempt during the holiday, it must pay taxes on income generated by holiday investments once the holiday is finished. If the firm must write down the value of its assets for tax purposes during the tax holiday, the tax depreciation writeoffs after the tax holiday may be inadequate in relation to the true cost of depreciation. For example, suppose capital is written off at a 100 percent rate for tax purposes but has an economic life that goes well beyond the holiday period. A firm that undertakes an investment during the holiday must expense the capital for tax purposes yet pay taxes on profits generated by the remaining capital after the holiday period. In fact, the "rule" can be described as follows: the effective tax rate on depreciable capital during the holiday is positive (or negative) if the tax depreciation rate (plus inflation rate with historical cost valuation of capital) is more (or less) than the true economic depreciation rate.[3] Indeed, it is possible, in the case of long-term depreciable capital, that the tax holiday may be no holiday at all in that the effective tax rate on investments during the holiday is higher than that on investments after the holiday! This does not imply that the tax holiday is of no value to the firm. Short-lived assets and labor (compensated by profits) bear no tax during the tax holiday. It is only long-lived assets that may be penalized by the tax holiday.

The remainder of this chapter is divided as follows. In the following section I survey details regarding the tax law in five countries that use tax holiday incentives. I then present the theory used to derive the cost of capital and the effective tax rate on capital for each year during and after a tax holiday. Some effective tax comparisons follow for the countries surveyed earlier. The last section concludes with a discussion of the distortions that arise from tax holidays.

A Detailed Description of Tax Holidays

In this section I describe the details of the corporate income tax law as öf 1987 that are relevant to tax holidays used in five countries: Bangladesh, Côte d'Ivoire, Malaysia, Morocco, and Thailand. Table 3-1 provides a summary of various tax provisions in these countries. Instead of describing the tax regimes in each country, I outline the general features of the tax law that apply to qualifying holiday investments. Many countries give other forms of tax relief during the holiday, such as a remission of import duties on inputs, export taxes on goods, sales taxes, and personal taxes on dividends. Because this chapter concentrates on the firm's investment decision, only the remission of import duties on capital goods and the remission of dividend taxes are considered.

Tax Holiday Provisions

In the five countries listed in table 3-1, tax holidays officially last from three to fourteen years, depending on the law. In general the firm is fully exempt from corporate income taxes during the holiday, although this is not always true. Côte d'Ivoire only partly exempts the firm during the last three years of the holiday, and certain Moroccan investments are given only a 50 percent exemption. In each of the countries, firms must apply for a tax holiday status, and not all firms qualify.[4]

The tax holiday provisions for the treatment of depreciable assets vary considerably among countries. Morocco and Thailand require assets to be depreciated for tax purposes during the holiday, whereas Malaysia explicitly permits the firm to depreciate assets after the holiday. Depreciation deductions in Côte d'Ivoire are not mandatory; these can be deferred indefinitely. Thus a Côte d'Ivoire firm may elect to defer its depreciation allowances until after the holiday. Bangladesh requires that depreciation deductions be claimed in the year, but unused deductions may be carried forward indefinitely.[5] As shown later, in the theoretical section, the deferral of depreciation deductions makes the tax holiday much more generous to the firm.

If the firm is granted a holiday, it usually does not qualify for other tax incentives, such as accelerated depreciation. Depreciation, except in Bangladesh, is based on the straight-line method, unindexed for inflation. In some countries, such as Bangladesh and Malaysia, an initial allowance is given. Morocco and Thailand require tax depreciation to conform to accounting depreciation. These rates of depreciation are applied to assets purchased both during and after the holiday period. Table 3-1 provides the rates of depreciation and initial depreciation or investment allowances. In most cases annual tax depreciation is based on the original cost of assets, and the asset base is not written down by the initial allowance.

Table 3-1. *Tax Holiday Provision for Industrial Enterprises*

Feature	Bangladesh	Côte d'Ivoire	Malaysia	Morocco	Thailand
Period	4–12 years	7–11 years	5–10 years	10–14 years	3–8 years, plus an optional 5 years
Exemption	100 percent	100 percent for 4, 6, or 8 years, depending on region; 75 percent 3 years before end, 50 percent year before last, 25 percent last year	100 percent	100 percent Zone IV, 50 percent Zone III	100 percent; 50 percent for 5 additional years
Treatment of depreciation	Unused mandatory deductions carried forward	Depreciation deductions not mandatory; can be deferred indefinitely	Depreciation delayed until end of holiday	Depreciation mandatory; carried forward in loss periods only	Depreciation mandatory
Rates of depreciation	Declining balance: buildings 15 percent, machinery 30 percent; initial allowance: buildings 10 percent, machinery 20 percent	Straight line: buildings 5 percent, machinery 10–33 percent	Straight line: buildings 2 percent, machinery 12 percent (average); initial allowance: buildings 20 percent, machinery 20 percent	Straight line: conformity with book	Straight line: conformity with book
Treatment of losses	Not carried forward after holiday	Carried forward 3 years	Mandatory deduction of associated nonpioneer loss; pioneer loss only carried forward indefinitely	Carried forward 4 years	Pioneer and associated nonpioneer income and loss aggregated

Other features	5–30 percent of income invested in government bonds; dividends of public firms exempt from personal tax	National Investment Fund levy: 10 percent tax fully recoverable at rate varying with type of investment	Dividends exempt from personal tax	None	Dividends exempt from personal tax
Postholiday					
Corporate tax rate	40 percent public, 45 percent private	40 percent plus 10 percent (NIF)	43 percent less 5 percent abatement	49.5 percent	30 percent public, 35 percent private
Depreciation rates	Same as above; recapture rules apply	Same as above	Same as above; recapture rules apply	Same as above	Same as above; recapture rules apply
Other tax incentives					
After holiday	Investment allowance 25 percent; depreciation base not adjusted	None	None	None	None
Not available during holiday	Accelerated at 100 percent or at 80 percent plus 20 percent	Accelerated at twice the normal rate	Accelerated at 40 percent; investment tax allowance of 100 percent	Investment reserve: 20 percent of profits abated, up to 30 percent of investment	None

Source: Data from *International Bureau of Fiscal Documentation Bulletin* (1987) and (1988).

If one ignores inflation, tax depreciation rates seem to be higher than economic depreciation rates, particularly for buildings and machinery in Bangladesh and, as a result of the initial allowances, Malaysia.

Another important provision regarding tax holidays is the treatment of tax losses. Thailand requires losses incurred by a pioneer firm to be written off against the income of a related nonpioneer company. The same applies to the tax losses of the nonpioneer business; they must be set off against the income of the pioneer firm. Malaysia also requires losses of associated nonpioneer firms to be written off against the income of pioneer firms but, unlike Thailand, not the converse (the tax losses of the pioneer firm are carried forward indefinitely). Bangladesh does not allow tax losses of holiday firms to be carried forward after the holiday, and in Côte d'Ivoire and Morocco there is a limit on the time permitted for losses to be carried forward. In Côte d'Ivoire, depreciation deductions can be deferred indefinitely, so it is unlikely that the restriction on the carryforward of losses is binding for many firms.[6]

A few other features apply to tax holidays. In Bangladesh a certain percentage of income earned during the holiday must be invested in government bonds (the rate varies from 5 to 30 percent, according to the region in which the investment is located). If the government bond rate is below the market rate, an "implicit" tax is imposed on the firm. Côte d'Ivoire has a similar provision associated with the National Investment Fund (NIF; this fund is financed by taxes levied on companies, and the taxes are recoverable if the firm purchases government bonds or undertakes sufficient levels of investment). The rate of corporate income tax is 10 percent and the rate of recovery depends on the region in which the investment is located.[7]

Another feature of tax holidays is that dividends paid by a firm to its shareholders may be exempt at the personal level during the holiday. Malaysia and Thailand fully exempt dividends; Bangladesh exempts only dividends of holiday firms listed on the stock exchange. An analysis of how dividend taxation affects the marginal investment decision of the holiday firm is presented in a later section, "Theoretical Analysis."

Post-Tax Holiday Provisions

When the holiday is terminated, the firm must pay corporate income taxes according to the normal tax code provisions. The statutory tax rate imposed in the five countries varies from 30 percent in Thailand (public firms) to about 50 percent in Morocco.

Tax depreciation rules, after the holiday is terminated, are the same as those described in the previous section. In general the rates of depreciation do not change except in Côte d'Ivoire, where accelerated depreciation (twice the normal rate) might be available for qualifying capital after the holiday period (for later analysis, I assume that post-tax holiday investments do not qualify for accelerated depreciation). An investment allowance not available to firms during a holiday is available after the holiday in Bangladesh. Otherwise, accelerated depreciation and investment allowance incentives are generally not available after the holiday period in most of the countries.

The corporate tax law reviewed above and outlined in table 3-1 is the basis for modeling in the next section and for estimating effective tax rates in the section following it, "Empirical Analysis." The information on the 1987 tax provisions was taken from published sources, so it is quite possible that the tax law has been misinterpreted in some cases.

Theoretical Analysis

In this section I analyze the effect of tax holidays on the investment decisions of price-taking firms. The assumption that there are no costs incurred by the firm in adjusting its capital stock simplifies the analysis.[8] In addition, the firm, when undertaking investments, anticipates no changes in the tax provisions that are applied during and after the holiday period. Personal taxation and debt finance are ignored, at least initially. These assumptions imply that the firm uses a time-invariant discount rate (the opportunity cost of shareholder funds) both during and after the holiday period to value its cash flows. Otherwise, in the presence of varying personal tax rates and financing policies, the firm's cost of finance, hence its discount rate, would be different during and after the holiday period. Time-varying discount rates are considered at the end of this section.

The first part of this section is devoted to the simplest model that can be formulated to evaluate the effect of tax holidays on investment. In this part, it is assumed that the holiday firm is not associated with a nontax holiday firm, that its depreciation deductions cannot be deferred, and that the firm has no accumulated losses at the end of the holiday period, thus being fully taxable when the holiday is finished. In the second part of this section, three complications are considered. The first is the possibility that depreciation deductions may be deferred. The second is the tax treatment of associated holiday and nonholiday firms. The third is incorporation of both debt and personal taxation in the model.

The Basic Theoretical Model

A competitive firm uses capital in each period with the objective of maximizing the value of shareholders' equity. With no debt, the payment made to shareholders is equal to the cash flow of the firm: revenues, net of expenditure, on gross investment and corporate taxes. Labor inputs are ignored because no tax consequences are associated with the use of current inputs (wages are fully deductible from the corporate tax base).

In each year, the firm earns nominal revenues equal to $(1 + \pi)^t F[K_t]$, where π is the rate of inflation and K_t is capital stock. Real revenues are thus output, which is represented by a strictly concave production function. The revenues are distributed as dividends to the shareholder or used for gross investment. Prices of capital goods rise with the general rate of inflation, and the price is equal to unity. Real gross investment, I_t, is physical depreciation (which is assumed to be of the declining-balance form) plus new investment:

$$(3\text{-}1) \qquad\qquad I_t = (\delta K_t + K_{t+1} - K_t).$$

The amount of corporate taxes paid by the firm in each period depends on whether the firm is operating during the tax holiday period or not. Let $t = 0$ be the time when the firm starts up and $t = t^*$ be the time at which the tax holiday ends and the firm becomes fully taxable. Prior to t^* ($t = 0 \dots t^* - 1$), the firm's taxable profits, revenues net of mandatory depreciation deductions, are taxed at the rate u_0 and, for $t \geq t^*$, at the rate u_1, with $u_1 > u_0$. The net-of-tax real revenues of the firm are thus equal to $F[K_t] (1 - u_0)$, and the real expenditure on gross investment net of the present value of tax allowances is equal to $I_t (1 - A_t)$. During the holiday, the tax value of depreciation allowances per dollar of gross investment (A_t) varies at each point of time, which is shown subsequently.

When the firm invests in capital at time t, it benefits from an initial allowance rate of β on gross investment. The investment allowance is deductible from corporate taxable income. An annual depreciation allowance is also given, based on the undepreciated capital cost (UCC) base, which is increased at time t, in real terms, by the amount $(1 - f\beta)I_t$, with f denoting the proportion of the initial allowance that is written off the UCC base. If there is full adjustment, $f = 1$, and if no adjustment, $f = 0$. At each point of time the annual allowance rate is α, which is assumed to be of the declining-balance form and based on the original purchase price of capital.[9] Thus at time $s > t$, the annual allowance deducted from profits is equal to $\alpha(1 - \alpha)^{s-t} (1 - f\beta) (1 + \pi)^t$, in nominal terms. Prior to t^*, the initial and annual allowances are written off at the rate u_0, and after t^*, the remaining annual allowance on the investments made prior to the termination of the tax holiday is written off at the rate u_1. Because these tax depreciation writeoffs are valued in nominal terms, they are discounted at the nominal interest rate i. Deflating by the price index at time t, the real value of tax depreciation allowances, A_t, is computed as follows:

$$(3\text{-}2) \quad A_t = u_0\beta + (1 - f\beta) \left\{ \sum_{s=0}^{t^*-1} u_0\alpha \left(\frac{1-\alpha}{1+i}\right)^{s-t} + \sum_{s=t^*}^{\infty} u_1\alpha \left(\frac{1-\alpha}{1+i}\right)^{s-t} \right\}.$$

Equation 3-2 yields a simpler expression for A_t:

$$(3\text{-}3)\ A_t = u_0\beta + Z\left\{u_0 + (u_1 - u_0)\left[(1 - \alpha)/(1 + i)\right]^{t^*-t}\right\} \qquad \text{for } t < t^*$$

and $Z = (1 - f\beta)(1 + i)\alpha/(\alpha + i)$. The tax value of depreciation writeoffs is thus equal to the value of the initial allowance $(u_0\beta)$ plus the present value of the annual allowances written off during and after the holidays. Given $u_1 > u_0$, the firm is given an additional tax benefit arising from the deduction of depreciation allowances after the holiday. The value of the deduction, however, is lower the earlier the investment takes place during the holiday because $\left[(1 - \alpha)/(1 + i)\right]^{t^*-t}$ is lower in value for t.

For investments undertaken after the holiday period is terminated, real revenues are equal to $F[K_t](1 - u_1)$, and the real cost of investment expenditure is $I_t(1 - A_t)$, where

$$(3\text{-}4) \qquad A_t = u_1\beta + (1 - f\beta)\left[\sum_{s=t}^{\infty} u_1\alpha\left(\frac{1-\alpha}{1+i}\right)^{s-t}\right]$$

$$= u_1(\beta + Z) \qquad \text{for } t \geq t^*.$$

After the holiday is finished, the present value of tax depreciation allowances is time invariant because β and Z are independent of t. This is the usual case found in the tax literature. Note that if $\beta = 0$, $A_t = u_1\alpha(1 + i)/(\alpha + i)$, which is the present value of annual tax depreciation on a declining-balance basis.

Given the above description of cash flows, one can formulate the value maximization problem. Let the real discount rate of the firm be $1 + r$, which is equal to $(1 + i)/(1 + \pi)$. Shareholders' equity is the discounted value of real cash flows earned during and after the holiday period:

$$(3\text{-}5) \qquad V = \sum_{t=0}^{\infty} \frac{1}{(1 + r)^t}\left\{F[K_t](1 - u_t) - (\delta K_t + K_{t+1} - K_t)(1 - A_t)\right\}$$

where A_t is defined by equations 3-3 and 3-4 and u_t denotes time-varying corporate tax rates. For convenience, let $A_t = A$ for $t \geq t^*$ because the present value of tax depreciation allowances on gross investment is shown to be time invariant after the tax holiday.

The firm maximizes its value by choosing K_t in each period. The first-order conditions are of three types. For $t < t^*$:

$$(3\text{-}6a) \qquad \frac{\partial V}{\partial K_t} = \frac{1}{(1 + r)^t}\left[F_t'(1 - u_0) - (\delta - 1)(1 - A_t)\right]$$

$$- \frac{1}{(1+r)^{t-1}} (1 - A_{t-1}) = 0 .$$

For $t = t^*$:

(3-6b) $$\frac{\partial V}{\partial K_{t^*}} = \frac{1}{(1+r)^{t^*}} [F'_{t^*} (1 - u_1) - (\delta - 1) (1 - A)]$$

$$- \frac{1}{(1+r)^{t^*-1}} (1 - A_{t^*-1}) = 0 .$$

For $t > t^*$:

(3-6c) $$\frac{\partial V}{\partial K_t} = \frac{1}{(1+r)^t} [F'_t (1 - u_1) - (\delta - 1) (1 - A)]$$

$$- \frac{1}{(1+r)^{t-1}} (1 - A_{t-1}) = 0 .$$

Equations 3-6a through 3-6c are rearranged using the expressions for A_t so that the familiar user cost of capital is derived as described below. Intuitively, the firm equates the discounted marginal value of capital in period t with purchase cost of acquiring capital in period $t - 1$. The discounted marginal value of capital is net-of-tax marginal revenues, $F'_t (1 - u_t)/(1 + r)$, plus the discounted resale value of capital net of the tax value of depreciation allowances that would be lost to the firm if capital is sold in period t: $(1 - \delta)(1 - A_t)/(1 + r)$. The cost of buying capital in period $t - 1$ is its purchase cost (net of tax depreciation allowances), $1 - A_{t-1}$. Each of the three cases is described according to when the investment takes place.

INVESTMENTS DURING THE HOLIDAY PERIOD. When $t < t^*$, the user cost obtained from equation 3-6a is

(3-7a) $$F'_t = \frac{(\delta + r) (1 - A_t)}{(1 - u_0)} + \frac{(1 + r) (A_t - A_{t-1})}{(1 - u_0)}$$

$$= \frac{(\delta + r) (1 - A_t)}{(1 - u_0)} + \frac{(u_1 - u_0) (1 - f\beta) Z (1 + r)}{(1 - u_0)} \left(\frac{1 - \alpha}{1 + i} \right)^{t^*-t} .$$

The user cost of capital during the tax holiday is composed of two parts, as shown in the first line of equation 3-7a. The first expression is quite familiar: the costs of holding a unit of capital are depreciation and financing costs adjusted for taxes. The expression $(1 - A_t)$ is the real purchase cost of capital net of the tax value of depreciation and investment allowances at time t^*. The expression is also divided by $(1 - u_0)$ because marginal revenues (gross of depreciation costs) are taxed at the rate u_0. The second part of equation 3-7a in the first line is the cost to the firm of purchasing capital in period $t - 1$ rather than t. Because depreciation writeoffs increase in value over time, the firm is better off waiting one period. The expression of equation 3-3 is substituted into equation 3-7a and rearranged by combining terms, yielding the second term of the right-hand side in line 2 of equation 3-7a. This expression is interpreted as the tax depreciation penalty of investing in assets during the holiday rather than waiting until the holiday ends.

In most cases, 100 percent of the firm's profits are exempt from taxation. This implies that $u_0 = 0$ and that the present value of tax depreciation allowances is based on writeoffs made after the tax holiday is completed: $A_t = u_1 Z\{(1 - \alpha)/(1 + i)\}^{t^* - t}$ (the value of tax depreciation allowances after the holiday is terminated). With a full exemption, the user cost of capital in equation 3-7a becomes the following:

$$(3\text{-}7b) \quad F' = \delta + r - [\delta\,(1 + \pi) - (\alpha + \pi)]\, u_1 Z\,[(1 - \alpha)/(1 + i)]^{t^* - t}/(1 + \pi).$$

Let $\delta\pi \to 0$. During the tax holiday, the user cost of capital is equal to the cost of depreciation and finance less the gain to the firm in tax depreciation allowances after the holiday is terminated. The interpretation of this formula is straightforward. By investing in capital in period $t - 1$ (yielding income in period t), the firm replaces δ units of capital in period t. This generates tax depreciation allowances per dollar of capital equal to $u_1 Z\,[(1 - \alpha)\,/(1 + i)]^{t^* - t}$ after the period. By investing in capital in period $t - 1$ rather than in t, however, the firm loses, in present value, tax depreciation that would be based on higher prices of capital goods. This is the term $\alpha + \pi$ multiplied by the present value of tax depreciation allowance later earned by the firm. Equation 3-7b leads to the following conclusion regarding a tax holiday that fully exempts a firm: *if the firm's economic depreciation rate were equal to the tax depreciation rate plus inflation, the capital good would be exempt from capital taxation during the holiday.*[10] If, however, the economic depreciation rate were more (less) than the tax depreciation rate plus the inflation rate, capital during the holiday would be subsidized (taxed).

The user cost of capital in equations 3-7a and 3-7b also shows that other distortions are associated with tax holidays. Nondepreciable assets such as nonspeculative land and inventories are fully exempt from taxation during the holiday (because $Z = 0$). If depreciable assets are written off quickly or if there is high inflation, the nondepreciable assets are favored by the tax holiday. Also, for a given tax depreciation rate, durable assets are favored less compared with nondurable assets during the tax holiday. It is also easy to determine that the cost of capital rises (falls) continuously during the tax holiday if $\alpha + \pi > \delta$ (or $\alpha + \pi < \delta$).

INVESTMENT AT THE END OF THE HOLIDAY PERIOD. When $t = t^*$, the tax holiday ends and the firm becomes fully taxable. Its income, however, is based on its capital stock held in period t^* but determined by the new investment decision taken in the previous period when the holiday was operating. Thus the present value of tax depreciation allowances is in part influenced by investment decisions taken in period $t^* - 1$ even though the income generated in period t^* is fully taxed. All this is determined by equation 3-6b, which is rearranged, with substitutions made for A_t, using the expressions in equations 3-3 and 3-4. The cost of capital in this case is the following:

$$(3\text{-}7b) \quad F'_{t^*} = \frac{(\delta + r)}{(1 - u_1)} (1 - A) + (1 + r) \frac{(u_1 - u_0) [\beta + (1 - f\beta)\, \alpha]}{(1 - u_1)}$$

$$A = u_1 (\beta + Z).$$

Intuitively, the user cost of capital stock for period t^* is equal to the cost of depreciation and finance adjusted for taxes in two ways. First, the corporate tax levied on revenues earned after the holiday is based on the postholiday statutory tax rate. Second, the purchase cost of holding capital is adjusted for the present value of tax depreciation allowances (A) that are incurred by the firm when it replaces capital at time t^*. Because the capital stock decision at time t^* is determined in the period before the end of the holiday, however, a correction must be made for the loss in the tax value of initial and annual allowances arising from investing too early in period $t^* - 1$. This tax penalty is captured by the second term of equation 3-7b.

INVESTMENTS MADE AFTER THE TAX HOLIDAY. When $t > t^*$, the firm is fully taxed both at the time of investment and when income is generated. In this case, the familiar user-cost-of-capital formula for a firm is derived:

$$(3\text{-}7c) \qquad F'_t = \frac{(\delta + r)}{(1 - u_1)} (1 - A) \qquad\qquad \text{for } t > t^*.$$

The postholiday user cost of capital is adjusted for the full statutory corporate tax rate and the tax value of investment allowances that are available after the holiday period.[11] Note that the cost of capital after period t^* is time invariant.

Some Complications

The above theory can be extended in three directions to take into account various complications in tax codes that are relevant to the effect of tax holidays on investment. The complications that are to be considered are the following: the deferral of depreciation deductions until after the tax holiday, the treatment of associated tax holiday (pioneer) and non-pioneer firms, and financial policy and time-varying personal tax rates.

DEFERRAL OF DEPRECIATION. When depreciation is deferred until after the holiday, the firm deducts the allowances from taxable income at the postholiday corporate tax rate. This could cause the firm to be nontaxpaying for a long time if unused holiday depreciation allowances are large in relation to postholiday net revenues. For convenience, it is assumed that the firm is taxpaying after the holiday, so deductions are used immediately, beginning at time t^*.

If deferral does arise, the present value of tax depreciation allowances is calculated beginning in period t as follows. At time $s = t^*$ (that is, when the holiday is over), the firm deducts the initial allowance at the value $u_1\beta$, or in present value terms at time $s = t$, at the value $u_1\beta[1 + i]^{-(t^*-t)}$. Investment expenditure in period t also adds $1 - f\beta$ dollars of investment expenditure to the UCC base that is used to calculate the annual allowance given at the rate α on a declining-balance basis.[12] The firm deducts an annual allowance only after the holiday is finished ($s \geq t^*$). The deduction for the annual allowance is equal to the nominal value $u_1\alpha(1 - \alpha)^{s-t^*}$ in each postholiday period. The present value of this deduction, at time t, is equal to $u_1\alpha(1 - \alpha)s - t^*(1 + i)^{-(s-t^*)}$. The tax benefit of depreciation allowances is thus equal to the following:

$$(3\text{-}8) \quad A_t = \left\{ u_1\beta + (1 - f\beta)\left[\sum_{s=t^*}^{\infty} u_1\alpha \left(\frac{1-\alpha}{1+i}\right)^{s-t^*} \right] \right\} (1 + i)^{-(t^*-t)}$$

$$= u_1 (\beta + Z) (1 + i)^{-(t^*-t)} \qquad \text{for } t \leq t^* .$$

The cost of capital is derived by following the same methodology as before except for the use of equation 3-8. The three expressions for the user cost of capital are the following:

Holiday period ($t < t^*$):

$$(3\text{-}9a) \qquad F_t' = \frac{(\delta + r)}{(1 - u_0)}\left[1 - u_1 (\beta + Z) (1 + i)^{-(t^*-t)} \right]$$

$$+ \frac{u_1 (\beta + Z) (1 + i)^{-(t^*-t)}}{(1 - u_0) (1 + \pi)} .$$

End of holiday ($t = t^*$):

$$(3\text{-}9b) \quad F_{t^*}' = \frac{(\delta + r)}{(1 - u_1)}\left[1 - u_1 (\beta + Z) \right] + \frac{iu_1 (\beta + Z)}{(1 - u_1) (1 + \pi)} .$$

Postholiday ($t > t^*$):

(3-9c)
$$F'_t = \frac{(\delta + r)(1 - A)}{(1 - u_1)}.$$

Equations 3-9a and 3-9b are similar to equations 3-7a and 3-7b, respectively, except for the treatment of the value of tax depreciation allowances. The value of tax depreciation allowances for investments during the holiday period is the discounted value of writeoffs that begin after the holiday is completed. This is quite unlike the situation (equation 3-7a) in which the firm must write off capital during the holiday—and thus has only $(1 - \alpha)^{t^*-t}$ units of capital invested at time t to write off. The second term in equation 3-9a is also similar in interpretation to that in equation 3-9b. Each one denotes the tax penalty of investing in capital prior to the end of the holiday and taking depreciation allowances afterward. If the firm could carry forward its tax deductions at a rate of interest, then this second term would disappear. Equations 3-9c and 3-7c are identical, as one would expect.

If the firm is able to defer its tax depreciation until after the holiday is completed, capital investment may be subsidized, especially if the firm is fully exempt ($u_0 = 0$). For example, in the first term of equation 3-9a the firm is able to deduct its depreciation allowances at the rate u_1, which is higher than the tax on revenues (u_0). The only cost to the firm of investing in capital at time t (depreciation allowances by investing in capital) is captured by the second term in equations 3-9a and 3-9b.

In some countries, such as Côte d'Ivoire, the firm may choose whether or not to deduct its depreciation allowances during the holiday period. The choice is determined by a comparison of the present value of tax depreciation allowances for each strategy. Under deferral the present value of tax depreciation (denote A_d) is equal to that shown in equation 3-8, and under no deferral the present value (A_{nd}) is that shown in equation 3-3. Deferral is preferred if $A_d - A_{nd} > 0$, implying $(\beta + Z)[u_1 - u_0(1 + i)^{t^*-t}] > (u_1 - u_0)(1 - \alpha)^{t^*-t} Z$. This is a useful result for empirical work presented later in that it can be assumed that a Côte d'Ivoire firm, given only a partial exemption during the last three years of the holiday, would still prefer to defer its depreciation deductions.

ASSOCIATED NONTAX HOLIDAY FIRMS. Tax holidays in many countries are given to designated firms that may be owned in association with other taxpaying firms. As a result, owners have a clear incentive to shift income from taxpaying to tax holiday entities and, similarly, to shift tax deductible costs from tax holiday to taxpaying firms to minimize corporate tax payments. For example, one strategy would involve intercorporate transfer pricing. Transacted prices of goods and services sold by a tax holiday firm to a taxpaying one can be overstated, thus allowing the firms to pass taxable income from the taxpaying firm to the tax holiday one (and vice versa if goods and services are sold from the associated taxpaying company to the tax holiday firm).

Unless tax administrators institute and enforce "tax-avoidance" rules, tax holidays provide significant advantages for investments undertaken by associated taxpaying firms. This argument can be elaborated on by considering the following case, in which it is assumed that the post-tax holiday regime is the same as that applying to all taxpaying firms.[13]

Suppose that the proportion, κ, of net revenues is shifted from taxpaying to nontaxpaying firms (but not so much that the taxpaying firm becomes a company with a tax loss). This implies that the effective statutory tax rate that is applied to the net revenues earned by the taxpaying company is $\mu = \kappa u_0 + (1 - \kappa)u_1$. Because tax depreciation is deductible at the rate u_1, the present value of tax allowances for the taxpaying firm is $A = u_1(\beta + Z)$. Thus the user cost of capital for the taxpaying firm takes into account the low tax on the firm's net revenues. This implies the following cost of capital:

$$(3\text{-}10) \qquad F' = \frac{(\delta + r)[1 - u_1(\beta + Z)]}{(1 - \mu)}.$$

The taxpaying firm has a lower cost of capital because $\mu < u_1$. In this case, the tax rate at which deductions are taken is greater than the tax rate at which operating income is taxed.

If a tax holiday firm is associated with a taxpaying firm, its investment decision is affected only to the extent that the firm can shift depreciation deductions to the taxpaying company. The discussion below applies to both cases, which involve either mandatory or permissive tax depreciation deductions. These can be achieved through leasing arrangements that allow the taxpaying company to own the capital (and deduct depreciation) and receive a taxable lease payment for use of the capital by the tax holiday firm. The tax holiday firm, however, can deduct the lease payment only at its effective statutory tax rate, which could, in fact, be zero. Thus because the asset held by the taxpaying company is fully taxed, the only tax-minimizing strategy that can work is for the lease payment to be less than the amount of depreciation deducted so that the taxpaying company incurs a taxable loss on the transaction. The incentive to use this tax-avoidance technique can be reduced by requiring lease payments to be no less than the deductible costs incurred by the taxpaying company that holds the asset.

In the above discussion it is assumed that neither type of associated firm incurs taxable losses. In some countries, associated firms may have to consolidate accounts when losses are incurred, which may influence the investment decisions of the two types of firms. If the taxable loss of the holiday firm is fully written off the income earned by an associated taxpaying firm, the holiday firm is able to transfer depreciation deductions to the nonholiday company. Income is also transferred, however, and is thus taxable because the taxpaying firm adds the income to its own to determine the overall tax liability. If this happens every year during the tax holiday, the holiday firm's investment is taxed as if it were not in the holiday (again, assuming that postholiday tax provisions are the same as those that apply to taxpaying firms in general). Thus the cost of capital for the tax holiday firm, in this particular case, is the same as that shown in equation 3-7c.

If the tax loss is incurred by the taxpaying company and is written off against the income of the associated tax holiday firm, investment decisions made by the taxpaying company could be significantly affected. Without consolidation, a tax loss company may carry forward its tax losses for a maximum number of years or, in some countries, indefinitely. With regard to present value, the tax benefit of marginal losses incurred in period t is the discounted value of tax writeoffs taken in the period t', when the firm becomes taxable. This implies that the tax on net revenues earned in period t by the tax loss firm is $v_{t = u_1} (1 + i)^{-(t'-t)}$. As for depreciation, initial and annual allowances and deductions are carried forward to t' and fully written off, and remaining allowances are written off income after t'. Thus the present value of depreciation deductions during the tax loss years is equal to $A_t = v_t \beta + v_t (1 - f\beta) [1 - (1 - \alpha)^{(t'-t)}] + v_t Z(1 - \alpha)^{t'-t}$. Without consolidation, the cost of capital for the tax loss company is the following (corresponding to equation 3-7a):

$$(3-11) \qquad F_t' = \frac{(\delta + r)}{(1 - v_t)} (1 - A_t) + (1 + r) \frac{(A_t - A_{t-1})}{(1 - v_t)}$$

If, however, the tax accounts of the associated companies must be consolidated, the nonholiday firm must deduct its loss against the income of the holiday firm that could be fully exempt from taxation. Because fewer losses are carried forward by the nontax holiday firm, it begins paying taxes earlier than t'. Thus consolidation affects the nontax holiday firm's decisions on both current and future investments because future income is less sheltered from taxation.

When losses are transferred to the tax holiday firm that is fully exempt, the tax on income earned by the nontax holiday firm is zero. As for depreciation deductions, some value is still left to the nontax holiday firm because nontransferred future annual depreciation allowances remain deductible against future income. All this implies that, in equation 3-11, the discounted tax rate is $v_t = 0$, and the present value of tax depreciation allowances is $A_t = u_1 Z[(1 - \alpha)/(1 + i)]^{t''-t}$ (t'' is the first year after t in which annual depreciation allowances are deductible by the taxpaying company). If assets, such as structures, are written off slowly over time, capital investment by the nontax holiday firm could be encouraged if losses must be transferred to the tax holiday firm. The nontax holiday firm's future investment, however, is no longer sheltered from tax writeoffs, so it becomes more highly taxed as a result of consolidation.

PERSONAL TAXATION AND DEBT POLICY. The analysis so far ignores both personal taxation and debt policy. To take both of these factors into account, the model must be revised accordingly. This is done by first reformulating the firm's maximization problem to be one in which the equity of shareholders is maximized rather than cash flows. The problem of equity maximization is then converted into a value maximization problem, which involves the firm's discounting its cash flows by a discount rate that is a weighted average of the costs of debt and equity finance. As is shown later, the discount rate actually varies over time because of the expected changes in tax rates after the holiday is terminated.

When a firm undertakes investment, it finances capital from three sources: retained earnings, debt, and new equity issues. (The latter source of finance is ignored to simplify the presentation.)[14] Investors face three types of personal taxation. The first is the tax on nominal interest income, which is assumed to be levied at the rate m. The second is tax on dividends, which is assumed to be levied at the rate θ_0 during the holiday and θ_1 after the holiday. (Note that the dividend tax rate is assumed to be net of dividend tax credits that may be paid for integration of corporate and personal taxes.) The third is the nominal capital gains tax that is assumed to be levied at the rate c on an accrual basis.[15] At the individual level, interest, dividends, and capital gains may be taxed at different rates, according to the individual's income and nationality. Below, it is assumed that investors in the tax holiday firm are identical and are residents of the country.

In a capital market facing no imperfections such as credit rationing, shareholders are willing to hold equity at the margin if the net-of-tax dividends and capital gains earned by investing in equity equals the net-of-tax return on investing the same funds in a bond. This capital market constraint holds each period during and after the holiday period and is written as follows:

$$(3\text{-}12) \qquad i\,(1-m)\,E_t = (1-\theta_{t+1})\,D_{t+1} + (1-c)\,(E_{t+1} - E_t)$$

where $\theta_t = \theta_0$ for $t < t^*$ and $\theta_t = \theta_1$ for $t \geq t^*$. The dividend in each period is equal to the nominal cash flow of the firm net of corporate taxes, X_t, plus new bond issues (used to finance capital acquired in period t) less interest payments, net of corporate taxes:

$$(3\text{-}13) \qquad\qquad D_t = X_t + B_{t+1} - B_t - i\,(1-u_t)\,B_t$$

where $u_t = u_0$ for $t < t^*$. Cash flow (arising from transactions in real goods) is equal to nominal revenues net of nominal gross investment and corporate tax payments (the latter is the tax on revenues net of capital cost allowances):

$$(3\text{-}14) \quad X_t = (1 + \pi)^t \, F[K_t]\,(1 - u_t) - (1 + \pi)^t\,(K_{t+1} - K_t + \delta K_t)$$

$$(1 - u_t\,\beta) + u_t\,\alpha K_t'\,.$$

Note that K_t' is the UCC base for annual depreciation allowances.[16]

With differential taxation of capital income both at the company and at the personal levels, there is an incentive for firms to issue securities that bear the least tax paid by investors. If equity income bears little tax compared with that for bonds, equity finance would be preferred, and vice versa. In the model below, only retentions and bond finance are considered. Because dividend taxes are capitalized in share values, they have no effect on the marginal finance decisions.[17] In contrast, capital gains taxes are relevant because the retention of profits increases the value of shares that are assumed to be taxed at the individual level at the rate c. Thus the effective tax on a unit of retained profit is $u_t + (1 - u_t)c$ and on bond interest, m. Because equity income is taxed less during the holiday, a firm would favor equity finance more at this time than during the period after the holiday.

If issuing different types of securities entailed no cost, only one least-taxed source of finance would be used: retentions or debt. Securities are issued at cost, however, so the firms must minimize the cost of financial funds, trading off tax benefits with other attendant costs. For example, debt may increase the cost of bankruptcy, so it is unlikely that debt would fully finance capital. This suggests that an optimal debt policy may exist, although differing in the pre- and postholiday periods. Without deriving an optimal debt policy, we assume that the firm finances itself, keeping its optimal debt-value ratio (denoted γ_t) constant in both the pre- and the post-tax holiday regimes. Note that the firm's value at each point of time, denoted V_t, is the sum of the "market" value of debt and equity.[18] There are thus two optimal financial policies in each period such that $(\gamma_0 < \gamma_1)$.

These assumptions regarding financial policy may be used to derive a value maximization problem for the firm. If equation 3-13 is substituted into equation 3-12, it can be rearranged to obtain:

$$(3\text{-}15) \quad E_t[1 + i\,(1 - m)] + B_t[1 + i\,(1 - u_{t+1})]\,\frac{(1 - \theta_{t+1})}{(1 - c)}$$

$$= \frac{(1 - \theta_{t+1})}{(1 - c)}\,X_{t+1} + E_{t+1} + B_{t+1}\,\frac{(1 - \theta_{t+1})}{(1 - c)}\,.$$

Let $V_t = E_t + B_t\,(1 - \theta_{t+1})/(1 - c)$ and $\gamma_t = B_t(1 - \theta_{t+1})/(1 - c)V_t$. The formulation of this problem requires one to interpret the "market" value of the firm carefully. The nominal value of bonds issued by the firm from the point of view of the equity investor must be corrected by the tax capitalization factor $(1 - \theta_{t+1})/(1 - c)$. The tax capitalization factor reflects the following. If the firm buys back in period $t + 1$, the bonds that it issued in period $t (B_t)$, the value of equity falls by $(1 - c)B_t$, but dividend payments increase by $(1 - \theta_{t+1})B_t$. Thus the firm's value rises by $(1 - \theta_{t+1})/(1 - c)$ when the firm buys back one dollar of its bonds B_t.

The definition of V_t is substituted into equation 3-15, yielding:

$$(3\text{-}16) \qquad V_t(1 + R_t) = \frac{(1 - \theta_{t+1})}{(1 - c)} \ X_{t+1} + V_{t+1}$$

where $R_t = \gamma_{ti}(1 - u_t) + (1 - \gamma_t) i (1 - m)/(1 - c)$, *the weighted average nominal cost of equity and debt finance net of corporate taxes.* Because tax rates and the weights have values that differ only according to when the firm is operating (pre- or post-tax holiday), R_t is only of two values, R_0 and R_1. Equation 3-16 holds at each point of time, so it is straightforward to obtain the value maximization problem for the holiday firm that starts up at time $t = 0$:

$$(3\text{-}17) \qquad V_0 = \sum_{t=0}^{t^*-1} \frac{X_t(1 - \theta_0)}{(1 + R_0)^t (1 - c)} + \sum_{t=t^*}^{\infty} \frac{X_t(1 - \theta_1)}{(1 + R_1)^t (1 - c)} \ \zeta_1$$

$$\text{with } \zeta_1 = \frac{(1 + R_1)^{t^*}}{(1 + R_0)^{t^*}}.$$

Equation 3-17 can be further manipulated by using the definition of the X_t and dividing terms by the price index $(1 + \pi)^t$ to yield:

$$V_0 = \sum_{t=0}^{\infty} \frac{(1 - \theta_t)\{ F[K_t] (1 - u_t) - (K_{t+1} - K_t - \delta K_t) (1 - A_t)\}}{(1 - c) (1 + r_t)^t} \ \zeta_t$$

with

$$\zeta_t = 1 \qquad\qquad \text{for } t < t_0 ; \ (1 + r_t)^t = [(1 + R_t) / (1 + \pi)]^t$$

and

$$A_t = u_0 \beta + \left[u_0 Z_0 (1 - \Upsilon_t) + u_1 Z_1 \frac{(1 - \theta_1) \Upsilon_t}{(1 - \theta_0)} \right] \qquad \text{for } t < t^*,$$

$$(3\text{-}18) \qquad A_t = u_1(\beta + Z_1) = A \qquad\qquad \text{for } t \geq t^*$$

where $Z_t = (1 - f\beta)(1 + R_t)\alpha/(\alpha + R_t)$ and $\Upsilon_t = ((1 - \alpha)/(1 + R_0))^{t^*-t}$.

One can repeat the analysis of the previous section by finding the optimal choices for capital, taking into account both personal taxes and financial policy. The user costs of capital for a firm during and at the end of its holiday are:

Holiday period:

$$(3\text{-}19a) \qquad F_t' = \frac{(\delta + r_0)(1 - A_t)}{(1 - u_0)} + (1 + r_0)\frac{(A_t - A_{t-1})}{(1 - u_0)}.$$

End of holiday:

$$(3\text{-}19b) \quad F_{t*}' = \frac{(\delta + r_0)(1 - A)}{(1 - u_1)} + (1 + r_0)\frac{[A - A_{t*-1}(1 - \theta_1)/(1 - \theta_0)]}{(1 - u_1)}.$$

The user cost of capital in the postholiday period is the same as that derived earlier for equation 3-7c except that r is replaced by r_1 (the cost of finance is the weighted average cost of funds in the postholiday period).

Expressions 3-19a and 3-19b are similar to equations 3-7a and 3-7b, respectively, except for three adjustments. First, the cost of finance is no longer the cost of equity finance; instead, it is now the weighted average cost of equity and debt finance during the holiday period. Second, the tax depreciation allowances are discounted by the weighted average cost of finance rather than the cost of equity finance (with the discount rate varying from the holiday to the post–tax holiday period). And third, the values of tax depreciation allowances are adjusted for the change in dividend tax rates from the holiday to the post–tax holiday period.

Although personal taxation and debt finance complicate the analysis, the results can be easily generalized. A few points are worth noting. First, when the personal tax on dividends changes at the end of the holiday period, the dividend tax is not a "lump sum" as found in the conventional analysis. A jump in the dividend tax directly affects the user cost of capital through depreciation deductions because they are less valuable after the holiday is terminated. Even though we began with the tax capitalization theory of dividend policy, we see that the dividend tax directly affects investment decisions. Second, the cost of capital is also affected by shifts in financial policy. Because deductions of interest from debt are less valuable during the holiday, the cost of funds is higher to the firm during the holiday than after it. This suggests that the firm's investments during the holiday may not receive as much benefit as one might believe.

Empirical Analysis

In this section, I estimate the user cost of capital and effective tax rates for depreciable capital investments undertaken during and after the holiday period for the five countries discussed earlier. These calculations are meant to be illustrative only because the data needed for a more careful measurement of the user cost of capital are lacking. In particular, no country-specific data except for interest rates and inflation rates were available. Instead, I used data, such as physical depreciation rates for capital, that were estimated for industrial countries. Certain corporate tax parameters specific to developing countries were also used, such as statutory corporate tax rates, dividend tax rates, and tax depreciation rates. No information was available, however, regarding such items as the average length of tax holidays, the weighted marginal dividend tax rate, and the distribution of machinery or building assets, which is needed to calculate the average tax depreciation rate. Thus I chose the length of holidays, dividend tax rate, and tax depreciation rates on the basis of the country's tax code. It is also not known to what extent governments limit the number of times that a firm can claim a tax holiday. It is quite possible that the effective holidays may last longer than is indicated in the statutes.

In the estimates below, I assume that the rate of depreciation of buildings is 5 percent and that of machinery 15 percent on a declining-balance basis.[19] I then convert straight-line physical depreciation rates into declining-balance rates using the well-known approximation formula $\alpha = 2/T$ (T denoting the life of the asset). As for debt-asset ratios of firms, I assume for one set of calculations that the firm finances capital 50 percent by debt during the holiday and 75 percent by debt after the holiday. Recent evidence suggests that this would be reasonable to assume, although it is clear that only country-specific information would be helpful in this regard.[20]

Corporate tax rates and depreciation rates are based on 1987 tax law as reported by the International Bureau of Fiscal Documentation. Tax depreciation rates of a straight-line form are converted to declining-balance depreciation rates when necessary. Depreciation is deferred until after the tax holiday for firms operating in Côte d'Ivoire and Malaysia.

Table 3-2 presents effective tax rates and user costs of capital for tax holiday investments that are assumed to be fully financed by equity. Note that personal taxes are ignored in this set of calculations.

For the five countries that are considered, effective tax rates on capital during a tax holiday (except for the final year) are generally below those that are faced by the firm after the holiday. This is not entirely surprising. What is surprising, however, is that the effective tax rates on capital during the holiday are generally high and positive in value. The implica-

Table 3-2. Effective Tax Rates and User Costs of Capital for Holiday and Postholiday Investments: 100 Percent Equity Finance
(percent)

| Period | Bangladesh (t* = 7) | | Côte d'Ivoire (t* = 7) | | Malaysia (t* = 7) | | Morocco (t* = 10) | | | | Thailand (t* = 5) | |
| | | | | | | | Zone 3 | | Zone 4 | | | |
	Buildings	Machinery	Buildings	Machinery	Buildings	Machinery	Buildings	Machinery	Buildings	Machinery	Buildings	Machinery
Effective tax rate [a]												
During holiday												
t = 0	15.7	6.3	-1.1	-909.8	-1.9	-44.1	28.0	28.8	1.4	0.8	8.0	n.a.
t = 3	30.9	22.4	1.5	610.4	-2.7	-76.3	28.3	29.2	2.5	2.1	0.7	1.0
t = 5	44.6	43.3	1.8	325.0	-3.4	-119.9	28.7	29.8	3.6	3.7	n.a.	n.a.
t = 8	n.a.	n.a.	n.a.	n.a.	n.a.	n.a.	29.7	31.7	6.3	8.9	n.a.	n.a.
End of holiday	88.1	93.0	56.0	61.6	51.5	51.1	59.1	68.2	63.9	75.7	41.9	51.7
Postholiday	44.6	46.7	45.2	34.9	36.9	8.4	53.0	54.3	53.0	54.3	34.6	32.9

User cost of capital

During holiday												
$t = 0$	8.6	18.2	10.1	30.5	13.0	20.6	16.5	26.7	13.4	23.4	21.2	31.2
$t = 3$	9.3	18.9	10.1	29.0	12.9	19.6	16.6	33.0	13.5	23.5	21.2	31.3
$t = 5$	10.4	20.3	10.1	27.7	12.9	18.7	16.7	26.8	13.6	23.6	n.a.	n.a.
$t = 8$	n.a.	n.a.	n.a.	n.a.	n.a.	n.a.	16.8	27.2	13.9	24.1	n.a.	n.a.
End of holiday	30.2	57.7	16.8	43.5	21.8	31.6	25.3	41.1	28.0	49.1	32.7	48.4
Postholiday	10.4	20.6	14.5	38.0	17.9	23.9	22.7	33.2	22.7	33.2	29.6	39.2
Nominal interest rate	14.0	14.0	9.9	9.9	12.2	12.2	15.5	15.5	15.5	15.5	18.6	18.6
Inflation rate	11.0	11.0	4.7	4.7	4.1	4.1	7.2	7.2	7.2	7.2	2.5	2.5

n.a. Not applicable.

t^* = period that holiday ends; t = year after which holiday begins.

a. Estimated as $t = (F' - \delta - r) / (F' - \delta)$ is the marginal gross-of-tax and r is the net-of-tax rate of return on capital. The user cost of capital is equal to F', the value of marginal product earned by capital.

Source: Authors' calculations.

tion of this is that a rather large tax penalty arises from insufficient tax depreciation deductions taken after the holiday for long-lived investments made during the holiday. This tax penalty is highest in those countries that have high inflation rates (Bangladesh and Morocco) and tax provisions that require capital to be written off quickly during the holiday (Bangladesh). If, however, a country allows firms to defer tax depreciation until after the holiday, capital is taxed at a lower rate or subsidized (as indicated by negative effective tax rates). This particularly applies to Côte d'Ivoire and to a lesser extent Malaysia.

The data in table 3-2 also indicate that effective tax rates imposed on firms at the end of the tax holiday are particularly high. At this point, the firms are investing in new capital just before the end of the tax holiday, but income earned is fully taxed after the holiday is terminated. Even in those countries that allow depreciation to be deferred, the firm does not get much benefit from this provision in the final year of the holiday because the allowances cannot be carried forward at a rate of interest. These extraordinarily high effective tax rates severely affect investment. In fact, the firm is selling off capital stock before the holiday is terminated and increases its capital stock after the holiday is completed.

These results can be quite sensitive to the financing decision. In table 3-3, I allow for debt finance, using the debt-asset ratios referred to earlier. In the case of Thailand, I also incorporate the exemption of dividends at the personal level during the tax holiday. Because the same exemption is not given to foreign investors, I effectively assume for these calculations that the cost of equity finance to the firm is affected by personal taxes imposed on domestic investors.[21] Otherwise, domestic personal taxes could be ignored because they affect only the ownership of domestic assets rather than investment decisions of firms.

Since nominal interest costs are deductible from the corporate tax base, it is not surprising to find that the user costs of capital and effective tax rates are much lower in table 3-3 than in table 3-2 in the postholiday period for all countries. It is well known that interest deductions can be quite generous to the firm because the deductibility of nominal interest payments allows the firm to write off part of the real value of the debt's principal. Of more interest, the incorporation of debt finance in the measures affects the relative ranking of tax rates during and after the firm's holiday. Because interest deductions are beneficial only after the holiday period, the effective tax rate may be higher during and at the end of the holiday than in the postholiday period. As seen in table 3-3, effective tax rates on capital during the holiday are higher than those after the holiday in Morocco (Zone 3) and Bangladesh. End-of-holiday investments also bear a high tax penalty for the same reasons as those cited earlier in the discussion of table 3-2.

Table 3-3. *Effective Tax Rates and User Costs of Capital for Holiday and Postholiday Investments: Debt Finance Case*
(percent)

Period	Bangladesh (t* = 7)		Côte d'Ivoire (t* = 7)		Malaysia (t* = 7)		Morocco (t* = 10) Zone 3		Zone 4		Thailand (t* = 5)	
	Buildings	Machinery	Buildings	Machinery	Buildings	Machinery	Buildings	Machinery	Buildings	Machinery	Buildings	Machinery
Effective tax rate [a]												
During holiday												
t = 0	30.9	13.0	-1.7	-532.8	-2.1	-48.9	5.9	8.6	2.7	1.4	0.5	0.4
t = 3	51.0	38.3	-2.2	-269.4	-3.0	-81.5	7.4	9.6	4.6	3.3	0.8	1.1
t = 5	64.6	61.6	-2.6	-212.8	-3.7	-124.0	8.8	11.6	6.5	5.8	1.3	2.1
t = 8	80.9	87.0	-3.4	-169.6	-5.1	-312.3	11.8	16.3	10.7	13.0	2.3	5.3
End of holiday	90.5	94.4	53.6	58.4	48.6	46.6	58.5	72.0	63.4	76.2	50.5	62.4
Postholiday	225.1	301.0	-13.8	-34.7	-17.2	-114.6	-29.3	-7.5	-29.3	-7.5	4.6	2.8
User cost of capital												
During holiday												
t = 0	7.3	16.8	9.1	29.0	11.8	19.6	12.2	22.4	11.9	21.8	19.3	29.3
t = 3	8.3	17.6	9.1	27.5	11.7	18.8	12.3	22.5	12.1	22.0	19.4	29.4
t = 5	9.5	19.2	9.1	26.3	11.7	18.1	12.4	22.6	12.2	22.4	19.4	29.6
t = 8	13.4	27.3	9.1	24.0	11.6	16.7	12.7	23.1	12.6	22.8	19.6	30.0
End of holiday	29.1	56.2	15.1	41.3	19.7	29.1	23.2	41.8	25.6	46.7	35.7	55.4
Postholiday	3.2	13.9	9.1	33.5	11.4	18.5	10.8	22.0	10.8	22.0	20.9	30.6

t* = period that holiday ends; t = year after which holiday begins.

a. Estimated as $t = (F' - \delta - r) / (F' - \delta)$ is the marginal gross-of-tax and r is the net-of-tax rate of return on capital. The user cost of capital is equal to F', the value of marginal product earned by capital.

Source: Authors' calculations.

Conclusions

The tax holiday provisions for long-term investment are not as generous to firms as one might initially conclude. Even if a firm is fully exempt during the holiday, its investment decision may be significantly affected by taxation during the holiday. As argued earlier, a firm that must write off tax depreciation allowances during the holiday may face a relatively high effective tax rate if the allowances that remain after the holiday are inadequate in relation to the income-generating capacity of the asset. Although effective tax rates during the tax holiday are generally lower than those imposed after the tax holiday, the effective tax rates during the holiday are far from zero. Only when the firm is allowed to defer depreciation until after the holiday do effective tax rates become low or negative. In some cases, when deferral is allowed, the effective subsidy is so large that authorities would perhaps be taken aback by the generosity of the tax holiday.

A corporate tax holiday may also be generous to firms that use non-depreciable factors of production, such as land and inventories, because these investments are generally tax exempt (except for the last period of the holiday). The holiday may be generous as well to labor if such labor is compensated by profit distributions that may be exempt at the individual level. Moreover, the holiday provides tax-planning opportunities for investors who may try to shift taxable income earned by associated companies into the tax holiday firm.

If the objective of a country is to encourage investment in structures and other durable capital, the tax holiday seems to be a poor tax incentive, at least in comparison with other potential tax incentives. Accelerated depreciation or an investment tax credit that leads to zero or negative effective tax rates encourages long-term investment. These tax incentives mean a significantly lower loss in tax revenue because, unlike the situation in a tax holiday, taxes remain on other assets used by the firm. In fact, an investment tax credit or an investment allowance that applies to capital expenditure can induce the same amount of new long-term investment as a tax holiday can but at less revenue cost because the tax holiday allows firms to earn rents without paying taxes. This issue, however, goes beyond the scope of this chapter.

Finally, a few technical issues should be briefly mentioned. The first is the effect of tax holidays on foreign investment that may be taxed by both the capital-importing and capital-exporting countries. Although the theory developed in this chapter could be easily generalized for this situation, an empirical application would require measuring the cost of funds for a foreign company. The second issue deals with imperfections in capital markets. The theory is based on households earning the same rates of return on assets net of taxes in perfect markets. If investors are constrained in borrowing funds to finance equity investments, the standard capital market equilibrium does not apply. This is a general issue that is relevant to the current effective tax rate literature as applied to developing countries. The third issue regards "recapture" rules that apply to the sale of assets by corporations. The theory in this chapter assumes that the sale of an asset by a firm reduces the base used to calculate depreciation writeoffs. The treatment of depreciation in most tax systems, however, is not symmetrical with regard to the sale and purchase of assets. If the firm sells an asset, a "balancing charge" is imposed that may require the inclusion of the sale value of the asset (net of unclaimed tax depreciation) in the income of the corporation, which is far less generous than writing down the undepreciated capital base. Because a tax holiday firm is expected to spin off its capital, particularly at the end of the holiday, a theory that was more carefully worked out would include "balancing charges." This suggests, however, that the effective tax rates estimated in this chapter are, if anything, underestimated if "recapture" rules have been modeled correctly.

Notes

This chapter is based on Mintz (1989).

1. The notions of the effective tax rate and the cost of capital are now fairly well known in the literature, so they are only briefly defined here. The user cost of capital is depreciation and financing costs, adjusted for taxes, which are incurred by the firm when it holds capital. Effective tax rates are conventionally defined as the difference between the marginal gross-of-tax rate of return (the user cost of capital net of depreciation costs) and the net-of-tax rate of return that savers earn when investing in the firm's capital. This difference may be divided by the gross-of-tax or net-of-tax marginal rates of return.

2. Two researchers who also try to answer this question are Agell (1982) and Bond (1981). Each measures the effective tax rate by taking into account that income earned by capital during the holiday is taxed at the end of the holiday and assuming that the value of the marginal product is constant during the tax holiday period. As I show in this chapter, this assumption, implying that the capital stock is constant until the end of the holiday, is incorrect. Tax depreciation allowances are also modeled incorrectly.

3. This rule applies when the firm cannot defer its tax depreciation writeoffs. As I discuss in the next section, some countries allow tax depreciation to be deferred until after the holiday. I show that capital is generally subsidized when income is fully exempt from taxation in the holiday period and firms are allowed to defer depreciation deductions.

4. Morocco grants tax holidays only for Zone III (50 percent exemption) and Zone IV investments (100 percent exemption) that are situated in rural areas. The length of Côte d'Ivoire tax holidays depends on the region in which the firm operates. Most countries do not allow tax holiday firms to claim other tax incentives (Bangladesh, Côte d'Ivoire, Malaysia).

5. If the firm earns taxable profits during the holiday, I interpret the rules to imply that these depreciation deductions during the holiday are fully used and thus not carried forward.

6. Canada, similar to Côte d'Ivoire, allows the firm to defer depreciation deductions. For this reason, most reported tax losses are written off during the seven-year maximum period in Canada. See Mintz (1988).

7. I have not been able to determine if the firm must pay the NIF tax during the holiday. I assume, if it does, that the tax does not affect the marginal investment decision, because the funds can be fully recovered by investing in qualifying capital.

8. It is straightforward to include adjustment costs as long as they are current and fully deductible from the corporate tax. If adjustment costs are capital in nature, the analysis is more complicated but adds little in theory to the model. For a discussion on effective tax rates and adjustment costs, see Boadway (1987).

9. The theory is easier to present with declining-balance tax depreciation. Straight-line depreciation is more common, as discussed earlier, so depreciation rates were adjusted for the empirical work presented in the following section, "Empirical Analysis."

10. If the tax depreciation allowances were indexed for inflation, the inflation term would drop out and all that would matter would be the relation between economic depreciation and tax depreciation.

11. Some tax holiday provisions also exempt the firm from paying sales taxes and import duties on their purchases of capital goods. If taxes are paid on capital goods, the price of capital in real terms is $1 + \tau$ instead of \$1 (let τ be the sales tax or import duty rate). The cost of capital is thus adjusted by multiplying the term $(1 - A)$ by $(1 + \tau)$ in expressions 3-7a through 3-7c where applicable, assuming that depreciation is based on the tax-inclusive price of the asset.

12. In some cases, the total amount of depreciation undeclared during the holiday may be expensed at the end of the holiday rather than written off in the postholiday period at the rate α. This practice does not seem to be followed in the countries that I deal with in this chapter.

13. As noted earlier, several of the countries may give other tax incentives to nontax holiday firms, thus making postholiday tax regimes different from the tax regime faced by associated taxpaying companies.

14. Because dividends may be exempt during the holiday, new equity may be a favored source of finance during a holiday. It is quite easy to adjust the cost of capital of a holiday firm for new equity finance by letting the cost of finance faced by the firm depend on the dividend tax rate faced by the shareholders. See Boadway (1987).

15. Unless capital gains are exempt from taxation, most countries tax capital gains on a realization basis. The accrual tax rate is derived by calculating the present value equivalent of capital gains taxes paid at disposal of the asset. See Auerbach (1983) for a discussion of this.

16. The UCC base at time t, assuming no deferral of allowance, is equal to the following:

$$K_t' = K_0 (1 - \alpha)^t + \sum_{s=0}^{t} (1 - f\beta) (1 + \pi)^s (K_{t+1} - K_t + \delta K_t) (1 - \alpha)^{t-s}.$$

This equation, describing the nominal value of the UCC base, is used to compute the present value of tax depreciation allowances.

17. The relevant personal tax rate on equity income depends on the view taken regarding the role of dividends in a financial model. One view is that the

dividend tax is fully capitalized in share values (Auerbach 1979). If the firm uses retentions as a source of finance, the relevant tax rate is *c*. If dividends convey information to the market, the effective personal tax rate on equity income may be a weighted average of personal dividend and capital gains taxes (Poterba and Summers 1985). Below, we assume "tax capitalization" of dividend taxes so that only the capital gains tax rate is relevant at the margin. If new equity is issued, the personal dividend tax will directly affect financial decisions.

18. The financial policy of the firm is thus determined independently of the capital stock decision. This procedure is valid only for particular financial models. See Bartholdy, Fisher, and Mintz (1987).

19. For Côte d'Ivoire, I assume that machinery, which generally includes vehicles and office furniture, depreciates at a rate of 30 percent on a declining-balance basis.

20. See Bartholdy, Fisher, and Mintz (1987), who estimate that a point increase in the corporate tax rate in Canada is associated with a three-quarter point increase in the debt-asset ratio.

21. In an open economy, equity financing may be available from the international market. If so, personal taxes imposed on domestic savers may affect only savings rather than the firm's cost of finance, which is determined exogenously in the international market.

References

Agell, Nils J. 1982. "Subsidy to Capital through Tax Incentives in the ASEAN Countries: An Application of the Cost of Capital under Inflation Situations." Fiscal Affairs Working Paper. International Monetary Fund, Washington, D.C.

Auerbach, Alan J. 1979. "Wealth Maximization and the Cost of Capital." *Quarterly Journal of Economics* 93 (3): 433–46.

———. 1983. "Taxation, Corporate Financial Policy, and the Cost of Capital." *Journal of Economic Literature* 21 (3): 905–40.

Bartholdy, Jan, Gordon Fisher, and Jack M. Mintz. 1987. "Taxation and the Financial Policy of Firms: Theory and Empirical Applications to Canada." Discussion Paper 324. Economic Council of Canada, Ottawa.

Boadway, Robin W. 1987. "The Theory and Measurement of Effective Tax Rates." In Jack M. Mintz and Douglas D. Purvis, eds., *The Impact of Taxation on Business Activity*. Kingston, Ont., Can.: Queen's University, John Deutsch Institute for the Study of Economic Policy.

Boadway, Robin W., and Neil Bruce. 1979. "Depreciation and Interest Deductions and the Effect of the Corporation Income Tax on Investment." *Journal of Public Economics* 11: 93–105.

Boadway, Robin W., Neil Bruce, and Jack M. Mintz. 1984. "Taxation, Inflation, and the Marginal Tax Rate on Capital in Canada." *Canadian Journal of Economics* 17 (1): 62–79.

Bond, Eric W. 1981. "Tax Holidays and Industry Behavior." *Review of Economics and Statistics* 63 (February): 88–95.

Bond, Eric W., and Larry Samuelson. 1986. "Tax Holidays as Signals." *American Economic Review* 76 (4): 820–26.

Doyle, Chris, and Sweder van Wijnbergen. Forthcoming. "Taxation of Foreign Multinationals: A Sequential Bargaining Approach to Tax Holidays." *International Tax and Public Finance* .

International Bureau of Fiscal Documentation Bulletin. 1987 and 1988. *Bulletin for International Fiscal Documentation*. Amsterdam: L. J. Veen.

King, Mervyn A., and Don Fullerton. 1984. *The Taxation of Income from Capital: A Comparative Study of the United States, the United Kingdom, Sweden, and West Germany*. Chicago, Ill.: University of Chicago Press.

Mintz, Jack M. 1988. "An Empirical Estimate of Corporate Tax Refundability and Effective Tax Rates." *Quarterly Journal of Economics* 102 (February): 225–31.

———. 1989. "Tax Holiday and Investment." WPS 178. World Bank, Country Economics Department, Washington, D.C.

Poterba, J. M., and L. H. Summers. 1985. "The Economic Effects of Dividend Taxation." In E. Altman and M. Subrahmanyam, *Recent Advances in Corporate Finance*. Homewood, Ill.: Richard Irwin.

Price Waterhouse. 1986. *Corporate Taxes: A Worldwide Summary*. New York.

TAXATION, INFORMATION ASYMMETRIES, AND THE FINANCING CHOICE OF THE FIRM

Andrew Lyon

THIS CHAPTER IS intended as a survey of the effects of taxation and asymmetric information on the financing choice of the firm. The literature on taxation posits a straightforward relationship between the pretax cost of funds and the required return on an investment project to cover the cost of finance that is a function only of tax rates. The real decisions of the firm are assumed in these analyses to be affected only by the after-tax cost of funds.

An alternative literature has focused on how the choice of financing can influence the real decisions of the firm. At least since Adam Smith, economists have recognized how managerial incentives may differ with outside ownership of the firm.[1] Two problems face outside debt and equity investors. First, they are unable to monitor completely the activities of the firm's managers. Second, they are less informed than the firm's managers as to the profitability of alternative actions. These monitoring and information problems affect the financing of enterprises ranging in scale from multinational corporations to single entrepreneurs. When there are outside equity holders, management may have a reduced incentive to take actions that maximize the value of the firm. This occurs because management bears the full cost of increasing its managerial effort yet receives only a portion of the benefit from this effort. With only outside debt finance, management may pursue excessively risky projects. Management captures the full marginal return to additional profit of successful projects but may bear no marginal loss in unsuccessful projects. Projects with extreme variance in outcomes may then be favored.

Outside investors are aware that management has the incentive to undertake activities that fail to maximize investors' wealth. Investors will factor these deviations into the price they are willing to pay for the firm's equity or the terms under which they will lend money to the firm. As a result, expected deviations from the maximization of the firm's value are at least partly borne by the management.

It would be in the interest of management to contract with the outside investors to operate the firm in the same manner as they would without outside ownership. Unless outside investors have complete information on all the activities of the managers, however, this contract is not enforceable. In the absence of the ability to convey symmetric information to potential investors, managers bear additional costs when outside finance is obtained.

The divergence in the cost of internal and external sources of finance may affect the efficiency with which investment is allocated. Firms that have access to sufficient internal funds or external funds without significant agency costs may be able to undertake all investment opportunities with positive net present value. Other firms, however, may face a divergence between the required return on internal funds and that required on external funds as a result of asymmetric information. In this case, investment opportunities that would be profitable to undertake with internal funds may not yield sufficient returns to allow external financing. Investment is misallocated because projects with high marginal returns may not receive financing, whereas projects available to firms with lower marginal returns are undertaken. Furthermore, the wrong amount of investment may be undertaken.

In the first part of this chapter, I examine how differential taxation of retained earnings, new share issues, and debt finance affects the financing choice of the firm in the absence of asymmetric information. Next, I examine the problems of asymmetric information that arise with external finance. I then briefly discuss mechanisms that have been created in rural sectors of developing countries to counter the problems of asymmetric information. In the final section of the paper, I examine policy options open to government to reduce the costs of the inefficiencies created by asymmetric information. Unfortunately, policy prescriptions appear to depend on the form of the information asymmetry. General government solutions to the problem of asymmetric information may not be possible without a precise understanding of the nature of the information problem.

Debt, Equity, and Taxes under Symmetric Information

A corporation can finance its initial investment by issuing either equity or debt. Equity represents ownership in the corporation. An equity investor receives a proportionate share of an uncertain future stream of income from the corporation. Assuming limited liability, the equity owner's potential loss is limited to the amount invested in the corporation. Debt represents a promise of a fixed payment to the lender. If the corporation defaults on this promise, the firm may be liquidated. The proceeds of the liquidation are paid to the firm's lenders up to the amount of the promised payment. If the liquidation payment is less than the promised payment, the lenders bear the loss.

These two different financing options have quite different return characteristics. Even in the absence of the confounding effects of taxation, one might expect that there is an optimal ratio of debt and equity for a firm—that is, some optimal mixture of debt and equity that maximizes the value of the firm. A surprising result of the theorem put forth by Modigliani and Miller (1958), however, is that the value of the firm is independent of the choice of financing. This fundamental theorem of corporate finance was derived in the absence of tax effects and assumes that the real activity of the firm is independent of its financing choice.

In the presence of taxes this result may no longer be true, as Modigliani and Miller (1963) subsequently demonstrated. I will first examine the initial financing choice of a firm in the presence of taxes. This analysis is developed along the lines of Modigliani and Miller (1958, 1963) and Miller (1977). Next, I will consider the role of retained earnings, a source of finance not available for the initial investment of the start-up firm. This analysis is intended to show how a firm would choose its mix of financing under Modigliani and Miller's assumptions, in which the real activity of the firm is not affected by the financing mix and there is no risk of bankruptcy. These assumptions are dropped in the section entitled "Financing Choices under Asymmetric Information," and the effects of bankruptcy and asymmetric information on the value of the firm are incorporated into the analysis.

The Modigliani-Miller Theorem

Under a classical or unintegrated system of corporate taxation, debt and equity income are treated differently. In such a tax system, a corporation may deduct payments of interest from taxable income but not payments of dividends. Interest income is taxable to the bondholder. A unit of pretax earnings of the corporation paid as interest yields net income of $(1 - \tau_b)$, where τ_b is the bondholder's tax rate on interest income. Dividend income, in addition to being taxed at the corporate level, is taxable to the stockholder. Dividend income is thus subject to a "double tax" in an unintegrated tax system.[2] One unit of pretax income to be distributed as a dividend is first reduced by corporate tax payments τ_c, and the remainder is then taxed at the stockholder tax rate τ_d. The net income to the dividend recipient is $(1 - \tau_c)(1 - \tau_d)$ per unit of pretax earnings.

Corporate income, net of corporate taxes and net of payments of interest, principal, and dividends, is retained by the firm. These retained earnings result in an appreciation in the value of the corporation. The appreciation is taxable as capital gains income to the shareholder. In many tax systems capital gains are taxed at a reduced statutory rate in relation to dividend and interest income. Even in the absence of an explicit statutory rate reduction for capital gains income, capital gains face a lower effective tax rate than dividend income. This is because capital gains are generally taxed only when the stock is sold rather than as the gains accrue. The deferral of taxation is equivalent to a rate reduction. The longer the period of time between the date of accrual and the date of realization, the greater is the equivalent rate reduction.[3] We can define τ_{re} as the tax rate at the shareholder level on retained earnings that would result in the same present value of tax collections as a capital gains tax paid when stock is sold.

If we assume a constant ratio of dividend payments to retained earnings, the effective rate of taxation of equity income at the shareholder level can be considered a weighted average of the effective tax rates applying to dividends, τ_d, and capital gains, τ_{re}. Assume that the corporation chooses a dividend payout ratio that results in an overall effective rate of taxation of τ_e on equity income, where $\tau_e = \beta \tau_d + (1 - \beta)\tau_{re}$ and β is the proportion of the firm's after-tax earnings paid as dividends.[4]

Let us consider the effect of the differential rates of taxation on debt and equity income on the initial financing choice of the firm. Assume initially that the investment project has a certain return. One can solve for the relation between the pretax returns this project must have to satisfy bondholders (r_b) or equity holders (r_e). If the entire project is financed with debt, no corporate tax liability will be assessed (because debt payments are deductible from corporate income), and after-tax income of bondholders is $r_b(1 - \tau_b)$. Alternatively, if the project is financed with a new equity issue, both corporate and personal taxes are paid on the income generated by the investment, yielding after-tax income of $r_e(1 - \tau_c)(1 - \tau_e)$ to the shareholders. The source of financing that results in the highest after-tax return will be chosen. Investors are indifferent to the source of financing if and only if $r_b(1 - \tau_b) = r_e(1 - \tau_c)(1 - \tau_e)$. If we assume that the pretax income of the project is independent of its source of financing $(r_b = r_e)$, debt will be preferred if the tax burden on interest income, τ_b, is less than the total of corporate and shareholder taxes paid on equity income, $\tau_c + \tau_e(1 - \tau_c)$. Alternatively, if $(1 - \tau_b) < (1 - \tau_c)(1 - \tau_e)$, then investors' incomes are maximized by the firm issuing equity.

Modigliani and Miller (1963) show that this same inequality governs the choice between debt and equity when the return to equity income is uncertain, provided there is no risk of bankruptcy. Modigliani and Miller propose a means by which a shareholder can borrow on his or her own to create an earnings stream from an unleveraged firm that is identical to that (in expectations) from a leveraged firm of the same risk. (A demonstration is given in appendix 4-1.)

The Modigliani and Miller proof suggests that under many plausible values for tax variables, a firm could increase its value by increasing its leverage. In the extreme a firm would be almost entirely financed by debt, except for some residual equity.

The Miller Equilibrium

Miller (1977) suggests a slightly different equilibrium relation between debt and equity. In this equilibrium there is a unique economy-wide optimal debt-equity ratio, yet no firm has an incentive to alter its own debt-equity ratio.

Miller notes that under a progressive tax system a wide range of potential tax rates exists on each source of financing. For tax-exempt investors, $\tau_b = \tau_e = 0$. Other investors may face high tax rates on interest income, such that $\tau_b > \tau_c$. Preferential tax treatment of capital gains may result in a higher after-tax return from corporate equity than from debt for these investors.

Let r be the pretax return on a project to be funded. Assuming the returns from both debt and equity are certain, investors will prefer the source of finance with the higher after-tax return. Both equity and debt will be issued in equilibrium if some investors receive a higher after-tax return by lending and others receive a higher return by purchasing equity. A marginal investor may exist who is just indifferent between holding debt and equity. For this marginal taxpayer, $(1 - \tau_b^*) = (1 - \tau_c^*)(1 - \tau_e^*)$, where the asterisk denotes the tax rate of this investor. The economy-wide ratio of debt and equity is determined by the quantity of investment undertaken by individuals with tax rates above and below those of the marginal investor. For investors with low tax rates, it is likely that $(1 - \tau_b) > (1 - \tau_c)(1 - \tau_e)$. These investors will prefer debt to equity. Investors in high tax brackets may find the inequality reversed and thus prefer holding equity to debt. Debt issued by the corporate sector is purchased by taxpayers in increasingly higher tax brackets. Equilibrium is achieved when the amount of investment in the economy is financed at its lowest possible cost. This will result in a unique debt-equity ratio for the economy, but there is no advantage to any firm of changing its own debt-equity ratio.

When Miller proposed this equilibrium theory of finance, the United States had personal tax rates on interest income as high as 70 percent, whereas the tax rate for large corporations was 48 percent. Investors who fell into these high tax brackets may have received a higher after-tax return through equity rather than debt. Subsequent tax changes in the United States in 1981 and 1986 lowered the rate of individual taxation in relation to that of corporations. By 1986 the highest personal tax rate on interest income was less than the statutory corporate tax rate. As a result the Miller equilibrium would now suggest a greater reliance on debt finance for newly established firms.

The Financing Choice of Existing Firms

The analysis by Modigliani and Miller (1958) and Miller (1977) can be viewed as an analysis of the choice of the optimal initial capital structure when a firm is first founded. If there is any equity at the time the corporation is first established, however, retained earnings may be an additional source of financing available to the firm when subsequent financing is needed.

Stiglitz (1973) suggests a life-cycle view of a firm. In return for contributing an initial idea of value, the founder of a corporation receives an equity share in the firm. The firm requires additional external funds to undertake the investment necessary to carry out this idea. Whether to finance this investment through debt or new shares is the focus of Modigliani and Miller (1958, 1963) and Miller (1977).

In subsequent periods, earnings of the initial investment may exceed interest payments on the firm's debt. These earnings constitute a third source of finance for further investment. The firm has three financing possibilities now: retained earnings, new share issues, or debt. King (1977) examines the consequences of the use of these alternative sources of financing.

King considers the real investment of the firm constant under each financing choice. Thus a decision to reduce the use of retained earnings during one period requires either an increase in new share issues or an increase in borrowing to keep investment constant. Each of these policies, although not affecting the real investment of the firm, alters the time path of dividends paid per share of stock and therefore will in general affect the share value of the firm. King examines the effects of small perturbations in the use of these sources of finance on share value. The firm is assumed to choose the source of finance that maximizes the current share value of the firm.

Consider the decision by the firm to increase the use of new share issues and reduce retained earnings by an equal amount in the present period, holding the firm's debt policy unchanged. This strategy causes dividends to increase today. In all subsequent periods, the total amount of dividends paid by the firm will be the same as they would have been without the perturbation. Dividends per share, however, will be lower because the firm's earnings are now distributed among a larger number of shares. If the after-tax present value of the flow of income per share is higher under this policy than the alternative, then share value will be maximized by adopting the policy. King (1977: chap. 4) shows that the policy of new share issues will be preferred to the use of retained earnings only if $\tau_d < \tau_{re}$. This is because a unit of earnings retained by the firm results in a tax liability of τ_{re}. A unit of earnings paid in dividends causes a tax liability of τ_d. Assuming τ_{re} is never greater than τ_d, the firm will always prefer the use of retained earnings to new share issues.

If retained earnings are always preferred to new share issues, then it is worthwhile for the firm to reduce new share issues to zero. Similarly, if the firm has retained earnings in excess of current investment needs, the firm could reduce shareholder tax liability by repurchasing shares rather than by paying dividends. Auerbach (1979), King (1977), and Stiglitz (1973) suggest that there may be legal restrictions on the ability of firms regularly to repurchase shares in lieu of paying dividends.[5] If share repurchases are restricted, a firm with no investment opportunities and positive earnings could acquire other companies as a means of disbursing the earnings in a manner designed to create capital gains rather than dividend tax liability. Finally, if there are restrictions on the acquisition of other firms, a firm will pay dividends only if a unit of retained earnings increases share value by less than $(1 - \tau_d)/(1 - \tau_{re})$.[6]

If new share issues are kept constant, a decision to reduce retained earnings in the present period requires an increase in corporate debt to maintain a constant level of investment. This policy will result in higher current dividends now but lower dividends in the subsequent period as a result of the firm's repayment of the principal and interest on this debt. The policy will increase share value if the shareholders value this stream of income at a greater present value than the alternative. If the shareholders' discount rate is greater than the cost of borrowing to the firm, this perturbation increases the value of the firm. King (1977) shows that this requires that $(1 - \tau_b)$ be greater than $(1 - \tau_{re})(1 - \tau_c)$. Alternatively, this inequality can be interpreted as requiring that the reduction in borrowing costs to a shareholder exceed the after-tax return from reinvesting the earnings in the corporation.

A sufficient condition for debt to be preferred to retained earnings is that the rate of personal taxation is less than the rate of corporate taxation. Debt may also dominate retained earnings when the personal tax rate is greater than the corporate tax rate, provided the tax rate on capital gains is sufficiently high. There would appear to be a range of tax rates throughout which debt is preferred to retained earnings.

A Tax-Induced Financing Hierarchy?

In this section I have focused only on the effects of taxation on the mix of financing for a firm. The results of my examination suggest that debt finance and retained earnings are preferable to new share issues in regard to taxes. For many tax systems, debt finance may be preferable to retained earnings as well.

Mayer (1990) presents a comparison of the extent to which retained earnings, debt, and new share issues were used to finance new investment in Canada, Finland, France, Germany, Italy, Japan, the United Kingdom, and the United States between 1970 and 1985. In all countries, despite varying tax treatment, the dominant source of finance was retained earnings, although their importance varied across countries. For example, retained earnings were the source of finance for virtually all net investment in the United Kingdom, whereas they financed just over half of net investment in Italy. In comparisons across countries, however, a correlation was not found between the tax treatment of each financing source and its use.

In developing countries internal finance is also the primary source of funds for most enterprises. The authors of studies surveyed by Kilby, Liedholm, and Meyer (1984) note that the original source of funds in rural manufacturing enterprises is predominantly from personal saving or informal loans from relatives. Future expansion is also largely financed from retained earnings. External finance is of limited importance, and that which is received is frequently from customers rather than from formal lending institutions.

Auerbach (1984) has examined differences between internal and external sources of investment at the firm level. He finds that ex post rates of return are generally higher when financed with new share issues than when financed with retained earnings. The finding supports the idea that each source of financing has a distinct opportunity cost. For example, firms may resort to new share issues only if the projects are sufficiently profitable to cover the higher tax costs of external finance. Auerbach's finding also suggests that certain firms may be unable to receive debt financing for these projects because debt would otherwise be preferred to new equity from a tax perspective.

Other researchers have examined differences in investment behavior across firms experiencing changes in cash flow. A tax-related theory would suggest that cash flow has no effect on investment behavior in firms that are presently paying dividends. These firms could finance any investment opportunity by reducing dividend payments. Increases in cash flow may give firms not paying dividends access to tax-favored retained earnings to finance investment. Fazzari, Hubbard, and Petersen (1988a) find that these predictions hold true for a large sample of publicly traded firms in the United States, even after they control for investment opportunities available to the firm using standard neoclassical models.

Fazzari, Hubbard, and Petersen believe that the strong effect of increases in the availability of internal funds for firms that pay low dividends is greater than would be predicted by taxes only. They argue that these firms are likely to face nontax constraints that limit the availability of external funds. They suggest that the cost of asymmetric information may preclude these firms from undertaking profitable investment opportunities.

Financing Choices under Asymmetric Information

As noted in the last section, the tax-guided view of corporate finance has been unable to explain adequately the observed mix of financing by corporations in different countries. Although consistent with the greater use of retained earnings than new share issues, it may not be a satisfactory explanation for the low use of debt finance. An alternative theory of finance is based on the assumption of asymmetric information. In this section I frequently talk of a *firm's* investment. This is not intended to preclude application of the material to family enterprises, single entrepreneurs, or farmers. Indeed, some of the earliest applications of the theory of information asymmetry were to small units of production, such as sharecroppers.[7] As noted by Hoff and Stiglitz (1990), the problems of asymmetric information may be even more severe in credit markets of developing economies, especially rural areas, where formal legal institutions are especially costly and ineffective, and formal information-sharing networks are scarce or nonexistent. Specific mechanisms in rural economies established to limit problems of asymmetric information are examined in the following section.

Under the theory of asymmetric information it is assumed that the managers of the firm have some information on the characteristics of the firm's assets and investment opportunities that investors do not have. This information asymmetry can cause managers to undertake activities that make some of the firm's claimants worse off.

If investors are aware that management may take actions from time to time that make them worse off, they will attempt to contract for this contingency. To monitor and enforce these restrictions, however, can be very costly. Thus the problems of asymmetric information can be only partly overcome.

One facet of the literature on asymmetric information has focused on the divergence of interests of the firm's managers from the shareholders of the firm. In this literature (for example, Jensen and Meckling 1976), managers are seen to act in their own interest as employees, rather than as agents for the owners of the firm. The managers may then fail to maximize shareholder value by pursuing goals that augment their own welfare.

Another part of the literature has focused on the potential conflicts of the different claimants of the firm, notably shareholders and bondholders. Here, even if the firm's managers act in the interest of the shareholders, actions that would maximize the value of the firm are not generally consistent with those actions that would maximize the value of shares. In many cases it can be shown that shareholders will favor this deviation from the maximization of firm value ex post. If the firm's debt holders can anticipate deviations from the maximization of the value of the firm, however, the shareholders will at least partly bear the cost of this deviation ex ante. Thus it can be in the shareholders' interest to find mechanisms that successfully limit the possibility for the firm's managers to undertake policies that deviate from the maximization of the value of the firm. If the firm is unable to control these deviations ex ante, the firm may find itself borrowing at costs greater than otherwise, or it may be denied credit entirely.

Bankruptcy Costs and Limits on Debt Finance

One traditional explanation for a limit on the quantity of a firm's investment financed by debt is the increasing probability of default as the firm's debt obligations increase. If operating income is uncertain, the firm is more likely to experience periods in which income is insufficient to service the firm's debt load when the debt is large. If changes in the firm's financing mix do not affect the firm's real investments, however, this increasing risk of bankruptcy will not affect the total value of the firm unless costs are incurred in the act of bankruptcy, that is, unless it is costly to transfer assets to the debt holders.

To understand this, recall the payoff structure of the debt and equity claims. Let $V(s)$ be the value of the firm for some outcome or "state of nature" s. The value of debt instruments of this firm in state s, V_d, is equal to $\min[V(s), P]$, where P is the promised payment of interest and principal. The value of equity, V_e, is equal to $\max[0, V(s) - P]$. Note that the sum of the payoffs to debt and equity in all states s is simply $V(s)$. The value of the firm is independent of its division between debt and equity claims. The firm could be financed entirely by debt or entirely by equity and its value would be unchanged. Thus a simple story of increasing the risk of bankruptcy cannot create a limit on debt finance if bankruptcy is costless.

If costs are incurred in bankruptcy, then ownership of the firm cannot be costlessly transferred to the firm's debt holders. These costs include the direct legal costs and the indirect costs of operating a firm near bankruptcy. Legal costs could be high if it is expected that the firm's shareholders will resist transfer of the firm. A firm near bankruptcy may find increased indirect costs if suppliers and customers are more reluctant to make commitments.

The direct costs of bankruptcy, however, have been found to be relatively small. For example, Warner (1977) examined the direct costs of bankruptcy for eleven U.S. railroads between 1930 and 1955. He found that the average cost of bankruptcy was equal to 1 percent of the value of the firm, where the firm value is established as that seven years prior to bankruptcy. The expected cost of bankruptcy is even less. Thus bankruptcy costs alone are an inadequate explanation for limits on debt finance.

Asymmetric Information and Bankruptcy Risk

The shortcoming of the pure bankruptcy story is in its failure to incorporate the effects of asymmetric information. Bankruptcy (and, more generally, limited liability) can alter the shareholders' preferred ordering of alternative projects from the ordering that would maximize firm value. Here, firm value is taken to be the sum of the value of the equity and debt claims. If the set of projects available to the firm at any point in time is not known to the firm's bondholders, then bondholders will be unable to write contracts that prevent this deviation from the maximization of firm value. In such a case, the firm may be unable to finance its projects.

One set of deviations from the maximization of firm value occurs because the value of the shareholders' equity claim is a convex function of the returns on the firm's investments. As a result the firm's shareholders will prefer riskier investments to safer investments with the same expected yield. The payoff to bondholders is a concave function of the firm's returns. Bondholders prefer investments that are less risky to those that are more so with the same expected yield. If the risk characteristics of projects available to the firm are not known to lenders, the firm can transfer wealth from bondholders to shareholders by undertaking riskier projects than those contemplated by the firm's lenders. The firm may have this incentive even if the riskier projects have a lower expected return. Furthermore, because the firm is not concerned with the return on its investments in states of bankruptcy, the expected return to shareholders from additional equity-financed investment can be less than the joint return to the firm's bondholders and shareholders. As a result the firm may fail to undertake investment opportunities that would have been profitable to undertake in the absence of debt.

Both of these factors—changes in the composition of the riskiness of investment and changes in the level of investment—can cause firm value to decrease in the presence of debt. Bondholders anticipate that shareholders will undertake all actions that maximize share value, not necessarily firm value. Thus debt can be obtained only if the expected return to debt holders is sufficient to compensate them for these anticipated actions. This compensation may take the form of higher interest rates. In this case, a firm's shareholders bear the cost of this anticipated deviation.

Higher interest rates, however, may lead the firm to shift to still riskier projects. As shown by Stiglitz and Weiss (1981), in this case an equilibrium can exist in which some firms are simply denied credit, whereas observationally equivalent firms receive credit. The excess demand for credit can persist in equilibrium. Lenders who raise interest rates receive lower returns on their loans because they attract a riskier set of borrowers.

Suboptimal Investment in the Presence of Asymmetric Information

Many different models have been developed to portray the inefficiencies that can occur under conditions of asymmetric information with debt finance. The developers of these models include Bernanke and Gertler (1990); Calomiris and Hubbard (1990); de Meza and Webb (1987); Leland and Pyle (1977); Myers (1977); and Stiglitz and Weiss (1981).

The models reveal that the presence of asymmetric information leads to either over- or underinvestment in relation to the social optimum. In the absence of asymmetric information, the first-best outcome could be achieved.

In these models, the firm is assumed to have better information on the distribution of returns from a potential project than the firm's lenders. In situations in which lenders cannot distinguish among firms, all firms must pay the same interest rate on their loans in equilibrium. As a result firms undertaking "better" projects (for example, projects with above-average expected rates of return to lenders because of the greater probabilities of their success) subsidize firms undertaking "worse" projects. Firms with better projects therefore pay a premium in relation to the rates they would pay if lenders were privy to the information known to the firm. Firms with better projects that are able to raise capital from internal funds to undertake the investment are then able to capture the full benefit of their projects.

Thus asymmetric information can cause a divergence between the yield required on a project funded from internal sources and that required on a project funded externally. A firm may be considered to be finance-constrained if internal funds are exhausted before the firm has been able to undertake all projects with yields in excess of the firm's opportunity cost of capital, and the yields from the projects are insufficient to cover the cost of external funds. Alternatively, the information asymmetry may lead to credit rationing. Funds may be denied to the firm despite the firm's willingness to pay the market rate of interest. In either case, a marginal change in the quantity of internal funds available for investment can have a positive effect on investment, whereas a marginal change in the cost of obtaining external funds may have no effect. Traditional analyses of the effects of taxation on investment behavior, such as the cost-of-capital model by Hall and Jorgenson (1967), focus on the effect of a tax change on the required marginal rate of return on capital, assuming the source of funds is perfectly elastic. As indicated by Fazzari, Hubbard, and Petersen (1988b), however, changes in the average profitability of capital may be more important in influencing investment for finance-constrained firms.

The effects of asymmetric information on the investment undertaken by a firm in the presence of debt finance can be shown by two models representing different types of financing decisions for the firm. Although these models cannot portray the full range of effects of asymmetric information on the financial and investment decisions of a firm, conclusions drawn from these models are representative of those based on more specialized models in the literature.

The first model is based on that of de Meza and Webb (1987).[8] In this model, a firm is seeking to borrow funds for a project with an uncertain probability of success. The second model is based on that of Myers

(1977).[9] A firm in this model uses both debt and equity. The firm has future projects that it may seek to undertake at a later date by issuing additional equity. These models encompass a wide variety of potential investment decisions of firms.

OVERINVESTMENT OR UNDERINVESTMENT WITH ASYMMETRIC INFORMATION. The assumption in a model commonly used to demonstrate the effects of asymmetric information on investment is that the population consists of a set of entrepreneurs, each with access to a unique risky project. The project of entrepreneur i is assumed to have two possible outcomes: success, in which case the project's return is R_i^s; or failure, in which case the project's return is R_i^f. The probability of success is p_i. A project requires total investment k. Each entrepreneur has the same wealth w, which is less than k. It is assumed that lenders know the joint distributions of project returns and the probabilities of success but cannot distinguish among entrepreneurs. As a result all entrepreneurs who receive loans borrow at the same interest rate r. Entrepreneurs are assumed to know more about their own risk characteristics than lenders, which creates a problem of asymmetric information.

The heterogeneity of investors is simplified by assuming either (a) the probability of success p_i is the same for all entrepreneurs but project returns R_i^s and R_i^f vary across entrepreneurs, or (b) the probability of success differs across entrepreneurs but project returns are identical. Let us first examine the model under this latter assumption, as assumed by de Meza and Webb (1987) and Bernanke and Gertler (1990). We will later examine an alternative assumption and see that the results of the model change, as shown by de Meza and Webb.

Assume that all entrepreneurs have identical wealth and identical project sizes. An entrepreneur borrows $B = k - w$ from lenders if the project is undertaken. It is assumed that $R^s > (1 + r)B > R^f \geq 0$. If the project fails, the entrepreneur defaults on the loan. Entrepreneurs are assumed to know their probabilities of success and are risk-neutral.

An entrepreneur undertakes his or her project provided the expected return from the project exceeds the opportunity cost. The opportunity cost is assumed to be the safe rate of interest ρ offered by a bank on its savings accounts in which the entrepreneur could have saved wealth w. An entrepreneur i then undertakes his or her project provided

$$(4\text{-}1a) \qquad p_i\left[R^s - (1 + r)B\right] \geq (1 + \rho)\, w .$$

The marginal project undertaken, that is, the entrepreneur for which equation 4-1a holds with equality, has the lowest probability of success of those projects undertaken. Let us denote this probability by p', so

$$(4\text{-}1b) \qquad p'\left[R^s - (1 + r)\, B\right] = (1 + \rho)\, w .$$

The profits to a competitive banking industry from lending to all entrepreneurs must be zero in equilibrium. If the banking industry earns profits on projects with high probabilities of success, it must lose profits on loans to projects with the lowest success probabilities. Thus the return to the bank on the marginal project with success probability p' is less than the cost of funds to the bank,

$$(4\text{-}2) \qquad p'(1 + r)\, B + (1 - p')R^f < (1 + \rho)\, B\, .$$

Finally, the socially optimal level of investment is to undertake all investment for which the expected return exceeds the opportunity cost, or

$$(4\text{-}3a) \qquad p_i R^s + (1 - p_i)R^f \geq (1 + \rho)\, k\, .$$

Note that for the marginal project with success probability p', adding equations 4-1b and 4-2 (and noting that $w + B = k$) shows that the expected return from this project is less than its opportunity cost,

$$(4\text{-}3b) \qquad p'R^s + (1 - p')R^f < (1 + \rho)\, k\, .$$

In this model, asymmetric information leads to overinvestment in relation to the social optimum. Poor investments—that is, investments with an expected return of less than the economy-wide opportunity cost of capital—are undertaken because the entrepreneur is not concerned with the return on the project in states of default. Banks lose profits on loans to entrepreneurs who have low probabilities of success. These losses are just offset by the profits earned on entrepreneurs who have high probabilities of success. Note that a bank in a competitive market cannot make greater profits either by rationing loans or by charging an interest rate different from the competitive rate on loans. Rationing holds no advantage because the expected profitability on each loan is zero. A bank cannot charge a higher rate than other banks charge either. If it charges a lower rate, it attracts all current entrepreneurs and new entrepreneurs who have even lower probabilities of success.

Entrepreneurs who have high probabilities of success pay higher interest rates than they would if their success probabilities were known to lenders. Because they are unable to identify themselves to banks, they end up subsidizing the entrepreneurs who have low probabilities of success. It is worth noting the effects of changes in the wealth of entrepreneurs on the equilibrium level of investment. A marginal increase in the wealth of an entrepreneur who has a high probability of success would allow the entrepreneur to increase the expected profit from undertaking the project.[10] This entrepreneur would reduce borrowing. In contrast, a marginal increase in the wealth of an entrepreneur with success probability p'

Table 4-1. Asymmetric Information with Debt Finance

Type of uncertainty in model	Outcome
Uncertain probability of success	Overinvestment
Uncertain payoff if successful	Underinvestment

Source: de Meza and Webb (1987); Stiglitz and Weiss (1981).

(from equation 4-1b) would cause this entrepreneur now to reject the project. If the wealth of each entrepreneur were greater than the project size, the optimal level of investment would always be undertaken.

Bernanke and Gertler (1990) and Calomiris and Hubbard (1990) further analyze the effects of changes in the amount and distribution of wealth in an economy. Entrepreneurs in developing economies, faced with a low level of personal wealth, may be able to undertake projects of only limited size, given their inability to raise sufficient collateral.

It is important to note, however, that no project with expected returns greater than the opportunity cost of capital is denied funds in the model presented above. De Meza and Webb (1987) show that this result is dependent on the assumption that all projects have the same return R^s if successful. If, alternatively, it is assumed that all projects have the same expected return, but both the probability of success p_i and the return if successful R_i^s vary, then the credit of entrepreneurs may be rationed. This replicates the finding of Stiglitz and Weiss (1981) that projects with expected returns greater than the opportunity cost of capital may go unfunded. The proportion of successful and unsuccessful entrepreneurs in the population who receive loans is the same as in the population of entrepreneurs denied loans.

In this modified model, the entrepreneur who is indifferent as to whether he or she undertakes the project or receives the safe return ρ on his or her wealth has the highest probability of success. (See appendix 4-2 for an explanation of this outcome.) As a result increases in the lending rate r cause the entrepreneurs with the highest probability of success not to undertake their projects. This increases the riskiness of the projects funded by the bank. If the increased riskiness of these projects reduces profits to the bank by more than the increase in profits from the higher rate paid by successful projects, an equilibrium with rationing results. Here, too little investment is undertaken when entrepreneurs require loans to undertake their projects. Table 4-1 is a summary of the different outcomes of these two models.

As in the earlier model presented, the entrepreneurs with projects that have a high probability of success subsidize entrepreneurs with projects that have lower probabilities of success. Because lenders are unable to distinguish among entrepreneurs, entrepreneurs with "better" projects are affected by credit rationing along with the entrepreneurs with "worse" projects. Although in the presentation of this model it was assumed that the expected returns to all projects are the same, it is possible that projects with the highest probabilities of success also have the higher expected rates of return. In this case, asymmetric information results in some poorer projects receiving funding, whereas better projects go unfunded. Although asymmetric information can result in either over- or underinvestment in these models, the models concur in the finding that there can be a divergence between the return required on internally generated funds and that required on funds that are sought externally.

MYERS'S MODEL OF DEBT AND UNDERINVESTMENT. Myers (1977) demonstrates how a firm that is partly financed by debt may undertake less than the optimal amount of investment in the presence of asymmetric information. In this model, firm value is composed of the value of existing assets and future growth opportunities. The growth opportunities require a future investment, and the returns from the future investment depend on the state of nature. The state of nature is revealed to the firm before the subsequent investment is made. The value today of these growth opportunities is the present value of the returns from these opportunities less the cost of undertaking the investment in those states of nature where the investment is undertaken. Myers shows that growth opportunities that would be undertaken by an unleveraged firm in some states of nature will not be undertaken by the leveraged firm. Thus the net present value of the growth opportunities is less in the leveraged firm. If bondholders can correctly anticipate the states of nature in which the firm will fail to exercise the growth option, then there can be no transfer of wealth from bondholders to shareholders. In this case, the loss in firm value is borne by the shareholders.

Consider an unleveraged firm with no existing assets in period zero that is valued for a single growth opportunity that can be exercised at the beginning of period one. The growth opportunity will require an equity-financed investment of I at that time and will yield returns of $V(s)$ in state s. Let the states of nature be ordered in increasing profitability of the investment opportunity. The growth option will be exercised then for all states s that are greater than or equal to s_a, where s_a is the state of nature such that $V(s_a) = I$. The value of the firm in period zero if investors are risk-neutral can then be written as

$$(4\text{-}4) \qquad V = E\left[\beta \cdot (V(s) - I \mid s \geq s_a)\right] \cdot \Pr(s \geq s_a)$$

where β is the one-period discount rate, and $\Pr(\cdot)$ denotes the probability of the event.

Now consider the effect on firm value if the firm issues debt to repurchase the shares belonging to initial equity owners before the state of nature is revealed to the firm. The firm value is unaffected by the issuance of debt in period zero if the debt holders are free to undertake the investment opportunity in the event that the shareholders default. The value of the firm's remaining equity after the debt is issued is

$$(4\text{-}5) \qquad V_e = E\left[\beta \cdot (V(s) - I - P \mid s \geq s_b)\right] \cdot \Pr(s \geq s_b)$$

where P is the payment of interest and principal, s_b is the state of nature such that $V(s_b) = I + P$, $s_b > s_a$. The shareholders choose to exercise the growth opportunity requiring equity contribution I only if it is sufficiently profitable to cover the cost of investment and the debt service.

The value of the firm's debt is

$$(4\text{-}6) \qquad V_d = E\left[\beta \cdot \min(P, V(s) - I \mid s \geq s_a)\right] \cdot \Pr(s \geq s_a).$$

If the shareholders default $(s < s_b)$ and $s \geq s_a$, the debt holders find it worthwhile to invest the quantity I required to carry out the project. If P is considered the face value of the firm's bonds, then the bonds are issued at a discount from their face value of $1 - (V_d/P)$.

Note that in this case the sum of the value of the debt and equity claims given by equations 4-5 and 4-6 is equal to the value of the unleveraged firm shown in equation 4-4. Here, debt does not reduce the value of the firm. The wealth of the initial equity owners is equal to V in both cases. Where debt is issued, the equity owners receive an immediate payment of V_d and have remaining equity equal to V_e. The wealth of the initial equity owners is the same in either case.

If, however, the investment opportunity is assumed to vanish if not undertaken by the firm's owners, then the value of the firm depends on the amount of debt borrowed. Consider the value to debt holders of bonds promising the same uncertain payment P in the next period under this alternative assumption. Bondholders know this payment will be received only if $s \geq s_b$. Further, if $s_b > s \geq s_a$, the bondholders receive nothing because they are unable to exercise the growth option. The value of the firm's debt, V_d', in this case is

$$(4\text{-}7) \qquad V_d' = E\left[\beta \cdot (P \mid s \geq s_b)\right] \cdot \Pr(s \geq s_b).$$

Note that V_d' is strictly less than V_d given by equation 4-6. The value of the remaining equity V_e', however, is the same as that given by equation 4-5. Thus the value of the leveraged firm $V' = V_d' + V_e'$ is less than the value of the unleveraged firm. The wealth of the initial equity owners, equal to their receipt of V_d' in cash and their remaining equity share V_e', is reduced by the issuance of debt.

Myers (1977) suggests that for many firms the value of future growth opportunities may constitute an important part of firm value. Additionally, the value of existing assets can be dependent on future discretionary spending by the firm on such activities as maintenance and advertising. To the extent that the proper level of the expenditure is known in advance, a contract could be written requiring these investments in amounts that would depend on the state of nature. It is unlikely, however, that the state of nature could be revealed sufficiently to outsiders to allow for proper legal enforcement of the contract. The alternative is to require a minimum level of investment independent of the state of nature. This requirement would avoid the problem of asymmetric information for these investments for states of nature $s \geq s_a$ but would result in overinvestment for $s < s_a$. The overinvestment in these activities in poor states of nature reduces the value of the growth options. Again, it is the equity holders who bear this loss.

Furthermore, for many activities the presence of an investment opportunity may be unknown to outsiders. Consider, for example, a firm's research and development (R&D) program. The R&D program may be expected to generate numerous growth opportunities, although the exact number and characteristics of the projects may be difficult to ascertain in advance. As a result the firm's managers may not pursue the results of discoveries that are known to lead to small, but positive, net present values. Bondholders could not contract for these discoveries to be carried out because by their very nature they are not known in advance. Even if, upon default, the bondholders did learn of the existence of a discovery, management could argue that the project was not expected to yield a positive present value.

Although the example presented above is based on a firm with no existing assets and only growth opportunities, the conclusions of the model apply to firms with existing assets and growth opportunities, provided there is some risk of bankruptcy. Because the leveraged firm will follow through on fewer of its profitable growth opportunities, the equity holders in a leveraged firm will value these opportunities at a reduced value in relation to the equity owners of an unleveraged firm. A firm will then ordinarily prefer not to issue risky debt if it wishes to take full advantage of potential future growth options. The firm will use internal funds first to finance its investments, and only if these are insufficient will it consider financing with debt. Any debt-financed investment must have a sufficiently high net present value that it increases share value by more than the loss in value resulting from the decline in value of the growth opportunities. Himmelberg and Petersen (1994) present empirical evidence that R&D investments are sensitive to the availability of internal funds, confirming the hypothesis that firms can raise outside funds for this purpose only at a higher cost.

The Myers model of asymmetric information, although formulated differently from the model presented in the previous section, leads to a similar conclusion—that the cost to the firm of using external funds is likely to exceed the cost of internal funds. If the firm's internal resources are low, it may be unable to undertake all investments that it would at a higher level of profitability. The divergence between the cost of internal and external funds may result in projects with positive net present values going unfunded.

Rural Credit Market Solutions to Asymmetric Information

Increasing attention has been given to the problems of information asymmetries in financing projects in the rural sectors of developing countries. Information problems in these sectors are severe. The mechanisms created to limit the effect of information asymmetries offer interesting insights on means of overcoming these problems.

Information asymmetries arise in a rural context in part because the productivity of borrowers (largely farmers) and that of their land differ. Lenders therefore have the problem of trying to ascertain the risk and possible collateral of different borrowers. Those with excellent collateral may be the most able to receive loans from the formal sector (Aleem 1990; Floro and Yotopoulos 1991). Poorer borrowers may receive loans only from the informal sector. Even where collateral might exist, poorly defined legal rights in property and high enforcement costs may preclude borrowing from the formal sector.

Aleem (1990) presents some evidence on the extent of imperfect information in these markets. He finds that a lender in the informal sector spends an average of one day to screen each loan applicant. After this screening, an average of 50 percent of the applicants are rejected. Administrative costs associated with these loans were estimated to represent 40 to 50 percent of the principal borrowed. Thus to a large extent, lenders in the informal sector are able to overcome the disadvantage of asymmetric information only by incurring significant costs to gain information on their borrowers. Other practices or mechanisms are intended directly to reduce the costs of information asymmetries. Two such mechanisms are discussed in the remainder of this section.[11]

Interlinkage between Credit and Other Markets

One manner by which lenders minimize these information costs is by lending only to those who have an additional relationship with the supplier of credit, such as a customer or a supplier of inputs. These interlinkages are intended to reduce the costs of obtaining information, monitoring behavior, or enforcing repayment. Bell (1989) notes how interlinkages can increase the ability of lenders to shape the behavior of borrowers without adversely affecting risk. Consider, for example, a loan to a supplier of inputs. Aleem (1990: p. 332) notes in his examination of rural credit markets in Pakistan, "In general, at least one end of the loan transaction involved the delivery of commodities, with the loan either extended or repaid in kind."[12]

Requiring a farmer's crop as repayment has several features that minimize the problems of information asymmetries. First, the lender is given a means of measuring the productivity of the borrower when considering loans in future growing seasons. This feature encourages the borrower to appear as productive as possible.

Second, the crop represents a form of collateral that can be collected by the lender at harvest time. For crops without fixed harvest periods, Siamwalla and others (1990) note that the land and standing crop may be transferred to the lender for a fixed period of time.

Finally, purchase of the farmer's output ensures that the lender and not other borrowers has access to information on the continuing productivity of the borrower. By limiting knowledge of the borrower's characteristics to other potential lenders, the lender may be better able to enforce repayment with the sanction of denial of credit in the event of default. This sanction has no effect in situations in which a borrower can quickly start anew with a new lender. If the lender will extend credit only after establishing a lengthy relationship with the potential borrower, however, the borrower may find that the possibility of default and the subsequent denial of credit are important incentives.

The practice of providing the initial loan in kind—for example, seed or other inputs rather than currency—also may reduce the costs of information asymmetries. This practice gives the lender greater control over the use of the loan proceeds for the stated purpose and knowledge of the production technique to be used.

Trade networks may result in credit being extended from one level to another through a series of trading relationships (Floro and Yotopoulos 1991). Intermediate firms in these relationships may not be net creditors but conduits through which credit flows to lower levels. This layering of credit makes use of personalized trading relationships between parties that reduce the riskiness of the loans. One disadvantage to the layering of credit is that transaction costs are incurred at each level, even though no net credit may occur at that particular level.

Interlinking can have ambiguous welfare consequences. Because a prior trading relationship may be necessary before a borrower can receive a loan, conditioning a loan on the requirement of an exclusive trading arrangement with the lender gives the lender a monopoly power. This allows the lender to charge a higher effective rate of interest than might occur in competitive markets.

The practice of interlinking is not unique to rural credit markets. Trade credit is common in industrial and developing countries. Producers of capital goods frequently provide financing for purchasing or renting these goods. Another type of interlinking is through a franchise, under which credit may be extended in return for an exclusive relationship with the parent firm.

Peer Monitoring

Siamwalla and others (1990) and Stiglitz (1990) discuss a mechanism under which a loan is received by individuals who form a group. Each member of the group is jointly liable for the debts of the other members of the group. As Stiglitz notes, the advantage of such a system is that the members of the group are better able to monitor the use of funds by an individual borrower than the lender would be. This monitoring can ensure that a farmer does not use risky methods (or methods riskier than those that other members of the group can tolerate) and does not shirk. Pressure can be applied by the fellow debtors on a noncompliant borrower. Furthermore, because borrowers of similar risk have an incentive to pool together, the lender may be able to ascertain the risk characteristics of the group more easily than the characteristics of any particular individual.

Peer monitoring can also lead to more efficient production decisions. Recall that in the Myers (1977) model a debt-financed firm may in future periods undertake suboptimal levels of investment. Consider the following example, patterned after the Myers model, taking place in a rural setting in the absence of peer monitoring. A farmer receives a loan to finance the planting of a crop. As the crop develops, insect damage ravages the crop. This state of nature—insect damage—is unobservable to the lender but not to the farmer. An application of pesticide might be cost-effective but perhaps would not save a sufficient amount of the crop to prevent default on the loan. In this case, the farmer does not apply the pesticide because it is not in his or her interest to do so. This outcome is inefficient if the cost of the pesticide is less than the value of the crops that could be saved through its application.

One way to prevent this inefficient behavior is to mandate application of pesticides at all times, regardless of whether or not it is necessary. Indeed, as noted by Thrup (1990), agricultural loans in developing countries often require application of pesticides whether they are necessary or not. This, too, is inefficient because the expenditure on pesticides is wasted when crop damage from insects is minimal.

The peer-monitoring group may be an alternative solution. Consider the situation in which a single farmer's crop could benefit from application of pesticide, even though the yield from the crop would be insufficient to prevent default on the farmer's loan. The group, since it is jointly liable for the farmer's loan, would have the appropriate incentive to apply the pesticide when it is cost-effective. The additional expenditure on the pesticide would reduce the group's liability when the individual farmer defaults. Only at high monitoring costs could a lender achieve the same outcome as the peer-monitoring group.

The peer-monitoring group may be able to prevent this sort of inefficiency only when the state of nature requiring subsequent investment is not strongly correlated across all members of the group. For example, if all farmers simultaneously experienced insect damage, it might be in the interest of the group not to apply pesticide and jointly default on the loan. This general lack of risk diversification is a disadvantage of the peer-monitoring system. There is a tradeoff between peer group members being located in the same area so as to maximize their ability to monitor and assist each other and the increased sensitivity of all members to common risks, such as environmental conditions. Stiglitz (1990) also notes that as the size of a peer-monitoring group expands, free-rider effects may reduce individual incentives to monitor the other members of the group. This disadvantage must be weighed against the benefits of risk diversification from expanding group size.

The experience with peer-monitoring groups of the Grameen Bank in Bangladesh has been quite successful. Loans through this program have experienced a default rate of only 3 percent (Biggs, Snodgrass, and Srivastava 1991). Braverman and Guasch (1989) note, however, that other types of cooperative credit programs have been less successful. They find that these failed programs are characterized by lack of joint responsibility and sense of belonging within the group, dishonesty, and poor administration and coordination both within the group and with the lending institution. These failures underscore the importance of carefully designing the structure and incentives within a cooperative credit group.

Policy Implications

This chapter has identified the effects of taxes and asymmetric information on financing choices. The classical corporate tax system is likely to create a lower opportunity cost on the use of retained earnings by the firm than new share issues. Asymmetric information may also create a financing hierarchy within the firm by which retained earnings are available at a lower cost to the firm than external financing. In the previous sections I discussed several ways in which the cost of obtaining debt finance could exceed the required return on additional internal financing.

These factors suggest that in the general case, in which firms do not all have equal access to retained earnings, investment is unlikely to be allocated in a manner that maximizes its return.

The important question facing policymakers is whether the government has instruments available to it that are not available to the financial markets and that could reduce the costs of asymmetric information. In this section I will examine possible government policies that could mitigate the effects of asymmetric information on investment. The policies to be examined can be grouped into (a) policies that promote equities markets, (b) regulation of the banking sector, (c) specific tax instruments, and (d) other measures.

Promotion of Equity Markets

Equity financing of investment represents one alternative to debt finance. In the absence of taxation and asymmetric information, risk-neutral agents would be indifferent to these sources of finance. A classical corporate tax system, by allowing a deduction for interest paid but not for dividends, creates one wedge favoring debt finance. To be examined here is whether, in the absence of this tax disadvantage, private markets would favor the use of equity financing of investment over debt. That is, are the costs of asymmetric information less with equity finance than with debt finance?

Problems of asymmetric information are different but still exist with equity finance. The inability of outside equity owners to monitor perfectly the effort of the firm's owner-manager may result in too little effort being provided by the manager (Jensen and Meckling 1976). In activities in which managerial effort is an important determinant of the success of the firm and not easily monitored, the costs of asymmetric information with equity contracts may be large.

Myers and Majluf (1984) note other costs that arise with equity finance when additional funds are required. Managers of the firm have better information on the value of the firm's existing assets and growth opportunities than outsiders. If managers seek to maximize the wealth of existing shareholders, they will prefer to issue new equity when the firm is overvalued. Outsiders, knowing this, discount the amount they are willing to pay for the shares. Truly good projects, then, must pay a premium to new investors because they cannot be distinguished from shares being issued by overvalued firms.

In both the Jensen and Meckling and the Myers and Majluf models, if a firm could borrow with riskless debt, the problem of asymmetric information would be overcome. In both cases a firm would use debt finance to undertake all projects with positive net present value. Whether the costs of issuing risky debt are less than the costs of issuing new equity is unclear. Myers (1984) suggests that a firm can minimize the riskiness of its debt by keeping debt burdens low. This allows the firm an option to issue debt at low cost if it is in need of financing a profitable project. A firm will forsake some positive net present value projects in order to leave this funding option open. Stiglitz and Weiss (1983) see a tradeoff between issuing risky debt and equity, depending on the degree to which the returns of the firm are dependent on managerial effort and on the scope the firm has to undertake projects with different degrees of risk. Where the former is dominant, debt is the optimal instrument. Where the latter is dominant, equity is the optimal instrument. In between, mixtures of debt and equity may minimize the costs of asymmetric information.

There is probably a role for both debt and equity securities. It is unlikely that government encouragement of an equities market could increase the costs of information asymmetries. Parties could always choose not to use instruments for which transaction costs, including the costs of asymmetric information, are high. De Meza and Webb (1987) point out that the inefficiencies of debt finance found in the model of Stiglitz and Weiss (1981), which does not incorporate moral hazard, would not exist with an equity contract. Certainly, government regulations should not restrict the range of contingencies over which parties contract.

A well-functioning equities market may initially require substantial investment in providing an institutional infrastructure. An efficient legal system to enforce contracts and to prosecute fraud is one such investment. Uniform accounting standards are necessary to value securities in an unbiased manner. Even in markets with highly developed financial and legal institutions, price volatility and outright fraud may exist.

Hybrid securities, or mixtures of debt and equity contracts, may also serve to reduce costs of asymmetric information. Tax rules may hinder the development of equity-like securities. For example, debt instruments with payment streams contingent on the level of earnings may be treated as equity, causing the firm to lose its deduction for these payments.

Although equity securities have some incentive advantages, other reasons exist for believing that financial institutions such as banks may be more successful at resolving problems of information asymmetries than decentralized securities markets. Mishkin (1990) and others have noted the advantages available to banks as lending institutions: information collection costs may decline with the scale of lending; a single lender is not subject to the free-rider problem of discovering the creditworthiness of a borrower that may be present in decentralized securities markets; and costs of monitoring are not duplicated.

In addition, as noted by Stiglitz and Weiss (1983), banks are free to engage in multiperiod contracts with a borrower. A multiperiod contract that makes the issuance of further loans subject to satisfactory payment of previous loans gives the lender more degrees of freedom in structuring incentives for the borrower. One criticism of the variety of models presented earlier is their focus on a single investment, whereas "financial relations are not a one-shot affair" (Hellwig 1989). Although multiperiod contracts may not be as explicit in open securities markets as they are in direct borrower-lender relationships, the long-term credit reputation of a firm can enhance a firm's ability to borrow at reduced cost in open securities markets as well.

Alternative means of reducing information asymmetries include conglomerate mergers and industrial groups like the Japanese *keiretsu,* which are loose affiliations of firms tied to a common financial intermediary. Industrial groups have been recognized as alternatives to traditional financial institutions (for example, Leff 1976). Recent research on the Japanese *keiretsu* has confirmed their ability to reduce the effects of credit rationing (Hoshi, Kashyap, and Scharfstein 1990, 1991). It should be noted, however, that in countries in which only some firms have access to group financing, the overall allocation of capital may not necessarily be improved. Firms within industrial groups may be able to undertake investment with low marginal returns, whereas firms outside industrial groups are unable to undertake projects with higher returns.

Regulation of the Banking Sector

The banking sector is frequently subject to a variety of regulations. As mentioned above, regulations restricting the contingencies under which borrowers and lenders may contract can limit the ability of lenders to modify the incentives of borrowers. One example of such a restriction is an inability by banks to take an equity position in their borrowers.

Other specific changes in regulations may be highly dependent on the form of the information asymmetry. For example, it was shown earlier that the existence of competitive lending markets can result in overinvestment. Perhaps surprisingly, regulations limiting the competitiveness of the banking sector can lead to more efficient allocation of investment funds. For example, a monopolist lender would never reduce lending rates to the point where the return on the marginal borrower was negative. Floors on lending rates could increase efficiency by limiting borrowing. The quantity of loanable funds could also be limited by ceilings on the rates that could be paid by banks.

In situations in which the information asymmetry causes underinvestment, policies restricting competition would only further reduce investment. Deposit insurance, which can encourage risk taking by banks, may result in excessive risk taking, as demonstrated in the United States in the 1980s. In the model leading to credit rationing, presented in an earlier section, deposit insurance would not improve the allocation of investment funds.

Competition may also limit the ability of a bank to engage in certain multiperiod contracts. For example, part of a bank's ability to enforce repayment of debt may be the sanction of denying future credit. Alternatively, in return for favorable treatment toward a borrower in the present period, the bank may increase the borrower's costs for subsequent loans. In a competitive loan market, the borrower may be able to avoid these costs or the sanction of credit denial by borrowing from a competing bank for the subsequent loan (Mayer 1988).

Tax Instruments

In the section entitled "Debt, Equity, and Taxes under Symmetric Information," I identified how the differing tax treatment of equity and debt can create divergent costs in the use of retained earnings, new share issues, and debt finance. In this section, I point out how specific tax instruments can improve the allocation of finance in the presence of asymmetric information.

Unfortunately, the use of tax instruments appears to depend greatly on the nature of the information asymmetry. In the model presented in the section "Financing Choices under Asymmetric Information," where there is overinvestment, de Meza and Webb (1987) show how a tax on interest paid on savings can lead to the first-best outcome. In a similar model, Bernanke and Gertler (1990) find that a tax on the return to successful projects reduces overinvestment. Both sets of authors note how this result is sensitive to the specification of the information asymmetry. In the model of Stiglitz and Weiss (1981), leading to rationing, de Meza and Webb show that an interest rate subsidy on savings is necessary to achieve optimality. Cho (1986) suggests that a tax paid on successful projects to compensate banks for losses they incur on additional loans beyond a rationing equilibrium may increase efficiency.

Hoff and Lyon (1994) present a variation of the model of de Meza and Webb. In this model, individuals make decisions on whether to invest in human capital through a program of higher education. Successful completion of the program depends in part on one's ability, which is learned only after expending effort in primary and secondary education. Hoff and Lyon show that if ability is known only to the individual, a problem of adverse selection results. Individuals who must borrow to finance their higher education "overinvest"; that is, individuals with low probabilities of success invest in higher education because the cost of default is shifted to others. In fact, the problem of adverse selection can be so severe that the loan market breaks down entirely. The cost of borrowing can be so high that the expected return from incurring effort in primary and secondary education is negative. Because without incurring this initial effort individuals cannot enroll in higher education, a problem of underinvestment emerges. Hoff and Lyon show that the solution of de Meza and Webb to tax interest can be ineffective in solving this problem. They find that a lump-sum grant to individuals, financed by a distortionary tax on future labor earnings, can increase efficiency and be more efficient than any tax or subsidy on borrowing. This runs counter to the traditional public finance literature that finds lump-sum grants financed by distortionary taxes to be welfare decreasing.

There may be systematic characteristics of the information asymmetries associated with certain projects as opposed to certain entrepreneurs. In this case it may be easier to identify types of projects that should receive favored tax treatment, rather than types of entrepreneurs. For example, Myers (1977) and Long and Malitz (1985) suggest that firms with significant intangible investments, such as R&D, may be less likely to support debt finance than firms with tangible assets. This is a result of the Myers model, where growth opportunities are less likely to be undertaken in the presence of debt finance. Debt finance can be obtained in this model only if lenders can anticipate the extent of the future underinvestment. Because future intangible investments are more discretionary and less easily monitored by lenders than the maintenance of tangible assets, firms with intangible investments may be unable to obtain debt finance. Long and Malitz also note that the moral hazard problem of debt finance is greater with intangible investments. Firms are able to shift intangible investments toward riskier projects more easily than they are tangible investments, the use of which is more easily monitored. If firms must finance intangible investments with equity, this may argue for more favorable tax treatment of intangible investments. Favorable tax treatment of R&D is frequently argued on the grounds that the social returns from this activity exceed the private returns. The information asymmetry argument suggests there may be underinvestment in this activity even in the absence of any divergence between social and private returns.

A number of other tax instruments, such as special tax rates for capital gains, could also be considered. In some cases, it may be desirable to tax investment gains and losses of lenders on an accrual basis rather than on realization. For example, if a bank suffers losses on its loan portfolio, it may have an incentive to sell this portfolio to realize the tax losses. (Accounting rules, however, may give banks an incentive not to realize the loss.) Still, if a continuing relationship between borrower and lender would result in certain efficiencies, taking the tax loss without selling the loan portfolio would be more efficient. Such a system is designated "mark-to-market" because the tax value of the securities is their current market value. The cost to the government of this favorable treatment of tax losses could be compensated for by marking to market all loans of the bank, not just those that have declined in value. The difficulty in such a proposal is that except for widely traded securities market valuation is difficult to ascertain.

One role government can play in the presence of a poorly functioning equity market is to become an equity partner. One way in which it can do this is to allow the immediate writeoff or expensing of new investment. This reduces the cost of an investment I to $(1 - \tau)I$, where τ is the tax rate of the entrepreneur. In situations in which the entrepreneur's wealth is a limiting factor, investments can be increased if the government is an equity partner. In cases in which equity is an inefficient instrument—for example, because the effort of the entrepreneur is variable—this inefficiency will also be present with the government as an equity partner. Moreover, the ability of the government to perform as a pure equity partner may be limited by imperfect loss offsets, minimum tax schedules, and graduated tax rates (see Lyon 1992).

Other Measures

Bernanke and Gertler (1990) note the important effects of entrepreneurs' endowments on the efficiency of investment. They suggest that the government can improve efficiency by redistributing wealth from entrepreneurs with projects that have an expected low return to entrepreneurs with projects that have an expected high return. The effects of marginal changes in wealth on projects with different probabilities of success were examined earlier. Such policies need not conflict with traditional notions of horizontal and vertical equity. The model of Hoff and Lyon (1994), considered in the last section, finds efficiency gains from lump-sum wealth transfers to low-wealth individuals that are financed either by labor taxes on the same individuals or by taxes on high-wealth individuals.

In some cases it is not clear whether the government is better able to identify creditworthy recipients than are financial markets. Tybout (1983) notes the failure of government credit schemes to allocate scarce financing to its most efficient use. He finds that firms rationed from credit have a higher marginal return on projects than firms favored under government credit schemes. He notes that rent-seeking activities to receive favored government treatment can further decrease efficiency. It should be mentioned that government provision of credit is not limited to countries without well-functioning financial institutions. One-third of all credit extended in the United States in the 1980s has been subsidized by the federal government (Gale 1991).

Stiglitz (1990) notes that direct government intervention in credit markets is unlikely to be successful: "If informational problems are the barrier to the development of an effective capital market, then there is no reason to presume that governmental lending agencies will be in a superior position to address these problems. Indeed, the lack of incentives for government bureaucrats to monitor loans may exacerbate the problem." Further, the political system may lack the willpower to enforce the collection of government debts, turning government loans effectively into government grants.

Instead, Stiglitz suggests that more basic government efforts to establish an infrastructure—both physical and legal—may do more to reduce credit risks. Physical improvement of transportation networks and irrigation can directly reduce the risks faced by agrarian economies. The establishment of a legal infrastructure can provide the legal means to enforce credit contracts.

Policies that increase the accessibility of collateral to borrowers may also be warranted. For example, land titling in rural areas might allow the use of land as collateral. This type of policy could reduce information costs of borrowing without the consequent distributional effects of policies such as those suggested by Bernanke and Gertler (1990). In this regard, policies that lead to the accumulation of wealth also lower the cost of asymmetric information. Furthermore, lending institutions that also serve as savings institutions may be able to develop better information regarding the creditworthiness of their borrowers through this linkage and better enforce repayment of loans.

Lenders who also have trading relations with their borrowers may have a greater ability to minimize costs of asymmetric information. Policies that promote the dissemination of credit through trade networks may be effective. Multinational corporations could be given incentives to make credit accessible to customers and suppliers. Efforts should encourage the transmission of credit from each level in these trade networks.

In the past many aspects of credit programs in developing countries have been criticized as being overly rigid and not taking local conditions into consideration. For example, Kilby, Liedholm, and Meyer (1984: 279) state: "Constraints placed on the use of rural credit should be removed so that rural households can more easily allocate their financial resources toward uses where they perceive the highest return." In a similar vein Thrup (1990) criticizes the mandated use of certain technical factors, such as fertilizers or pesticides. It is true that these restrictions are likely to result in suboptimal use of resources. But these authors frequently fail to point out that these restrictions are in part necessary because the borrowers and lenders do not share equally in risk and returns. The nature of the debt contract is likely to induce riskier projects than would otherwise be undertaken. Some restrictions on activities may be the only way that lenders can mitigate this tendency. Before criticizing credit programs as being overly restrictive, one must determine whether alternative means exist to overcome the problems of asymmetric information.

Given the variety of different problems caused by asymmetric information, it would be surprising if there were a single solution to these problems. Tradeoffs between alternative policies abound. The optimal form of finance for some activities may be debt, whereas for others it is equity, depending on the importance of effort by the entrepreneur and the risks of alternative techniques of production. Restrictions on the range of techniques that may be used by a borrower reduce the risk to the lender but may result in the use of inappropriate technology. Peer-monitoring groups offer one method of reducing monitoring costs, but they could also transfer risk to borrowers who may be more risk-averse than their lenders. The composition of peer-monitoring groups affects risk diversification and incentives to monitor other group members. The variety of tradeoffs suggests that experimentation with different methods of controlling the costs of asymmetric information may be productive.

Appendix 4A. Modigliani and Miller's Homemade Leverage and Firm Value

Modigliani and Miller (1963) show how any stream of income from a leveraged firm can be achieved from a similarly risky unleveraged firm and borrowing by the stockholder on his or her own personal account. Because the cash return from the two investments is the same, the value of either position must be equal. This allows a comparison between the value of the leveraged firm and that of the unleveraged firm.

Consider a leveraged firm with assets yielding an uncertain return, debt B, and an interest rate r. The amount of debt is assumed to be constant over time. An investor who owns a share α of the firm will have an after-tax cash flow of

$$(4A\text{-}1) \qquad C_L = \alpha\,(\tilde{x} - rB)\,(1 - \tau_c)\,(1 - \tau_e).$$

A shareholder in an unleveraged firm with the same uncertain return would have an after-tax cash flow of

$$(4A\text{-}2) \qquad C_U = \alpha(\tilde{x})(1 - \tau_c)(1 - \tau_e).$$

If the investor in the unleveraged firm borrows an amount equal to $\alpha B(1 - \tau_c)(1 - \tau_e)/(1 - \tau_b)$, the investor's net after-tax cash flow (after deducting the interest payments at τ_b) is identical to C_L.

Because the cash flow from both of these positions is identical, the dollar value of the positions must be identical or there would be unlimited arbitrage profits to be made. If αS_U is the dollar cost of the shares in the unleveraged firm, the investor's net capital invested is

$$(4A\text{-}3) \qquad \alpha S_U - \alpha B\,(1 - \tau_c)(1 - \tau_e)/(1 - \tau_b).$$

The investment in the leveraged firm, αS_L, must be equal to this amount, or

$$(4A\text{-}4) \qquad S_L = S_U - B\,(1 - \tau_c)(1 - \tau_e)/(1 - \tau_b).$$

Finally, the total value of the leveraged firm V_L is the sum of S_L and B, whereas the value of the unleveraged firm V_U is S_U. Substituting for S_L and S_U in equation 4A-4 yields

$$(4A\text{-}5) \qquad V_L - V_U = B\left[\,1 - (1 - \tau_c)(1 - \tau_e)/(1 - \tau_b)\,\right].$$

This is the increase in the value of the firm from leveraging when $(1 - \tau_b) > (1 - \tau_c)(1 - \tau_e)$.

To understand the size of the potential increase in the value of the firm from debt finance, consider the following parameters: $\tau_c = 0.40$, $\tau_b = 0.40$, and $\tau_e = 0.10$. In this case, each unit of capital financed through debt would increase the market value of the leveraged firm by 10 percent of the value of the capital acquired in relation to the unleveraged firm.

Appendix 4B. Rationing with Asymmetric Information

This model assumes that all projects have the same expected return, but both the probability of success p_i and the return if successful R_i^s vary. In such a model, the marginal entrepreneur who is indifferent concerning whether to undertake a project or to lend at the safe interest rate ρ has the highest probability of success of those projects receiving funding. As a result, increases in the borrowing rate r will cause the best credit risks to drop out. Banks may experience higher profits by rationing credit rather than increasing the rate at which they lend funds. The result that the marginal entrepreneur has the highest probability of success of those projects undertaken is presented here.

The assumption that the expected returns from all projects are identical,

(4B-1) $p_i R_i^s + (1 - p_i)R^f = \text{constant}$,

implies that $\partial R_i^s / \partial p_i < 0$. Entrepreneurs will choose to undertake their projects if the expected profits exceed the return that could be earned by lending their wealth at the safe interest rate ρ,

(4B-2) $p_i [\, R_i^s - (1 + r)\, B \,] \geq (1 + \rho)\, w$.

Note that because $(1 + r)B > R^f$, and because equation 4B-1 is unaffected by changes in p_i, the left-hand side of equation 4B-2 must be decreasing in p_i. Thus the entrepreneur for whom equation 4B-2 holds as an equality has the highest probability of success of those projects undertaken.

Notes

I wish to thank Karla Hoff for many useful suggestions and especially Anwar Shah for his guidance of this project.

1. Jensen and Meckling (1976) cite a particularly relevant passage from Adam Smith's *The Wealth of Nations* ([1776] 1937: 700): "The directors of such [joint-stock] companies, however, being the managers rather of other people's money than of their own, it cannot well be expected that they should watch over it with the same anxious vigilance with which the partners in a private copartnery frequently watch over their own."

2. A fully integrated tax system gives a dividend recipient credit for income taxes paid by the corporation. In this case the original Modigliani-Miller result found in the absence of taxation (indifference between debt and equity) holds.

3. Capital gains not realized before the death of the stockholder may even escape taxation entirely, as in the United States. The heir may be liable only for tax on the appreciation of the stock from the date the stock was inherited.

4. What factors a firm may consider in choosing whether to retain earnings or pay income as dividends will be examined later in this section. For now, how this choice is made will be ignored.

5. In the United States the effect of the legal restrictions is unlikely to con- strain most firms. The presence of dividend payments is then likely the result of nontax factors that are omitted from this analysis.

6. An important implication of this model noted by Auerbach (1979) is that a positive tax rate on dividends does not discourage corporate investment if re- tained earnings are sufficient to meet investment needs. The dividend tax in this case encourages investment to a point where a unit of new investment is valued at less than a unit by the stock market. Increases in the dividend tax rate could actually lead the firm to undertake greater investment by reducing the opportu- nity cost of retained earnings.

7. See Stiglitz (1974) for an early analysis of the role of information asymme- tries in sharecropping. Singh (1989) presents a recent survey on this subject.

8. With modifications, this model can also be used to analyze the findings of Bernanke and Gertler (1990); Calomiris and Hubbard (1990); and Stiglitz and Weiss (1981).

9. This model has been modified by Long and Malitz (1985).

10. The entrepreneur's expected profit from undertaking the project in rela- tion to his opportunity cost is (from equation 4-1a) $p_i[R^s - (1 + r)B] - (1 + \rho)w$. Differentiating with respect to w yields $p_i(1 + r)dw - (1 + \rho)dw$, where use of the identity $B = k - w$ has been made. Let us assume here that $R^f = 0$. Because the banking sector in equilibrium makes zero profit, $\rho = r\bar{p}$, where $\bar{p}$ is the average probability of success. Thus entrepreneurs whose $p_i > \bar{p}$ have an increase in expected profit, whereas those whose $p_i < \bar{p}$ have a decrease in expected profit.

11. For further discussion of these and other mechanisms, see the overview paper by Hoff and Stiglitz (1990).

12. Aleem notes that the high occurrence of loans repaid or lent in kind in Pakistan may also be a way of avoiding loans bearing fixed interest rates, which would be considered un-Islamic. This interlinkage, however, is also found in other, non-Islamic developing countries (see Siamwalla and others, 1990).

References

Aleem, Irfan. 1990. "Imperfect Information, Screening, and the Costs of Infor- mal Lending: A Study of a Rural Credit Market in Pakistan." *World Bank Economic Review* 4 (3): 329–50.

Auerbach, Alan J. 1979. "Share Valuation and Corporate Equity Policy." *Journal of Public Economics* 11 (3): 291–305.

———. 1984. "Taxes, Firm Financial Policy and the Cost of Capital: An Empiri- cal Analysis." *Journal of Public Economics* 23 (1/2): 27–57.

Bell, Clive. 1989. "A Comparison of Principal-Agent and Bargaining Solutions: The Case of Tenancy Contracts." In Pranab Bardhan, ed., *The Economic Theory of Agrarian Institutions.* New York: Oxford University Press.

Bernanke, Ben, and Mark Gertler. 1990. "Financial Fragility and Economic Performance." *Quarterly Journal of Economics* 105 (1): 87–114.

Biggs, Tyler S., Donald Snodgrass, and Pradeep Srivastava. 1991. "On Minimalist Credit Programs." *Savings and Development* 15 (1): 39–52.

Braverman, Avishay, and J. Luis Guasch. 1989. "Institutional Analysis of Credit Co-operatives." In Pranab Bardhan, ed., *The Economic Theory of Agrarian Institutions.* New York: Oxford University Press.

Calomiris, Charles W., and R. Glenn Hubbard. 1990. "Firm Heterogeneity, Internal Finance, and 'Credit Rationing.'" *Economic Journal* 100 (399): 90–104.

Cho, Yoon Je. 1986. "Inefficiencies from Financial Liberalization in the Absence of Well-Functioning Equity Markets." *Journal of Money, Credit, and Banking* 18 (2): 191–99.

de Meza, David, and David C. Webb. 1987. "Too Much Investment: A Problem of Asymmetric Information." *Quarterly Journal of Economics* 102 (2): 281–92.

Fazzari, Steven, R. Glenn Hubbard, and Bruce Petersen. 1988a. "Financing Constraints and Corporate Investment." *Brookings Papers on Economic Activity* 1 (1): 141–95.

———. 1988b. "Investment, Financing Decisions, and Tax Policy." *American Economic Review* 78 (2): 200–05.

Floro, Sagrario L., and Pan Yotopoulos. 1991. *Informal Credit Markets and the New Institutional Economics: The Case of Philippine Agriculture.* Boulder, Colo.: Westview Press.

Gale, William G. 1991. "Economic Effects of Federal Credit Programs." *American Economic Review* 81 (1): 133–52.

Hall, Robert, and Dale W. Jorgenson. 1967. "Tax Policy and Investment Behavior." *American Economic Review* 57 (3): 391–414.

Hellwig, Martin. 1989. "Asymmetric Information, Financial Markets, and Financial Institutions: Where Are We Currently Going?" *European Economic Review* 33 (2/3): 277–85.

Himmelberg, Charles P., and Bruce Petersen. 1994. "R&D and Internal Finance: A Panel Study of Small Firms in High-tech Industries." *Review of Economics and Statistics* 76 (1): 38–51.

Hoff, Karla, and Andrew S. Lyon. 1994. "Non-Leaky Buckets: Optional Redistributive Taxation and Agency Costs." National Bureau of Economic Research Working Paper 4652. Cambridge, Mass.

Hoff, Karla, and Joseph E. Stiglitz. 1990. "Introduction: Imperfect Information and Rural Credit Markets—Puzzles and Policy Perspectives." *World Bank Economic Review* 4 (3): 235–50.

Hoshi, Takeo, Anil Kashyap, and David Scharfstein. 1990. "Bank Monitoring and Investment: Evidence from the Changing Structure of Japanese Corporate Banking Relationships." In R. Glenn Hubbard, ed., *Asymmetric Information, Corporate Finance, and Investment.* Chicago, Ill.: University of Chicago Press.

——. 1991. "Corporate Structure, Liquidity, and Investment: Evidence from Japanese Industrial Groups." *Quarterly Journal of Economics* 106 (1): 33–60.

Jensen, Michael C., and William H. Meckling. 1976. "Theory of the Firm: Managerial Behavior, Agency Costs, and Ownership Structure." *Journal of Financial Economics* 3 (4): 305–60.

Kilby, Peter, Carl Liedholm, and Richard Meyer. 1984. "Working Capital and Nonfarm Rural Enterprises." In Dale W. Adams, D. H. Graham, and J. D. Von Pischke, eds., *Undermining Rural Development with Cheap Credit*. Boulder, Colo.: Westview Press.

King, Mervyn A. 1977. *Public Policy and the Corporation*. London: Chapman and Hall.

Leff, Nathaniel H. 1976. "Capital Markets in the Less Developed Countries: The Group Principle." In Ronald I. McKinnon, ed., *Money and Finance in Economic Growth and Development*. New York: Marcel Dekker.

Leland, Hayne E., and David H. Pyle. 1977. "Informational Asymmetries, Financial Structure, and Financial Intermediation." *Journal of Finance* 32 (2): 371–87.

Long, Michael S., and Ileen B. Malitz. 1985. "Investment Patterns and Financial Leverage." In Benjamin M. Friedman, ed., *Corporate Capital Structure in the United States*. Chicago, Ill.: University of Chicago Press.

Lyon, Andrew S. 1992. "Tax Neutrality under Parallel Tax Systems." *Public Finance Quarterly* 20 (3): 338–58.

Mayer, Colin. 1988. "New Issues in Corporate Finance." *European Economic Review* 32 (5): 1167–83.

——. 1990. "Financial Systems, Corporate Finance, and Economic Development." In R. Glenn Hubbard, ed., *Asymmetric Information, Corporate Finance, and Investment*. Chicago, Ill.: University of Chicago Press.

Miller, Merton H. 1977. "Debt and Taxes." *Journal of Finance* 32 (2): 261–75.

Mishkin, Frederic S. 1990. "Asymmetric Information and Financial Crises: A Historical Perspective." National Bureau of Economic Research Working Paper 3400. Cambridge, Mass.

Modigliani, Franco, and Merton H. Miller. 1958. "The Cost of Capital, Corporation Finance, and the Theory of Investment. *American Economic Review* 48 (3): 261–97.

——. 1963. "Corporate Income Taxes and the Cost of Capital: A Correction." *American Economic Review* 53 (3): 433–43.

Myers, Stewart C. 1977. "Determinants of Corporate Borrowing." *Journal of Financial Economics* 5 (2): 147–75.

——. 1984. "The Capital Structure Puzzle." *Journal of Finance* 39 (3): 575–92.

Myers, Stewart C., and Nicholas S. Majluf. 1984. "Corporate Financing and Investment Decisions When Firms Have Information That Investors Do Not Have." *Journal of Financial Economics* 13 (2): 187–221.

Siamwalla, Ammar, Chirmsak Pinthong, Nipon Poapongsakorn, Ploenpit Satsanguan, Prayong Nettayarak, Wanrak Mingmaneenakin, and Yuavares Tubpun. 1990. "The Thai Rural Credit System: Public Subsidies, Private Information, and Segmented Markets." *World Bank Economic Review* 4 (3): 271–95.

Singh, Nirvikar. 1989. "Theories of Sharecropping." In Pranab Bardhan, ed. *The Economic Theory of Agrarian Institutions*. New York: Oxford University Press.

Smith, Adam. [1776] 1937. *An Inquiry into the Nature and Causes of the Wealth of Nations.* New York: Modern Library.

Stiglitz, Joseph E. 1973. "Taxation, Corporate Financial Policy, and the Cost of Capital." *Journal of Public Economics* 2 (1): 1–34.

———. 1974. "Incentives and Risk-Sharing in Sharecropping." *Review of Economic Studies* 41 (2): 219–55.

———. 1990. "Peer Monitoring and Credit Markets." *World Bank Economic Review* 4 (3): 351–66.

Stiglitz, Joseph E., and Andrew Weiss. 1981. "Credit Rationing with Imperfect Information." *American Economic Review* 71 (3): 393–410.

———. 1983. "Incentive Effects of Terminations: Applications to the Credit and Labor Markets." *American Economic Review* 73 (5): 912–27.

Thrup, Lori Ann. 1990. "Inappropriate Incentives for Pesticide Use: Agricultural Credit Requirements in Developing Countries." *Agriculture and Human Values* 7 (3/4): 62–69.

Tybout, James R. 1983. "Credit Rationing and Investment Behavior in a Developing Country." *Review of Economics and Statistics* 65 (4): 598–607.

Warner, Jerold. 1977. "Bankruptcy Costs, Absolute Priority, and the Pricing of Risky Debt Claims." *Journal of Financial Economics* 4 (3): 239–76.

RESEARCH AND DEVELOPMENT INVESTMENT, INDUSTRIAL STRUCTURE, ECONOMIC PERFORMANCE, AND TAX POLICIES

5

Anwar Shah

THIS CHAPTER PROVIDES a selective survey and synthesis of the theoretical and empirical literature on the economics of research and development. I have organized it into several sections. The first section contains an overview of the theoretical underpinnings of the relation between research and development (R&D) capital and the structure of production and a summary of empirical evidence concerning this relationship. Highlighting the special nature of the R&D capital as a factor of production, I survey the nature of lags in R&D capital accumulation, the adjustment process, the relation between R&D capital and other factors of production, and the rate of technological progress and output. In addition, I discuss the nature of R&D capital spillovers, the channels for their transmission, their effect on incentives to undertake R&D, and possible mechanisms to internalize these externalities.

The next section deals with the contemporaneous relation between R&D capital and product market structure. The focus is on the following types of issues: the relation between R&D capital, firm size, stock market value of the firm, product demand, and the nature of competition; the effects of R&D spillovers on the industry performance; and the effect of asymmetric information on R&D project financing as well as on the R&D firm's ability to profit from its output.

I then outline the case for government intervention in the R&D capital market, provide critical comments, indicate instruments of government support for R&D investment, and discuss the Canadian government's current initiatives for technology development. I also provide an overview of tax incentives for R&D in major industrial societies, review the effect of tax policy on the cost of R&D capital, and survey the broad empirical approaches to evaluating the effectiveness of government tax incentives for R&D investment. The rationale and limitations of each approach are presented. The section concludes with a description of the overall research strategy adopted in the present study.

In the next section, I outline the empirical approach and discuss the econometric results, drawing some conclusions regarding the effectiveness of tax measures in promoting R&D investment in Canada. The chapter concludes with a summary of the entire study.

Appendix 5A provides a description and lists sources of data used in this study. Several procedures used in constructing various series are also documented. Appendix 5B provides the definition of the R&D capital adopted in the Canadian Income Tax Act.

R&D Capital and the Structure of Production: Theory and Evidence

Formalizing the role of R&D capital in the production process raises many issues. These issues include the lags in R&D capital accumulation; the effect of R&D capital on productivity growth, input proportions, and output expansion; and the effect of R&D capital spillovers on incentives to undertake own R&D investment. These issues are discussed and the empirical evidence is summarized in the following subsections.

R&D Capital, Factor Substitution, and Adjustment

R&D projects create new knowledge as a result of accumulated expenditure over time. The cumulative results of all R&D projects constitute our stock of knowledge or the stock of R&D capital.[1] Because R&D capital plays a fundamental role in promoting productivity growth and output expansion in any economy, it is important to have as accurate a measure of such capital as possible. R&D expenditure is usually considered a convenient measure of R&D capital. Nominal R&D expenditure is, however, an imperfect guide because it incorporates the effect of price inflation and does not reveal true changes in the level of R&D activity. Furthermore, R&D expenditure relates to projects in the current year, but knowledge capital is a result of the accumulated expenditure from past projects at any point in time. An appropriate deflator must therefore be used to derive real R&D expenditure. Bernstein (1986a) pointed out the limitations of the gross national expenditure (GNE) implicit price index and the consumer price index (CPI) as deflators for R&D expenditure and stressed the need for developing a specific R&D deflator.[2] He argued that a time-varying bias was associated with deflating R&D expenditure by the GNE or the CPI deflators because these deflators reflected changes in output prices, and R&D expenditure related to inputs in the production process.

R&D investment projects, if successful, result in new products and processes. But there may be several lags between the initial undertaking of investment and the final development of product and process. Research and development takes time, and it may take several years for a project to proceed from proposal to development stage. Process innovations typically are introduced gradually, and product innovations require time for advertising strategy to command consumer acceptance. For any industry there may be a large number of projects that came on stream at different time periods, are currently in varying stages of implementation, and are likely to be completed at a sequence of time periods. R&D capital represents an aggregation and accumulation of these projects. The overall adjustment process could take several years. The transformation of R&D expenditure into R&D capital is affected by the speed with which new ideas are translated into product and process development and the rate at which this knowledge is acquired by rivals in the industry. Nelson (1982) argues that an R&D capital accumulation process is costly and time consuming. One learns about efficacious R&D projects through one's successes and failures, which guide one's future search efforts. One round of technological advance lays the foundation for the next round. The process of technical advancement is cumulative, but translation of results into processes and products is subject to lags.

The available empirical evidence suggests that the overall adjustment process from the initiation of the R&D project to the development of the product and process often takes several years. Nadiri (1980) and Nadiri and Bitros (1980) estimate the intervening period to be three to five years, and Bernstein and Nadiri (1988) found it to be even longer—four to eight years. Ravenscraft and Scherer (1982) estimated that a mean lag of R&D on net pretax profits for U.S. businesses ranged from four to six years. Mohnen, Nadiri, and Prucha (1986) obtained a mean lag in the adjustment of R&D of five years in the United States, eight years in Japan, and ten years in Germany.

The evidence supports the hypothesis that adjustment costs for R&D capital exceed those for physical capital. For the United States, Bernstein and Nadiri (1989) estimated that marginal adjustment costs for R&D exceeded those for plant and equipment. They further observed that this difference was more pronounced in industries that exhibited higher propensities to spend on R&D. For Canada, Bernstein (1986b) estimated that the marginal adjustment costs for R&D were higher than those for plant and equipment. Griliches (1979) estimated that the short-term nature of commercial research and development served to make the development lag peak between three and five years and rapidly decline afterwards, with most of the original R&D output becoming public knowledge in about ten years.

R&D Capital, Output Expansion, and Productivity Growth

R&D capital combines with traditional inputs in production to facilitate output expansion by reducing the cost per unit of output. Changes in the level of R&D capital change factor intensities by allowing substitution from relatively scarce factors. This serves to decrease the cost of production. The demand for R&D capital as an input in the production process is influenced by relative factor prices and output quantities. Many empirical studies have examined the influence of changes in the prices of conventional inputs on the demand for R&D capital. The results from a few selected studies are presented here.

Most of the studies found that the demand for R&D capital was price inelastic—that is, an increase of 1 percent in its own price led to a decrease of less than 1 percent in quantity demanded. Furthermore, the long-run own-price elasticity of demand for knowledge capital was found to be higher than the short-run estimate. Nadiri (1980) developed estimates of rental rates for R&D capital for U.S. manufacturing industries. He observed that an increase of 1 percent in this rental rate caused a decline of 0.6 percent in the demand for R&D capital. Bernstein and Nadiri (1988) estimated own-price elasticity of demand for knowledge capital to be −0.45. Bernstein (1984b) estimated long-run own-price elasticity of demand for R&D capital to be −0.35. The short-run elasticity was about one-third of this estimate. Bernstein (1984a) examined the effects of factor prices for Canadian-controlled private corporations as well as U.S. subsidiaries. He estimated long-run own-price elasticities of demand for R&D capital for the two subsamples as −0.28 and −0.42, respectively. The short-run elasticities were nearly half of the above estimates. Mohnen, Nadiri, and Prucha (1986) found the own-price elasticity of R&D capital for the U.S. manufacturing industries to be −0.04, −0.06, and −0.15 in the short, intermediate, and long runs, respectively.[3]

The empirical evidence suggests that physical and R&D capital complement each other but substitute for labor in the long run. The short-run evidence is mixed. Rasmussen (1973) found that the demand for R&D capital was sensitive to changes in the prices of labor and physical capital. Schwartz (1983) studied the relation between R&D capital and three other factors of production—labor, physical capital, and energy—for fourteen manufacturing industries in Canada. His results suggest that exogenous changes in R&D capital lead to increased requirements for all three of the remaining factors of production studied. Bernstein and Nadiri (1989a) found physical and R&D capital to be complements. The demand for R&D capital on average declined by 0.2 percent for a one percentage point increase in the rental rate on physical capital. The labor and R&D capital, however, were substitutes. A one percentage point increase in the rental rate of R&D capital in the long run resulted in a decline of 0.25 percent in labor demand. Bernstein (1988) also found evidence of the complementarity between R&D and physical capital and substitutability between R&D capital and labor inputs in the Canadian context. In the long run a decrease of one percentage point in the rental rate for R&D capital resulted in an increase of about 0.05 percent in the demand for physical capital but a decrease of about 0.40 percent in the demand for labor. In the short run the same estimates were 0.01 and 0.25, respectively. This study showed that R&D and physical capital inputs complemented each other but substituted for labor both in the short and the long runs. Mohnen, Nadiri, and Prucha (1986) estimated that labor and R&D capital were substitutes in production, whereas labor and capital were complements in Japan and Germany but substitutes in the United States. Capital and R&D capital were complements in the United States and Japan and substitutes in Germany.

R&D CAPITAL AND OUTPUT EXPANSION. Output expansion has been considered an important determinant of the demand for R&D capital in much of the empirical work. For example, for a sample of firms in five U.S. industries Nadiri and Bitros (1980) observed that, on average, a 1 percent increase in output generated a 0.7 percent increase in R&D capital. This figure was smaller for the subsample of large firms only. For four U.S. industries Bernstein and Nadiri (1987) found the long-run output elasticity of demand for R&D capital to be greater than unity. On the basis of a sample of major R&D performing firms in Canada, Bernstein (1984b) found this elasticity to equal unity. The short-run estimate for this measure was about one-quarter of that for the long run. Bernstein (1984a) concluded that the short-run output elasticity was higher for Canadian-controlled private corporations than for U.S. subsidiaries in Canada but that the long-run elasticity was invariant to the control or ownership of the firms. Bernstein (1986d) estimated the output elasticities of demand for R&D capital to equal 1 and 0.2 in the long and the short runs, respectively. Mohnen, Nadiri, and Prucha (1986) estimated short-, intermediate-, and long-run output elasticity of demand for R&D capital in U.S. manufacturing industries to be 0.16, 0.31, and 1.00, respectively. Thus we conclude that although in the short run the output expansion induces an increase in demand for R&D capital that is less than proportionate, in the long run it leads to almost a one-to-one increase in the demand for R&D capital.

R&D capital is generally shown to have a positive effect on output. Mansfield (1968), Minasian (1969), and Griliches (1973) estimated that for U.S. manufacturing and other industries a 1 percent increase in R&D capital led, on average, to a 0.1 percent increase in output. In an early study of the subject in Canada, Globerman (1972) did not find any significant effect of R&D capital on output, but in a more recent study Switzer (1984) found results similar to those from the U.S. studies.

Quite a large number of studies have empirically investigated the relation between R&D capital and productivity growth. Summary results of a few selected studies are presented here.

R&D CAPITAL AND TOTAL FACTOR PRODUCTIVITY GROWTH. Mansfield (1965, 1968) found that the rate of technological change is directly related to the growth rate of R&D capital. This result is invariant to the nature of technological change. For ten chemical and petroleum firms he found that 20 percent of the productivity growth could be attributed to growth in R&D capital when the technical change was disembodied. With a capital-embodied technical change, the growth in R&D capital explains nearly 70 percent of the total factor productivity growth.

Griliches (1964) found that the R&D capital contributed to about 30 percent of total factor productivity growth in agriculture. In a subsequent study of U.S. manufacturing at two-, three-, and four-digit Standard Industrial Classification (SIC) levels, R&D growth explained about 40 percent of the total factor productivity growth.

Terleckyj (1974, 1980) considered both the direct and indirect effects of R&D for twenty U.S. manufacturing industries. He defined direct effects as those arising from intraindustry R&D investment and indirect effects as those associated with interindustry transactions. His analysis credited privately financed R&D capital for 30 percent growth in total factor productivity. The indirect effects associated with privately financed R&D were found to account for nearly 78 percent of total productivity growth. The government-financed R&D did not show any significant direct or indirect effects on productivity growth.

Griliches (1980b) related total factor productivity growth measures for 883 large U.S. companies during the 1957–65 period to various measures of the growth in R&D capital and found a sizable and significant positive effect of R&D on productivity growth. He obtained an elasticity of output with respect to R&D investments of about 0.07 and an implied average gross excess return of 27 percent (as of 1963), a significantly lower rate of return to federally financed R&D expenditure, and no clear evidence of scale effects either in R&D investment policies or the returns from it. The positive contribution of R&D to total factor productivity growth was also confirmed by Griliches (1980a).

Working with a sample of twenty U.S. manufacturing industries for 1948–66 and sixteen U.S. petroleum and chemical firms for 1960–76, Mansfield (1980) found that the growth rate of both the basic and applied privately financed R&D capital had a positive and significant influence on total factor productivity growth. In support of the Terleckyj results he found that government-financed R&D did not have any significant effect on productivity growth. He found a significant premium on basic research, on the order of two to one at the industry level and sixteen to one at the firm level.

Nadiri and Schankerman (1981) decomposed total factor productivity growth into four components: factor price effect, product demand effect, R&D effect, and autonomous technical change effect. This decomposition was carried out for U.S. manufacturing at total, durable, and nondurable levels of aggregation for four subperiods between 1958 and 1978. They found that R&D and exogenous technical change (the *technology effect*) dominated productivity growth in the earlier years and that the factor price and product demand (the *scale effect*) were the prime motivators for productivity growth in the later years of the period studied.

Jaffe (1988), instead, suggests decomposing the total factor productivity growth into the following three factors: technological opportunities, market demand, and R&D spillovers. Using data compiled at the National Bureau of Economic Research in relation to 573 firms during 1965–77, the author concludes that all three factors have an effect on R&D demand. At the same time, in explaining total factor productivity growth, Jaffe (1988) cannot separate the effects of technological changes and demand. More robust is the result in relation to R&D spillovers: in the innovation process, the R&D spillovers show a positive externality on the level of R&D investment and costs of neighbor firms.

Scherer (1982) found that both the intraindustry and interindustry effects of R&D capital on productivity growth during 1945–65 were strong but appear to have weakened during the 1970s. Furthermore, he found interindustry effects of R&D capital to be much stronger than the intraindustry effects. Scherer (1982) concluded that 0.20 to 0.28 percent of the decline in productivity in 1978 could be attributed to less R&D.

Levy and Terleckyj (1983) estimated that private sector R&D capital had a large effect on private sector productivity, with elasticity of about 0.28. The comparable elasticity estimate for R&D under government contract was 0.065. No significant effect of all other government R&D on private sector productivity was found. These findings for government contract R&D were consistent with those of Scott (1984), indicating small but significant stimulative effects of government support for R&D.

Griliches and Mairesse (1984) studied 100 large U.S. firms during 1966–77. They found that the contribution of R&D capital to productivity growth was higher than that of physical capital. Clark and Griliches (1984) found a statistically significant relation between R&D intensity and the growth in total factor productivity, implying a gross excess rate of return to R&D of about 20 percent. This return is bigger for process R&D than for product R&D. These returns, however, crucially depend on the presence of previous major technological changes in the respective industries, which implies that spillovers from the previous R&D efforts of other firms and industries play an important role.

Griliches and Lichtenberg (1984b) found that the statistical relation between productivity growth and R&D intensity grew stronger in the 1970s for U.S. manufacturing industries at two- and three-digit SIC levels. Lichtenberg (1984) found a negative and statistically significant relation between government contracted R&D and private-sector productivity growth. Baily and Chakrabarti (1985) found a positive relation between innovation and productivity patterns from case studies of chemical and textile industries in the United States. They attributed the slowdown in the U.S. manufacturing industries in the 1970s partly to a slowdown in innovation.

Griliches (1986), using a sample of 911 large (1,000 or more employees) U.S. manufacturing companies that performed R&D during 1966–77, reported three major findings: R&D contributed positively to productivity growth and seemed to have earned a relatively high rate of return; basic research appeared to be more important as a determinant of productivity than other types of R&D; and R&D expenditure that was privately financed was more effective, at the firm level, than that which was federally financed.[4]

Two earlier Canadian studies on the subject did not support U.S. findings. Lithwick (1969) did not find any significant relation between productivity growth and industry R&D expenditure. Globerman (1972) estimated a negative and statistically significant relation between R&D capital and overall productivity growth. A recent study by Switzer (1984) of fourteen industries in Canada attributed nearly 60 percent of the growth in factor productivity to the growth in R&D capital. Switzer further found that government-financed R&D had no significant effect on productivity growth. Switzer's results, however, must be considered tentative because he did no tests to determine whether the value added or total output (output inclusive of intermediate inputs) is the appropriate output measure. He also treated R&D capital and conventional factors of production asymmetrically. Profit maximization framework was used for the latter only.

Goto and Suzuki (1989) analyzed the effect of R&D on total factor productivity growth in Japan. Moving away from the previous research, which used data based on financial statements, the authors constructed and used data based on R&D expenditure. The empirical findings support the hypothesis that the productivity growth of a firm is stimulated by other industries' R&D.

Robert Solow (1957) suggested that only 10 percent of the rise in per capita output in the United States during the years 1909–1949 was due to growth in the capital-labor ratio. To explain the remainder of the increase, the more efficient use of inputs or the presence of technological changes needed to be considered. During the past few decades, many researchers who have explored the determinants of the latter have suggested two explanations. In particular, R&D investment is generally regarded as having a strong effect on growth in total factor productivity. Moreover, the links between technological change and productivity growth have been documented by numerous recent studies, which generally use R&D expenditure as an indicator of the intensity of technological change.

Englander, Evenson, and Hanazaki (1988) tested whether an increase of the R&D capital stock translates into an improvement in technology and productivity. Using industry-level data across countries for the years 1970 to 1983, the authors found that part of the deceleration in total factor productivity recorded in the 1970s may have been caused by a reduction in the generation of new technologies. In addition, they highlighted the unequal distribution of innovation across sectors, which can be considered as one of the possible causes for the divergent trends in growth in total factor productivity and price inflation in manufacturing and service industries observed in many Western economies.

Whereas the strong positive correlation between R&D investment and growth in total factor productivity at the industry level is supported by several empirical studies, the results at the firm level have been much less robust. A significant improvement of the state of knowledge is due to Lichtenberg and Siegel (1991). Using confidential census longitudinal microdata, the two researchers found that a significant cause of the growth in total factor productivity during the years 1972–85 was the investment in R&D. Furthermore, it appears that investments in different types of R&D had different effects on productivity growth; among all investments, only the investment in basic research strongly affected the growth in total factor productivity. Another important finding was the strong positive correlation between the rate of growth of total factor productivity and privately funded R&D. Federally funded R&D, however, cannot be considered as a significant determinant of productivity growth.

The most important conclusion from this body of studies is that the R&D spending was not responsible for the productivity slowdown of the 1970s because it has been proved that both aggregate R&D intensity and the (estimated) effect of R&D on productivity growth experienced no decline during this period. Because both the size and the efficacy of R&D investment increased during the 1980s, however, we must take into account R&D investment to elucidate the rise in total factor productivity growth in those years.

As suggested earlier, capital accumulation is stimulated by technological change, and it is responsible for the increase in output per hour worked. Romer (1990) suggested, however, that the technological change observed was more likely to be endogenous than exogenous because it is primarily the consequence of rational actions taken by people in response to market incentives. This implies that market incentives have a central role in the process of translation of new knowledge into goods. Moreover, the good "new knowledge," an imperfect public good, has different features from other economic goods because it comports only an initial fixed cost for its use.

The most important result from Romer's study is that not only the level of income and welfare but also the rate of growth are affected by increases in the size of the market—that is, larger markets are more conducive to more research and faster growth (Romer 1990). In addition, the author suggested that the growth rate is an increasing function of the stock of human capital but not of the total size of the labor force nor of the population. This result helps to explain why countries with a stock of human capital too low may not experience any growth.

R&D CAPITAL AND LABOR PRODUCTIVITY. Most studies on the subject found that private R&D capital had a positive and significant effect on the growth rate of labor productivity. Griliches (1980b) attributed 30 percent of the growth in labor productivity in six U.S. industries to R&D capital accumulation. Nadiri (1980) placed the same figure at 35 percent for the aggregate U.S. private sector. Canadian results were somewhat mixed. Postner and Wesa (1983) and Hartwick and Ewan (1983) concluded that there was no significant relation between growth rate of labor productivity and R&D capital accumulation in Canada. When Postner and Wesa (1983) considered interindustry effects, however, they found that the indirect effect of R&D investment on labor productivity was positive and significant. Longo (1984) estimated that the growth in R&D capital accounted for 16 to 60 percent of labor productivity growth in major R&D performing industries.

R&D CAPITAL AND SPILLOVERS. A special feature of R&D activities is that a firm can augment its R&D capital stock simply by profiting from the R&D results of another firm. The knowledge that is acquired in the absence of a market transaction is commonly referred to as an R&D spillover. The presence of spillovers suggests that the firm generating the spillover cannot completely appropriate the returns associated with its R&D capital. Thus R&D spillovers arise because of the inability of the R&D performers to exclude others from obtaining the benefits of new R&D capital at no or lower cost. In the presence of these spillovers the R&D investor may not be able to earn sufficient return on investment, and thereby the incentive to undertake R&D is diminished.

Spillovers diffuse knowledge by a wide variety of channels. Foremost among these channels are patents, licensing agreements, R&D personnel mobility, and input purchases. Patents enable firms to receive vital information that could be used to develop further patents around the original invention. Royalty payments would not reflect the social value of a patented invention if the ideas of the patentee were being successfully exploited to their own ends by other firms. Cross-licensing agreements also serve to transmit spillovers. Licensing fees may not fully reflect the benefit received from this knowledge transfer because the initial recipient may recover fully or partially his initial costs through cross-licensing. The mobility of R&D personnel from one firm to another is potentially an important source of spillovers. The formation of AMDAHL by a former engineer for the International Business Machines Corporation (IBM) illustrates the importance of this mechanism in knowledge transmission. Input purchases also have the potential of generating spillovers if the input prices do not fully reflect the R&D costs of the sellers. For example, the purchase price of computers in general does not reflect all the cost-reducing possibilities open to downstream or purchasing firms.[5]

It was noted earlier that the existence of these spillovers leads to imperfect appropriability of returns to R&D capital and acts as a disincentive to undertake own R&D investment (see also Arrow 1962). Reinganum (1981) and Spence (1984) formally showed that, as R&D spillovers in a given industry increase, the incentive to undertake R&D diminishes. Thus the larger the spillover, the lower will be the incentive to undertake R&D investments. Spillovers also affect productivity by diffusing the knowledge relating to less costly production processes. More recently, Bernstein and Nadiri (1989b) and Cohen and Levinthal (1989) argued that Spence and others assume that the technical knowledge that spilled over is a public good like a radio signal or smoke pollution in that its effects are costlessly realized by all affected agents. They argue that this assumption is not valid for industrial R&D because the assimilation or absorption of this knowledge by other firms is not well recognized.[6] This process depends on a firm's capacity to assimilate or absorb externally generated knowledge. Mowery (1983a, 1983b) states that a firm must invest in its own R&D to be able to use information that is available externally. He observed that the more sophisticated the externally generated knowledge, the greater is the need for complementary in-house research to exploit it.

Cohen and Levinthal (1989) present a formal model to demonstrate that the overall effect of R&D capital spillovers is ambiguous because of two offsetting effects: the negative effect that is associated with imperfect appropriability of returns from own R&D investments and the positive effect that arises from the incentive to assimilate the scientific and technological findings generated by firms, universities, and public agencies.[7] Bernstein and Nadiri (1989b) examine three effects associated with the intraindustry R&D spillover: first, costs decline for the externality receiving firms as a consequence of the increase of knowledge; second, changes in factor demands in response to spillovers have an effect on production structures; third, R&D spillovers affect the rates of capital accumulation. Nelson and Winter (1982) also suggest that because much of the detailed knowledge of organization routine is acquired only through experience within the firm, the internal R&D capability to recognize the value of, to assimilate, and to use externally generated knowledge in a timely fashion is essential for success in a competitive and technologically progressive environment. The existence of the positive incentive effect helps resolve the paradox posed by the electronics and chemical industries, where high levels of spillovers do not appear to impede the level of investment in research and development. The results of Nelson and Winter's study suggest that the high level of spillovers, combined with rapid scientific and technological advances from sources both inside and outside the industries, provides an incentive for firms to maintain high levels of absorptive capacity, which, in turn, elicits levels of R&D that are high enough to more than offset the negative appropriability effect.

Empirical evidence on the R&D spillovers is scant, and only a few studies have estimated their effects with any rigor. Mansfield and others (1977) calculated social and private returns for seventeen innovations. They found that the median social return was twice as large as the private return (56 percent in contrast to 25 percent). Furthermore, they found that the private rate of return in one-third of the cases "was so low that no firm, with the advantage of hindsight, would have invested in the innovation, but the social rate of return from the innovation was so high that, from society's point of view, the investment was well worthwhile" (Mansfield and others 1977: p. 235). Bernstein and Nadiri (1988) also reached similar conclusions. Using U.S. data, they found that the excess of social return over private return varied from a low of 9 percent for machinery to a high of 76 percent in petroleum products industries. The average was 40 percent for the sample as a whole.

A Canadian study on the subject by Bernstein (1988) employed a production structure methodology and data on seven industries for the period 1978 to 1981 to estimate the effect of R&D spillovers. Bernstein concluded that the social rate of return on R&D projects greatly exceeds the private rate of return. In industries with a high propensity to spend on R&D, the real social rate of return, net of depreciation, was 25 percent in 1981, or more than double the net real private rate of 11.5 percent. In industries whose spending on R&D tends to be low, the social rate of return was 20 percent, or more than two-thirds greater than the private rate. He attributed the high rates of social returns to spillovers associated with R&D investment. He found the society's overall demand for R&D projects to be 75 percent greater than the actual demand observed for 1981. These results are consistent with Longo (1984), who found high rates of return to R&D capital. Bernstein attributed the high rates of return found by Longo to spillovers.

More recently, Bernstein and Nadiri (1989) estimated the cost reduction, factor bias, and capital adjustment effects of the spillover for four industries (chemicals, petroleum, machinery, and instruments) between 1965 and 1978. The existence of R&D spillovers implies that the social and private rates of return to R&D capital differ: even in this case, as in the one examined by Bernstein (1988), the social return exceeds the private return in each of the four industries analyzed.

A later Canadian study focusing on the subject supports the U.S. findings. Using data for nine major Canadian industries, Bernstein (1989) estimates the effects of interindustry R&D spillovers on production costs: all nine industries are influenced by R&D spillovers and, in particular, six of them are affected by multiple spillover sources. The author also computes the rate of return to R&D capital for each industry and finds that it is generally two and a half to about four times greater than the private rate of return on physical capital. Furthermore, as for the U.S. industries, the private rate of return generated by R&D capital is between three and four times smaller than the rate of return inclusive of the interindustry spillover effects.

Since the 1960s, the United States and other Western countries have experienced a decline in the ratio of the number of registered inventions both to real R&D expenditure and to the number of scientists and engineers engaged in R&D. The magnitude of the decline by 1990 is impressively large: for the United States, the United Kingdom, Germany, and France the ratio between the number of patents and the number of scientists and engineers was only 55, 44, 42, and 40 percent of their levels in 1969–70. Some explanations advanced are as follows.

Griliches (1989, 1990) believes that the rising costs of dealing with the patent system are the main reason. Because of the increased expense, researchers have patented fewer of their inventions. From this prospective, the decline in the ratio between patents and R&D can be viewed as the result of "a decline in the propensity to patent inventions, rather than a decline in the actual number of inventions" (Griliches 1990).

Evenson (1984, 1991, 1993), in contrast, has argued that the productivity of the research sector has decreased because of the depletion of technological opportunities. Using a search-research model of invention potential, Evenson tests whether there are common economy-wide effects on changes in the ratios between the number of patents and the amount of capital invested in R&D and the number of patents and the number of scientists and engineers and whether there are common industry effects. The results (Evenson 1993), based on a data set of four countries and seven industries, provide strong support for the "demand-side explanation" and particularly for the importance of the foreign demand. In the pooled-industries specification, growing domestic demand and growing foreign demand are associated with lower ratios between the number of patents and the number of scientists and engineers.

Kortum (1993) emphasizes that Evenson's demand-side story is not capable of explaining a relevant fraction of the decline in the ratio between patents and R&D. From his point of view, the value of patents has been raised by the expansion of the markets, and competition in the research sector has implied a greater R&D expenditure per patent. In particular, his equilibrium model of industry growth predicts that an industry converges to a steady state in which the ratio between invention and R&D continually falls if there is sufficient growth in demand. But this result is not robust: data from twenty U.S. manufacturing industries show a growth in demand not rapid enough to explain the decline in the ratio between patents and R&D. Still, the data corroborate his intuition that the expansion of markets translates into increasing value of an invention and higher research expenditure per invention.

Part of the empirical evidence in relation to R&D has been described earlier. The objective of the next paragraphs is to highlight a few studies that estimate R&D, their features, and their effect on the economic system.

The R&D costs during 1970–82 for twelve U.S.-owned pharmaceutical firms were estimated by DiMasi and others (1991): the cost estimates were substantially higher than in previous studies because of the inadequate measure of R&D costs (Hansen 1979). In particular, the average cost of development at New Chemical Entities was estimated to be US$231 million, 2.3 times higher in real terms than previous estimates.[8]

Data from 191 U.S. manufacturing firms are used to analyze the direction of causality between R&D and investment for the period 1973–81 (Lach and Schankerman 1989). There are two interesting findings from this study. First, the relation between R&D and investment is unidirectional, in the sense that R&D causes investment but not vice versa. Second, the firm's investment program and R&D program are affected in the long run by some "common factors." Moreover, the response to a change of these common factors is persistent over time.

The relation between trade flows and R&D is described in a study by Charos and Simos (1988). Using a multi-input, multioutput model, the authors estimate the import demand and export supply functions for the United States. The results of the study highlight the positive relation between R&D and level of imports; moreover, exports are found to be human capital intensive, whereas investment goods are R&D intensive.

R&D Capital and Product Market Structure: Theory and Evidence

This section focuses on the following issues: the relation between R&D capital, firm size, and the nature of competition; the effect of R&D spillovers on industry performance; and the effect of asymmetric information on the financing of R&D projects as well as on the R&D firm's ability to profit from its output. Some tentative conclusions are presented at the end of the section.

R&D Capital and Technological Competition

It has long been recognized that technological innovations affect market structure and, since Schumpeter's important work (1950), that market structure influences both the level of spending and the appropriability of the R&D. In his *Capitalism, Socialism, and Democracy,* Schumpeter (1950) argued that a market structure involving large firms with a considerable degree of market power is the price that society must pay for rapid technological advance. The Schumpeterian hypothesis has been contested in the subsequent literature. For example, Kamien and Schwartz (1975) and Scherer (1980) pointed out that it was unclear whether highly concentrated markets enhanced the appropriability of R&D investment or whether the opposite was true (Arrow 1962; Fellner 1951). Levin and Reiss (1984) investigated the relation between market structure and R&D investment using a detailed industry equilibrium model in which concentration, R&D intensity of output, and advertising intensity were all jointly determined. They found a strong positive effect of R&D on industry concentration and a negative effect of concentration on R&D intensity, which became positive for industries with a high share of product rather than process R&D.

Nelson and Winter (1982) also postulated a model of Schumpeterian competition and focused on the competitive contest among innovators and imitators. They observed that not only would a relatively concentrated industry tend to provide a higher level of R&D but production and technical advance would be more efficient in that setting. They stated that, where innovative R&D is profitable, the firms that spend on innovative R&D (and hence have a higher ratio of R&D expenditure to output) tend to grow faster than the imitators, but in such a competition small firms are eliminated. Where innovative R&D is not profitable but is permitted to survive by market structure, however, the R&D-intensive firms tend to be small.[9]

Dasgupta (1986) has questioned the causal interpretation given to the relation between R&D investment and the structure of industries. He reasoned that innovative activity and industrial structure are simultaneously determined by technological opportunities, conditions of product demand, and the structure of financial capital markets.

Technical advancement may create a "success breeds success" spiral, sometimes termed as the Matthew effect in reference to the passage in the Gospel according to Saint Matthew describing how the rich will get richer and the poor, poorer. Many empirical studies have investigated the "success breeds success" hypothesis and concluded that past successes of R&D investment lead to greater current R&D efforts. The successful firms tend to produce further innovations and widen the gap between themselves and their rivals.

Philips (1966) could not find support for this hypothesis in data for eleven U.S. industry groups. A subsequent study (Philips 1971) of the commercial aircraft market in the United States during 1932–65, however, provided some support for it. The latter study concluded that the stream of innovations resulted in a decrease in the number of manufacturers and large shifts in market shares. Comanor (1964, 1967) found that R&D was a significant element of interfirm rivalry in the pharmaceutical industry, with profits largely dependent on firms' continued innovative success. Pavitt and Wald (1971) concluded that opportunities for small firms diminish as technological competition becomes more intense. Grabowski (1968) found that for the chemical, drug, and petroleum industries past R&D success led to greater current R&D effort and resulted in widening the gap between technologically successful firms and their competitors.

Many studies have investigated the relation between R&D capital and industrial concentration. Horowitz (1962) and Hamberg (1966) found a weak positive correlation with R&D expenditure per sales dollar and industrial concentration. Freeman (1965) found R&D to be a barrier to entry in the oligopolistic international electronic capital goods industry. Mellor and Tilton (1971) observed that in technological competition, R&D costs act as a barrier to entry in the semiconductor and photocopying industries. (The stage is set for technological competition when the industry is composed of many firms, the basic science is well understood, and the research is relatively sophisticated and specialized.) Scherer (1967) and Kelly (1969) suggested that industrial concentration and R&D were positively correlated up to "moderate" levels of concentration. Comanor (1967) suggested that concentration is also associated with R&D capital in industries in which technological and innovative opportunities are weak. Philips (1971) concluded that, in Belgium, concentration and R&D effort tended to be positively associated in those industries with greatest technological opportunities—that is, R&D-intensive industries. Globerman (1973) found that, for R&D-intensive industries in Canada, research intensity varied inversely with concentration (and directly with both foreign ownership and government financing). For other industries, no significant relation between research and concentration was discovered. Rosenberg (1976) found that the percentage of R&D employees in a firm increased with industry concentration. He also discovered that concentrated industries with firms of equal size (market share) were more R&D intensive. He further found that entry barriers, as measured by capital requirements, necessary advertising levels, and economies of scale, tended to have a positive effect on R&D intensity. Shrieves (1978) concluded that firms in concentrated industries tend to be more R&D intensive, as measured by R&D-associated personnel, than firms in less concentrated ones. Levin and Reiss (1984), on the basis of three years (1963, 1967, and 1972) of data for twenty U.S. manufacturing industries, established a strong positive effect of R&D on industry concentration and a negative effect of concentration on R&D intensity that becomes positive for industries with a high share of product rather than process R&D. A recent study by Mansfield (1984) of twenty-four U.S. firms in the chemical, petroleum, steel, and drug industries, covering sixty-five innovations introduced in the past fifty years, indicated that less than half of the product innovations in all four industries seemed to increase the four-firm concentration. He observed that the concentration-increasing effects of R&D may be much weaker than is commonly perceived.

A large number of studies have addressed the relation between R&D capital and firm size. The overall conclusion in these studies is that larger firms do not engage in greater R&D activity in relation to their size than smaller firms.[10] Furthermore, the technological possibilities between R&D inputs and innovative output do not display any economies of scale with respect to the size of the firm in which R&D is undertaken.[11] It is further indicated that industries facing greater technological opportunities tend to be more concentrated.[12] Howe and McFetridge (1976) studied the determinants of R&D spending in eighty-one Canadian firms in the chemical, electrical, and machinery industries during 1967–71. They found that R&D spending increased more proportionately than sales in the chemical and electrical industries only for intermediate-size firms. Link (1978) found that size is not especially conducive to R&D in the electric utility industry beyond some modest level. Bound (1984) concluded that the elasticity of R&D expenditure with respect to firm size (measured by sales and gross plant) is close to unity with some indication of slightly higher R&D intensities for both very small and very large firms in the sample.[13]

Many empirical studies have confirmed that growth in demand for the products of an industry stimulates R&D activity within it. Mairesse and Siu (1984), Pakes and Schankerman (1984), Rosenberg (1976), and Schmookler (1966), support this result. Pakes and Schankerman (1984), however, established that very little of the observed differences in R&D intensity across firms can be explained by either past or even expected rates of growth of sales or by transitory fluctuations in these variables. At the industry level of aggregation, however, they found that the variance in the growth rate does account for much of the variance in R&D intensity.

R&D Capital Spillovers and Industry Performance

As it relates to spillover effects, appropriability has two prominent facets. On the one hand, it has positive effects on industry costs both in the R&D-performing industries and in related ones. Imperfect appropriability ensures that the outcomes of R&D are disseminated elsewhere and result in decrease in costs. Because R&D involves major fixed costs and relatively minor variable costs, the marginal cost of R&D would be small, if not zero, and allocative efficiency requires that it be priced so. For R&D receivers the relevant costs are the transmission costs of R&D. These are not expected to be significantly different from zero, and hence R&D should be provided free. This problem is analogous to the provision of a public good, and nonappropriability serves to price it correctly. Thus lack of appropriability has positive effects on R&D dissemination and industry costs. On the other hand, the appropriability problem generates two opposing incentive effects for the R&D performer. A negative incentive effect works to discourage the firm from making large investments in R&D because it may not be able fully to appropriate the returns associated with such investments.[14] A positive incentive effect arises because of the complementarity of its own R&D to spillover benefits. The net effect of these two opposing influences will determine whether the appropriability problem induces firms to undertake a lower or higher level of R&D investment. Thus the presence of imperfect appropriability may not necessarily lead to underinvestment in innovative activity.[15]

Levin and Reiss (1984) modeled spillover effects as the influences of a firm's own R&D expenditure on costs in all other firms in the industry. They specified spillovers as a function of share of R&D devoted to new or improved products and the ratio of government R&D to sales. They estimated that the share of R&D devoted to new and improved products had a positive effect on the interfirm spillovers but that government funding diminished spillovers. The latter result was unexpected, but the authors argued that it may be plausible because the government support for R&D in the United States is mostly for large-scale, capital-intensive defense systems, which are not cheaply replicable for private-sector applications.

Bernstein (1986b, 1988), using Canadian data, found that the intra- and interindustry spillovers reduced the average production costs of the firms receiving the spillovers. The interindustry spillovers resulted in significant cost savings to Canada because of the lower R&D investment needed. He further established that spillovers from the industries with high R&D propensities stimulated those industries to further R&D investment. The industries with low R&D inclinations, in contrast, substituted the knowledge from these spillovers for their own projects. His overall conclusion was that in industries that exhibit relatively rapid technological developments, Canadian firms need to carry out their own R&D projects to remain competitive.

Jaffe (1986) modeled R&D spillovers by examining whether the R&D of neighboring firms had an observable effect on the firm's R&D success. He found that U.S. firms whose neighbors did much R&D produced more patents per dollar of their own R&D, and that a positive interaction existed that gave the high R&D firms the largest benefit from spillovers. In regard to profit and market value, however, the R&D of nearby firms produced both positive and negative effects. The net effect was positive for firms whose R&D was intensive, but firms with R&D about one standard deviation below the mean were made worse off overall by the R&D of others.

R&D Capital and Information Asymmetry

It is frequently argued that returns from investment in R&D are more uncertain than they are from traditional investment. As a result, risk-averse individuals discount these returns more heavily than investment in other forms of capital. This argument is plausible but may be of minor importance because the differentials in after-tax returns from R&D are often greater than the returns from traditional investment by margins that cannot be explained by risk premium alone. Furthermore, most firms undertake a diversified portfolio of R&D projects and as a result, although the risk of failure associated with any particular project may be quite large, the group of projects as a whole may hold little risk.

Simply because R&D is risky does not mean that it should be treated differently from other risky investments—for example, oil exploration and development or futures markets. What is special about R&D is information asymmetry between the performer of R&D and the financier. It is in the interest of the performer of R&D not to release vital information relating to the project to an outside party because of the possibility that release of such information will jeopardize the chances of success (for example, input costs for very large projects may be affected by such a release of information) or that someone else will capitalize on the information. But to raise capital for a project requires releasing information about the prospective returns from the project. In the absence of detailed information, necessary financing for the project may not be forthcoming. The situation mimics an adverse selection problem. Because information about the project is withheld from the financier, he or she cannot determine whether the project will be a good risk. As a result, there emerges an imperfect market for financing R&D projects, which provides an inadequate level of financing. This problem arises in a variety of situations and is commonly referred to as the *agency paradigm*. As an example, suppose an inventor seeks to initiate a project and offers to sell shares in the project to obtain necessary financing. A potential investor would be uncertain as to the success of this project in the absence of adequate data on project feasibility and the commitment of the inventor. To inspire greater confidence in the project by outside investors, the investor must assume a substantial share of risk by buying a majority interest. This insures potential investors against any moral hazard associated with the project. It means, however, that the project may not be undertaken at all.

Shapiro (1985) has argued that asymmetric information limits a firm's ability to achieve the licensing gains from trade in R&D. Asymmetric information stands in the way of parties striking a deal. Furthermore, it may be difficult for the innovator to let others use his or her invention without giving them useful information in the ongoing competition to acquire additional patents. It may also be costly or impossible for the licenser to monitor the licensee's output so as to charge per unit royalties.

Asymmetric information can be viewed not only as a constraint in the patent acquisition's process (Shapiro 1985) but also as an entry barrier (Chen 1991). In a model with incomplete information, in fact, a new firm faces an externality because the quality of its products is unknown to the customers. As a consequence, the firm cannot quantify the effects of its R&D investment on the average quality of production. The optimal way to internalize this externality is to implement R&D subsidies jointly with an entry fee. If firms can signal the quality of their products, then the previous policy becomes not socially optimal because it reduces the incentives for new firms to enter the market.

The positive effects of R&D subsidies and their relation to market structure are also recognized by Nakao (1989). Using a model with Bertrand competition among firms, the author suggests that R&D subsidies would be the socially optimal policy only in the case of cooperative oligopoly. In the case of competitive oligopoly, taxes would be the optimal instruments to internalize the externality present in the economy. Furthermore, the noncooperative Bertrand behavior of the firms or the joint R&D ventures lead to a decline in the level of welfare of a society.

An interesting finding in relation to the determinants of market structure is suggested by Belman and Heywood (1990). Testing the correlation between high quality of workers and concentration of the market, the authors estimate that including R&D measures leads to a breakdown of such relation: workers of better quality are employed in industries with a large R&D expenditure that happen to be concentrated because of the dynamism and the technological opportunities of such industries. To analyze the dynamic effects of product innovation and R&D investment on market structure, researchers have often assumed the R&D technology to be stochastic. Using this approach, Aoki (1991) compares a deterministic R&D model with a stochastic one. The results suggest that the deterministic feature of R&D investment can help to explain the continual leadership of one firm in a particular industry. It follows that in this setup the only effect of stochastic R&D (combined with the uncertainty of a successful outcome) is to increase the duration of the competition among rival firms.

Isaac and Reynolds (1988) employ a stochastic model of R&D investment to determine the effects of market structure and degree of appropriability on R&D spending. The simulations run by the authors suggest that both the size of the market and the degree of appropriability are negatively correlated with the level of R&D spending per firm (but a rise in the size of the market will affect positively the aggregate R&D spending).

The costs and the benefits deriving from a new technology are key variables in the innovation process. Lane (1991), using an adjustment model, tries to isolate the factors that affect the investment decision for the coal mining sector in the United States between 1945 and 1975. The main results suggest that there exists a positive relation between a high level of captive production and leaders in the innovation process. Moreover, the degree of vertical integration has a positive incentive on the adoption decision.

How investors evaluate the market value of a firm is the focus of the work done by Shevlin (1991). His starting point is the consideration of whether the assets and liabilities of an R&D firm are affected (positively) by a particular type of off-balance sheet financing, the R&D limited partnerships. Empirical analysis of a sample of 103 R&D limited partnerships for five years suggests that the existence of limited partnerships (usually reported in footnotes to the balance sheet) provides significant information to capital market agents in the investment process.

On the same line of research, Chan, Martin, and Kensinger (1990) examine the effect of the announcements of changes in the level of R&D expenditure on stock prices. During 1979 through 1985, U.S. stock markets responded to announcements of R&D changes with a long-term perspective: the share value of a firm appears to be positively correlated with the rise in R&D, even if the earnings of a few firms initially decline. This result does not hold for firms defined as "technologically mature" (as steel, oil refining, or nonferrous metals), for which the announced change in R&D expenditure has a negative effect.

Public Policy and R&D Investment

In this section I examine a theoretical case for public support of R&D investment and present an overview of instruments of government support for R&D in Canada and other industrial countries. I also review various empirical methods of examining the effectiveness of public policies in support of R&D investment.

Rationale for Public Intervention

The case for government intervention in R&D activities is well known: the social rate of return from R&D is higher than the private rate of return, so if decisions on what R&D to undertake are left solely to private initiative and investment, resources will be underallocated to innovative activities. Several reasons have been cited for the disparity between social and private returns. These include externalities and information asymmetries.

EXTERNALITIES. The presence of spillovers prevents the R&D performer from fully appropriating the benefits associated with his or her R&D

activity. Because of large numbers either of generators of externalities or of those affected by the externalities, a privately negotiated settlement is almost never reached. The situation can be alleviated only by government action. The same argument for public intervention is sometimes termed the public-good nature of R&D capital. Once knowledge has been created, it is almost freely appropriable. Hence strong incentives for free ridership are created.

This line of reasoning has not escaped criticism. For example, Dasgupta and Stiglitz (1980) showed that firms would undertake socially excessive R&D expenditure in their attempts to deter entry to markets through patents. Their analysis, however, ignores both the positive and negative effects of R&D spillovers on incentives. Hirschleifer (1971) has also argued that R&D expenditure in general would be undertaken beyond the optimal level because too many firms would be fishing for the same piece of information. Spence (1984) also argued against restoring appropriability. He stated that restoring appropriability not only may create monopoly or monopoly power, but also it incorrectly prices the good that R&D has created. An alternative effect of nearly perfect appropriability, he argued, would be the creation of redundant and hence excessive levels of R&D at the industry level. Thus there is a tradeoff between positive incentives of appropriability on the one hand "and the efficiency with which the industry achieves the levels of cost reduction it actually does achieve, on the other" (Spence 1984: 102). Spillovers, therefore, have a positive partial effect on industry's costs and a negative effect on incentives. On the whole, Spence argued that potential industry performance is significantly better with high spillovers (or low appropriability) because the output R&D is essentially a public good, and if it is implicitly priced as a private good, the performance of the system will be adversely affected. Cohen and Levinthal (1989) also discount the negative effect of spillovers on incentives. They argued that other firms' spillovers provide a firm with greater incentive to conduct its own R&D, because only through its own R&D can a firm tap into the knowledge and associated benefits generated by other firms.

The validity of this argument is considerably weakened by patents and the requirement to have internal R&D capability to benefit from external R&D knowledge. The existing patent systems confer property rights for defined periods, thereby restricting the use of new knowledge. Also, the patent system ensures greater social benefits with wider use of knowledge after the expiration of the initial patent. The problem is that patents do not necessarily confer perfect appropriability because patents can be invented around (that is, minor variations can be made to existing patents to create new patents), or in some instances they may not withstand a legal challenge or may simply be unenforceable because of the difficulty of establishing infringement. Levin (1986), however, notes that substantial resources are required to imitate an innovation even if it is not legally protected. Furthermore, a mere failure of the patent system to confer full appropriability does not necessarily represent a policy problem. In fact strengthening the patent system might result in almost complete capture of property rights. As a result, too much effort might be devoted to patents to capture any rents associated with future use of an invention. In any case powerful incentives to innovate, even in the absence of a patent system, exist in many high-technology industries, for example, the aircraft industry, in which multicomponent systems provide built-in protection against imitation.

INFORMATION ASYMMETRIES. It is frequently argued that returns from R&D investment are more uncertain than they are from traditional investment. As a result, risk-averse individuals discount these returns more heavily than may be warranted by proper calculation of riskiness of investment. Thus R&D investment is underprovided by the private sector.

The above argument is plausible but may be of minor importance because the differentials in after-tax returns from R&D are often greater than the returns from traditional investment by margins that could not be explained by risk premium alone. Furthermore, most firms undertake a diversified portfolio of R&D projects and as a result, although the risk of failure of any particular project may be quite large, the group of projects as a whole may hold little (average) risk.

Perhaps the most powerful argument for public support of R&D is the presence of asymmetric information. The presence of asymmetric information between R&D performer and financier limits the financing of R&D projects. Project success warrants secrecy, but project financing requires release of vital information. As a result many projects lapse, lacking financing. The asymmetric information in the R&D output market also limits the R&D firm's ability to achieve the licensing gains from trade.

Tax Incentives for R&D in Large Industrial Societies

Government endeavors to stimulate R&D activities take a variety of forms. These include patent protection; government-owned laboratories; government contracts for new products and processes; grants and loans; technical information services; support of education and training of scientists, engineers, and technicians; and tax incentives. Here, the focus is on the provisions in the tax code that are intended to stimulate R&D spending by corporations in the private sector.

The government of Canada has a long history of using the tax code to encourage R&D investment. A few significant landmarks are reported below.

BRIEF HISTORY OF TAX INCENTIVES FOR R&D.

Pre-1961   Current expenditure on R&D was made fully deductible in the year incurred.

One-third of the capital expenditure on R&D during the two preceding years was deductible in the current year.

The total deduction for R&D was limited to 5 percent of the previous year's taxable income unless the expenditure was approved by Revenue Canada (the Canadian tax collection and administration department).

1961   Capital expenditure was made fully deductible in the year incurred or any year thereafter.

1962   The requirement for approval by authorities of expenditure in excess of 5 percent of previous year's taxable income was eliminated.

50 percent of an increase in R&D expenditure (current or capital) over the base, defined as expenditure in 1961, was deductible from taxable income.

1967   The 50 percent deduction for all R&D expenditure in excess of the 1961 base was replaced by grants under the Industrial Research and Development Incentives Act. This act provided a cash grant of 25 percent of capital expenditure and 25 percent of current expenditure in excess of the average expenditure made during the base period. The latter period was defined as the five years preceding the grant year. The 25 percent tax grant was nontaxable.

1975   The deferral privilege for capital R&D expenditure was extended to current expenditure. Now both current and capital R&D expenditure could be written off in the year incurred or any year thereafter.

1976   The Industrial Research and Development Incentives Act was repealed.

1977   The R&D investment tax credit was introduced. The credits ranged from 5 to 10 percent, depending on the region. The credit applied to all current and capital expenditure for R&D.

The higher (10 percent) credit was applied to R&D expenditure in the Atlantic provinces and the Gaspé area of Quebec.

1978   R&D investment tax credits were raised to 10 percent for most of Canada and 20 percent in Atlantic Canada and the Gaspé region, and a 25 percent credit for small business was introduced.

A tax allowance of 50 percent of total R&D expenditure in addition to the average amount over the previous three years was introduced.

1983   The rates of credit for scientific research expenditure were increased by 10 percentage points. The basic rate was raised to 20 percent of the R&D expenditure, except for expenditure made in the Atlantic provinces and the Gaspé, where it was 30 percent. The small business credit rate was increased to 35 percent.

The limit on the amount of tax credit a taxable firm could claim in a year was removed.

Unused credits were permitted to be carried forward for seven years and carried back three years to offset federal taxes. Forty percent of unused credits earned in the year by small businesses and 20 percent of those earned by large corporations could be refunded. This refundability provision was set to expire in May 1986.

The 50 percent additional allowance was eliminated.

As a temporary measure, tax credits not claimed by corporations were allowed to be transferred to individuals who purchased new issues of the corporation's stock.

As a temporary measure, a portion of the value of unused credits was paid in cash to nontaxable corporations and unincorporated businesses.

A new financing mechanism called Scientific Research Tax Credit (SRTC) was unveiled in April 1983 and made law in January 1984. Its principal elements were as follows:

- Investors earned the 50 percent tax credit by purchasing shares, or debt, or an interest in the products or revenues of the R&D performing company (whether related to R&D or not).
- For every dollar raised by the R&D corporation under such tax credit financing, the corporation was liable for a refundable tax equal to the credits given by the investors.
- The company performing the R&D was permitted, at any time after raising capital, to renounce its claim to R&D tax deductions and tax credits it could otherwise claim. The corporation performing R&D was able to claim a rebate of its refundable tax credit at the rate of 50 percent of the amount of R&D expenditure for which it renounced its claim to tax incentives.
- If the investor was an individual, the credit was set at 34 percent of the amount designated in respect of the qualifying investment made, to be offset against basic federal

taxes. The computation of provincial income taxes meant that a total effective rate of credit of approximately 50 percent was provided. For a corporate investor, the credit was 50 percent, to be applied against federal taxes.

1984   A moratorium on certain "quick flip" SRTC investments was announced on October 10, 1984. Nearly 60 percent of the SRTC claimed involved "quick flip" transactions, in which investors and the companies bought and sold the credits. In a typical quick flip transaction an investor would lend a research company $100, $55 of which was to be repaid on demand. The investor would then receive $50 from the federal government as a credit. After a short period, the investor's loan would be repaid. The repayment of $55 plus the receipt of $50 of the credit when the tax return was processed provided the investor with a gain of $5.

1985   The SRTC was repealed in May 1985.
Tax credits earned by small Canadian-controlled private corporations for current expenditure on R&D were made 100 percent refundable. This provision was made effective May 23, 1985, with no expiry date.
The provision that the expenditure eligible for the R&D incentives must be "wholly attributable" to R&D was replaced by a provision that an expenditure "all or substantially all" of which was attributable to R&D would qualify.
The term *scientific research* was changed to *scientific research and experimental development*. This change was made to recognize that the bulk of industrial R&D is concentrated on the experimental development of new products or processes rather than pure and applied research.

R&D TAX CREDITS CURRENTLY AVAILABLE IN CANADA. Section 37 of the Income Tax Act allows taxpayers to deduct all current and capital expenditure for R&D in the year in which it is incurred. In addition, an investment tax credit for R&D is also available to Canadian industry. The basic credit is 20 percent of the taxpayer's expenditure on R&D, except for expenditure made in the Atlantic provinces and the Gaspé, where it is 30 percent. A 35 percent credit applies on the first $2 million (1986 Canadian dollars) of current expenditure on scientific research and experimental development by small business.

Credits may be used to fully offset federal taxes otherwise payable. Any balance of the tax credit in the year may be carried back for three years or carried forward for five years to offset federal taxes. A portion of any credit that is unused in the year it is earned is refundable to businesses. Large corporations are entitled to a 20 percent refund of unused credits in the year, whereas small corporations and unincorporated businesses are entitled to a 40 percent refund.

Tax Incentives for R&D in Major Industrial Societies

In this section I present an overview of tax provisions relating to R&D investment in France, Germany, Japan, the United Kingdom, and the United States.

FRANCE. Government grants of up to 50 percent of the cost of a project are provided for R&D investment. For tax purposes the grant is treated as a loan rather than as income to the company. Expenditure for R&D is fully deductible in the year incurred. R&D plant and equipment investment also qualifies for accelerated depreciation. Firms that do R&D exclusively receive special tax treatment. Royalties and patent sales are not taxed if reinvested within three years.

GERMANY. All R&D expenditure can be deducted in the year incurred. Plant and equipment devoted to R&D are subject to accelerated depreciation allowances. A cash grant of 7.5 percent of R&D capital investment is available to qualifying R&D investment. Further cash or credit assistance is available to many R&D-intensive industries. Individual and corporate donations for scientific purposes are tax deductible, and corporate support of research organizations that execute a program of cooperative R&D for an industry receives a generous tax allowance.

JAPAN. All R&D expenditure and costs of developing patent rights can be either expensed immediately or amortized over several years. A 25 percent tax deduction is allowed on the R&D expenditure that represents an increase over the highest R&D expenditure incurred by the company in any year since 1967. Special accelerated depreciation allowances are provided to approved investments in new technology. Joint research associations in certain industries can immediately expense the cost of new machinery and equipment or a new facility. Special tax incentives are provided to small and medium-size enterprises. A large number of government agencies provide direct support for approved scientific projects.

The UNITED KINGDOM. R&D current and capital expenditure can be deducted in the year incurred. Corporate and individual donations for R&D do not qualify for tax deduction. Direct support for R&D investment is available from various government departments and agencies.

THE UNITED STATES. The U.S. government has tried to lower the cost of private R&D through a combination of tax policy, direct spending, and patent legislation.[16] Major tax incentives include, first, allowing firms to deduct qualified R&D expenses in the year incurred. Section 174 of the Internal Revenue Code permits business taxpayers to deduct all research or experimental expenditure in the year it is incurred. Businesses also have the option to capitalize R&D expenditure and amortize it over a five-year period or longer. Expenditure on capital assets such as land, building, and equipment used for R&D is not eligible for immediate expensing. Because R&D expenditure is presumed to lead to an asset with a useful life in excess of one year, immediate expensing provides a tax incentive. A second incentive gives firms a 25 percent credit on increases in qualified research and experimentation (R&E) expenses above the previous three years' average, and a third incentive permits firms to fund research through limited partnership. It is to be noted that the U.S. tax code makes a distinction between basic research and product development. Whereas basic research costs are eligible for the credit and other tax benefits, only development costs incurred in the course of experimentation in the laboratory are eligible for special tax consideration. Other development costs must be capitalized.

The R&D tax credit passed by Congress in 1981 has been criticized on the grounds that it provides only weak incentives for research and could potentially induce firms to defer such projects. For example, a firm that steadily increases its R&D spending will receive less credit per dollar of incremental R&D spending than the firm that raises its R&D spending for only one year. Perhaps most important, the credit does not help firms reverse a downward trend or even a one-year drop in R&D spending. Fifteen percent of firms fit into this category. The tax credit is also not of much use to new firms.

The R&D limited partnership reduces the cost of R&D to high-technology firms by permitting tax shelters for R&D projects. An R&D limited partnership is typically sponsored by a corporation that may also serve as a general partner, seeking to fund research projects without incurring the disadvantages of more conventional financing. The limited partners, who are usually persons in high tax brackets, provide the funds; they can immediately deduct most of their investment from income and receive their return in the form of tax-advantaged long-term capital gain. Like most such shelters, R&D limited partnerships use the tax laws to drive a wedge between what investors earn and what the issuing firms must pay; the wedge is revenue loss to the treasury. If the research pays off, the revenue loss may be as high as 80 percent of the research costs.

Scientific research organizations are also exempted from paying taxes as a measure of support for scientific research carried out by these institutions. In addition, individual and corporate contributions to such organizations are tax deductible up to certain limits.

The U.S. tax code also treats revenues from the sale of patents by individual investors as capital gains, and thus such revenues qualify for preferential tax treatment. Corporate transactions of patents and licenses also frequently qualify for capital gains treatment.

A disproportionate share of R&D investment is done by small businesses in the United States. Thus the preferential tax treatment of small firms as opposed to large firms indirectly provides incentives for R&D investment. Finally, almost all incentives for investment also encourage R&D investment and affect the speed at which technical change is embodied in capital stock.

Tax Policy and the Cost of R&D Capital

It was noted in the previous section that two types of tax incentives are currently available in Canada. First, the cost of R&D capital is reduced by allowing immediate expensing of R&D expenditure. This is equivalent to a 100 percent capital consumption allowance. Second, current and capital R&D expenditure is eligible for a tax credit that varies by size of business and location of activity. Thus both measures lower the cost of R&D and provide incentives to undertake more of such investment. To understand the effects of these measures more clearly, consider a $1.00 expenditure on R&D. This expenditure would reduce the taxable income by $1.00, and assuming a marginal tax rate of 46 percent, the tax deduction will be $0.46. The post-tax cost of a dollar of R&D expenditure is thus $0.54. Contrast this to the case in which R&D expenditure is eligible for a capital consumption allowance rate of 30 percent, and assume that future depreciation deductions are discounted at 15 percent. Under these assumptions, the present value of depreciation deductions is $0.67. The tax reduction is obtained by multiplying this number by the tax rate and equals $0.31. The post-tax cost of a dollar of R&D expenditure is then $0.69, which is greater than the $0.54 under the immediate expensing provision.[17]

Next, consider the combined effects of the deductibility provision and the tax credit on the cost of R&D capital. Suppose the credit rate is 10 percent. The deductibility provision in the absence of a tax credit reduces taxes by $0.46 per $1.00 ($1.00 x marginal tax rate) of R&D expenditure. The credit reduces the tax liability by $0.10 but reduces eligible R&D expenditure for deductibility purposes by the same amount. Thus the tax reduction from the deductibility provision in the presence of a 10 percent tax credit is $0.41 ($0.90 x $0.46), and the total tax reduction from both measures is $0.51. The tax credit, therefore, contributes about $0.06 to tax reduction per $1.00 of R&D expenditure. The post-tax cost of $1.00 of R&D capital under this scenario is $0.49. Thus the subsidy rate is more than $0.50 per $1.00 of R&D expenditure. According to Bernstein (1986a), the post-tax cost of a dollar of R&D expenditure is lowest for large nonmanufacturing industries in the Atlantic region (62 percent subsidy) and the highest for small firms anywhere in Canada (51 percent subsidy).

Although the rate of subsidy is important, the effectiveness of subsidy is also determined by the tax status of the firm. Incentives are much less attractive to firms in a nontaxable position. In 1980, such firms undertook 47 percent of total R&D capital expenditure

The Effect of Tax Incentives on Investment: A Survey of Empirical Approaches and Research Findings

Empirical approaches to evaluation of tax incentives have varied from opinion surveys to rigorously derived testable models and from partial equilibrium to general equilibrium analysis. In this section, I provide an overview of the principal approaches, note their key assumptions and caveats, and survey research findings of selected studies.

SURVEY OF FIRMS. Opinion surveys of company executives have frequently been used to evaluate the effectiveness of R&D tax incentives. A study by Mansfield and Switzer (1985), using Canadian data, represents an example of such an approach. The authors divided Canadian R&D firms into two groups: (a) the 65 corporations doing most of the R&D in 1981 and (b) the remaining 1,305 R&D-performing firms. They chose a stratified random sample of 55 firms and interviewed the company officials to ascertain their views on the effectiveness of the two R&D tax credits in place during the early 1980s. An analysis of these responses suggests that the incentive effect of the two tax credits was much smaller than the revenue forgone as a result of these measures ($50 million of additional R&D at a cost to the federal treasury of $130 million in 1982).

An objective assessment of the effect of tax measures is not possible through opinion surveys. Opinion surveys do not provide any data on observed behavior both before and after a policy change, and hence the validity of their results is doubtful.

ESTIMATION OF AD HOC AND ECLECTIC EQUATIONS. This approach usually specifies R&D spending as a function of a host of independent variables, including R&D tax credit. The selection of variables and specification of the model are most often based on a fishing expedition for a high coefficient of multiple determination, R^2.

Mansfield and Switzer (1985) specify an ad hoc model to estimate the effect of R&D tax credits on R&D spending by the Canadian industry. In their model, R&D spending by industry is a function of industry sales during the current year and a time trend. Parameters obtained in this equation were then related to the nature of prevailing tax incentives in each year. The results indicate that $132 million of federal tax expenditure for R&D produced $30 million of new R&D capital.

INVESTMENT MODELS. Five principal models have been used to analyze tax incentives.

- The flexible capital stock adjustment model, or the accelerator theory of investment
- The Q-theory model
- Forward-looking models
- Effective tax rate and return-over-cost models
- The production structure, or the adjustment cost, approach

A brief description of these approaches follows.

The flexible capital stock adjustment approach. The simple, or naive, form of the acceleration principle postulates a certain fixed relation between the desired capital stock and output. It is argued that tax incentives affect investment through changes in desired capital stock by reducing the relative price of capital. For illustrative purposes the Hall-Jorgenson approach is outlined here.

Employing a Cobb-Douglas production technology, one can obtain the desired capital stock, K, as follows:

$$K_t^* = \alpha \, (P_t \, Q_t \, / \, c_t)$$

where P = price of output; Q = quantity of output; c = user cost of capital; and α = elasticity of output with respect to capital. Net investment (I_t) is a weighted average of past changes in the desired capital stock, such that

$$I_t = \sum_{s=0}^{\alpha} w_s \, \Delta K_{t-s}^* \, .$$

By imposing restrictions on the sequence (w_s), net investment becomes

$$I_t = w_0 \, \Delta K_t^* + w_1 \, \Delta K_{t-1}^* - w_2 \, I_{t-1}.$$

Recalling the equation for the desired capital stock, one can write the investment function as follows:

$$I_t = \alpha \, w_0 \, \Delta \frac{P_t \, Q_t}{c_t} + \alpha \, w_1 \, \Delta \frac{P_{t-1} Q_{t-1}}{c_{t-1}} - w_2 I_{t-1} + \varepsilon_t$$

where e_t is the error term.

Changes in tax incentives alter the user cost of capital, which in turn changes the desired stock of capital. Changes in the desired stock of capital then lead to changes in net investment (or disinvestment).

Braithwaite (1975), Harman and Johnson (1978), and May (1979) used this general approach in evaluating Canadian tax incentives. Braithwaite and May focused on the effect of the accelerated capital consumption allowances and reduced corporate tax rates for manufacturing and processing. Harman and Johnson looked at the capital consumption allowances and deferred allowances. Harman and Johnson employed the Coen model, a variant of the Hall-Jorgenson model that better specifies the production technology and the speed of adjustment in response to changes in the user cost of capital. Harman and Johnson concluded that, although the incentives influence investment, the associated revenue loss is often greater than the investment gains.

The Q-theory approach. The essence of James Tobin's Q-theory model is that a firm will invest as long as a dollar spent buying capital raises the market value of the firm by more than one dollar. Because Q is defined as the ratio of the market value of existing capital to its replacement cost, then investment will take place as long as Q is greater than unity.

Summers (1981) employed this general approach to examine the effect of various tax policies on investment. He assumes constant returns to scale technology and a constant ratio of debt to capital stock (b).

Firms maximize the market value of equity and bonds at time t:

$$V_t = \int_{t=0}^{\infty} \frac{(1-\theta)}{(1-c)} \, \mathrm{DIV}_s \, \mu_s \, ds + B_t$$

where

θ	= dividend tax rate
c	= capital gains tax rate
DIV_s	= after-tax profits minus investment expenses

$$[\, pF(K, L) - wL - pbK\,]\, (i - \tau) - (1 - \mathrm{ITC} - z - b)$$

$$+\, (1 - \tau)\, \phi\, p_k\, I \,+\, p_k\, bK\, (\pi - \delta)$$

p	= overall price level
p_k	= nominal price of capital
i	= nominal interest rate
τ	= corporate tax rate
z	= present value of depreciation allowances on a dollar of new investment
ITC	= investment tax credit
b	= present value of depreciation allowances on existing capital
ϕ	= adjustment cost function
I	= investment
π	= inflation rate

δ = rate of economic depreciation of the capital stock

$$\mu_s = \exp \int_t^s -\frac{(\rho + \pi)}{(1 - c)}\, du$$

ρ = fixed real after-tax return.

Firms choose an investment and financial policy to maximize the value of equity and bonds, subject to the constraint that capital accumulation equals net investment. Solving the optimization problem generates the following investment function:

$$\frac{I}{K} = h \left[\frac{\dfrac{(V - B)(1 - c)}{pK(1 - \theta)} - 1 + b + \text{ITC} + z}{(1 - \tau)} \right] = h\,(Q).$$

If an adjustment cost function of the following form is employed:

$$\phi = \frac{B\!/\!2\,(I\!/\!K - v)^2}{I\!/\!K}$$

then an investment function that is linear in Q results:

$$\frac{I}{K} = v + \left(\frac{1}{B} \right) Q.$$

This is the basic equation estimated by Summers (1981).

Forward-looking models. The decision rule governing investment in forward-looking models is identical to that in the Q-theory, but the two theories differ in how the unobservable expectations are related to observable variables. Unobservable expectations have been defined in either two-step, one-step, or transformation procedures. The two-step procedure is based on a decomposition of the investment problem into expectation formation and, given these expectations, the decision to acquire investment goods. Expectations are based on lagged variables, and the parameters derived from expectations equations are used to forecast future variables that replace unobservable expectations. These variables are then used to estimate production and adjustment parameters.

Effective tax rate and return-over-cost models. Feldstein (1980) is the proponent of the effective tax rate approach to incentives evaluation. Feldstein posits that net investment is dependent on the net-of-tax real return to capital. Real return, net of taxes, depends on the effective tax rate, which is defined as the ratio of a comprehensive measure of all taxes assessed on capital income to operating income less depreciation.

The return-over-cost model (also presented by Feldstein) quantifies investment incentives by contrasting the maximum potential net return on a standard investment project with the cost of funds. The maximum potential net return is influenced by tax incentives. Whenever the maximum potential net return exceeds the cost of funds, firms have an incentive to acquire more capital.

The production structure, or the adjustment cost, approach. The essence of this approach is that capital is subject to adjustment costs in that investment causes output to be forgone when factors of production are diverted to install the additions to the capital stock. As a result, firms cannot move instantaneously to a new level of the capital stock but instead must adjust over time to the desired level. For this reason the capital input is termed a quasi-fixed factor, whereas the labor input (which adjusts instantaneously) is a variable factor.

To illustrate an application of this approach, a study by Bernstein (1984a, 1984b) is summarized here. Bernstein develops a dynamic model of corporate production, which integrates financial and production decisions. Output is a function of physical capital, R&D capital, labor, and time trend, where both capital inputs are subject to adjustment costs. The production technology is represented by

$$y(t) = F\left[L(t), K_r(t), K_p(t), I_p(t), I_r(t), t\right]$$

where F is the production function with the usual properties, y = input, L = labor, K_p = physical capital, K_r = R&D capital, I_p = physical investment, I_r = R&D investment, and t = time trend.

Firms minimize costs subject to appropriate restraints. Inverting the production function yields the labor requirement function:

$$L = G(K_p, K_r, I_p, I_r, y)$$

and so the cost minimization problem is:

$$\text{Min } I_r, I_p \int_0^\infty e^{-\rho t} [w_L\, G(K_p, K_r, I_p, I_r, y) + w_p K_p + w_r K_r]\, dt$$

$$\text{s.t.} \quad \dot{K}_i = I_i - \delta_i K_i \quad i = p, r \quad \left.\begin{array}{l} \\ \\ \end{array}\right\} \begin{array}{l}\text{capital} \\ \text{accumulation} \\ \text{conditions}\end{array}$$

$$K_i(0) = K_i^c > 0$$

where ρ = cost of equity capital; $w_{L,p,r}$ = factor prices on labor, physical capital, and R&D capital, respectively; and δ_i = the depreciation rate of the *i*th capital stock.

Solving the minimization problem generates a system of equations for L, K_p, and K_r. Bernstein estimates this system of three equations.

Bernstein (1986a) considered the effect of Canadian R&D tax incentives (the R&D investment tax credit and the special research allowance) on R&D investment. Note that this model could also be employed to analyze the effect of incentives on physical investment (see Bernstein 1986d). Bernstein used a pooled set of cross-section and time series data for twenty-seven firms for the period 1975–80. He evaluated the incentives in regard to increased R&D expenditure per dollar of lost revenue for a realistic range of price elasticity of product demand. He found that one dollar increase in tax expenditure resulted in more than one dollar of new R&D capital.

APPLIED GENERAL EQUILIBRIUM ANALYSIS. A large majority of complex interactions in an economy are assumed away by partial equilibrium analysis. An applied general equilibrium model, however, can provide a disaggregated view of the economy and thereby yield quantitative estimates of all important interactions. It is, therefore, a more valuable tool in assessing the relative merits of alternative tax policy changes.

Applied general equilibrium analysis entails several sequential steps. First, basic data are collected from a variety of sources. These data are then adjusted for microconsistency. Next, the choices of model, functional forms, and elasticity parameters are specified. Parameter values for model functions are then determined through calibration. A replication test is carried out to check that the calibrated parameter values are consistent with the original data on quantities and prices and the assumed model structure. Once this replication test is passed, a policy change is specified and a new (counterfactual) equilibrium is computed. Policy evaluation is then based on pairwise comparison between benchmark and new equilibrium.

The applied dynamic sequenced model developed by Hamilton, Shah, and Whalley (1986) estimates the effect of tax changes on investment, factor use, output, savings, public revenues, and overall welfare gains and losses. This model could be applied to evaluate the effect of R&D tax incentives.

Directions for the Present Study

The above discussion suggests that a production structure approach yields important insights into the effect of tax policy on business production, investment, and financing decisions. In this chapter, I specify a rigorous production structure framework and estimate it using flexible functional forms. The superiority of the empirical approach adopted in this chapter is demonstrated using theoretical criteria.

Tax Policy, Production Structure, and R&D Capital

In this chapter, I examine production relations in Canadian industries using a model that incorporates R&D capital as an input in addition to the usual factors of production—namely, physical capital, labor, and intermediate inputs. The analysis of production relations traditionally has been carried out through use of a production function approach by specifying output as a function of inputs and by using functional forms that impose restrictions on factor substitution possibilities. Recent developments in production economics have resulted in improved representation of production technology through use of the dual relation between cost and production and through use of flexible functional forms in econometric estimation.

Given a production function, there exists a corresponding cost function. This dual relation was formally established by Shephard's lemma. The duality theory implies that if the firm minimizes costs, if input prices are exogenous, and if the product transformation function—$T(Q, X) = 0$, where Q denotes output, and X denotes a vector of inputs—satisfies the usual regularity conditions (that is, strictly convex isoquants), there exists a dual cost function, $C(Q, P)$, where P is a price vector, which is as good a representation of the firm's production technology as the product transformation function and which satisfies the following regularity properties:

- C is nonnegative, differentiable, nondecreasing, linearly homogeneous, and concave on P for fixed nonnegative output Q.
- C is strictly positive for nonzero output Q and is strictly increasing in Q.

Thus for well-behaved relationships, one can deduce the structure of production technology directly from the cost function.

Works of Diewert (1971) and others have demonstrated that the application of the duality theorem and the specification of a flexible functional form eliminate the need for a priori restrictions on the production set. Furthermore, flexible functional forms allow us to test for separability (a firm's decision on the use of one or more inputs is independent of the rest of the inputs), homotheticity (relationship between scale and factor intensities), and consistency in aggregation. In view of these features, I have adopted a flexible functional form approach here.

From the duality correspondence between the production and cost functions, one can use either of the two methods of deriving input demand and cost share equations.

- Postulate a functional form for the production function, satisfying certain regularity conditions, and then solve for the output-constrained cost minimization problem, which is used in deriving the input demand function and hence the cost share equations.
- Postulate a differentiable functional form for the industry cost function, satisfying certain regularity conditions, and obtain the derived input demand functions by applying Shephard's lemma.

The cost function approach is more commonly used than a production function approach in estimating parameters because it has the following advantages:

- Estimation of parameters is much easier using a cost function than a production function.
- Tests on elasticities of substitution between factor inputs are more easily carried out with the cost function approach because the required standard errors are readily available.
- The production function method uses inputs as arguments, whereas cost function has output and input prices as arguments. Thus a cost minimization approach implicitly assumes that entrepreneurs make decisions on factor use according to exogenous prices, which makes the factor levels endogenous decision variables. Because the choice of inputs is endogenous to the firm and the production function method is concerned with the direct use of inputs, this approach needs endogenous treatment of the input variables, leading to a simultaneous estimation problem. The cost function method avoids this problem but requires that one assume that individual producers cannot influence prices.
- Given an exogenous shock on input prices, it would be easier to use an estimated cost function than a production function to examine the effect on factor demands.
- Recent productivity studies measure total factor productivity growth as a sum of technical change effects and scale effects. In order to estimate it, however, or to separate scale effects from technological change effects, an estimate of the scale elasticity is required. The scale elasticity can be obtained directly from an estimated cost function.
- Cost functions are homogeneous in prices regardless of the properties of homogeneity in the production function.
- Prices are likely to be less collinear than inputs. This implies that a cost function approach may encounter less multicollinearity than a production function approach.

Because of the above advantages, I have implemented the cost function approach in this study. Although the issue of choice among various flexible functional forms is far from settled, translog function is often shown to be preferable to alternative forms. I use the nonhomothetic translog cost function as the maintained hypothesis in this study.

The Model

A five-input production model is used in the specification of the translog cost function. The inputs are:

1. Capital stock—structures (land and buildings) (S)
2. Capital stock—machinery (M)
3. R&D capital stock (RDK)
4. Intermediate inputs (II)
5. Labor (L).

A translog cost function of the usual form incorporating these inputs can be represented as follows. In

$$C = \alpha_0 + \alpha_Q \ln Q + \tfrac{1}{2} \gamma_{QQ} \ln Q^2$$

$$+ \sum_{i=1}^{5} \alpha_i \ln P_i + \tfrac{1}{2} \sum_{i=1}^{5} \sum_{j=1}^{5} \gamma_{ij} \ln P_i \ln P_j$$

$$+ \sum_{i=1}^{5} \gamma_{Q_i} \ln Q \ln P_i$$

$$+ \phi_t\, t + \tfrac{1}{2}\, \phi_{tt}\, t^2$$

(5-1)
$$+ \sum_{i=1}^{5} \phi_{tP_i}\, t \ln P_i + \phi_{tQ} t \ln_Q + \varepsilon$$

where

C = total cost

$$= \sum_{i=1}^{5} P_i X_i$$

P_i = price of input i, where i = S, M, RDK, II, L
X_i = quantity of input i
t = technological change.

The translog cost function (equation 5-1) is a second-order logarithmic Taylor series expansion of a twice differentiable analytic cost function around unity. Cost-minimizing derived-demand equations for the various inputs are obtained from equation 5-1 by logarithmically differentiating this function with respect to input prices and applying Shephard's lemma, that is, $\partial C/\partial P_i = X_i$.

The derived-demand equations obtained from this process can be written as

$$(5\text{-}2) \quad \frac{\partial \ln C}{\partial \ln P_i} = \frac{P_i X_i}{C} = S_i = \alpha_i + \sum_{j=1}^{5} \gamma_{ij} \ln P_j + \gamma_{Q_i} \ln Q + \phi_i P_i t$$

where S_i is the share of the ith input in total cost. A "well-behaved" cost function must satisfy the following conditions:

- Hicks-Samuelson symmetry conditions

$$\gamma_{ij} = \gamma_{ji} \qquad \text{(Slutsky symmetry)}$$

- Linear homogeneity condition (or zero homogeneity in prices); that is, when all factor prices are doubled, the total cost will double. It can be shown that linear homogeneity implies the following restrictions:

$$\sum_{i=1}^{5} \alpha_i = 1$$

$$\sum_{j=1}^{5} \gamma_{ij} = 0$$

$$\sum_{i=1}^{5} \gamma_{ji} = 0$$

$$\sum_{i=1}^{5} \gamma_{Q_i} = 0$$

$$\sum_{i=1}^{5} \phi_i P_i = 0 \qquad \text{for all } i, j$$

- Monotonicity: the function must be an increasing function of input prices, that is,

$$\frac{\partial \log C}{\partial \log P_i} \geq 0, i = S, M, \text{RDK}, \text{II}, L.$$

Because of the homogeneity constraint, only $(n-1)$ share equations 5-2 are linearly independent and can be estimated simultaneously. Therefore one of the five share equations is to be deleted, leaving a system of five equations (the translog cost function and four share equations) to be estimated through use of either a nonlinear multivariate system estimator or Arnold Zellner's seemingly unrelated regression technique (see Kamenta 1971: 518).

ELASTICITIES OF SUBSTITUTION. The elasticities of substitution (σ_{ij}'s) are specific to pairs of inputs (for example, between inputs i and j) and as such summarize economic interrelations between two inputs only. In a two-input specification, (σ_{ij}) must denote substitutability, whereas in the case of more than two inputs at least one of them may denote either substitutability or complementarity. Estimates of partial elasticities of substitution σ_{ij} can be obtained directly from the parameters of the cost function as follows:

$$\sigma_{ij} = \frac{\sum_{i=1}^{5} P_i X_i}{X_i X_j} \cdot \frac{\partial^2 C}{\partial P_i \partial P_j} = \frac{C}{X_i X_j} \cdot \frac{\partial^2 C}{\partial P_i \partial P_j}.$$

The Hicks-Allen-Uzawa partial elasticity of substitution between inputs i and j can be written as

$$\sigma_{ij} = C C \cdot C_{ij} / C_i \cdot C_j$$

where

$$C_i = \frac{\partial C}{\partial P_i}$$

$$C_j = \frac{\partial C}{\partial P_j}$$

and

$$C_{ij} = \frac{\partial^2 C}{\partial P_i \partial P_j}.$$

For the translog cost function the parameters γ_{ij} can be shown to be related to σ_{ij} and the factor shares as follows:

$$\sigma_{ij} = 1 + (\gamma_{ij} / S_i S_j) \qquad \text{for all } i, j, i = j$$

$$\sigma_{ii} = (\gamma_{ii} + S_i^2 - S_i) / S_i^2 \qquad \text{for all } i.$$

The above elasticities are not constrained to be constant as in the Cobb-Douglas and the constant elasticity of substitution (CES) functions but depend on factor share and input coefficients.

ELASTICITIES OF FACTOR DEMAND. The price elasticities of input demand in respect to both own and other prices are also derived from the estimated gamma coefficients. The concepts of elasticity of substitution and elasticity of input demand are closely related. For the translog cost fraction the input demand elasticities are given as follows:

$$S_{ij} = S_j \sigma_{ij} \quad \text{(cross-price elasticity)}$$

and

$$S_{ii} = S_i \sigma_{ii} \quad \text{(own-price elasticity)}$$

The production structure specified in equations 5-1 and 5-2 imposes no a priori restrictions on the elasticities.

Empirical Estimation

The system of expressions specified in equations 5-1 and 5-2 was estimated by a nonlinear iterative system method using Gauss-Newton algorithm. The system converged in ten iterations with a criterion of .01. Parameter estimates are presented in table 5-1. Asymptotic *t*-statistics reported in the same table imply that most of the coefficients are significant. In particular, coefficients of most interest to us in this study, namely, γ_{RR}, γ_{QR}, and γ_Q are significant at the .05 level.

The parameter estimates presented in table 5-1 enable us to calculate both partial and total own-price elasticity of demand. The partial own-price elasticity of factor demand is given by

$$\xi_{ii} = \sigma_{ii} S_i = (\gamma_{ii} + S_i^2 - S_i) / S_i^2.$$

For R&D capital, partial own-price elasticity of demand can be written as

$$\xi_{RR}^c = S_R \sigma_{RR} = (\gamma_{RR} + S_R^2 - S_R) / S_R^2.$$

By substituting numerical values for the parameter,

$$\xi_{RR}^c = -0.8034.$$

The total own-price elasticity of R&D capital, however, is given by

$$\xi_{RR} = \xi_{RR}^c + \frac{\partial X_R}{\partial Q} \cdot \frac{P_Q}{X_R} \cdot S_R = \xi_{RR}^c + N_{RQ} \cdot S_R = -0.1615.$$

To obtain the effect of changes in tax credits on additional R&D expenditure, we also need to develop an estimate of the elasticity of the user

Table 5-1. Estimation Results

Parameter	Estimate	t-statistic
α_Q	1.718	12.4
γ_{QQ}	−0.080	−4.5
γ_{QS}	0.015	1.9
γ_{QM}	0.007	2.7
γ_{QI}	−0.014	−1.4
γ_{QR}	−0.003	−11.2
γ_{QL}	−0.004	−0.8
α_S	−0.285	−4.2
α_M	−0.135	−5.9
α_I	1.122	13.2
α_R	0.036	12.5
α_L	0.261	5.3
γ_{SS}	−0.062	−7.4
γ_{MM}	−0.001	−0.4
γ_{II}	−0.075	−5.3
γ_{RR}	0.001	5.1
γ_{LL}	−0.001	−3.0
γ_{SM}	−0.002	−0.5
γ_{SI}	0.065	7.0
γ_{SR}	0.001	5.1
γ_{SL}	−0.002	−3.0
γ_{MI}	0.004	0.6
γ_{MR}	0.001	5.1
γ_{ML}	−0.002	−3.0
γ_{IR}	−0.001	−2.0
γ_{IL}	0.007	3.0
γ_{RL}	−0.002	−3.0
ϕ_t	0.033	2.7
ϕ_{tt}	−0.001	−3.4
ϕ_{tS}	0.006	2.5
ϕ_{tM}	0.001	0.2
ϕ_{tI}	0.012	4.3
ϕ_{tR}	0.000	0.2
ϕ_{tL}	0.019	−9.0
ϕ_{tQ}	−0.006	−0.4
α_0	−3.600	−6.6

Note: Log of likelihood function = 3410.9.
Source: Model results.

cost of R&D capital with respect to the credit rate. This estimate can be obtained from the expression for the user cost of R&D capital given in appendix 5A (data appendix) as follows:

$$\frac{\partial W_R}{\partial V} \cdot \frac{V}{W_R} = -P_R\,(\rho + \delta_v)\,(1 - u_c)\,\frac{V}{W_R} = \Psi \text{ (say)}.$$

By substituting parameter values and the sample mean values in the above expression, we obtain $\Psi = -0.49248$.

Now additional R&D expenditure can be obtained by multiplying the R&D capital stock by Ψ and ξ_{RR}. Total R&D capital stock for 1983 is estimated to be $10 billion. Thus additional R&D expenditure = $10 \times (-0.16150)\,(-0.49248) = 0.7959$ billion = $795 million.

The total cost of R&D tax credits ($194 million) and R&D allowances ($247 million) in 1983 was $441 million. Thus additional R&D expenditure per dollar cost would be $1.80 (795/441 = $1.80). This suggests that R&D tax credits had a significant positive effect on R&D investment in Canada, and for every dollar of revenue forgone by the national treasury, $1.80 worth of additional R&D investment was undertaken. Thus R&D tax credit is a cost-effective instrument for the promotion of R&D in Canada.

Summary

This concluding section is a summary of the conclusions of earlier sections. I present the main themes that have emerged from an analysis of R&D and production structure, R&D and product market structure, rationale for public intervention for R&D investment, and the effectiveness of tax policies for R&D investment.

R&D Capital and the Structure of Production

R&D capital, as an input, includes scientific and engineering personnel, laboratories and equipment, and related inputs. R&D capital serves as an input in a joint production of multiple outputs, which include product and process development. R&D capital facilitates the mapping of technological possibilities into economic opportunities.

R&D takes time to accumulate and uses up scarce resources. It may take several years for a project to proceed from proposal to development stage. R&D capital accumulation serves to create new knowledge relating to new production techniques. Thus it ensures that the process of technical change is evolutionary and cumulative in character. Technological change widens production opportunities for the economy by enabling it to obtain greater outputs with given inputs or relatively cheaper inputs in place of relatively more expensive ones.

A special feature of R&D capital is the imperfect appropriability of returns as a result of intra- as well as interindustry capital spillovers. Spillovers diffuse knowledge by channels such as patents, cross-licensing agreements, R&D personnel mobility, and input purchases. The overall effect of R&D capital spillovers on incentives to undertake additional R&D investment is unclear in view of two opposing influences. First, the imperfect appropriability of returns from own R&D has a disincentive effect. Second, the desire to tap into the external knowledge and associated benefits provides incentives to undertake own R&D to develop an internal capability to benefit from externally generated knowledge. The net effect of the above varies by industry and explains the paradox posed by some R&D-intensive industries such as electronics and chemicals, where the high levels of spillovers do not seem to have any detrimental effect on the incentive to undertake additional R&D investment.

The following broad conclusions emerge from a survey of the available empirical evidence relating R&D capital to the structure of production.

- The overall adjustment process from R&D project initiation to product and process development takes three to five years.
- The marginal adjustment costs for R&D are higher than those for plant and equipment.
- The own-price elasticity of demand for R&D capital is less than unity regardless of the time period considered.
- R&D capital is a complement to physical capital but a substitute for labor in the long run.
- The long-run output elasticity of demand for R&D capital is close to unity. Short-run elasticities are much smaller than those for the long run.
- U.S. subsidiaries in Canada and Canadian-controlled private corporations show similar responses in the long run, but the effect of output changes on R&D capital in the short run is more pronounced in the Canadian-controlled companies.
- Output changes exert a much stronger influence on R&D capital than vice versa.
- The contribution of R&D capital to the productivity growth is inconclusive, but more recent work confirms U.S. findings of a positive and significant relation.
- R&D capital spillovers are large and significant, and as a result the social rate of returns on R&D projects exceeds the private returns by at least two-thirds of the private return in Canada.

R&D Capital and Product Market Structure

The value of cost-reducing R&D is determined by its profitability. Because private returns from R&D understate true social returns from such investments, R&D will be underprovided. Furthermore, because R&D investments often represent large fixed costs, market structure in R&D-intensive industries is going to be concentrated. The above situation is, however, not unique to R&D. What is unique about the R&D is the nature of spillovers. These spillovers reduce industry costs, but because they result in inappropriability of returns for the R&D performer, incentives to do R&D are reduced. Restoring appropriability does not help matters either because it results in industrial concentration, incorrect pricing of R&D, and resulting social costs. Perfect appropriability may also result in excessive R&D because too many firms may be fishing for the same information.[18]

The information asymmetry between an R&D performer and a financier distinguishes R&D investment from traditional risky investment. It is in the interest of the R&D performer to keep vital project information secret, but in the absence of detailed information, project financing may not be forthcoming. Asymmetric information also limits the R&D firm's ability to profit from its output.

The following broad conclusions emerge from a survey of empirical evidence on the relation between R&D capital and market structure.

- Success breeds success. Because learning involves costs, successful firms possess an advantage over their rivals in enjoying greater possibilities for further success. Thus monopoly persists in the R&D capital market. Past successes of R&D investments lead to greater current R&D efforts on the part of the successful firms. These firms, thereby, tend to produce further innovations and thus widen the gap between themselves and their rivals.
- The relation between R&D and firm size is much looser and more obscure than is implied by the usual statements of Schumpeterian hypothesis. Although much of the R&D capital is concentrated in large firms, it is more likely that they have become large because of their R&D successes than that they do more and more fruitful R&D because they are large.
- R&D capital and industrial concentration are positively correlated up to moderate levels of industrial concentration.
- Intraindustry spillovers drive a wedge between the social and the private return in an industry, as well as between the social rates across industries. Social rates of return diverge from the private rates by 50 to 150 percent, depending on the R&D intensiveness of the industry.
- In the presence of spillovers, society's demand for R&D capital at the existing market rates of return significantly exceeds private demand.

Public Policy and R&D Investment

It has been argued that the social rate of return from R&D is higher than the private rate of return either because of the presence of spillovers or because of information asymmetries. Because of the presence of spillovers, the R&D performer is not able fully to appropriate benefits associated with his or her activity. The presence of asymmetric information between R&D performer and financier limits financing of R&D projects. Project success warrants secrecy, but project financing requires release of vital information. As a result, many projects lapse, lacking financing. The asymmetric information in the R&D output market also limits the R&D firm's ability to achieve licensing gains from trade.

Most industrial nations see the need to intervene through the tax code to encourage R&D activities. Empirical evidence on the effectiveness of such initiatives is quite limited. In this chapter, I examined the effect of Canadian R&D tax credits on R&D investment using a production structure framework. This framework makes it possible to trace the effect of tax policies on production and investment decisions of an industry. The framework was implemented by using detailed data on inputs, outputs, factor and output prices, and the tax regime for eighteen Canadian industries for the period 1963 to 1983. Provisions in the tax code were used to develop estimates for the user cost of capital. A system of simultaneous equations incorporating the cost function and derived input demand functions was estimated by nonlinear interactive methods in translog form. The estimated cost function fitted the data well and was also "well-behaved." An analysis of parameter estimates for this cost function suggests that R&D tax credits had a significant positive effect on R&D investment in Canada and that for every dollar of revenue forgone by the national treasury, $1.80 worth of additional R&D investment was undertaken. These results indicate that a properly designed tax incentive can further public policy objectives cost-effectively.

Appendix 5A.   The Data

Most of the data used in this study are drawn from the Economic Council of Canada data bank for the Candide model and cover the period 1963 to 1983. A three-digit level of aggregation is used for a sample of eighteen industries. The following industry aggregates are included in the sample.

1.   Communications and transportation
2.   Crude petroleum
3.   Mining
4.   Utilities
5.   Furniture and fixtures
6.   Iron and steel
7.   Nonferrous metals

8. Metal fabricating
9. Machinery except electrical machinery
10. Nonauto transport equipment
11. Motor vehicles except parts and accessories
12. Electrical products
13. Nonmetallic mining products
14. Food and beverages
15. Rubber and plastics
16. Textiles
17. Petroleum and coal products
18. Chemical and chemical products

The following series were obtained either from the Candide model 3.0 data bank or from other sources in the Economic Council of Canada.

- Gross output in current dollars
- Gross output in constant (1971) dollars
- Man-hours: these series were developed by P. S. Rao, and the details of construction are given in Ostry and Rao (1980: 59–62).
- Wages
- Capital stock—structures
- User cost of structures: estimates are from Lodh (1984), who used a modified Hall-Jorgenson (1967) approach to take into account sector-specific depreciation rates, tax parameters, and debt-equity ratios.
- Capital stock—machinery and equipment
- User cost of machinery and equipment: estimates are from Lodh 1984.
- Intermediate inputs in current dollars
- Intermediate inputs in constant (1971) dollars
- Energy consumption in current dollars
- Energy price indexes: the data are from Rao and Preston 1983.

In addition, data were also collected or estimated for the following series:

- R&D price indexes: previous studies on the subject have invariably used the GNE implicit deflator, the GNE implicit price index for machinery and equipment, or the consumer price index to deflate R&D expenditure. The GNE deflator or the CPI are inappropriate deflators for the R&D expenditure because they relate to output measures of economic activity, whereas R&D serves as an input in the production process. The GNE implicit price index is also inappropriate as a deflator because more than 80 percent of R&D expenditure represents operating as opposed to capital expenditure. Fortunately, Bernstein (1986c) has developed price indexes for Canadian industrial R&D expenditure. These are the series used in this chapter.

- R&D tax credits, R&D allowances, and R&D expenditure: these series were compiled from various releases of Statistics Canada, Ottawa, and from unpublished data files of Statistics Canada.
- R&D capital stock: I used a perpetual inventory method to construct these data series (see Mohnen, Nadiri, and Prucha 1986). The benchmark data are obtained from the first-period R&D expenditure as follows:

Period 1:

R&D expenditure (1)/price index (1) = R&D investment (1)

R&D capital (1) = public investment (1)/($n + \delta$), where n = rate of growth of real output, and δ = depreciation rate

Period 2:

R&D capital stock (2) = R&D expenditure (2)/R&D price index (2) + (1 − δ) R&D capital (1) and so on.

- User cost of R&D capital (P_r): to estimate this I used the following formula (see Bernstein 1986a):

$$P_r = q(r + \delta)\left[(1 - u_c)(1 - v) - d_r\right]$$

where q = acquisition price of R&D capital, r = discount rate, δ = depreciation rate, u_c = corporate income tax rate, v = effective tax credit rate, and d_r = present value of investment allowances for R&D expenditure.
- Total cost: I estimated the total cost of output by applying input prices (user costs) to input quantities. For this purpose, five inputs are considered, namely, structure capital, machinery capital, R&D capital, intermediate inputs, and labor.

Appendix 5B. Definition of Scientific Research and Experimental Development

Regulation 2900 of the Canadian Income Tax Act (section 37) defined "scientific research and experimental development" (SRED) as a "systematic investigation or search carried out in a field of science or technology by means of experiment or analysis." The technology was defined as a systematic study of the application of scientific knowledge to industrial processes or product development.

(a)   basic research, namely, work undertaken for the advancement of scientific knowledge without a specific practical application in view,

(b)   applied research, namely, work undertaken for the advancement of scientific knowledge with a specific practical application in view, or

(c)   development, namely, use of the results of basic or applied research for the purpose of creating new, or improving existing materials, devices, products, or processes.

Activities in engineering or design, operations research, mathematical analysis or computer programming, and psychological research are eligible only if such activities are undertaken directly in support of basic or applied research or eligible development activities.

The following activities are excluded from SRED:

- Market research and sales promotion
- Quality control or routine testing of materials, devices, or products
- Research in the social sciences or the humanities
- Prospecting, exploring, or drilling for or producing minerals, petroleum, or natural gas
- The commercial production of a new or improved material, device, or product or the commercial use of a new or improved process
- Style changes
- Routine data collection

Revenue Canada circular 86-4 provides a detailed interpretation of section 37 and regulation 2900 of the Income Tax Act relating to tax provisions for scientific research and development.

Notes

The author is grateful to Jeffrey Bernstein and James Tybout for comments on earlier drafts of the chapter and to Francesca Recanatini for assistance in updating the literature review.

1. Conventionally defined, knowledge capital, or R&D capital inputs, primarily refers to the aggregation of expenditure for scientists, engineers, other R&D personnel, laboratories and associated equipment, and related items into a single or a few broad categories. See Bernstein and Nadiri (1987), Griliches (1979), and Mansfield (1968). Following Mansfield (1968), I define *research* in this chapter as original investigations directed to the discovery of new scientific knowledge, and I define *development* as entailing all technical activities geared to translating research findings into products and processes. Mansfield (1968) also argued that the amount of R&D capital in a particular industry depends on the resources devoted by firms, independent investors, and governments to the improvement of the industry's technology.

2. See Bernstein (1986a: 2–5).

3. Mohnen, Nadiri, and Prucha (1986) found that the rates of return (net of depreciation and adjustment costs) for R&D capital were higher than those for physical capital and that the rates for Japanese industries were higher than those for the United States and West Germany. One structural explanation concerns the financing of R&D. In 1975 only 1.7 percent of the gross expenditure on R&D performed by the manufacturing sector was funded by the government in Japan compared with 13.5 percent in Germany and 35.4 percent in the United States. The authors suggest that the absence of adequate government support may be a motivating factor for Japanese managers to direct their R&D efforts to more profitable projects. See Mohnen, Nadiri, and Prucha (1986: 765).

4. Similar results were found by Lichtenberg and Siegel (1991) for a more recent sample.

5. This discussion of spillover transmission covers only some better-known formal mechanisms and omits important informal processes. For example, the U.S. National Aerospace Program and the Pentagon do not sell anything to hospital supplies industries, but major advances in medical technology have been a spinoff of the R&D done by the former institutions. See Bernstein (1985a: 25–26) for further insights into R&D spillover mechanisms.

6. See also Nelson (1982).

7. Nelson (1982) notes that even rival firms make *logy* (theory as opposed to technique, which refers to a way of doing something) public, although the technique is kept private. This practice serves to reduce the deadweight loss associated with keeping R&D efforts completely secret.

8. In 1987 dollars.

9. See Nelson and Winter (1982: 130–31).

10. See Kamien and Schwartz (1975: 16–18); also see Kamien and Schwartz (1982: 75–84).

11. See Kamien and Schwartz (1975: 8–11); also see Dasgupta (1986: 8).

12. See Scherer (1967).

13. Following Mansfield (1968), I define *research* as original investigations directed to the discovery of new scientific knowledge, and *development* as entailing all technical activities geared to translating research findings into products.

14. A recent example of "inventing around" is Eastman Kodak's instant cameras. A superior court ruled that the cameras infringed on the patent rights of the Polaroid Corporation.

15. See also Spence (1984) for a formal treatment of this problem.

16. This section is based on United States Congressional Budget Office (1985: 19–29).

17. This section draws heavily from Bernstein (1986d).

18. See Scherer (1967).

References

Allen, J. A. 1967. *Studies in Innovation in the Steel and Chemical Industries.* Manchester, U.K.: Manchester University Press.

Aoki, Reiko. 1991. "R&D Competition for Product Innovation: An Endless Race." *AEA Papers and Proceedings* 81 (2): 252–56.

Arrow, K. J. 1962. "Economic Welfare and the Allocation of Resources of Invention." In Richard R. Nelson, ed., *The Rate and Direction of Inventive*

Activity: Economic and Social Factors. Universities–National Bureau of Economic Research Conference Series 13. Princeton, N.J.: Princeton University Press for the National Bureau of Economic Research.

Baily, Martin Neil, and Alok K. Chakrabarti. 1985. "Innovation and Productivity in U.S. Industry." *Brookings Papers on Economic Activity* (2): 609–32.

Belman, Dale, and John S. Heywood. 1990. "Market Structure and Worker Quality." *Journal of Industrial Economics* 39 (2): 155–68.

Bernstein, Jeffrey I. 1984a. "Corporate Ownership, Production, Tax Policy, and Research and Development." Report to the Department of Regional Industrial Expansion, Ottawa, Can.

———. 1984b. "Patents, Production, and Tax Incentives." Report to the Federal Department of Consumer and Corporate Affairs, Ottawa, Can.

———. 1985a. "R&D Spillovers, Rates of Return, and Costs of Production in Canadian Industries." Science Council of Canada, Ottawa, Can.

———. 1985b. "Research and Development, Patents, Production, and the Effectiveness of Grant and Tax Policies." In D. G. McFetridge, ed., *Technological Change in Canadian Industries*. Prepared for the Royal Commission on the Economic Union and Development Prospects for Canada. Toronto, Can.: University of Toronto Press.

———. 1986a. "The Effect of Direct and Indirect Tax Incentives on Canadian Industrial R&D Expenditures." *Canadian Public Policy* 12 (3): 438–46.

———. 1986b. "Issues in the Determinants and Returns to R&D Capital in Canada." Ministry of State for Science and Technology, Ottawa, Can.

———. 1986c. "Price Indexes for Canadian Industrial Research and Development Expenditures." Statistics Canada, Ottawa.

———. 1986d. *Research and Development, Production, Financing, and Taxation*. Toronto, Can.: Ontario Economic Council and University of Toronto Press.

———. 1988. "Costs of Production, Intra- and Interindustry R&D Spillovers: Canadian Evidence." *Canadian Journal of Economics* 12 (2); 324-47.

———. 1989. "The Structure of Canadian Interindustry R&D Spillovers and the Rates of Return to R&D." *Journal of Industrial Economics* 37 (3): 315–28.

Bernstein, Jeffrey I., and M. Ishaq Nadiri. 1987. "Corporate Taxes and Incentives and the Structure of Production: A Survey." In Mintz and Purvis, eds., *The Impact of Taxation on Business Activity*. John Deutsch Institute, Queen's University.

———. 1988. "Interindustry R&D Spillovers, Rates of Return and Production in High-Tech Industries." *American Economic Review Papers and Proceedings* 78 (2): 429-34.

———. 1989a. "Rates of Return, Research and Development, and the Structure of Production: Cross Section and Time Series Evidence." In B. Raj, ed., *Advances in Econometrics and Modelling*. London: Kluwer.

———. 1989b. "Research and Development and Intraindustry Spillovers: An Empirical Application of Dynamic Duality." *Review of Economic Studies* 56 (2): 249–67.

Bound, John. 1984. "Who Does R&D and Who Patents?" In Zvi Griliches, ed., *Research and Development, Patents, and Productivity*. Chicago, Ill.: University of Chicago Press for the National Bureau of Economic Research.

Braithwaite, Carleton. 1975. *The Effects of Recent Tax Policy Changes on Investment in Canadian Manufacturing: Further Results*. Ottawa: Economic Council of Africa.

Chan, Su Han, John D. Martin, and John W. Kensinger. 1990. "Corporate Research and Development Expenditures and Share Value." *Journal of Financial Economics* 26 (2): 255–76.

Charos, Evangelos N., and Evangelos O. Simos. 1988. "The Effect of Human Capital and R&D upon International Trade Flows: Evidence from a Multi-input, Multi-output Model for the United States." *Weltwirtschaftliches Archiv* 124 (4): 701–12.

Chen, Mah-Lih. 1991. "The Role of R&D Subsidies When Incomplete Information Is an Entry-Barrier." *Journal of International Economics* 31 (3-4): 251–70.

Clark, K., and Zvi Griliches. 1984. "Productivity Growth and R&D at the Business Level: Results from the PIMS Data Base." In Zvi Griliches, ed., *Research and Development, Patents, and Productivity*. Chicago, Ill.: University of Chicago Press for the National Bureau of Economic Research.

Cohen, Wesley M., and Daniel A. Levinthal. 1989. "Innovations and Learning: The Two Faces of Research and Development." *Economic Journal* 99 (September): 569–96.

Comanor, William S. 1964. "Research and Competitive Product Differentiation in the Pharmaceutical Industry in the United States." *Economica* 31 (November): 379–80.

———. 1967. "Market Structure, Product Differentiation, and Industrial Research." *Quarterly Journal of Economics* 81:639–57.

Comanor, William S., and Frederic M. Scherer. 1969. "Patent Statistics as a Measure of Technical Change." *Journal of Political Economy* 77 (3): 392–98.

Dasgupta, Partha. 1986. "The Theory of Technological Competition." In Joseph E. Stiglitz and G. Frank Mathewson, eds., *New Developments in the Analysis of Market Structure*. Cambridge, Mass.: MIT Press.

Dasgupta, Partha, and J. E. Stiglitz. 1980. "Industrial Structure and the Nature of Innovative Activity." *Economic Journal* 90 (358): 266–93.

Diewert, W. E. 1971. "An Application of the Shephard Duality Theorem: A Generalized Leontief Production Function." *Journal of Political Economy* 79(3): 481–507.

DiMasi, Joseph A., Ronald W. Hansen, Henry G. Grabowski, and Louis Lasagna. 1991. "Cost of Innovation in the Pharmaceutical Industry." *Journal of Health Economics* 10 (2): 107–42.

Englander, Steven A., Robert E. Evenson, and Masaharu Hanazaki. 1988. "R&D, Innovation and the Total Factor Productivity Slowdown." *OECD Economic Studies* (11): 7–42.

Evenson, Robert E. 1984. "International Invention: Implications for Technology Market Analysis." In Zvi Griliches, ed., *Research and Development, Patents, and Productivity*. Chicago, Ill.: University of Chicago Press for the National Bureau of Economic Research.

———. 1991. "Patent Data by Industry: Evidence for Invention Potential Exhaustion?" In *Technology and Productivity: The Challenge for Economic Policy*. Paris: OECD.

———. 1993. "Patents, R&D and Invention Potential: International Evidence." *AEA* Papers and Proceedings 83 (2): 463–68.

Feldstein, Martin. 1980. "Fiscal Policies, Inflation, and Capital Formation." *American Economic Review* (September): 636–50.

Fellner, W. J. 1951. "The Influence of Market Structure on Technological Progress." *Quarterly Journal of Economics* 65 (1): 556–77.

Freeman, Christopher. 1965. "Research and Development in Electronic Capital Goods Industry." *National Institute Economic Review* (United Kingdom) 34 (November): 40–91.

Globerman, Steven. 1972. "The Empirical Relationship between R&D and Industrial Growth in Canada." *Applied Economics* 4 (3): 181–95.

————. 1973. "Market Structure and R&D in Canadian Manufacturing Industries." *Quarterly Review of Economics* 13 (2): 59–67.

Goto, Akira, and Kazuyuki Suzuki. 1989. "R&D Capital, Rate of Return on R&D Investment, and Spillover of R&D in Japanese Manufacturing Industries." *Review of Economics and Statistics* 71 (4): 555–64.

Grabowski, Henry G. 1968. "The Determinants of Industrial Research and Development: A Study of the Chemical, Drug, and Petroleum Industries." *Journal of Political Economy* 76 (2): 292–306.

Griliches, Zvi. 1964. "Research Expenditures, Education, and the Aggregate Agricultural Production Function." *American Economic Review* 54 (6): 961–74.

————. 1973. "Research Expenditures and Growth Accounting." In B. R. Williams, ed., *Science and Technology in Economic Growth*. New York: Halstead Press.

————. 1979. "Issues in Assessing the Contribution of Research and Development to Productivity Growth." *Bell Journal of Economics* 19 (1): 92–116.

————. 1980a. "Research and Development and the Productivity Slowdown." Papers and Proceedings. *American Economic Review* 70 (2): 343–48.

————. 1980b. "Returns to Research and Development in the Private Sector." In J. W. Kendrick and B. N. Vaccara, eds., *New Developments in Productivity Measurement and Analysis*. Chicago, Ill.: University of Chicago Press for the National Bureau of Economic Research.

————. 1986. "Productivity, R&D, and Basic Research at the Firm Level in the 1970s." *American Economic Review* 76 (1): 141–54.

————. 1989. "Patents: Recent Trends and Puzzles." *Brookings Papers on Economic Activity* (Special issue): 291–319.

————. 1990. "Patent Statistics as Economic Indicators: A Survey." *Journal of Economic Literature* 28 (December): 1661–1707.

————. 1994. "Productivity, R&D, and the Data Constraint." *American Economic Review* 84 (1): 1–23.

Griliches, Zvi, and Frank R. Lichtenberg. 1984a. "Interindustry Technology Flows and Productivity Growth: A Re-examination." *Review of Economics and Statistics* (May): 324–29.

————. 1984b. "R&D and Productivity Growth at the Industry Level: Is There Still a Relationship?" In Zvi Griliches, ed., *Research and Development, Patents, and Productivity*. Chicago, Ill.: University of Chicago Press for the National Bureau of Economic Research.

Griliches, Zvi, and Jacques Mairesse. 1984. "Productivity and R&D at the Firm Level." In Zvi Griliches, ed., *Research and Development, Patents, and Productivity*. Chicago, Ill.: University of Chicago Press for the National Bureau of Economic Research.

Grossman, Gene M., and Carl Shapiro. 1974. "Dynamic R&D Competition." National Bureau of Economic Research Working Paper. Cambridge, Mass.

Hall, Robert E., and Dale W. Jorgenson. 1967. "Tax Policy and Investment Behavior." *American Economic Review* 57 (June): 391–414.

Hamberg, Daniel. 1966. In *Economic Concentration, Part 3: Concentration, Invention, and Innovations.* Hearings before the Subcommittee on Anti-Trust and Monopoly, U.S. Senate.

Hamilton, Bob, Anwar Shah, and John Whalley. 1986. *A Dynamic General Equilibrium Model for Corporate Tax Policy Evaluation in Canada.* Ottawa: Government of Canada, Department of Finance, Tax Policy and Legislation.

Hansen, R. W. 1979. "The Pharmaceutical Development Process: Estimates of Current Development Costs and Times and the Effects of Regulatory Changes." In R. I. Chien, ed., *Issues in Pharmaceutical Economics.* Lexington, Mass.: Lexington Books.

Harman, Francis J., and James A. Johnson. 1978. "An Examination of Government Tax Incentives for Business Investment in Canada." *Canadian Tax Journal:* 691–97.

Hartwick, J., and B. Ewan. 1983. "On Gross and Net Measures of Sectoral R&D Intensity for the Canadian Economy." Queen's University, Kingston, Ont., Can.

Hirschleifer, Jack. 1971. "The Private and Social Value of Information and the Reward of Inventive Activity." *American Economic Review* 61 (4): 561–74.

Horowitz, Ira. 1962. "Farm Size and Research Activity." *Southern Economic Journal* 28 (January): 298–301.

Howe, J., and D. G. McFetridge. 1976. "The Determinants of R&D Expenditures." *Canadian Journal of Economics* 9 (1): 57–71.

Isaac, Mark R., and Stanley S. Reynolds. 1988. "Appropriability and Market Structure in a Stochastic Invention Model." *Quarterly Journal of Economics* 104 (4): 647–71.

Jaffe, Adam B. 1986. "Technological Opportunity and Spillovers of Research and Development: Evidence from Firms' Patents, Profits, and Market Value." *American Economic Review* 76 (5): 984–1001.

———. 1988. "Demand and Supply Influences in R&D Intensity and Productivity Growth." *Review of Economics and Statistics* 70 (3): 431–37.

Kamenta, Jan. 1971. *Elements of Econometrics.* New York: Macmillan.

Kamien, Morten I., and Nancy L. Schwartz. 1975. "Market Structure and Innovation: A Survey." *Journal of Economic Literature* 13 (1): 1–37.

———. 1982. *Market Structure and Innovation.* Cambridge University Press.

Kelly, Thomas M. 1969. "The Influence of Size and Market Structure on the Research Efforts of Large Multiple-Product Farms." Ph.D. dissertation, Oklahoma State University.

Kortum, Samuel. 1993. "Equilibrium R&D and the Patent-R&D Ratio: U.S. Evidence." *AEA Papers and Proceedings* 83 (2): 450–57.

Lach, Saul, and Mark Schankerman. 1989. "Dynamics of R&D and Investment in the Scientific Sector." *Journal of Political Economy* 97 (4): 880–904.

Lane, Sarah J. 1991. "The Determinants of Investment in New Technology." *AEA Papers and Proceedings* 81 (2): 262–65.

Levin, Richard C. 1986. "New Look at the Patent System." *American Economic Review, Papers and Proceedings* 76 (2): 199–202.

Levin, Richard C., and P. C. Reiss. 1984. "Tests of a Schumpeterian Model of Research and Development and Market Structure." In Zvi Griliches, ed., *Research and Development, Patents, and Productivity.* Chicago, Ill.: University of Chicago Press for the National Bureau of Economic Research.

Levy, David M., and Nestor E. Terleckyj. 1983. "Effects of Government R&D Investment and Productivity: A Macroeconomic Analysis." *Bell Journal of Economics* (Autumn): 551–61.

Lichtenberg, Frank R. 1984. "The Relationship between Federal Contract R&D and Company R&D." *American Economic Review* (May): 73–78.

Lichtenberg, Frank R., and Donald Siegel. 1991. "The Impact of R&D Investment on Productivity—New Evidence Using Linked R&D-LRD Data." *Economic Inquiry* 29 (April): 203–28.

Link, Albert N. 1978. "Optimal Firm Size for R&D Innovations in Electric Utilities." *Journal of Economics and Business* 31 (1): 52–56.

Lithwick, N. H. 1969. *Canada's Science Policy and the Economy.* Toronto, Can.: Methuen.

Lodh, B. K. 1984. "Disaggregated Investment Functions of Canadian Non-Residential Business Sector, 1961–81: Candide Model 3.0." Economic Council of Canada, Ottawa.

Longo, F. 1984. "Industrial R&D and Productivity in Canada." Science Council of Canada, Ottawa.

Mairesse, Jacques, and Alan K. Siu. 1984. "An Extended Accelerator Model of R&D and Physical Investment." In Zvi Griliches, ed., *Research and Development, Patents, and Productivity.* Chicago, Ill.: University of Chicago Press for the National Bureau of Economic Research.

Mansfield, Edwin. 1965. "Rates of Return from Industrial Research and Development." *American Economic Review* 55 (2): 310–22.

———. 1968. *Industrial Research and Technological Innovation.* New York: Norton.

———. 1980. "Basic Research and Productivity Increase in Manufacturing." *American Economic Review* 70:863–73.

———. 1984. "R&D and Innovation: Some Empirical Findings." In Zvi Griliches, ed., *Research and Development, Patents, and Productivity.* Chicago, Ill.: University of Chicago Press for the National Bureau of Economic Research.

Mansfield, Edwin, and Lorne Switzer. 1985. "How Effective Are Canada's Direct Tax Incentives for Research and Development?" *Canadian Public Policy* (June): 241–46.

Mansfield, Edwin, John Rapoport, Anthony Romeo, Samuel Wagner, and George Beardsley. 1977. "Social and Private Rates of Return from Industrial Innovations." *Quarterly Journal of Economics* 91 (2): 221–40.

May, Douglas. 1979. "Investment Incentives as Part of an Industrial Strategy." *Canadian Public Policy* 5 (1): 70–79.

Mellor, John, and John E. Tilton. 1971. *International Diffusion of Technology: The Case of Semi-Conductors.* Washington, D.C.: Brookings Institution.

Minasian, J. 1969. "Research and Development Production Functions and Rates of Return." *American Economic Review* 59 (2): 80–85.

Mintz, Jack M., and Douglas D. Purvis, eds. 1987. *The Impact of Taxation on Business Activity.* Kingston, Ont., Can.: Queen's University, John Deutsch Institute for the Study of Economic Policy.

Mohnen, P. A., M. I. Nadiri, and I. R. Prucha. 1986. "R&D, Production Structure, and Rates of Return in the U.S., Japanese, and German Manufacturing Sectors." *European Economic Review* 30 (4): 749–71.

Mowery, David C. 1983a. "The Relationship between Intrafirm and Contractual Forms of Industrial Research in American Manufacturing, 1900–1940." *Explorations in Economic History* 20 (4): 351–74.

———. 1983b. "Industrial Research and Firm Size, Survival, and Growth in American Manufacturing, 1921–1946: An Assessment." *Journal of Economic History* 43 (4): 953–80.

Nadiri, M. I. 1980. "Contributions and Determinants of Research and Development Expenditures in the U.S. Manufacturing Industries." In G. M. von Furstenberg, ed., *Capital, Efficiency, and Growth*. Cambridge, Mass.: Ballinger.

Nadiri, M. I., and G. C. Bitros. 1980. "Research and Development Expenditures and Labor Productivity at the Firm Level: A Dynamic Model." In J. W. Kendrick and B. N. Vaccara, eds., *New Developments in Productivity Measurement*. Chicago, Ill.: University of Chicago Press for the National Bureau of Economic Research.

Nadiri, M. I., and M. A. Schankerman. 1981. "Technical Change, Returns to Scale, and the Productivity Slowdown." *American Economic Review* 71 (2): 314–19.

Nakao, Takeo. 1989. "Cost-reducing R&D in Oligopoly." *Journal of Economic Behavior and Organization* 12 (1): 131–48.

Nelson, Richard R. 1959. "The Simple Economics of Basic Scientific Research." *Journal of Political Economy* 67 (3): 297–306.

———. 1982. "The Role of Knowledge in Research and Development Efficiency." *Quarterly Journal of Economics* 97 (3): 453–70.

Nelson, Richard R., and Sidney Winter. 1982. "The Schumpeterian Trade-Off Revisited." *American Economic Review* 72:114–32.

Ostry, S., and P. S. Rao. 1980. "Productivity Trends in Canada." In J. Kendrick, ed., *Lagging Productivity Growth: Causes and Remedies*. Cambridge, Mass.: Ballinger.

Pakes, Ariel. 1984. "Patents, Research and Development, and the Stock Market Rate of Return: A Summary of Some Empirical Results." In Zvi Griliches, ed., *Research and Development, Patents, and Productivity*. Chicago, Ill.: University of Chicago Press for the National Bureau of Economic Research.

Pakes, Ariel, and M. Schankerman. 1984. "The Rate of Obsolescence of Patents, Research Gestation Lags, and the Private Rate of Return to Research Resources." In Zvi Griliches, ed., *Research and Development, Patents, and Productivity*. Chicago, Ill.: University of Chicago Press for the National Bureau of Economic Research.

Pavitt, Keith, and Solomon Wald. 1971. *The Conditions for Success in Technological Innovations*. Paris: OECD.

Philips, Almartin. 1966. "Patents, Potential Competition, and Technical Progress." *American Economic Review* 56:301–10.

Postner, H., and L. Wesa. 1983. *Canadian Productivity Growth*. Study prepared for the Economic Council of Canada. Ottawa: Ministry of Supply and Services.

Rao, P. S., and R. S. Preston. 1983. "Inter-Factor Substitution and Total Factor Productivity Growth: Evidence from Canadian Industries. Discussion Paper 242. Economic Council of Canada, Ottawa.

Rasmussen, J. 1973. "Applications of a Model of Endogenous Technical Change to U.S. Industry Data." *Review of Economic Studies* 40 (2): 225–38.

Ravenscraft, D., and F. M. Scherer. 1982. "The Lag Structure of Returns to Research and Development." *Applied Economics* 14 (6): 603–20.

Reinganum, J. 1981. "Dynamic Games of Innovation." *Journal of Economic Theory* 25 (1): 21–41.

Romer, Paul M. 1990. "Endogenous Technological Change." *Journal of Political Economy* 98 (1): S71–S102.

Rosenberg, Joel B. 1976. "Research and Market Share: A Reappraisal of the Schumpeter Hypothesis." *Journal of Industrial Economics* 25 (2): 101–12.

Scherer, Frederick M. 1967. "Market Structure and the Employment of Scientists and Engineers." *American Economic Review* 57 (3): 524–31.

———. 1980. *Industrial Market Structure and Economic Performance.* 2d ed. Chicago, Ill.: Rand-McNally.

———. 1982. "Interindustry Technology Flows and Productivity Growth." *Review of Economics and Statistics* 64 (4): 627–34.

———. 1983a. "Concentration, R&D, and Productivity Change." *Southern Economic Journal* (July): 221–25.

———. 1983b. "The Propensity to Patent." *International Journal of Industrial Organizations* 107–28.

———. 1983c. "R&D and Declining Productivity Growth." *American Economic Review* (May): 215–18.

Schmookler, J. 1966. *Invention and Growth.* Cambridge, Mass.: Harvard University Press.

Schumpeter, J. A. 1950. *Capitalism, Socialism, and Democracy.* New York: Harper.

———. 1966. *The Theory of Economic Development.* Oxford, U.K.: Oxford University Press.

Schwartz, S. I. 1983. *An Assessment of the Impact of R&D in Canadian Manufacturing.* Vancouver, Can.: University of British Columbia.

Scott, John T. 1984. "Firm versus Industry Variability in R&D Intensity." In Zvi Griliches, ed., *Research and Development, Patents, and Productivity.* Chicago, Ill.: University of Chicago Press for the National Bureau of Economic Research.

Shapiro, Carl. 1985. "Patent Licensing and R&D Rivalry." *American Economic Review* (May): 25–30.

Shevlin, Terry. 1991. "The Valuation of R&D Firms with R&D Limited Partnerships." *Accounting Review* 66 (1): 1–21.

Shrieves, Ronald E. 1978. "Market Structure and Innovation: A New Perspective." *Journal of Industrial Economics* (June): 329–47.

Solow, Robert. 1956. "A Contribution to the Theory of Economic Growth." *Quarterly Journal of Economics* 70 (1): 65–94.

———. 1957. "Technical Change and the Aggregate Production Function." *Review of Economics and Statistics* 39 (3): 312–20.

Spence, M. 1984. "Cost Reduction, Competition and Industry Performance." *Econometrica* 52 (1): 101–21.

Summers, Lawrence H. 1981. "Taxation and Corporate Investment: A Q-Theory Approach." *Brookings Papers on Economic Activity* 67–127.

Switzer, Lorne. 1984. "R&D and Total Factor Productivity Growth in Canada." Paper presented to a meeting of the Canadian Economics Association, Guelph, Ont., June.

———. 1985. *The Financing of Technological Change.* Ann Arbor, Mich.: University of Michigan Press.

Terleckyj, Nestor E. 1974. *The Effects of R&D on Productivity Growth of Industries: An Exploratory Study.* Washington, D.C.: National Planning Association.

———. 1980. "Direct and Indirect Effects of Industrial Research and Development on the Productivity Growth of Industries." In J. W. Kendrick, B. N. Kendrick and B. N. Vaccara, eds., *New Developments in Productivity Measurement.* Chicago, Ill.: National Bureau of Economic Research.

United States Congressional Budget Office. 1985. *Federal Financial Support for High Technology Industries.* Washington, D.C.: U.S. Government Printing Office.

Williams, B. R. 1973. *Science and Technology in Economic Growth.* New York: Halstead Press.

TAX POLICY TOWARD FOREIGN DIRECT INVESTMENT IN DEVELOPING COUNTRIES IN LIGHT OF RECENT INTERNATIONAL TAX CHANGES

Joel Slemrod

THE WAVE OF tax reform that swept over industrial countries in the late 1980s has profound implications for the tax treatment of foreign direct investment (FDI) by developing countries. In particular the rate-reducing and base-broadening reforms of corporate taxation have increased the potential effectiveness of tax incentives to FDI. At the same time, they have reduced the ability of host countries to take advantage of overlapping tax jurisdictions to attract taxable income, holding constant real activity.

In this chapter, I review how tax reform in the industrial world has changed the economic calculus involved in setting tax policy toward foreign direct investment in developing countries. The first section includes a brief overview of host and home country taxation of FDI. In the next section, I review the normative theory of host country taxation of FDI and stress the role of the interaction with home country tax policy. The following section is a review of the principal changes in the taxation by the home countries of multinational corporations' (MNCs') income from foreign sources. I concentrate on the U.S. tax changes, not only because this is the case with which I am most familiar, but also because the reforms of other important capital-exporting countries, particularly Japan and the United Kingdom, have followed a similar pattern. In the final section, I discuss how policy considerations in host countries change in light of the changes made in tax policies in home countries.

An Overview of Host and Home Country Taxation of the Income from FDI

Each country in the world asserts the right to tax the income that is generated within its borders, including the income earned by foreign MNCs. Countries do, however, differ widely in the tax rates they apply, their definition of the tax base, and the special incentives they offer for investment. Thus the first (and quantitatively most important) tax burden on FDI comes from the government of the country (known as the host country) where the investment is located.

Many countries, including Japan, the United Kingdom, and the United States, also assert the right to tax the worldwide income of their residents, including their resident corporations. As a rule, the income of foreign subsidiaries is recognized only on repatriation of earnings through dividends, interest, or royalty payments. In order to avoid the potentially onerous burden of two layers of taxation, those countries that tax on a worldwide basis also offer a credit for income and withholding taxes paid to foreign governments. The total credit available in any given year is usually limited to the home country's tax liability on the income from foreign sources, although credits earned in excess of the limitation may often be carried forward or backward to offset excess limitations in other years. Several other countries, including France and the Netherlands, operate a "territorial" system of taxing their resident corporations, under which foreign-source business income is completely exempt from home country taxation.[1]

This would be the end of the story if the geographical location of income were not a matter of dispute. In fact, even if all the information necessary to ascertain the location of income were available at no cost, the conceptual basis for locating income would still be controversial (Ault and Bradford 1990). In reality, corporations do not have the incentive to reveal in full all the information necessary to determine the geographical source of income. For any pattern of real investment decisions, an MNC has the incentive to shift the apparent source of income out of high-tax countries into low-tax countries. This can be accomplished, for example, through the pricing of intercompany transfers of goods and intangible assets or by borrowing via subsidiaries in high-tax countries. Note that this incentive applies regardless of whether the home country operates a territorial or worldwide system of taxation.

Much of the complexity of the taxation of foreign-source income arises from the attempt of countries to defend their revenue base against the fungibility of income tax bases. Complex rules cover standards for acceptable transfer pricing, allocation rules for interest expense and intangibles, and taxation on an accrual basis of certain types of income. It is impossible to summarize concisely the variety of rules that countries employ to determine the location of income. In some countries the statutes are not as important as the outcomes of case-by-case negotiations between representatives of the MNCs and the countries involved. In other countries the source rules are governed by bilateral tax treaties. What is clear, however, is that the de facto rules that govern the sourcing of income are at least as important in understanding the effective taxation of FDI as the tax rates, depreciation rules, and tax credits.[2]

The United States operates a worldwide system of taxation. Thus the income of its MNCs from both domestic and foreign sources is subject to U.S. taxation. The income of foreign subsidiaries is not, however, taxed as accrued but instead enters the tax base of the U.S. parent only on repatriation of dividends, which are then "grossed up" by the average tax rate paid to foreign governments to yield the before-tax income that corresponds to the dividends paid.[3] The grossed-up dividends, minus certain expenses of the MNC allocated to foreign-source income, enter into the taxable income of the parent. Foreign-source income of the parent also includes interest and royalty payments from subsidiaries and certain types of "passive" income on an accrual basis, plus the foreign-source income of foreign branch operations.

In general income taxes paid by foreign affiliates to foreign governments can be credited against U.S. tax liability. This credit is, however, limited to the U.S. tax liability on the foreign-source income, which is equal, with certain exceptions, to the U.S. statutory corporation tax rate multiplied by the net foreign-source income of the subsidiary. MNCs whose potentially creditable foreign taxes exceed the limitation on credits are said to be in an "excess credit" position. These excess credits may be carried forward for five years (or backward for two years) without interest to be used if and when the parent's potentially creditable taxes fall short of the limitation. If the potentially creditable taxes are less than the limit on credits to be taken in a given year, the corporation is said to be in an "excess limitation" (or "deficit-of-credit") position. Distinguishing the excess credit and excess limitation situation is critically important because the tax-related incentives for real and financial behavior are often quite different for a corporation, depending on which situation it is in.

The Normative Theory of Host Country Taxation of FDI

In this section, I review briefly the normative theory of the taxation of FDI by developing countries. Throughout I assume that the host country is small enough that its tax policy cannot affect the opportunity cost of foreign investors. Furthermore, I assume that each developing country is small enough to take the tax policy of the capital-exporting countries and other developing countries toward MNC's foreign-source income as exogenous to its own policy choices.

Host Country Taxation without Home Country Taxation

I begin with a stark result from a simple model that includes many assumptions, some of which will be discussed later: in the absence of home country taxation, a small open economy should impose no distorting taxes on FDI. The reasoning behind the result is straightforward. Because there is a fixed alternative return available to foreign investors, they will bear none of the burden of the tax. If the world return is r, distorting taxation by the host country will drive out capital until its pretax return is $r/(1 - t)$, where t is the effective tax rate on FDI. The tax will be borne by immobile factors in the host country, such as land and labor, as their marginal product falls when the capital stock declines. There will be an excess burden because the capital whose marginal social product lies between $r/(1 - t)$ and r will be forgone, although the opportunity cost to the country is only r. Taxes on FDI are dominated by taxes imposed directly on the fixed factors of land and labor because such taxes can raise the same amount of revenue with the same incidence without reducing the amount of capital below the efficient amount. Note, however, that a nondistorting tax on capital can be achieved either by levying no tax or by levying a cash-flow tax, which levies zero tax on marginal investment in net present value terms but which may collect some tax on rents earned by foreign business.

Host Country Taxation with Home Country Taxation

Suppose that a single capital-exporting country taxes its single resident company on its income as it accrues on a worldwide basis and offers a foreign tax credit for income and withholding taxes paid to foreign governments. To be consistent with the small-country model, assume that the foreign MNC has many overseas investments, so the investment in this particular host country is negligible. In particular, whether the firm is in excess credit or deficit-of-credit status is independent of host country policy.

Now assume that the MNC is permanently in a deficit-of-credit position. This means that any additional taxes paid (or deemed to have been paid) to foreign governments will be matched by increased foreign tax credits offered by the home government. Thus the MNC is indifferent to the tax policy of the host government because its worldwide tax liability is unaffected by the host country's policy. From the point of view of the host country, increasing the tax rate on FDI raises revenue (at the expense of the home country's treasury) but does not discourage investment. Therefore high tax rates are called for. Note that the optimal tax rate is not bounded above by the home country's tax rate, as would be true if the foreign tax credit were limited to the tax due on foreign-source income based on home country rates *and* the MNC invested only in the host country.[4] But the small-country assumption of a multiple of foreign investments in other host countries diminishes the force of this argument because tax payments to the host country are so small that they do not endanger the deficit-of-credit position of the MNC. Thus from the point of view of the host country, offsetting foreign tax credits are in unlimited supply.

Home countries do not, however, tax the foreign-source income of foreign subsidiaries on accrual. Instead, the income is taxed only on repatriation, at which time a foreign tax credit is available for withholding taxes and for corporate income taxes deemed to have been paid on the income from which the repatriations are made.[5] Unless all foreign-source income is immediately repatriated (so that the home country tax is in effect on an accrual basis), corporate taxes imposed by the host government do not give rise to the immediate offsetting of foreign tax credits. The credits are postponed, and are therefore of lower present value, until such time as the income is repatriated. Thus host country taxes do lower the after-tax rate of return on investment and therefore provide a disincentive to FDI. Still, the tax rate should be positive because of the partial subsidy offered by the home country's foreign tax credit. At the optimal rate the marginal revenue transfer from the home country should equal the marginal excess burden caused by the reduced FDI.

The story is different, however, for withholding taxes. These are payable only on repatriation of income rather than on accrual of income. They thus trigger a foreign tax credit that is concurrent with the tax payment to the host country, incurring no additional present value of tax liability.

Now consider the other extreme case—that the MNC is in a permanent excess credit position. An increase in taxes would generate no incremental foreign tax credits, and thus any tax imposed by the host country would discourage FDI. In this case it is optimal to levy no tax on the marginal investment.

What if the MNC is likely to alternate between excess credit and deficit-of-credit years? Remember that excess credits can be carried forward, without interest, to be used in deficit-of-credit years. If, on average over time, potential credits exceed the credit limit, then, including credit carry-forwards, the MNC is effectively in an excess credit situation, so host country taxes are fully distorting. If, on average, potential credits fall short of the credit limit so that in certain years the MNC is in a deficit-of-credit position even when the carrying forward of credit is considered, then the effect of host country taxation depends on the flexibility of timing repatriations. If repatriations can be timed to coincide precisely with years in which there is a deficit of credit, then the effect is the same as the permanent deficit-of-credit position, where the credits do not offset host country taxation to the extent that repatriations are deferred. If repatriations cannot be timed so precisely, then the offsetting effect of the credit is further diminished because the potential credit must be carried forward and thus reduced in present value.

Most of the capital-exporting countries that tax worldwide income, with the notable exception of the United States, are willing to include "tax-sparing" provisions in their tax treaties with developing countries. Under tax sparing, the home country allows the foreign affiliate of its resident MNC to take a foreign tax credit for taxes as if the host country had levied taxes at a rate specified by treaty, even if the taxes are not in fact assessed by the host country. If the host country levies no tax at all, then the result is a subsidy to FDI that is financed by the home country's government.

What policy should the host country adopt if it is dealing with an MNC from a tax-sparing home country? (Immediate repatriation of all earnings is assumed.) Because the tax credit received by the MNC is independent of the actual tax assessed by the host country, and therefore does not at the margin offset host taxation, any tax imposed by the host country increases the cost of capital to the MNC and will discourage investment.

Note that the foregoing argument applies regardless of the credit status of the MNC. For an MNC permanently in an excess limitation position, the credits earned have a positive value that is independent of the host country's true tax rate. For an MNC permanently in an excess credit position, the credits earned have no value that is independent of the host country's true tax rate. The key point is that in either case the foreign tax credits offered by the home country do not offset the taxes imposed by the host country. In the excess limitation case, the cost of FDI to the host country is fixed at $r/(1 - \bar{t})$, where $\bar{t}$ is the rate of tax-sparing credit; in the excess credit case, it is fixed at r.

If not all profits are immediately repatriated, then the tax-sparing credit will not exactly offset, in present value terms, a corporate income tax imposed at the tax-sparing rate. The above argument still holds, however, because the value of the credit offered by the home country remains independent of the actual rate of tax collected.

In sum, the message so far is that a small open economy should consider (apparently) distorting taxes on FDI only to the extent that the home country treasury, and not the MNC itself, pays the tax. This can happen only if the MNC is from a country that taxes worldwide income—and only to the extent that the MNC is in a deficit-of-credit position. Even in this case, withholding taxes are more attractive than corporate income taxes because they can be credited immediately rather than on repatriation of income.

Implementation Problems: Discriminating among MNCs

One problem with implementing this normative theory is that a developing country is likely to attract FDI from MNCs both from countries with a territorial system of taxation and from those with a worldwide system and from MNCs both in excess credit positions and in deficit-of-credit situations. In practice it is difficult to design tax policy that would, for example, levy low taxes on MNCs from territorial countries and high taxes on FDI from deficit-of-credit MNCs resident in worldwide system countries. In fact, tax treaties explicitly prohibit discriminatory treatment of one country's firms over another's. Moreover, the United States may disallow the creditability of a tax if its application depends on the availability of a foreign tax credit in the taxpayer's country of residence. Of course, discriminating tax (or other) treatment can be difficult to detect.

If discrimination is impossible, then the appropriate policy should be a compromise between the no-tax policy that is appropriate for FDI from territorial or worldwide excess credit MNCs and the high-tax policy that is appropriate for deficit-of-credit MNCs, with weighting depending on the mix of potential investors likely to invest in the host country.

Implementation Problems: Interaction with Domestic Tax Policy

Suppose that, using the above reasoning, a developing country decides to impose a low (zero, for the sake of argument) tax on the income from FDI. This will conflict with the desire to impose a corporate income tax on domestic corporations because differentiating the tax treatment on the basis of ownership is not straightforward. De facto domestic corporations could set up as foreign corporations (presumably domiciled in territorial countries) to receive preferential treatment. Joint ventures will be difficult to tax.

This is a serious issue because a domestic corporation income tax is often an important component of domestic tax policy—as a backstop to individual taxation of residents' capital income in the absence of accrual taxation of capital gains, as a tax "handle" in countries with high tax administration costs, and also as a way to tax rents.[6] If the corporation income tax is worth defending, the question then becomes how to offer preferential taxation of income from FDI in the context of an operative corporate income tax. One common answer is to offer tax holidays on a selective basis to FDI. The selectivity can be used to exempt domestically owned corporations but could also be used to target the holiday to MNCs whose governments do not offer offsetting tax credits for taxes paid to the host government. Many of the same implementation problems discussed above, however, apply to tax holidays, and therefore it is not clear that tax holidays are always the best way to provide incentives to FDI.

Income Shifting by Transfer Pricing and Other Financial Strategies

One key assumption maintained heretofore is that the location of income is observable by all parties at no cost; this is of course false. Moreover,

MNCs have an incentive to move the apparent source of income to their tax advantage. The worldwide fungibility of taxable income implies that developing countries should be concerned not only with the marginal effective tax rate on new investment but also with the statutory rate on income, because it is the statutory rate that applies to taxable income moved into a country by, say, transfer pricing. For this reason a low-rate, low-allowance system is preferable to a high-rate, high-allowance system, if the marginal effective tax rate on new investment is held constant. A low statutory rate acts as a magnet for fungible taxable income. A high statutory rate acts as a repellent, inducing affiliates to shift away profits through debt finance and transfer pricing.

Recent Changes in Home Country Taxation of FDI

Above I have outlined the theory of how home country tax policy affects appropriate host country tax policy. In what follows I discuss the important recent changes in United States tax rules governing outward FDI and develop their implications for developing country policy.

The U.S. Tax Reform Act of 1986

The three most important aspects of the Tax Reform Act of 1986 (TRA86) for FDI from the United States, in order of importance, are as follows:[7]

   1. The reduction in the statutory rate from 46 percent to 34 percent, and the resulting increase in the number of firms in an excess credit situation[8]
   2. The change in the rules governing the sourcing of income and the allocation of expenses (most significantly, interest) between domestic and foreign-source income
   3. The tightening of the foreign tax credit that limits the averaging of different types of income.

The single most important aspect of the TRA86 for outward FDI was the reduction in the statutory rate of corporation income tax from 46 percent to 34 percent. Many of the repercussions of the new law follow from this change. To explain this, I must make a brief digression on the effect of the TRA86 on domestic investment. It is well known that the net effect of the tax system on the incentive to invest depends not only on the statutory rate but also on, among other things, the schedule of depreciation allowances, the rate and scope of investment tax credits, the source of financing, and the rate of inflation. The TRA86 eliminated the investment tax credits that previously applied to equipment and machinery, and it provided generally less generous depreciation allowances. Both actions tended to offset the tax rate reduction. Most analysts concluded that their net effect was to increase slightly the effective corporate-level tax on new domestic investment, an important alternative to FDI.

An analysis of how these same changes affected the effective tax rate on FDI must proceed quite differently because, with certain exceptions, foreign-source income of foreign subsidiaries enters the parent company's tax base only to the extent that dividends and other payments are repatriated. There is thus no calculation of foreign-source taxable income from which depreciation allowances are deducted and against which investment tax credits can be offset. The tax base is simply dividends received minus allocable deductions, grossed up by the average rate of foreign taxation (calculated by use of an earnings and profits measure of taxable income, which is not sensitive to legislated changes in the tax depreciation schedules used for domestically located assets, investment credits, and so on).[9] To that base is applied the corporate statutory tax rate.

Thus leaving aside for now the source-of-income rules discussed below, the corporate tax changes of the TRA86 reduced the statutory rate from 46 percent to 34 percent but did not broaden the tax base. This resulted in an unambiguous reduction in the tax rate on income from FDI. If we assume that the taxes imposed by the foreign governments remained unchanged, it follows that the amount of additional taxation imposed by the United States on repatriation either stayed the same or declined.[10] It stayed at zero for MNCs whose average tax rate paid to foreign governments exceeds 46 percent.[11] Any MNC subject to an average tax rate by foreign governments between 34 and 46 percent had formerly been paying taxes on repatriation; under the new rate it would no longer be liable for any additional taxes. For firms paying less than a 34 percent average tax rate to foreign governments, the tax due on repatriation would fall substantially, although not to zero.[12]

The other important implication of the reduction of the U.S. statutory rate from 46 percent to 34 percent is that a much higher fraction of U.S. firms are likely to be in an excess credit situation, because the average tax paid to foreign governments exceeds 34 percent.[13] For a firm with excess credits, every additional dollar paid in tax to a foreign government generates a foreign tax credit that cannot be used immediately. The credit has some value to the firm only if the firm will be in an excess limitation position in the next five years (the carryforward limit) or had been in an excess limitation position in the previous two years (the carryback limit). Thus a U.S. corporation in an excess credit position is likely to be much more sensitive to differences in foreign effective tax rates than a firm in an excess limitation situation.[14] This increases the attractiveness of investment in a low-tax foreign country compared with that in a high-tax country.

Many of the policy implications discussed below depend on the TRA86's making excess credit status a more typical situation for MNCs. It is therefore worthwhile to examine the empirical underpinning of this conclusion. Goodspeed and Frisch (1989) analyzed individual corporation tax return data for 1985 and concluded that the change in the statutory rate from 46 percent to 34 percent would increase the overall percentage of foreign-source income subject to excess credits from 50 percent to 78 percent, and from 32 percent to 82 percent in manufacturing. It is important to note that their calculations did not take into account the new source allocation rules or the separate "baskets," discussed below. In addition the analysis does not consider any changes in other countries' tax systems that may have been induced by the changes in the U.S. law. Perhaps most important, the analyses do not take into account any behavioral response of the MNCs.

Broadly speaking, a home country's MNCs are likely to be in excess credit status if the home country's tax rate is less than the average of all host countries. From this perspective it seems likely that when country A decreases its own tax rate, the tendency for country A's MNCs to go into an excess credit position should be offset by the fact that other countries' MNCs, for which country A is a host country, are likely to go into an excess limitation position. Or, in other words, how can all countries' tax rates be (or move in the direction of being) below average? The answer to this apparent paradox is made clear by referring to the U.S. TRA86. The TRA86 decreased the statutory corporation tax rate from 46 percent to 34 percent but increased the tax base for income from U.S. sources enough to approximately offset the rate decrease. Thus the average tax rate paid by MNCs investing in the United States was not likely to fall much and would therefore not affect the excess credit status of non-U.S. multinational corporations investing in the United States. For capital-exporting U.S. corporations the story is different. The tax base on which the foreign tax credit limit is calculated was not directly changed, but the rate applied to that base was reduced from 46 percent to 34 percent. So the effect of the rate-reducing, base-broadening tax reforms in the United States was to increase the number of U.S. multinationals with excess credits, without increasing the number of non-U.S. multinationals with excess limitations.

As discussed later in the context of developing countries, the increase in excess credit status puts pressure on host countries to lower their effective tax rates on inward FDI. This would tend to reduce the prevalence of excess credit status. The reduction of the statutory rate, however, puts pressure on other countries to reduce their statutory rates in order to offset the tendency for accounting profits to seek the lowest statutory rate. Reductions in statutory rates will tend to increase the prevalence of excess credit status. The combination of the pressure for average effective rates to come down to other countries' statutory rates and the pressure for countries' statutory rates not to diverge suggests that, in time, most companies will be operating with a balance between taxes paid to foreign governments and allowable credits. The TRA86 may have created a temporary disequilibrium, in which excess credit status for U.S. multinationals prevails, but it is likely to diminish over time.

The actions of the U.S. multinational firms themselves are also likely to reduce the projected increase in their excess credit status. Companies that find themselves in an excess credit status because of a change in the tax laws have the incentive to eliminate that status by using one (or both) of two broad classes of strategies—increasing the limit on foreign tax credit and decreasing the taxes paid to foreign governments. If such strategies were available without cost, then there would be no excess credits. More likely, however, there are costs to the use of financial and accounting strategies that would not have been employed in the absence of the pressure of excess credits.

A firm with excess credits can reduce the present value of its tax burden to the extent that it can increase the limit on foreign tax credits. This increases the importance of the rules concerning the source, for U.S. tax purposes, of worldwide income. With worldwide income held constant, if a dollar of income is shifted from a domestic source to a foreign source, it increases the foreign tax credit limitation by $1.00 and allows $0.34 more of foreign taxes to be credited immediately against U.S. tax liability. Only to the extent that foreign governments enforce the same source rules will there be an offsetting increase in foreign tax liability.

One existing source rule that becomes more important applies to production for export. According to current regulations, between 40 and 50 percent of the income from domestic U.S. production of export goods can effectively be allocated to foreign-source income. For an MNC in an excess credit position, this in effect reduces the effective tax rate on domestic investment for export by as much as a half. Thus if a contemplated FDI is to produce goods for sale outside the United States, the alternative of domestic U.S. production has become relatively tax favored for those firms that have shifted into excess credit status, in spite of the base-broadening aspects of the TRA86. This reasoning would not, however, apply to FDI designed to reexport to the United States; the alternative of domestic production for internal consumption does not benefit from the export source rule.

Interest expenses of the U.S. parent corporation must be allocated to either U.S. or foreign-source income. The general rule is to allocate on the basis of the book value of assets so that interest expenses deductible from foreign-source income are equal to total interest payments multiplied by the fraction of worldwide assets expected to generate foreign-source income. Although the TRA86 did not significantly alter this allocation formula, it did add a "one-taxpayer" rule, under which corporations that are members of an affiliated group are consolidated for the purpose of allocating interest expenses between U.S. and foreign sources.[15] In the absence of this rule an MNC could load its debt into a

U.S. subsidiary with no foreign-source income and have the interest expense be allocated entirely to income from the United States, thus maximizing foreign-source income and the limitation on foreign tax credits. With the one-taxpayer rule, a fraction of these interest payments has to be allocated to foreign-source income regardless of the legal structure of the MNC.

For MNCs in an excess credit position that are forced to reallocate interest payments, this provision increases the average cost of capital of domestic or foreign investment to the extent that debt finance is used. It also increases the marginal cost of foreign investment because foreign investment increases the amount of interest payments that must be allocated abroad, which decreases foreign-source income and therefore the amount of foreign taxes that are immediately creditable.[16] This provision is obviously most important for MNCs that have a high debt-to-capital ratio.

The TRA86 also changed the operation of the foreign tax credit by creating separate limitations ("baskets") for certain categories of income. Foreign taxes imposed on taxable income in a particular basket can offset only those U.S. taxes that are due on that category of income. There are eight separate baskets, including passive income, high withholding tax interest, and financial services income. In addition, a separate basket is needed for each foreign company in which the parent has a 10 to 50 percent ownership stake. In some cases (for example, passive income) the objective was to prevent fungible income from being earned in foreign jurisdictions with low tax rates and thus increasing the amount of available foreign tax credits that could offset taxes paid on other income to foreign governments. In other cases (for example, high interest on withholding taxes) the objective was to prevent MNCs (often banks) in an excess limitation position from paying effectively high withholding taxes (which, because of the excess limitation, could be immediately credited against U.S. tax liability) in return for favorable pretax terms of exchange (that is, higher pretax interest rates on loans than otherwise). These objectives share the common thread of limiting the revenue loss to the United States that can arise from manipulation of the foreign tax credit mechanism.

In general the creation of separate foreign tax credit baskets increases the effective taxation of foreign-source income because it makes it more difficult in certain cases to credit foreign income taxes against U.S. tax liability. In addition the baskets can add significant complexity to the typical MNC's compliance procedure, and to this extent the provisions add a hidden tax burden to multinational operation. From the point of view of a host country, the basket provisions make it more difficult to shift the true burden of revenue raised from U.S. multinationals to the U.S. treasury.

One other change in the calculation of the foreign tax credit is worth mentioning. Prior to the enactment of the TRA86, in calculating the amount of taxes paid on income associated with remitted dividends, the rules traced a dividend to the most recently accumulated earnings and profits of the foreign affiliate paying the dividend. This allowed MNCs to manipulate the timing of their foreign-source income by paying dividends in those years in which the average tax rate was high (the "rhythm" method of repatriation), thus maximizing the foreign tax credit. This rule gave host countries the incentive to subject MNCs to average tax rates that varied widely over time. By repatriating dividends only in the years with high average taxes, the amount of foreign tax credit earned per dollar of earnings could easily exceed the true average tax rate imposed over the lifetime of the investment. In this case the U.S. treasury was effectively subsidizing the tax incentive to investment provided by the host country.

Since 1987, dividends paid by a foreign affiliate to its U.S. parent corporation have been traced to a pool of its post-1986 undistributed earnings, and post-1986 foreign income taxes are allocated pro rata to those earnings and profits.[17] This eliminates much of the potential gain to MNCs from manipulating the timing of dividend repatriations and reduces the incentive of host countries to provide the possibility of time-varying average tax rates.

Corporate Tax Reform in Japan and the United Kingdom

In Japan and the United Kingdom, the other two principal capital-exporting countries that operate a worldwide tax system, corporate tax reform has proceeded along a path similar to that of the United States. To be specific, the reforms have featured reduced statutory tax rates, limitation of investment incentives that applied only to domestic investment, and, in Japan, tightening of the limitations on the foreign tax credit.[18] Thus in qualitative terms, many of the arguments made here also apply to FDI from these countries, although the details differ. Note, however, that Japan and the United Kingdom have tax-sparing treaties with many developing countries, and for these host countries the home country changes in taxation are not directly comparable.

Rethinking Host Country FDI Tax Policy in Light of Home Country Policy Changes

The principal implication of the changes in U.S. tax policy made in 1986 is that, because of the probable increased prevalence of MNCs in positions of excess credit, host country taxation of FDI is more likely to be effective at the margin. This means that the disincentive effect of taxation on FDI is likely to be larger than in the past, and low rates of tax on FDI are more appealing. Even in the new tax regime, however, some MNCs that operate predominantly in low-tax countries will not have excess credits. For these companies, the importance of offsetting foreign tax credits will continue, and the possibility that host countries will export some of their tax burden remains.

Tax reform in the home country also affects several other issues in the taxation of FDI. In what follows I examine briefly its effect on five important issues.

Tax Holidays

The more MNCs there are in an excess credit position, the more likely it is that tax holidays will be effective in attracting FDI. Increased FDI is desirable as long as the pretax national return of the investment exceeds the opportunity cost of capital. The fact that the prevalence of excess credit status is likely to decline over time suggests that the tax holidays should be limited in duration because, after a certain period, tax exemptions granted are more likely to be offset by reduced foreign tax credits granted by the home country. Of course, tax holidays offered in the start-up stage of operation of a foreign affiliate are likely to be less attractive (and perhaps even inhibiting; see Mintz 1990) because net earnings often are low or negative during this period.

Different reasoning applies to joint ventures with U.S. partners. Recall that under the TRA86 there is, for foreign tax credit limitation purposes, a separate basket for each foreign company in which the parent company has a 10 to 50 percent stake in ownership. This implies that the overall excess credit status of the MNC is irrelevant. In this case effective taxes up to the U.S. rate of 34 percent will be creditable, but effective taxes over that will not be. The policy prescription in this case is to set the average tax rate no higher than 34 percent but clearly at a positive rate in order to soak up the foreign tax credits offered by the home country. What is, from the perspective of the MNC, an unfavorable tax treatment of joint ventures presents an opportunity to collect taxes from MNCs in an excess credit position without discouraging investment as much as otherwise. The change in the tracing of dividends to earnings from a rule of the LIFO (last in, first out) type to one of the pooling type has potentially important implications regarding the attractiveness and the appropriate structuring of a tax holiday. Under the law before the TRA86, if a foreign affiliate postponed repatriation until the tax holiday had expired, it could then receive foreign tax credits based on the (postholiday) rate of tax paid. Under the law of the TRA86, in the same situation the foreign tax credit would be calculated by averaging the postholiday rates of taxation with the tax rates paid during the holiday, which would yield lower foreign tax credits. The reduced attractiveness of tax holidays under the new rules is an example of the general proposition, discussed earlier, that variability in average tax rates over time has lost some of its pre-TRA86 benefits to host countries. In this case the variability refers to the change between the preholiday and postholiday periods. Of course, reducing the available amount of foreign tax credits may not be a big loss to an MNC faced with excess credits in the foreseeable future.

The fact that U.S. tax reform has reduced the ability of MNCs to take advantage of tax holidays, and variable tax rates in general, suggests that tax systems with these features have become less attractive as a means of attracting FDI compared with a stable low-tax regime.

High Statutory Tax Rates as against Low Statutory Tax Rates

For a given effective tax on investment, a statutory rate above a percentage in the mid-30s now prevalent in the principal capital-exporting countries will encourage outmovement of taxable income. Rates above that level will give MNCs the incentive to use transfer pricing and other mechanisms to move profits from the host country to the lower-rate home country tax base.[19] The increased prevalence of excess credit status underlines this proposition because it implies that tax liability incurred in the host country is less likely to be offset by credits offered by the home country.

Creditable Taxes as against Noncreditable Taxes

As long as there is a prevalence of MNCs with excess credits, the advantage of creditable taxes over noncreditable taxes is diminished. This suggests that tax policy can be designed to meet other fiscal objectives that may not be well served by creditable (income-based or withholding) taxes. On the list of noncreditable taxes that become relatively more attractive are taxes based on consumption, cash flow, or assets.

Tax Subsidies as against Nontax Subsidies

It makes sense for a host country, when dealing with MNCs in an excess limitation situation, to provide subsidies to FDI in nontax vehicles—for example, by providing training to workers or infrastructure improvements, rather than via explicit tax reductions. The reasoning behind this argument is straightforward. Because taxes could be credited against home country tax liability, reductions in taxes could be worth less than direct reductions in the cost of doing business. Gersovitz (1987) argued that if subsidies to FDI could be offered outside of the tax system (so that the amount of foreign tax credits earned was based on gross-of-subsidy taxes), then the optimal strategy of a small open economy dealing with excess limitation MNCs was simultaneously to tax their profits (with tax revenues offset by home country foreign tax credits) and offer nontax subsidies so that on net there was a fiscal incentive to invest.[20] This is the optimal strategy because the true cost of capital to the host country in this case is $r(1 - t)$, where t is the rate at which the home country is willing to offer foreign tax credits to its firms' FDI.

For MNCs that are predominantly in an excess credit situation, tax subsidies are likely to be as valuable as nontax subsidies. If there are other reasons to prefer tax subsidies, then tax subsidies may be strictly preferable.

Tax Treaties and Tax Sparing

Germany, Japan, and the United Kingdom, but not the United States, have entered into tax-sparing agreements with many developing countries. Under such an agreement, the home country agrees to grant foreign tax credits for taxes paid to foreign governments at an agreed-upon rate, even if the actual taxes paid to the host government are below that rate. The intent of tax sparing is to ensure that tax incentives granted by the host country are effectively lowering the taxation of MNCs, rather than merely being offset by reduced foreign tax credits offered by the home country. The refusal by the United States to enter into tax-sparing agreements has long been a significant cause of the lack of successful treaty negotiations with developing countries. This lack contrasts with the wide network of treaties between most other industrial countries and developing nations.

U.S. taxpayers are, since the enactment of the TRA86, unlikely to derive substantial benefits from tax-sparing credits. Now that an excess credit position is more likely to be the norm, the primary concern of U.S. taxpayers is to reduce their actual foreign tax burden (for example, through reductions of withholding rates by treaty) and not to generate potentially unusable tax-sparing credits.

The diminished value of tax sparing makes tax treaties without tax sparing more acceptable to developing countries. Consistent with the reduced opposition, the United States is expected this year to complete treaties with India, Indonesia, and Tunisia, and negotiations are currently under way with Mexico and Thailand. (Negotiations with Indonesia and Tunisia had begun in earnest before 1986, but the Indian treaty was accelerated only in 1987.)

Tax treaties generally provide for reductions in withholding taxes, a move that could be made unilaterally by any country and one that is made more appealing by the changes in home country taxation. The principal benefit of having a treaty with a country like the United States is the expectation of a stable tax regime. The promise of a stable, explicit set of tax rules undoubtedly improves the attractiveness of a country as a host for FDI. Treaties also generally contain provisions for exchange of tax information, which can be helpful to a developing country in its efforts to enforce a residence-based tax on capital income.

Notes

The views expressed in this chapter are mine alone and should not be attributed to the World Bank. I am grateful to Daniel Frisch, Peter Merrill, Jack Mintz, and John Mutti for helpful comments on an earlier draft.

1. By statute, Canada and Germany have a worldwide system of taxation. Their tax treaties, however, generally provide that dividends repatriated from affiliates satisfying a test of minimum share of ownership are subject to no further tax liability.

2. See Slemrod (1989) for a framework for measuring the effective tax rate on an FDI by a multinational firm.

3. The income of foreign branches of U.S. corporations is taxed as accrued. Partly for tax reasons, most foreign activity of U.S. corporations is carried out by subsidiaries rather than branches.

4. By statute, the United Kingdom uses a per-country limitation on its foreign credit, but the use of offshore companies to "mix" foreign-source income before repatriation renders it effectively like the overall limitation system of the United States.

5. There are exceptions to this statement. In the U.S. tax code the rules under subpart F subject U.S. taxpayers to current tax whenever a significant purpose of earning income through a foreign corporation is the avoidance of U.S. or foreign income taxes. In addition the income of foreign branches of U.S. corporations is taxed on accrual.

6. On these issues see Mintz and Seade (1989). Note that if the host country is unable to tax its residents' foreign-source income, then owners of domestic wealth will not bear the burden of taxes on (domestically located) capital. Instead, it will be shifted to fixed domestic factors such as labor and land. In this case an apparent capital income tax is dominated by a tax on these domestic factors, so the importance of the corporation income tax as a backstop for taxation of capital income is less salient.

7. Some of the material in this section is drawn from Slemrod (1990a).

8. To be precise, the U.S. corporate tax rate structure is graduated, 34 percent being the rate that applies to the top bracket. Although for a large fraction of firms lower rates apply, the top rate applies to the great majority of corporate income. This is particularly true for MNCs, which are on average much larger than the typical firm with purely domestic operations.

9. The depreciation rules used in the calculation of earnings and profits do, however, change. For example, since 1980 the depreciation rules that apply to property used overseas have been made less generous. These schedules affect the calculation of tax deemed paid by subsidiaries to foreign governments and the amount of foreign tax credit available for any given amount of dividends remitted.

10. Since the passage of the TRA86, many other countries have enacted tax reforms that share some of the corporate-rate-reducing, base-broadening aspects of the TRA86. To the extent that the TRA86 *caused* these reforms (or increased their likelihood), the effective tax rate in the host country was influenced by the U.S. tax reform. The analysis that follows holds constant the foreign tax system.

11. The average tax rate paid to foreign governments is subject to a degree of control by the MNC via its repatriation policy. By repatriating income primarily from high-tax countries, the average tax rate on its foreign-source income is high and less likely to attract additional U.S. tax liability.

12. Hartman (1985) has argued that, regardless of the excess credit status of the U.S. parent company, the level of repatriation tax is irrelevant for the incentive to undertake FDI financed by earnings of the foreign subsidiary. This is because the repatriation tax reduces equally both the return to investment and the opportunity cost of investment (reduced dividends). This argument would not apply to the infusion of new equity capital from the parent company. See Jun (1989) and Leechor and Mintz (1990) for a critique of this view.

13. Grubert and Mutti (1987) quote U.S. Treasury Department estimates that the fraction of manufacturing MNCs (weighted by worldwide income) with excess credits would increase from 20 percent to 69 percent.

14. Of course, Hartman's argument implies that, for investment financed by retained earnings, only the host country's tax rate matters even for firms in an excess limitation position, so no post-TRA86 increased sensitivity to host country tax rates should be observed.

15. The one-taxpayer rule already effectively applied to the allocation of expenses on research and development.

16. This analysis presumes that the interest allocation rules of foreign governments have not changed.

17. See McIntyre (1989: 4–39).

18. For more details on the Japanese tax treatment of foreign direct investment, see Slemrod and Timbers (1990).

19. Regardless of the statutory tax rates of other countries, a lower statutory rate tends to increase the tax base, holding real activity constant. A host country with a 46 percent statutory tax rate, however, was, before TRA86, unlikely to encounter nearly as much effort from MNCs to reroute taxable income as it is now.

20. Note, however, that the U.S. tax code can disallow the credibility of taxes when the tax revenues are rebated, directly or indirectly, to the investor. It is unclear how effective this provision is in limiting the strategy outlined in the text.

References

Ault, Hugh J., and David Bradford. 1990. "Taxing International Income: An Analysis of the U.S. System and Its Economic Premises." In Assaf Razin and Joel Slemrod, eds., *Taxation in the Global Economy*. Chicago, Ill.: University of Chicago Press.

Gersovitz, Mark. 1987. "The Effects of Domestic Taxes on Foreign Direct Investment." In David Newbery and Nicholas Stern, eds., *The Theory of Taxation for Developing Countries*. New York: Oxford University Press.

Goodspeed, Timothy, and Daniel Frisch. 1989. "U.S. Tax Policy and the Overseas Activities of U.S. Multinational Corporations: A Quantitative Assessment." U.S. Treasury Department, Washington, D.C.

Grubert, Harry, and John Mutti. 1987. "The Impact of the Tax Reform Act of 1986 on Trade and Capital Flows." In *Compendium of Tax Research 1987*. Washington, D.C.: Department of the Treasury, Office of Tax Analysis.

Hartman, David G. 1985. "Tax Policy and Foreign Direct Investment." *Journal of Public Economics* 26:107–21.

Jun, Joosung. 1989. "What Is the Marginal Source of Funds for Foreign Investment?" Working Paper 3064. National Bureau of Economic Research, Cambridge, Mass.

Leechor, Chad, and Jack M. Mintz. 1990. "On the Taxation of Multinational Investment When the Deferral Method Is Used by the Capital Exporting Country." Working Paper 9013. University of Toronto, Toronto, Can.

McIntyre, Michael J. 1989. *The International Income Tax Rules of the United States.* Stoneham, Mass.: Butterworth Legal Publishers.

Mintz, Jack M. 1990. "Corporate Tax Holidays and Investment." *World Bank Economic Review* 4:81–101.

Mintz, Jack M., and Jesus Seade. 1989. "Cash Flow or Income: The Choice of Base for Company Taxation." Working Paper 177, PPR Working Paper Series. World Bank, Washington, D.C.

Slemrod, Joel. 1989. "A Framework for Measuring the Effective Tax Rate on Foreign Direct Investment." University of Michigan, Ann Arbor.

———. 1990a. "The Impact of the Tax Reform Act of 1986 on Foreign Direct Investment to and from the United States." In Joel Slemrod, ed., *Do Taxes Matter?: The Impact of the Tax Reform Act of 1986.* Cambridge, Mass.: MIT Press.

Slemrod, Joel, and Kenneth Timbers. 1990. "Japanese and U.S. Tax Treatment of Their Resident Multinationals: Who Has the Competitive Advantage?" Paper presented at the U.S.–Japan Symposium on Tax Policy and Politics, April 1–3, Princeton University, Princeton, N.J.

WHY TAX INCENTIVES DO NOT PROMOTE INVESTMENT IN BRAZIL

7

Antonio Estache and Vitor Gaspar

ACCORDING TO *World Development Report 1989,* Brazil's ratio of invest-ment to gross domestic product (GDP) is below the average for upper-middle-income countries (World Bank 1989). In 1987 Brazil's investment was below 20 percent of GDP, whereas the average for upper-middle-income countries was 25 percent. Simultaneously, Brazil's taxes on capital income yielded roughly 2.4 percent of GDP in revenue, or 12 percent of the investment volume. This is less than half the average revenue from taxes on capital income in similar countries.[1] In addition to a weak tax administration, the poor revenue performance is explained by the erosion of the tax base and tax rates resulting from an unusually large number of tax incentives granted to corporate investors. These programs are widely used and cost annually about 1.5 percent of GDP in direct federal revenue loss. This represents about 20 percent of the federal tax revenue.

In view of this heavy reliance on tax incentives, Brazil's poor invest-ment performance seems paradoxical. Several factors can explain this ap-parent paradox. The most obvious one is uncertainty with respect to the direction of economic policy in Brazil. A more subtle, complementing explanation is the low effectiveness of these tax incentives as policy instru-ments to promote investment. It may be that even with tax incentives, the Brazilian taxation of capital is too high at the margin. The second explanation is the focus of this chapter.

First, we develop an analytical framework illustrating the tax design issues that reduce the incentive to invest in Brazil. The framework ac-counts for all the major characteristics of the Brazilian tax system leading to distortions in the capital market. It allows the computation of the marginal effective tax rates (METRs) on capital. The METR measures the size of the distortion. The simulations show that the level of taxation of capital in Brazil in 1989 was unusually high by international standards, with and without tax incentives. Second, the computation of the METR for various types of investment projects is used to identify the key sources of distortions in the Brazilian taxation of capital. Furthermore, the simulations show why the plethora of tax incentives introduced over time to alleviate that burden have led to complex, inefficient, and largely evaded taxes on capital, yielding little revenue and not increasing investment. The simulations are used to rank the incentives programs by their effectiveness at promoting investment. They also point to an agenda for reforming the taxation of capital if Brazil is to recover investment and tax revenue.

The section that follows summarizes the methodology we used to assess quantitatively the size of the distortion that the major taxes impose on the capital market. We then assess the deterrence effect the Brazilian tax system has on investment with and without tax incentives. In conclusion we suggest a direction for a reform of the taxation of capital in Brazil.

A Methodology to Assess Tax-Driven Distortion in the Capital Market

Excessive tax levels are believed to be among the major sources of Brazil's weak investment performance during the 1980s. It is important, then, to be able to quantify the distortions they create. Concerns about the effects of the high tax rates on capital have often focused on personal and corporate income tax (CIT) rates, as well as on the total and average tax burden imposed on capital. The analysis of tax-induced distortions, however, requires an assessment of the combined effect of all taxes, direct and indirect. The concept of the METR has become widely used to assess these effects.[2] The METR measures the size of the intertemporal distortion imposed by the tax system on marginal investment projects with a return just sufficient to cover costs. In fact, it measures the deterrence effect of taxes on the investment decision.

The focus is on marginal tax rates rather than average tax rates because for most allocational decisions average tax rates are less relevant than marginal tax rates. Marginal rates determine the tax wedges that affect factor demand and supply decisions. More specifically, the marginal tax rate applicable to a given factor income measures (a) the tax liability that results from an increase of one cruzado in income, and (b) the distortion imposed by taxation on the decision to earn income in that particular way. Average tax rates are relevant only for the computation of tax revenues and for the distributional content of taxes. They have no effect on the demand and supply decisions.

The METR expresses the tax wedge created by taxes in the capital market as a percentage of the pretax rate of return on an investment project, p. The tax wedge, in turn, is defined as the difference between p

(demand for capital) and the after-tax return, *s,* to those who supply the capital to finance it, the savers (supply of capital). The pretax rate of return is derived from the neoclassical model of investment by a competitive firm. It can be interpreted as the social return on an investment project. The computation of the METR also requires the derivation of the appropriate discount rate faced by the firm because that rate varies for the differing sources of financing for the project. Finally, the after-tax rate of return needs to be computed. It measures the opportunity cost of funds to the savers. It is easier to derive than the pretax rate because it requires only the deduction from the market rate of return of the taxes faced by savers. Formally, the METR on the income from capital, t_e, is defined as

$$(7\text{-}1) \qquad\qquad t_e = \frac{p-s}{p}.$$

Taxes affecting capital are responsible for various types of distortions. Therefore the METR can be computed for various types of investment goods (machinery and building), for various types of industries, and for different financing instruments. Although these measures are largely indicative (they do not reflect the general-equilibrium effects resulting from the shifting of the tax burden between agents), they provide important information on the various sources of distortions caused by taxes on capital, as well as information on the major victims and beneficiaries. The four major types of distortions caused by taxes on capital are (a) the intertemporal distortion, the extent of which is measured by the size of the METR; (b) the interindustry distortion, measured by the dispersion of the METR across sectors; (c) the interest distortion, measured by the dispersion of the METR across sectors; (d) the financing distortion, measured by the dispersion in the METR across financing instruments.[3]

The importance of the assumptions underlying this methodology needs to be emphasized. The firm is a price taker in all markets, and all markets are perfectly competitive. The firm selects its stock of debt to minimize its cost of finance. The firm's financial policy is assumed to be exogenously given. Inflation is not an issue because the relevant components of the tax system are perfectly indexed. The firm maximizes profits by investing until the marginal rate of return on capital is equal to the cost of capital. The cost of capital is a function of depreciation, capital gains, financing costs, and the effective purchasing price of capital, and it accounts for the tax provisions affecting the price of capital—CIT, indirect taxes, depreciation rules, and fiscal incentives. In the computation of the METR, all projects are assumed to offer savers the same after-tax rate of return, *s*. There are at least two interpretations of a constant after-tax rate of return to savers. The first is that it reflects the conventional closed economy assumption. The second is an open economy interpretation, in which savers have access to the world capital markets with an after-tax rate of return of *s*.

Derivation of the Pretax Rate of Return in a Tax-Free World

The basic idea gained from the neoclassical model of investment is that an investment project is worthwhile when the net present value of its revenues exceeds its acquisition cost. The costs associated with an investment are usually expressed on a per-unit base and referred to as the user cost of capital. This user cost of capital is the sum of the real cost of financing the investment and depreciation. The relevant rate of return in this context is the real user cost. The idea is that for any private entity, physical capital and financial capital are alternative ways of acquiring future income. Therefore the acquisition cost of physical capital must equal at the margin the price of financial assets that generate the same path of future income.

More formally, the assumption underlying this framework is that the firm maximizes its market value or, equivalently, its net present value (NPV). In a continuous-time approach and in a world without taxes, the net present value may be written as

$$(7\text{-}2) \qquad \text{NPV} = \int_0^\infty e^{-\rho(t)} \left\{ P(t)\, F[K(t)] - q(t)\, I(t) \right\} dt$$

where ρ = the discount factor, P = the price of output, $F(\cdot)$ = the production function, q = the price of capital goods, I = the investment level, and t = time.

Without taxes, the discount factor ρ equals the market rate of interest r ($\rho = r$). The firm is assumed to be competitive and hence takes the path of prices as given. The firm faces an initially given level for the capital stock:

$$(7\text{-}3) \qquad\qquad K(0) = K_0$$

and the capital stock evolves according to

$$(7\text{-}4) \qquad\qquad \dot{K}(t) = I(t) - \delta K(t)$$

where $\dot{K} = dK/dt$ and δ is the rate of (exponential) economic depreciation.

The firm maximizes equation 7-2 subject to equations 7-3 and 7-4, that is,

$$(7\text{-}5) \qquad \max \int_0^\infty e^{-\rho(t)} \left\{ P(t)\, F[K(t)] - q(t)\, I(t) \right\} dt$$

$$\text{s.t.} = \dot{K}(t) = I(t) - \delta K(t) \ \text{ and } \ K(0) = K_0 \,.$$

The current Hamiltonian for this problem may be written as

$$H = P(t)\, F[K(t)] - q(t)\, I(t) + \lambda(t)\, [I(t) - \delta K(t)].$$

The first-order conditions for an interior solution for this problem imply that

$$(7-6) \qquad P\,\frac{\partial F}{\partial K} = q\,(\rho + \delta - \dot{q}/q).$$

The right-hand side of equation 7-6 is the user cost of capital *c:*

$$(7-7) \qquad c = q\,(\rho + \delta - \dot{q}/q).$$

Finally, *p*, the required real rate of return, net of real depreciation, on a marginal investment, is derived by rearranging equation 7-6 to define the cost of capital in real terms and subtracting depreciation:

$$(7-8) \qquad p = \frac{P \cdot (\partial F/\partial K)}{q} - \delta,$$

which, in equilibrium, may be written as

$$(7-9) \qquad p = \frac{c}{q} - \delta.$$

Without taxes, inflation, or relative price changes, the real rate of return to the saver would be equal to the interest rate, or *p = r*.

The Pretax Rate of Return in a World with Taxes

If the CIT were comprehensive and fully integrated with other taxes on capital and with the taxation of individuals, if there were no tax rate differentiation, and if depreciation were accounted for correctly, the tax system would have no effect on decisionmaking by firms.[4] Firms would maximize profit by choosing the most efficient means of production and financing. Savings would go to the most efficient investments. The various differences between the desirable and the actual design of the CIT, however, combined with interactions with the other major taxes on capital, result in significant price distortions in the capital market and lead to an inefficient allocation of resources in the economy. So the next step is to introduce taxes into this framework. This step requires the identification of the various taxes that need to be accounted for. In Brazil, capital is taxed (a) at the personal level under the personal income tax or through withholding taxes; (b) at the firm level under the CIT; and (c) through various indirect taxes and surcharges levied at both the federal and the state levels.

With taxation, the decision problem of the firm is similar to equation 7-4, but the expression for NPV is now given by

$$(7-10) \quad \text{NPV} = \int_0^\infty e^{-\rho t}\left\{P(t)\,F[K(t)] - q(t)\,I(t) - T(\cdot)\right\}dt\,.$$

Once taxes are accounted for, the firm's discount factor reflects its financial policy and might differ from the interest rate, r. This issue is addressed separately later in this section. For the time being, the firm's financial policy will initially be assumed to determine exogenously ρ. $T(\cdot)$ denotes the tax function that determines the firm's tax liability net of any fiscal credits that may apply. The firm's objective may be written more explicitly as

$$(7\text{-}10') \ \text{NPV}^* \ = \ \max \int_0^\infty e^{-\rho t}\left\{ (1-\tau)\left[PF(K, L)/(1+\xi)\right] - q(1+\phi)I\right\} dt$$

$$+ \int_0^\infty \int_t^\infty e^{-\rho s}\tau q(1+\phi)\, D(s-t)\, I\, ds\, dt$$

$$\text{s.t. } \dot{K}(t) \ = \ I(t) - \delta K(t) \text{ and } K(0) = K_0$$

where τ = the effective business income tax rate, ϕ = the rate of taxes on capital goods, ξ = the rate of the product-based value added tax (the ICM [Imposto sobre a circulação de mercadorias—sales turnover tax or value-added consumption tax] and the IPI [Imposto sobre produtos industriais—a tax on industrial products] are both product-based).

We also introduce the following definitions:

$$(7\text{-}11) \qquad\qquad \int_t^\infty e^{-\rho s}\, \tau D(s-t)\, ds \ = \ A.e^{-\rho t}$$

where A is the present value (at time t) of tax savings from depreciation allowances permitted by the tax law.

The current Hamiltonian for this problem may be written as

$$H = (1-\tau)\left[PF(K, L)/(1+\xi)\right] - q(1+\phi)(1-A)I + \lambda(I-\delta K).$$

The first-order conditions for an interior solution for this problem imply that

$$(7\text{-}12) \qquad P\, \frac{\partial F}{\partial K} = \frac{q(1+\phi)(1+\xi)(1-A)(\rho+\delta-\dot{q}/q)}{(1-\tau)}.$$

The user cost of capital now equals the right-hand side of equation 7-10:

$$(7\text{-}13) \qquad c = \frac{q(1+\phi)(1+\xi)(1-A)(\rho+\delta-\dot{q}/q)}{(1-\tau)}.$$

This expression of the user cost of capital accounts for all the taxes levied on Brazilian firms. As earlier, the real pretax rate of return is found by rearranging the cost-of-capital equation and subtracting depreciation. The resulting formula for the pretax rate of return, p, is

$$(7\text{-}14) \quad p = \frac{c}{q} - \delta = \frac{(1+\phi)(1+\xi)(1-A)(\rho+\delta-\dot{q}/q)}{(1-\tau)} - \delta.$$

Because the Brazilian taxation of capital is perfectly indexed for inflation:

$$(7\text{-}15) \qquad\qquad \dot{q}/q = 0.$$

The Pretax Rate of Return for Firms with Tax Holidays

The existence of a plethora of fiscal incentives in Brazil is one of the most remarkable characteristics of its tax system. The range and variety of their objectives are exceptionally wide. They include export promotion, sectoral promotion, regional promotion, input promotion, and many types of specific activities. Sixty-six incentive programs are available against business income taxes alone for different kinds of sectors and assets. Almost every tax in Brazil is associated with its own set of fiscal incentives.[5]

Because the Brazilian tax law includes so many tax holidays, their modeling deserves special attention. In general it is fairly simple to model the tax preferences within the framework just described by selecting the appropriate value for the tax variable. The modeling of tax holidays is, however, more complex because they alter the time path faced by the firm for its investment decision. Here we discuss the alteration of the previous framework needed to assess tax holidays.[6]

Consider a firm that in the interval from 0 to t^* faces the business income tax τ^* and that, after t^*, faces the tax with rate τ. The firm's problem for this case may be written as

$$(7\text{-}16)\ \mathrm{NPV}^* = \max \int_0^{t^*} e^{-\rho^* t} \left\{ (1-\tau^*)\left[PF(K,L)/(1+\xi)\right] - q(1+\phi)I \right\} dt$$

$$+ \int_0^{t^*} \int_t^{t^*} e^{-\rho^* s}\, \tau^* q\,(1+\phi)\, D\,(s-t)\, I\, ds\, dt$$

$$+ \int_{t^*}^{\infty} e^{-\rho t}\left\{ (1-\tau)\left[PF(K,L)/(1+\xi)\right] - q(1+\phi)\,I \right\} dt$$

$$+ \int_{t^*}^{\infty} \int_t^{\infty} e^{-\rho s}\, \tau q\,(1+\phi)\, D\,(s-t)\, I\, ds\, dt$$

$$\text{s.t. } \dot{K}(t) = I(t) - \delta K(t) \text{ and } K(0) = K_0.$$

As before, A* is defined as

$$(7\text{-}17) \qquad \int_0^{t^*} e^{-\rho^* s}\, \tau^* q\,(1+\phi)\, D\,(s)\, I\, ds$$

$$+ \int_{t^*}^{\infty} e^{-\rho s}\, \tau q\,(1+\phi)\, D\,(s)\, I\, ds = q\,(1+\phi)\, A^*I$$

where A^* is the present value of the tax savings that follow from depreciation allowances. The current Hamiltonian for the firm's problem is then

$$(7\text{-}18) \quad H = (1 - \tau^*) \left[PF(K, L)/(1 + \xi) \right] - q(1 + \phi)(1 - A^*) I + \lambda (I - \delta K)$$

for the interval from 0 to t^*. The user cost of capital may then be written at time zero as

$$(7\text{-}19) \quad c = \frac{q(1 + \phi)(1 + \xi)(1 - A^*)(\rho^* + \delta - \dot{q}/q)}{(1 - \tau^*)} + \frac{q(1 + \phi)(1 + \xi) \cdot A^*}{(1 - \tau^*)}.$$

The other steps needed to conclude the computations are exact replicates of those already presented. One important difference, however, stems from the fact that the cost of capital is not constant for this case even if the tax law does not change. That happens because depreciation allowances are a function of time (the postponement of investment allows larger depreciation allowances for the firm). In the numerical computations firms are assumed to depreciate their capital stock at the same rate during the holiday period. As shown in Mintz 1989, this is a crucial assumption.

After-Tax Rates of Return

The modeling of the supply side of the capital market requires the derivation of the net rate of return of savings, s. This is analytically much simpler than the derivation of the gross rate of return relevant to the demand side of the market. Under Brazilian law the only relevant tax for the savers is the personal tax or the final withholding tax levied at the source on capital income. In most cases, these two taxes have the same rate and are perfect substitutes. They can be viewed as a single tax. Because this aspect of the tax system is appropriately indexed, the after-tax rate of return to the savers is expressed as

$$(7\text{-}20) \qquad\qquad s = (1 - m) r$$

where m is the personal tax rate on interest income. Equation 7-20 also assumes perfect indexation for inflation.

The Firm's After-Tax Discount Rate

The last issue to be dealt with is the alteration of the firm's discount rate to account for taxes. Once taxes are introduced, the discount rate is no longer equal to the market interest rate. This discount rate will, however, vary according to the financing source of the investment project. Financing can be acquired through equity, retained earnings, or debt. In many countries the tax treatment of these three sources differs. In Brazil, however, since 1989, retained earnings and equity are subject to the same tax treatment and are, hence, equivalent within the framework used here.

For debt finance, because interest income is taxed but is tax deductible at the firm level, the appropriate discount factor for after-tax cash flows is the interest rate, net of taxes:

$$(7\text{-}21) \qquad\qquad \rho = r(1 - \tau).$$

For new share issues and retained earnings, the relevant expression is

$$(7\text{-}22) \qquad\qquad \rho = \frac{1-m}{1-d}\, r$$

where d is the personal tax rate on distributable dividends (dividends actually distributed and retained earnings). Equation 7-22 ensures that the net-of-tax return on dividend income $(1 - d)\,\rho$ equals the net-of-tax return on interest income $(1 - m)r$.

Effective Tax Rates on Capital in Brazil

We begin this section with a brief overview of the tax provisions relevant to the derivation of the METR. Next, we present the results of the computation of the METRs for investment projects under the normal tax regime. We then turn to the assessment of the major tax incentive programs in regard to their effect on the METR.

The Major Taxes on Capital

This section distinguishes between direct and indirect taxes levied on capital. The complexity of the Brazilian tax system requires detailed assessment of the specific design of each tax.

PROFITS TAXES. Until 1988, business profits were subject only to the CIT and to a withholding tax on distributed profits.[7] In 1989 the Brazilian tax law began to allow four different taxes on business profits: the CIT, a surcharge levied by states on the tax revenue collected by the federal government from the CIT, a social contribution earmarked to finance social expenditure, and withholding taxes on dividends and retained earnings. Because they are all levied in sequence on business profits, we combine their description and assessment.

Tax base. The generic base for each one of these taxes is business income. The definition of income for tax purposes includes, in principle, any increase in the firm's net worth. Thus the adopted definition conforms to the accepted convention of identifying income with increments in wealth. This means that, for instance, the deduction of the depreciation of productive assets is allowed in calculating income and that debt interest is tax deductible. There are, however, some differences for the exact base in each case.

The computation of taxable income for the CIT follows several steps. It defines taxable profits as the difference between gross receipts from sales and services and all production and financial costs, as well as many specific deductions allowed by the law. The actual tax base, however, is narrower because it also allows a large set of deductions that reflect the many tax incentives granted to corporations. The tax base for the social contribution is essentially taxable profits, except for one major difference: it also allows the exclusion of export profits. No other fiscal incentive is allowed against the social contribution. The tax base for the state tax is simply the tax revenue collected by the federal government from the CIT and from the withholding tax on capital.

Sequencing of bases. Because the three taxes are levied in sequence, their order matters for the computation of the effective tax rate on business profits. The social contribution is the first tax to be levied on all profits—except exports—before deductions for tax incentives. The amount paid for this social contribution is then deducted, along with eventual incentives from the base, to obtain the taxable base for the CIT. The revenue from this computation is the base for the state tax. Once these taxes have been accounted for, equity income can be computed by deducting them from taxable profit. The withholding taxes are levied on the residual. The state tax is then levied on that withholding tax revenue.

Tax rates. The standard rate for the CIT is 30 percent, with an additional surcharge of 5 percent for income between 150,000 BTNs (Bonus do tesouro nacional, or national treasury bonds) and 300,000 BTNs and 10 percent for profits over 300,000 BTNs (financial institutions pay surcharges of 10 percent and 15 percent, respectively). Agriculture continues to receive favored tax treatment. The sector pays a 6 percent tax rate, is allowed a generous acceleration of depreciation (investments are costed at two to five times their actual value), and can deduct actual costs up to nine times their actual value in the computation of their taxable income. This reduces the sector's effective tax rates to zero on a fairly permanent basis.

The social contribution tax is levied at a rate of 8 percent for most firms (12 percent for financial institutions), on net profits as computed for the CIT, before any fiscal incentive has been taken into account. The state tax on capital income is levied at a rate of up to 5 percent on the federal revenue collected within the state from capital income taxes (essentially the CIT and the withholding taxes on dividends and retained earnings in this case). With a CIT rate of 30 percent, the maximum effect that the local tax may have on business income is 1.5 percent. States can allow a discount on that rate, but few have so far decided to do so. The withholding tax on equity income is levied at 8 percent.

Depreciation. Depreciation rates allowed for tax purposes are determined by the tax authorities. The most important are machinery and equipment, 10 percent; installations, 10 percent; buildings, 4 percent. These rates apply to the useful life of a fixed asset in normal use in eight-hour shifts. Depreciation rates are increased by 50 percent and 100 percent for machinery and equipment used in two and three eight-hour shifts, respectively. Higher rates can be permitted given appropriate evidence.

Accelerated depreciation. Accelerated depreciation is allowed for new capital assets produced in Brazil and for capital assets necessary for projects in certain industries. As a rule, the rate of accelerated depreciation is twice the normal rate and is to be added to normal depreciation. The sum of ordinary and accelerated depreciation is not permitted to exceed the acquisition cost of goods, adjusted for inflation.

Indexation for inflation. Brazilian law recognizes that inflation produces an appreciation of permanent assets and distorts net worth. The indexation procedure ("monetary correction") allows for the restatement of specific items of the balance sheet: all permanent-asset accounts (fixed assets, investments, depreciation, and amortization accounts) and net worth accounts (defined as capital, capital reserves, retained earnings, and accumulated deficits).

The difference between the corrected value of adjustable items and their previous value was added to the corresponding account and compensated for with a corresponding entry in the income statement (a special adjustment account) labeled, as a rule, "monetary correction." The adjustment of permanent-asset accounts is registered as a credit in the special-adjustment accounts, and the adjustment of net worth counts as a debit.

Any loss appearing in the monetary correction account is deductible for tax purposes. Corporations may, however, choose to defer the tax on unrealized inflationary gains. The definition of realized inflationary gains was provided in the Brazilian tax law. The adjustment for inflation does not apply to inventories (other than immovable property held for sale by enterprises engaged in the real estate business).

INDIRECT TAXES. In Brazil, capital goods are subject to indirect taxes. Domestic machinery is subject to the IPI, a 7.5 percent (on average) federal tax on manufactured products, and to the ICM, a 20.5 percent state tax on industry and service transactions and a 12.5 percent (on average) import tax. Buildings are subject only to the ISS (Imposto sobre serviços, or tax on services), a tax on service of 5 percent. Both the IPI and the ICM are product-based (rather than consumption-based) value added taxes, which is why they introduce a tax wedge into the capital market. Imported capital goods are subject to the IPI and the ICM as a rule but may be exempted if they benefit from incentives.

TAX INCENTIVES. Brazilian tax law uses tax incentives intensively. In 1989, sixty-six different incentive programs reduced CIT liability, mainly to promote sectoral or regional growth. Another forty-one sets of incentives also allow reductions in IPI indirect tax liabilities. They lead to a revenue loss to the federal government of at least 1.6 percent of GDP. They include rate reductions (most notably in the agriculture sector), increases in deductions allowed (again in agriculture), reductions in taxable profits (mostly for certain regional operations like the Manaus Free Zone, or Zona Franca de Manaus [ZFM], and for exports), and accelerated depreciation for approved projects. Many of these incentive programs can be used cumulatively, and are intensively used by firms to decrease their tax liabilities. A detailed description is provided in the appendix.

Because there is such a wide variety of incentives in Brazil, we will concentrate on analyzing the tax preferences leading to the largest revenue losses. These include various types of regional tax incentives (0.3 percent of GDP in revenue loss) and export incentives (0.1 percent of GDP in revenue loss). The relevant technical details are introduced as needed in the next section.

The Normal Tax Treatment as the Base Case

The base case characterizes a marginal investment project by a firm that is subject to a normal tax treatment, without the benefit of any fiscal incentive but with a net profit sufficient for its profits to be subject to a 10 percent additional federal tax—a surcharge—on its income. The firm benefits from straight-line depreciation at rates of 10 percent for industrial machinery and 4 percent for buildings. The appropriate economic depreciation is assumed to be exponential at the same rates. The firm is also subject to a state surcharge on income from capital and to the new social contribution. It pays the tax on retained earnings and dividends. Interest income is also taxed. The firm pays indirect taxes—the IPI, the ICM, and import tax—on all its purchases of capital goods. The IPI and the ICM have to be included in the computation in spite of being value added taxes because their base is product rather than, as in most other countries using value added taxes, consumption. The METRs are computed for two types of productive capital (machinery and buildings) and three types of financing (debt, equity, and retained earnings), with the last two being equivalent under the tax system in 1989.[8] Table 7-1 summarizes the data requirements for the computation of the METR in the base case. The METRs obtained from these data illustrate the set of issues resulting under the most straightforward application of the tax law.

The results of the computation in the base case, summarized in table 7-2, confirm one of the tentative conclusions drawn from the macroeconomic stylized facts. Brazilian METRs derived from the normal tax

Table 7-1. Data for Computation of Brazilian METR
(percent)

Feature	Value in base case
Tax liability invested in special funds	0.000
Effective social contribution rate	0.080
Profits earned from exports	0.000
Real interest rate	0.100
Effective CIT [a]	0.380
Effective total tax rate on profits [b]	0.460
Depreciation allowance (straight line)	
Industry machinery	0.100
Buildings	0.040
Indirect taxes	
Machinery: federal [c]	0.200
Machinery: state (ICM)	0.205
Buildings (ISS)	0.050
Tax on interest income	0.250
Tax on distributed dividends	0.080
Tax on capital gains	0.080

a. Excluding social contribution. Computed as CIT rate (30 percent) plus federal rate (10 percent) plus state rate (5 percent on 40 percent); additional correction for reduced rate (6 percent) on export profits.

b. Effective CIT plus effective social contribution rate.

c. IPI = 7.5 percent; import = 12.5 percent.

Source: Brazilian tax law.

treatment of investment projects are high by international standards. This may explain the relatively low level of investment in Brazil. Although the METRs in the countries belonging to the Organization for Economic Cooperation and Development (OECD) presented in table 7-2 are not strictly comparable and are presented here for purely illustrative purposes, they allow us to conclude that the Brazilian METRs are too high.[9] Only the Netherlands, Denmark, and Norway were, on average, worse off than Brazil among the nineteen OECD countries covered by the OECD average. The major factors explaining Brazil's outlier status are of two types. First, Brazil levies a much larger number of taxes on profits than most other OECD countries. Second, Brazil's value added taxes are product-based, whereas in most other countries, indirect taxes are not levied on capital goods, and when value added taxes are adopted, they are levied on consumption, not production.

In addition, the results from the base case reveal two more problems due to the current design of the taxation of capital in Brazil. First, the tax treatment of assets is differentiated by type of asset. The Brazilian METRs are systematically smaller for buildings than for machinery. This results

Table 7-2. METR in Brazil before and after 1989 Reform, Compared with METR in the OECD and East Asia
(percent)

Financing mean	Machinery		Buildings	
	Brazil 1989	*OECD 1983*	*Brazil 1989*	*OECD 1983*
Debt	55.0	11.0	39.8	19.4
New share	68.1	52.8	60.4	64.4
Retained earnings	68.1	32.5	60.4	46.0

Note: Normal values for Brazil; averages for OECD.

Source: For Brazil, World Bank staff calculations; for OECD, McKee and Visser 1986: table 11, average inflation.

from much smaller indirect taxes levied on buildings. As noted earlier, buildings are subject only to the ISS, the tax on services. Machinery is subject to the IPI, the ICM, and the import tax. Second, taxes also distort financing decisions in Brazil. Debt should be the preferred instrument because it benefits from lower tax rates. These are two important items to be included in any tax reform agenda in Brazil.

Accounting for Tax Incentives

As just illustrated, the normal tax treatment of capital leads to unusually high METRs. One of the outstanding characteristics of Brazil's tax system, however, is that it provides potential investors with a plethora of tax incentives. These incentives are expected to reduce the deterrence to invest because of the high METRs resulting from the normal tax treatment. Intuitively, it would seem that because investment is not growing as fast in Brazil as it is in comparable countries, it must be that these incentives do not reduce the Brazilian METRs enough. In this section we show the results of simulations of the effects on the METR of Brazil's major tax incentive programs.

We assessed three major types of fiscal incentives: accelerated depreciation, benefits granted to exporters, and regional development. This third type is composed of two categories: tax benefits granted for investment in regional development funds (FINOR, Northeast Investment Fund, FINAM, Amazon Investment Fund, and FISET, Sectorial Investment Fund) and tax holidays granted for investment in particular regions, mainly the Amazon (SUDAM, Amazon Development Authority), the Northeast (SUDENE, Northeast Development Authority), and the Zona Franca de Manaus (ZFM), which, in addition, benefits from the exemption from IPI and import taxes.[10]

MAJOR SOURCES OF DISTORTIONS IN THE BRAZILIAN CAPITAL MARKET. Table 7-3 summarizes the results of simulations of the effects of all the major tax incentive programs. Figure 7-1 provides a visualization of the relative differences in METRs. The METR on a hypothetical investment project ranges from 10.4 percent to 68.1 percent. It varies by type of asset (machinery or buildings), sector, region, market orientation (domestic or export), country of origin of capital goods (domestic or foreign), and means of financing (debt or equity). The highest METR falls on an investment in industrial machinery financed by new share issues or retained earnings and subject to the normal direct and indirect tax treatment—that is, without the benefit of any fiscal incentive. The lowest rate falls on the same machine financed through debt and freed from any indirect tax liability—that is, subject to true zero-rating for all value added taxes.

The results show that few tax incentives can effectively reduce the deterrence effect on investment caused by taxes. In fact, tax incentives need to be targeted to the major source of the distortion because of taxes in the capital market. Table 7-3 shows that indirect taxation, not the CIT, is the most important source of effective taxation on a marginal investment project. This suggests that the simplest way for Brazil to reduce its METR to international levels would be to transform its product-based value added taxes into consumption-based value added taxes. None of the other incentive programs work as efficiently. Generally, the incentives targeted at the taxes on profits do little to reduce the deterrence effect. In some cases they even have a perverse effect and lead to an increase in the METR rather than a decrease. For example, regional incentives may raise rather than reduce the METR on capital. But these are only the main conclusions emerging from the results of the simulations. In the rest of this section we present a detailed discussion of each one of these results.

Table 7-3. Marginal Effective Tax Rates on Investment, 1989
(percent)

	Financed through debt		Financed through equity	
Tax status of firm	*Machinery*	*Buildings*	*Machinery*	*Buildings*
Base case	55.0	39.8	68.1	60.4
Normal corporate tax, no indirect taxes	10.4	16.7	42.6	46.9
Regional investment funds	55.9	40.8	66.2	57.2
Zona Franca de Manaus	47.4	43.2	35.2	33.2
Accelerated depreciation	48.1	33.1	62.4	56.0

Source: Authors' calculations.

Figure 7-1. Marginal Effective Tax Rates on Investment in Brazil, 1989

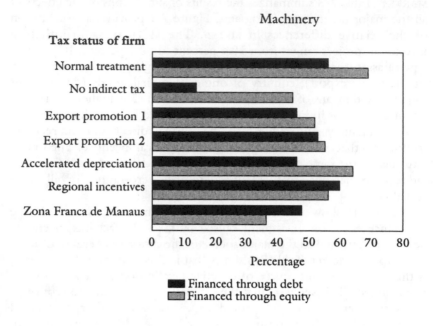

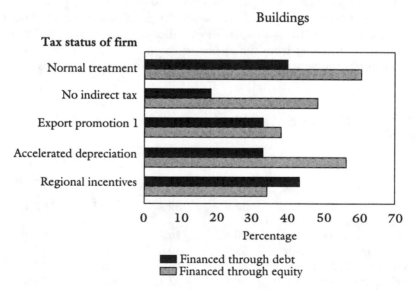

Note: Export promotion 1 is to users of domestic capital; export promotion 2 is to users of foreign capital.

Source: Authors' calculations.

INDIRECT TAXES AS THE MAJOR ISSUE. A simulation suppressing all indirect taxes on capital—with the rest of the data as in the base case—shows that the METR on machinery declines from 55 percent to 10.4 percent when the machinery is financed by debt and from 68.1 percent to 42.6 percent when financed by equity or retained earnings. For buildings, the suppression of indirect taxes cuts the METR from 39.8 percent to 16.7 percent when financed by debt and from 60.4 percent to 46.9 percent when financed by equity.[11] The cut is lower for buildings for two reasons. First, current indirect taxes on buildings are lower than those levied on machinery. In addition, both the IPI and the value added tax are essentially product-based taxes that, implicitly, include depreciation in their base. The longer the life of the asset, the lower the relative importance of the depreciation. All in all, however, the differences in rates explain why indirect taxes in Brazil discriminate against short-lived assets.

INVESTMENT IN REGIONAL DEVELOPMENT FUNDS. This first type of regional incentive allows any Brazilian firm to invest up to 40 percent of its income tax liability in special investment funds—basically, FINOR, FINAM, and FISET. This is modeled as a reduction in the effective CIT rate, computed as follows: if the rates of return on these investments were the same as those the firm could obtain elsewhere, this would be equivalent to a 40 percent reduction in the CIT rate. The returns on these investments, however, are widely believed to be very low, and, hence, the rate reduction is not that high. For illustrative purposes we assumed that the rate of return on these regional funds was a third of the normal rate of return. It could be argued that this represents an upper limit rather than an approximation of the actual rate of return. In any case the METR computed then provides an upper limit for the reduction in the METR through these incentive programs. The computations are for a firm investing up to the limit in those special funds.

We arrive at two conclusions concerning investments in regional development funds. First, they do not alter the METR significantly. Second, and more surprising, whereas the METR falls somewhat in equity financing, it increases in debt financing. In other words the size of the distortion increases rather than decreases, reducing the incentive to invest. This result may seem counterintuitive. It derives from the tax treatment of interest payments. Because they are deductible as a cost, the firm's discount factor increases, causing the effective rate to increase as well.

REGIONAL TAX HOLIDAYS AND THE ZFM. This second type of regional incentive takes the form of tax holidays.[12] Two significant results emerge here. First, the maximum reduction in the METR that can be obtained from SUDAM or SUDENE is not significant. In debt financing, an increase in the METR can occur. Hence the second major conclusion is that equity financing should always be preferred to debt financing. The explanation is somewhat complex, but it is worth discussing.

The distinguishing features of this type of incentive is that it is time dependent. The METR is likely to be different for each year during the tax holiday period. A full awareness of the time path of the METR resulting from the tax holiday may provide an incentive to postpone investment. Hence the effects of tax holidays on investment are hard to assess.[13] To obtain time invariance of the investment decision, the model assumes perfect foresight by the firm of the length of the holiday and of the future tax regime. The METR can then be computed for each year for the full duration of the tax holiday. For illustrative purposes, figure 7-2 shows the METR under debt financing for a fifteen-year tax holiday granted to an investment in the ZFM. In the long run, as shown by Mintz (chapter 3, this volume), if the firm must write down the value of its assets for tax purposes during the holiday period, the tax depreciation writeoffs after the tax holiday may be inadequate in relation to the true depreciation cost. As a rule, if there are no deferrals of tax depreciation writeoffs, as is the case in Brazil, the METR on depreciable capital during the holiday is positive (or negative), if the tax depreciation rate is more (or less) than

Figure 7-2. Regional Incentives in Brazil for Industrial Machinery under Debt Financing, Zona Franca de Manaus

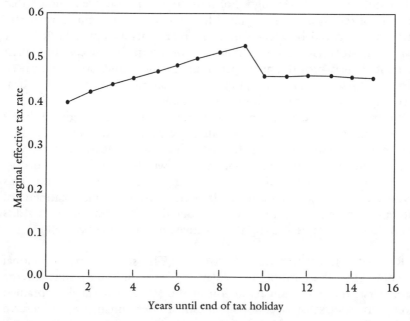

Source: Authors' calculations.

the true economic depreciation rate. The results assume fifteen-year holidays and a zero CIT rate.

In applying the model to Brazilian tax law, the only difference between the ZFM and the other regional holidays is that the latter pay indirect taxes while the former does not. This also explains why investments in the ZFM have a lower METR. Without this tax break tax holidays would, on average, result in increases in the METR in the case of debt financing for an investment in SUDENE or SUDAM, in which the average METR increased from 55 percent to 61 percent. The reason for this counterintuitive increase in the METR is explained in the previous paragraph. On average, the tax depreciation rate during the holiday is much higher than the actual depreciation rate, whereas the opposite holds after the holiday. As a result, a penalty is imposed for the remaining life of the asset after the tax holiday. The relative importance of this penalty increases with the duration of the life of the asset. The importance of this effect in the case of the ZFM is fully dominated by the indirect tax reduction. An investment in machinery in the ZFM has a METR of 46.4 percent as against 55 percent in the base case for debt financing. The tax break is even larger— an almost 50 percent reduction—in the case of an equity-financed asset because the spurious effect resulting from the allowance of deductions for interest payments is no longer present.

ACCELERATED DEPRECIATION. In general the rate of accelerated depreciation is twice the normal rate and is added to normal depreciation. This is the assumption built into the results provided in table 7-3. As expected, accelerated depreciation reduces the METR. The reduction is not dramatic, however. The METR declines only by 7 to 17 percent, depending on the type of asset and on the financing used. Note, however, that the new tax law has resulted in a minor increase in the METR for debt financing. This is explained by the fact that accelerated depreciation is not available for the new social contribution levied on profits.

EXPORT INCENTIVES. The assessment of the effect of export incentives on the METR is unusually complex. It is best illustrated by a set of simulations for varying shares of export sales in total sales. With respect to the model, the relevant variable is the share in regard to sales revenue, not profits. The results of those simulations are presented in table 7-4. Exporters also benefit from an exemption from the new social contribution. Exports are assumed to be exempt from the ICM and federal indirect taxes.

Table 7-4 suggests the following conclusions. First, and somewhat unexpectedly, the method of financing that minimizes the METR differs for producers with a small share of exports in their production and for those with a large share of exports. The exact turning point was calcu-

Table 7-4. Marginal Effective Tax Rates on Exporters' Investment, 1989
(percent)

Percentage of exports in total sales	Financed through debt		Financed through equity	
	Machinery	*Buildings*	*Machinery*	*Buildings*
0 (= base case)	55.0	39.8	68.1	60.4
10	49.9	35.3	59.4	50.3
40	48.7	33.5	53.2	40.8
50	48.2	32.9	51.0	35.5
100	45.1	28.5	37.6	17.0

Note: The CIT rate on profits from exports is assumed to be 6 percent.
Source: Authors' calculations.

lated to be at 65 percent. The preferred financing means for firms exporting less than 65 percent of their output is debt, whereas it is equity or retained earnings for firms producing 65 percent or more. This result is explained by the deductibility of debt-financed investment. The value of such distortions is larger, the larger the effective tax rate on the firm.

Second, reductions in the METR can be significantly larger for equity financing than for debt financing and are therefore more likely to lead to a stimulation of investment for the former financing means. Under equity financing, the METR for machinery could drop from 68.1 percent to 37.4 percent, and that for buildings could fall by as much as 43 percent (from 60.4 percent to 17 percent). Under debt financing the maximum cut would be only 10 percent for any asset type.

Third, and maybe most important, in the case of machinery, for a relatively small drop in the METR (10 percent at the most), the revenue costs of a reduction in the effective CIT rate are very high. To understand this, assume that a firm decides to specialize fully either in domestic consumption or in exports. If it is domestically oriented, it faces the base case METR. If it is fully outward oriented, it faces the 100 percent case shown in table 7-4. The decision to move from one extreme to the other results in a cut in the CIT rate from 30 percent to 6 percent and an exemption from the new social contribution. These translate into a reduction in tax revenue on profits of over 80 percent.

IMPORTED AS OPPOSED TO DOMESTIC CAPITAL GOODS. So far, the firms have always been assumed to invest in domestic capital goods. There are two major differences for firms that invest in foreign capital goods instead: (a) foreign capital goods are burdened with larger indirect taxes (from which export firms may be exempted in Brazil); (b) foreign capital goods cannot benefit from accelerated depreciation. This results in

Table 7-5. *Comparison of Domestic and Foreign Capital Goods*
(percent)

Tax status of the firm	Machinery financed through debt	Machinery financed through equity
Accelerated depreciation and regional funds for domestic-oriented user of domestic capital goods	50.2	61.2
Accelerated depreciation and regional funds for domestic-oriented user of foreign capital goods	71.7	77.6
Accelerated depreciation, regional funds, and export promotion to user (exports = 50 percent of sales)	51.9	54.5
Accelerated depreciation, regional funds, and export promotion to user of foreign capital (exports = 50 percent of sales)	52.6	51.5

Source: Authors' calculations.

discrimination against the use of foreign capital goods, as illustrated by table 7-5.

SECTORAL DISTORTIONS. The discussion to this point has focused on the individual effect of tax provisions on the METR for a theoretical investment project. To assess the differentiation of METRs across sectors, the Brazilian publication *Conjuntura Econômica* computed average METRs for the firms included in the manufacturing sector of the *Balanço das mil maiores sociedades por ações* (Conjuntura Econômica 1988). The results are likely to show some systematic bias because the survey covers only the larger firms. In addition, the marginal tax rate on the various means of financing had to be assumed to be equal to the average tax rates computed from the sample because the publication only provides data on averages. Finally, with respect to incentives, comparable sectoral data provided by the SRF (revenue service) were used when possible. Not all incentives could be assessed. No data were available on accelerated depreciation, for example. The results of the computations are presented in table 7-6 and figure 7-3.

Aside from the clear differences between debt and equity financing, and between investments in machinery and buildings, the spread of the METR across sectors can also be significant. To illustrate the effect of these differences, an investment in buildings in the leather product sector,

Table 7-6. Marginal Effective Tax Rate on Industry
(percent)

	Industrial Machinery			Buildings		
	Debt	Equity	Average	Debt	Equity	Average
Theoretical base case	55.0	68.1	n.a.	39.8	60.4	n.a.
Manufacturing	54.7	64.5	61.1	39.5	55.0	49.8
Basic metals	54.4	63.7	59.1	39.2	53.9	46.9
Mechanical equipment	55.1	65.8	61.5	39.9	56.9	50.4
Electrical machinery	55.1	66.1	62.5	40.0	57.3	51.9
Transport equipment	54.7	64.7	59.8	39.6	55.4	47.7
Chemicals	54.9	65.4	63.3	39.8	56.3	53.2
Textiles	54.8	64.9	62.1	39.6	55.6	51.3
Leather products	53.0	59.3	57.5	37.8	47.5	44.7
Foods and beverages	53.7	61.5	59.1	38.5	50.7	47.0

n.a. Not applicable.
Source: Authors' calculations.

financed with debt, has a METR of 37.7 percent, whereas an investment in industrial machinery in the electrical machinery industry is subject to a METR of 63.3 percent. Table 7-6 also shows that equity financing is relatively more costly combined with the use of tax benefits in the table because only in that case is the difference between the theoretical base case and the actual figures significant. It is also in the case of equity financing that divergences from the manufacturing mean are more significant.

AN IMPORTANT NOTE ON TAX INCENTIVES AND TAX EVASION. An important implicit assumption underlying the analysis so far has been that firms comply with the tax law. The assumption is clearly strong in the current Brazilian context. Tax evasion can, however, usefully be related to tax holidays. In fact, tax holidays provide an easy opportunity for tax arbitrage when there is an association between tax holiday firms and normal tax-paying firms. Income from tax-paying units can be shifted into tax holiday units and tax deductible costs can follow the opposite trajectory in order to minimize corporate tax payments.[14]

The differential tax treatment across assets, industries, or modes of financing provides many incentives for tax arbitrage. The multiplicity of opportunities for tax avoidance and evasion also increases tax administration costs and reduces its efficiency. In addition, tax arbitrage essentially results in reductions in average tax rates, which in turn means lower tax revenue. For instance, a form of arbitrage that could take place in Brazil involves interest payments. A firm subject to a high effective tax rate, such as an industrial firm, borrows from a firm subject to a low tax rate,

Figure 7-3. Marginal Effective Tax Rates on Industry

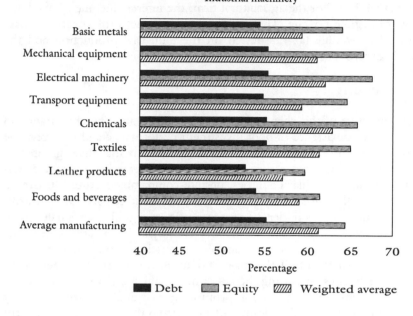

Industrial machinery

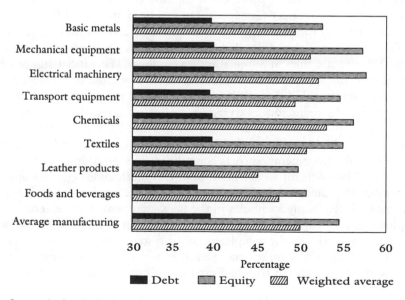

Buildings

Source: Authors' calculations.

such as one in the agricultural sector. Since interest paid is deductible from the CIT, it reduces the tax base and hence the tax liability for the industrial firm. For the agricultural firm, the interest income is taxed at a lower marginal tax rate. The two firms split the net profit of the transaction. The average tax rate levied on the industrial production and the total tax revenues are both lower.[15]

Conclusions

The objective of this chapter has been to explain an apparent paradox in Brazil: the coexistence of poor investment performance and little revenue from the taxation of capital because of multiple tax incentives granted to investors. As indicated earlier, the taxation of profits in Brazil yields less revenue than in similar countries, despite comparable statutory tax rates. In spite of this, according to *World Development Report 1989,* Brazil's investment rate was under 20 percent, a figure significantly smaller than the average for upper-middle-income countries. To a large extent the results presented here allow a plausible explanation of this paradox.

The assessment of all the major tax incentive programs in regard to their effectiveness at cutting the METR on capital shows that most are not very powerful instruments for promoting marginal investment. They often do not provide significant METR cuts from the normal tax treatment of an investment, or they provide a tax break only to investors already installed. In fact, incentives are unlikely to be the decisive factor in the decision to invest, except, perhaps, for the case of the ZFM, in which the benefits from the indirect tax exemptions can be quite critical for certain sectors. The only successful incentives are those targeted at indirect taxes.

The assessments also show that fiscal incentives are more efficient at reducing revenue than at stimulating investment. The official figure of 1.5 percent of GDP for the loss in federal revenue because of fiscal incentives is underestimated. Even if it covers the major programs, it does not account for the reduction in average tax rates obtained through incentives. Many producers decrease their average tax liability by offsetting profits in the highly taxed profitable sectors with losses in the low-taxed less profitable investments, such as agriculture. The procedure is, in general, illegal but difficult to detect without thorough auditing. This illustrates that the multiplicity of fiscal incentives (there are sixty-six different programs) leaves many loopholes in the tax system, which are extensively exploited by taxpayers to reduce their tax burden. The multiplicity of incentives also adds to the complexity of the system and results in opaque tax accounting, which makes tax evasion easier. In sum, although most tax incentives do not cut marginal tax rates, all reduce average tax rates, which helps explain the coexistence of the low revenue yield of the Brazilian CIT and a poor investment performance.[16]

Besides resolving the paradox emerging from the stylized facts, the analysis also permitted the identification of other distortions that reduce the growth potential of the economy. The simulations illustrated that, through interactions with other taxes and as a result of the extensive use of fiscal incentives, the taxation of capital introduces several types of distortions, discriminating between

- Means of financing (debt as opposed to equity or retained earnings)
- Assets (machinery as opposed to buildings or, equivalently, short-lived as opposed to long-lived assets)
- Sectors (agriculture as opposed to others)
- Regions—SUDAM, SUDENE, and SUFRAMA (Zona Franca de Manaus) as opposed to others
- Market orientation (domestic as opposed to foreign)
- Origin of capital goods (domestic as opposed to foreign).

Finally, the results show that the current system of depreciation allowances is also a source of distortion. Diversification of rates at the corporate level implies that the value of depreciation rules is lower to firms facing lower tax rates than to those facing higher rates when there are provisions limiting the carrying forward of losses. This is a major factor in explaining interasset, interfinancing, and intersectoral distortions; finally, progressivity at the source differentiates unduly by ignoring the actual ability of the owners of capital to pay.

In conclusion, if it is to recover revenue and investment simultaneously, Brazil can hardly avoid a reform of its tax system and, in particular, a revision of most of the rules defining the tax treatment of capital. In such a reform the country's highest priority will have to be a reform of its major indirect taxes. Only consumption-based value added taxes would significantly reduce the METR and hence the deterrence to invest. They would do so more efficiently than any of the incentive programs. Value added taxes based on consumption would also restore Brazil's attractiveness to international investors by making its METR comparable to those observed in the OECD countries. An agenda for reform should also include a dramatic simplification of the corporate tax law. Its current complexity leads to avoidance and evasion. This simplification is unlikely to be achieved unless most of the incentive programs are suppressed. This suppression would not further deter investment because, in most cases, tax incentives do not reduce the METRs significantly. It would, however, have the advantage of increasing tax revenue.

Appendix. Description of the Principal Brazilian Fiscal Incentives Available in 1989

The Brazilian definition of fiscal incentives was clarified during the debates in 1988–89 that preceded the preparation of the first annual budget for fiscal incentives mandated by the new constitution. The Brazilian team that helped prepare the budget defined a fiscal incentive as a public expenditure implemented through the tax system to achieve economic and social objectives. The incentive can be identified in the tax law as an exemption to the normal law, leading to a reduction in the tax liability of the taxpayer. These reductions identified in the budget are classified according to five types:

- Exemptions or tax reductions: revenues totally or partially excluded from the base and reductions in tax rates. The tax treatment of profits from exports comes under this category.
- Tax deductions: additional deductions from the base of a tax that should not take place under the normal tax law. Accelerated depreciation would come under this category.
- Tax credits: credits against the tax liability that partially, fully, or more than fully offset the tax liability. An example of such credits is provided by the legal treatment of employees' training costs paid by the employer.
- Tax rate reductions on customary tax rate scales: for example, many imports benefit from rate reductions on their IPI or import tax.
- Deferrals of the tax liability: the Brazilian incentives budget will also include the deferral of tax liabilities, unlike many other countries preparing similar budgets. The justification for this is that the budget is annual and for any given year the deferral is equivalent to a reduction in the tax liability. The documents available describing the budget preparation do not mention whether late payments of tax liabilities authorized under this "incentive" scheme would be treated symmetrically, that is, whether they would be included in the budget for the year they were actually paid as a "subsidy" to the government and entered as a negative item in that budget.

Incentives to Regional Development

The core of the regional incentives is provided by a set of programs aimed at the development of the north and northeast. The exhaustive list of regions intended to benefit from incentives programs is provided hereafter. Regional incentives can be granted to projects leading to the following goals:

- The creation of industrial or agricultural firms and the modernization or development of existing firms in the north or northeast.
- The creation of industrial firms in the Zona Franca de Manaus in the northern region. For those firms, the incentives come in addition to those granted through the program for the northern region.
- The development of western Amazonia.
- The economic recovery of the state of Espírito Santo, the least-developed state in the southern part of the country.
- The development of Grande Carajás.

TAX INCENTIVES. The incentive programs are specific to each region. They are of two main types. One reduces an investor's income tax liability due for activities elsewhere in the country. The other reduces the investor's tax liability arising from the project promoted by the incentive program. As was seen before, the principal tax break obtained is a total or partial reduction in the corporate income tax liability. Ten of sixteen fiscal incentive programs are granted against the CIT. But within each region these incentives can be cumulated with other regional or sector-specific incentives. The major incentives for each region are listed below. Some restrictions apply on the volume of tax reduction due to incentives. For instance, the entire amount of the CIT liability that can be invested through incentive schemes is limited to 50 percent of such liability. If that limit prevents a firm from taking a benefit in a particular year, it can be carried forward for up to five years.

SUDENE AND SUDAM. For both the northeastern region and the Amazon region, the incentive programs are the same. The first type of incentive works through the reduction of the total income tax liability of the firm investing in an incentive-endowed region. Since 1974 the two regions have benefited from a financing allowed by the earmarking of a share—24 percent, including the share allocated to the sectoral fund—of the CIT liability of businesses to two funds: FINAM for the north (the Amazon) and FINOR for the northeast. The funds are deposited with special banks, administered and controlled by special agencies, and finally invested in the purchase of shares issued by companies operating in the region concerned. The total share of the income tax liability that can be deposited to finance incentive programs—whatever their purpose—is limited to a total of 50 percent of the total liability. The limit is reduced when combined with sectoral incentives granted for investments in agriculture in the north and northeast. The use of investment fund resources in a single project is also limited to 50 percent of the total investment programmed for new projects, 40 percent for the others. In exchange for their investment taxpayers receive securities, representing an interest in the relevant funds. Some of these shares have a stock market listing and quotation.

The second type of incentive consists of a reduction in the income tax liability arising from the project installed in the incentive region. For projects initiated before December 31, 1988, a total exemption of income tax liability for ten years has been granted. Firms can obtain an exemption or rate reduction on the import tax and the IPI on any imported machinery, equipment, or foreign material required for the implementation of the project if no similar Brazilian item exists. In August 1988 the tax incentives for investors in industrial and agricultural projects in the SUDAM and SUDENE areas were extended to December 31, 1993.

In the Zona Franca de Manaus, the benefits are added to those obtained through SUDAM. All sales to the rest of the country and all sales from industrial projects within the ZFM benefit from a full exemption from the IPI. In this case, the incentive benefits both the firm installed in Manaus and its customer who uses inputs produced in Manaus. Local producers can purchase equipment and raw materials exempt from the IPI and the import tax and sell their products with the same exemption. The distance between producers in Manaus and their major customers in the south is such that the major beneficiaries of the incentive program are firms that manufacture products subject to high IPI rates. Finally, Brazilian sellers of inputs to producers in Manaus also benefit from an IPI credit for taxes paid on inputs used in products sent to Manaus.

Tax preferences are also available for investments in the state of Espírito Santo, Carajás, the western Amazon, and a few free export processing zones. The tax incentives may take the form of tax holidays, exemption from indirect taxes, or rate reductions. Because these programs are much less significant in regard to revenue losses for the government, they are not covered in this chapter.

Incentives to Sectors

For three sectors—tourism, fisheries, and reforestation—the concession of tax preferences to sectors follows the structure used for regional incentives. Investment funds are made up of parts of the CIT paid by firms. The sectoral funds are managed by FISET. The first parts, created through the incentive program, do not pay income tax and benefit from exemption or reductions from the IPI and the import tax on imports of parts, machinery, and equipment. For many other sectors, the programs are specific, as will be discussed below. Many of the programs have been eliminated for the next fiscal year (1990) or are in the process of being eliminated. If known, their status will be specified in their description, given below.

Sectoral incentives cover a wide area, including aeronautics, agriculture, energy, fisheries, forestry, mining, shipbuilding, steel, tourism, and transportation. Some of the incentives could equally apply to agriculture, industry, or services, depending on the particular circumstances of the firm. The objectives of these programs are also rather diversified. In some cases the incentives are used to promote imports; in others they are based on the infant industry argument, or they are simply used to fix some market failure that has resulted in production that is socially less than optimal in a given activity. Often, sectoral incentives are also the result of intense lobbying by well-organized producers' associations.

TAX INCENTIVES. The sectoral incentive programs all have specific characteristics. Nearly half (thirty-one of sixty-four) of the sectoral incentives are granted against the IPI. Also, the IPI incentive is often extended to the import tax or the CIT. The standard type of tax preference is the pure and simple exemption of the liability.

TOURISM, FISHERIES, AND REFORESTATION. In addition to the two regional funds, the taxpayer could opt to allocate part of his or her CIT liability to a sectoral investment fund that finances investment in tourism, fisheries, and reforestation. The creation of the sectoral investment funds led to a competition for the tax dollars obtained from the CIT. Taxpayers had the option of allocating them to the sectoral or regional funds. The activities financed by the FISET funds included tourism, fisheries, and reforestation. The first two options were eliminated in 1988. The third one was eliminated in 1989. In addition, a limit of 6 percent of the CIT was imposed on the use of remaining options. Under specific conditions, tourism and fisheries continue to benefit from a total or partial exemption of their income tax liability.

INFRASTRUCTURE. The sectors linked to the development of infra-structure, generally dominated by public enterprises, enjoy the most important benefits. Firms producing or distributing electric energy (ELETROBRAS), firms in telecommunications (TELEBRAS), and firms involved in water cleaning benefit from a reduced CIT. Currently, they pay 6 percent and are exempted from any surtax. Other firms producing public services and transport of passengers pay a rate of 17 percent and are also exempted from any surtax.

AGRICULTURE. Firms engaging in agricultural activities are subject to a 6 percent income tax, as opposed to the 30 percent tax imposed for most others. Individual farmers may take a deduction of up to 80 percent of their agricultural income. The deduction is calculated by applying coefficients ranging from one to six to expenditure for farm improvement or contributions to the advancement of Brazilian agriculture. Individual farmers enjoy an additional incentive. Only 50 percent of net farming income (that is, income after the deduction above has been taken), with a limit of 15 percent of gross receipts from farming, is included in taxable income. Furthermore, agricultural projects approved for SUDENE and SUDAM areas are eligible for the investment tax credit on new investment in these areas.

Incentives to Exports

Abundant incentives were granted to promote exports during the mid-1970s and later. Some of these incentives, covering both general and specific exports, were then progressively phased out. Many remained in 1989 but in a milder form.

Capital goods imported by exporting companies in accordance with special export programs approved by CACEX (the foreign travel department of the Bank of Brazil) or BEFIEX (a special program of fiscal incentives for exporters) are fully or partially exempt from the import tax and the IPI. This incentive is expected to be in force up to 1991. Other incentives are available through BEFIEX. These include the allowance for an averaging of losses and profits over several years. A firm with a loss can include it in its operating costs for up to the next six years (as against the usual three years).

Components for the production of articles to be exported can be imported under the drawback regime, provided the import duty involved is equal to at least five minimum salaries and the value of exports exceeds at least 40 percent of the value of imports. The drawback may be implemented by means of tax deferral, exemption, or reimbursement.

Until 1988, profits from export activities were exempt from the CIT. In 1988, the tax rate became 3 percent and will be doubled each year after until exports profits are taxed at the same rate as profits from inward-oriented activities.

Many incentives are also granted against the value added taxes. Exports of industrial products are exempt from the IPI. In addition, a tax credit for the tax paid on components of exported products is available to exporters. Exports of industrial products were exempt from the ICM, the states' value added tax, until 1989. With the shift of the jurisdiction of the ICM to the states, some changes have been observed. Exports of semifinished products, for example, now are subject to the ICM.

Notes

This chapter was written in 1989 as a background paper for a World Bank report assessing the Brazilian tax system at the time. Most of the issues raised for the 1989 tax system remain relevant under the current tax system.

1. Brazil's collection of taxes on capital has been improving since the mid-1980s but is still far from the collection of similar countries.

2. The methodology followed was popularized by King and Fullerton (1984) and is now widely used to assess the tax treatment of capital. For surveys, see Boadway (1987) and Boadway, Bruce, and Mintz (1987).

3. For a longer discussion of these issues, see Jog and Mintz (1989).

4. Atkinson and Stiglitz (1980: 142–59). Actually, the CIT would still have an intertemporal effect on the investment decision of the firm.

5. The appendix to this chapter summarizes the major incentive programs relevant for investment projects.

6. The modeling of tax holidays within the framework of King and Fullerton (1984), in general, and the case of temporary business income tax reductions has been dealt with by Mintz (1989) in a discrete time framework. The version used here is a continuous-time version based on Gaspar and Alpalhoa (1989).

7. The summary in this section of the Brazilian CIT identifies the data to be used to assess its role as a form of capital income taxation. It covers the most important provisions of the CIT that directly affect the cost of capital and introduce a wedge between the gross and net of return in the capital market.

8. The rates were computed assuming that Brazil was equivalent to a closed economy with respect to the price of capital.

9. We do not explicitly address the issue of sustainability of such high rates. It is, however, clearly related to the Brazilian protection level. Tax policies whose goal is to increase the well-being of residents of a net demander of capital may justify restriction in net demand if the country faces a nonhorizontal supply curve. See Hartman (1985a; 1985b).

10. See appendix for details.

11. Note that this simulation provides the results that would obtain if the Brazilian value added taxes were to be fully consumption-based rather than consumption-based and product-based, with the characteristics of the second dominating, as currently is the case.

12. A tax holiday allows a firm operating in a given region or sector to be fully or partially exempt from the CIT during a specified period of time. Full taxation applies after the end of the holiday.

13. Mintz provides a fuller discussion in chapter 3.

14. See Mintz (1989).

15. To understand this, assume that the industrial firm—X—has a profit of 100 from its production activity. Assume the agricultural firm—Y—has no profit. The corporate tax rate on industry is 50 percent, and the rate on farming is 10 percent. Hence X's normal tax liability would be 50, Y's would be 0. Now assume the industrial firm borrows 200 from the agricultural firm at an interest rate of 10 percent. X can deduct 20 (10 percent of 200) from its profit and has now a taxable base of 80 (100 − 20). Its new tax liability is 40 (50 percent of 80) instead of 50 under the normal tax regime. Y owes a tax of 2 (10 percent of 20, its interest income), which will be picked up by X, informally. Total tax revenue declines from 50 to 42, the average tax on X's production moves from 50 percent to 42 percent, and there is no additional production in agriculture as a result of its preferential tax treatment.

16. There are two additional important explanations for the poor revenue performance. First, Brazil's tax administration system is weak. Unlike Argentina and Mexico, Brazil has not yet modernized its system. It is still understaffed and underequipped. In sum, Brazil's tax administration system cannot afford the

complexity of its tax structure. Second, there is little evidence that revenue forgone today because of tax incentives is collected later.

References

Atkinson, A. B., and J. E. Stiglitz. 1980. *Lectures on Public Economics.* New York: McGraw-Hill.

Boadway, Robin W. 1987. "The Theory and Measurement of Effective Tax Rates." In Jack M. Mintz and Douglas Purvis, eds., *The Impact of Taxation on Business Activity.* Kingston, Ont., Can.: John Deutsch Institute for the Study of Economic Policy.

Boadway, Robin W., Neil Bruce, and Jack M. Mintz. 1987. "Taxes on Capital Income in Canada: Analysis and Policy." Canadian Tax Paper 80. Canadian Tax Foundation, Toronto, Can.

Conjuntura Econômica. 1988. *Balanço das mil maiores sociedades por ações.* March. Rio de Janeiro, Brazil.

Gaspar, Vitor, and R. Alpalhoa. 1989. "Taxes marginais efetivas de tributação sobre o rendimento do capital em Portugal." Universidade Nova Lisboa, Lisbon. Mimeo.

Hall, R. E., and D. W. Jorgenson. 1967. "Tax Policy and Investment Behavior." *American Economic Review* 57 (June): 391–414.

———. 1971. "Application of the Theory of Optimum Capital Accumulation." In Gary Fromm, ed., *Tax Incentives and Capital Spending.* Washington, D.C.: Brookings Institution.

Hartman, D. G. 1985a. *On the Optimal Taxation of Capital in the Open Economy,* Working Paper 1550. National Bureau of Economic Research, Cambridge, Mass.

———. 1985b. *The Welfare Effects of a Capital Income Tax in an Open Economy,* Working Paper 1551. National Bureau of Economic Research, Cambridge, Mass.

Jog, V. M., and Jack M. Mintz. 1989. "Corporate Tax Reform and Its Economic Impact: An Evaluation of the Phase 1 Proposals." In Jack M. Mintz and John Whalley, eds., *The Economic Impacts of Tax Reform.* Canadian Tax Paper 84. Toronto: Canadian Tax Foundation.

King, Mervyn A., and Don Fullerton. 1984. *The Taxation of Income from Capital: A Comparative Study of the United States, the United Kingdom, Sweden, and West Germany.* Chicago, Ill.: University of Chicago Press.

McKee, Michael T., and Jacob T. C. Visser. 1986. "Marginal Tax Rates on the Use of Labour and Capital in OECD Countries." *OECD Economic Studies* 7. OECD, Paris.

Mintz, Jack M. 1989. "Tax Holidays and Investment." Country Economic Department. Policies, Planning, and Research Working Paper 178. World Bank, Washington, D.C.

World Bank. 1989. *World Development Report.* New York: Oxford University Press.

INVESTMENT INCENTIVES AND THE CORPORATE TAX SYSTEM IN MALAYSIA

8

Robin W. Boadway, Dale Chua,
and Frank Flatters

DIRECT TAXES, AT both the company and personal levels, accounted for about one-third of total Malaysian federal government revenue and one-half of its tax component in 1988.[1] The purpose of this chapter is to measure the effect of this direct tax system on investment decisions. The main tool we use for this purpose is the marginal effective tax, a measure of the investment distortions attributable to taxes.

Like many other developing countries, Malaysia makes extensive use of the tax system to alter investment incentives. Tax holidays and rapid tax writeoffs of investment costs are among the most important instruments. But also, like many other countries, Malaysia has made many alterations in the form and conditions of these incentives in recent years. Tax reform is an important item on the fiscal agenda. Unlike Indonesia, Malaysia has not yet gone so far as to abolish investment incentives based on the income tax.[2] Nevertheless, the changes, and the possibility of further reforms, make Malaysia an interesting country in which to study the use of such incentives.

The use of investment incentives based on the income tax, such as rapid depreciation and tax holidays, has been widespread in Malaysia. Several important changes, however, were made in these incentives in the tax reform implemented in the 1989 budget. First, the budget provided what might be regarded as the most general and broadly based of investment incentives—a significant reduction in corporate tax rates. And second, it changed the terms associated with the granting of tax holidays by prohibiting the carrying forward of certain allowances to the post–tax holiday period. One of the purposes of this chapter is to measure how these changes affected incentives to investment.

We begin with a brief outline of relevant features of Malaysia's direct taxes.[3] The system comprises taxes on personal and corporate incomes. Personal incomes are taxed under a progressive rate structure in which rates rise from 5 percent to 40 percent. In addition there is an excess profits tax on incomes over M$300,000.[4] The treatment of interest income and dividends under the personal income tax is important in determining the effects of investment incentives. Both these forms of household income are, in effect, fully taxable in the period received, just like ordinary wage income. The principal exception to this is in respect to dividends from companies that are operating under a tax holiday and, hence, not taxable at the time the dividends are issued. In such cases the dividends are not taxable in the hands of the shareholder either. This is consistent with the integration of the personal and corporate income taxes as practiced in Malaysia and as described later in this chapter in connection with the corporate tax.

Prior to the 1989 budget all companies in Malaysia were subject to a 40 percent income tax and an additional 5 percent development tax. For companies with income in excess of M$2 million, there was a further 3 percent excess profits tax. The 1989 budget reduced the income tax rate to 35 percent and announced the phasing out of the development tax at a rate of one percentage point per year. All forms of normal business income are subject to tax. Except for a 2 percent real property gains tax, capital gains are not taxed.

Taxable income is gross business income less (a) dividends paid out, (b) deductible business expenses, (c) depreciation and other investment allowances, (d) eligible losses and other allowances carried forward from previous periods, and (e) gifts and bad debts. The deduction of dividends from taxable income, together with their full taxation in the hands of recipients, means that Malaysia has a full imputation system and that dividend income is taxed only once. Deductible business expenses include only expenses of a current, not a capital, nature. Interest payments are allowable current expenses. Any business losses can be deducted from gross income in calculating taxable income. Any unabsorbed tax losses in any year may be carried forward indefinitely for use in future years but without interest. Depreciation allowances of various types are available in respect to capital assets used to generate business income. They vary according to the type of physical asset and the industry in which it is used. The basic forms include initial, annual, balancing, accelerated, agricultural, and forestry allowances. Unused depreciation allowances also may be carried forward in the same way as unabsorbed business losses.

A variety of special investment incentives is available to encourage particular types of investments. Among the most important of these are the tax holidays granted to firms that apply successfully for pioneer status.[5] Firms granted pioneer status are free of corporate income tax for a period of time (usually five years) following the investment in question.

Prior to the 1989 budget, pioneer firms were permitted to carry forward initial and annual depreciation allowances from the pioneer period to future years. As with other carryforward provisions, these allowances did not accumulate interest. The 1989 budget eliminated this carryforward provision.

In order to evaluate alternative tax structures, we have undertaken empirical estimates for several different scenarios. These cases vary according to (a) whether the firm has been granted pioneer status in respect to the investment under consideration, (b) whether, in the case of a pioneer firm, it is generating a positive cash flow in the tax holiday period, (c) the sector in which the firm is investing, and (d) whether the firm is operating under the pre- or post-1989 tax regime.

We find that the tax system plays a major role in determining the profitability of investments in Malaysia. For some investments, it provides a considerable net subsidy. But many others are faced with sizable tax penalties. The overall pattern of incentives and disincentives—whether according to method of finance, type of capital good being purchased, or sector in which the investment occurs—bears no obvious relation to any conceivable social or economic goals that might in principle guide the construction of an incentive system. The unintended consequences of these distortions, therefore, almost certainly include significant waste in the use of Malaysia's investment resources.

Although pioneer status is used to promote investment in desirable activities and to assist infant industries and disadvantaged economic and social groups, it almost certainly has failed to achieve these goals. Pioneer status actually imposes a net penalty on investors in many cases. It is of possible value only to firms with sufficient taxable profits against which to use the benefits of the tax holiday; that is, it is highly unlikely to be of value to the weak or infant investors or to the industries that are claimed to be the intended beneficiaries of the measures.

Definition of the Marginal Effective Tax

The marginal effective tax is defined as the difference between the gross (before-tax) rate of return on a marginal investment and the net (after-tax) rate of return on domestic savings to finance such investments.[6] A small open economy such as Malaysia, with relatively free international capital flows, can lend and borrow at prevailing (risk-adjusted) world interest rates. Thus the determination of the marginal effective tax can be broken conveniently into two components, illustrated in figure 8-1, in which the prevailing real world interest rate is shown by r^*. The corporate tax drives a wedge between the rate of return on capital and the world interest rate so that the gross return on investment, r_g, is r^* plus the *effective marginal corporate tax* rate. The effective marginal corporate tax, t_c, is the difference between r_g and r^*. At the same time, the personal

Figure 8-1. Effective Tax Wedge for an Open Economy

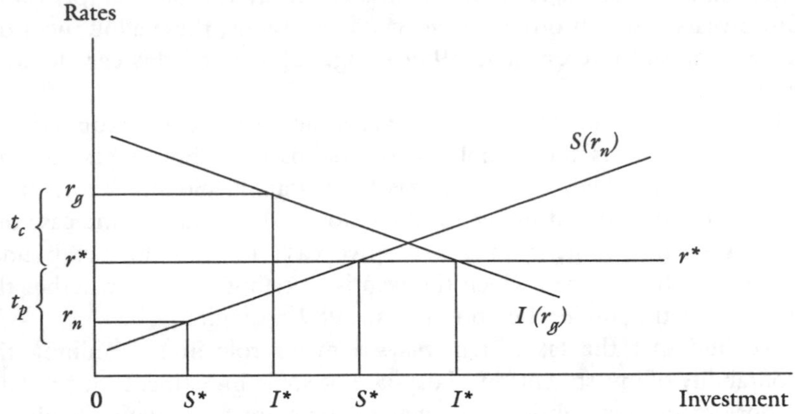

Rates

Note: t_c = marginal effective corporate tax; t_p = marginal effective personal tax; r^* = world interest rate; S^* = domestic savings; I^* = domestic investment.

income tax introduces a wedge between r_n and r^*. The *effective marginal personal tax*, t_p, is the difference between r_n and r^*. The sum of t_c and t_p is the marginal effective tax.

The principal effect of a direct personal or corporate income tax is to drive a wedge between the gross return to investment and the net return to savings. The diagram depicts the "normal" case, in which the marginal effective tax is positive, that is, in which the tax system effectively imposes a net tax on investment. Many corporate tax systems, however, including Malaysia's, contain provisions that have the net effect of subsidizing marginal investments. For example, the present value of immediate tax savings resulting from accelerated depreciation provisions might well exceed the future tax burdens on the income from an investment. In cases such as this, the marginal effective tax on the investment would be negative.

The Measurement of r_g and r_n

The after-tax rate of return to domestic savings can be measured from observed market prices. Pretax returns can be obtained from corporate bond rates, rates of return to equity, and weighted combinations of both of them. The main difficulty in estimating the net returns is that various assets and persons are subject to different tax rates. For our purposes it is sufficient to take the case of a "representative" saver's portfolio and personal income tax rate. The after-tax nominal rate of return to savers must also be converted into real terms by subtracting the expected rate of inflation. We used two different estimates of inflation rates, one based on time series estimates and the other simply the actual annual inflation rate. The results reported below are based on the actual inflation rate.

The required before-tax rate of return on a marginal investment is not directly observable. Because a marginal investment, by definition, is one whose rate of return is just sufficient to cover all its costs after taxes, however, we can infer its pretax rate of return by measuring the user cost of capital. This is the standard method of estimating marginal effective tax rates.

Several adjustments are required to take account of the effect of taxes on the user cost of capital. First, deductions must be made for the cost of holding capital. These include interest deductibility for the portion of the capital financed by debt, and depreciation deductions (or their equivalent on forms of capital such as inventory and depletable resources). The interest deduction affects the cost of finance, whereas the depreciation deduction affects the rate of economic depreciation. Second, the tax on revenues generated by the capital must be accounted for. And third, the effect of any other special tax allowances, such as investment tax credits, must be included.

Pretax rates of return are derived for several general cases, which differ according to whether (a) the firm is currently making a profit or sustaining losses (measured by current taxable income) and (b) it has been granted pioneer status. Firms that are experiencing losses are assumed to be in this position only temporarily. They are in the process of setting up or expanding and have insufficient revenues against which to offset capital costs. Typically, these would be small, growing firms. Large firms would be more likely to have revenues from other parts of their operations against which to offset investment expenditure.

For a profit-maximizing competitive firm the user cost of capital is equal to the pretax value of the marginal product of capital per dollar of gross investment in each period. This can be shown to be equal to equation 8-1.

$$(8\text{-}1) \qquad \text{VMP}(t) = \left(\frac{1}{1-u_t}\right) \left\{ [r_t - \pi_t + \delta - (\Delta q/q)_t] \, (1 - Z_t) \right.$$

$$\left. + \, [1 + r_t - \pi_t - (\Delta q/q)_t] \, (Z_t - Z_{t-1}) \right\}$$

where $\text{VMP}(t)$ is the gross value of the marginal product of capital per dollar of gross investment in time period t, u_t is the firm's corporate tax rate, r_t is the firm's nominal posttax cost of finance, π_t is the expected inflation rate at t, δ is the (proportional) physical depreciation rate of the capital good whose investment is being considered, q_t is the real price of investment goods at t, and Z_t is the present value at time t of future tax depreciation allowances per dollar of investment.

The user cost of capital represents the cost of using one dollar's worth of capital for one period, taking full account of taxes. Its components may be explained as follows: In the absence of taxes, the user cost is just $r_t - \pi_t + \delta - (\Delta q/q)_t$. This is the sum of the real cost of financing the dollar of capital $(r_t - \pi_t)$ and the economic depreciation on the dollar of capital $(\delta - \Delta q/q)_t$. The remaining terms capture the effects of taxes. The term $(1 - Z_t)$ represents the effective price of acquiring one dollar's worth of capital after allowing for future tax savings on depreciation. The second term in parentheses is the additional tax cost the firm bears as a result of investing in period $t - 1$ rather than period t. Note that the present value of tax depreciation allowances, Z_t, is an increasing function of time. This is because the nonlinearity in the calculation of Z_t discounts the stream of tax savings accruing to investment taken at time t more heavily than if the investment were undertaken a period later at $t + 1$. Finally, the entire equation is "grossed up" by the effective corporate tax rate, u_t, reflecting the fact that the revenues generated by the investment must cover the tax liabilities on the revenues generated.

Alternatively, VMP(t) can be thought of as a return to investment that can be divided into three parts: that going to the tax authority, that which is used to maintain the real capital stock of the firm, and the remainder, which is a net return on investment. We define the pretax rate of return on investment as what remains after accounting for the second of the above components, economic depreciation. In other words, we define r_g using equation 8-1 as follows:

(8-2) $$r_g(t) = \text{VMP}(t) - \delta + (\Delta q/q)_t \qquad \text{for all } t$$

$$= \left(\frac{1}{1 - u_t}\right)\left\{[r_t - \pi_t + \delta - (\Delta q/q)_t]\,(1 - Z_t)\right.$$

$$\left. + \,[1 + r_t - \pi_t - (\Delta q/q)_t]\,(Z_t - Z_{t-1})\right\} - \delta + (\Delta q/q)_t.$$

By subtracting $(\delta - \Delta q/q)$ from VMP(t), we are effectively calculating the rate of return (before taxes) that must be earned by a profitable investment in order to maintain the real value of capital stock. The return r_g is then split between the tax authority and savers.

Equation 8-2 serves as the basis for calculating pretax rates of return and the marginal effective tax rates for all our scenarios. What distinguishes one type of firm from the other is the way in which taxes affect the right-hand side of the expression. Each of the cases will now be considered. The key in each instance will be to derive expressions for u_t, r_t and Z_t that incorporate the provisions of the Malaysian tax laws facing that type of firm.

Case 1: Profit-Making Nonpioneer Firms

We begin with the case of a well-established firm that earns positive taxable income in the current and all future periods. Apart from the initial and annual tax depreciation allowances, the firm does not enjoy any other special tax treatment. It is taxed at the full rate in each period. Therefore the effective statutory corporate tax rate is simply the statutory rate, u, for all periods.

The nominal cost of funds to the firm, $r(t)$, is a weighted average of its after-tax borrowing costs and the cost of raising equity. For simplicity we assume that the costs of debt and equity are both constant over time, as is the debt-equity ratio.[7] Then the nominal cost of funds is given by

$$(8\text{-}3) \qquad r = \beta i (1 - u) + (1 - \beta) \rho$$

where β is the debt-asset ratio of the firm, i is the corporate lending rate, and ρ is the firm's cost of equity.[8] This rate, r, is the one at which the firm discounts its cash flows. It reflects the interest deductibility provisions of the corporate tax system, as well as the absence of analogous provisions for equity financing.

Consider now the present value of tax savings due to depreciation, Z_t. It is common for firms in Malaysia to enjoy both an initial tax allowance on gross capital investment and, subsequently, an annual capital depreciation allowance on the remaining undepreciated capital cost base. The depreciation allowance is based on the straight-line method, according to which the asset is written off in equal amounts over its depreciation life. Thus if the depreciation life is T periods, a proportion $1/T$ of the original asset cost, net of initial allowance, is written off each period. Given the tax rate u and the discount rate r, the present value of future tax savings from the initial allowance and future depreciation on one dollar of investment is given by[9]

$$(8\text{-}4) \qquad Z = u\gamma + (1 - \gamma) u \left[1 - \left(\frac{1}{1+r} \right)^T \right] (rT)^{-1}.$$

where γ is the initial tax allowance rate and T is the deemed writeoff period for the investment. Thus the depreciation rate is $100/T$ percent. The first term, $u\gamma$, is the tax saving from the initial allowance, and the second term is the present value of future tax savings from $\$(1 - \gamma)$ of depreciable cost.[10] The term multiplying $(1 - \gamma)u$ is the present value of depreciation deductions arising from a per period depreciation deduction of $1/T$.

Case 2: Profit-Making Pioneer Firms

We now consider firms operating under a tax holiday. Such tax holidays are usually granted for five years. This is the case we consider here. No taxes are paid by the firm during the tax holiday period. Moreover, until the 1989 budget, the Promotion of Investment Act of 1986 allowed the use of initial and depreciation allowances to be delayed until the end of the tax holiday. All accumulated tax savings from the initial and annual depreciation allowances then could be set off against revenues earned by the firm after the tax holiday period. The privilege of postponing unused depreciation writeoffs has been withdrawn with the tax reform of 1989.

Here we consider the prereform provisions, postponing discussion of the effects of the 1989 budget until later. We assume that the profits in the period immediately following the tax holiday are sufficiently large to absorb all depreciation allowances that have accumulated over the tax holiday period. Should the firm decide to distribute any profits during the holiday period, the dividends received by its shareholders are also exempted from personal income taxes. Exempting the dividends from personal taxes implies a reduction in the effective personal tax rate.

The tax holiday provisions make Z_t, r_t, and u_t all vary over time. The present value of tax savings, Z_t, from investing in period t will be different from that of period $t + 1$. Similarly, the effective corporate tax rate will vary by period, and this variation will affect the cost of debt finance and therefore r_t. The variability of these terms will imply a time-varying rate of return on capital. This will alter the firm's time pattern of investment. We consider u_t, r_t, and Z_t in turn.

The effective statutory corporate tax will be zero over the tax holiday period and 40 percent plus a 5 percent development tax afterward; that is,

$$(8\text{-}5) \qquad\qquad u_t = \begin{cases} 0 \text{ for } 0 \leq t \leq 4 \\ u \text{ for } t > 4 \end{cases}$$

The cost of finance is given by

$$(8\text{-}6) \qquad\qquad r_t = \beta i(1 - u_t) + (1 - \beta)\,\rho \ .$$

where, again, we treat the parameters β, i, and ρ as fixed. This cost of finance will differ between pioneer and nonpioneer firms (and between the tax holiday and later time periods for pioneer firms) because of the differences in u_t.

The calculation of the present value of tax savings resulting from depreciation must take into account the carryforward from the pioneer to the taxpaying period of accumulated initial allowances and depreciation expenses as well as the variable discount rate. The value of Z_t will vary, depending on when the investment is undertaken. For investments made during the pioneer period, Z_t is given by

$$(8\text{-}7) \quad Z_t = \left(\frac{1}{1+r_t}\right)^{5-t} \left\{ u\gamma + \frac{(5-t)\,u\,(1-\gamma)}{T} + \frac{u\,(1-\gamma)}{rT} \right.$$

$$\left. \cdot \left[1 - \left(\frac{1}{1+r}\right)^{T-5+t} \right] \right\} \quad 0 \le t \le 4 .$$

For $t > 4$ the expression for Z_t is the same as in equation 8-4. Note that Z_t is monotonically increasing over time during the holiday period. Equations 8-5, 8-6, and 8-7, along with equation 8-2, can be used to calculate the time profile of the pretax rate of return on capital $r_g(t)$ for a pioneer firm. It will vary over the pioneer period and will become constant after the transition to full taxpaying status.

Firms may also apply for an investment tax allowance in lieu of the usual initial and annual depreciation allowances. Like the latter, it is just an offset against revenue and is not refundable but may be carried forward. The investment tax allowance is offered on a discretionary basis and at varying rates by the government. Because of this, and because of a lack of information, we have not incorporated the investment tax allowance into our initial set of computations. Given the data, it would be quite straightforward to do so because it has effects that are similar to the initial allowance.

Case 3: Firms in Temporary Loss Positions

Here we look at a firm that is experiencing a temporary tax loss (that is, earning negative taxable income) during the first few periods of its operation and a profit thereafter. Any unabsorbed losses can be carried forward indefinitely, without interest, until they are set off fully against future income. Unused depreciation allowances may also be carried forward without interest and set off against income in the following year. We consider the case of a firm that is experiencing losses in the first five years of its operations; these losses are carried forward into year 6 and set off against income in that year before taxes are paid.

Note that we have not specified whether this is a pioneer firm. The reason is that under the pre-1989 tax provisions a loss-making firm such as this gained no additional benefit from being granted pioneer status. Under the 1989 tax reform measures, a firm such as this one actually would be worse off under pioneer status because of its inability under the new laws to carry forward unused depreciation and investment allowances from the tax holiday period. The only possible exception would be if the period of temporary losses were shorter than the tax holiday. In any case, for the purpose of this section we assume that the tax incentives facing firms in temporary loss positions are independent of whether they have been granted pioneer status. We postpone a discussion of the implications of the tax reform measures for pioneer firms in a temporary loss position.

We first consider the cost of finance. Because the firm is in a loss position, it cannot obtain the full benefits of the deduction of interest costs in the years in which the costs are incurred. Instead, the benefit is deferred until future periods when the loss carryforward can be offset against taxable income. This deferral reduces the value of the tax saving from the interest deduction and therefore increases the after-tax cost of finance. Consider a firm that finances new investment entirely with debt. In this case the effective tax rate that applies to the interest deduction will be less than 45 percent because of the deferral of the interest writeoff. Recall that all writeoffs from the loss period can be offset against profits in period 6. The cost of interest finance in a period in which the firm is making losses, therefore, is given by

$$(8\text{-}8) \qquad r_t = i\left[1 - \frac{u}{\Pi_{s=t}^{4}(1 + r_s)}\right] \qquad t = 0, \ldots, 4 \, .$$

This expression reflects the fact that the tax savings from interest costs incurred in an early time period are postponed until period 6. This tax saving must be discounted back to period t to yield its present value as of the time that the interest cost is incurred. The tax saving in period 6 is evaluated at the full corporate tax rate, u.

Equation 8-8 gives relations for each of the five loss periods, which must be solved simultaneously for the values of r_t in each period. This system can be solved recursively backward. After period 6, once the firm is profit-making, the usual expression for r_t applies.

Similar principles apply when the firm uses some equity finance. In this case, r_t is given by $r_t = \beta i_t + (1 - \beta)\rho$, $t = 0, \ldots, 4$, where

$$i_t = i\left[1 - \frac{u}{\Pi_{s=t}^{4}(1 + r_s)}\right].$$

As above, this equation can be solved recursively for r_t during each loss period.

Analogous amendments must be made with respect to the effective corporate tax rate. Although tax loss firms do not pay taxes during these loss periods, their effective tax rate is not zero. Any additional revenues during the loss period have the effect of reducing tax losses that can be carried forward into the future—in effect, they still bear taxes but at a later date. Because these liabilities are carried forward without interest, the effective tax rate faced during the loss period is less than the statutory rate. To capture this effect, a discount factor must be applied to the corporate tax rate in equation 8-2. This gives a set of time-varying effective statutory corporate rates over the initial loss period. Using the discount rate as derived in equation 8-8, we find that the effective corporate tax rate is

(8-9) $$u_t = \frac{u}{\Pi_{s=t}^{4}(1 + r_s)} \qquad t = 0, \ldots, 4.$$

The present value of tax depreciation allowances will also be modified slightly to account for the fact that the unabsorbed depreciation allowance may also be carried forward, but without interest, to be set off against profits from the same business source at a later date. We continue to assume that all depreciation allowances accumulated in the first five loss periods can be written off against income in period 6. The present value of depreciation deductions in respect to investments in each of the temporary loss periods in this case is given by

(8-10) $$Z_t = \Pi_{s=t}^{4-t}\left(\frac{1}{1 + r_s}\right)\left\{ u\gamma + \frac{(5 - t)\, u\, (1 - \gamma)}{T} + \frac{u\, (1 - \gamma)}{rT} \right.$$

$$\left. \cdot \left[1 - \left(\frac{1}{1 + r}\right)^{T-5 + t}\right]\right\}, \qquad t = 0, \ldots, 4.$$

The first term is the initial allowance discounted back from period 6 to loss period t, when the firm undertakes the investment. The second is the cumulated depreciation writeoffs between periods t and 5, also discounted back to t. The third is the usual depreciation writeoffs incurred from period 6 onward, when the firm is earning positive profits. For $t \geq 5$, the expression for Z_t is again given by equation 8-4. As before, it can be shown that Z_t is increasing with time during the loss period. Using equations 8-8, 8-9, and 8-10 along with equation 8-2, the time profile of the rate of return on capital for the tax loss firm can then be calculated. For $t \geq 5$, the value of $r_g(t)$ will be as in case 1.

Posttax Returns on Savings: The Effective Marginal Rate of Personal Tax

So far we have concentrated on the marginal effective rate of corporate tax, t_c. For investments that are domestically financed, this represents only part of the effect of income taxes on marginal investments. Returns to domestic asset owners are also taxed under the personal tax system. This gives rise to an effective personal tax, which adds to the tax wedge on investments. Given the limited coverage of the capital gains tax and the imputation of corporate taxes against personal tax liabilities on dividends, we need only consider the distortionary effect of the personal income tax applied against interest income.

This simplifies the task of calculating the marginal effective personal tax. The effective personal tax is given by

$$(8\text{-}11) \qquad\qquad t_p = r^* - r_n$$

where r_n is the real rate of return to savers net of taxes. This rate depends on the source of financing. A person holding corporate bonds receives an after-tax nominal rate of return of $i(1 - m)$, where m is the individual's personal tax rate. In the case of equity, the after-tax rate of return depends on whether the financing comes from retained earnings or new equity issues. New equity issues give rise to a stream of dividends that are taxed at the personal level after being credited for corporate taxes paid. The after-tax nominal rate of return on the new shares is $(1 - m + u)\rho$, where ρ is the before-tax nominal rate of return from equity. In financing by retained earnings, the return is in the form of a nontaxable capital gain. Therefore the after-tax rate of return to savers on retained earnings is simply ρ.

The overall after-tax rate of return on savings is a weighted average of those rates on the three types of finance:

$$(8\text{-}12) \quad r_n = \beta i(1 - m) + (1 - \beta)\,[a(1 - m + u)\,\rho + (1 - a)\,\rho] - \pi$$

where a is the proportion of equity finance coming from new share issues.[11]

Estimates: The Marginal Effective Personal Tax

This and the following section present our estimates of the marginal effective distortions to savings and investment decisions resulting from Malaysia's direct tax system. The information on the tax system is derived from the laws themselves as well as from interpretations of Malaysian tax practitioners wherever necessary. We attempt to capture the principal effects of both the pre- and postreform tax systems. Estimates are based on actual Malaysian economic data regarding interest rates, inflation, financial structure of firms, and so on. In general we have used data for the period 1983 to 1987 and report estimates for this time period.

We begin with the marginal effective personal tax. This tax, t_p, is given by $r^* - r_n$, where r^* is the real cost of funds in the international capital market and r_n is the after-tax rate of return to savers (equation 8-12). The latter is affected by the graduated personal income tax structure as well as by the integration of the corporate and personal tax systems. Our estimates of the effective personal tax for five different patterns of financing are presented in tables 8-1 and 8-2. The five patterns are 100 percent debt or bond, 100 percent new share issues, 100 percent retained earnings, mixed bonds and new issues, and mixed bonds and retained earnings. The effects of the pre-1989 tax system are shown in table 8-1, and some of the principal effects of the reforms introduced in the 1989 budget are shown in table 8-2.

Pre–Tax Reform Savings Incentives

We present estimates of the marginal effective personal tax rate for various sources of financing before the 1989 tax reform.

FULL DEBT FINANCING. The effective taxes are calculated under the assumption that the real bond rate is constant at approximately 7.7 percent, corresponding to the nominal rate of 12 percent in 1983. The average personal tax rate used in our calculations is 20 percent. The differences in the personal tax wedge in the first column of table 8-1 simply reflect variations in the inflation rate over the period. Because personal taxes are levied on nominal interest earnings, the wedge increases with the rate of inflation.

NEW SHARE FINANCING. For new share issues the effective personal tax wedge is negative throughout the period. This is because of the integration between the personal and corporate tax systems, which provides full imputation at the personal level for taxes paid at the corporate level, and the fact that the corporate tax rate is generally greater than the personal rate. The distortion is given by $-(u - m)\rho$, where u is the corporate (inclusive of development tax) rate, m is the

Table 8-1. *Effective Personal Tax at a Full Corporate Tax Rate of 45 Percent and a Personal Tax Rate of 20 Percent, 1983–87*

Year	Bond financing	New issues	Retained earnings	Debt and new issues	Debt and retained earnings
1983	0.0240	−0.0174	0	0.0078	0.0146
1984	0.0240	−0.0156	0	0.0088	0.0148
1985	0.0164	−0.0083	0	0.0078	0.0107
1986	0.0168	−0.0070	0	0.0082	0.0107
1987	0.0174	−0.0128	0	0.0030	0.0091

Source: Authors' calculations.

Table 8-2. Effective Personal Tax at a Full Corporate Tax Rate of 35 Percent and a Personal Tax Rate of 20 Percent, 1983–87

Year	Bond financing	New issues	Retained earnings	Debt and new issues	Debt and retained earnings
1983	0.0240	−0.0104	0	0.0105	0.0146
1984	0.0240	−0.0093	0	0.0112	0.0148
1985	0.0164	−0.0049	0	0.0089	0.0107
1986	0.0168	−0.0042	0	0.0092	0.0107
1987	0.0174	−0.0076	0	0.0055	0.0091

Source: Authors' calculations.

average personal tax rate, and ρ is the rate of return on equity financing. The fluctuations in this distortion across time (table 8-1, column 2) are due entirely to variations in the rate of return during the period. In general the higher the rate of return on equity and the greater the excess of the corporate over the personal tax rate, the higher is the subsidy to this form of savings.

FINANCING BY RETAINED EARNINGS. Financing by retained earnings yields a return in the form of a capital gain to shareholders. No distortion is imposed on this form of savings because capital gains are not taxed. Retained earnings can be allowed to accumulate free of the personal tax as long as they are retained and reinvested rather than being paid out as dividends.

FINANCING BY DEBT AND NEW SHARE ISSUES. The fourth column in table 8-1 indicates the tax distortion on the rate of return to personal savings if the firm finances its investments by a combination of bonds and new shares. The proportion used in our estimates is given by the average industry debt-asset ratio for each year. In this case, the tax wedge is determined by the firm's debt-asset ratio as well as by the tax system. The fluctuations across the years are therefore a result of variations in the debt-asset ratio of the representative firm and in the rate of return to equity. The net effect is a tax-induced disincentive to this method of finance.

FINANCING BY DEBT AND RETAINED EARNINGS. The figures in the fifth column of table 8-1 show the tax wedge on mixed debt and retained earnings finance, using the same debt-asset ratios as in the previous case. Once again, taxes discourage this form of finance. The wedge is generally greater than in the previous case because of the absence of a tax subsidy to retained earnings finance.

In summary the principal effects of the pre-1989 direct tax system on the incentive to save are as follows. It has no effect on savings that finance investment through retained earnings. It distorts savings decisions in all other cases, however. It subsidizes savings in the form of new share issues because of the differential between corporate and personal tax rates. And it taxes savings used to purchase corporate debt. Hence, the tax system may either promote or discourage mixed debt and equity finance on balance according to the actual debt-asset ratio chosen by firms. On average, for the aggregate debt-equity ratios observed in Malaysia, the tax system discourages savings.

Effects of Tax Reform

The 1989 budget included an immediate reduction in the basic corporate tax rate to 35 percent and a gradual elimination of the 5 percent development tax. These measures would have the net effect of reducing the basic corporate tax rate from 45 percent to 35 percent. The effects of these changes on the effective personal tax rates are given in table 8-2.

The qualitative patterns in tables 8-1 and 8-2 are similar. Nothing changes if the firm continues to use only bond financing, or if it finances its investment by retained earnings. The reduction in the gap between the personal and corporate tax rates, however, means that the marginal distortion is reduced for pure new issue finance. In the case of financing by mixed debt and new share issues, the previously existing tax disincentive is increased slightly. This is because of the reduction in the tax subsidy given to new share issues. Last, the disincentive to financing by mixed debt and retained earnings is unaffected by the tax changes. This is because the reduction in the corporate tax rate has no effect on either retained earnings or bond finance.

Estimates: Effective Corporate Taxes

We turn now to the effect of direct taxes on firms' capital investment decisions, that is, t_c. The principal results, which can be divided into three groups according to the same categories used in the previous estimates of t_p, are summarized in tables 8-3 through 8-12. In tables 8-3 to 8-6 we present the "normal" case of a firm making positive taxable profits throughout the period. In tables 8-7 to 8-10 we examine the case of a pioneer firm, and in tables 8-11 and 8-12 we look at the case of a firm in a temporary tax loss position. As before, we show the effective tax rate under different financing scenarios and over a period of five years of varying economic conditions in the country.

We consider only three possible financing scenarios, two less than for our estimates of t_p. The reason for this is that the tax implications to the

Table 8-3. *Effective Corporate Tax for Profit-Making Firms
at a Full Corporate Tax Rate of 45 Percent, 1983–87*

Year	Bond financing	Retained earnings	Debt and retained earnings
Investment in buildings			
1983	–0.0289	0.0275	–0.0069
1984	–0.0273	0.0243	–0.0076
1985	–0.0025	0.0247	0.0069
1986	–0.0020	0.0209	0.0062
1987	–0.0140	0.0274	0.0056
Investment in machinery			
1983	–0.0436	0.0112	–0.0223
1984	–0.0433	0.0098	–0.0231
1985	–0.0272	0.0066	–0.0155
1986	–0.0277	0.0054	–0.0158
1987	–0.0308	0.0091	–0.0118

Source: Authors' calculations.

Table 8-4. *Effective Corporate Tax for Profit-Making Firms
at a Full Corporate Tax Rate of 35 Percent, 1983–87*

Year	Bond financing	Retained earnings	Debt and retained earnings
Investment in buildings			
1983	–0.0202	0.0181	–0.0052
1984	–0.0191	0.0161	–0.0057
1985	–0.0017	0.0162	0.0045
1986	–0.0014	0.0137	0.0040
1987	–0.0098	0.0181	0.0034
Investment in machinery			
1983	–0.0031	0.0073	–0.0173
1984	–0.0329	0.0064	–0.0179
1985	–0.0207	0.0043	–0.0121
1986	–0.0211	0.0035	–0.0123
1987	–0.0235	0.0060	–0.0095

Source: Authors' calculations.

Table 8-5. Disaggregated Effective Corporate Tax for Profit-Making Firms at a Full Corporate Tax Rate of 45 Percent, 1983

Sector earnings	Bond financing	Retained earnings	Debt and retained earnings
Investment in buildings			
Food	–0.0289	0.0896	0.0522
Building materials	–0.0289	0.0317	0.0101
Services	–0.0289	0.0929	–0.0074
Plantation	–0.0289	0.0360	0.0261
Construction, tin	–0.0289	–0.0013	–0.0172
Manufacturing	–0.0289	0.0764	0.0370
Investment in machinery			
Food	–0.0368	0.0615	0.0293
Building materials	–0.0368	0.0211	0.0004
Services	–0.0368	0.0640	–0.0199
Plantation	–0.0389	0.0210	0.0118
Construction, tin	–0.0449	0.0005	–0.0198
Manufacturing	–0.0389	0.0463	0.0084

Source: Authors' calculations.

Table 8-6. Disaggregated Effective Corporate Tax for Profit-Making Firms at a Full Corporate Tax Rate of 35 Percent, 1983

Sector earnings	Bond financing	Retained earnings	Debt and retained earnings
Investment in buildings			
Food	–0.0202	0.0590	0.0341
Building materials	–0.0202	0.0209	0.0062
Services	–0.0202	0.0611	–0.0056
Plantation	–0.0202	0.0237	0.0170
Construction, tin	–0.0202	–0.0009	–0.0124
Manufacturing	–0.0202	0.0502	0.0198
Investment in machinery			
Food	–0.0275	0.0404	0.0185
Building materials	–0.0275	0.0139	–0.0009
Services	–0.0275	0.0421	–0.0155
Plantation	–0.0292	0.0138	0.0072
Construction, tin	–0.0342	0.0003	–0.0153
Manufacturing	–0.0292	0.0305	0.0043

Source: Authors' calculations.

firm of financing an investment by new issues and by retained earnings are equivalent.[12] In the case of profit-making firms we also report estimates of the variability of the effective tax rate across broad industrial sectors. In all cases we investigate differences in the distortions facing investments in buildings and in machinery.

Case 1: Profit-Making Firms

Effective corporate tax rates are presented for firms with positive taxable profits, before and after the 1989 tax reform.

PRE–TAX REFORM. The effective corporate tax estimates for profit-making firms are shown in tables 8-3 and 8-6. The first column of table 8-3 shows that the effective marginal corporate taxes for all bond-financed investments are consistently negative; that is, these investments are subsidized at the margin in every year. The size of the tax subsidy varies somewhat and is smallest in 1985 and 1986. This variation is because of differences in the rate of inflation over the period.

The effect of inflation on t_c is a priori ambiguous. On the one hand, the basing of depreciation deductions on historic cost means that inflation reduces their real value and increases the effective corporate tax rate. On the other hand, the deductibility of the *nominal* interest cost of borrowing means that inflationary increases in nominal interest rates make this deduction more valuable and, hence, reduce the effective tax rate. In this case the estimated tax rates for the relatively low inflation years of 1985 and 1986 are higher than for the other years. For Malaysia, therefore, the effective tax rate on bond-financed capital investments tends to vary inversely with the rate of inflation.[13]

The second column of table 8-3 shows that investments financed by retained earnings (or new issues) are taxed at the margin. This is because of the nondeductibility of the costs of financing by new issues or retained earnings. The actual size of this disincentive ranges from about two to three percentage points for buildings, and from about one-half to one percentage point for machinery. Unlike the bond-financing case, the effect of lower inflation (as occurred in 1985 and 1986) is to lower the effective corporate tax slightly.

The third column of table 8-3 shows the effective corporate tax on a marginal investment financed by a mixture of debt and equity. For buildings the tax-induced distortion is less than one percentage point in all years; in the relatively high inflation years of 1983 and 1984 the tax system provides a small subsidy, and in the subsequent years, with lower inflation, it provides a small disincentive. The distortion in the case of machinery is larger in all years, with a subsidy of about two percentage points throughout the period. This is explained by the shorter economic life of machinery in relation to buildings, which increases the relative importance of the tax savings from depreciation allowances.[14]

The direct tax system also distorts the intersectoral allocation of investment. Direct taxes are likely to have a much smaller effect in this regard than indirect taxes, especially import and export duties, which explicitly discriminate among sectors. Intersectoral differences in financial characteristics and in the economic lives of capital goods, however, will also cause differential intersectoral incentive effects. In tables 8-5 and 8-6 we disaggregate the earlier results into six industrial subsectors from data for twenty-three subsectors from the Kuala Lumpur Stock Exchange. Because the relevant data were available only for 1983, we report effective corporate tax estimates for only that year.

Under bond financing we continue to assume that each subsector borrows at a 7.7 percent real interest rate. Because building investment attracts the same depreciation allowances in all sectors and the buildings in each are assumed to endure the same physical wear and tear, the (negative) tax wedge is identical across sectors. Because of intersectoral differences in the rates of initial investment allowance and annual depreciation allowances, the size of the tax distortion for machinery is not identical. For example, the construction and tin sector, with the highest writeoff rate, receives the highest tax subsidy.

Greater intersectoral variations occur if financing is by retained earnings. Because the cost of finance to the firm is not tax deductible in this case, all sectors except construction and tin are taxed at the margin. The highest tax distortion falls on services, followed closely by food and manufacturing. These patterns are similar for both buildings and machinery.

Under financing by mixed debt and retained earnings, the tax-induced investment distortion is once again some combination of those imposed by the two forms of finance separately. But because debt-equity ratios vary between sectors, the intersectoral differences in tax rates depart from those seen in the previous calculations. It turns out that investments in the construction and tin sector remain the most generously treated. The service sector, however, which is quite heavily taxed under retained earnings financing, is now less heavily taxed in relation to, say, food. This is the result of the relatively higher debt-equity ratios observed in this sector.

POST-TAX REFORM. Tables 8-4 and 8-6 show the effect of the corporate tax rate reductions in the 1989 budget. The general conclusions are quite straightforward. First, the qualitative results for all financing schemes remain unchanged; and second, the quantitative effect of a lower corporate tax rate is to reduce the absolute magnitude of the distortions. If a subsidy existed before, that subsidy is now reduced; and similarly, if the tax system discouraged investment previously, the size of the disincentive is also reduced.

Table 8-7. *Effective Corporate Tax for Pioneer Firms at a Full Corporate Tax Rate of 45 Percent, 1983: Pre-1989 Budget Deferral and Carryforward Regulations*

Time of earnings profile	Bond financing	Retained earnings	Debt and retained earnings
Investment in buildings			
Year 1	−0.0032	−0.0035	−0.0033
Year 2	−0.0036	−0.0039	−0.0037
Year 3	−0.0042	−0.0043	−0.0042
Year 4	−0.0048	−0.0047	−0.0047
Steady state	−0.0289	0.0275	−0.0069
Investment in machinery			
Year 1	−0.0118	−0.0135	−0.0124
Year 2	−0.0158	−0.0176	−0.0165
Year 3	−0.0204	−0.0219	−0.0209
Year 4	−0.0255	−0.0263	−0.0258
Steady state	−0.0436	0.0112	−0.0223

Source: Authors' calculations.

Table 8-8. *Effective Corporate Tax for Pioneer Firms at a Full Corporate Tax Rate of 35 Percent, 1983: Pre-1989 Budget Deferral and Carryforward Regulations*

Time of earnings profile	Bond financing	Retained earnings	Debt and retained earnings
Investment in buildings			
Year 1	−0.0026	−0.0027	−0.0027
Year 2	−0.0030	−0.0030	−0.0030
Year 3	−0.0035	−0.0033	−0.0034
Year 4	−0.0039	−0.0036	−0.0038
Steady state	−0.0202	0.0181	−0.0052
Investment in machinery			
Year 1	−0.0095	−0.0105	−0.0099
Year 2	−0.0130	−0.0137	−0.0133
Year 3	−0.0169	−0.0170	−0.0170
Year 4	−0.0213	−0.0204	−0.0210
Steady state	−0.0331	0.0073	−0.0173

Source: Authors' calculations.

Table 8-9. Effective Corporate Tax for Pioneer Firms at a Full Corporate Tax Rate of 45 Percent, 1983: Post-1989 Budget, No Tax Deferral for Depreciation Allowances

Time of earnings profile	Bond financing	Retained earnings	Debt and retained earnings
Investment in buildings			
Year 1	0.0011	0.0014	0.0012
Year 2	0.0012	0.0015	0.0014
Year 3	0.0013	0.0016	0.0015
Year 4	0.0015	0.0017	0.0016
Steady state	−0.0289	0.0275	−0.0069
Investment in machinery			
Year 1	0.0393	0.0470	0.0421
Year 2	0.0397	0.0454	0.0418
Year 3	0.0399	0.0436	0.0413
Year 4	0.0406	0.0417	0.0407
Steady state	−0.0436	0.0112	−0.0223

Source: Authors' calculations.

Table 8-10. Effective Corporate Tax for Pioneer Firms at a Full Corporate Tax Rate of 35 Percent, 1983: Post-1989 Budget, No Tax Deferral for Depreciation Allowances

Time of earnings profile	Bond financing	Retained earnings	Debt and retained earnings
Investment in buildings			
Year 1	0.0007	0.0011	0.0008
Year 2	0.0008	0.0012	0.0009
Year 3	0.0009	0.0013	0.0010
Year 4	0.0010	0.0014	0.0011
Steady state	−0.0202	0.0181	−0.0052
Investment in machinery			
Year 1	0.0302	0.0365	0.0325
Year 2	0.0301	0.0353	0.0320
Year 3	0.0300	0.0339	0.0315
Year 4	0.0296	0.0324	0.0307
Steady state	−0.0331	0.0073	−0.0173

Source: Authors' calculations.

Case 2: Pioneer Firms

Next, we present effective corporate tax rates for firms that have been granted pioneer status.

PRE-TAX REFORM. Recall that a pioneer firm is given tax-free status for a period of five years and, under the pre-1989 tax laws, tax depreciation allowances could be deferred to the end of the holiday period. In table 8-7 we show the results of the effective tax rate calculations for a firm granted pioneer status in 1983. Ideally, we would show the rates that apply to marginal investments undertaken in each of the five years of the tax holiday period; but absence of pertinent data for 1982 precluded our doing so, and therefore we report rates for only the final four years of the tax holiday. For purposes of comparison we also show at the end of each column the effective corporate tax rate that would apply to the same firm's 1983 investments in the absence of the tax holiday and other provisions arising from pioneer status. These estimates are taken from tables 8-1 to 8-6.

The first observation is that all marginal investments undertaken by pioneer firms, regardless of type and method of finance, are subsidized. The second observation is that the size of this subsidy is rather small. Except for investments in machinery in the fourth and fifth years of the tax holiday period, the subsidy is less than two percentage points (and often less than one). Furthermore, in the case of debt-financed investments, the tax-induced subsidy for pioneer firms is *less* than that for nonpioneer firms; that is, the granting of pioneer status actually penalizes firms for such investments. In the case of equity finance, however, the granting of pioneer status has the effect of turning a tax-induced disincentive into a subsidy.

These results arise from two opposing effects of pioneer status for a firm. On the one hand, as intended, the granting of the tax holiday relieves the firm of the burden of any taxes during the holiday period. This relief acts as a subsidy. On the other hand, pioneer firms lose the ability to deduct interest expenses, and initial and annual depreciation allowances must be postponed, without interest, until after the end of this period. These provisions serve as investment disincentives for a pioneer firm.

Thus pioneer status might serve, in principle, either to increase or to decrease investment incentives. If the tax burden on current revenues less interest deductions is larger (in present value) than the tax savings from depreciation allowances, pioneer status would increase investment incentives, and vice versa. This is exactly what is observed in comparing the first two columns of table 8-7. For debt-financed investments, we see that, in the absence of the tax holiday, investment receives a net subsidy; that is, the tax savings effect is most important. The reduction of this benefit under pioneer status, therefore, reduces the subsidy. But if the investment is financed by equity, the tax savings are less than the burden of taxes on current revenues; the granting of pioneer status thus reduces the disincentives provided by the tax system. In this case the net tax imposed by the tax system is turned into a subsidy.

The general conclusion is that pioneer status tends to reduce the effect of the tax system on marginal investment decisions. If investment is penalized under the general tax laws, then pioneer status reduces this disincentive. But if investments are subsidized, pioneer status reduces the size of the subsidy. For Malaysian firms it turns out that pioneer status (a) eliminates the bias of the tax system in favor of marginal investments financed by debt rather than equity and (b) provides a net additional subsidy only to investments with sufficiently low debt-equity ratios.

Disaggregated sectoral estimates (not reported in detail here) showed patterns of distortions for most individual sectors that were qualitatively similar to those for aggregate investment. As is true for nonpioneer firms, the range of intersectoral variation in distortions is greater for machinery than for buildings and greater under equity financing than debt financing. For all investments involving equity financing, however, the range of intersectoral variation in tax distortions is less for pioneer than for nonpioneer firms.

The other interesting observation from the disaggregated analysis is the divergence of some sectors from the norm with respect to the overall pattern of investment incentives for pioneer firms. For instance, in the case of equity-financed investment in buildings, it was found that pioneer status turns a tax-induced investment disincentive into a subsidy for five of the sectors. But for the construction and tin subsector, the opposite occurs; that is, a small investment subsidy received by nonpioneer firms becomes a small marginal tax on investments by pioneer firms. For investments in machinery, where marginal investments in all sectors are subsidized by the tax system, the magnitude of the "improvement" in incentives is far from uniform across sectors. In particular, the construction and tin subsector experiences by far the smallest such improvement for either debt or equity-financed investments.

POST–TAX REFORM. The most important effects of the tax reform measures in the 1989 budget related to pioneer firms. The tax rate reduction from 45 to 35 percent affected all firms, including those with pioneer status. But more significant was the removal of the opportunity for pioneer firms to defer initial and annual depreciation allowances until the end of the tax holiday period. The net effects of these changes on pioneer firms are shown in table 8-10.

As a result of the reforms, pioneer firms now face a small tax-induced investment *dis*incentive as compared with the net subsidy received under the previous system. For buildings, the tax system is now essentially neutral; the wedge during the pioneer years is less than 10 percent of a percentage point under debt financing and only slightly more under equity financing. The effective tax on machinery investments is now considerably higher than this—on the order of 3 to 4 percentage points. The much shorter investment lives of machines in relation to buildings means that the value of the tax savings on investment allowances in the pioneer period is a much greater portion of the total of such tax savings over the life of the investment. This makes the loss of this tax allowance of much greater cost to investment in machinery than to investment in buildings.

As was true before the reforms, debt-financed marginal investments are treated more favorably for nonpioneer than for pioneer firms. Equity-financed building investments continue to receive better treatment if they are made by pioneer rather than nonpioneer firms, but investments in machinery are now slightly better treated if made by nonpioneer firms. Investment allowances made during the pioneer period are also more important for machinery. In addition the tax reforms reduce the differences in distortions between pioneer and nonpioneer firms in equity-financed investment in machinery (see the second column of tables 8-7 and 8-9) and equity-financed investment in buildings. Although the size of the distortion for debt-financed investment has been reduced, the differential treatment of pioneer and nonpioneer firms has not been altered appreciably (see the first column of tables 8-7 and 8-9).

The changes in the tax treatment of pioneer firms are the net effect of two measures—the rate changes and the modification of carryforward provisions. The data in tables 8-8 and 8-9 show the separate effects of each of these reforms. The figures in table 8-8 show the size of the distortions resulting only from the rate change, whereas those in table 8-9 show what would have happened with the change in the carryforward provisions and no rate change. It is apparent that it is the removal of the carryforward provisions for depreciation and initial investment allowances that is primarily responsible for the reversal in the tax incentives for pioneer firms.

Intersectoral variations in the effective tax wedges in different types of investments by pioneer firms following the 1989 tax reform were also investigated. Although intersectoral variations continue to exist, in most cases they are less for pioneer than for nonpioneer firms. This is another manifestation of the greater neutrality of the tax system for pioneer firms after the tax reform. Interestingly enough, however, in debt-financed investments in machinery the intersectoral range of tax distortions is considerably greater for pioneer than for nonpioneer firms. In other words, even though the average level of tax distortion is smaller for pioneer than for nonpioneer firms under the new tax system, the extent of intersectoral investment distortions is actually greater for this particular type of investment.

Table 8-11. Effective Corporate Tax for Tax Loss Firms at a Full Corporate Tax Rate of 45 Percent, 1983

Time of earnings profile	Bond financing	Retained earnings	Debt and retained earnings
Investment in buildings			
Year 1	−0.0097	0.0216	0.0025
Year 2	−0.0071	0.0238	0.0049
Year 3	−0.0042	0.0264	0.0077
Year 4	−0.0011	0.0294	0.0108
Steady state	−0.0289	0.0275	−0.0069
Investment in machinery			
Year 1	−0.0022	0.0294	0.0101
Year 2	−0.0041	0.0277	0.0083
Year 3	−0.0064	0.0259	0.0061
Year 4	−0.0092	0.0240	0.0037
Steady state	−0.0436	0.0112	−0.0002

Source: Authors' calculations.

Table 8-12. Effective Corporate Tax for Tax Loss Firms at a Full Corporate Tax Rate of 35 Percent, 1983

Time of earnings profile	Bond financing	Retained earnings	Debt and retained earnings
Investment in buildings			
Year 1	−0.0064	0.0151	0.0020
Year 2	−0.0042	0.0164	0.0038
Year 3	−0.0018	0.0179	0.0059
Year 4	0.0008	0.0197	0.0081
Steady state	−0.0202	0.0181	−0.0052
Investment in machinery			
Year 1	−0.0018	0.0205	0.0069
Year 2	−0.0030	0.0191	0.0056
Year 3	−0.0045	0.0176	0.0041
Year 4	−0.0062	0.0160	0.0024
Steady state	−0.0331	0.0073	−0.0173

Source: Authors' calculations.

As with the situation before reform, it was also found that the intersectoral structure of tax incentives differs between pioneer and nonpioneer firms. Once again, the construction and tin subsector showed several such reversals. For debt-financed machinery investments, for instance, this sector faces the highest marginal investment subsidy among nonpioneer firms, although it faces the highest rate of tax among pioneer firms.[15] And for equity-financed machinery investment this same sector faces a higher rate of tax for pioneer than for nonpioneer firms, whereas the pattern is the opposite for all other sectors.[16] Also, in equity-financed machinery investment, the food and services subsectors, which face the highest marginal tax rates among nonpioneer firms, turn out to face the lowest rates among pioneer firms.

Case 3: Firms with Tax Deductible Losses

Finally, we consider the case of a firm that, during an initial five-year start-up period, is assumed to experience tax losses; thereafter, its cash flow improves to the point where it enters into a taxpaying position. We take 1983 as the presumed initial year of the firm's operations. As we did in the case of the pioneer firm, we calculate the effective tax wedge during the final four years of the loss period and, for purposes of comparison, the tax wedges on similar investments had the firm been in a taxpaying position in 1983.

PRE-TAX REFORM. The figures in table 8-11 show that under the pre-1989 tax rules debt-financed investments in buildings and machinery receive a small subsidy during the tax loss period. In both cases the magnitude of the subsidy is considerably less than that received by a firm in a taxpaying position.[17] The differential between the tax loss and taxpaying situations is greater for machinery. It should be noted also that the size of the subsidy decreases over time (during the tax loss period) in the case of buildings and increases over time for machinery.[18]

For equity-financed investments, the difference in the distortions facing tax loss and taxpaying firms is much smaller. As in the case of taxpaying firms, equity-financed investments are taxed at the margin, whereas debt-financed investments are subsidized. For buildings the differential between taxpaying and nontaxpaying firms is small, with the marginal tax wedge for loss firms starting in the early years of the loss period just below that for taxpayers and rising slowly over time until it slightly exceeds that for taxpayers.[19] For machinery, the marginal tax wedge falls during the loss period but remains more than double that facing taxpaying firms.[20] For firms financing investments through a combination of debt and equity, the tax system discourages investment for loss firms while subsidizing it for taxpaying firms.

POST–TAX REFORM. The data in table 8-12 show that the tax reforms do not change any of the qualitative patterns of investment distortions facing tax loss firms. But they have the uniform effect of reducing the magnitude of all the positive and negative tax incentives. This is the same as was observed for taxpaying firms.

Conclusions

Direct taxes in Malaysia distort investment decisions in many significant and often quite unintended ways. We begin this last section with a brief summary of the principal effects of these taxes under both the pre- and the post-1989 regimes. We conclude with some comments on the policy implications of these findings.

Summary of Results

The more or less complete integration of the personal and corporate taxes is a desirable feature of the tax system that succeeds in avoiding the double taxation of corporate income. This, together with the nontaxation of capital gains, means that the personal tax system imposes a minimal distortion on investment financed through retained earnings. But the personal tax system does distort savings decisions in the form of purchases of new debt or new equity issues. The differential between personal and corporate tax rates (the latter are generally higher for taxpaying firms), together with the integration of personal and corporate taxes, means that the tax system provides a significant subsidy to new equity finance. The reduction in corporate tax rates in the 1989 budget reduces the size of this subsidy. The taxation of interest income, in contrast, means that the personal tax system imposes a net tax on bond finance. Furthermore, the nonindexation of interest taxation means that the size of this disincentive increases with the rate of inflation. For typical investments in Malaysia that are financed by some combination of debt and new equity, personal taxes provide a net disincentive to savings. This distortion is decreased by the 1989 reforms.

The effects of the corporate tax system on firms' investment decisions are much more complex and depend on a variety of considerations, including the type of capital good being purchased, the method of finance, the treatment of depreciation in relation to true economic depreciation for different types of investments, the treatment of tax losses, and the granting of various types of investment incentives. We have estimated the effects of the tax system on investments by three types of firms: those making taxable profits throughout the time period under consideration, those experiencing temporary tax losses during the relevant time period, and those that have been granted pioneer status. We summarize the results for each of these cases in turn.

PROFIT-MAKING FIRMS. Because of the tax deductibility of interest costs and the nondeductibility of equity costs to the firm, bond-financed investments are treated much more favorably than those that are equity-financed. In fact, the corporate tax system provides a net subsidy to bond-financed investments and a net disincentive to equity finance. Machinery investments generally are given more favorable treatment than buildings. As is true for personal taxes, the 1989 tax reform, by lowering the marginal tax rate, reduces the magnitudes of all these investment distortions. Differences in initial investment allowances and in annual depreciation allowances produce corresponding intersectoral differences in the tax distortions facing investments in different sectors. These differentials are greater for equity-financed than for bond-financed investments. The tax reform reduces the magnitudes of these differential investment distortions.

PIONEER FIRMS. Under the Malaysian tax system, a firm would derive no benefit from pioneer status unless it was making what otherwise would be taxable profits during the pioneer period. Pioneer status provides no additional benefits to firms that have no taxable profits against which to use the tax holiday. For profit-making firms, pioneer status provides a small subsidy to all types of investments. But in debt-financed investments, the tax-induced subsidy is less than that for nonpioneer firms; that is, the granting of pioneer status penalizes investment in these cases. This happens because the postponement of the use of depreciation allowances costs firms more than they gain from the reduction in taxes during the tax holiday period. In general pioneer status tends to reduce the effect of the tax system—whether positive or negative—on investment. It tends to eliminate the bias of the tax system in favor of debt-financed investments and to provide a net additional subsidy only to investments with sufficiently low debt-equity ratios. As is true for their nonpioneer counterparts, pioneer firms face differential investment distortions according to the sectors in which they invest. For all equity-financed investments, however, the range of intersectoral variation in distortions is less for firms under pioneer status.

The 1989 tax reforms both reduced tax rates and removed the ability of pioneer firms to carry forward unused depreciation allowances to the end of the tax holiday. This has reduced the value of any subsidies provided to pioneer firms. The number of instances in which pioneer status imposes a net penalty has increased. The removal of the carryforward provisions is the major reason for these results. There is, however, wide intersectoral variation in both the magnitude and the direction of these effects. One frequently observed result of the reforms, nevertheless, is a smaller range of variation in distortions for pioneer than for nonpioneer firms.

TAX LOSS FIRMS. Firms in a temporary tax loss position generally receive a small net subsidy on debt-financed investments, although this subsidy is considerably less than for taxpaying firms. Equity-financed investments, however, face a net disincentive; but the difference in the treatment of taxable and tax loss firms is very small. As with taxpaying firms, the 1989 reforms have the effect of reducing both the size and the range of tax-induced investment distortions.

Some Policy Implications

The tax system plays a major role in determining the profitability of investments in Malaysia. For some investments, it provides a considerable net subsidy. But many others are faced with sizable tax penalties. The overall pattern of incentives and disincentives, whether according to method of finance, type of capital good being purchased, or sector in which the investment occurs, bears no obvious relation to any conceivable social or economic goals that might in principle guide the construction of an incentive system. The unintended consequences of these distortions, therefore, almost certainly include significant waste in the use of Malaysia's investment resources.

Various specific incentives have been introduced in an attempt to achieve particular goals. These include export, regional, and employment incentives. One of the major incentives of this type in Malaysia has been the granting of pioneer status to selected investments. This type of measure has been used in many different countries in order to promote investment in desirable activities and to assist infant industries and disadvantaged economic and social groups.

If Malaysia has set these objectives as the goals of pioneer status, it almost certainly has failed to achieve them. Pioneer status imposes a net penalty on many investors. It is of possible value only to firms with sufficient taxable profits against which to use the benefits of the tax holiday; it is highly unlikely to be of value to the weak or infant investors or to the industries that usually are the intended beneficiaries of the measures.[21]

Another clear result arising from both this work and the experience of other countries, is that broadly based taxes, levied at low marginal rates, are quite possibly the most effective form of investment incentive available. Such systems have far fewer unintended consequences and produce smaller, less variable, and more predictable investment distortions. The 1989 tax reform was a useful step in this direction.

Appendix. Description of Data

Two types of data were used in the calculation of the user cost of capital and the effective marginal tax rate. The first set concerns all general tax and macroeconomic variables that are not specific to any firm. The second includes all firm-specific tax and financial variables. Time series as well as cross-sectional estimates were made from the two groups.

Economywide Data

The following data apply for the economy as a whole.

CORPORATE TAX RATE. Prior to the 1989 budget all companies were taxed at the normal rate of 40 percent. A development tax of 5 percent was also imposed on all companies. Until recently, an excess profits tax of 3 percent was chargeable on income in excess of M$2 million. Petroleum income is subject to a 45 percent gasoline income tax only.

PERSONAL TAX RATE. Individuals are subject to a graduated tax rate. The lowest taxable income bracket is taxed at 5 percent. At the top end, income in excess of M$100,000 attracts a 40 percent tax rate. In addition a 3 percent excess profits tax is levied on individuals whose annual incomes are over M$300,000. In our calculations we assumed that the average personal tax rate was 20 percent.

DIVIDEND AND CAPITAL GAINS TAX RATES. An imputation system is used in Malaysia, so the same source of corporate income is taxed only once. In effect, therefore, the dividend tax rate is zero. Capital gains are not taxed in general. The only exception is the real property gains tax that imposed a graduated tax rate on all gains from the disposal of real assets. The rate is affected by the number of years from acquisition to disposal. We have ignored the taxation of capital gains in the analysis because capital gains arising from holding financial assets are not taxed. A 2 percent share transfer tax on the gross market value of each disposal of shares in a land-based company has been scrapped.

INFLATION RATE. The actual inflation rate was used in the calculations over the entire time period. The assumption of perfect foresight was employed so that the expected inflation rate was equal to the observed inflation rate. The data were obtained from the various issues of *Bank Negara Statistical Bulletin* (quarterly).

Firm-Specific Data

The following data are based on individual firms.

FINANCING RATIOS. Time series as well as cross-sectional data on the sources of financing of capital investment were obtained from the Kuala Lumpur Stock Exchange (unpublished data). The firms' total liabilities were used as a proxy for debts. Because the corporate lending rate was not readily available, a base case was used, in which the lending rate was assumed to be 12 percent. The shareholders' fund was used to calculate the return to equity.

TAX DEPRECIATION RATES. We used a straight-line tax depreciation method. *Income Tax Act 1967 and Supplementary Income Tax Act 1967 and 1982* (Ministry of Finance 1980 and 1982) was the source of the initial and annual tax depreciation allowances for industrial building and plant and equipment. The rates are specific to each type of investment as well as the sector in which those investments are undertaken.

PHYSICAL DEPRECIATION RATES. No data were available on depreciation rates. Some estimates were used from Canadian sources.

Notes

This chapter derives from a study prepared by the authors for the Tax Reform Project of the Malaysian Institute of Economic Research. We are indebted to members of the institute's Tax Reform Group for much valuable input. Our greatest debt is to Tan Hui Gek, a senior research officer of the institute, who worked closely with us and provided invaluable assistance at every stage of our work. The work of the Tax Reform Group, and of this study in particular, received financial support from the Canadian International Development Agency as part of a collaboration program between the Malyasian Institute of Economic Research and Queen's University.

1. See Ministry of Finance (1988: 74).

2. See Gillis (1985) and (1989) for a description and discussions of the recent Indonesian tax reforms.

3. Good sources of information about the Malaysian tax law are the International Bureau of Fiscal Documentation (Amsterdam, Netherlands) and the Asian-Pacific Tax and Investment Research Centre (Singapore). See also Subramaniam (1984).

4. In mid-1991 the Malaysian dollar was worth approximately U.S.$0.35.

5. Bardai (1987) estimated that the cost of government subsidies to each pioneer firm is about M$2.3 million over the average of 5.2 tax relief years. Comparing this with the average investment value of paid up capital, it means that the government has been subsidizing about 31 percent of those investments.

6. For a review and discussion of the marginal effective tax rate literature, see Boadway (1987).

7. We are assuming that the firm holds static expectations, which are realized, with respect to those parameters.

8. Firms might use both retained earnings and new issues as sources of equity financing. We might expect, therefore, the cost of equity financing, ρ, to be some weighted combination of the cost of retained earnings and of new issues. Given that capital gains from holding corporate shares are not taxed and that the full imputation system essentially exempts dividends from being taxed again at the

personal level, the cost of equity to the firm becomes independent of the way in which it is raised.

9. Because the firm in this situation is operating under the long-run, steady-state conditions, Z_t and Z_{t-1} are the same. Furthermore, expectations of cost of finance, inflation, changes in the capital goods price, and the statutory corporate tax rate are all assumed to be stationary. Hence, we can drop all time subscripts.

10. It is assumed that depreciation begins the first period after the initial allowance is taken.

11. Although the after-tax rate of return to savers is given by equation 8-12, data limitation permits only the consideration in which the proportion of equity finance coming from new issues is either zero or unity. We therefore report only on the two extreme cases in which $a = 0$ or 1.

12. See note 8 above.

13. The inverse relation between the effective tax rate and the rate of inflation is the opposite of what has been found for the U.S. and Canadian economies. See, for example, Auerbach 1983; Boadway, Bruce, and Mintz 1984; and King and Fullerton 1984.

14. The writeoff period for machinery typically ranges from four to twelve years, whereas that of a building is about fifty years.

15. This situation occurs because machinery investments in this sector attract one of the highest depreciation writeoff rates. Thus the postponement of these benefits under pioneer status is a considerable disadvantage to investors.

16. This somewhat peculiar result is because the real cost of finance in the construction and tin sector, in the period under consideration, is negative, giving rise to the possibility that the tax wedge, which could be either positive or negative under any status, has a higher probability of being larger for a pioneer firm than a nonpioneer one.

17. Three factors influence the results: first, the incentive that comes from the deferral of tax liability on revenues, if the firm is in a loss position; second, the disincentive that arises from the deferral of the interest deduction from bond financing; and third, the disadvantage that comes from the deferral of depreciation allowances without interest. The smaller subsidy for a pioneer firm suggests that the combined disincentive effects outweigh the advantages gained from deferring tax payment on revenues.

18. The reason for this is best explained when interest deductibility is not an issue, which is the case under equity financing. Therefore we defer the explanation to the next paragraph.

19. Two opposing factors affect the tax wedge. The advantage to a pioneer firm is the incentive from the deferral of tax payment on revenue accruing in the holiday period. The disincentive is the deferral of depreciation allowances, without interest. Our results suggest that, because equity-financed investments are taxed at the margin, the incentive effect is small in relation to the disincentive effect. Further, the small increment in the tax wedge for building investment suggests that the cumulative advantage from not paying taxes in the pioneer period in relation to the cumulative disadvantage of depreciation deferral increases as the length of the pioneer status increases in this case.

20. The time-decreasing tax wedge during the pioneer period for machinery is primarily a result of the short writeoff periods and, hence, the high depreciation rates for such investments. This being the case, the cumulative disincentive effect of depreciation deferral is strongest in the earlier periods.

21. For some recent estimates that show the futility of using corporate tax incentives to encourage private reforestation activities in Malaysia, see Flatters 1991.

References

Auerbach, Alan J. 1983. "Corporate Taxation in the United States." Brookings Papers on Economic Activity 2. Brookings Institution, Washington, D.C.

Bardai, Barjoyai. 1987. "Evaluation of Malaysian Corporate Tax Incentives." Malaysian Institute of Economic Research, Kuala Lumpur.

Boadway, Robin W. 1987. "The Theory and Measurement of Effective Tax Rates." In Jack M. Mintz and Douglas D. Purvis, eds., *The Impact of Taxation on Business Activity.* Kingston, Ont., Can.: Queen's University, John Deutsch Institute for the Study of Economic Policy.

Boadway, Robin W., Neil Bruce, and Jack M. Mintz. 1984. "Taxation, Inflation, and the User Cost of Capital in Canada." *Canadian Journal of Economics* 17 (February): 62–79.

Flatters, Frank. 1991. "Fiscal Incentives for the Development of Forest Plantations in Sabah, Malaysia." Malaysian Institute for Economic Research, Kuala Lumpur.

Gillis, Malcolm. 1985. "Micro and Macro Economics of Tax Reform in Indonesia." *Journal of Development Economics* 19:221–54.

———. 1989. "Comprehensive Tax Reform: The Indonesian Experience, 1981–88." In Malcolm Gillis, ed., *Lessons from Fundamental Tax Reform in Developing Countries.* Durham, N.C.: Duke University Press.

King, Mervyn A., and Don Fullerton. 1984. *The Taxation of Income from Capital: A Comparative Study of the United States, the United Kingdom, Sweden, and West Germany.* Chicago, Ill.: University of Chicago Press.

Ministry of Finance, Malaysia. 1980 and 1982. *Income Tax Act 1967 and Supplementary Income Tax Act 1967 and 1982.* Kuala Lumpur: Jabatan Percetalcan Negara.

———. 1988. *Economic Report.* Kuala Lumpur: National Printing Department.

Subramaniam, Arjunan. 1984. *The Law of Personal and Business Taxation.* Kuala Lumpur, Malaysia: Dasaratha Raja (M) Sdn. Bhd.

INDIRECT TAXES AND INVESTMENT INCENTIVES IN MALAYSIA

9

Robin W. Boadway, Dale Chua,
and Frank Flatters

INDIRECT TAXES ACCOUNT for about one-half of the government tax revenues in Malaysia. Most of them are levied on only particular subsets of activities or goods, and often at quite different rates across taxed commodities. Import taxes, consisting of import tariffs and surcharges on a broad range of commodities, have been diminishing in importance but still account for the largest share of indirect tax revenues. These import taxes have the greatest degree of rate variation across commodities. The other main types of indirect taxes, in decreasing order of importance, are excise duties, export duties, and sales taxes. Excise and export duties are both quite narrow in their commodity coverage, whereas the coverage of the sales tax is more similar to that of import duties. For all of these indirect taxes, but especially the two more general ones (import tariffs and sales taxes), there are many different types of exemptions.

   Such an assortment of taxes, accounting for a considerable portion of government tax revenues and exhibiting large variations in rates, coverage, and exemptions, might be expected to have many unanticipated distortionary effects on economic incentives. Our objective in this chapter is to give some broad indications of the nature and magnitude of the distortions in investment incentives arising from this indirect tax system. To do this we first estimate the differential price effects of these taxes across sectors of the economy, in a manner analogous to the measurement of effective rates of protection (ERPs). We then adapt the methodology of the literature on marginal effective tax rates (METRs), usually used to estimate the distortionary investment incentives caused by direct taxes, to estimate the investment distortions caused by indirect taxes. The results are used to evaluate the effects of tax reforms, including the introduction of a value added tax for Malaysia.

We have divided the chapter into four main sections. The first section provides a brief overview of Malaysia's indirect tax system. In the second section we describe the methodology for estimating the investment incentive effects of indirect taxes. The third section is a presentation of our estimates of these distortions for Malaysia. In the last section we make some concluding observations about the policy implications of our findings.

Indirect Taxes in Malaysia

As indicated, the indirect tax system comprises many different taxes. For ease of exposition we describe them separately, in order of decreasing importance as revenue. A summary of the evolution of the major components of the indirect tax system from 1970 through 1989 is presented in table 9-1.

Table 9-1. Indirect Tax Collections

Year	Direct and indirect	Indirect taxes					
		Total	Import	Export	Sales	Excise	Other
Millions of ringgit							
1970	1,840	1,156	557	259	0	249	91
1975	4,256	2,266	801	625	272	450	118
1980	12,059	6,564	2,061	2,567	696	973	267
1985	16,699	7,441	2,518	1,839	1,234	1,376	475
1989	16,674	8,882	2,899	1,588	1,913	1,932	550
As a share of all tax revenues (percent)							
1970	100	63	30	14	0	14	5
1975	100	53	19	15	6	11	3
1980	100	54	17	21	6	8	2
1985	100	45	15	11	7	8	3
1989	100	53	17	10	12	12	3
As a share of indirect tax revenues (percent)							
1970	n.a.	100	48	22	0	22	8
1975	n.a.	100	35	28	12	20	5
1980	n.a.	100	31	39	11	15	4
1985	n.a.	100	34	25	17	19	6
1989	n.a.	100	33	18	22	22	6

n.a. Not applicable.
Source: Bank Negara Malaysia (1990).

Import Taxes

Since 1960, import taxes, consisting of import duties and import sur-
taxes, have fallen in relative importance from 52 to 32 percent of indirect
taxes, or from 40 to 16 percent of total tax revenues (Salleh 1988: table
2). Import duties are levied on a broad range of imported commodities,
at rates ranging from 0 to 100 percent, with the majority of rates falling
between 10 and 35 percent. The import surtax is imposed at a uniform
rate of 5 percent, except on raw materials and certain forms of machinery,
which are taxed at a rate of 2 percent. Exemptions to both types of
import taxes are granted on the basis of the type of end user (for example, government departments and public enterprises) to encourage certain types of investments or to promote certain types of activities,
especially exports. In recent years, petroleum and fuel oils have been the
single most important source of import duties, accounting for over 30
percent of the total in 1987. Until 1983, tobacco products had been
most important; they still account for over 8 percent of import tax collections (Salleh 1988: table 7).

Excise Duties

Excise duties have accounted for about 10 percent of total tax revenues
since the mid-1960s but have grown from 15 to 23 percent of indirect
tax collections during this period (Salleh 1988: table 2). They are levied
on a small number of domestically manufactured commodities, principally petroleum products and fuel oils, alcoholic beverages, motor vehicles, and tobacco products. Petroleum products and fuel oils alone
account for 56 percent of excise revenues, with alcohol and motor vehicles each contributing about 15 percent (Salleh 1988: table 2). As with
import taxes, there is provision for granting full or partial exemptions to
particular users, activities, and goods.

Export Duties

Export duties, levied on many primary export products, have yielded
cyclically variable revenues, depending on world market conditions for
the taxed products. The ad valorem duty rates vary across commodities
and are progressive with respect to their world selling prices. They are
now levied on a "cost-plus" basis, that is, on the excess of the export
price over some notional cost of production. Export duty collections in
1987 accounted for only 10 percent of total tax revenue, or 20 percent of
indirect taxes. Even after taking account of the commodity slump of the
1980s, this is still a considerably less important revenue source than it was
in the 1960s and 1970s (Salleh 1988: table 2). Rubber and tin, which

together accounted for 95 percent of export duty revenues in 1961, 81 percent in 1970, and 65 percent in 1980, have now been completely eclipsed in importance by crude petroleum. In 1987 crude petroleum accounted for 94 percent of collections (Salleh 1988: table 6).

Sales Taxes

The sales tax, introduced in 1972, is a relatively new revenue source in Malaysia. Originally levied at a rate of 5 percent, the basic rate is now 10 percent. In 1989 it accounted for 11 percent of all tax revenues, or about 22 percent of indirect tax collections. The tax is imposed on manufactured goods, at the level of the manufacturer for domestic production and of the importer (on the basis of the customs valuation plus import duties) for foreign goods. Exempt goods include personal and professional services; sales of real and intangible property; exports; certain specific goods, such as food and other necessities; petroleum products; construction building materials; and certain industrial raw materials and machinery. Small manufacturers (with turnover of less than M$100,000) are also exempted. Finally, under the "ring system," licensed manufacturers (those who are "in the ring") are entitled to a credit against taxes owing on sales of products any sales taxes paid on materials used in their production. The share of sales taxes collected on imports fell from 57 percent, when the tax was introduced in 1972, to 42 percent in 1987.

Other Indirect Taxes

Other indirect taxes, accounting in total for about 3.5 percent of total tax revenues, or 7 percent of indirect taxes, include a road tax, stamp duties, and a 5 percent service tax on certain hotel, restaurant, and entertainment services. (Percentages were calculated from Salleh 1988: table 2.)

Methodology for Estimating Incentive Effects of Indirect Taxes

For expository purposes, the mechanism whereby indirect taxes affect investment incentives can be thought of in three distinct steps. The first, and most immediate, effect of an indirect tax is on the relative prices of different goods and services. An export tax, for instance, lowers the domestic price in relation to that in world markets of the taxed good; and an import duty raises the domestic price of the taxed good. Thus the first step in estimating the effects of indirect taxes is to determine these relative effects on prices.

The second step is to take account of the fact that most activities involve the use or production of a variety of taxed goods. This makes it necessary to estimate the net effects of indirect taxes on the prices of all of a firm's inputs and outputs. To do this requires information, not only on the relative price effects on all relevant goods (the first step), but also on the relative importance of these goods in the costs and revenues of all producers affected by indirect taxes. This information is provided by the Malaysian *Input-Output Tables* (Ministry of Finance 1983). These I-O tables enable us to estimate the effects of indirect taxes on the value added prices of all production activities. This is a standard procedure that is often used in the analysis of the effects of trade policies by estimating "effective rates of protection."

The third and final step is to make estimates of the marginal returns to investment in Malaysia and to determine how these returns are affected by changes in value added prices resulting from the indirect tax system. The basic methodology for estimating returns to investment is the same as that used in estimating METRs on different types of investments due to the direct tax system (see chapter 8, this volume). In this chapter we adapt this methodology to determine the METRs on different types of investments due to indirect taxes. Because indirect taxes discriminate primarily on the basis of commodity types, this exercise will be much more sharply focused on intersectoral investment distortions than is normally the case with direct taxes.

Price Effects of Indirect Taxes

We now consider the effects of the four main types of indirect taxes on the prices of taxed commodities faced by Malaysian producers. The most important features of the Malaysian economy from this viewpoint are its relative openness to international trade and its relatively small size in world markets. This means that Malaysia cannot, by its own actions, including changes in its tax system, affect the world prices of tradable commodities. This simplifies considerably the analysis of the effect of taxes on prices to domestic producers.

Import taxes have the effect of raising domestic consumer and producer prices over the world price by the amount of the tax. If the world price (and the domestic price in the absence of taxation) of a commodity is P_w, and it is subject to an import tax at a rate of t percent, then the domestic price facing both sellers and buyers of the commodity will be $P_w(1 + t)$. To the producer of such a good for the domestic market, this acts like a production subsidy (in relation to imports); but to a user of the good, it acts as a tax. Producers of this good for the export market do not benefit from the tariff on their export sales because they must continue to sell in export markets at the prevailing world price. To the extent that duty drawback and exemption schemes for exporters are effective, exporters will not suffer the penalty of higher input prices due to import taxes.

For nontradable goods, an excise tax and a sales tax will have the same effect of lowering the price received by producers of the good and raising the price paid by its users. The relative sizes of these two burdens will depend on the elasticities of demand and supply of the good. But for tradable goods, the effects of these taxes are easier to determine. Because they are applied equally to imports and domestic production, they impose no net subsidy or tax on producers of the good. But users of taxed goods bear a burden in the form of an increase in the cost of the good by the full amount of the tax. On the input side, therefore, sales and excise taxes are just like import taxes, whereas on the output side, they have no effect on investment incentives.

Export taxes have precisely the opposite effect of import taxes; they lower the domestic price, to both producers and users of the taxed commodity, by the amount of the tax. With a world market price (and, hence, domestic price in the absence of taxes) of P_w, and an export tax at a rate of t percent, the domestic price facing both producers and users would fall to $P_w(1 - t)$. The tax is a subsidy to domestic users of the good and a penalty on its domestic producers.

Value Added Price Effects of Indirect Taxes

Most producers are affected by a variety of indirect taxes on both their inputs and their outputs. The first step in determining the net incentive effect of all these taxes is to estimate their effect on the value added of the firm's activities. Suppose that the relevant price facing a firm for an input or output, i, in the absence of any indirect taxes is given by P_i^w, and the price of the same good in the presence of a particular set of indirect taxes is P_i^d. Then, if the amount of good j used to produce a unit of output of good i is given by a_{ji}, we could define value added for production of good i in the absence of indirect taxes and in the presence of these taxes, respectively, as

$$VA_i^d = P_i - \sum a_{ji} P_j^d$$

and

$$VA_i^w = P_i^w - \sum a_{ji} P_j^w.$$

The change in value added for producers of good i as a result of the indirect tax system, then, is simply the difference between these two numbers. To estimate this change in value added for good i, it is necessary to know (a) the changes in each of the input and output prices for this sector as discussed above and (b) the sector's input-output coefficients, which can be obtained from the *Input-Output Tables*.

A commonly used method for estimating the distortionary effects of indirect taxes, especially in the case of international trade taxes, is to calculate the ERP due to these fiscal measures in each sector. The ERP is defined as the percentage change in the sector's value added as the result of taxation:[1]

$$\text{ERP}_i = \frac{VA_i^d - VA_i^w}{VA_i^d}.$$

Although this measure indicates the short-run incentive effects of indirect taxes, it is an imperfect indicator of their marginal distortionary effects on investment decisions. To capture these latter effects, it is necessary to combine the information provided by (a) ERP-type measures of changes in net cash flows arising from tax-induced changes in current revenues and costs and (b) rates of return in the economy to marginal investments of various types in the different sectors. The methodology we use for this purpose is described in the following section.

Investment Incentive Effects of Indirect Taxes

In order to estimate the distortionary effects of taxation on investment decisions, it is necessary to determine the increase (or decrease) in the gross rate of return required on a marginal investment as a result of the tax(es) in question. If the net effect of a tax is to force investors to require a higher (lower) gross rate of return, then the tax acts as a disincentive (subsidy) to that type of investment. There is now a well-developed methodology for measuring the distortionary effects of direct taxes in this manner. Under this method, the METR is defined simply as the difference between the rate of return on a marginal investment, gross of taxes, in the presence of the direct tax system (r_d) and the rate of return available in world capital markets (r_w). We denote this by t_d.

By altering the prices of a firm's inputs and outputs in the manner described above, the indirect tax system also causes changes in the rates of return of different investments. If the required gross rate of return in the presence of both direct and indirect taxes is defined as $r_{d\&n}$, then we can define the following additional METRs. The METR due to both direct and indirect taxes is ($r_{d\&n} - r_w$), or $t_{d\&n}$. And the METR due to indirect taxes alone, t_n is ($r_{d\&n} - r_d$). Using information derived from the (assumed) long-run profit-maximizing behavior of the firm, we can show that

$$t_n = (-\text{ERP})(\text{VMP})$$

where ERP is the effective rate of protection (and thus its negative, the effective rate of taxation) resulting from indirect taxes, as defined above, and the value of the marginal product (VMP) is the value to the firm, after taking account of all direct tax implications, of the additional output from a marginal investment of one dollar.[2] The main thing to note is that, as might have been expected, the METR resulting from indirect taxes is negatively related to the ERP provided to the sector by these taxes. The ERP in each sector can be calculated along the lines suggested in the previous section. And the method for estimating the VMP for different types of investments is the same as that used in calculating METRs from direct taxes. For the purposes of this study, we draw on estimates obtained in our previous study of Malaysia's direct tax system (see chapter 8, this volume).

Indirect taxes distort investment decisions in a manner somewhat different from that of direct taxes. It is well known, for instance, that a fully general sales tax on consumption does not distort the intertemporal decision at all and so does not impose a distortion on investment. In other words, a proportional value added tax on consumption should have a zero METR on investment. The measure of the indirect tax wedge that we have derived here has this property.

The actual indirect tax system in Malaysia is not perfectly general; indeed, it is very far from it. Some consumer goods or services are exempt, and others face differential rates; intermediate purchases are not all exempt; and some capital goods bear the tax. Furthermore, a major part of the indirect tax system consists of levies on trade, which are highly selective and which, in particular, tend to tax final goods at higher rates than intermediate inputs. Therefore the indirect tax system ends up distorting investment decisions in some sectors in relation to others. Our measures of METRs in various sectors might best be interpreted in this manner—that is, as indicating the extent of intersectoral investment distortions due to Malaysia's indirect tax system. The *intersectoral* variations in METRs resulting from indirect taxes will tend to be much greater than those resulting from the direct tax system.

Estimates of Distortionary Effects of Malaysia's Indirect Tax System

We present here calculations of the way in which the indirect tax system distorts output and investment decisions in Malaysia.

The Data

The data used for our estimates of the intersectoral structure of indirect taxes and of the economy are from the Malaysian *Input-Output Tables* for 1983. The financial and economic data necessary for estimating gross rates of return to investments of different types are also, as much as possible, from the same year, as estimated in our earlier study of the incentive effects of the direct tax system. For the purpose of the current exercise, we used the 60 by 60 sector version of the *Input-Output Tables* and further simplified the estimations by concentrating on the economy's tradable goods sectors.

As is suggested from the earlier discussion of the effects of commodity taxes on relative prices, it is important to distinguish between those sectors that produce exports and those that produce primarily import substitutes. Because, especially at the level of aggregation of the *Input-Output Tables,* many of the sectors comprise both types of producers, we based the import-export distinction on the sign of the net trade balance of each sector.

With respect to the structure and incentive effects of different types of indirect taxes, the theory indicates that the most important distinction is between taxes that apply only to internationally traded goods (import duties and export taxes) and those levied equally on imports and domestic production (sales and excise taxes). The Malaysian *Input-Output Tables* distinguishes only between "taxes on imported commodities" and "taxes on domestic goods." Unfortunately, at least for the purpose of this exercise, the former comprises import duties, sales taxes, and excises, whereas the latter includes sales taxes and excises on domestic products only. To estimate the effects of Malaysia's indirect taxes, therefore, it is necessary to separate the import duty from the sales and excise tax components of the "taxes on imports." The obvious way to do this is to assume that the sales and excise tax rates on imports are the same as those on domestic goods, which is true for any particular commodity, before taking account of differences in exemption practices between imports and domestic goods. If this assumption is correct, then the import duty component of the "taxes on imports" can be calculated as the residual after estimating and subtracting from total commodity taxes the sales and excise tax payments on each import group on the basis of the rate applied to domestic goods. But if the commodity composition of the import component of any input-output sector differs from that of its domestic component, or if the two groups differ in regard to exemption practices, then this method will be an imperfect way to estimate import duty collections by sector. Our estimates of import duties and surcharges derived by this method yielded some results, such as negative rates of import duty on some goods, that were clearly incorrect. Fortunately, the number of such obvious anomalies was rather small. The procedure in such anomalous cases was to make some rough adjustments to the tariff rate estimates based on the statutory tariff rates.

Effective Rates of Protection from Indirect Taxes

The estimated ERPs provided to all tradable goods sectors by Malaysia's indirect taxes are shown in table 9-2. The first thing that is apparent is the considerable intersectoral variation in both sets of ERPs. We begin with the variations from all indirect taxes. The wide range of ERPs can be seen in various ways. It can be seen that, although many sectors receive protection in excess of 30 percent, many others actually receive negative

Table 9-2. Effective Protection Rates from Indirect Taxes
(percent)

I-O table sector number	Trade status	All indirect taxes	Indirect trade taxes[a]	Sales and excise taxes
1	Import substitution	4.50	4.50	0.00
2	Export	−19.83	−19.83	0.00
3	Export	−2.21	−2.21	0.00
4	Import substitution	1.70	1.70	0.00
5	Export	−88.49	−64.22	−24.22
7	Export	−187.43	−180.29	−7.14
8	Import substitution	7.06	7.75	−0.69
9	Import substitution	21.08	21.35	−0.27
10	Export	−4.88	−4.88	0.00
11	Import substitution	6.92	6.92	0.00
12	Export	−3.36	−0.38	−2.98
13	Import substitution	5.57	6.38	−0.81
16	Import substitution	309.92	315.51	−5.59
17	Import substitution	50.73	55.17	−4.44
18	Export	−8.42	−3.94	−4.48
19	Export	−8.23	−5.79	−2.44
20	Import substitution	44.13	48.30	−4.17
21	Import substitution	178.70	187.49	−8.79
22	Import substitution	21.43	30.79	−9.36
23	Import substitution	−10.76	1.48	−12.24
24	Import substitution	8.77	12.19	−3.42
25	Import substitution	−50.77	22.02	−72.79
26	Export	−24.76	−23.88	−0.88
27	Export	−11.05	−3.73	−7.32
28	Import substitution	23.17	29.09	−5.92
29	Import substitution	37.30	38.49	−1.19
30	Import substitution	6.22	6.22	0.00
31	Import substitution	15.32	15.32	0.00
32	Import substitution	19.03	35.92	−16.89
33	Import substitution	26.13	29.08	−2.95
34	Import substitution	2.30	8.15	−5.85
35	Import substitution	11.54	20.65	−9.11
36	Import substitution	52.64	60.46	−7.82
37	Import substitution	−2.74	2.86	−5.60
42	Export	3.84	3.84	0.00
44	Export	2.60	2.60	0.00

a. Indirect taxes on international trade (import duties and surcharges, export duties).
Source: Authors' calculations.

protection from indirect taxes. Negative protection arises when the cost-raising effect of taxes on inputs more than offsets the protective effect of import protection on outputs (and, where applicable, the cost-reducing effect of export restrictions on a sector's inputs). Of the thirty-six tradable goods sectors, twelve turn out to have negative protection and twenty-four positive. Of those with negative protection, more than half (seven) face a net tax exceeding 10 percent. And of those sectors with positive protection, ten (more than 40 percent) have ERPs of more than 20 percent; and six sectors, fully a quarter of those with positive protection, receive in excess of 40 percent. The general pattern, as is the case in many similar protection regimes, is that export-oriented industries face low or negative effective protection, whereas import-substitution industries receive high positive protection.

The second general observation is that a large part of the variation in ERPs stems from the taxes on international trade. A comparison of the last two columns of the table shows that the ERPs from indirect taxes on foreign trade alone explain a large part of the intersectoral distribution of ERPs. In fact, by raising the costs of intermediate inputs for most sectors, the domestic sales and excise taxes tend to reduce (slightly) the highest ERPs caused by trade taxes. (The opposite is true for sectors with negative ERPs.) Overall, the variations in ERPs tend to be reduced slightly by the taxes on domestic goods. The few exceptions to the variance-reducing effect of the domestic taxes occur in the cases of excise taxes on important inputs in a few sectors. The dominance of trade taxes in explaining the variance of ERPs is a result of their slightly greater importance in government revenues and, of greater importance, the relatively greater dispersion in their rates across sectors.

METRs, or Estimated Investment Distortions

The effect of indirect taxes on investment incentives is best measured by their effect on the rate of return on marginal investments—that is, on investments that are on the margin of yielding a normal rate of return. This is precisely what is measured by the METR. In table 9-3 we present the results of our estimates of the METRs due to Malaysia's indirect tax system. The estimates represent the number of percentage points by which the rate of return is raised or lowered as a result of these taxes. An METR of, say, 2 means that the rate of return is lowered by 2 percentage points. A negative METR means that the indirect tax system provides a subsidy to that activity and, hence, raises the rate of return.

Not surprisingly, an examination of this table reveals many of the same patterns that appeared earlier with the ERP estimates. There is considerable dispersion in the METRs, with the range being greater for taxes on trade than for sales taxes and excises. The data in table 9-4 show the frequency distributions of METRs corresponding to the last three columns

Table 9-3. *METRs from Indirect Taxes*
(percent)

I-O table sector number	Trade status	All indirect taxes	Indirect trade taxes[a]	Sales and excise taxes
1	Import substitution	−0.51	−0.51	0.00
2	Export	2.24	2.24	0.00
3	Export	0.25	0.25	0.00
4	Import substitution	−0.19	−0.19	0.00
5	Export	10.00	7.26	2.74
7	Export	18.98	18.25	0.72
8	Import substitution	−1.07	−1.18	0.10
9	Import substitution	−3.20	−3.24	0.04
10	Export	0.74	0.74	0.00
11	Import substitution	−1.05	−1.05	0.00
12	Export	0.51	0.06	0.45
13	Import substitution	−0.85	−0.97	0.12
16	Import substitution	−103.69	−105.55	1.87
17	Import substitution	−15.16	−16.49	1.33
18	Export	2.52	1.18	1.34
19	Export	0.55	0.39	0.16
20	Import substitution	−2.96	−3.24	0.28
21	Import substitution	−30.23	−31.72	1.49
22	Import substitution	−3.45	−4.95	1.50
23	Import substitution	1.73	−0.24	1.97
24	Import substitution	−1.41	−1.96	0.55
25	Import substitution	13.25	−5.75	19.00
26	Export	7.89	7.61	0.28
27	Export	3.52	1.19	2.33
28	Import substitution	−4.55	−5.71	1.16
29	Import substitution	−7.32	−7.55	0.23
30	Import substitution	−0.46	−0.46	0.00
31	Import substitution	−1.14	−1.14	0.00
32	Import substitution	−2.29	−4.33	2.03
33	Import substitution	−3.15	−3.50	0.36
34	Import substitution	−0.12	−0.42	0.30
35	Import substitution	−0.60	−1.07	0.47
36	Import substitution	−27.54	−31.63	4.09
37	Import substitution	0.59	−0.62	1.21
42	Export	−0.49	−0.49	0.00
44	Export	−0.14	−0.14	0.00

a. Indirect taxes on international trade (import duties and surcharges, export duties).

Note: METR applicable to investment in capital equipment (not buildings). Debt-equity ratios are assumed to be the same in all sectors considered.

Source: Authors' calculations.

Table 9-4. *Distribution of METRs from Indirect Taxes*

METR	All indirect taxes Frequency	All indirect taxes Median METR (percent)	Trade taxes Frequency	Trade taxes Median METR (percent)	Sales and excises Frequency	Sales and excises Median METR (percent)
Less than –7	5	–27.54	5	–31.63	0	n.a.
–7 to –3.5	1	–4.50	7	–4.33	0	n.a.
–3.5 to –1.75	5	–3.15	1	–1.96	0	n.a.
0 to –1.75	12	–0.56	13	–0.51	0	n.a.
0 to 1.75	6	0.57	6	0.57	29	0.23
1.75 to 3.5	2	2.38	1	2.24	5	2.03
3.5 to 7	2	5.69	0	n.a.	1	4.09
More than 7	4	11.63	3	7.61	1	19.00

n.a. Not applicable.
Source: Authors' calculations.

in table 9-2. Trade taxes are the only ones that result in negative
METRs—that provide subsidies to some activities. Domestic taxes on trad-
ables can only raise input costs and, hence, cannot result in subsidies.
Therefore the sales and excise taxes tend to reduce the magnitudes of the
subsidies provided to industries that are protected by trade policies. But
in this regard sales taxes seem mainly to affect industries with relatively
low rates of subsidy from trade taxes. At the other end of the distribution, sales and excise taxes tend to increase the effective tax rates of
activities on which import and export taxes have already been imposed.
The incidence of high METRs is much greater for sales and excise taxes
than for trade taxes.

Median METRs were calculated in aggregate for all tradable goods and
separately for export and import-competing sectors (that is, industries
that produce goods that are also imported). The median METRs were
calculated for all indirect taxes and separately for trade taxes and other
indirect taxes. The results of these calculations are shown in table 9-5.

Table 9-5. *Median METRs from Indirect Taxes*
(percent)

Goods	All taxes	Trade taxes	Sales and excise taxes
All	–0.50	–0.80	0.33
Importables	–1.27	–2.60	0.42
Exportables	1.50	0.96	0.22

Source: Authors' calculations.

For all tradable goods the median METR is –0.50, which results from a median METR from trade taxes of –0.80 and a median METR from sales and excise taxes of 0.33. In other words, as measured by the median rates, trade taxes provide a net subsidy on average, and "domestic" taxes impose a net tax, with the effects of trade taxes dominating in determining the overall sign of the aggregate METR. The pattern of tax burdens differs considerably, however, between export and import-competing sectors, especially in the case of trade taxes. Sales and excise taxes tend to impose a heavier burden on import than on export sectors, with the median METR being 0.42 for imports and 0.22 for exports. Trade taxes, on the other hand, impose a median METR of 0.96 on exports and –2.60 on import-competing sectors. In other words, trade taxes impose a much heavier burden on export sectors than do sales and excise taxes. And they provide a substantial subsidy to import-competing activities. This latter result is caused by the escalating pattern of tariff rates, which imposes much higher rates on final products produced in Malaysia than on their imported inputs. Trade taxes, therefore, are a serious impediment to the development of efficient export industries in Malaysia. And at the same time they provide a substantial subsidy to less efficient import-competing industries.

A more accurate method of aggregating METRs across all sectors is to calculate an average in which sectors are weighted by their importance in the economy. For METRs the most useful weights would be the levels of the capital stock in each sector. In the absence of such data, however, the next best alternative is to use the corresponding levels of sectoral value added. Calculated this way, the weighted average METR from all indirect taxes turns out to be 2.26. In other words, the net effect of all indirect taxes is to lower the average rate of return to marginal investments in Malaysia by 2.26 percentage points. The weighted average METR from sales and excise taxes alone is only 0.70 percentage point. The difference between this and the total, 1.56 percentage points, is the METR from import duties and export taxes. What is also more readily apparent from table 9-6 is the wide range of investment incentive effects across sectors resulting from indirect taxes. The discrepancies between the treatment of

Table 9-6. Weighted Average METRs from Indirect Taxes
(percent)

Goods	All taxes	Trade taxes	Sales and excise taxes
All	2.26	1.56	0.70
Importables	–7.89	–9.15	1.26
Exportables	6.30	5.82	0.48

Source: Authors' calculations.

importables and exportables are much more obvious when sectors are weighted by their contribution to national output than when median values are simply observed, as in table 9-5. The net effect of all indirect taxes is a subsidy of almost 8 percentage points on the rate of return to investments in import substitution industries and a tax of more than 6 percentage points on the rate of return in export sectors. The differentials from trade taxes alone are even greater than this. Sales and excise taxes partially offset the high subsidies to importables caused by trade taxes, and they add to the burden placed by trade taxes on investments in exportables.

Conclusions and Policy Implications

Indirect taxes make roughly the same contribution as direct taxes to Malaysia's government budget. Although these indirect taxes are seldom thought of as providing or altering investment incentives, they actually have distortionary effects on investment decisions that are, on average, of about the same order of magnitude as all the distortions and incentives contained in the direct tax system. Furthermore, the investment distortions caused by indirect taxes have a much greater variance across industrial sectors than those caused by direct taxes. For example, indirect taxes impose a severe penalty on efficient export sectors and provide substantial subsidies to less efficient import-competing activities. These are the sorts of differentials that make the distortions especially pernicious and threatening to the continued rapid development and competitiveness of the Malaysian economy.

Trade taxes, which account for about 50 percent of indirect tax revenues, account, in aggregate, for about 70 percent of the investment distortions caused by indirect taxes. They also account for a disproportionate share of the intersectoral variability in these investment distortions. The reason is that trade taxes have much higher and more variable rates than do sales and excise taxes. The solution to this problem is simple. Rates of trade taxes, and especially import duties, must be lowered and the rate structure drastically simplified. A sensible goal would be to aim for an import duty rate structure consisting of, rather than a large number of rate categories between 0 and 100 percent, only one or two rates in the neighborhood of 15 percent. This structure might better be achieved in a series of preannounced stages than in a single once-and-for-all change.

Sales and excise taxes, despite accounting for about 45 percent of indirect tax revenues, cause only about 30 percent of the aggregate investment distortions from indirect taxes. These distortions are also far less variable across different types of activities. To some extent they tend to offset some of the biases in investment incentives resulting from indirect taxes on trade. None of this is surprising because sales taxes, especially, are fairly general in nature and are levied at a relatively uniform rate. In fact, in light of this, what is most surprising is that their distortionary effects are so large. The reasons they are so large are that (a) the ring system is far from perfect in ensuring the absence of tax cascading and uniform tax treatment of different activities and firms and (b) there are many sales tax exemptions granted to particular firms and activities. The principal solution is to replace the current sales tax and ring system with a uniform value added tax. At the same time, the use of arbitrary exemptions from sales and excise taxes should cease. And the government should explore the possibilities of replacing some of the current excise taxes with the new value added tax to take advantage of the noncascading characteristics of the latter. All these possibilities have been under discussion for some time within Malaysian policymaking circles. There is no doubt that moving ahead swiftly to enact these reforms, to set up the necessary administrative framework, and to educate the taxpaying public about the benefits of the reforms and the means of compliance will considerably help the treasury and the economy.

Appendix. Measuring METRs in the Presence of Indirect Taxes

In this appendix we provide a description of the theoretical underpinnings of the expressions used to calculate METRs in the presence of indirect taxes.

The Model

In each of a sequence of periods a firm chooses a vector of intermediate inputs $M_t = (M_t^1, M_t^2, \ldots, M_t^m)$ and an investment good I_t to produce an output X_t. Its production technology,

$$(9A\text{-}1) \qquad X_t = X(K_t, M_t^1, M_t^2, \ldots, M_t^m)$$

is assumed to be concave. The firm's objective function for maximizing the present value of discounted cash flows is

$$(9A\text{-}2) \qquad \underset{K_t, M_t}{\text{Max}} \ V = \sum_{t=0}^{\infty} R_t \Big\{ [P_t^o X(K_t, M_t) - P_t^m] (1 - u_t)$$
$$- Q_t [K_{t+1} - (1 - \delta) K_t] (1 - Z_t) \Big\}$$

where R_t is the nominal discount factor, P_t^o is the output price, P_t^m is a $(1 \times M)$ row vector of intermediate input prices, u is the corporate tax rate, Q_t is the price of the capital good K_t, and Z_t is the present value of tax savings from depreciation allowances evaluated at time t. The firm is a price taker in both input and output markets.

Because we are concerned with the capital investment behavior of the firm, we can consider this decision conditional on the optimal choice of the intermediate goods. The optimal use of intermediate goods will be governed by

(9A-3)
$$\frac{\partial X_t}{\partial M_t^j} = \frac{P_t^j}{P_t^o} \cdot$$

This is the standard marginalist rule that equates, for each period t, the marginal product of intermediate good j to its relative marginal cost. Note that this gives a set of m equations in regard to $m + 1$ unknowns (m intermediate inputs and one capital input) and fixed prices of inputs and the firm's output. For each period t, by using these m first-order conditions, it is possible to define an optimal choice for each intermediate input implicitly in regard to the capital input and all prices. That is, we can write the intermediate input demand as

(9A-4) $M_t^{j*} = M(K_t, P_t^1, P_t^2, \ldots, P_t^m, P_t^o)$ for $j = 1, 2, \ldots, m$ and $\forall t$.

Substituting these optimal intermediate input demands into the firm's objective function, we have

(9A-5)
$$P_t^o X(K_t, M_t^*) - P_t^m M_t^* \equiv X^*(K_t, P_t^o, P_t^m)$$

where the function $X^*(.)$ may be interpreted as a "revenue" production function.

Conditional on the optimal choices of intermediate inputs, the discounted cash flow of the firm's objective function can now be written with respect to all known parameters (such as price, tax, and other macroeconomic parameters) and the choice variable K_t. That is, the firm chooses K_t to maximize

(9A-6)
$$\operatorname*{Max}_{K_t} \quad V = \sum_{t=0}^{\infty} R_t \Big\{ X^*(K_t, P_t^m, P_t^o)(1 - u_t)$$
$$- Q_t [K_{t+1} - (1 - \delta) K_t](1 - Z_t) \Big\}$$

where the function $X^*(.)$ is conditional on optimal intermediate inputs.

Assuming that the *revenue* production function $X^*(.)$ has a separable form and that the production process requires a fixed input-to-output ratio, we can write:

(9A-7)
$$X^*(K_t, P_t^o, P_t^m) = \Big(P_t^o - \sum_{j=1}^{m} a_j P_{jt}^m \Big) F(K_t)$$

where a_j is the fixed input-output coefficient. Adopting standard practice, we define the indirect tax-free value added, VA_t^o, as

(9A-8)
$$VA_t^o = P_t^o - \sum_{j=1}^{m} a_j P_{jt}^m .$$

If, however, the firm is subject to some indirect taxes that cannot be passed onward, then the tax-affected value added the firm receives, VA_t^T, will be

(9A-9)
$$VA_t^T = P_t^T - \sum_{j=1}^{m} a_j P_{jt}^T$$

where P^T denotes indirect tax-affected prices.

If a firm is affected by both direct and indirect taxes, then to account for these taxes the firm's maximization problem becomes

(9A-10)
$$\text{Max}_{K_t} \quad V = \sum_{t=0}^{\infty} R_t \Big\{ VA_t^T F(K_t)(1 - u_t)$$
$$- Q_t [K_{t+1} - (1-\delta) K_t](1 - Z_t) \Big\}.$$

Solving this problem and imposing steady-state conditions, we obtain

(9A-11)
$$\frac{(VA^T) F'(K_t)(1 - u)}{Q} = \frac{1}{1 - u}[r - \pi + \delta - (\Delta q/q)](1 - Z)$$

where r is the cost of finance, π is the expected inflation rate, and $\Delta q/q$ is the rate of change of capital goods prices in real terms.

This equation solves for an indirect tax-affected optimal capital stock at period t, K_t^*. It is the tax-affected condition that equates the marginal value product of capital (left-hand side of the equation) to its user cost (right-hand side). Direct and indirect taxes influence this equation in different ways. The direct tax system affects the right-hand side of this equation via u, r, and Z, that is, through the corporate tax rate, the interest cost deduction, and the depreciation allowances. In contrast, indirect taxes affect the left-hand side via the value added term VA^T.

In the absence of indirect taxes, the first-order condition for investment is

(9A-12)
$$\frac{(VA^o) F'(K^0)}{Q} = \frac{1}{1 - u}[r - \pi + \delta - (\Delta q/q)](1 - Z).$$

If we compare the two first-order conditions (equations 9A-11 and 9A-12), we see that the demand for capital is affected by the indirect tax system. Whether the level of investment demand induced by indirect taxes is greater or less than the level without indirect taxes will depend on how the firm's value added is affected by the indirect tax system. In other words, the demand for the capital good will be adjusted to reflect the indirect taxes that are borne by the firm. For example, an excise tax on a firm's output will reduce investment, whereas a protective tariff will probably increase it.

The Indirect Tax Wedge

Before deriving an algebraic expression for the indirect tax wedge, we first illustrate the idea with a diagram. In figure 9A-1 we show an investment market in an open economy in which the savings schedule has been suppressed. The world interest rate is r^*. Let us assume that the direct tax system imposes an investment disincentive measured by the positive corporate tax wedge $t_c = r_g - r^*$, where r_g is the required rate of return on investment gross of corporate taxes. Let us further suppose that without indirect taxes the equilibrium investment level distorted by direct taxes is I^0, where the demand for investment curve $\text{VMP}(K^0)$ cuts the required rate of return gross of corporate taxes, r_g. Suppose the firm sells its output in the world market and faces an output demand that is perfectly elastic at the prevailing world price. Now suppose a production tax is levied on the firm. The full brunt of this tax will be borne by the firm. Thus the value added it receives falls, and this feeds into its demand for capital investment. Other things being equal, the firm's investment demand (indirect tax affected) will shift to the left, to $\text{VMP}(K^T)$. In this

Figure 9A-1. Positive Direct and Indirect Wedges ($t_c > 0$ and $t_i > 0$)

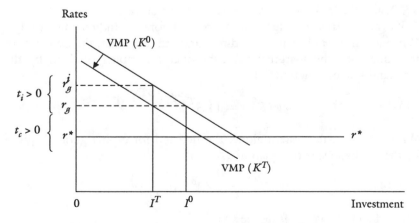

Note: t_i = indirect tax wedge; t_c = corporate tax wedge; r_g^i = gross-of-total-tax rate of return; r_g = gross-of-corporate-tax rate of return; r^* = world interest rate.

case, we deduce the indirect tax wedge as follows: With the indirect tax, the firm is in equilibrium at I^T, where the new demand for investment curve $\text{VMP}(K^T)$ cuts the required gross-of-corporate-tax rate of return, r_g. This is so because the methodology in the derivation of the direct corporate tax wedge ensures that r_g is independent of indirect taxes. Therefore the corporate tax wedge t_c must remain the same, independent of indirect taxes. We can ask under what conditions this level of investment I^T will be undertaken in the absence of indirect taxes. The answer is that the required rate of return gross of corporate taxes must rise to a level higher than r_g. Let this new level be r_g^i. Turning the question around, instead of conceptualizing a shift in the investment demand from $\text{VMP}(K^0)$ to $\text{VMP}(K^T)$ when the production tax is imposed, we can think of the resulting fall in the level of investment $(I^0 - I^T)$ as if it were caused by a higher required rate of return. Arguing along this line, we can interpret the gap between the new and old required rate of return as the indirect tax wedge, t_i. That is, $t_i = r_g^i - r_g$, where we define r_g^i as the required rate of return to investment gross of total taxes. The required rate of return gross of total taxes refers to the return that a marginal investment must earn in order to meet the combined direct and indirect tax cost of the investment, as well as maintaining the real capital stock and paying an acceptable rate of return to savers. The required rate of return gross of total taxes, r_g^i, differs from the required rate of return gross of corporate taxes, r_g, in that the former includes all relevant indirect tax costs that must be borne by the firm in making its investment. Note that in this particular case the indirect tax wedge, t_i, is positive because the production tax penalizes the firm.

Of course, if an indirect tax, such as an import tariff on a firm's output, encourages investment by such a firm, then the investment demand schedule would shift in the direction opposite to that shown in figure 9A-2, and the indirect tax wedge would be negative.

We now derive an algebraic expression for the indirect tax wedge. When a firm is subject to both direct and indirect taxes, the demand for investment or the marginal value product for capital is given by the left-hand side of equation 9-11:

$$(9A\text{-}13) \qquad \text{VMP}(K^T) = (VA^T)\frac{F'(K^T)}{Q}.$$

With the direct tax system alone, the demand for capital goods is given by the left-hand side of equation 9A-12:

$$(9A\text{-}14) \qquad \text{VMP}(K^0) = (VA^o)\frac{F'(K^0)}{Q}.$$

The indirect tax wedge is defined as

$$(9A\text{-}15) \qquad t_i = r_g^i - r_g$$

Figure 9A-2. Positive Direct Tax Wedge and Negative Indirect Tax Wedge
$(t_c > 0$ and $t_c > 0)$

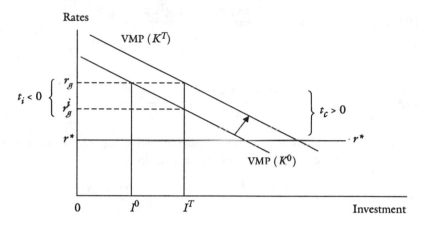

Note: t_i = indirect tax wedge; t_c = corporate tax wedge; r_g^i = gross-of-total-tax rate of return; r_g = gross-of-corporate-tax rate of return; r^* = world interest rate.

where the required rate of return gross of total taxes, r_g^i, is evaluated at the new investment level I^T under the investment demand schedule exclusive of indirect taxes VMP(K^T) and the required rate of return gross of corporate taxes, r_g, is evaluated at the new investment level I under the investment demand curve inclusive of indirect taxes VMP(K^T). Equivalently, r_g can be evaluated at the investment schedule exclusive of indirect taxes VMP(K^0) under the old investment level I^0. This is because the corporate tax wedge confronting the firm is independent of the indirect tax system.

The required rate of return gross of corporate taxes, r_g, is equal to the user cost of capital less the quantity $(\delta - \Delta q/q)$. That is, r_g is the real rate of return that must be earned by a profitable investment before corporate taxes are paid and after enough has been subtracted to maintain the real value of the capital stock. So, rewriting the definition of the indirect tax wedge, we have

$t_i = \{$VMP$[I^T$ evaluated under the investment demand schedule exclusive of indirect taxes, VMP(K^0)$] - (\delta - \Delta q/q)\} - \{VMP[I^T$ evaluated under the investment demand schedule inclusive of indirect taxes, VMP(K^T)$] - (\delta - \Delta q/q)\}$

or

$t_i = \{$VMP$[I^T$ evaluated under the investment demand schedule that is exclusive of indirect taxes, VMP(K^0)$] - \{$VMP$[I^T$ evaluated under the investment demand schedule that is inclusive of indirect taxes, VMP(K^T)$]\}$.

Using the demand for investment equations and evaluating them appropriately at the new investment level, we get

$$(9A\text{-}16) \qquad t_i = \frac{(VA^0)\, F'\,(K^T) - (VA^T)\, F'(K^T)}{Q}.$$

This yields

$$(9A\text{-}17) \qquad t_i = \frac{(VA^0 - VA^T)}{VA^T} \cdot \frac{(VA^T)F'(K^T)}{Q}.$$

Substituting equation 9A-12 into equation 9-17, we can express the indirect tax wedge t_i strictly in observable quantities:

$$(9A\text{-}18) \qquad t_i = \frac{(VA^0 - VA^T)}{VA^T} [r - \delta - (\Delta\, q\, /q\,)] \frac{(1 - Z)}{(1 - u)}.$$

This is the basic equation for calculating the indirect tax wedge, t_i. There are two points to note. First, the initial main term in the expression is the effective rate of protection, in which the change in value added resulting from the tax system is measured in relation to its tax-distorted level rather than its undistorted value. Note that if effective protection is positive, which means that the firm is being protected, the indirect tax wedge will be negative. Conversely, if effective protection is negative, t_i will be positive, which suggests a tax on the marginal investment. Second, the other major term in the expression indicates that the size of the indirect tax wedge depends as well on the corporate tax system. Only if the direct tax system is completely neutral will the indirect tax wedge be independent of corporate taxes.

Notes

This chapter is a summary of part of a project undertaken in collaboration with the Tax Reform Group of the Malaysian Institute of Economic Research (MIER). Funding was provided by the Canadian International Development Agency as part of an Institutional Cooperation Agreement between MIER and the John Deutsch Institute for the Study of Economic Policy at Queen's University.

1. The most common formulation of the ERP uses the free trade, or undistorted, value added in the denominator of the expression that follows in the text. This can cause difficulties, however, in cases in which free trade value added turns out to be negative. As we show in the appendix, the correct formulation of the ERP for measuring changes in investment incentives due to indirect taxes requires using tax-distorted value added in the denominator of the expression. This is the method we use throughout this chapter.

2. See appendix to this chapter for an explanation of the derivation of this result.

References

Bank Negara Malaysia. 1990. *Buletin Suku Tahunan,* May–June.

Ministry of Finance, Malaysia. 1983. *Input-Output Tables.* Kuala Lumpur: National Printing Department.

Salleh, Ismael Md. 1988. "Consumption and Trade-Related Taxes in Malaysia." Discussion Paper. Malaysian Institute of Economic Research, Kuala Lumpur.

FISCAL INCENTIVES FOR INVESTMENT IN THAILAND

10

Robert Halvorsen

THIS CHAPTER IS an analysis of the structure and effectiveness of fiscal incentives for private investment in Thailand. I focus on the activities of the Board of Investment, which is the government agency with the primary responsibility for the promotion of private investment. The overall effect of the fiscal system on private investment, including the general structure of taxes and duties as administered by the Ministry of Finance, is considered only insofar as it directly relates to the activities of the Board of Investment.[1]

The Board of Investment was established in 1960 to grant incentives to private investment under the Promotion of Industrial Investment Act, B.E. 2503. A series of subsequent acts enhanced the powers and flexibility of the Board of Investment and expanded the scope of incentives available to private investment.

Fiscal incentives offered by the Board of Investment include the exemption from or reduction of corporate income taxes and import duties and business taxes on machinery and raw materials. The Board of Investment is also able to grant important nonfiscal incentives, including the relaxation of restrictions on business activities by foreign investors and of restrictions on the employment of foreign employees.

I have organized the chapter in sections. In the following section, I discuss the theoretical rationale for investment incentives. Next, I provide a brief history of the Board of Investment and describe its current priorities, incentives, and criteria for promotion. I go on to discuss the historical data on the magnitude and characteristics of promoted activities, and then, in the next section, I analyze the cost-effectiveness of the Board of Investment's incentives. In the last section, I summarize the findings and discuss their implications for possible improvements in the Board of Investment's promotion process.

Theoretical Rationale for Investment Incentives

The basic theoretical rationale for offering fiscal incentives for investment is to offset market imperfections that distort the aggregate amount or the composition of private investment. In many developing countries, including Thailand, the most important source of market imperfections is the government itself. When this is the case, the most direct route for improving the incentives for private investment is to reform the government policies that distort the functioning of the market. If this is not possible, then a second-best case exists for an agency such as the Board of Investment to provide investment incentives designed to offset the existing distortions, including those introduced by other government policies.

Aggregate Amount of Investment

The most important nongovernmental source of distortions affecting the aggregate amount of investment is the existence of positive and negative externalities from investment. Positive externalities include benefits to other firms arising from expenditure on the training of labor and on research and development as well as the creation of external economies of scale. Negative externalities include adverse effects on the environment and the costs of infrastructure congestion. In recent years the negative externalities of investment have become all too apparent, especially in Bangkok, and it is reasonable to assume that they now outweigh the positive externalities for investment located in and around Bangkok and may do so in the aggregate as well.

Governmental policies that distort the aggregate amount of investment have both negative and positive effects. Policies that have negative effects on the aggregate amount of investment include high rates of import duties on machinery and equipment, restrictive licensing of large-scale investment projects in some industries, bureaucratic red tape, and discouragement of foreign investment through restrictions on the employment of foreign workers and ownership of land. The most important source of positive effects on aggregate investment is the existence of high rates of effective protection against imports of final goods. On balance it is likely that until recently in Thailand the net effect of market imperfections has been to decrease the aggregate amount of investment in relation to the efficient amount. Given the serious strains on the Thai economy and environment imposed by the investment boom of the last several years, however, it is unlikely that an investment incentive program aimed primarily at increasing the aggregate amount of investment would be justified at the present time.

Before considering the effects of market imperfections on the composition of investment, it is useful to note two ways in which the need for, and effectiveness of, investment incentives intended to affect the aggregate amount of investment interact with incentives intended to affect the composition of investment. First, to the extent that investment incentives are successful at improving the composition of investment, the justification for providing incentives for increased aggregate investment is increased. For example, if a major share of new investment could be induced to locate in the less-developed provinces, the aggregate balance of positive and negative externalities might be improved.

Second, a reduction in government distortions that negatively affect the aggregate magnitude of investment will reduce both the desirability of incentives intended to increase aggregate investment and the effectiveness of incentives intended to affect the composition of investment. For example, the recent lowering of import duties on imported machinery has reduced the desirability of positive incentives at the aggregate level and the effectiveness of selective exemptions from import duties intended to affect the composition of investment.

Composition of Investment

A much stronger case can be made for investment incentives intended to offset market imperfections that distort the composition of investment than for incentives intended to increase the aggregate amount of investment. It is important to note from the outset, however, that the most appropriate incentives might be negative rather than positive. That is, if market imperfections distort the composition of investment toward a less desirable type of investment at the expense of a more desirable type, the most appropriate incentive might be a tax on the less desirable type of investment, rather than a subsidy to the more desirable type.

This is particularly likely to be the case for nongovernmental distortions of the composition of investment, the most important of which arise from the existence of varying amounts of negative externalities from different types of investment. Although several alternative instruments exist for offsetting these distortions by making the investing firms "internalize the externalities," the use of taxes or user charges for environmental and infrastructure externalities has many important advantages, not least of which is that they relieve, rather than exacerbate, the government's revenue constraints.[2] Therefore it is unfortunate that the Board of Investment is limited to using subsidy instruments.

The principal ways in which market imperfections distort the composition of investment include their effect on the location of firms, orientation toward domestic in contrast to export markets, the size of firms, and the sources of capital.

LOCATION. The net effect of positive and negative externalities is likely to be more centralization of investment in and around Bangkok than would occur if the externalities were fully taken into account in investment decisions. One reason is that external economies of scale are likely to be greater in the less-developed parts of Thailand. Also, marginal costs of infrastructure congestion are probably greater in Bangkok. Last but not least, the high population density in Bangkok will generally result in a given amount of pollution causing more damage than if it occurred in a less densely populated area.

MARKET ORIENTATION. The level and structure of tariff rates in Thailand result in effective rates of protection that distort the market orientation of investment projects, production for the domestic market being favored at the expense of production for export. Although effective protection rates for industries producing final goods for the domestic market tend to be high, several important export industries actually experience negative effective rates of protection (Thailand 1984).

SIZE OF FIRMS. One of the most important sources of revenue in Thailand is a business tax that is levied on the gross value of output at each stage of production with no credit given for taxes paid at prior stages. Because the effective rate of business tax can be decreased by vertical integration, this tax introduces a bias in favor of large firms at the expense of small ones.

SOURCE OF CAPITAL. The Thai legal structure imposes several important restrictions on foreign investors and thereby distorts the source of investment capital in favor of domestic sources. The major restrictions include limitations on foreign ownership in certain activities under the Alien Business Law, restrictions on the employment of foreign nationals under the Alien Employment Act, and restrictions on foreign ownership of land under the Land Code.

The Board of Investment

The Board of Investment has the primary responsibility for the promotion of private investment in Thailand. In this section I briefly review the history of the board and then discuss its current priorities, incentives, and criteria for project approval.

History

The Board of Investment was established in 1960 to grant incentives to private investment under the Promotion of Industrial Investment Act, B.E. 2503.[3] The 1960 act was soon found to be largely ineffective and was superseded in 1962 by the Promotion of Industrial Investment Act, B.E. 2505. The new act substantially increased the flexibility and independence of the Board of Investment by allowing it to grant promotioncertificates and alter the conditions for promotion subject only to the approval of the prime minister. The 1962 act also provided more incentives, including the exemption from business taxes and import duties on machinery and the extension of exemption from income tax to five years from two years.

The 1962 act also provided for different incentives according to type of activity. The highest level of incentives was available mainly to capital-intensive industries, the next highest was available mainly to industries engaged in assembly of machinery and equipment, and the lowest level of incentives was available to a group of about eighty industries, including agricultural processing and textiles.

The 1962 act was amended in 1965 and 1968 and then replaced in 1972 by the National Executive Council Announcement 227. The 1972 act extended the scope of promotion to include more nonmanufacturing industries; required that a promoted firm be a limited company or a cooperative; changed the period of income tax exemption from five years to a period of from three to eight years, to be specified by the Board of Investment; and offered special rights and benefits to firms operating in specific areas and engaged in exporting.

The 1972 act was replaced in 1977 by the Investment Promotion Act, B.E. 2520, which remains in effect. The main changes in the 1977 act were a reduction of the full exemption from business taxes and import duties on machinery to 50 percent, and an allowance of a reduction of up to 90 percent of business taxes and import duties on imported materials and components. The 1977 act also increased the power of the Board of Investment, which now consists of the prime minister as chairman, the Minister of Industry as vice chairman, and thirteen members, including the ministers of various important ministries and the governor of the Bank of Thailand.

In 1977 the Board of Investment also established the Investment Service Center, commonly referred to as the One-Stop Service Center, to provide information to potential investors and, more important, to help new enterprises deal with the considerable bureaucratic red tape involved in establishing a business in Thailand. The actual power to issue the necessary company registrations, factory permits, work permits for foreign employees, and so on remained, however, with the ministries concerned.[4]

The intent of the *Announcement of the Board of Investment, No. 1/2526,* published in 1983, was "to ensure that investment promotion supports and relates to the objectives of national economic and social development policies" (Thailand 1983). It made the Board of Investment's criteria for approving investment promotion and providing fiscal incentives easily available to the public for the first time.

In 1989 the current definitions of the Investment Promotion Zones were introduced along with revised criteria for fiscal incentives for projects located in each zone. Projects located in Zone 1, which consists of Bangkok and five neighboring provinces, receive the lowest level of incentives. Projects located in Zone 2, which consists of a ring of ten provinces around Zone 1, receive an intermediate level of incentives, and projects located in Zone 3, which consists of all provinces not included in Zones 1 or 2, receive the highest level of incentives.

Priorities

The Office of the Board of Investment (Thailand 1990) lists its priorities in regard to the characteristics of projects to which it gives special consideration. These are projects that

- Significantly strengthen the balance of payments, especially through export production
- Support the country's resource development
- Substantially increase employment
- Locate operations in the (less-developed) provinces
- Conserve energy or replace imported energy supplies
- Establish or develop industries that form the basis for further stages of industrial development
- Are considered important and necessary by the government.

Although it is not included in its list of priorities, the Board of Investment also clearly places a high priority on the participation of Thai investors in foreign investment through the formation of joint ventures. This is indicated by the restrictions placed on the allowable percentage of foreign ownership. For example, if production is mainly for domestic consumption, Thai nationals are required to own at least 51 percent of the registered capital.[5]

Giving special consideration to the projects that satisfy the stated priorities can affect the characteristics of the projects by one of two means. First, the structure of different incentives can affect the average characteristics of projects applying for promotion. The effective structure of different incentives depends on both the types of incentives used and the criteria for qualifying for different levels of incentives. As discussed below, the structure of different incentives is generally consistent with the stated priorities.

Second, after the stock of applications is received, projects that satisfy the priorities can be provided special consideration at each stage of the review process. Such consideration can mean that the average characteristics of the projects actually receiving promotion certificates become more consistent with the Board of Investment's priorities than would be the case if a more neutral approval process was used. The extent to which the data on project characteristics at each stage of the promotion process are consistent with the Board of Investment's stated priorities is discussed in a later section of this chapter.

Incentives

The incentives currently available from the Board of Investment are listed in table 10-1. The incentives include various guarantees and permissions as well as tax and tariff incentives.

GUARANTEES. The guarantees offered by the Board of Investment should have significant incentive value because they reduce the degree of risk facing promoted firms. In particular, the guarantees against competition from new state enterprises and against price controls are likely to result in greater security even for firms from nations with which Thailand has investment protection treaties.

PROTECTION MEASURES. The Board of Investment can provide protection to promoted firms against competition from imported products by imposing surcharges of up to 50 percent of the value of their cost, insurance, and freight (CIF). The surcharges can be imposed for only one year at a time but are renewable.[6] If it is believed that a surcharge would provide insufficient protection, an import ban on competitive products can be imposed.

PERMISSIONS. The permissions offered by the Board of Investment have limited incentive value for domestic firms but can be important for foreign firms. In particular, permission to bring in foreign nationals both to undertake feasibility studies and to work in the promoted activities can be valuable to foreign investors.

TAX INCENTIVES. The major fiscal incentives offered by the Board of Investment are an exemption from or a 50 percent reduction in import duties and business taxes on machinery, a reduction of up to 90 percent of import duties and business taxes on imported raw materials and components, and several types of tax holidays, including the exemption from corporate income taxes for three to eight years. Not all promoted projects qualify for these incentives, however, and variation in the extent of the incentives is the primary instrument used to provide different incentives related to the location and export orientation of promoted firms.

Duties and taxes on machinery. The exemption from or reduction of import duties and business taxes on machinery is generally considered to have been the most effective fiscal incentive offered by the Board of Investment. As discussed later, this observation is supported both by the amount of revenue forgone under this incentive and by a ranking of the importance of incentives in a survey of promoted and nonpromoted

Table 10-1. Incentives under Investment Promotion Act B.E. 2520

Category	Incentive
Guarantees	Against nationalization
	Against competition from new state enterprises
	Against state monopolization of sale of products similar to those produced by promoted person
	Against price controls
	Permission to export
	Against imports by government agencies or state enterprises with taxes exempted
Protection measures[a]	Surcharge on foreign products at rate not exceeding 50 percent of CIF value for 1 year or less
	Import ban on competitive products
	Chairman's authority to order assisting actions or tax relief measures for benefit of promoted projects
Permissions	To bring in foreign nationals to undertake investment feasibility studies
	To bring in foreign technicians and experts to work on promoted projects
	To own land for carrying out promoted activities
	To take foreign currency or remit it abroad
Tax incentives	Exemption or 50 percent reduction of import duties and business taxes on imported machinery
	Reduction of import duties and business taxes of up to 90 percent on imported raw materials and components
	Exemption of corporate income taxes 3—8 years, with permission to carry forward losses and deduct them as expenses for up to 5 years

firms. It has also been the most commonly granted fiscal incentive.[7] Although this incentive has been effective in stimulating investment, it also has had the effect of favoring relatively capital-intensive projects.

By varying the extent to which this incentive has been offered, the Board of Investment has been able to vary to a great extent the total incentives available to promoted firms based on their location or export orientation. For example, projects located in Zone 1 do not generally qualify for any exemption unless they export 80 percent or more of their output; projects located in Zone 2 generally receive only a 50 percent reduction unless they export 80 percent or more, in which case they receive full exemption; and projects located in Zone 3 receive full exemption.[8]

The value of the exemption from or reduction of import duties on imported machinery, however, has recently been greatly reduced because the import duty on most types of machinery was reduced to 5 percent as

Category	Incentive
	Exemption of up to 5 years on withholding tax on goodwill, royalties, or fees remitted abroad
	Exclusion from taxable income of dividends derived from promoted enterprises during income tax holiday
Additional incentives for enterprises in special investment promotion zones	Reduction of up to 90 percent of business tax on sale of products for up to 5 years
	Reduction of 50 percent of corporate income tax for 5 years after termination of normal income tax holiday or from date of income earning
	Allowance to double cost of transportation, electricity, and water supply for deduction from taxable corporate income
	Allowance to deduct from taxable corporate income up to 25 percent of investment costs of installing infrastructure facilities, for 10 years from date of income earning
Additional incentives for export enterprises	Exemption of import duties and business taxes on imported raw materials and components
	Exemption of import duties and business taxes on re-exported items
	Exemption of export duties and business taxes
	Allowance to deduct from taxable corporate income 5 percent of increase in income derived from exports over previous years, excluding costs of insurance and transportation

Note: CIF = cost, insurance, and freight.
a. Subject to justification and needs.
Source: Thailand (1990).

of September 18, 1990. In addition to reducing the general effectiveness of this incentive, the reduction in the import duty has reduced the Board of Investment's ability to offer different incentives related to the location or export orientation of promoted projects.

Duties and taxes on raw materials. The exemption from up to 90 percent of the import duties and business taxes on raw materials has been of substantial benefit only to a relatively few firms. The reasons for the limited effect of this incentive are that only a small percentage of promoted firms qualify for it, and of those that do qualify, the incentive has little value to firms producing for export because alternative methods of obtaining exemption from import duties on raw materials are available to them from the Customs Department.[9]

Tax holidays. The potentially most important tax holiday offered by the Board of Investment is the exemption from corporate income taxes for a period of three to eight years, with permission to carry forward losses for up to five years. In addition, promoted firms may receive an exclusion from taxable income of dividends paid during the income tax holiday, and the withholding tax on payments remitted abroad for goodwill, royalties, and fees can be exempted for up to five years.

Variations in the length of the corporate income tax holiday are used to provide different incentives according to the location, export orientation, and size of the promoted projects, as well as a number of other characteristics. Projects located in Zone 1 generally do not qualify for any exemption unless they export 80 percent or more of their output and are located in an industrial estate or promoted industrial zone, in which case they can receive a three-year exemption.[10]

Projects located in Zone 2 can receive an exemption for three years, extendable yearly up to a maximum of five years, if they satisfy one of several alternative criteria, including being located in an industrial estate or saving or earning net foreign exchange of at least US$2 million a year. Projects located in Zone 3 can receive exemptions of four or five years, extendable yearly up to a maximum of eight years, if they satisfy one of several alternative criteria, including being located in an industrial estate, employing more than two hundred full-time workers, or saving or earning net foreign exchange of at least US$1 million a year.[11]

Still, the general effectiveness of the corporate income tax holiday as an incentive, and therefore also the effectiveness of providing different tax holiday incentives in order to affect the composition of investment, does not appear to have been very great. One reason for this is that the reported taxable income of promoted firms during the tax holiday period, and therefore the amount of corporate income taxes actually forgone, has been quite small. The extent to which this reflects underreporting of income, rather than actual low profitability, may be substantial, especially for domestically owned firms.

Also, of the amount of corporate income taxes forgone, a substantial fraction has represented transfers to foreign governments, rather than benefits to the promoted firms, because much of the revenue forgone has not been covered by tax-sparing agreements. As discussed further below, Japan, Taiwan (China), and the United States have together accounted for more than 70 percent of total foreign investment promoted by the Board of Investment. Thailand has not yet negotiated tax-sparing agreements with the United States or Taiwan (China), and the tax-sparing treaty with Japan was suspended during the period when most of the corporate income tax holidays were granted.[12]

The effectiveness of the tax holiday incentive has recently been enhanced by the signing of a new tax-sparing agreement with Japan on August 2, 1990. Japan has been the source of more than half the foreign investment promoted by the Board of Investment. Also, even when a tax-sparing agreement is not in effect, a promoted firm may benefit from having taxes deferred until profits are repatriated.

ADDITIONAL INCENTIVES FOR LOCATION IN ZONE 3. In addition to the more favorable application of tax incentives, discussed above, projects locating in Zone 3 may qualify for the special additional incentives listed in table 10-1. The effectiveness of extending the corporate income tax holiday for five years in the form of a 50 percent reduction in tax is subject to the same limitations as the tax holiday itself. Still, the reduction of business taxes by up to 90 percent for a period of five years, and the tax allowances for infrastructure services and investment may provide significant benefits to the promoted firms.

ADDITIONAL INCENTIVES FOR EXPORT ENTERPRISES. The effectiveness of the additional incentives for export enterprises over and above the more favorable application of tax incentives discussed above is likely to be quite limited because alternative sources exist for most of the incentives offered.

Criteria for Project Approval

The criteria for project approval include minimum requirements for investment capital, Thai ownership, and export levels that vary with the type of activity applying for promotion. Other requirements, which apply more uniformly, include the value added being no less than 20 percent of the value of sales, unless the output is exported; a maximum debt-to-equity ratio of five to one; the ability to compete with imports subject to an import duty of 30 percent or the existing rate, whichever is higher; the use of modern production processes and new equipment, unless an older process is certified as efficient; and adequate market demand to absorb the increased production capacity. Except for the market demand criterion, these criteria have the merit of being capable of objective application.

Investment projects not eligible for promotion include projects that would produce a product that was already being produced by viable firms without promotional privileges; projects that use entirely imported raw materials in production mainly for the domestic market, if the existing import duty for the product exceeds 40 percent; and projects that could earn a reasonable rate of return and no longer need promotion.

The rate-of-return criterion is obviously important for the cost-effectiveness of the investment incentive program because fiscal incentives given to a project that would occur without them would be largely without effect, except possibly in influencing the characteristics of a project in a desirable direction. As discussed further below, however, estimates of the rates of return for a sample of promoted projects indicate that this criterion is not consistently applied in practice.

Magnitude and Characteristics of Promoted Activities

From its establishment in 1960 through June 1990, the Board of Investment issued promotion certificates for 4,487 projects, involving an estimated employment of 1.1 million Thais.[13] The total registered capital for the promoted projects was $5.8 billion, and the estimated total investment was $23.1 billion.[14] The data for total investment have the advantage of being more inclusive than the data on registered capital, but they have the disadvantage of including an unknown degree of double counting because investment by firms with foreign investment from more than one country is fully attributed to each of the countries.

It should be noted that the data on promotion certificates that were issued overstate the magnitude of the investment promotion program because not all of the projects promoted actually started operations. The number of promoted projects reported to be in operation was only 53 percent of the number of projects promoted.

The promoted projects tended to be quite large, with an average investment per project of $5.2 million and average employment per project of 256. The projects were also quite capital intensive, with an average investment of $20,128 per Thai employee, of which $9,283 represented the cost of machinery and equipment.

Of the total number of firms promoted through 1990, only 7.0 percent were entirely owned by foreigners, with the rest of the firms being approximately equally divided between entirely Thai-owned firms and joint ventures of Thai and foreign owners. As shown in table 10-2, however, the distribution of ownership of the registered capital of firms granted promotion certificates was quite different. Firms entirely under foreign ownership accounted for 11.8 percent of the total registered capital; those entirely under Thai ownership accounted for 32.8 percent; and joint ventures accounted for 55.7 percent.

The distribution of registered foreign capital by country of origin is also shown in table 10-2. Japan is by far the dominant source of foreign capital, accounting for more than half of the total and almost three-fourths of the capital of firms entirely under foreign ownership. Taiwan (China) is the second most important source of foreign capital, with 11.2 percent of the total, followed by the United States with 6.6 percent.

Level of Promotional Activity

As shown in table 10-3, the promotional activities of the Board of Investment increased rapidly after 1986. The number of applications received

Table 10-2. *Registered Capital of Firms Granted Promotion Certificates,*
1960 through June 1990

Nationality of ownership	100 percent owned	Joint venture	Total[a]
Dollars (millions)[b]			
Thai	1,910.2	1,719.9	3,614.1
Foreign	685.8	1,524.3	2,205.4
Total	2,595.9	3,244.2	5,819.6
Percent of total			
Thai	32.8	29.6	62.1
Foreign	11.8	26.2	37.9
Total	44.6	55.7	100.0
Foreign capital (percent)			
Australia	1.2	0.6	0.8
Denmark	0.0	0.2	0.2
France	0.7	0.6	0.6
Germany	0.3	0.7	0.6
Hong Kong	2.1	3.9	3.4
India	0.0	0.7	0.5
Israel	0.1	0.1	0.1
Japan	72.3	45.3	53.8
Malaysia	0.1	1.0	0.7
Netherlands	1.4	0.9	1.1
Panama	0.4	0.8	0.7
Philippines	0.0	0.4	0.3
Portugal	0.0	0.1	0.1
Singapore	2.2	3.6	3.1
Switzerland	0.9	3.5	2.7
Taiwan (China)	9.8	11.9	11.2
United Kingdom	0.9	3.9	2.9
United States	2.8	8.3	6.6
Other countries	4.7	13.4	10.7

a. Sum of 100 percent owned plus joint ventures, minus certificates withdrawn in 1990.
b. Converted at 25.5 baht per U.S. dollar.
Source: Thailand (1989–90): report for June 1990.

and approved, as well as the number of promotion certificates issued, peaked in 1988. The number of projects starting operations continued to increase through the first half of 1990, reflecting the lag between project approval and commencement of operations.

The number of applications received more than doubled between 1986 and 1987 and doubled again between 1987 and 1988. The number of

Table 10-3. Applications, Certificates, and Projects, 1972 through July 1990
(number)

Year	Applications[a]			Certificates issued	Approvals canceled	Projects started
	Received	*Approved*	*Rejected*			
1972–73	366	221	13	93	12	53
1974–75	170	130	17	169	42	89
1976–77	192	82	17	68	19	67
1978–79	340	218	48	141	16	64
1980–81	255	165	42	132	41	84
1982–83	271	125	40	113	28	107
1984–85	351	238	73	173	28	86
1986	431	295	41	191	73	145
1987	1,058	626	34	378	44	168
1988	2,127	1,463	83	913	74	224
1989	1,284	1,175	72	850	283	277
1990[b]	1,046	993	n.a.	785	n.a.	456
Total[a]	9,832	6,906	725	4,892	845	2,367

n.a. Not applicable.

Note: Data for 1972–73 through 1984–85 are biennial averages.

a. Applications rejected and approvals canceled are for 1972–89.

b. Extrapolated from data for January through July.

Source: Thailand (1989–90): reports for December 1989, June and July 1990.

applications received decreased substantially in 1989 but was still almost three times as large as in 1986. The pattern is similar for applications approved and certificates issued, the number of certificates issued in 1989 being more than four times the number in 1986.

The explosive growth of applications received presumably placed considerable strain on the Board of Investment's project review process. As shown in table 10-4, the percentage of applications approved tended to be somewhat higher, and the number of applications rejected substantially lower, in the more recent years than previously.

For the period as a whole, the number of certificates issued was almost one-third less than the number of applications approved, and the number of projects started was equal to only about one-half the number of certificates issued. The cumulative effect was that the number of projects started was equal to only about one-fourth the number of applications received. Given the substantial differences in the number of projects at each stage from receipt of applications to the start of operations, it is useful to investigate whether there are significant differences in the average characteristics of projects at each stage of the promotion process.

Table 10-4. Distribution of Applications, Certificates, and Projects
(percent)

Year	Applications		Certificates issued as percentage of approvals	Projects started as percentage of	
	Approved	Rejected		Certificates issued	Applications
1972–73	60.2	3.4	42.2	56.5	14.3
1974–75	76.4	10.0	130.1	52.5	52.2
1976–77	42.6	8.6	82.8	99.3	35.0
1978–79	64.0	14.0	64.8	45.4	18.8
1980–81	64.7	16.5	80.0	63.6	32.9
1982–83	46.2	14.6	90.0	95.1	39.6
1984–85	67.9	20.7	72.7	49.4	24.4
1986–87	61.9	5.0	61.8	55.0	21.0
1987–88	65.6	3.7	61.8	30.4	12.3
1988–89	77.3	4.5	66.8	28.4	14.7
1989–90	93.0	n.a.	75.4	44.8	31.5
Total[a]	70.2	7.4	70.8	48.4	24.1

n.a. Not applicable.

Note: Data for 1972–73 through 1984–85 are biennial averages. Data for 1986–87 through 1989–90 are two-year moving averages.

a. Applications rejected and approvals canceled are for 1972–89.

Source: Thailand (1989–90): reports for December 1989, June, and July 1990.

Project Characteristics

Because of the rapid increase in the level of promotion activities in the late 1980s, a disproportionate amount of the Board of Investment's total promotion activities over its lifetime occurred in those years. For example, the amount of registered capital for which promotion certificates were issued in 1986 or later is more than three-fourths of the total since the Board of Investment was established. Accordingly, the cumulative characteristics of the projects promoted by the Board of Investment over its lifetime have been largely determined by the characteristics of projects promoted in 1986 or later.

Cumulative data for 1986 through June 1990 on domestic and foreign registered capital, the distribution of foreign capital by country of origin, and selected project characteristics are presented in table 10-5. The amount of capital in projects actually started was only 10.7 percent of the total amount in the applications received, but this low percentage was partly due to the effects of lags during a period of rapid growth in applications received.

Table 10-5. Registered Capital, 1986 through June 1990

Factor	Applications		Certificates issued	Projects started
	Received	Approved		
Dollars (millions)[a]				
Thai	9,453.7	4,006.4	2,721.3	819.8
Foreign	6,207.5	4,198.7	1,814.2	867.3
Total	15,661.4	8,205.1	4,535.5	1,687.0
Thai employees (number)				
Estimated total	1,525,379	1,114,151	746,630	206,654
Per project	282	276	275	198
Location of factories (percent)[b]				
Zone 1	47.0	49.1	54.5	62.0
Zone 2	24.5	23.4	21.1	17.8
Zone 3	28.5	27.5	24.4	20.1
Export (percentage of projects)[b]				
80–100 percent	57.0	64.9	68.2	64.0
30–79 percent	7.7	9.6	5.6	4.4
Foreign capital (percent)[b]				
Australia	3.0	0.5	0.2	0.3
Belgium	0.1	0.9	0.4	0.1
Canada	0.0	0.0	0.0	0.0
France	0.5	0.4	0.2	0.2
Germany	1.3	0.6	0.4	0.2
Hong Kong	6.0	4.2	2.9	5.5
India	3.3	1.6	0.3	0.2
Italy	1.0	1.5	0.0	0.1
Japan	35.8	36.0	59.2	62.5
Korea, Rep. of	2.1	2.1	1.1	0.6
Malaysia	1.0	0.5	0.4	0.3
Netherlands	1.3	1.2	0.6	1.3
Singapore	2.3	3.3	2.9	3.3
Switzerland	0.2	0.6	2.1	1.5
Taiwan (China)	12.8	10.5	11.9	7.1
United Kingdom	4.1	3.0	2.0	1.8
United States	7.2	5.0	4.4	3.4

a. Converted at 25.5 baht per U.S. dollar.
b. Data are for 1987 through June 1990, except for capital for Japan, Taiwan (China), and the United States.
Source: Thailand (1989–90): reports for June and July 1990.

LOCATION OF INVESTMENT. One of the Board of Investment's stated priorities is the geographic decentralization of investment. To this end, as stated earlier, smaller incentives are offered for investment in Zone 1 (Bangkok and five neighboring provinces) than Zone 2 (a ring of ten provinces around Zone 1), for which the incentives are in turn smaller than for investment in Zone 3 (the rest of Thailand). Although the applications received reflect the effects of different incentives on firms' choices of location, the priorities actually applied by the Board of Investment in the approval process are also important in determining the final effects of the incentives.

As shown in table 10-5, the data for applications received indicate that the different incentives did affect the location decisions of firms applying for promotion during this period. In sharp contrast to the high concentration of investment in and around Bangkok historically, Zone 1 was the planned location for only 47.0 percent of factories, whereas Zone 3 was the planned location for 28.5 percent.[15]

Still, the percentage of factories increased in Zone 1 and decreased in Zone 3 at each subsequent stage of the promotion process. As a result, for the projects actually starting operations during the period, 62.0 percent of factories were located in Zone 1 and only 20.1 percent were located in Zone 3. The finding that the percentage of factories increased in Zone 1 and decreased in Zone 3 at each stage of the promotion process under the direct control of the Board of Investment (that is, from applications received to certificates issued) is surprising, given that, as officially stated, geographic decentralization of investment is a high priority.

Annual data for the location of factories, as well as other characteristics of investment, at each stage of the promotion process are shown in tables 10-6 through 10-9. As shown in tables 10-6 and 10-7, in 1987 the percentage of factories intended to be located in Zone 1 was unusually high and the percentage in Zone 3 unusually low, both on applications received and on applications approved. During the later years the percentages in each zone were similar to the cumulative figures, with no apparent tendency to increase or decrease.

In contrast, as shown in table 10-8, the substantial decrease over time in the percentage in Zone 1 suggests that the Board of Investment placed an increasing priority on geographic decentralization of promoted investment. It is important to note, however, that most of the decrease in the percentage of factories located in Zone 1 reflects an increase in the percentage located in the nearby Zone 2, rather than the more remote Zone 3. Also, as shown in table 10-9, for projects starting operations during the period there is no clear trend in the percentage of factories located in Zone 1 and, contrary to the Board of Investment's stated priorities, there is a clear tendency for the percentage located in Zone 2 to increase at the expense of Zone 3.

Table 10-6.   Registered Capital: Applications Received, 1986 through June 1990

Factor	1986	1987	1988	1989	Jan.–June 1990
Dollars (millions)[a]					
Thai	429.9	1,249.7	3,099.9	3,267.3	1,406.9
Foreign	189.9	987.7	2,368.9	1,902.6	758.5
Total	619.8	2,237.4	5,468.8	5,169.9	2,165.5
Thai employees (number)					
Estimated total	100,681	332,495	532,602	409,701	149,900
Per application	234	314	250	319	297
Location of factories (percent)					
Zone 1	n.a.	63.1	41.6	43.2	44.9
Zone 2	n.a.	18.1	27.4	24.9	25.1
Zone 3	n.a.	18.8	31.1	31.9	30.0
Export (percentage of projects)					
80–100 percent	n.a.	69.6	66.3	54.4	47.1
30–79 percent	n.a.	5.7	11.1	6.6	6.9
Foreign capital (percent)					
Australia	2.1	3.3	6.0	0.1	0.5
Belgium	0.0	0.0	0.3	0.1	0.0
Canada	0.0	0.0	0.1	0.1	0.0
France	0.0	0.0	0.4	1.0	0.0
Germany	2.0	0.3	0.4	3.1	0.6
Hong Kong	1.8	3.4	2.7	8.2	15.4
India	2.7	3.4	1.9	5.0	3.3
Italy	0.0	0.0	2.0	0.2	1.1
Japan	34.9	37.3	35.2	34.3	40.1
Korea, Rep. of	0.1	1.7	1.3	3.7	1.5
Malaysia	1.2	0.4	0.5	1.1	2.8
Netherlands	0.1	0.3	0.8	2.8	0.6
Singapore	0.7	2.2	2.3	2.9	1.4
Switzerland	0.0	0.0	0.2	0.5	0.0
Taiwan (China)	12.4	8.3	15.9	13.0	9.0
United Kingdom	4.0	0.9	3.8	3.4	10.9
United States	11.3	7.4	8.4	6.7	3.3

n.a. Not applicable.
a. Converted at 25.5 baht per U.S. dollar.
Source: Thailand (1989–90): reports for June and July 1990.

Table 10-7. Registered Capital: Applications Approved, 1986 through June 1990

Factor	1986	1987	1988	1989	Jan.–June 1990
Dollars (millions)[a]					
Thai	237.8	410.3	1,113.6	910.7	1,333.9
Foreign	123.1	328.0	1,255.7	1,826.1	665.9
Total	360.9	738.2	2,369.3	2,736.8	1,999.8
Thai employees (number)					
Estimated total	60,231	206,432	352,964	332,194	162,330
Per approval	204	330	241	283	336
Location of factories (percent)					
Zone 1	n.a.	70.9	44.6	45.5	43.4
Zone 2	n.a.	12.7	23.7	27.3	27.0
Zone 3	n.a.	16.5	31.7	27.2	29.6
Export (percentage of projects)					
80–100 percent	n.a.	77.2	72.0	67.3	61.3
30–79 percent	n.a.	5.9	11.1	13.9	5.0
Foreign capital (percent)					
Australia	0.5	0.5	0.7	0.4	0.5
Belgium	0.0	0.0	3.1	0.1	0.0
Canada	0.0	0.0	0.1	0.1	0.0
France	0.0	0.0	0.3	0.8	0.0
Germany	3.9	0.4	0.6	0.7	0.2
Hong Kong	7.3	4.2	2.8	2.7	10.6
India	0.9	0.6	0.3	1.5	5.1
Italy	0.0	0.0	0.1	3.4	0.0
Japan	53.4	43.6	57.1	21.4	29.2
Korea, Rep. of	0.1	1.3	1.7	1.5	5.2
Malaysia	4.1	0.2	0.7	0.2	0.5
Netherlands	1.2	0.6	0.1	0.4	5.9
Singapore	3.1	0.6	3.0	2.3	7.8
Switzerland	0.0	0.0	0.5	0.9	0.0
Taiwan (China)	1.5	18.4	12.4	8.5	10.1
United Kingdom	9.3	1.3	5.2	2.2	0.9
United States	4.6	6.9	5.8	2.2	10.2

n.a. Not applicable.

a. Converted at 25.5 baht per U.S. dollar.

Source: Thailand (1989–90): reports for June and July 1990.

Table 10-8.   Registered Capital: Certificates Issued, 1986 through June 1990

Factor	1986	1987	1988	1989	Jan.–June 1990
Dollars (millions)[a]					
Thai	125.1	290.5	573.8	1,095.1	636.7
Foreign	31.3	198.8	588.0	638.2	357.8
Total	156.4	489.3	1,161.8	1,733.4	994.6
Thai employees (number)					
Estimated total	46,456	104,624	245,411	230,717	119,422
Per certificate	243	277	269	271	311
Location of factories (percent)					
Zone 1	n.a.	65.4	58.2	48.8	47.3
Zone 2	n.a.	12.0	21.3	22.5	26.5
Zone 3	n.a.	22.7	20.5	28.7	26.2
Export (percentage of projects)					
80–100 percent	n.a.	73.3	78.1	68.8	72.1
30–79 percent	n.a.	5.8	6.1	7.6	2.6
Foreign capital (percent)					
Australia	n.a.	0.5	0.2	0.2	0.2
Belgium	n.a.	0.0	0.0	1.1	0.0
Canada	n.a.	0.0	0.1	0.0	0.0
France	n.a.	0.0	0.3	0.4	0.0
Germany	n.a.	0.6	0.2	0.3	0.6
Hong Kong	n.a.	1.9	5.5	1.4	2.2
India	n.a.	0.3	0.5	0.2	0.4
Italy	n.a.	0.0	0.1	0.0	0.0
Japan	9.9	66.3	61.0	63.9	48.1
Korea, Rep. of	n.a.	0.0	1.8	1.3	0.5
Malaysia	n.a.	0.5	0.3	0.6	0.3
Netherlands	n.a.	0.2	0.3	1.0	0.7
Singapore	n.a.	0.5	3.3	4.0	1.8
Switzerland	n.a.	0.0	0.6	5.5	0.0
Taiwan (China)	21.5	6.3	14.3	10.3	13.3
United Kingdom	n.a.	4.2	2.2	1.4	1.8
United States	18.9	4.6	6.1	2.2	4.4

n.a. Not applicable.
a. Converted at 25.5 baht per U.S. dollar.
Source: Thailand (1989–90): reports for June and July 1990.

Table 10-9. Registered Capital: Projects Started, 1986 through June 1990

Factor	1986	1987	1988	1989	Jan.–June 1990
Dollars (millions)[a]					
Thai	93.6	137.1	135.8	168.7	284.5
Foreign	60.6	60.9	187.8	234.5	323.4
Total	154.2	198.1	323.7	403.2	607.9
Thai employees (number)					
Estimated total	26,178	39,209	50,395	53,354	37,518
Per project	181	233	225	193	164
Location of factories (percent)					
Zone 1	n.a.	57.9	66.5	65.5	56.7
Zone 2	n.a.	16.9	13.7	18.0	22.5
Zone 3	n.a.	25.3	19.8	16.5	20.8
Export (percentage of projects)					
80–100 percent	n.a.	64.9	75.4	79.1	74.2
30–79 percent	n.a.	5.4	5.4	5.4	4.4
Foreign capital (percent)					
Australia	n.a.	0.9	0.3	0.6	0.2
Belgium	n.a.	0.0	0.1	0.2	0.0
Canada	n.a.	0.0	0.0	0.1	0.0
France	n.a.	0.0	0.9	0.0	0.0
Germany	n.a.	0.0	0.6	0.1	0.1
Hong Kong	n.a.	25.2	7.8	5.9	1.0
India	n.a.	0.3	0.7	0.0	0.2
Italy	n.a.	0.0	0.0	0.4	0.0
Japan	44.3	32.4	62.4	65.0	69.8
Korea, Rep. of	n.a.	0.0	0.0	1.4	0.6
Malaysia	n.a.	0.6	0.3	0.4	0.1
Netherlands	n.a.	3.8	0.3	2.7	0.7
Singapore	n.a.	10.4	2.0	3.3	3.2
Switzerland	n.a.	0.0	4.7	1.8	0.0
Taiwan (China)	4.7	3.3	5.8	11.1	6.1
United Kingdom	n.a.	2.3	3.9	0.6	1.6
United States	8.8	10.1	4.0	3.5	0.6

n.a. Not applicable.
a. Converted at 25.5 baht per U.S. dollar.
Source: Thailand (1989–90): reports for June and July 1990.

EXPORT ORIENTATION. Another major priority of the Board of Investment has been the promotion of production for export. Cumulative data for the period 1987 through June 1990 on the planned export orientation of projects are shown in table 10-5, and annual data for each stage of the promotion process are shown in tables 10-6 through 10-9. The cumulative share of the most export-oriented projects (80 to 100 percent of output exported) increased at each stage of the promotion process under the direct control of the Board of Investment, suggesting that the priority on exports does affect the selection process. The cumulative data on the share of moderately export-oriented projects (30 to 79 percent) are less consistent, but the range in this category is too wide to draw conclusions concerning differences in the average export orientation of projects at each stage of the promotion process.

The annual data for the most export-oriented projects provide some cause for concern in that there is a clear downward trend in applications received for these projects (table 10-6) and, despite the apparent preference given to these projects, in applications approved (table 10-7). For projects starting operation, there has been some tendency for the share of the most export-oriented projects to increase (table 10-9). To some extent this is probably simply the result of lags between the approval of projects and the commencement of operations, in which case a downward trend of the most export-oriented projects in projects started can be expected in the near future. It is also possible that the most export-oriented projects have greater commercial viability and therefore are more likely actually to use their promotion certificates.

SOURCE OF FOREIGN INVESTMENT. As discussed earlier, Thailand does not have tax-sparing agreements with the United States and Taiwan (China), and the tax-sparing agreement with Japan was not in effect between 1977 and mid-1990. Because the absence of a tax-sparing agreement greatly decreases the incentive value of exemptions from and reductions of corporate income taxes and withholding taxes, the distribution of foreign investment by country of origin affects the overall cost-effectiveness of investment promotion by the Board of Investment.[16]

The distribution of foreign registered capital by country of origin for the full period of operation of the Board of Investment is shown in table 10-2. Japan was the dominant source of foreign investment, followed by Taiwan (China) and the United States. Together these three countries have accounted for 71.6 percent of the total foreign registered capital granted promotion certificates by the Board of Investment since its establishment.

Data on the distribution of foreign registered capital by country of origin for 1986 through June 1990 are contained in tables 10-5 through 10-9.[17] As shown in table 10-5, Japan's share in cumulative foreign capital during this period was much lower at the applications received and approved stages of the promotion process than at the certificates issued and projects started stages.

The reason for the increase of almost two-thirds in Japan's share in going from the applications approved to certificates issued stage is not clear but appears to be partly due to the rapid increase and subsequent decrease in the amount of foreign capital included in applications received during this period, coupled with a decrease in Japan's share in applications received in relation to its share in applications approved (tables 10-6 and 10-7).

The share of Taiwan (China) in foreign capital exhibits no clear pattern either from stage to stage of the promotion process (table 10-5) or over time (tables 10-6 through 10-9). The share of the United States shows a tendency to decline both from stage to stage of the promotion process and over time.

The combined shares of Japan, Taiwan (China), and the United States follow the same basic patterns as the share of Japan alone. The cumulative combined shares of these three countries in foreign registered capital is approximately one-half at the applications received and approved stages of the promotion process and approximately three-fourths at the certificates issued and projects started stages.

Although their combined share of the corporate income tax holidays provided by the Board of Investment was probably not as large as their share of total foreign capital promoted, the cost-effectiveness of this incentive must be considered to have been considerably reduced by the absence of tax-sparing agreements for these three countries. In addition, the ability to attract such a large proportion of promoted capital from these countries despite the reduced incentive effects of tax holidays suggests that exemptions from corporate income taxes are not a critically important element of the incentives that the Board of Investment offers to promoted projects.

Among the other foreign countries whose firms have received investment promotion, the cumulative share of Hong Kong at each stage of the promotion process is comparable to that of the United States (table 10-5), and the share of Hong Kong at the applications received stage has shown a strong upward trend, in contrast to the downward trend for the United States (table 10-6). Singapore and the United Kingdom also have shares in cumulative capital at each stage of the promotion process that are not insignificant, but neither country exhibits a clear upward trend at the applications received stage.

AVERAGE INVESTMENT. The structure of the Board of Investment's incentive system tends to favor larger projects by imposing minimum capital requirements, requiring that promoted firms be limited companies or cooperatives, and offering special incentives for projects with more than two hundred full-time employees. Cumulative data on the average size of investment at each stage of the promotion process are shown in table 10-10 for 1987 through June 1990, and the annual data for each stage are shown in tables 10-11 through 10-14.

Cumulative average investment per project decreases at each stage of the promotion process, with the result that average investment for projects started is less than half that at the applications received stage. The annual data, however, indicate upward trends in the average size of investment at each stage of the promotion process.

CAPITAL INTENSITY. One of the Board of Investment's stated priorities is to increase employment. Other things being equal, the amount of employment created by a given amount of investment will be inversely related to the capital intensity of the promoted projects. The average capital intensity of projects, measured by both total investment per employee and the cost of machinery and equipment per employee, decreased at each stage of the promotion process (table 10-10). Both measures of capital intensity, however, exhibit a tendency to increase over time at every stage of the promotion process of the Board of Investment (tables 10-11 through 10-14).

An alternative measure of capital intensity is the share of capital equipment in total investment. For 1987 through June 1990, the average share of machinery and equipment in total investment was approximately 46 percent for each of the first three stages of the promotion process and was 42 percent for projects started.[18] The annual data indicate some tendency for the share of machinery and equipment to decrease over time for the first three stages of the promotion process but not for projects actually started.

Cost-Effectiveness of Investment Incentives

The cost-effectiveness of alternative fiscal incentives for investment depends on both the net loss of revenue to the government and the extent to which the incentives actually alter the behavior of private investors. An incentive that resulted in a net loss of revenue without altering investor behavior in the desired direction—that is, by either increasing the aggregate amount of investment or favorably altering its composition—would clearly be simply a transfer of wealth and have zero cost-effectiveness. It is also possible for incentives to have a negative cost-effectiveness. This would be the case if the incentives were effective in inducing investment but the investment was not in fact socially desirable.

Net Revenue Forgone

The net loss of revenue attributable to an investment incentive is equal to the revenue forgone minus the revenue generated from investments that

Table 10-10. *Total Investment, 1987 through June 1990*

Factor	Applications Received	Applications Approved	Certificates issued	Projects started
Dollars (millions)				
Thai	14,852.7	7,727.5	4,847.7	968.2
Foreign	39,328.2	20,789.6	10,505.1	3,119.6
Total	54,180.9	28,517.1	15,352.8	4,087.8
Average investment				
Per application (millions of dollars)	10.9	7.7	6.1	4.5
Per employee (dollars)	38,030	27,058	21,927	22,650
Machinery and equipment				
Total cost (millions of dollars)	25,204.9	13,118.0	7,074.9	1,715.1
Cost per application (millions of dollars)	5.1	3.5	2.8	1.9
Per employee (dollars)	17,691	12,447	10,104	9,503
Share of investment (dollars)	46.5	46.0	46.1	42.0
Foreign investment (percent)				
Australia	3.9	1.1	0.8	1.3
Belgium	2.0	2.7	3.9	1.7
Canada	0.2	0.3	0.3	0.3
France	3.5	1.1	0.9	0.4
Germany	2.5	1.6	0.8	1.0
Hong Kong	8.0	8.2	5.4	10.2
Italy	5.0	3.4	1.1	0.1
Japan	36.1	43.9	61.2	54.7
Korea, Rep. of	1.8	2.4	0.8	0.4
Malaysia	1.4	1.0	1.0	0.8
Netherlands	0.8	1.1	1.1	13.2
Singapore	4.4	5.9	7.6	9.4
Switzerland	1.0	1.9	3.7	2.6
Taiwan (China)	10.8	11.2	8.9	6.8
United Kingdom	5.0	4.9	6.2	6.2
United States	15.3	10.4	9.5	8.0

Note: Currency converted at 25.5 baht per U.S. dollar. Firms with foreign investment from more than one country are counted for each investment.

Source: Thailand (1989–90): reports for December 1989 and June 1990.

Table 10-11.   Total Investment: Applications Received, 1987 through June 1990

Factor	1987	1988	1989	Jan.–June 1990
Dollars (millions)				
Thai	1,786.6	5,336.5	4,688.5	3,041.1
Foreign	6,410.6	15,459.3	13,392.0	4,066.3
Total	8,197.2	20,795.8	18,080.5	7,107.5
Average investment				
Per application (millions of dollars)	7.7	9.8	14.1	14.1
Per employee (dollars)	24,654	39,046	44,131	47,415
Machinery and equipment				
Total cost (millions of dollars)	4,464.1	10,232.0	7,328.5	3,180.2
Cost per application (millions of dollars)	4.2	4.8	5.7	6.3
Per employee (dollars)	13,426	19,211	17,887	21,216
Share of investment (dollars)	54.5	49.2	40.5	44.7
Foreign investment (percent)				
Australia	4.5	7.6	0.1	1.3
Belgium	9.4	0.9	0.2	0.4
Canada	0.4	0.2	0.1	0.1
France	0.0	7.6	1.4	0.3
Germany	0.4	1.4	4.7	2.7
Hong Kong	4.3	5.1	10.6	16.3
Italy	0.7	11.3	0.2	3.9
Japan	28.7	37.6	39.8	29.6
Korea, Rep. of	1.4	0.9	2.8	2.2
Malaysia	0.5	1.1	1.3	4.5
Netherlands	0.7	0.5	1.4	0.3
Singapore	3.0	4.3	5.4	3.4
Switzerland	1.4	0.9	1.0	0.5
Taiwan (China)	9.0	13.8	8.9	8.6
United Kingdom	2.6	3.2	4.6	16.9
United States	11.8	23.5	9.2	9.9

Note: Currency converted at 25.5 baht per U.S. dollar. Firms with foreign investment from more than one country are counted for each investment.

Source: Thailand (1989–90): reports for December 1989 and June 1990.

Table 10-12. Total Investment: Applications Approved, 1987 through June 1990

Factor	1987	1988	1989	Jan.–June 1990
Dollars (millions)				
Thai	690.6	1,715.5	3,229.4	2,092.0
Foreign	1,966.2	6,198.7	8,058.6	4,566.1
Total	2,656.8	7,914.2	11,288.0	6,658.1
Average investment				
Per approval (millions of dollars)	4.2	5.4	9.6	15.2
Per employee (dollars)	12,870	22,422	33,980	41,016
Machinery and equipment				
Total cost (millions of dollars)	1,429.0	4,065.1	4,701.2	2,922.6
Cost per approval (millions of dollars)	2.3	2.8	4.0	6.7
Per employee (dollars)	6,922	11,517	14,152	18,004
Share of investment (percent)	53.8	51.4	41.6	43.9
Foreign investment (percent)				
Australia	2.0	0.8	1.1	1.1
Belgium	2.9	7.4	0.4	0.1
Canada	1.0	0.4	0.1	0.2
France	0.1	0.8	1.2	1.5
Germany	0.8	2.2	1.6	1.2
Hong Kong	6.4	7.2	7.0	12.4
Italy	1.2	0.2	8.3	0.2
Japan	49.5	48.7	44.1	34.8
Korea, Rep. of	0.7	1.7	2.1	4.4
Malaysia	0.6	1.6	0.9	0.5
Netherlands	0.8	0.2	0.9	2.9
Singapore	3.3	4.4	5.1	10.4
Switzerland	3.4	1.0	2.3	1.5
Taiwan (China)	15.3	13.6	10.9	6.7
United Kingdom	4.0	5.3	6.1	2.5
United States	8.8	10.8	6.9	16.7

Note: Currency converted at 25.5 baht per U.S. dollar. Firms with foreign investment from more than one country are counted for each investment.

Source: Thailand (1989–90): reports for December 1989 and June 1990.

Table 10-13.   Total Investment: Certificates Issued, 1987 through June 1990

Factor	1987	1988	1989	Jan.–June 1990
Dollars (millions)				
Thai	625.7	1,046.6	2,051.1	1,124.3
Foreign	1,362.0	2,369.8	5,082.8	1,690.5
Total	1,987.7	3,416.4	7,133.9	2,814.8
Average investment				
Per certificate				
(millions of dollars)	5.3	3.7	8.4	7.3
Per employee (dollars)	18,998	13,921	30,921	23,570
Machinery and equipment				
Total cost				
(millions of dollars)	993.6	1,790.9	2,971.0	1,319.5
Cost per certificate				
(millions of dollars)	2.6	2.0	3.5	3.4
Per employee (dollars)	9,497	7,297	12,877	11,049
Share of investment				
(percent)	50.0	52.4	41.6	46.9
Foreign investment (percent)				
Australia	2.0	1.4	0.4	0.4
Belgium	10.6	0.1	5.0	0.5
Canada	0.2	0.3	0.2	0.5
France	0.4	1.1	0.8	1.6
Germany	1.5	0.8	0.4	1.5
Hong Kong	5.7	7.4	3.3	8.7
Italy	7.4	0.4	0.0	0.3
Japan	54.5	59.1	70.6	41.3
Korea, Rep. of	0.0	1.2	0.9	0.6
Malaysia	0.6	1.1	1.3	0.5
Netherlands	0.1	0.6	1.4	2.1
Singapore	4.6	13.7	4.3	11.1
Switzerland	1.8	1.2	4.1	7.5
Taiwan (China)	5.3	14.4	6.3	11.9
United Kingdom	12.5	10.5	2.0	7.6
United States	5.9	15.5	6.4	13.2

Note: Currency converted at 25.5 baht per U.S. dollar. Firms with foreign investment from more than one country are counted for each investment.

Source: Thailand (1989–90): reports for December 1989 and June 1990.

Table 10-14. Total Investment: Projects Started, 1987 through June 1990

Factor	1987	1988	1989	Jan.–June 1990
Dollars (millions)				
Thai	230.2	158.2	215.6	364.1
Foreign	501.3	581.5	820.1	1,216.7
Total	731.5	739.7	1,035.8	1,580.9
Average investment				
Per project (millions of dollars)	4.3	3.3	3.7	6.9
Per employee (dollar)	18,656	14,677	19,413	42,136
Machinery and equipment				
Total cost (millions of dollars)	310.0	305.9	416.6	682.5
Cost per project (millions of dollars)	1.8	1.4	1.5	3.0
Per employee (dollars)	7,907	6,070	7,808	18,192
Share of investment (percent)	42.4	41.4	40.2	43.2
Foreign investment (percent)				
Australia	1.8	2.0	0.4	1.2
Belgium	0.0	0.6	0.1	3.9
Canada	0.0	0.0	0.7	0.3
France	0.0	1.9	0.0	0.1
Germany	0.5	1.8	1.4	0.5
Hong Kong	19.4	18.2	9.4	3.1
Italy	0.0	0.0	0.5	0.0
Japan	44.6	50.7	66.5	52.8
Korea, Rep. of	0.0	0.0	1.3	0.1
Malaysia	0.8	1.3	1.1	0.5
Netherlands	2.9	0.9	5.1	28.7
Singapore	23.0	7.1	4.1	8.6
Switzerland	0.7	2.3	4.0	2.5
Taiwan (China)	3.1	4.9	11.4	6.1
United Kingdom	4.9	11.6	4.0	5.5
United States	12.2	14.4	8.1	3.0

Note: Currency converted at 25.5 baht per U.S. dollar. Firms with foreign investment from more than one country are counted for each investment.

Source: Thailand (1989–90): reports for December 1989 and June 1990.

would otherwise not have been made. Therefore the net loss of revenue is itself partially a function of the effectiveness of the incentive. If the incentive mainly went to investments that would have occurred even in its absence, it would generate little or no additional revenues, and the net loss of revenue would be approximately as large as the revenue forgone. The ability of a fiscal incentive to generate revenues also depends in part on the nature of the tax instrument being used. For example, a corporate tax holiday will begin to generate new revenue from the corporate income tax immediately after the holiday, provided that it has been successful in inducing additional profitable investment. In contrast, even if it is successful in inducing additional investment, a reduction of import duties on machinery may generate new customs revenues from machinery imports only if and when the original capital equipment is replaced.

Because the true net revenue generated by an incentive depends on the total revenue generated from all existing tax instruments, however, the main determinant of the net revenue loss from a fiscal incentive is its effectiveness in stimulating investment that would otherwise not have occurred. One measure of the effectiveness of fiscal incentives is the redundancy rate, defined as the proportion of promoted investment that would have occurred without promotion. The aggregate redundancy rate for the Board of Investment's promotion activities has been estimated to be 70 percent (Thailand 1984).

The actual redundancy rate for a particular fiscal incentive will not necessarily be equal to the aggregate redundancy rate because the effectiveness of an incentive in stimulating additional investment will depend on the type of incentive involved. For example, as discussed above, the effectiveness of the tax holidays offered by the Board of Investment was greatly reduced by the absence of tax-sparing agreements with countries accounting for more than three-fourths of the promoted investment, and therefore the redundancy rate for this incentive may be substantially higher than average. Nevertheless, it is interesting to consider the estimates of net revenue losses obtained for alternative fiscal incentives using the estimated aggregate redundancy rate of 70 percent.

Table 10-15 contains a summary of the estimates of net revenue losses for 1980 published in Thailand (1984); in addition, the percentage share of each incentive in total revenue forgone, total revenue generated, and total net revenue forgone is shown. The estimated revenue forgone because of exemptions from corporate income taxes was relatively small, and the estimated revenue generated was larger by far than for the other incentives, resulting in the estimated net revenue forgone being the smallest of all the fiscal incentives considered. The assumption that the redundancy rate for this incentive was no higher than the aggregate rate probably biased the estimate of revenue generated upward and therefore the estimate of net revenue loss downward.

Table 10-15. Revenue Forgone and Generated, 1980

Category	Revenue forgone	Revenue generated	Net revenue forgone
Dollars (thousands)			
Corporate income tax	15,531	8,778	6,753
Import duties			
Machinery	25,547	97	25,449
Raw materials	45,183	483	44,700
Total	70,730	580	70,149
Business tax			
Machinery	10,013	31	9,983
Raw materials	15,912	166	15,746
Total	25,925	197	25,728
Total taxes and duties	112,186	9,555	102,631
Percentage			
Corporate income tax	13.8	91.9	6.6
Import duties			
Machinery	22.8	1.0	24.8
Raw materials	40.3	5.1	43.6
Total	63.0	6.1	68.4
Business tax			
Machinery	8.9	0.3	9.7
Raw materials	14.2	1.7	15.3
Total	23.1	2.1	25.1

Note: Currency converted at 25.5 baht per U.S. dollar.
Source: Thailand (1984): 124–31.

The exemption from or reduction of import duties and business taxes on machinery together accounted for 31.7 percent of total revenue forgone and only 1.3 percent of revenue generated. As a result they accounted for more than one-third of total net revenue forgone. The estimate of revenue generated may be biased downward both because the redundancy rate for the machinery incentive may be lower than the estimated aggregate rate and because no credit was given for revenue generated by other tax instruments from the additional investment stimulated by these incentives.

The net revenue forgone from the reduction of import duties and business taxes on raw materials was estimated to be the largest of all. A large part of the net revenue forgone, however, might have been experienced even in the absence of these incentives because exporting enterprises had available alternative means of obtaining reductions in these taxes.

Effectiveness

The aggregate redundancy rate provides only a rough estimate of the aggregate effectiveness of the Board of Investment's promotion activities and does not provide any information on differences in effectiveness across different types of incentives. There are two other sources of information on the effectiveness of incentives that, although flawed, provide some light on the issue. First, survey data are available on how the investors themselves viewed the incentives. These data have the drawback of being subjective but do offer some insight into the relative importance of alternative incentives.

The second source of information on the effectiveness of incentives consists of comparisons of the private and social rates of return on promoted projects. These data are limited in scope and do not distinguish between the effectiveness of alternative incentives. They do have, however, the important advantage of indicating not only whether the promoted investments *would* have occurred in the absence of promotion but also whether the investments *should* have occurred, with or without promotion.

SURVEY DATA. Table 10-16 is a summary of the relative importance placed on five types of incentives by executives of fifteen firms that were being promoted at the time of the survey. The first three columns report the number of executives ranking each incentive as first, second, or third most important to their firm. The final column, which does not appear in the original source, contains a simple aggregate ranking for each incentive, calculated on the basis of three points for each time an incentive is ranked first, two when it is ranked second, and one when it is ranked third.

The results indicate that the exemption from or reduction of import duties and business taxes on machinery was by far the most important incentive to promoted firms. Exemption from the corporate income tax is essentially tied for second place with the reduction of import duties and business taxes on raw materials. Interestingly, a nonfiscal incentive, the permission to bring in foreign technicians, was also ranked as one of the three most important incentives for three of the firms.

RATES OF RETURN ON PROMOTED PROJECTS. The estimated private and social rates of return on seven promoted projects are shown in table 10-17. The private rates of return are based on the firm's revenues and costs calculated from market prices. They measure the profitability of the

Table 10-16. Ranking of Board of Investment Incentives: Fifteen Selected Firms

Incentive	*First*	*Second*	*Third*	*Total points*[a]
	Ranking incentive (number of responses)			
Exemption/reduction of import duties and business taxes on machinery	10	3	1	37
Reduction of import duties and business taxes on raw materials	4	1	0	14
Exemption from corporate income tax	1	5	0	13
Foreign technician allowance	0	1	2	4
Import surcharge[b]	0	1	0	2

a. Calculated as three points for first, two points for second, one point for third.
b. Only two firms in the sample had this incentive.
Source: Thailand (1984): 100.

project from the point of view of its investors. The social rates of return are calculated by applying shadow prices to inputs and outputs; they measure the profitability of a project from the point of view of society as a whole.[19] Thus the private rate of return for a project determines whether or not it will be undertaken, whereas the social rate of return indicates whether or not it should be undertaken.

The available data for projects 1 through 6 in table 10-17 do not provide direct information on whether or not the projects would have been undertaken without Board of Investment incentives because the only data published on the private rates of return include the effects of the incentives. If no incentives were provided, the private rates of return for these projects would have been lower than those shown in table 10-17 but still might have been higher than the return required for the firm to invest.

It seems likely, however, that projects 2, 4, and 5, which have relatively low private rates of return even with the incentives, would not have occurred without promotion. Unfortunately, the social rates of return indicate that neither project 2 nor 4 should have been undertaken. The social rate of return for project 2 is negative, and the social rate of return for project 4 is positive but much lower than normally required for a project to be acceptable. Thus the Board of Investment's incentives may have had a negative cost-effectiveness with respect to these projects.

The information available for project 7 is more complete than for projects 1 through 6 in that it includes an estimate of the private rate of return without Board of Investment incentives.[20] The social rate of return is 69 percent, indicating that the project was in fact socially desirable. The cost-effectiveness of the Board of Investment's incentives was most likely zero, because the private rate of return without the incentives

Table 10-17. Private and Social Rates of Return for Selected Projects

Product	Market orientation	Rates of return	
		Private[a]	Social
Polyethylene pipes	Domestic	0.23	−0.38
Paper	Domestic	0.15	−0.23
Animal feeds	Domestic	0.27	−0.02
Glass bottles	Domestic	0.13	0.03
Iron and steel products	Domestic	0.17	0.16
Castor oil	Export	0.36	0.49
Electronics[b]	Export	0.61[c]	0.69

a. With Board of Investment incentives.
b. Assuming pessimistic case.
c. Rate of return without Board of Investment incentives is 0.42.
Source: Data for projects 1 through 6: Thailand (1984); data for project 7: Kanpairoh (1988).

was 42 percent, indicating that the project would have been undertaken even if it had not been promoted. Therefore the substantial incentives provided by the Board of Investment, which increased the private rate of return from 42 to 61 percent, were essentially merely transfers from the government to the private investors.

Conclusions

A review of the theoretical rationale for investment incentives indicates that there is currently little justification for promotion aimed at increasing the aggregate amount of investment in Thailand but that there remains a need for incentives aimed at altering the composition of investment. In seeking to alter the composition of investment, the emphasis should be on providing the correct incentives, rather than promotion as such. In many cases, the appropriate instruments for providing the correct incentives may be negative incentives for the less desirable types of investment, rather than increased subsidies for the more desirable types.

The particular distortions in the composition of investment that an incentives program should try to correct include excessive centralization of investment in and around Bangkok, too great an orientation toward producing for the domestic market rather than for export, excessive firm size, and discouragement of foreign sources of investment.

The stated priorities of the Board of Investment are consistent with the need to correct the first two of these distortions but are silent regarding the last two. Also, the implicit priority placed on joint ventures is at least partially inconsistent with the correction of the last of these distortions.

The structure of different incentives used by the Board of Investment is largely consistent with its stated priorities. The incentives offered to firms employing at least two hundred full-time workers, however, may actually run counter to the stated priority of increasing employment, and they tend to reinforce, rather than offset, the existing distortion toward excessive firm size. The restrictions placed on minimum capital requirements and on unincorporated firms tend to have the same effect.

Although the structure of incentives and formal criteria is potentially important in influencing the characteristics of projects put forth for promotion, the evaluation standards applied in deciding which of the projects are granted promotion certificates are also important in determining the actual composition of promoted investment. A review of the data on the average characteristics of projects at each stage of the promotion process indicates that the results of the review process have tended to run counter to the priority placed on increased decentralization of investment but are consistent with the priority of increased export orientation.

The evidence concerning the cost-effectiveness of the Board of Investment's fiscal incentives is quite negative. The cost-effectiveness of all incentives has been reduced by the tendency to promote projects that would have occurred even if they had not been promoted. In addition, some projects have been promoted that had negative social rates of return, implying negative cost-effectiveness.

The cost-effectiveness of tax holidays appears to have been particularly low because of the absence of tax-sparing agreements with the dominant sources of foreign capital. This situation has been improved by the recent signing of an agreement with Japan.

The exemption from or reduction of import duties and business taxes on machinery appears to have been effective but costly. The recent reduction of duties on imported machinery, however, greatly reduces the effectiveness of this incentive and therefore decreases the ability of the Board of Investment to offer substantial differences in incentives to induce favorable alterations in the composition of investment.

Several possibilities exist for increasing the future cost-effectiveness of the Board of Investment's system of incentives. First, there is a strong need to decrease the extent to which fiscal incentives are made available to projects that are capable of earning adequate rates of return without the incentives. This could be accomplished by the formal incorporation in the review process of information on the rate of return of projects, with and without proposed fiscal incentives, and the disqualification of projects that clearly do not require promotion to be financially viable.

Second, there is a similar need to decrease the extent to which fiscal incentives are made available to projects with low or negative social rates of return. Although it might not be feasible formally to incorporate the calculation of social rates of return in the review process, considerable improvement might be obtained by placing stronger restrictions on the granting of incentives to projects that rely heavily on imported inputs for the production of products aimed at the domestic market. Given the existing system of tariff rates, these types of projects are particularly likely to earn negative social rates of return. In implementing such restrictions, it would be desirable to base the criteria for eligibility on effective rates of protection, rather than nominal tariff rates.

Last, the existing nonfiscal incentives, such as facilitating the employment of foreign nationals, appear to have been quite cost-effective. The further strengthening of the ability of the Board of Investment to offer nonfiscal incentives appears both feasible and desirable. In particular, increasing the information and facilitation capacities of the One-Stop Service Center could be an especially cost-effective use of the board's resources.

Notes

I am grateful to Atchaka Sibunruang Brimble, Neil Bruce, Supote Chunanuntathum, Wisarn Pupphavesa, and Somsak Tambunlertchai for discussions of the subject matter in this chapter and to Naree Boontherawara for her excellent research assistance. All opinions expressed here, as well as any errors of commission or omission, are solely my own responsibility. The final draft of this chapter was written in December 1990.

1. For an analysis of the effects of the Thai system of taxation on the financing and investment decisions of multinational companies, see Leechor and Mintz (1991).

2. See, for example, Baumol and Oates (1988).

3. The historical summary in this section is mainly based on material in Thailand (1984: 7–10).

4. Section 51 of the 1977 Investment Promotion Act states, "In the case where the promoted person encounters any problem or obstacle in the course of carrying out the promoted activity and lodges his complaints to secure the assistance of the Board, the Chairman shall have the power to render any appropriate assistance or to order the related government agencies, government organizations, or state enterprises to proceed with the assistance without delay" ("Investment Promotion Act" 1977). It is not clear, however, how effective this provision has been in practice.

5. Given that the distribution percentages of registered capital do not necessarily represent the distribution of control, which may remain almost entirely with the foreign investors (Sibunruang and Tambunlertchai 1986: 17), the priority on Thai participation may largely reflect rent-seeking behavior.

6. During 1978–83 the Board of Investment imposed surcharges ranging from 10 to 50 percent on eighty-six commodities. In thirty-seven cases the surcharge had been renewed at least once, and in five cases the surcharge had been renewed five times (Thailand 1984: 11).

7. For example, during 1978–83, an average of 93 percent of promoted activities received an exemption from or a reduction of import duties and business taxes on machinery, approximately 2 percent (based on incomplete data) received a reduction of import duties and business taxes on raw materials, and 73 percent received an exemption from corporate income tax (Thailand 1984: 122).

8. Projects located in Zones 1 or 2 that export less than 80 percent of their output can nevertheless qualify for exemptions if they are located in an industrial estate or promoted industrial zone or if their output is supplied mainly to producers of capital equipment that are located in the same zone.

9. See note 7.

10. Projects located in Zone 1 can also receive a three-year exemption if their output is supplied mainly to producers of capital equipment in the same zone and they are located in an industrial estate or promoted industrial zone.

11. The priority placed on increasing employment may not be well served by the special incentives available to projects employing more than two hundred full-time workers. A given amount of total investment generates more total employment if it is distributed over a large number of small, labor-intensive projects than if it is distributed over a smaller number of large, capital-intensive projects.

12. Mintz (chapter 3, this volume) has pointed out that the effectiveness of corporate income tax holidays may also be reduced by the treatment of depreciation, which may result in high effective tax rates on long-lived investments. His calculations indicate that the treatment of depreciation in Thailand does not have this effect, and therefore effective tax rates in Thailand for domestic investors are in fact low during the tax holiday. He does not, however, consider the effect of the absence of a tax-sparing agreement on foreign investors.

13. All data are based on the estimates contained in the applications for promotion, as reported in the monthly activity reports of the Office of the Board of Investment (Thailand 1989–90). The available data on the actual characteristics of promoted projects in operation are incomplete. Given the incompleteness of subsequent auditing, firms have an incentive to misstate the characteristics of projects to increase the amount of incentives received. There is some evidence that firms applying for promotion have understated assets and the import content of inputs and overstated employment and domestic inputs (Thailand 1984: 69–71).

14. Thai baht are converted to U.S. dollars using an exchange rate of 25.5 baht per dollar.

15. From 1960 through 1981, 71.3 percent of promoted firms were located in an area smaller, by one province, than Zone 1, and only 14.2 percent were located in the rough equivalent of Zone 3 (Thailand 1984).

16. See, for example, Leechor and Mintz (1991).

17. Tables 10-10 through 10-14 report data on the distribution of foreign investment by country of origin. As noted earlier, these data are more inclusive than the data on registered capital but include double counting of investment by firms with foreign investment from more than one country. The basic conclusions concerning the distribution of foreign registered capital also apply to the distribution of foreign investment.

18. The share of machinery and equipment in total investment at the certificates issued stage for 1987 through June 1990, 46.1 percent, was identical to the share over the full period that the Board of Investment had been in operation.

19. The data for projects 1 through 6 are from Thailand (1984), and the data for project 7 is from Kanpairoh (1988). The principal source of differences between shadow and market prices in both studies is an adjustment for the overvaluation of the baht in relation to the free-trade level. The Thailand (1984) study used 1981 data to estimate a foreign exchange rate premium of 4.95

percent, and the Kanpairoh study used a later World Bank estimate of 8.7 percent. Projects 1 through 5 primarily produced importable commodities, whereas projects 6 and 7 primarily produced for export.

20. Rates of return were calculated under both optimistic and pessimistic assumptions concerning the project's future revenues. The rates of return discussed here are for the pessimistic case.

References

Baumol, William J., and Wallace E. Oates. 1988. *The Theory of Environmental Policy.* 2d ed. Cambridge, U.K.: Cambridge University Press.

"Investment Promotion Act B.E. 2520." 1977. *Government Gazette,* May 4.

Kanpairoh, Abhinya. 1988. "An Analysis of BOI Promotion in Electronics Products: A Case Study." M.S. thesis, National Institute of Development Administration, School of Development Economics, Bangkok.

Leechor, Chad, and Jack M. Mintz. 1991. "Taxation of International Income by a Capital Importing Country: The Perspective of Thailand." In Javad Khalilzadeh-Shirazi and Anwar Shah, eds., *Tax Policy in Developing Countries.* Washington, D.C.: World Bank.

Sibunruang, Atchaka, and Somsak Tambunlertchai. 1986. "Foreign Direct Investment in Thailand." Background paper for United Nations Center on Transnational Corporations seminar on the Role of Transnational Corporations in Thailand, Pattaya, Thailand, August 29–30.

Thailand, Ministry of Finance, Fiscal Policy Office, Fiscal and Tax Policy Division. 1984. *Study on Fiscal Implication of Investment Incentives and Promotion Efficiency.* Prepared by Industrial Management Co., Ltd., in association with IMG Consultants Pty., Ltd., Bangkok.

Thailand, Office of the Prime Minister. 1983. "Announcement of the Board of Investment 1/2526." Office of the Board of Investment, Bangkok.

_____. 1989–90. Monthly Activity Reports. Office of the Board of Investment, Bangkok.

_____. 1990. *A Guide to Investing in Thailand.* Office of the Board of Investment, Bangkok.

PATTERNS IN INVESTMENT TAX INCENTIVES AMONG DEVELOPING COUNTRIES

Ngee Choon Chia and John Whalley

IN THIS CHAPTER we attempt to evaluate the effectiveness of investment tax incentives in the developing world.[1] We briefly summarize developments in the use of investment tax incentives in a sample of developing countries and provide an overview of trends and patterns, setting out what is known about their effectiveness in light of various global factors, such as foreign tax credits in the source country—that is, the industrial country from which the investment originates. Then we trace the effects of the tax competition that underlie the growth in the use of investment incentives in the countries belonging to the Association of Southeast Asian Nations (ASEAN), excluding Indonesia.[2] In doing so, we assess whether there is scope for transnational cooperation through nonemulation pacts or other similar arrangements between subgroups of countries.

The picture that emerges reveals not only higher corporate tax rates in developing countries than in industrial nations but also seemingly more pervasive investment incentives. The incentives go substantially beyond the acceleration in depreciation allowances and investment tax credits common until recently in most countries of the Organization for Economic Cooperation and Development (OECD) countries. They include tax holidays for inward investment, regional investment incentives, tax-free processing zones, and other arrangements. Moreover, in some parts of the developing world the use of investment tax incentives continues to grow, although in others it has begun to recede.

Recent growth in the use of tax incentives has come mainly in Asia—in some of the ASEAN countries and in South Asia—seemingly driven in part by intercountry tax competition designed to attract or maintain inward foreign investment at the expense of other recipient countries. In Africa, in contrast, incentives seem to focus on company-specific arrangements and tax holidays, and their use, if anything, seems to have changed little in recent years. In Latin America, the use of incentives seems to be receding, reflecting general liberalization policies as well as the influence of tax reforms in industrial countries (especially the United States), which phased out investment incentives in the 1980s. In all or most OECD countries, recent years have seen investment tax credits eliminated and acceleration in depreciation allowances sharply curtailed.[3]

Investment Tax Incentives in Developing Countries

Investment tax incentives in developing countries differ from those commonly used in industrial countries in many key respects. In general, most developing countries have continued to move in the direction of increasing their incentives in the last few years, whereas industrial countries have been phasing them out (removing investment tax credits and withdrawing acceleration in depreciation allowances; see Whalley 1990). Incentives in industrial countries usually take the form of accelerated depreciation allowances and investment tax credits (see King and Fullerton 1984 for documentation of individual country arrangements). In developing countries the range of instruments is larger. Shah and Toye (1978) surveyed the different fiscal incentives schemes available in twenty-eight developing countries. In their study, they found tax holidays, accompanied by generous loss carryover periods, to be the most popular with developing countries. Except for Tanzania and Zambia, all countries in the survey have tax holidays. The second most popular scheme is one that is dependent on the scale of investment, such as accelerated depreciation, and investment tax credits. Sixteen of the twenty-eight countries in the sample have one of these incentives. Exemption of imported plant and machinery from custom duties or other import taxation is the next most frequently observed incentive scheme, with ten of the twenty-eight countries employing it.

The objective of these incentives is to attract investment to particular regions, key sectors, export-earning activities, small firms, pioneer industries, and other targeted purposes (see chapter 3, this volume). In many countries, significant amounts of discretion are vested in the local officials who administer these schemes. In addition, in most countries a significantly larger fraction of investment is undertaken by the public sector through central direction than is the case in industrial countries. Such public sector investment shows little responsiveness to such schemes.

The situation differs from one developing country to another. There has been a trend toward enhancement of incentives in the Asia-Pacific region and in particular in ASEAN countries and South Asia, where growth in use of incentives seems, in part, to have been sparked by tax competition among countries. The governments in this region seem to believe that in order to continue to attract inward foreign investment, any enhancement of incentives by any other country in the region has to be matched, or more than matched. Thus in response to incentives introduced by Singapore first in 1959, and later in 1967 and 1986, comparable incentives have been introduced in the Philippines, Malaysia, and Thailand. Each response, in turn, has sparked Singapore to enhance its incentives further.

Africa remains the region where generalization across countries is difficult, but heavy reliance on tax holiday arrangements (negotiated between companies and the government) remains as a means to attract inward foreign investment by resource and other companies. By way of contrast, the larger Latin American economies (Argentina, Brazil, and Mexico) have recently all been moving in the direction of reducing or phasing out their investment incentives. This behavior reflects both the general policy approach toward market-based arrangements in these countries and the direction taken by the United States in its 1986 tax reform.

Table 11-1 provides information on incentive schemes in seven countries, chosen to provide continental balance. Besides conventional investment tax credit and accelerated depreciation schemes commonly found in industrial countries, tax holidays, sectoral incentives of various kinds, and regional and export incentives are important in this group of countries. Export incentives include duty drawbacks (tariffs remitted on imported inputs) as well as special incentives designed to encourage investment in export processing zones. In table 11-2 we present comparative chronologies contrasting an incentive-accelerating country (Singapore) and an incentive-decelerating country (Mexico). The chronologies emphasize the differences in the direction of change in the use of these incentives across countries.

The reasons for this widespread use of incentives and the differing experiences by country lie principally in the domestic regulatory regimes characteristic of developing countries. Inward foreign investment is seen

Table 11-1.   Investment Tax Incentives in Selected Developing Countries

Country	Invest- ment tax credit (percent)	Acceler- ated deprecia- tion	Sectoral incen- tives	Export incen- tives	Regional incen- tives	Carry- over of losses (years)	Length of tax holiday (years)
Korea	6–10	Yes	Yes	Yes	No	3	5
Brazil	None	Yes	Yes	Yes	Yes	4	15
Mexico	19–25	Yes	Yes	Yes	Yes	4	None
Nigeria	5–20[a]	No	Yes	Yes	No	4	3–5
Egypt	None	Yes	Yes	No	No	5	5–8
Singapore	33.3/ 3–50[a]	Yes	Yes	Yes	No	Unlimited	5–10
Philippines	75–100[a]	No	Yes	Yes	No	6	4–6

a. Investment allowance.
Source: Bauman (1988); Choi (1988); Majd (1988); Pinto (1989); Price Waterhouse (1988).

Table 11-2.   Chronologies for Selected Developing Countries with Accelerating or Decelerating Uses of Incentives

Singapore (accelerating incentives)

1959: Introduction of pioneer industry status
- Designated pioneer industries granted relief from prevailing 40 percent company profit tax for 5 years
- Unlimited loss carryforward and accelerated depreciation

1967: Export industry incentives
- 90 percent of profits from export activities tax free 3–5 years
- Double tax deduction schemes introduced for expenses incurred in overseas trade fairs and missions, for establishing overseas trade offices and overseas market development

1975: Pioneer incentives expanded
- Tax holiday for pioneer industries extended from 5 years to 10 years
- End of requirement that company must incur fixed capital expenditures of not less than $1m to be eligible for pioneer status

1979: Investment tax credits and servicing industry export tax incentive
- Introduction of investment credit of 10–50 percent for approved projects in manufacturing industries. Investment credit for year in which investment expenditure incurred; can be carried forward.
- Concessional 20 percent tax rate for overseas-oriented sales and servicing companies for 5 years

1980: Research and development tax incentives
- Accelerated depreciation (over 3 years) for all plant and machinery used for research and development
- 50 percent investment tax credit for all plants and machinery used for research and development
- Double deduction from taxable income for approved research and development

1983: Offshore tax incentives
- Offshore income earned from funds managed by Singapore-based financial institutions exempt from income taxes
- 10 percent tax on profits arising from management services (instead of 40 percent)

1986: Operational headquarters incentives
- New concessionary tax rate of 10 percent on domestic income derived from providing qualifying services (as opposed to normal 33 percent)
- Incentives granted initially for 10 years, with possible extension to follow

1987: Tax incentives expanded further
- Tax incentive schemes under 1967 Economic Expansion Incentives Act expanded to include export of services such as consulting, management, construction, technical, and engineering services

- 90 percent of income derived from these services tax exempt for initial period of 5 years

1988: Service incentives
- Incentives for service companies and overseas investment, including double tax deduction for research and development expenses
- New incentive for overseas investments, with 100 percent tax writeoff for losses from sale of share in or liquidation of approved overseas investments

Mexico (decelerating incentives)

1972: Tax Reform Bill
- Increases in accelerated depreciation allowances and more favorable treatment of ordinary depreciation
- Tax relief for capital reinvestment in industrial enterprises
- Tax exemption on corporate income derived from sale of fixed assets by firms investing in areas of low industrial concentration

1975: Reduction in tax incentives for exports and manufacturing
- Level of domestic components that exporters must use for duty rebate reduced from 50 percent to 40 percent
- Domestic component on temporary imports reduced from 40 percent to 20 percent on goods manufactured for export

1977: Machinery acquisition tax relief
- Tax credits up to 10 percent of costs of acquisition of new machinery for approved industrial activities and for enterprises that export at least 50 percent of their products

1978: Excess profit tax
- Up to 50 percent tax on profits exceeding average of previous 3 years' profits

1989: Finance law
- Introduction of 2 percent net worth tax assessed on company's net equity creditable against income tax, with 3-year carryover for unused credits
- Repeal of 75 percent deduction for investments in low income rental housing
- Reduction of advanced deductions of investments in fixed assets to 60 percent, when made in Mexico City, Guadalajara, and Monterrey

1990: Incentive reductions
- Investment in metropolitan area of Federal District and in Guadalajara and Monterrey not eligible for investment allowances
- Coverage of net worth tax extended to include civil companies and associations. In calculating net equity, fixed assets on which investment allowance is taken are valued as if investment allowance had not been taken

Source: IBFD (various volumes); Lee (1986); and various materials collected by authors (available on request).

as necessary for development (although limited in many cases to a few sectors or to nonsensitive sectors). But because inward investment flows are controlled through licensing restrictions, and repatriation of earnings is further restricted through foreign exchange controls, it becomes necessary to offset the effects of these restrictions to encourage inward investment. Hence, investment incentives in developing countries can be seen as offsets to the disincentives to investment that accompany the regulatory and control regimes that typically operate in these countries, as well as policies that are designed to stimulate investment more positively. Hence, investment incentives in developing countries are both more widespread by instrument and more extensive than in industrial countries because the negative effects of the domestic regulatory regimes are themselves more pervasive.

Budget costs of these investment incentives also vary by country, and firm estimates are available for only a few of them. For the Philippines, Manasan (1988) has estimated these costs to be in the region of 1 percent of the gross domestic product, which is a significant fraction of revenues because many developing countries collect less than 10 percent of the gross domestic product in revenues.

Several issues naturally arise from this description. How effective are investment incentives in developing countries, and why do they not seem to be tracking developments in the industrial world? To what extent do incentives actually stimulate new investment, and specifically, how far do they stimulate new inward foreign investment? If large budget costs are involved with these measures, are they the only costs that should be taken into account? And, if tax competition drives some of the developing countries to escalate their use of incentives, how best can these competitive effects be contained?

The Effect of Tax Incentives in Developing Countries

Evaluating the effects of investment incentives has long been a preoccupation of applied economists in industrial countries. Attempts go back to the 1950s and earlier, some using the cost-of-capital method popularized by Jorgenson (1963) after his formulation of a neoclassical theory of investment behavior. Jorgenson based his work on the assumption that firms operate to maximize the discounted present value of the return to investment net of taxes. In such a regime, firms invest up to the point at which the marginal revenue product from an additional unit of capital (investment) equals the expected marginal cost of capital. This approach was taken further in subsequent production function formulations of firm activity, generating the well-known user cost of capital—that is, the current dollar rental price of one unit of capital, including asset purchase costs, depreciation, and taxes.

The user-cost-of-capital strategy captures the effect of investment incentives through the influence of taxes on the user cost of capital. The effect is usually captured in a tax rate term, as well as in the depreciation component of tax rules. Such a method underlies the work of King and Fullerton (1984), which compares tax influences on the cost of capital across four OECD countries. This method has also been used in other empirical studies on the effects of tax policies on investment, especially in the United States. Results from some of these are summarized in table 11-3; they all seem to suggest that the effects of investment incentives are to increase investment, although only by relatively small amounts.

In developing countries a similar cost-of-capital strategy has been used to investigate the effects of investment incentives. In these studies, analyses have been executed for single countries or groups of countries; results from some of these are summarized in table 11-4. They generally come to the same conclusion, sometimes even more strongly, that tax incentives have a small or even insignificant effect on investment.

One shortcoming of the cost-of-capital strategy is its treatment of expectations that are backward-looking. An alternative formulation that has been widely used in the literature is based on Tobin's Q, where forward-looking expectations enter the econometric specification of investment behavior directly through the market value of the firm. In this

Table 11-3. Studies of U.S. Tax Incentives on Investment, Using Cost-of-Capital Approach

Study	Effects of U.S. tax policy
Hall and Jorgenson (1967)	Investment increased by 6.89 percent
Bischoff (1971)	Investment increased by 1.46 percent
Coen (1975)	Investment increased by 2.02–3.87 percent[a]
Chirinko and Eisner (1982)	Results varied widely according to specifications of investment equations
Green (1980)	With 2 percent increase in investment tax credit, ratio of nonresidential fixed investment to total investment increased
Chirinko and Eisner (1983)	Fixed investment increased to $11.7 million, and net federal budget deficit increased by $10.2 billion in 1982

a. Investment influences depend on whether cash flow defects enter the model. Results also depend on the method assumed for tax depreciation (double-declining balance or sum-of-the-years digits) and length of lag for user cost. Estimated effects can vary by as much as 80 percent.

Source: Chirinko 1986.

Table 11-4. Cost-of-Capital Studies of Investment Incentives in Developing Countries

Study	Country	Result
Manasan (1988)	ASEAN	Fiscal incentives did not have significant effect on relative competitiveness of ASEAN
Kwack (1988)	Korea	Tax incentives played minor role in promoting exports in Korea
Manasan (1986)	Philippines	Fiscal incentives had significant effects on rate of return and user cost of capital
World Bank (1980)	Thailand	Investment incentives had little effect. Share of exports in total production of firms awarded incentives no higher than average for all industrial firms

Source: Kwack (1988); Manasan (1986); World Bank (1980).

formulation, investment is an increasing function of Q, which is the ratio of the stock market valuation of existing capital to its replacement cost. For any increase in the rate of return on physical capital, there will be an increase in the market value of capital, which will cause new investment to occur until equilibrium is restored.

Thus, in this approach, investment depends on the stock market valuation of corporate capital, which, in turn, represents the present value of firms' dividend streams. In a tax-free world, firms tend to invest as long as each dollar spent on purchasing capital raises the marginal value of the firm by more than one dollar. Analyzing the effects of investment incentives using this framework involves the two steps of relating changes in tax parameters to changes in asset returns, which, in turn, affect investment through the estimated coefficients of investment equations. In most of the studies based on this strategy (see Chirinko 1986), Q is significant in explaining investment, bringing into doubt both traditional neoclassical theories of investment and the mechanisms through which investment incentives are supposed to work.

Hence, even in developed countries, ambiguities exist as to the appropriate framework for the analysis of investment incentives. The literature that uses a neoclassical method suggests that investment may be only slightly responsive to incentive. And whether this translates into potentially significant effects on investment in developing countries remains uncertain.

Developing countries' circumstances, however, reveal other complications, both of which are neglected by these strands of literature and which potentially further complicate analysis of the effects of investment incentives. First and foremost is the issue of the foreign tax credit in source countries. If the investing firm is located in a country that allows either a foreign tax credit or an exemption from domestic taxes on account of taxes paid abroad, then foreign taxes generally will have little or no effect on marginal investment behavior by subsidiary firms; that is, efforts to stimulate inward investment by foreign-owned firms through incentives will be ineffective. In the presence of such credits, if the developing country tax rate is below the rate that applies to parent firms in the industrial country, taxes paid in developing countries will typically have no marginal effect on investment activity. Such taxes are effectively paid by the foreign treasury rather than by the firm investing in the developing country. In such circumstances developing country investment incentives have little effect on the investment activity of foreign firms.

But other developing country features also complicate the analysis of investment incentives. One is credit rationing. In many developing countries credits are allocated by the central bank to qualifying firms, and prioritization of credits determines both the pattern and size of investment. With credit-constrained firms, investment activity will be largely unaffected by investment incentives. Similar arguments also apply to the effects of other forms of intervention, including protection and the allocation of scarce foreign exchange. With such quantity and other constraints in developing countries, what is at issue are rents. In such circumstances, investment incentives largely reallocate rents rather than providing instruments that have a marginal effect on investment behavior by firms.

Hence, although the available literature on cost of capital might seem to suggest that investment incentives could have small but potentially significant effects on investment in developing countries, in actually evaluating the effects of incentives one finds that things are more complicated. Alternative methods for industrial countries (Tobin's Q) offer a different interpretation of the effectiveness of incentives. And once special features of developing countries are taken into account, such as foreign tax credits in industrial countries and quantity and other controls in developing countries, their effectiveness comes even more into question.

Tax Competition and Investment Incentives in ASEAN Countries

A particularly important factor in understanding why tax incentives are used in certain developing countries is tax competition. Tax competitive effects operate with varying intensity in different parts of the developing world. In the ASEAN countries and elsewhere in Asia, these pressures are widely seen as key to fueling the growth of these incentives in recent years. In Africa they are thought to be mild, or even of no consequence. In Latin America they are thought to be stronger than in Africa but milder than in Asia.

The spread of these incentives among the ASEAN countries is summarized in table 11-5. It began with the adoption of investment incentives

Table 11-5. Spread of Investment Incentives in ASEAN Countries

Decade	Singapore	Malaysia	Philippines	Thailand
1950s	1959: Pioneer Industries Ordinance	1958: Pioneer Industries Ordinance	1967: Investment Incentive Act (RA 5186)	None
	Tax holiday of 5 years Depreciation, net operating loss carryover		Incentives for pioneer and preferred enterprises Includes accelerated depreciation, net operating loss carryover, tax exemption on imported capital equipment, tax credit on domestic capital investment, and double deduction of promotional expenses and shipping costs of exporting firms	None
1960s	1967: Economic Expansion Incentives Act	1968: Investment Incentive Act	1970: Export Incentives Act (RA 6135)	1972: Promotion of Industrial Investment Act
	90 percent tax concession on profits from export activities Double tax deduction schemes for expenses incurred in promotion of export overseas	Promotes labor-intensive and export-oriented industries New incentives include invest-ment tax credit, export allowance, accelerated depreciation allowance, and double deduction for expenses incurred on promotion of exports overseas	Tax and duty-free importation of capital equipment and spare parts Credit for taxes paid on domestic capital equipment, raw material, and semi-manufactured products used in production for export	Provides tax incentives to export industries, including tax holiday of 3–8 years, reduction in import duty and business taxes, and accelerated depreciation of 25 percent of invested capital, in addition to normal depreciation

Period				
1970s	1975: Tax holiday extended to 10 years 1979: Investment credit scheme — 10–50 percent	1973: Export-oriented industries — Entitled to tax holiday, ranging from 4–10 years	1973: Amendments to Investments and Exports Incentives Act (PD 62) — Liberalizes conditions for deduction of expansion reinvestment from taxable income. Tax credit on sales, duties on imports in export production extended indefinitely from start of operation. Abolishes double deduction of promotional expenses. Limits expansion reinvestment allowance from 100 percent to 25 [to] 50 percent and 50–100 percent for nonpioneer and pioneer projects, respectively	1977: Investment Promotion Act (BE 2520) — Decentralizes industries from Bangkok area. Incentives given to Investment Promotion Zone, including maximum reduction of 90 percent of business tax on sale of products for up to 5 years, reduction of 50 percent of corporate income tax for 5 years upon expiration of tax holiday. Incentives for export promotion by tax and duty exemption or reduction
1980s	None	1986: Promotion of Investments Act — Pioneer companies entitled to tax holidays for 5 years, with possible extension for 5 years	1983: Investment Incentive Policy Act (BP 391) — Withdraws accelerated depreciation and reinvestment allowance. Nonexporting firms allowed to defer payment of duties and taxes on machinery and capital equipment	None

Source: IBFD (various volumes) and various materials collected by authors (available on request).

Table 11-6. *Fiscal Incentives in ASEAN Countries, 1978–89*

Year	Incentive	Philippines	Indonesia	Malaysia	Singapore	Thailand
1978	Tax holiday (years)	Nil	2–3	2–5	5–10	n.a.
	Loss carryover	n.a.	Indefinite	n.a.	n.a.	n.a.
	Investment allowance	n.a.	n.a.	25 percent tax credit	n.a.	n.a.
	Import duty exemption	n.a.	Plant, machinery, raw materials	n.a.	n.a.	n.a.
1983	Tax holiday (years)	None	2–6	2–8	5–10	3–8
	Loss (years)	6	Unlimited	Unlimited	Unlimited	5
	Carryover of investment tax credit	75–100 percent investment allowance	20 percent investment allowance	25 percent investment tax credit	33.3–50 percent investment allowance	20 percent investment allowance
1989	Tax holiday (years)	4–6	Nil	5–10	5–10	3–8
	Loss carryforward	Nil	n.a.	Withdrawn	Available	Available
	Investment tax credit (percent)	100	None	100	10–50	None
	Exemption on capital equipment	100 percent if acquired before 8/12/90	Exempt from value added tax	100 percent	n.a.	50–100 percent
	Accelerated depreciation	None	50 percent, 25 percent, 10 percent for asset life less than 4 years, 8 years, more than 8 years, respectively	For assets not qualified for investment tax allowance, written off in 3 years	Plant and machinery written off in 3 years, computers and automation in 1 year	20 percent for nonland or plant equipment

n.a. Not applicable.
Source: For 1978, Shah and Toye (1978); for 1983, Modi (1987); for 1989, various materials collected by authors (available on request).

by Singapore in 1959 and continued with subsequent extensions of coverage in that country in 1967, 1979, and 1986. Each of these changes in incentives in Singapore was replicated in other ASEAN countries, which added pressure for further subsequent increases by Singapore. The net effect was that by the mid-1980s, substantial increases in incentives had taken place in all of the ASEAN countries except Indonesia. Other ASEAN countries attributed these increases largely to Singapore's repeated increases in incentives, which they felt had to be matched. This leader-follower behavior seems most marked in the case of Malaysia and Singapore, second most marked in the case of the Philippines and Singapore, and weakest in that of Thailand and Singapore.

An indication of the quantitative orders of magnitude involved in the growth of these incentives between 1978 and 1989 can be seen in table 11-6. During this period, tax holidays lengthened, investment tax credits grew, and import duty exemptions on equipment entered the system.

This process of accelerating investment incentives in ASEAN countries both parallels and differs from what some international trade literature sees as the underlying forces generating an escalation of protective barriers toward trade in goods in the global economy in the 1930s. During this time, when world trade collapsed by 70 percent following the recession of 1929 and the adoption of the Smoot-Hawley tariff in the United States, trade barriers increased rapidly in European countries and in other countries that had been trading partners of the United States, as collective retaliation took place.[4] Trade theorists are fond of characterizing this process as one of tit-for-tat retaliation, exchanging optimal tariffs one for another, with the eventual outcome being a Nash equilibrium (see Gorman 1957; Johnson 1953). In such an outcome, cooperative incentives exist for joint actions to be taken to improve on the Nash equilibrium through an agreed-on policy of restraint. The General Agreement on Tariffs and Trade (the GATT) is sometimes taken as the clearest example of such a cooperative agreement because, when drafted in the 1940s, it sought to improve on the retaliatory Nash equilibrium that accompanied the collapse in world trade in the 1930s.

This discussion raises the question of whether in the case of tax competition between subsets of developing countries (such as the escalating use of investment incentives by ASEAN countries) there are also incentives to negotiate cooperative arrangements that jointly improve on the current outcome. Can this be achieved in the area of investment incentives? Or are these investment incentives relatively ineffective, and hence supply little motivation for joint action? Are there joint arrangements that the ASEAN countries could enter into to achieve a cooperative agreement guaranteeing mutual restraint? How might they restrain each other from competition with the intent of attracting new inward foreign investment that would have gone to their rivals?

A GATT-type process in this area would involve an international agreement with incremental steps. There would be clear rules limiting the ways in which investment incentives could be applied, typically stressing non-discrimination, and binding agreements above the level of investment incentives. The countries, in this case the ASEAN countries involved, could then mutually agree to lower their incentives.

Could a GATT-type arrangement eventually be negotiated and implemented with respect to investment incentives among the ASEAN countries? First, the question must be answered as to whether policy reform with respect to investment incentives can best be achieved by unilateral action in each country. If many of these incentives are as ineffective as some of the literature suggests, this unilateral action may be the best way forward. Second, a danger with collective action of the GATT-type arrangement suggested above is that countries may keep their incentives in place as bargaining chips; they would see them as useful because they could be bargained away for restraint by neighboring rivals. Under this scenario collective action by the ASEAN countries may be an inferior approach.

A GATT-type arrangement covering investment incentives among ASEAN countries is, however, somewhat more complicated than it appears at first sight. In this particular case, there is, for example, no direct exchange of concessions involved as there is in a GATT-type arrangement in which reciprocally driven access to partner markets for trade in goods occurs. In this case competitors are seeking out new inward foreign investment through packages of increasing attractiveness to third-party investors outside of the group of countries involved that drives the competitive process.

In addition, it is clear from experience in ASEAN countries that the competitive process is not a traditional tit-for-tat retaliation, as trade theorists often characterize the 1930s. Instead, it is closer to a Stackelberg situation with leader-follower characteristics. Thus Singapore, being the largest exporter of manufactured goods in ASEAN since the 1960s, has been in a leader situation, typically taking steps that other countries then followed. The issue, therefore, is more how to constrain the leader so as to reign in the competitive process. No doubt joint cooperation may improve things, as in the GATT, but a nonemulation pact is what would be needed for the ASEAN countries. Because of the leader-follower situation, it may well be that to obtain meaningful discipline on use of investment incentives other ASEAN countries have to make concessions to the leader to persuade Singapore to comply.

What these concessions might be in the investment area seems unclear, and hence how to obtain meaningful direct discipline in regard to the use of investment incentives by ASEAN countries may be elusive. A more fruitful approach may be to bring a negotiation on investment incentives into the wider trade and integration negotiations now under way in ASEAN. When first formed in 1964, ASEAN was a defense, not a trade arrangement; a group of countries adopted common defense strategies in light of the Vietnam War and concerns over the domino effect at that time. ASEAN has, by and large, remained a strategic rather than an economic arrangement, but in the last five or so years various efforts to move to closer economic integration have made headway.

ASEAN countries have attempted to speak with one voice in the Uruguay Round negotiations in the GATT, for example, working out common positions before negotiations were engaged in various negotiating groups, allowing only one country from the ASEAN countries to speak, and representing a common point of view. In addition, ASEAN countries have now initiated tariff reductions between member countries with the intent of stimulating inter-ASEAN trade. These tariff reductions have made relatively little headway thus far and have focused on coverage of trade with regard to the number of items on which a tariff has been imposed rather than on major trade categories. As a result, tariff reductions have concentrated on relatively inconsequential items. Nonetheless, this process is likely to accelerate during the next ten years, and it may well be that it would make sense for the ASEAN countries to incorporate a working group on investment incentives into this wider set of negotiations.

Because Singapore is the one country in the ASEAN region that effectively has free trade, and because it is the largest exporter of manufactured goods, it is seen as the greatest beneficiary of any reduction in tariffs on manufactured goods. The perception that Singapore would reap all the benefits of inter-ASEAN trade negotiations has thus made the other ASEAN countries generally reluctant to engage in talks. Were Singapore willing to undertake disciplines on the use of investment incentives, which would be seen as beneficial to the Philippines, Malaysia, and Thailand, in return for trade concessions on manufactured goods trade by these countries, a sufficient basis may be provided to obtain meaningful ASEAN agreement in the use of investment incentives. The side benefit of allowing for more forward progress on trade negotiations may also accrue. Thus beyond a simple GATT-type approach to investment incentives, linking an arrangement on investment incentives to other areas of policy that would allow more forward progress may be a good strategy for ASEAN.

Conclusion

In this chapter we discuss some of the factors underlying the current use of investment incentives by developing countries. We stress the current global bifurcation between industrial and developing countries. Industrial countries were phasing out their investment incentives during the 1980s, removing both accelerated depreciation in investment incentives and investment tax credits. In contrast, in a surprisingly large number of countries in the developing world, predominantly in Southeast Asia and South

Asia, acceleration rather than deceleration in investment incentives has been the norm. In Latin America many countries have tended to follow the path of industrial countries and have attempted to phase out or at least reduce investment incentives. In Africa investment incentives continue to be dominated by company-to-government negotiations on tax holidays.

These developments have all taken place in spite of research that has questioned the effectiveness of most, if not all, investment incentives. Even when analyzed by the traditional cost-of-capital method, the effectiveness of these investment incentives seems questionable. And when additional special features of developing countries are taken into account, such as the presence of price, quantity, and other restrictions and foreign tax credits in industrial countries, then their effectiveness seems all the more in doubt.

In the final section of the chapter, we contrast this picture of dubious effectiveness of investment incentives with what seems to be the increasing use of them in developing countries. The tax competition between countries, using ever larger incentives, is ostensibly justified on the basis of attracting even more inward investments into these countries and is the reality in some regions such as that of ASEAN.

In the ASEAN case, we suggest that collective rather than unilateral actions may be needed to arrest this trend. We briefly discuss the use of cooperative arrangements on a regional basis among ASEAN countries, perhaps reminiscent of the kinds of arrangements that evolved in the 1940s under the GATT, with joint concessions, binding agreements, and restrictions on the use of trade-distorting measures. We suggest that such joint actions could forestall the spread of further tax competition in the area, which, in turn, we suggest may be based as much on the perception as on the reality of the effectiveness of these measures.

Notes

1. The effectiveness of many if not most of these incentives has long been questioned on many grounds. (See, for example, the discussion of the Philippine incentives in Manasan 1988.) One is that with rationed credit, financial, not tax, factors determine investment decisions. Another is that if the investment at issue is by a corporation under foreign control from a foreign tax credit country, any taxes paid will be creditable abroad, and, hence, investment tax incentives in the host country will be ineffective.

2. We excluded Indonesia from the analysis because beginning in 1984 Indonesia abolished all incentives. Undoubtedly, Indonesia has felt the effects of tax competition in the region. Recently, the country has made changes in its tax structure to increase its attractiveness to its investors. These changes include capping the individual and corporate tax rates at a maximum of 30 percent, with the long-run rate set at 25 percent (the same long-run rate set by Singapore), and tax incentives for small businesses, exporters, investments in remote areas, and enterprises geared to research and development.

3. See Whalley 1990 for more details.
4. See Kindleberger 1975.

References

The word "processed" describes informally reproduced works that may not be commonly available through libraries.

Bauman, R. 1988. "Fiscal Incentives in Brazil." Processed.

Bischoff, Charles W. 1971. "Business Investment in the 1970s: A Comparison of Models." *Brookings Papers on Economic Activity*, pp. 13–58. Brookings Institution, Washington, D.C.

Chirinko, Robert S. 1986. "Business Investment and Tax Policy: A Perspective on Existing Models and Empirical Results." *National Tax Journal* 39 (2):139–66.

Chirinko, Robert S., and Robert Eisner. 1982. "The Effects of Tax Parameters in the Investment Equations in Macroeconomic Econometric Models." In Marshall E. Blume, Jean Crockett, and Paul Taubman, eds., *Economic Activity and Finance*. Cambridge, Mass.: Ballinger.

———. 1983. "Tax Policy and Investment in Major U.S. Macroeconomic Econometric Models." *Journal of Public Economics* 20:139–66.

Choi, Kwang. 1988. "Tax Policy and Tax Reforms in Korea." In Javad, Khalilzadeh-Shirazi, and Anwar Shah, eds., *Reforming Taxes in Developing Countries*. Washington, D.C.: World Bank.

Coen, Robert M. 1975. "Investment Behaviour, the Measurement of Depreciation, and Tax Policy." *American Economic Review* 65 (March): 59–74.

Gorman, W. M. 1957. "Tariffs, Retaliation, and the Elasticity of Demand for Imports." *Review of Economic Studies* 25:133–62.

Green, R. Jeffery. 1980. "Investment Determinants and Tax Factors in Major Macroeconometric Models." In George M. von Furstenberg, ed., *The Government and Capital Formation*. Cambridge, Mass.: Ballinger.

Hall, Robert E., and Dale W. Jorgenson. 1969. "Tax Policy and Investment Behavior: Reply and Further Results." *American Economic Review* 59 (June): 388–401.

IBFD (International Bureau of Fiscal Documentation). Various volumes. *Tax News Service*. Netherlands.

Johnson, H. G. 1953. "Optimum Tariffs and Retaliation." *Review of Economic Studies* 21:142–53.

Jorgenson, Dale W. 1963. "Capital Theory and Investment Behavior." *AEA Proceedings* 53 (May): 247–59.

Kindleberger, Charles P. 1975. *The World in Depression 1929–1939*. Berkeley: University of California Press.

King, Mervyn A., and Don Fullerton, eds. 1984. *The Taxation of Income from Capital: A Comparative Study of the United States, the United Kingdom, Sweden, and West Germany*. Chicago, Ill.: University of Chicago Press.

Kwack, Taewon. 1988. "Public Finance, Trade, and Economic Development: The Role of Fiscal Incentives in Korea's Export-Led Economic Growth."

Paper presented at the Forty-fourth Congress of the International Institute of Public Finance, Istanbul, Turkey, August.

Lee, Fook-Hong. 1986. "A Summary of Singapore's 1986 Budget." *Bulletin for International Fiscal Documentation* (IBFD, Netherlands) 40 (July): 319–25.

Majd, Nader. 1988. "Characteristics of Major Tax Instruments Used in Sub-Sahara Africa." World Bank, Macroeconomic Adjustment and Growth Division, Country Economics Department, Washington, D.C.

Manasan, Rosario G. 1986. "Impact of BOI Incentives on Rate of Return, Factor Prices, and Relative Factor Use." PIDS Staff Paper Series 86-01. Philippine Institute for Development Studies, Manila.

————. 1988. "A Review of Investment Incentives in ASEAN Countries." PIDS Working Paper Series 88-27. Philippine Institute for Development Studies, Manila.

Modi, Jitendra R. 1987. "Major Features of Corporate Profit Taxes in Selected Developing Countries." *Bulletin for International Fiscal Development* (IBFD, Netherlands) 41 (February): 65–74.

O'Reilly, David, ed. 1989. *Income Taxation in the ASEAN Countries.* Singapore: Asian-Pacific Tax and Investment Research Centre.

Pinto, Luiz Fernando Teixeira. 1989. "Brazilian Tax Treatment of Foreign Investments." *Bulletin for International Fiscal Documentation* (IBFD, Netherlands) 43 (August–September): 376–79.

Price Waterhouse. 1988. *Corporate Taxes: A Worldwide Summary.* New York.

Shah, S. M. S., and J. F. J. Toye. 1978. "Fiscal Incentives for Firms in Some Developing Countries: Survey and Critique." In J. F. J. Toye, ed., *Taxation and Economic Development.* Cambridge, U.K.: University of Cambridge.

Sinaga, Simon. 1994. "Jakarta to Change Tax Structure to Attract Investors." *Straits Time Weekly Edition* (Singapore), September 10.

Subramanian, Arjunan. 1990. "Malaysia: An Outline of Tax Incentives." *Bulletin for International Fiscal Documentation* (IBFD, Netherlands) 44 (July): 334–39.

Whalley, John. 1990. "Foreign Responses to U.S. Tax Reforms." Paper presented at the conference on the 1986 U.S. Tax Reform Act held at the University of Michigan, November 10–11.

World Bank. 1980. *Thailand: Industrial Development Strategy in Thailand.* Washington, D.C.

CORPORATE INCOME TAXATION AND FOREIGN DIRECT INVESTMENT IN CENTRAL AND EASTERN EUROPE

12

Jack M. Mintz and Thomas Tsiopoulos

THE EFFECT OF taxation on flows of foreign direct investment must be judged in the context of the many other factors that determine how much foreign investment is made, and where. For most decisions, effective corporate income tax levels are not the make-or-break factor. There are, however, two important exceptions. First, extremely high taxes will deter foreign direct investment. Second, to attract so-called footloose investments—such as the labor-intensive assembly of garments, electronics, and toys, which can be done in many satisfactory locations—it is necessary to have a highly competitive corporate income tax regime, as well as other factors important to such activities. But apart from these two exceptions, normally small intercountry differences in profit taxes are unlikely to affect company decisions significantly, especially in the Central and Eastern European (CEE) countries, where many economic and political factors influence the decisions of investors.

Investors find that corporate income tax regimes can have varying effects on profitability. The current statutory rates of such taxation range from as low as 15 percent in some economies (Hong Kong, for example) to more than 50 percent in others (such as Japan). As any astute investor knows, however, the tax treatment of depreciation and inventory costs, interest deductions, and losses also can affect the amount of profits, net of corporate taxes, obtainable from a foreign investment. In addition, many governments provide special incentives such as investment allowances, investment tax credits, and tax holidays (temporary tax exemptions or reductions) that influence the company's obligations.

The country's economic climate can also be a factor. For example:

- If the interest rate that a company uses to discount future benefits is high, then the current value of writeoffs given for depreciation will be low. In general, when interest rates are high, a company has less incentive to spread deductions over a period of time.
- Similarly, if inflation rates are high and accounting does not allow assets and liabilities to be revalued accordingly, future deductions such as those for depreciation or losses carried forward are less valuable than in situations in which inflation is low or amounts carried forward are indexed for inflation.
- High inflation can, however, reduce taxes for companies that finance investments by debt unindexed for inflation. With the deductibility of high nominal interest, unadjusted for inflation, the business is able to write off not only the "real" portion of the interest but also the rest, which is in fact an adjustment for inflation's effect on the value of the principal.

Because of these effects, the actual value of taxes paid usually differs from the tax rate specified in the law. Actual tax burdens can be higher or lower than the statutory rate, depending on the presence and the relative importance of the effects mentioned. To take all these effects into account, a useful summary measure called the effective tax rate is commonly employed. The effective tax rate indicates the degree to which the tax system in all its ramifications, and in its interactions with the economic environment, reduces the after-tax rate of return from a given before-tax return. For example, if an investment earns 10 percent before taxes and the effective tax rate is 40 percent, the net-of-tax rate of return is 6 percent. The appendix contains an explanation of the methodology used to calculate effective tax rates in this chapter.

Calculations were made for two kinds of investments, a typical light manufacturing company and a hotel. Results are presented only for an investor whose home country is the United States.[1] The same calculations were made for an investor based in Germany, but the results were so similar that they are not presented here. The calculations are based on the assumption, among other things, that the investments are financed with typical debt-equity mixes and that the debt is borrowed locally. This assumption affects the results in some of the countries; if no local debt is used in the financing, the effective tax rates in some countries change considerably, as shown in the sensitivity analysis.

The base case results for each of the five CEE countries, presented in table 12-1, show the effective tax burdens of the systems as they actually performed (as closely as we were able to model them) in mid-1991. (Assumptions and parameters are shown in table 12-2.) Effective tax burdens were also calculated, and the results presented, for the same

Table 12-1. *Effective Tax Rates, Mid-1991*
(percent)

Country	Manufacturing	Services
Bulgaria	10.2	9.8
Czechoslovakia	22.2	19.8
Greece	15.1	–8.8
Hungary	6.0	5.1
Poland	7.6	14.3
Portugal	31.3	19.8
Romania	12.2	9.8
United States	41.9	29.7

Source: Authors.

investments in two other countries, Greece and Portugal, and also for investments in the home country, the United States.

Variations on the base case results are shown in tables 12-3 through 12-8. These variations apply only to the five CEE countries; for Greece, Portugal, and the United States only the actual situation was analyzed.

Results of the Analysis

The conclusions of the analysis can be summarized as follows:

- All five of the CEE countries impose rather uniform tax burdens on foreign investors. The differences among them in effective tax rates are unlikely to make one country more attractive than another (table 12-1).
- Effective tax rates in CEE countries are competitive with those of other countries and are not high enough to deter foreign investors (table 12-1).
- Eliminating tax holidays would make Romania and Bulgaria much less tax competitive for investments in manufacturing. The effective tax rates in these countries would be high enough to deter some investors. The effective rates also would go up to some extent in Czechoslovakia if it stopped offering holidays, but probably not enough to deter many investors (table 12-3).[2]
- In Hungary and Poland the tax holidays are essentially redundant to investors who borrow locally. The full deductibility of high nominal interest rates in these countries makes the corporate income tax burdens so low that the holidays are irrelevant. For investors who do not borrow locally, however, eliminating the tax holiday would also reduce the tax competitiveness of these two countries significantly (tables 12-3 and 12-4).

Table 12-2. *Input Data*
(percent)

Rate	Greece	United States	Czechoslovakia	Poland	Hungary	Bulgaria	Romania	Portugal
Statutory corporate income tax	40.0	40.0	40.0	50.0	39.0	39.0	46.0	38.0
Inflation	10.0	55.0	20.4	36.0	15.0	10.3	15.9	4.2
Interest	14.1	59.1	24.5	40.1	19.1	14.4	20.0	8.3
Dividend withholding tax for								
United States	25.0	5.0	0.0	15.0	10.0	25.0	2.0	n.a.
Annual depreciation allowance								
Structures	2.3	2.5	2.0	1.5	1.5	4.0	5.0	2.2
Machinery	12.5	15.0	13.0	7.0	7.0	14.0	15.0	9.3
Tax holiday (years)	3	5	10	5	5	0	0	0
Inventory valuation system	LIFO	LIFO	LIFO	FIFO	FIFO	LIFO	LIFO	LIFO
Debt-to-total-asset ratio	38.0	38.0	38.0	38.0	38.0	38.0	38.0	29.0

n.a. Not applicable.
Source: World Bank.

458

Table 12-3. *Effective Tax Rates: No Tax Holiday*
(percent)

Country	Manufacturing	Services
Bulgaria	241.7	−128.0
Czechoslovakia	37.4	25.9
Hungary	4.2	−31.7
Poland	−239.1	−326.4
Romania	60.9	32.4

Source: Authors.

Table 12-4. *Effective Tax Rates for Manufacturing,*
without Tax Holiday: Varying Debt-Asset Ratios
(percent)

Country	Debt-asset ratio		
	40.0	20.0	0.0
Bulgaria	213.1	534.3	1,006.9
Czechoslovakia	34.8	55.7	63.9
Hungary	−5.8	52.0	62.7
Poland	−266.7	−18.4	77.4
Romania	59.4	72.0	80.5

Source: Authors.

Table 12-5. *Effective Tax Rates, Tax Holiday: Mid-1991,*
with 3 Percent Inflation
(percent)

Country	Manufacturing	Services
Bulgaria	18.4	−4.3
Czechoslovakia	22.9	14.3
Hungary	7.3	4.7
Poland	17.7	13.8
Romania	14.9	5.8

Source: Authors.

Table 12-6.   Effective Tax Rates: No Tax Holiday, 3 Percent Inflation
(percent)

Country	Manufacturing	Services
Bulgaria	62.3	52.9
Czechoslovakia	43.1	35.2
Hungary	42.4	37.2
Poland	41.1	36.2
Romania	53.3	42.9

Source: Authors.

Table 12-7.   Effective Tax Rates, No Tax Holidays, 20 Percent Corporate Income Tax
(percent)

Country	Manufacturing	Services
Bulgaria	58.7	−36.9
Czechoslovakia	18.5	11.1
Hungary	0.5	−12.7
Poland	−92.3	−127.6
Romania	38.1	15.6

Source: Authors.

Table 12-8.   Effective Tax Rates: No Tax Holidays, 20 Percent Investment Tax Allowance for Depreciable Assets
(percent)

Country	Manufacturing	Services
Bulgaria	197.7	−182.5
Czechoslovakia	11.6	−35.9
Hungary	−59.3	−358.4
Poland	−270.1	−361.4
Romania	53.1	5.0

Source: Authors.

- The assumption of low inflation moves the base case results in the same direction as the assumption of no local borrowing—but not as much. With low inflation the countries remain tax competitive with their existing rules (table 12-5). But if the tax holiday were to be eliminated, then under low inflation the effective tax burdens of all five countries would rise to the range of 35 to 60 percent—somewhat high, in the range where they might deter some investors (table 12-6).
- Eliminating the tax holidays but compensating with either a reduction in the corporate income tax rate to 20 percent or a 20 percent tax allowance for new investments in depreciable assets would maintain tax competitiveness for Czechoslovakia, Hungary, and Poland. Bulgaria and Romania would, however, have to take stronger measures to remain tax competitive if they were to eliminate tax holidays (tables 12-7 and 12-8).

Comparability of the CEE Tax Regimes

The effective tax rates on manufacturing and service industries are summarized in table 12-1 under the existing rules in each of the CEE countries. The rates range from 6 percent to 22 percent in manufacturing—a wide range. But more important, all these rates are reasonably competitive—not high enough to deter most investors from making an investment. From this point of view, the rates are not significantly different in regard to their effects on investment decisions. For services qualifying for the holiday (for example, hotels), a similar range—from 5 percent to 20 percent—in effective tax rates is observed. Still, the effective tax rate for investments in the Polish service industry, with a two-year holiday, is much higher than that for Polish manufacturing, with a five-year holiday.

The similarity of the effective tax rates across the countries (except to some extent for Czechoslovakia) is somewhat surprising, given the significant differences in corporate tax provisions from country to country. As discussed earlier, many factors affect effective tax rates, and some of these offset some others. These factors include the following (besides the length of the holiday):

- The higher the corporate tax rate, the more taxes the company might pay on income earned after the holiday. Bulgaria has the highest corporate tax rate (50 percent) compared with the other CEE countries. Its effective tax rate on manufacturing investments is higher than that in Poland, even though both countries have a five-year holiday period and similar inflation experience.
- The more a company uses long-lived assets, the more taxes the company pays after the tax holiday expires. In all CEE countries except Poland, manufacturing and services have the same length of holiday.

The higher effective tax rates in manufacturing than in services in the other four countries are in part due to the greater use of long-lived depreciable capital in manufacturing than in service activities, in which more short-lived capital is used.

- If the company depreciates assets during the holiday, tax depreciation allowances available after the holiday can be reduced in value. Thus for a given asset, the more depreciation claimed during the holiday, the more taxes paid after the holiday. All five CEE countries require companies to depreciate assets during the holiday. If companies could delay their claim of depreciation until after the holiday, effective tax rates would be much lower than those illustrated in table 12-1.[3]

Tax Competitiveness of CEE Countries

The effective tax rates in the CEE countries compare well with those of other countries who may compete for the same foreign direct investment (table 12-1). Moreover, the effective tax rate is much smaller than for investments in the United States itself. The United States now has few incentives available for capital investment because the 1986 tax reforms abolished the investment tax credit and scaled back deductions for depreciation. At the same time, however, the United States reduced its corporate tax rate from more than 50 percent to less than 40 percent, a rate comparable to that of most CEE countries (except Bulgaria, which has a 50 percent corporate tax rate).[4]

The CEE countries are also tax competitive with Greece (manufacturing only) and Portugal in attracting foreign capital in manufacturing.[5] Although neither country provides tax holidays for investments, both permit companies to expense a large portion of their capital expenditure. Greece, for example, allows services to write off at least 40 percent the first year, in addition to annual depreciation allowances.

Elimination of Holidays

Table 12-3 provides effective tax rate measurements, assuming no tax holidays are available in the CEE countries. Under these assumptions, three of the countries would not lose their tax competitiveness, given a typical project's debt-equity ratio. In this instance the effective tax rates for Bulgaria (services only), Hungary, and Poland are actually lower than they are in the tax holiday case.[6]

In Bulgaria (manufacturing), Czechoslovakia, and Romania, however, eliminating tax holidays would mean that investments would face higher effective tax rates than investments made in Greece and Portugal. This results primarily from the substantial deductions that Greece and Portugal give for capital expenditure by existing as well as new businesses. By contrast, incentives in the CEE countries benefit new companies only. Bulgaria and Romania, especially, would need to take other steps to reduce effective tax burdens if they eliminated tax holidays.

Debt Finance as a Tax Shelter

Interest deductions for debt in highly inflationary environments largely account for the somewhat surprising conclusions of the previous section. The writeoff of high nominal interest rates drastically reduces tax burdens, having the same effect as tax holidays. So the holidays are important only if investments are financed by equity or foreign borrowing in low-inflation countries or, as discussed in the following section, when the host countries experience low inflation.

For investments financed in significant degree by local debt (at least 40 percent), the holiday incentive does little to encourage foreign investment in Bulgaria (services only), Hungary, and Poland. In the absence of the tax holidays, companies can use interest deductions to shield investments from corporate taxation. This can intensify the effect of inflation on the value of depreciation and other deductions that are based on the historical cost of assets. As discussed previously, when inflation increases interest rates and there is no indexation, the foreign investor can virtually eliminate any corporate tax paid to the host country on investments. Thus the effective tax rates in the three higher-inflation CEE countries—Bulgaria (services only), Hungary, and Poland—are significantly less than in the tax holiday case.

The influence that varying debt-asset ratios have on the effective tax rates for manufacturing across the CEE countries is illustrated in table 12-4. (Results are similar for services and are not reported.) The higher the debt-asset ratio, the lower the effective corporate tax rate in the absence of the tax holiday.[7] When companies finance investments without using money borrowed at high nominal interest rates, the effective tax rates are quite high compared with other countries. This is especially true for countries such as Bulgaria, Hungary, and Poland, where high inflation reduces the value of depreciation deductions. It is also true for Romania and Bulgaria, which provide an inadequate deduction for inventory costs in the presence of inflation.[8]

Even without a tax holiday, however, when debt-asset ratios are normal (such as the 40 percent assumed here), Poland and Hungary have competitive effective tax rates on manufacturing that are similar to or lower than those of Greece, Portugal, and the United States. Czechoslovakia and Romania, however, would have relatively high effective tax rates. The reason is that the latter countries have relatively low inflation, so the deductibility of interest is of less value. As for Bulgaria, its effective tax rate on manufacturing remains high because of its inadequate treatment of inventory costs for tax purposes under inflation. Table 12-3 shows that Bulgaria's effective tax rate on services, however, is quite low in the presence of inflation. Unlike manufacturing, services use little inventory.

All this variation illustrates some of the unpredictable effects of interest deductibility and inflation on the effective tax rate that companies face in high-inflation countries. Further effects of inflation are discussed in the following section.

Inflation and Corporate Tax

As stated previously, the tax holidays in the CEE countries do little to reduce effective tax rates when companies use some local debt to finance investments. This may happen particularly in countries with high rates of inflation because the interest deductions, unadjusted for inflation, shield corporate income from taxation.

The importance of inflation can be illustrated by a hypothetical situation in which these countries experience an inflation rate similar to those of the countries belonging to the Organization for Economic Cooperation and Development (OECD). Assuming 3 percent inflation, we compare, in tables 12-5 and 12-6, the effective tax rates that could be expected under tax holiday and nonholiday situations.

As shown in table 12-5, with the tax holiday, the effective tax rates on manufacturing and services in the five CEE countries are much lower than those in Greece, Portugal, and the United States. Without the holiday, however (table 12-6), the effective tax rates in the CEE countries are much higher, somewhat surpassing those in the other countries. Thus with low rates of inflation, removal of the tax holiday would significantly reduce the tax competitiveness of the CEE countries.

These results are especially important for Romania and Bulgaria, which impose much higher effective corporate tax rates on manufacturing and services in the absence of a tax holiday. In these two countries, depreciation and inventory deductions are less generous than those in the other CEE countries as well as in Greece, Portugal, and the United States.

The calculations in tables 12-5 and 12-6 raise an important policy issue that the CEE countries face. The data in tables 12-1 and 12-3 show that the corporate tax holidays may have little effect on foreign investment if inflation remains high and the companies are able to shelter income from taxes by deducting financing costs that are unadjusted for inflation. Thus if high inflation continues, the corporate tax holidays will be of little value to the investor who borrows locally. Moreover, inflation can have various unplanned and undesirable effects on investments, especially in the absence of tax holidays, depending on how the investments are financed. For projects financed by low debt, inflation results in high effective tax rates, if depreciation and inventory deductions are not indexed for inflation. For projects financed by high debt, effective tax rates can be extraordinarily low because interest deductions are not adjusted for inflation. Therefore, if for any reason inflation continues, the tax system would need to be adjusted to avoid these effects.

If, however, inflation is only temporary and price stability or a low rate of inflation eventually occurs, the corporate tax holidays will be more effective in reducing the income tax burden. Without the tax holiday the effective tax rates on capital will be quite high unless corporate tax policies change in some compensating way. Thus the evolution of corporate tax policy in the CEE countries will depend on their long-term experience with inflation.

Policy Options for Tax Incentives

The CEE countries are focused on their change from centrally planned to market-oriented economies. A significant objective of their policies, unlike those of industrial nations, is to attract not only foreign capital but also technology and managerial talent for industry. Rightly or wrongly, these governments often consider corporate tax incentives a major tool for the transformation process. They see the reduction of taxes on foreign direct investment—for example, by tax holidays—as easier than other methods, such as improving infrastructure, to make their economic climate more hospitable. This objective for corporate tax policy is not without its costs, however. Government activities, such as education, public safety, social services, and construction of roads and bridges, still must go on and tax revenues are needed to pay for them.

Specialists suggest that a tax system should meet three criteria in raising revenue:

- *Efficiency.* The system should have a minimal effect on the allocation of resources achieved by a market economy.
- *Equity.* The system should treat similar taxpayers in a similar way.
- *Simplicity.* The system should be easy to comply with and to administer.

Efficiency, equity, and simplicity all favor taxing investments at the same rate (not discriminating, for example, among investors of different nationalities), with a broad tax base (that is, few exemptions) and a moderately low tax rate. Many government officials in CEE countries, however, are concerned that such a strategy may not be effective in attracting more foreign direct investment. In the short run they may fear that their tax systems will appear unfriendly until they can complete comprehensive reform measures. Or, in the long run, they may feel that their countries need lower rates to compete effectively for foreign capital.

Corporate tax policy in CEE countries must concentrate on two objectives weighed against each other: (a) revenue raising and (b) economic policy—specifically, the attraction of foreign capital.[9] The policymakers must ask themselves: what is the best type of tax incentive to attract foreign investment without losing considerable revenue? There are three types of incentives they could consider: (a) tax holidays, already employed in each of the countries studied in this report; (b) fast writeoffs for investments, such as accelerated depreciation, LIFO accounting for inventories, investment allowances, or investment tax credits; and (c) a low corporate tax rate applied to a broad corporate tax base. (Other steps, such as employment tax incentives, could be considered, but these are not particularly aimed at foreign investment and go beyond the analysis of this chapter.)

Tax Holidays

The tax holiday is the principal form of corporate tax incentive now available in the CEE countries. It operates by exempting, or taxing at a preferential rate, income earned during the first years of the founding of the company. In principle, when the holiday ends, the company must begin to pay taxes—the company is not allowed to transform itself into a new company that would qualify for a new holiday. Thus tax holidays require that the tax authority monitor the development of the enterprise. The holiday incentive is infrequently used in the industrial nations.

The tax holiday offers several benefits as a means of attracting foreign investments, including the following:

- It provides large benefits as soon as the company begins earning income. Although the holiday is of little immediate help to an unprofitable company, its prospective benefits are more valuable than an incentive such as a lower corporate tax rate that accrues more slowly over a longer time.
- The holiday primarily benefits short-term investments, which often are undertaken in so-called footloose industries, companies that can quickly disappear in one jurisdiction and reappear in another. Thus footloose investments, which use capital that quickly depreciates or is easily disposed of, benefit most from the tax holiday.[10] The prospect of no or reduced taxes for a limited time encourages footloose projects to locate in such a place, and therefore many countries compete for such investment with generous tax holidays.
- With a tax holiday, interest deductions are of little tax value. Thus the holiday removes an incentive for corporations to finance investment by borrowing. Indeed, if the holiday also implies that company shareowners need not pay personal income taxes on dividends and capital gains, equity finance will be encouraged instead. This reduces the prospect of bankruptcy because the company will likely be more financially viable.

The following are some of the drawbacks to using tax holidays:

- When assets must be written down for tax purposes during the holiday, the incentive discriminates against investments that rely on long-lived depreciable capital. Although holidays may attract footloose industries, they are less likely to attract industries bringing more significant capital commitment. Discouragement of investments having a long-term stake could hurt the economy.
- The holiday can lead to a large erosion of the tax base as taxpayers learn how to escape taxation of income from other sources. During the holiday years, companies operate at a preferential corporate tax rate (zero in the case of the CEE countries). If corporate taxpayers have a choice, it is to their advantage to shift income into a company enjoying the tax holiday and take more deductible expenses in another company they may own that must pay taxes. They would prefer to have the taxpaying company incur interest costs on borrowed finance and the tax holiday company to be financed with equity. In fact, the tax holiday company could hold debt in the nonholiday company. The nonholiday company can deduct interest while the tax holiday company earns the interest tax-free.
- Company turnover adds another complexity. A company can try to lengthen its holiday term by closing down in one location and restarting (under the guise of new ownership) in another location. Tax authorities may try to guard against such abuses, but it may be difficult to eliminate them entirely.
- The tax holiday is a difficult incentive to target and thus can have unintended distorting effects on the economy. It may help non-qualifying companies to shift away taxable income. A tax holiday given in a CEE country could ultimately benefit investments in other countries if the parent company can shift its own income into its CEE company through transfer pricing, financing, and other tax arbitrage techniques.

In summary, tax holidays have significant advantages and disadvantages. A disadvantage to the government is that they can reduce needed revenues. They create tremendous opportunities for multinational companies to engage in tax-planning strategies that result in steady erosion and leakage of revenues normally available to the government. The revenue cost may be particularly large even if some new investment is encouraged. As for attracting more foreign direct investment, the tax holiday is of limited usefulness: the incentive is more effective in attracting footloose industries than in enticing those that would take a long-term interest in the economy. Finally, the tax holiday benefits the formation of new companies rather than investment in new productive assets, although what the CEE countries want is the new assets. Whether the investors are new or existing companies should not matter.

Low Corporate Tax Rate

CEE countries might well consider eliminating tax incentives, such as the holiday, and levying a low corporate tax rate on all industrial activities. The tax base could be chosen to correspond roughly with the corporation's income.[11] As currently being practiced in several CEE countries, companies would deduct labor costs, depreciation, inventory costs, and interest expense from revenues earned. And countries experiencing high inflation could index income and costs. As argued earlier, however, indexation would not be necessary if inflation were reduced.

In table 12-7 we show the effective tax rate on manufacturing and service investments in the five CEE countries, assuming a corporate tax rate of only 20 percent and no tax holiday.[12] As indicated in the table, all except Bulgaria would be tax competitive.

A low corporate tax rate on a broad base would have three advantages over the current system of tax holidays:

- Compliance and administration would be much simpler. Governments would be able to maintain corporate tax revenues because investors would have few tax-planning opportunities.
- Investors would look favorably on a country offering a low statutory tax rate, especially one well below the worldwide norm of 35 to 40 percent. Also, a low corporate tax rate with few other incentives signals to foreign investors that the government is interested in letting the market determine the most profitable investments without undue governmental influence.
- A low corporate tax rate is, in itself, an incentive. It allows investors to keep a larger portion of profits. Also, in inflationary climates, an unindexed corporate tax system has less effect on investment activities.

Although a low corporate tax rate on a broad base is consistent with the current philosophy of industrial economies, this strategy has limitations:

- International linkages can undermine a country's efforts to make its tax system relatively neutral. In fact, a country with a corporate tax system greatly out of line with other countries' might be better off having a less neutral system to minimize distortions.[13] When corporate tax bases and rates are not uniform, multinational corporations can exploit the differences to their own advantage. For example, a multinational could issue debt in a country with a high tax rate to finance investments in a country with a low tax rate. This would provide a benefit for multinational companies that would not be available to local businesses.

- Because they face economic and political uncertainties, the CEE countries may need to offer an incentive that provides immediate benefits to foreign investors. A low corporate tax rate may not suffice because the benefits largely accrue in later years. Also, a cut in rates reduces taxes paid on old investments, resulting in a windfall gain to owners of old capital and a considerable revenue loss to the government.
- Most OECD countries give preferential corporate tax treatment to activities that may bring long-term benefits, such as research and development. Investments in advanced-technology machinery also are encouraged.[14]

Investment Tax Allowances or Credits

A third form of tax incentive, found in many OECD countries, is a fast writeoff for investment expenditure. These allowances take three forms: (a) accelerated depreciation, which allows companies to write off capital more quickly for tax purposes than for accounting; (b) an investment expenditure allowance, which lets companies write off a percentage of qualifying investment expenditure from their taxable income; and (c) an investment tax credit, which allows companies to reduce taxes paid by a percentage of investment expenditure. The second and third types are tax incentives that immediately benefit the investing company. Actual use may be limited, however, if the company cannot write off the allowance (for example, if it were in a loss position for tax purposes and the government does not refund the allowance in such a case).[15]

In table 12-8 we show estimated effective tax rates for manufacturing and service projects, assuming a fully refundable 20 percent investment tax allowance for machinery and structures, with no tax holiday.[16] As indicated in the table, the effective rates in all CEE countries are lower than those in Greece, Portugal, and the United States—except for manufacturing in Romania and Bulgaria.[17] Thus a country can substitute investment tax allowances for tax holidays and still maintain its competitive tax position; Bulgaria and Romania would have to lower their tax rate or provide larger allowances than those assumed here.

Investment tax allowances have distinct advantages over other incentives the CEE countries could provide. They include the following:

- An investment tax allowance permits the company to receive the benefit of lower corporate taxes only if it makes an investment. The incentive is correctly targeted at the desired activity (that is, additional investment, rather than formation of a new company).
- The investment tax allowance, if targeted toward long-lived capital such as structures and machinery, encourages investments that are

expected to be profitable for many years. It encourages companies to take a long-term view when planning investments.

- The investment allowance costs the government less than alternatives such as tax holidays and reduced corporate tax rates. By targeting current capital spending, the allowance causes less revenue leakage than would a tax holiday. And it promotes new investment instead of giving a windfall gain to owners of old capital, as does a reduction in corporate tax rates.

Like the other tax incentives, the investment tax allowance has its limitations and drawbacks.

- In many OECD countries, the allowance applies only to machinery and perhaps structures. If some types of capital, such as inventories, do not qualify, the allowance discriminates against those industries that use them intensively.
- A company that must replace capital often can claim the investment allowance frequently. Thus the allowance favors assets that have higher rates of economic depreciation. If governments did not want to favor certain assets, they would have to gear allowance rates to the expected rate of capital depreciation.
- If the investment tax allowance is not refundable, existing companies reap the full benefits, whereas start-up companies must first earn enough income before they can take the allowance. Also, projects with long gestation periods suffer in comparison with those that begin earning income quickly.
- When inflation is high, the allowance aggravates the tax system's uneven effect on the investment behavior of companies. Companies in high-inflation countries will benefit more if they borrow to finance capital, because tax deductions for capital expenditure are more valuable. This is the reverse of the tax holiday and of lower corporate tax rates, which reduce the advantages of interest cost deductions for tax purposes during high inflation.

Like any other tax incentive, the investment allowance reduces the government's revenue. But the allowance probably is the most cost-effective strategy because it is targeted more precisely toward the type of activity wanted—that is, additions to productive capacity. It can also be made refundable, allowing the government to share the investment costs, and risks, with the foreign entrepreneur.

Conclusion

In tables 12-7 and 12-8 we illustrate how alternatives to tax holidays can maintain tax competitiveness in the CEE countries. Either of the particular alternatives chosen for the examples, a 20 percent statutory rate or a 20 percent investment tax allowance, would by itself be sufficient for Czechoslovakia, Hungary, and Poland. For Bulgaria and Romania, additional changes would be necessary (for example, allowing LIFO inventory accounting).

Given the strengths and weaknesses of the various incentives discussed here, we suggest that the CEE countries seriously consider reducing or completely eliminating tax holidays and maintaining their tax competitiveness with some kind of investment credit or allowance (as well as permitting LIFO and liberal loss-carryforward rules, a topic not analyzed in this chapter). The same tax rules should apply to all private enterprises, regardless of the nationalities of the owners. Such changes would leave the countries as attractive to foreign direct investment as they are now, or even more so, and they would be more cost-effective in inducing more additional investment per unit of revenue loss to their treasuries.

Appendix. Calculating the Effective Tax Rates

In this appendix we supply additional details of the methodology, assumptions, and data sources used to calculate the effective tax rates. The methodology is based on the open economy analysis of Boadway, Bruce, and Mintz (1984, 1987). The work is similar to that of King and Fullerton (1984), Andersson (1991), and the OECD (1991). The main differences in the methodology used here and that of the OECD, for example, is that here we use actual interest rates and inflation rates to measure the effective tax rates. Also, risk is incorporated in the analysis following Bulow and Summers (1984) and McKenzie and Mintz (1990).

The methodology used to estimate the effective tax rates rests on several assumptions. First, companies are assumed to maximize profits, which implies that they invest in capital to the point at which the return on capital equals the cost of capital. It is also assumed that companies choose the level of debt and equity needed to minimize their cost of finance. Cost minimization of financing implies that companies issue debt until the tax benefits from additional debt equals the bankruptcy and agency costs associated with incremental debt. In addition, the seven host countries of this study—Bulgaria, Czechoslovakia, Greece, Hungary, Poland, Portugal, and Romania—are treated as small open economies. In a small open economy, corporations have the option of acquiring financing from domestic and international markets while, at the same time, the domestic market interest rate for a country is determined by the international trading of currencies.

Furthermore, the analysis throughout this chapter explicitly deals with those investments of multinational corporations whose home country is the United States of America. Whereas the United States is the capital-exporting country, Bulgaria, Czechoslovakia, Greece, Hungary, Poland, Portugal, and Romania are the host, or capital-importing, countries.

The effective tax rates were estimated for two different tax incentive schemes (tax holidays and post–tax holiday regimes) and under three different simulations (actual inflation, 3 percent inflation for all countries, and three different debt-asset ratios, 40 percent, 20 percent, and 0 percent). The calculation of r_n, the net-of-tax return required to compensate savers for their savings, remains the same for each industry and within each country and across the two tax incentive schemes. The different tax incentives, however, require us to make considerable modifications in formulating the gross-of-tax return (r_g) to capital formulas and estimating the effective tax rates.

The multinational corporation is assumed to use two sources of money to finance capital in the host country. The first is debt raised in the host country. The second is equity invested by the multinational parent in the subsidiary operating in the host country. In turn, the multinational finances equity acquired in the subsidiary with equity and debt raised in the home country. The mathematical expression for the net-of-tax, risk-adjusted, rate of return on capital, for each industry is

$$(12A\text{-}1)\ r_n = [\ \beta i'\,(1-u') + (1-\beta)\,g' - p'\ ]\,(1-\gamma) + \gamma\,(i-p).$$

All home (capital-exporting) country variables are denoted by the prime symbol ('). Those characters without the prime symbol represent host (capital-importing) country variables. The term i is the nominal interest rate; β is the portion of the multinational parent's capital financed by debt in the home country; γ represents that portion of the multinational subsidiary's investment financed by debt in the host country; g' is the nominal cost of equity finance in the home country; and p' is the expected rate of inflation of the home country (p is also the inflation rate of the host country). The rate of return on capital held by the owners of the multinational parent, as formulated above, is essentially a weighted average of the rate of return available to owners of debt, $\gamma(i-p)$, and owners of equity, $[(1-\beta)g' + \beta i'(1-u') - p']$. The host country rate of return on capital from holding equity is itself a weighted average of both home country equity, $(1-\beta)g'$, and the rate of return on corporate bonds in the home country, $\beta i'(1-u')$.

It is assumed that international interest rates are determined in the long run by arbitrage in international markets. Under the assumption that purchasing power parity will hold in the long run, we can determine the host country's interest rate in relation to the home country by the following equation:

$$(12A\text{-}2) \qquad\qquad i = i' - (p' - p).$$

The owner of a multinational parent corporation is assumed to be a typical G-7 country investor. The investor is assumed to face a weighted average of tax rates imposed at the personal level across the G-7 countries. It is important to note that the rate of return, net of personal taxes, earned on bonds is assumed to equal the rate of return earned on equity held by the marginal investor in the U.S. parent. This relation between the rate of return earned by bonds and equity implies the following expression:

(12A-3) $g = i'(1 - m')/(1 - \theta')$.

The variable m' is the personal income tax paid on interest (the rate used was 31 percent). The variable θ' is the tax on equity income for the average OECD investor. This tax rate, assumed to be a weighted average of personal tax rates on dividends and capital gains, equals 13.6 percent.

The nominal interest rate is operationally defined as the 1990 lending rate, whereas the annual change in the consumer price index was used as the inflation rate. Both variables for all countries were collected from the *IMF International Financial Statistics* (IMF 1989). The rates used for each country are presented in tables 12A-1 and 12A-2.

The data used for the ratio of debt to total assets (β), the ratio of debt to assets of the multinational company's investment within the host country (γ), and the economic depreciation rates (δ) were estimated from World Bank project data for all countries except the United States. The U.S. statistics are based on estimates obtained by McKenzie and Mintz (1990). The components of the debt data included debentures and loan stocks, loans from financial institutions, loans and advancements from headquarters and subsidiaries, short-term borrowing, and other creditors. The debt-to-asset ratio was estimated for each of the three industries. The debt-to-asset and economic depreciation parameters used are summarized in table 12A-1.

Table 12A-1. Debt-to-Asset and Economic Depreciation Parameters

Parameter	Manufacturing	Services
Debt to total assets (β)	29	44
Debt to assets of multinational company in host country (γ)	38	50
Building depreciation (δ)	3	4
Machinery depreciation (δ)	14	22

Note: The statutory annual depreciation rates and relevant tax rates, such as the corporate, income, and dividend tax rates, were obtained from the *International Bureau of Fiscal Documentation,* 1990 edition. Actual rates used are provided.

Source: Authors.

Table 12A-2. *Capital Stock Weights*

Category	Manufacturing	Services
Land	4.51	2.86
Buildings	22.54	6.41
Machinery	33.28	6.36
Inventory	23.16	0.89
Total	83.49	16.51

Source: Authors.

Absence of Incentives: Postholiday Period

For a profit-maximizing company, capital is acquired until the return on capital, gross of taxes and depreciation, equals the rental price of capital. The rental price of capital, for buildings and machinery, is mathematically defined as

$$(12A\text{-}4) \qquad F' = (\delta + r + h)\,(1 - A)/(1 - u)$$

where F' represents the return per dollar of capital (gross of depreciation and taxes), h is the risk premium on capital, and δ is the economic depreciation rate. The term A is the tax value of initial and annual depreciation allowances per dollar of capital expenditure:

$$(12A\text{-}5) \qquad A = u \left\{ a_1 + (1 - a_1 f)\, a_2 \,/\, [a_2 + R - (p' - p)] \right\}$$

where a_1 is the initial writeoff of capital and a_2 is the annual declining balance (or equivalent) depreciation rate. The variable f captures the proportion of the initial allowance written off the capital cost base; f was assumed to be zero for all countries. The term R is the company's nominal cost of financing, net of corporate taxes, which is defined as

$$(12A\text{-}6) \quad R = (1 - \gamma)\,[\beta i'(1 - u') + (1 - \beta)g\,']\,/\,(1 - x) + \gamma\,[i\,(1 - u) + p' - p]$$

and $r = R - p'$.

The cost of finance is similar to the net-of-tax return on capital (equation 12A-1) except for two terms. The first, $i(1 - u)$, incorporates the interest deductibility of debt in the host country. The second incorporates the term x, which represents the weighted average host country withholding tax. The real cost of financing is r.

For inventories, the user cost of capital, assuming a FIFO system, is made up of the cost of financing and the additional corporate taxes that apply to the inflationary appreciation of a company's inventories adjusted for the interest deductibility of the cost of borrowing. The user cost of capital for inventories is defined as

$$(12A\text{-}7) \qquad F'_{inv} = (r + up\ \phi)\ /\ (1 - u)$$

such that $\phi = 1$ for FIFO and $\phi = 0$ for LIFO.

Finally, if we eliminate physical depreciation and tax depreciation allowances, the user cost of capital for land is expressed as follows:

$$(12A\text{-}8) \qquad F'_{Land} = r\ /\ (1 - u).$$

The effective corporate tax rate (U), defined as the difference between the risk-adjusted cost of capital, net of economic depreciation, r_g, and the net-of-tax rate of return required to compensate savers for their savings that are to be invested in the company's particular capital, is for the purpose of this study defined as in the following equation:[18]

$$(12A\text{-}9) \qquad U = (r_g - r_n)/r_g$$

where

$$(12A\text{-}10) \qquad r_g = F - \delta - h$$

and

$$(12A\text{-}11) \qquad r_n = (1 - \gamma)\ [\beta i\ (1 - u') + (1 - \beta)\ g' - p'] + \gamma\ (i - p).$$

As stated previously, the host country economic depreciation rate used, δ, for buildings and machinery was derived from World Bank project data, and the rate for the United States was derived from McKenzie and Mintz (1990). The risk premium, h, was set at 4.5 percent for all countries, based on the estimates used by McKenzie and Mintz (1990).

Tax Holidays

Of the tax incentive schemes analyzed, tax holidays complicate the analysis because the methodology must explicitly account for the time, before the tax holiday expires, when the investment was undertaken.

We will consider the final-form equations without deriving the methodology underlying the cost of capital and effective tax rates during the tax holiday. (See chapter 3, this volume, for such discussion.) Assuming no deferral of depreciation allowances until after the tax holiday period expires, we estimated the cost of capital and effective tax rates based on the following formulas:

$(12A-12) F' = (\delta + r_0 + h)(1 - A_t)/(1 - u_0) + (1 + r_0)(A_t - A_{t-1})/(1 - u_0)$

where

$(12A-13) \quad A_t = u_0 \alpha_1 + \left[u_0 Z_0 (1 - \Upsilon_t) + u_1 Z_1 (1 - \theta_1)/(1 - \theta_0) \Upsilon_t \right]$

for $t^* - t > 0$.

$(12A-14) \quad Z_t = (1 - f\alpha_1)[1 + R_t - (p' - p)] a_2 / \left[a_2 + R_t - (p' - p) \right]$

and

$(12A-15) \qquad \Upsilon_t = (1 - a_2)/[1 + R_0 - (p' - p)]^{t^*-t}.$

The term u_0 represents the corporate tax rate for the tax holiday period ($t^* - t > 0$), which is set to zero. The variable f represents the proportion of the initial allowance written off the undepreciable capital cost base (which is set equal to zero). R_t is the nominal weighted average net-of-corporate tax cost of equity and debt financing at each point of time. The expression A_t represents the present value of the tax depreciation allowances, and Υ_t captures the value of the depreciation deduction after the holiday; the earlier the investment, the lower the depreciation deduction ($\Upsilon_t > \Upsilon_{t-1}$).

The user cost of capital during the tax holiday, equation 12A-12, essentially consists of two terms. The first expression represents the real cost of holding a unit of capital, composed of economic depreciation and financing cost adjusted for the tax value of investment and depreciation allowances at time t^* ($1 - A_t$). The second expression captures the loss in depreciation deductions by investing in period $t - 1$ rather than period t.

The rate of return on capital, net of taxes, for tax holidays is identical to the postholiday rate of return, net of taxes, except that the host country level of debt is lower during the tax holiday period, given the reduced tax benefits of interest deductions taken during the holiday. For this study we reduced the tax holiday host country debt-asset ratio, γ_0, by one-third of the postholiday host country debt-asset ratio (γ), based on empirical results of Bartholdy, Fisher, and Mintz (1987).

We followed the same set of equations used in the absence-of-incentive case to estimate effective tax rates for all tax holiday situations.

Aggregation

The aggregation of the effective tax rates for each industry for each country involved the individual weighting of r_g and r_n by the corresponding capital stock weight, then using equation 12A-9 to determine the effective tax rates. The aggregation of the effective tax rates can be more formally expressed as

$$U'_{ij} = \left[\sum_{ij} (r_{gij} \, \text{csw}_{ij}) - \sum_{ij} (r_{nij} \text{csw}_{ij}) \right] \Big/ \sum_{ij} (r_{gij} \, \text{csw}_{ij})$$

where i represents the three industries and j the capital stocks. The capital stock data used for the United States and Germany for each industry were obtained from McKenzie and Mintz (1990). The capital stock weights used for the CEE countries were derived from World Bank project data.

Notes

This report is based on a detailed analysis of the effect that corporate income tax regimes in Central and Eastern Europe have on the profitability of foreign investment. The results were presented at a workshop sponsored by the Foreign Investment Advisory Service (FIAS), held in the United Nations Industrial Development Organization (UNIDO) Center in Vienna on November 7 and 8, 1991. Participants included representatives of five countries (Bulgaria, Czechoslovakia, Hungary, Poland, and Romania), as well as experts from the Foreign Investment Advisory Service, the Organization for Economic Cooperation and Development (OECD), and UNIDO. Country delegates considered changes to existing corporate income tax policy and analyzed them in regard to their effect on the profitability of foreign investments.

The expenses of this work were shared by FIAS, the Europe and Central Asia Region of the World Bank, the Europe Department of International Finance Corporation (IFC), and the Economics Department of IFC. Staff from these units, as well as from the OECD, contributed to the project. We wish to thank Joel Bergsman for his helpful comments, which much improved our argument.

1. It is assumed that the U.S. company is in an excess foreign tax credit position. That is, the amount of taxes paid to the U.S. government, after application of foreign tax credits, is zero. Because of the 1986 tax reform, many U.S. companies are in this position, so this assumption is the most relevant. For an analysis of the case in which a U.S. multinational corporation pays taxes on remitted income to the U.S. government (deficient tax credit position), see Leechor and Mintz (1991).

2. In table 12-3 and some subsequent ones, the effective tax rate as calculated is negative for some countries. This means that the company would pay no corporate income tax in the host country unless its rate of return was above its cost of capital. Furthermore, it would have a loss on its books for tax purposes that could potentially be used to reduce taxes on other income, which could be either its own future income if losses can be carried forward or income of other linked companies if they could transfer income to it through transfer pricing or other means. The size of the calculated negative tax rate is an indication of the importance of this potential benefit in relation to the income of the company.

3. Indeed, the tax holiday would encourage the use of long-lived capital if companies could delay claiming depreciation deductions until after the holiday. Mintz (1990) compares the effect of mandatory and discretionary depreciation allowances on the investment decisions of companies during and after the tax holiday. See also Mintz and Tsiopoulos (1992), in which effective tax rates in Singapore are compared with those in Taiwan (China) and Thailand for similar holiday investments. Singapore, unlike the latter two countries, allows companies

to delay depreciation deductions until after the holiday. As a result, Singapore's effective tax rate for holiday investments is much lower than the rates in Taiwan (China) and Thailand.

4. The United States has a 34 percent corporate tax rate at the federal level. States increase the statutory tax rate by another 4 percent on average, if we take into account the deductibility of state taxes from the federal tax base.

5. The negative effective tax rate in services for Greece (table 12-1) implies that the tax system subsidizes marginal investment. Any tax losses generated by a marginal investment are being used to reduce taxes paid on inframarginal investment. If the company cannot apply all the tax losses to income earned on other investments, then the losses must be carried forward and charged against future income. The effective tax rate therefore will be higher, possibly zero, or even positive, for a company that expects to pay taxes only in the future. For further discussion, see McKenzie and Mintz (1990).

6. For the investment to have a higher effective tax rate with a tax holiday than it would with no tax holiday, the investment must incur some tax losses during the holiday period. Without the holiday, the company can use tax losses to reduce income earned on other investments, whereas a holiday restricts the full use of the tax losses to reduce taxes paid on other investments. Therefore the effective tax rate when there is a holiday can be higher than it would be when there is not.

7. Note that with the tax holiday the debt-asset ratio has little influence on the effective tax rate in each of the five CEE countries.

8. Romania and Bulgaria have a relatively high effective tax rate in manufacturing because inventories are valued according to the price of the oldest inventory purchased by the company (this is known as the first-in, first-out, or FIFO, method of accounting). When prices are rising, most inventory deductions are valued at historical costs and are unindexed for inflation. Hungary, Czechoslovakia, and Poland allow companies to write off the value of the last-dated unit of inventory purchased by the company (the last-in, first-out, or LIFO, method). This can be similar to a deduction of the replacement cost of inventories.

9. See Leechor and Mintz (1991) for a lengthy discussion of the principles involved in the tax treatment of foreign investment in developing countries.

10. As noted previously, this statement is true only if companies must write down assets for tax depreciation purposes during the tax holiday. If they can delay depreciation until afterward, the holiday provides a significant benefit to depreciable long-lived capital.

11. For developing economies, McLure and others (1989) advocate a cash flow tax that would require expensing capital instead of deducting depreciation and interest at the corporate and personal levels. The cash flow base has several attractive features, particularly its simple treatment of depreciation and financial income. Many complexities are associated with cash flow taxation, however; especially important are those that arise from international transactions and the incentives for tax evasion that are evoked when other countries continue to levy income taxes. See Mintz and Seade (1991) for a discussion of the implementation problems associated with both income and cash flow taxation.

12. Note that we do not analyze whether the government would gain or lose corporate tax revenue under a 20 percent corporate tax rate compared with the current tax holiday system.

13. The international linkages undermine the ability of a CEE country to pursue a cash flow tax when other governments rely on income taxation. For

example, multinational companies can take advantage of the expensing of capital and interest by using debt raised by the parent to finance investment undertaken in the country with the cash flow tax. See Mintz and Seade (1991) for further discussion.

14. See De Long and Summers (1991).

15. A refundable investment allowance would imply that the government gives the company a refund, or its equivalent, equal to the tax value of the incentive. For example, suppose that a company invests $100 and faces a corporate tax rate of 40 percent. If fully used, the investment allowance tax benefit is $40. If the credit is refundable, the government would give a $40 rebate or grant if the company has no tax payable during the year. Alternatively, the government could allow the company to carry back deductions or credits against taxes paid in previous years or carry forward deductions at an interest rate to preserve their value over time.

16. The investment tax allowance would allow a company to write off 20 percent of qualifying investment expenditure from taxable income. We also assume that annual tax depreciation allowances would not be affected. If the corporate tax rate is 40 percent, the 20 percent investment tax allowance is equivalent to an 8 percent investment tax credit.

17. These results reflect the effect of high inflation rates in Bulgaria, Hungary, and Poland. The negative effective tax rates imply that the investments would be subsidized, although the subsidy would be reduced if inflation went much lower or companies used debt less to finance their investments.

18. For the CEE countries that have high inflation rates (Bulgaria, Hungary, and Poland), the effective tax rate is modified slightly to the following formula:

$$(12A\text{-}9')\qquad\qquad U' = (r_g - r_n)/r_n .$$

For those three countries, equation 12A-9' was preferred to equation 12A-9 to avoid a technical complexity associated with a negative cost of capital. The gross return to capital (r_g) for many assets was negative and with equation 12A-9 the effective tax rate would turn out positive, when it should be negative.

References

Andersson, Krister. 1991. "Taxation and the Cost of Capital in Hungary and Poland." *International Monetary Fund Staff Papers* 38 (2): 327–55.

Bartholdy, Jan, Gordon Fisher, and Jack M. Mintz. 1987. "Taxation and the Financial Policy of Firms: Theory and Empirical Applications to Canada." Discussion Paper 324. Economic Council of Canada, Ottawa.

Boadway, Robin W., Neil Bruce, and Jack M. Mintz. 1984. "Taxation, Inflation, and the Effective Marginal Tax Rate on Capital in Canada." *Canadian Journal of Economics* 15: 278–93.

Boadway, Robin W., Neil Bruce, and Jack M. Mintz. 1987. *Taxes on Capital Income in Canada: Analysis and Policy.* Toronto, Can.: Canadian Tax Foundation.

Bulow, J., and L. H. Summers. 1984. "The Taxation of Risky Assets." *Journal of Political Economy* 92: 20–39.

De Long, J. Bradford, and Lawrence H. Summers. 1991. "Equipment Investment and Growth." *Quarterly Journal of Economics* 106 (2): 445–502.

IMF (International Monetary Fund). 1989. *International Financial Statistics.* Washington, D.C.

King, Mervyn A., and Don Fullerton. 1984. *The Taxation of Income from Capital: A Comparative Study of the United States, the United Kingdom, Sweden, and West Germany.* Chicago, Ill.: University of Chicago Press.

Leechor, Chad, and Jack M. Mintz. 1991. "Taxation of International Income by a Capital Importing Country: The Perspective of Thailand." In Javad Khalilzadeh-Shirazi and Anwar Shah, eds., *Tax Policy in Developing Countries.* Washington, D.C.: World Bank.

McKenzie, Kenneth J., and Jack M. Mintz. 1990. "Tax Effects on the Cost of Capital: A Canada-United States Comparison." In John Shoven and John Whalley, eds., *Canada-U.S. Tax Comparisons.* Chicago, Ill.: University of Chicago Press.

McLure, Charles E., Jr., Richard Bird, Victor Thuryoni, and George Zodrow. 1989. *The Taxation of Income from Business and Capital in Colombia.* Durham, N.C.: Duke University Press.

Mintz, Jack M. 1990. "Corporate Tax Holidays and Investment." *The World Bank Economic Review* 4 (1): 81–102.

Mintz, Jack M., and Jesus Seade. 1991. "Cash Flow or Income? The Choice of Base for Company Taxation." *The World Bank Research Observer* 6 (2): 177–90.

Mintz, Jack M., and Thomas Tsiopoulos. 1992. "Contrasting Corporate Tax Policies: Canada and Taiwan." Toronto, Can.

OECD (Organization for Economic Cooperation and Development). 1991. "Taxation and International Capital Flows." Paris.

13

DO TAXES MATTER FOR FOREIGN DIRECT INVESTMENT?

Anwar Shah and Joel Slemrod

THE 1980s SAW a remarkable growth in foreign direct investment (FDI). Along with this growth came a renewed interest in the effect of FDI on economic performance (of both the host and the home countries) and in the question of appropriate government policy toward FDI. Not surprisingly, a critical consideration in this discussion is the responsiveness of FDI to taxation of the income that it generates. If FDI is not responsive to taxation, then it may be an appropriate target for taxation by the host country, which can raise revenue without sacrificing the economic benefits of FDI. If, however, the volume of FDI declines with taxation, the host country must consider the tradeoff between the possible revenue gains from increased taxation and the economic costs of discouraging FDI. This issue is important for countries in which FDI has penetrated deeply and the revenue raised from taxing FDI represents a significant fraction of total tax revenues. For example, in Ecuador, Egypt, Indonesia, Nigeria, Peru, and Trinidad and Tobago, tax payments by U.S. corporations alone as a share of host country corporate tax revenues exceed 10 percent (Alworth 1988: 33).

Because of the ready availability of data on investment to and from the United States, most of the empirical literature since 1980 on the tax sensitivity of FDI has focused on U.S. inward FDI. In this chapter we extend the standard methodology used in these studies to examine the effect of taxation on FDI in Mexico. We proceed as follows. In the first section we review the empirical literature on FDI since the early 1980s in the United States. We then discuss the salient features of the environment for FDI in Mexico that are relevant for extending the research done on U.S. FDI. After presenting an empirical framework, we go on to outline the data issues and review the empirical results. Last, we offer some concluding comments.

Review of the Existing Empirical Literature

The empirical study of the effects of taxation on inward FDI in the United States was pioneered by Hartman (1984). Using annual data from 1965 to 1979, he estimated the response of FDI, both for investment financed by retained earnings and for transfers from abroad, to three variables: the after-tax rate of return realized by foreign investors in the United States, the overall after-tax rate of return on capital in the United States, and the ratio of the tax rate on U.S. capital owned by foreigners to that on U.S. capital owned by U.S. investors. The first two variables are proxies for the prospective return to new FDI, the first term being more appropriate for firms that are considering expanding their current operations and the second more applicable to the acquisition of existing assets. The third variable captures the possibility that tax changes that apply only to U.S. investors will, by affecting the valuation of assets, alter the foreign investor's cost and, therefore, the return from acquisition of the asset. Hartman does not measure an effective withholding tax rate or the foreign income tax rate applied to the aggregate of FDI. He defends the absence of these variables by noting the likelihood that the average values of these tax rates are relatively constant over time. Furthermore, no attempt is made to measure the rate of return available abroad to foreign investors.

Hartman's (1984) regressions show a positive association of both after-tax rate of return variables with the ratio of FDI financed by retained earnings to U.S. gross national product (GNP). They show a negative association of this FDI/GNP ratio with the relative tax rate on foreign-owned capital as compared with that on domestically owned capital. The model does not explain investment financed by transfers from abroad nor that financed from retained earnings, although coefficients of all three variables have the expected sign and are significantly different from zero. Hartman (1984) concludes that the effect of taxes on FDI, regardless of the source of financing, is quite strong.

Subsequent studies of U.S. FDI have essentially followed Hartman's approach, differing primarily in the data series used. Boskin and Gale (1987) use the updated tax rate and rate of return series from Feldstein and Jun (1987) to reestimate Hartman's equations. Although the estimated elasticities of FDI to the rates of return on capital are somewhat smaller, none of the point estimates changes by more than one standard deviation. Boskin and Gale also extend the sample forward to 1984, and in some cases backward to 1956, and experiment with a variety of alternative explanatory variables and functional forms. The empirical results are somewhat sensitive to sample period and specification, but they show that Hartman's qualitative conclusions are robust.

Young (1988) uses revised data on investment, GNP, and rates of return earned by foreigners to estimate similar equations. The estimated elasticities with respect to the rate of return realized by foreigners and the relative tax rate are larger, but the equations for new transfers of funds estimated by using the 1956–84 data yield very poor results.

Newlon (1987), while attempting to replicate Hartman's and Boskin and Gale's results, discovered that the series measuring the rate of return on FDI, used in all earlier papers, had been miscalculated from the original Bureau of Economic Analysis data for the years 1965 to 1973. If the corrected series is used, the equation explaining FDI from retained earnings does not fit as well, although the equation explaining FDI from transfers fits better. In the former case, the estimated coefficients on the return to FDI and the tax ratio are slightly larger in absolute value and remain statistically significant, although the estimated coefficient on the net return in the United States is smaller and is no longer statistically significant. For transfers of funds, the estimated coefficient on the return to FDI is much larger and becomes significant, although the estimated coefficient on the net return in the United States becomes smaller and insignificant. When the sample containing the corrected series is extended, Newlon's results also differ from those of Hartman and Boskin and Gale; in particular, the equation explaining FDI from the transfer of funds fits poorly, and all estimated coefficients are insignificant.

The narrow focus of the previous empirical research is reason enough to explore alternative methodologies. Furthermore, the standard method is problematic and could be improved. In the studies cited, the disincentive to investment caused by the tax system is implicitly measured by an average tax rate, computed as total taxes paid divided by a measure of profits. The incentive to undertake new investment, however, depends on the effective marginal tax rate, which, as is well known, can deviate substantially from an average tax rate concept. Slemrod (1990) extends and updates a Hartman-style model of aggregate FDI in the United States. He does so in part by replacing the average rate of tax by a measure of the marginal effective tax rate on new investment; U.S. effective rates of taxation are found to have a negative effect on total FDI and on new transfers of funds, but not on FDI from retained earnings.

A second problem is that none of the studies estimates the effect of the home country's tax system on FDI in the United States. Of course, collecting the appropriate data is difficult and perhaps, as Hartman argued, these tax rates have not varied much. The observed stability of tax rates, though, applies to statutory rates and not necessarily to the more appropriate effective marginal tax rates. Hartman (1985) has also argued that because the home country's tax reduces the parent company's return to an investment and the opportunity cost of making an investment, remitting a dividend to the parent, only the host country's tax system matters for investment coming from subsidiaries' earnings. For any subsidiary whose desired investment exceeds earnings, however, the tax due upon repatriation of earnings does matter. This situation is likely to arise for newly formed subsidiaries, rendering investigation of the effect of both the home country's rate of taxation and its system of taxing foreign source income worthwhile.

Finally, as stressed by Newlon, the interpretation of the coefficient on the rate of return to FDI is problematic. This rate of return is defined as the after-tax income from direct investment divided by the stock of direct investment. When the home country has a foreign tax credit with deferral, it is often optimal for the subsidiary to finance investment by first using retained earnings and to use funds transferred from the parent firm only when these earnings are exhausted. This hierarchy of financing implies that whenever a subsidiary's investment exceeds its retained earnings, its retained earnings will exactly equal its income. In these cases we would expect a direct association between the calculated rate of return on FDI (in which after-tax income is the numerator) and retained earnings, regardless of whether the average rate of return in fact influences decisions concerning new FDI. As Newlon notes, if subsidiaries were following a fixed dividend payout rule (for example, paying out a fixed fraction of income), a direct association between income and retained earnings would also be observed.

FDI in Mexico

Historically, because foreign investment was viewed as a vehicle used by other countries to gain political and economic domination of Mexico, government policy through the National Foreign Investment Commission has emphasized regulating rather than promoting foreign investment. From 1948 to 1982 the policy toward foreign investment became increasingly restrictive. First, important industries such as telecommunications, electric power, timber, and film distribution were nationalized. Second, foreign investment in most industries was restricted to minority participation subject to prior authorization from the central government. The discouragement of foreign participation by this regulatory environment resulted in an annual average net FDI flow of less than 1 percent of gross domestic product from 1950 to 1985. A dramatic reversal of these policies began to take place in 1986 with the initiation of a debt-to-equity conversion scheme and the exemption of small-to-medium levels of investment from government approval for foreign majority participation. Beginning in 1987, majority FDI participation in specified sectors was permitted on a case-by-case basis. In a press release on May 19, 1989, President Carlos Salinas de Gortari announced a major shift in Mexican policy toward foreign investment, stating:

We are a mature country with the judicial, intellectual and economic capacity to assimilate the largest flow of foreign investment. On behalf of all Mexicans, we will institute new regulations to encourage the types of foreign investment that support our economic policy objectives without compromising our sovereignty and freedom of action.

Major changes in the foreign investment regulations soon followed. Under the new regulations, majority investment in nonrestricted sectors meeting all of the following six criteria is eligible to receive automatic approval:

- The investment must be less than 250 billion pesos (in 1989 pesos; about US$100 million).
- The capital must originate from outside Mexico.
- The project must be located outside the country's three major industrial cities (Mexico City, Monterrey, and Guadalajara).
- The foreign exchange cost must be spread evenly over a period of three years.
- The investment must provide permanent jobs and training.
- The project must use technologies satisfying existing environmental regulations.

Furthermore, limited access to the Mexican stock market is permitted through special trust funds. Temporary access to some sectors normally reserved for Mexican citizens is allowed under twenty-year trusts for investment in Mexican companies that have high export potential or are in financial distress. Thirty-year trust funds provide access to otherwise restricted geographical zones such as coastal and border areas. New regulations stipulate automatic approval of applications on which the National Foreign Investment Commission fails to reach a decision within forty-five days of initial submission.

It is clear that whatever the demand for FDI in Mexico has been in the postwar period, the supply of available opportunities for FDI was severely limited until changes were initiated in the mid-1980s. Thus it will be important to control for this in the analysis. If demand were always limited by these regulations in a binding way, there would be no interesting story to tell about taxation. Data on FDI flows indicate a positive correlation between FDI flows and after-tax rates of return in FDI. This suggests that these limitations were not always binding and therefore that tax influences on demand did play a role in the volume of FDI into Mexico.

The instability of the Mexican economy also poses analytical problems. High inflation rates (114 percent in 1987) and nominal interest rates (92 percent in 1987) have dramatic consequences for the calculations of effective tax rates on new investment. The standard assumption used in such calculations—that current values for inflation, interest rates, tax rates, and tax depreciation rates will persist in the future—is unlikely to be accurate, but reasonable alternative assumptions about expectations are not obvious. This problem suggests that some measure of the average rate of taxation (taxes paid divided by a measure of economic income) may be a more accurate measure of the tax system's disincentives than an analytically constructed marginal tax rate.

Mexico taxes nonresidents only on the income originating from Mexican sources. Mexico is a member of the Latin America Integration Association, which is designed to provide preferential treatment to member countries in matters of trade and taxation. Mexico has not yet concluded any comprehensive treaty on avoidance of double taxation or tax sparing with any other country.

One important change in the tax code concerned the treatment of income of subsidiaries and branches of foreign companies. Until 1989, establishing a subsidiary rather than a branch office in Mexico was a tax-preferred alternative, since the retained earnings of a subsidiary of a foreign corporation were exempt from taxation, dividends being taxed upon distribution to a parent. All income of a branch office, in contrast, was taxed upon accrual. Following changes in the Mexican tax code in 1989, the different treatment of subsidiary and branch income was eliminated. The major features of the taxation of income earned in Mexico by foreigners, as revised in 1989, are summarized in appendix 13A.

Some Theory and the Empirical Model

The modern theoretical literature has, for the most part, concluded that the demand for FDI is primarily an issue of industrial organization. Dunning (1985: 6–7) argues that foreign investment by firms is more likely if the firms (a) possess ownership-specific advantages in relation to host country firms in sourcing markets; (b) find it profitable to use these advantages themselves rather than to lease them to host country firms; and (c) find it profitable to use their ownership-specific advantages in the host country rather than at home. This theory of international production, usually referred to as the "eclectic" theory, has been tested in a large body of empirical literature (see Dunning 1985). Much of this research has been cross-sectional, relating the extent of foreign investment in a given sector to characteristics of that sector representing ownership-specific and location-specific advantages. The authors of studies of the effects of taxation on FDI have generally taken the view that firms must weigh the benefits of foreign investment against the tax consequences of carrying out FDI. We hypothesize that the tax systems of both Mexico and the firm's home country affect not only the incentives to invest but also the best way to finance a given level of FDI.

Mexico asserts the right to tax income originating within its borders, including income generated by multinationals. The effective tax rate on this income depends in a complicated way on the statutory tax rate on corporate income; the extent of tax credits granted; and the definition of the tax base, including the system of depreciation and the way in which gross income and deductions are allocated between Mexican source and foreign source. There are two ways to measure the effective tax rate on new investment. In the analytical method pioneered by Jorgenson (1963), the level of pretax return required for a stylized investment to yield a given after-tax return is calculated. The wedge between the pretax and the after-tax rates of return is a measure of the tax-related disincentive to invest. This procedure requires details on the tax code, the rate of inflation, economic depreciation rates, and the proportion and costs of debt and equity finance. Thus the effective tax rate on FDI from equity transfers and retained earnings would be different.

The alternative method is to calculate the ratio of taxes paid in a given year to a measure of income that is independent of the definition of taxable income. This method may capture some of the features of the tax law that are left out of the analytical method. It also may capture more accurately some features that are present in the analytical models but are inadequately represented by the stylized assumptions that must be made to calculate marginal effective tax rates. As argued above, because of the extreme volatility of the Mexican inflation rate, such an average tax.rate may be more appropriate.

The multinational's country of residence may also tax the income that is generated in Mexico. Not all countries do so, however. Some countries, notably France, the Netherlands, and Mexico itself, operate a "territorial" system for active (in other words, nonportfolio) income earned abroad. Under a territorial system, the home country levies no tax of its own on the foreign source income. Under the "worldwide" system of taxation, used by Canada, Japan, the United Kingdom, and the United States, among other countries, the home country asserts the right to tax the multinational's income regardless of where it is generated. In order to avoid two tiers of taxation, these countries offer their multinationals a limited credit against domestic tax liability for certain taxes paid to foreign governments. The credit is generally limited to the tax liability that the foreign source income would incur if home country tax rules were applied. Finally, in most cases the tax liability (and credit) on subsidiaries' foreign source income is deferred until dividends are repatriated to the parent company, but foreign source income of branch operations is taxable upon accrual.

Let τ_m be the effective rate of tax on new investment imposed by the Mexican tax system. For a multinational from a country using the territorial system, τ_m is also the total tax burden imposed. For a multinational from a country with a worldwide system of taxation, the home country's taxation must also be considered. The "old" view of this extra level of taxation is given by $\max[\alpha(t_u - \tau_m),0]$, where t_u is the tax rate of the home country and α is a value between zero and one that reflects the benefits of being able to defer the tax liability on subsidiaries' foreign source income until the earnings are repatriated. Note that t_u is generally closer to a statutory rate than to an effective tax rate on investment, since the home country tax base for foreign source income generally does not allow such things as accelerated depreciation and investment tax credits that affect taxable income from domestic operations. In cases in which earnings are never repatriated (α is equal to zero) or when the firm is in an excess credit position ($\tau_m > t_u$), so taxes paid to the host country generate foreign tax credits that may be used to completely offset the tax that would otherwise be due upon repatriation, the home country tax is irrelevant. An opposite extreme case occurs when α is equal to one, which implies that the host country tax liability of the multinational can be fully offset by the home country tax credits.

The "new" view of the total tax burden on FDI, expounded by Hartman (1984, 1985), distinguishes between debt and equity financing. If investment is financed by the retained earnings of the foreign subsidiary, then the home country tax rate is irrelevant and the total tax burden is τ_m. Any taxes due upon repatriation to the home country are also irrelevant to the investment decision. The home country tax rate would be relevant for multinationals that are contemplating a transfer of funds to a foreign subsidiary, so the total tax burden on FDI in this case is $\tau_m + \alpha \cdot (t_u - \tau_m)$.

Scholes and Wolfson (1989) have suggested that the ownership of a given stock of domestic capital depends on the relative tax rate paid by alternative owners. This implies that, in the contest for ownership of Mexican capital, foreign owners are more likely to be successful the lower the ratio $[\tau_m + \alpha \cdot (t_u - \tau_m)]/\tau_m$. (This, of course, applies only if the home country operates a worldwide system of taxation.) The surprising implication of this analysis is that, as long as α is greater than zero and t_u exceeds τ_m, an increase in τ_m, the tax rate in Mexico, will increase foreign ownership of Mexican capital. This would be so because an increase in τ_m, although fully borne by potential Mexican owners, is partly offset for foreign owners by foreign tax credits. Thus the relative tax burden on foreign owners from countries with worldwide tax systems is reduced. Of course, to the extent that τ_m reduces the incentive to undertake investment in Mexico, both domestically owned and foreign-owned investment will decline. The overall effect on FDI thus depends on the relative strength of the Scholes-Wolfson ownership effect and the volume effect. Furthermore, the ownership effect applies only to investment from countries with a worldwide tax system and only to the extent that home country tax rates exceed those in Mexico. Additional taxes paid to the Mexican government thus do in fact generate additional foreign tax credits.

The foregoing discussion suggests that a general empirical model of the effect of taxation on FDI in Mexico has the following form:

(13-1) $$\text{FDI}_s = f_s\left[\tau_m \,;\, L\,(t_u - \tau_m),\, X\right]$$

where X is a vector of nontax factors that affect FDI, the subscript s refers to the source of investment financing, and L is an (inverse) index of the excess credit status of the investing countries. The presumption is that the greater the extent of excess credit status, the smaller the effect of the home country's tax rate. For empirical estimation, equation 13-1 is specified as follows:

(13-2a) $$\text{FDI}_T = a_0 + a_1\tau_m + a_2\,(t_u - \tau_m) + a_3 \cdot L \cdot (t_u - \tau_m) + a_4 X + u_T$$

(13-2b) $$\text{FDI}_R = b_0 + b_1\tau_m + b_2\,(t_u - \tau_m) + b_3 \cdot L \cdot (t_u - \tau_m) + b_4 X + u_R$$

where the subscript T denotes FDI financed by transfers of funds and the subscript R denotes FDI financed by retained earnings.

The Data and Estimation

Aggregate data on stocks and flows of FDI and other relevant variables for the period 1965–85 have been assembled from a variety of sources. A few key variables used in the study are described here, and details of variable construction are given in appendix 13B.

Data on FDI levels come primarily from the Banco de Mexico, which provides substantial details on the financial flows of firms with foreign capital, including the amount of transfers and reinvested earnings, and a breakdown of FDI by economic sector and the country of origin. FDI from 1965 to 1987 is shown in figure 13-1. From 1965 to 1977, FDI increased slowly but steadily. The beginning of the oil boom in the late 1970s led to dramatic increases in FDI, which peaked in 1981 at US$2 billion. The end of the oil boom in 1981 coincided with a sharp drop in FDI. FDI growth accelerated again in 1984 with the initiation of debt-equity conversion schemes and the exemption of small-to-medium FDI from the government control and approval process. Figures 13-2 and 13-3 show details of FDI financed by transfers and retained earnings, respectively, during the period 1965 to 1987. Both types of FDI follow

Figure 13-1. Foreign Direct Investment in Mexico, 1965–87

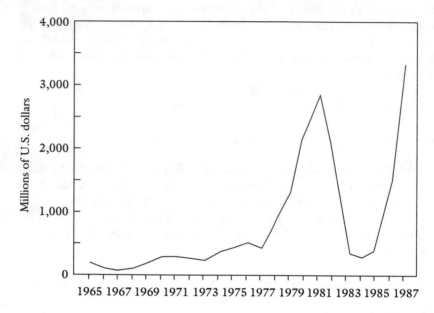

Source: Banco de México (various issues).

Figure 13-2. Foreign Direct Investment in Mexico Financed by Transfer of Funds from Parent Company, 1965–87

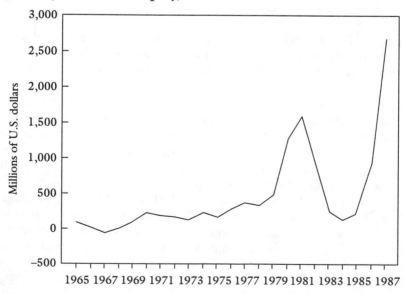

Source: Banco de México (various issues).

Figure 13-3. Foreign Direct Investment in Mexico Financed by Retained Earnings of Multinationals, 1965–87

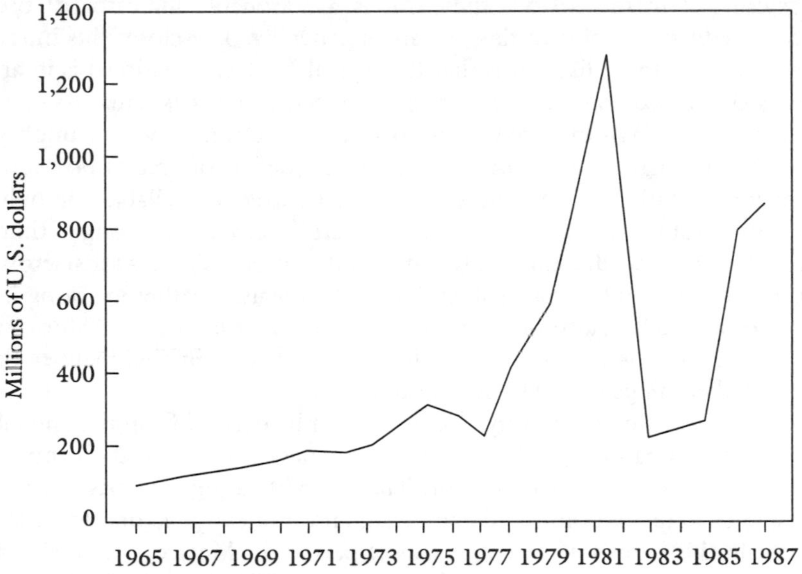

Source: Banco de México (various issues).

the same broad trends, but transfers become the dominant source of financing in the mid- to late 1980s.

We compute several tax concepts as measures of tax disincentives in this chapter, beginning with the simple Mexican (t_m) and U.S. (t_u) statutory tax rates. We also develop four alternative measures of the tax disincentive to new investment in Mexico, three marginal and one average (see appendix 13B for details). First, using the standard Auerbach-Hall-Jorgenson methodology, we compute a historical series on the marginal effective tax rate on new aggregate investment in Mexico (τ_m). We obtain a comparable series for the United States from Auerbach and Hines (1988). Then we calculate marginal effective tax rates for transfers and for retained earnings. The marginal effective tax rate measures are conceptually attractive but, as discussed above, a highly inflationary environment with financing constraints diminishes their usefulness. Therefore we calculate an average effective tax rate measure based on corporate tax liability per dollar of value added for Mexico (T_m) and the United States (T_u). The choice of this particular formulation of the average effective tax rate is based primarily on the completeness of the data series for this measure.

The index of the excess foreign tax credit position of investing multinationals (L) is calculated as the ratio of aggregate foreign tax credit claimed to foreign tax credits available to U.S. multinationals investing in Mexico. Because U.S. investment has accounted for about two-thirds of Mexican FDI in the period studied, it is a reasonable indicator of the excess credit status of investing countries generally. The closer this index is to zero, the more likely it is that the typical U.S. multinational is in an excess credit position. At the extreme where this index is equal to one, all available foreign tax credits are immediately claimed, which implies that the multinationals are in an excess limit (deficit of credit) position. A major limitation of this measure is that data were available for only five years; values for the remaining years are interpolated. Longer time series data are available on an alternative but conceptually less satisfactory measure—the credit status of all U.S. multinationals, whether investing in Mexico or not. Because of the presence of some firms with no Mexican investment in this sample, use of this latter measure in the analyses of reinvested earnings would be subject to caveats.

A useful measure of country risk factors can be derived from the annual country credit ratings published by the Business International Corporation and the Institutional Investor. These credit ratings are based on a composite index of political, commercial, and monetary factors. In order to obtain this index for the entire sample period for Mexico, the Business International Corporation index for 1965 to 1979 was spliced with the Institutional Investor index for 1979–87.

Black market exchange rate premia are used as an index of regulation in Mexico. Exchange rate premia in Mexico correlate well with the past history of regulation and, therefore, serve as a reasonable proxy of the regulatory environment. This is, however, not a fully satisfactory measure of regulations because it may simply be capturing the effects of import restrictions. To capture the effects of protective trade barriers on inward investment, we calculate effective tariff rates using data on import duties and the value of imports from various Mexican government publications.

A wide array of variables is available to implement the empirical models specified in equations 2a and 2b. The modeler must choose among several measures of tax disincentives; two measures of multinationals' excess credit status; and a host of nontax factors, including quantitative restrictions, unemployment rates in the host and home countries, and exchange rate and price movements.

The biggest dilemma in model estimation is presented by the choices available for the tax rate variable. Economic theory does not provide much guidance in this respect beyond a preference for marginal tax rates, so final variable selection was done primarily on the basis of model selection tests. Mexican data show a great deal of variability from 1977 to 1987 because of oil booms and busts. We first used an intercept dummy variable with a value of one for the oil boom and bust period and zero otherwise in various regressions, but when it was found to be insignificant, we dropped it from further analysis. Note that the economic environment associated with oil boom and bust cycles is well captured by credit ratings, and thus it is possible to isolate tax effects from the effects associated with a general deterioration or amelioration of economic activity. Furthermore, the marginal effective tax rate incorporates the rate of return to FDI and therefore captures the variability of profits over time.

As a first step, in model specification we use the Lagrangian multiplier test to screen regressors. Subsequently, we formulate several alternative models and conduct standard model selection tests to pick the "best" model. These tests take the general form of the residual sum of squares multiplied by a penalty factor. The penalty factor varies directly with the number of estimated parameters, so an increase in model complexity would reduce the residual sum of squares but raise the penalty. Two of the better regressions based on these tests are presented in table 13-1.[1]

FDI from transfers is very sensitive to the Mexican marginal effective tax rate. The estimated coefficient on τ_m implies a startlingly high elasticity of –6.25 of FDI transfers with respect to the marginal effective tax rate when

Table 13-1. Estimated Foreign Direct Investment Equations for Mexico, 1965–87

Independent variable	Dependent variable	
	FDI financed by transfers[a]	FDI financed by retained earnings[b]
Marginal effective tax rate in Mexico (τ_m)	–6,766.7 (–2.4)	–2,593.7 (–2.9)
U.S. statutory tax rate minus Mexican tax rate ($t_u - \tau_m$)	–3,994.5 (–0.8)	–6,687.5 (–2.7)
Excess credit status of multinationals $[L(t_u - \tau_m)]$	–3,012.1 (–0.6)	5,166.0 (2.5)
Country credit rating	34.6 (3.8)	17.1 (3.0)
Index of regulations	–394.6 (–1.6)	–340.0 (–1.9)
Effective tariff rate	2,507.9 (1.1)	–1,573.9 (–0.9)
Constant	2,341.1 (1.7)	3,415.6 (5.1)

Note: t-statistics are in parentheses.
a. R^{-2} = .89; log likelihood = –157.7.
b. R^{-2} = .69; log likelihood = –146.9.
Source: Authors' calculations.

evaluated at the mean values over the period; a more reasonable elasticity of -0.79 is obtained when evaluated at 1987 values. Since the elasticity of marginal effective tax rates with respect to the Mexican statutory tax rate is only -0.2, the elasticity of FDI transfers with respect to changes in Mexican statutory tax rates is -1.24 at mean values and -0.16 at 1987 values. The large difference in elasticities calculated at mean and 1987 values results from the increased magnitude of FDI in Mexico after the mid-1980s. What would have been a large change in FDI in previous years represents a much smaller change in relative magnitude in the later years. This same fact implies that the behavior of FDI after the mid-1980s is critical to the estimation results. For example, if the years 1985–1987 are excluded in estimating the equation for FDI transfers, the large negative coefficient on τ_m disappears. This suggests that future research should focus on whether the surge in FDI transfers and decline in τ_m in the late 1980s were in fact causally related or coincidental.

The tax differential variable, $t_u - \tau_m$, and the composite variable on the credit status of multinationals, $L(t_u - \tau_m)$, have signs consistent with a priori expectations but are not statistically significant. It is, however, interesting to note that the coefficients imply that for the extreme excess limit case $(L = 1)$, it is approximately true that the t_u but not the τ_m provides a disincentive to investment; in general, though, both home and host country tax rates mattered. The empirical results weakly suggest that the regulatory environment in Mexico discourages foreign investment but that protective trade barriers have a positive effect on FDI.

The estimated equation for FDI from retained earnings indicates that such FDI is sensitive to the Mexican marginal effective tax rate, Mexican and U.S. tax differences, the credit position of the multinationals, and Mexico's credit ratings and regulations. The elasticity of reinvested earnings with respect to τ_m is -1.5; the elasticity with respect to the Mexican statutory tax rate is -0.56 and with respect to Mexican and U.S. tax differences is -2.8 (all calculated at 1987 values). A change in the credit status of multinationals toward excess limit positively influenced their decisions to reinvest rather than to repatriate their earnings, with an estimated elasticity of 1.9 at 1987 values. These results are qualitatively robust even if the 1985–87 period is eliminated.

It should be noted that in various formulations of the models, the marginal effective tax rate variable showed a great deal of consistency as a determinant of transfers and retained earnings. Estimated coefficients of average tax rate and statutory tax rate variables, in contrast, were sensitive to model specification. This instability of coefficients was partly attributable to a degree of collinearity among a subset of variables. An unexplained aspect of this instability is that the coefficient estimates for regressions on retained earnings were less robust than those for transfers.

Thus the conclusions reached in the following sections merely represent our best judgments based on available, imperfect data. It is conceivable that different conclusions could be reached if a better set of data were used.

Overall, the results are consistent with the old view that the source of financing is not critical to the tax sensitivity of FDI and suggest that both the host and home country tax regimes matter for FDI in Mexico. Because of the difficulty in accurately measuring effective tax rates and the sensitivity of the results to alternative forms of the tax rate variables, however, these results concerning tax sensitivity must be interpreted with great caution. In addition to taxation, the regulatory framework and the overall economic and political climate in the country appear to influence FDI transfers and reinvestments in Mexico.

Policy Implications

Our analysis suggests that FDI in Mexico shows a great deal of sensitivity to the Mexican tax regime. If this conclusion stands up in further investigations, it implies that Mexico must aim for tax rates neither higher nor lower than the U.S. rates. Higher rates would discourage investment, whereas lower rates would allow a transfer of revenue from Mexico to the U.S. treasury through the operation of U.S. foreign tax credit provisions. Note, however, that the U.S. Tax Reform Act of 1986 pushed more U.S. multinationals into excess credit status, thus increasing the likely disincentive effects of Mexican taxation of FDI and reducing the possibility that reductions in Mexican tax rates will simply transfer revenues to the United States. This implies that, for U.S. multinationals that operate globally, a Mexican tax rate below that of the United States may be appropriate (see chapter 6 in this volume).

Mexico has already implemented tax reforms to make its tax regime competitive with those of the United States and Canada. Furthermore, effective taxes on reinvestments in Mexico are lower than the tax on repatriations, which provides incentives for increasing retained earnings. Still, the 2 percent assets tax initiated in 1989 may, because of its partial noncreditability against U.S. tax liabilities, discourage potential investors. This tax could be replaced by an alternative minimum tax with an adjusted base that would include tax preferences as part of taxable income. Such a tax could function the same as the assets tax but would be fully creditable against U.S. tax liabilities. Because the tax changes introduced in 1989 do not contain any special disincentives for foreign investment, perhaps public policy attention in Mexico should focus on accelerating the process of deregulation of FDI that has already been initiated.

Appendix 13A. Taxation of Foreign Investment Income in Mexico

The corporate income tax base is now indexed. Taxable profits (defined as gross receipts minus costs, business expenses, dividends corresponding to previous periods of earnings, and net losses carried forward from other periods) are subject to tax at a rate of 35 percent (the rate was 42 percent before 1987). Depreciation deductions are indexed, or alternatively, the present value of depreciation calculated at a discount rate of 7.5 percent may be deducted fully in all regions except major metropolitan areas and in all sectors except for the automobile industry. In major metropolitan areas only 60 percent of the present value of depreciation can be deducted in the first year; the remaining 40 percent is subjected to capital consumption allowances over time. An assets tax of 2 percent of the average value of total assets of business enterprises is levied, but it may be credited to income tax liability. Dividends are no longer deductible by the corporation distributing them nor includable in the gross income of the recipient. The withholding tax on dividend distributions varies from 0 percent to 40 percent, depending on the tax regime faced by the recipient and on whether the dividends are paid from accumulated earnings already taxed—the "net tax profit account"—or from previously untaxed sources.

In 1991 the withholding tax rate on interest income paid to nonresidents was set at 35 percent, and the rate on payments for technical assistance, transfer of technology, and fees (including royalties for patents when licensed in connection with the rendering of technical assistance) was set at 21 percent. Payments for the use of other royalties, such as for the licensing of trademarks or trade names, and for the use of patents without the rendering of technical assistance are taxed at 40 percent. Goods in bonded warehouses are subject to a 3 percent tax either on the value on which import duties are assessed or on the declared value, whichever is greater. All businesses in Mexico are obliged to share 10 percent of their profits with employees. Employers are obliged to contribute 11 percent of workers' weekly wages to social security coverage, 1 percent of wages to children's nurseries, and from 5 to 167 percent of wages to an occupational risk fund. In addition, employers contribute 5 percent of wages to the National Housing Fund and 1 percent of wages in support of education. The general 15 percent value added tax is applicable to all transactions concluded in the border and free zones.

In 1991, immediate full expensing of the present value of capital consumption allowances, calculated at a 7.5 percent discount rate, became available to all investors in nonmetropolitan areas, regardless of their resident status. Incentives in the form of investments and employment tax credit certificates for priority industries and special regions are available but only to Mexican residents. The "inbond assembly" industries established in border areas may be completely owned and operated by foreigners, provided Mexicans are hired to process the imported raw materials using imported equipment and the processed goods are exported back to the country of origin. Table 13A-1 provides a comparative perspective on taxation of business income in Mexico and the major source countries for foreign investment. It shows that the Mexican tax system is fully competitive with the tax regime in the home countries of foreign investors. Mexico has also moved some distance toward adoption of a full cash flow taxation in a future year.

Appendix 13B. Data Definitions

In the following, brief descriptions of various data series used in this chapter are presented.

Index of Excess Credit Status (L)

These data are obtained from the U.S. Department of Commerce. The index is calculated as follows:

$$L = \frac{A}{B + C - D + E}$$

where A = foreign tax credit claimed; B = foreign taxes paid or accrued; C = foreign taxes deemed paid; D = deductions for certain foreign taxes; and E = taxes carried over.

Marginal Effective Tax Rates

The following formulation, developed by Auerbach (1990), is used in the calculation of marginal effective tax rates.

$$\tau = \frac{[(r + \delta)(1 - \Gamma)/(1 - t) - \delta] - s}{(r + \delta)(1 - \Gamma)/(1 - t) - \delta}$$

where τ = the effective corporate tax rate; r = the weighted average cost of capital; δ = the capital depreciation rate (assumed value); Γ = the

Table 13A-1. Taxation of Business Income: A Comparative Perspective

Tax	Mexico (1991)	United States (1990)	Canada (1990)
Corporate income tax rate: general[a]	35 + 3.9 = 38.9	34 + 6 = 40	28 + 15 = 43
Withholding rates			
Interest	35	30	28
Dividends	0–40	30	25
Technology transfer fees	21	30	25
Royalties	40	30	25
Indexation of deductions	Full	No	No
Loss carryforward	5	15	7
Loss carrybackward	0	3	3
Minimum or alternative minimum	2 percent on assets	20 percent on taxable income, including tax preferences	0.175 percent on capital in excess of $10 million creditable against 3 percent surtax on corporate profits
Capital gains			
Coverage	Full	Full	Two-thirds
Indexation	Full	No	No
Rate	35	34	28
Dividends deduction	No	Yes	Yes
Full expensing of investment	No	No	No
Investment tax credits	Regional, priority sectors	Energy, rehabilitation of real estate, targeted job credit	Regional, research and development

a. The profit-sharing rate in Mexico and the average provincial or state tax rates in the United States and Canada are added to the basic federal rate.

Source: Gil-Diaz (1990); IBFD (1991); Mancera Hermanos (1989); Price Waterhouse (1988, 1989); and Ugarte (1988).

present value of investment credits and depreciation deductions (based on a sample of twenty-three firms reported in Schwartzman 1987); t = the corporate tax rate (Mexico); s = the rate of return to the supplier of funds (calculated based on data from IMF, various years).

MARGINAL EFFECTIVE TAX RATE FOR TRANSFERS (τ_t). The following expression is used for the weighted average cost of capital (r).

$$r = b \frac{[i_u(1 - t_u^p) - (\pi_u - \pi_m) - XRRC]}{1 - t_{max}}$$

$$+ (1 - b)\left[\frac{\mu}{1 - \phi}\right]\left[1 - \frac{t_{min}}{1 - t_u}\right]$$

where b = the fraction financed by debt; μ = the real discount rate for equity; t_m = the Mexican corporate tax rate; t_u^p = the U.S. personal tax rate; i_u = the U.S. nominal interest rate; π_u = the U.S. rate of inflation; π_m = the Mexican rate of inflation; $XRRC$ = the rate of depreciation of Mexican pesos against the dollar; t_{max} = the higher of U.S. personal income tax rate and the Mexican withholding tax on interest payments; t_{min} = the smaller of Mexican and U.S. corporate tax rates; and ϕ = the effective tax rate on real equity return.

MARGINAL EFFECTIVE TAX RATE FOR RETAINED EARNINGS. $r = \mu/1 - \phi$ is used in the formula for the effective tax rate for retained earnings.

Regulations

Exchange rate premia are used as proxies for regulation. They are defined as: $REGU = (XRM - XRN)/XRN$, where XRM = the market exchange rate; XRN = the official exchange rate; and $REGU$ = the index of regulations.

Note

1. Note that only regressions incorporating the aggregate marginal effective tax rate are presented here. This formulation allows us to test the two alternative views on tax sensitivity of FDI in a simple and transparent manner. Results from regressions incorporating the marginal effective tax rate on transfers and retained earnings are close to this simple formulation.

References

Alworth, Julian. 1988. *The Financial Decisions of Multinationals*. Oxford: Basil Blackwell.

Auerbach, Alan. 1990. "The Cost of Capital and Investment in Developing Countries." Policy, Research, and External Affairs Working Paper 410. World Bank, Country Economics Department, Washington, D.C.

Auerbach, Alan J., and James R. Hines, Jr. 1988. "Investment Tax Incentives and Frequent Tax Reforms." *American Economic Review* 78 (2): 211–16.

Banco de Mexico. Various issues. *Indicadores Economico*. Mexico, D.F.

Boskin, Michael J., and William G. Gale. 1987. "New Results on the Effects of Tax Policy on the International Location of Investment." In Martin Feldstein, ed., *The Effects of Taxation on Capital Accumulation*. Chicago, Ill.: University of Chicago Press.

Dunning, John H., ed. 1985. *Multinational Enterprises, Economic Structure, and International Competitiveness*. Colchester, U.K.: John Wiley and Sons.

Feldstein, Martin S., and Joosung Jun. 1987. "The Effect of Tax Rules on Nonresidential Fixed Investment: Some Preliminary Evidence from the 1980s." In Martin Feldstein, ed., *The Effects of Taxation on Capital Accumulation*. Chicago, Ill.: University of Chicago Press.

Gil-Diaz, Francisco. 1990. "Reforming Taxes in Developing Countries: Mexico's Protracted Tax Reform." World Bank, Country Economics Department, Washington, D.C.

Hartman, David G. 1984. "Tax Policy and Foreign Direct Investment in the United States." *National Tax Journal* 37 (4): 475–88.

———. 1985. "Tax Policy and Foreign Direct Investment." *Journal of Public Economics* 26 (1): 107–21.

IBFD (International Bureau of Fiscal Documentation). 1991. "Mexico: The Tax System." Supplement 71 (June). Washington, D.C.

IMF (International Monetary Fund). Various years. *International Financial Statistics Yearbook*. Washington, D.C.

Jorgenson, Dale. 1963. "Capital Theory and Investment Behavior." *American Economic Review* 53 (2): 247–59.

Mancera Hermanos y Cia, S.C. 1989. "Circular á clientes. Tax Brief." Mexico, D.F.

Newlon, Timothy Scott. 1987. "Tax Policy and the Multinational Firms' Financial Policy and Investment Decisions." Ph.D. diss., Princeton University, Department of Economics, Princeton, N.J.

Price Waterhouse. 1988. *Corporate Taxes: A Worldwide Summary*. New York.

———. 1989. *Highlights of the Amendments to Mexican Tax Laws for 1989*. Mexico, D.F.

Scholes, Myron, and Mark A. Wolfson. 1989. "The Effect of Changes in Tax Laws on Corporate Reorganization Activity." Stanford University, Stanford Business School, Palo Alto, Calif.

Schwartzman, Aaron. 1987. "Exchange Rate, Investment and Tax Adjusted Q." Ph.D. diss., Massachusetts Institute of Technology, Cambridge, Mass.

Slemrod, Joel. 1990. "Tax Effects on Foreign Direct Investment in the U.S.: Evidence from a Cross-Country Comparison." In Assaf Razin and Joel

Slemrod, eds., *Taxation in the Global Economy.* Chicago, Ill.: University of Chicago Press.

Ugarte, Fernando Sanchez. 1988. "Taxation of Foreign Investment in Mexico: The North American Perspective." International Economics Program Working Paper DP88-7. University of Toronto, Toronto, Canada.

Young, Kan H. 1988. "The Effects of Taxes and Rates of Return on Foreign Direct Investment in the United States." *National Tax Journal* 41 (1): 109–21.

CORPORATE TAX STRUCTURE AND PRODUCTION

14

Jeffrey I. Bernstein and Anwar Shah

FISCAL INCENTIVES FOR investment promotion are in wide use in most developing countries. The effectiveness of these instruments in meeting stated policy goals is an important area of public policy concern. Nevertheless, rigorous empirical evidence from developing countries to guide policy in this area is almost completely lacking. To address these concerns in the past, policymakers relied on opinion surveys of firms (see, for example, Guisinger and Associates 1985); more recently, they have depended on analyses of marginal effective tax rates (see, for example, chapter 1, this volume). None of these methods, however, is able to provide analyses of the effects of tax policy changes on the structure of production and the rate of capital accumulation.

In this chapter we develop and estimate a dynamic model of production with which to examine the effect of taxes on an array of production decisions regarding inputs and outputs. We examine six industries in three developing countries: Mexico, Pakistan, and Turkey. We evaluate investment tax credits (ITCs), investment tax allowances (ITAs), capital cost (or consumption) allowances (CCAs), and corporate income taxes (CITs) as instruments for investment promotion. Under an ITC, corporations are allowed to deduct against their tax liabilities a fraction of expenditure on new additions to physical capital stock. Tax credits provide a direct subsidy to such activities. An ITA allows a deduction from taxable income based on a fraction of investment expenditure. CCAs permit depreciation for tax purposes as a deduction from taxable income. Reductions in CITs permit a lower rate of taxation on corporate income.

We have organized this chapter into eight sections. In the first, we present illustrative calculations on the post-tax cost of capital expenditure under alternative tax policy provisions and a history of tax changes in three countries. Next we introduce the theoretical model. After specifying the empirical framework and deriving relevant elasticity formulas, we discuss the effect of tax policy on investment and government revenue. In the following two sections we present the empirical results for selected industries in the sample countries, and in the final section we summarize the results.

Cost of Capital Expenditure

Four tax instruments that affect the purchase prices of capital stocks are considered here: the CIT rate, the CCA rate, the ITA rate, and the ITC rate. To see the effect of tax policy on after-tax, or post-tax, purchase prices, consider a machine that has a price of one unit denominated in the local currency. Dealing first with the CCA rate, suppose that depreciation occurs at an annual rate of 30 percent. In addition, because the expenditure on the machine must be capitalized, assume that the future depreciation deductions are discounted at the rate of 15 percent. The present value of depreciation deductions based on declining-balance depreciation is $z = d(1 + \rho)/(\rho + d)$, where d is the CCA rate and ρ is the discount rate. Thus the tax deduction attributable to depreciation is 0.77.

Next, consider the CIT rate. In the present example the tax reduction due to depreciation equals $0.77u_c$, where u_c is the CIT rate, and the post-tax cost of the unit value of the machine is $1 - 0.77u_c$. If the CIT rate is 0.46, and there is taxable income, then the post-tax cost is 0.65 and the tax reduction is 0.35 on a machine of unit value in the local currency.

It is of interest to compare the tax reduction resulting from a CCA with the reduction resulting from the immediate writeoff of the machine. In the latter case, assuming there is taxable income, the tax reduction is u_c and the post-tax cost is $1 - u_c$. Hence, with a CIT rate of 0.46 the post-tax cost is 0.54 and the tax reduction is 0.46. The tax reduction in the CCA case is 24 percent smaller than the tax reduction from immediate writeoff.

Next, consider the ITC. Let the credit rate be υ. The tax reduction on the unit value of the machine is $zu_c(1 - \upsilon) + \upsilon$. This tax reduction has three aspects. The first is zu_c, which is the depreciation or capital cost part. The second is $-zu_c\upsilon$, which is the amount that the tax credit reduces the depreciation base. The third is υ, which is the ITC rate. Thus the post-tax cost of the unit value of the machine is $1 - [zu_c(1 - \upsilon) + \upsilon]$. If $z = 0.77$, u_c is 0.46 and υ is 0.10, then the tax reduction is 0.42, and the post-tax cost of the machine is 0.58.

Some countries—for example, Turkey—rather than offering a credit for investment expenditure, allow a fraction of this expenditure to be deducted from taxable income in the year the outlay is made. This is an ITA. Under such a regime, the post-tax cost of the unit value of the machine is $1 - (zu_c + u_c\psi)$. If $z = 0.77$, $u_c = 0.46$, and ψ (the allowance rate) $= 0.10$, then the tax allowance contributes 0.40 to tax reduction, with the final cost of the machine equal to 0.60.

Table 14-1. Cost of a Unit Value of Capital Expenditure, Mexico, Pakistan, and Turkey

	Discount rate	
Country	0.05	0.15
Mexico[a]	0.46	0.53
Pakistan[b]	0.43	0.52
Turkey[c]	0.46	0.53

a. $u_c = 0.42$; straight-line depreciation at 0.10; this is an average rate; $\upsilon = 0.30$; $z = 0.811$ for $\rho = 0.05$, and $z = 0.577$ for $\rho = 0.15$.

b. $u_c = 0.55$; this includes the supertax rate; declining balance depreciation at 0.10; $\upsilon = 0.30$; and $z = 0.7$ for $\rho = 0.05$, $z = 0.46$ for $\rho = 0.15$.

c. $u_c = 0.46$; declining balance depreciation at 0.25; ITA rate $= 0.30$; this is the minimum rate allowed and $z = 0.875$ for $\rho = 0.05$, $z = 0.719$ for $\rho = 0.15$.

Source: Authors' calculations.

Examples of the post-tax cost of the unit value of machinery and equipment for three countries—Mexico, Pakistan, and Turkey—are shown in table 14-1. We observe that the post-tax cost of a unit value of capital expenditure is not too different in the three countries. As future depreciation deductions are discounted at a higher rate, their value diminishes and the post-tax cost of the expenditure rises. This can be seen in the table, because the figures in the second column are higher than those in the first column.

Tax Structure and Production: A Dynamic Theoretical Model

The technology of a representative firm within an industry can be defined as

$$(14\text{-}1) \qquad y_t = f(K_{t-1}, v_t, \Delta K_t, A_t)$$

where y is the output quantity, K is the m-dimensional vector of quasi-fixed factors, v is the n-dimensional vector of variable factors, and A is the indicator of the level of technology. The production function is denoted by f, which is defined for nonnegative input quantities, and is nonnegative with positive marginal products. The production function also declines with respect to the net investment vector, $\Delta K = K_t - K_{t-1}$. Adjustment costs are represented through the net investment vector in the production function and are measured as forgone output. The cost of changing a quasi-fixed factor is the loss in output that could have been produced. Adjustment costs are thereby internal to the production process (see, for example, Epstein 1981; Mortensen 1973; Treadway 1971, 1974). The subscript t represents the time period.[1]

Quasi-fixed factors are also referred to as capital inputs. In this model, capital inputs relate to various types of plant and equipment. The stocks of the capital inputs accumulate according to

$$(14\text{-}2) \qquad\qquad K_t = I_t + (I_m - \delta)\, K_{t-1}$$

where I is the m-dimensional investment vector, δ is an m-dimensional diagonal matrix of fixed depreciation rates such that $0 \le \delta_i \le 1$, $i = 1, ..., m$. It is assumed that capital services are proportional to the capital stocks (see Bernstein and Nadiri 1988).[2] In addition, I_m is the m-dimensional identity matrix.

Firms sell their products, hire or purchase factors of production, invest in capital stocks, and finance their operations such that the flow of funds is given by

$$(14\text{-}3)\; p_t\, y_t - w_t^T\, v_t - q_t^T\, I_t + \Delta B_t + p_{st}\, \Delta N_{st} - r_{bt}\, B_{t-1} - T_{ct} - D_t = 0.$$

The product price is denoted by p; w is the vector of variable input prices; q is the vector of capital purchase prices; B is the value of outstanding bond issues; $\Delta B_t = B_t - B_{t-1}$ is the value of net bond issues (net of retirements); p_s is the price of shares; N_s is the quantity of outstanding shares; $\Delta N_{st} = N_{st} - N_{st-1}$ is the quantity of new share issues; r_b is the interest rate on bonds; T_c represents income taxes; and D is the value of dividends.

The flow of funds can be further decomposed by considering income taxes. First, investment incentives are often in the form of credits such that at time t with a credit rate of $0 < v_{it} < 1$, $1 = 1, ..., m$, the ith capital stock ITC is

$$(14\text{-}4) \qquad\qquad \text{ITC}_{it} = v_{it}\, q_{it}\, I_{it} \qquad i = 1, \ldots, m.$$

Second, CCAs are associated with the depreciation of the capital stocks. In general, depreciation deductions equal $d_{i\,\tau}$ on a unit value of the original cost of the ith capital stock of age τ. Because capital must be fully depreciated, then it must be the case that $\sum_{\tau=0}^{\infty} d_{i\tau} = 1$ $\quad i = 1, \ldots, m$. The CCA at time t for the ith capital stock installed at different times is

$$(14\text{-}5) \quad \text{CCA}_{it} = \sum_{\tau=0}^{\infty} q_{it-\tau}\, I_{it-\tau}\, (1 - \varphi_{it}\, v_{it})\, d_{i\tau} \qquad i = 1, \ldots, m$$

where $0 \le \varphi_{it} \le 1$ is the proportion of the ITC that reduces the depreciation base for tax purposes.

The income tax is defined at time t by the rate $0 < u_{ct} < 1$, based on revenue that is net of the cost of the variable inputs net of interest payments, net of CCAs, and net of ITCs.[3] Thus income taxes at time t are

$$(14\text{-}6) \qquad T_{ct} = u_{ct} \left(p_t y_t - w_t^T v_t - r_{bt} B_{t-1} - i_m^T \text{CCA}_t \right) - i_m^T \text{ITC}_t$$

where i_m is the m-dimensional unit vector and CCA and ITC are m-dimensional vectors of CCAs and ITCs, respectively. If we substitute equation 14-6 (the income tax equation) into the flow of funds, equation 14-3 yields

$$(14\text{-}7) \quad \left(p_t y_t - w_t^T v_t \right)(1 - u_{ct}) - q_t^T I_t + i_m^T (u_{ct} \text{CCA}_t + \text{ITC}_t)$$

$$= \left[D_t / (p_{st-1} N_{st-1}) + \Delta p_{st} / p_{st-1} \right] p_{st-1} N_{st-1} + r_{bt}(1 - u_{ct}) B_{t-1}$$

$$- \Delta(p_{st} N_{st}) - \Delta B_t .$$

The left side of equation 14-7 shows revenue, net of tax, net of variable input cost, and net of investment expenditure. The right side of the equation shows the flow of funds to bondholders and shareholders. Equations 14-1, 14-2, and 14-7 summarize the technology, capital accumulation, and flow of funds for the representative firm in the industry.

Turning to the nature of market structure, we will consider the product market first. Product demand is represented by

$$(14\text{-}8) \qquad\qquad p_t = H(Y_t, e_t)$$

where $Y = \sum_{j=1}^{f} y^j$ is industry output, with the superscript representing the particular firm, and e is a vector of exogenous variables affecting product demand. The inverse product demand function is given by H, which is defined for nonnegative industry output, and the function is nonnegative and decreasing in industry output. Implied by the inverse product demand function, firms within an industry produce homogeneous products. Moreover, depending on the conjectural relation between the output of a firm and an industry, the product market in the model can be competitive, monopolistic, or oligopolistic (see Bernstein and Mohnen 1991).

The next markets to be considered are the variable and capital input markets, which are assumed to be competitive. Thus firms face exogenous variable and quasi-fixed input prices.

The last set of markets are the financial markets. Given the less-developed nature of the economy, firms are not able to affect the rates of return on their shares or bonds. These rates of return are essentially constrained by world financial markets. If we define financial capital as $V_t = p_{st} N_{st} + B_t$, then $\Delta V_t = \Delta(p_{st} N_{st}) + \Delta B_t$, and equation 14-7 can be rewritten as

$$(14\text{-}9) \qquad F_t = \left[r_{st} + r_{bt}(1 - u_{ct}) \, l_{t-1} \right] (1 + l_{t-1})^{-1} \, V_{t-1} - \Delta V_t$$

where F_t is the left side of equation 14-7, which is net after tax revenue; the rate of return on the shares of a firm is $r_{st} = (D_t / p_{st-1} N_{st-1}) + (\Delta p_{st}/p_{st-1})$; and the leverage ratio is $l_{t-1} = B_{t-1}/p_{st-1} N_{st-1}$. The rate of return on shares consists of the payout ratio, which is dividends per value of outstanding shares, plus the capital gains (or losses) on the share prices. The leverage of a firm, l, is the ratio of debt to equity capital. Define ρ as the coefficient of V_{t-1} in equation 14-9. It is the rate of return on financial capital, which is a weighted average of the rates of return on equity and debt. It is assumed that the rate of return on financial capital issued by a firm is exogenous.[4]

The objective of a firm is to operate in the interest of its owners by maximizing the expected present value of the flow of funds to its shareholders. In the context of the present model, because the rates of return on equity and debt capital are exogenous, and therefore cannot be influenced by shareholders, the objective is equivalent to maximizing the expected present value of the flow of funds to shareholders and bondholders. In other words, a firm maximizes the expected present value of financial capital. The objective can be obtained from equation 14-9. Solving for V_t and applying the conditional expectations operator yields

$$(14\text{-}10) \qquad J_t = E_t \sum_{s=1}^{\infty} \alpha\,(t,\, s) \left(P_s y_s - W_s^T v_s - Q_s^T I_s - i_m^T M_s \right)$$

where E_t is the expectations operator conditional on information known at time t; the discount rate is the rate of return on financial capital; $\alpha\,(t,\, t) = 1$, $\alpha\,(t,\, t+1) = (1 + \rho_t)^{-1}$, $P = p\,(1 - u_c)$ is the after-tax product price; $W_j = w_j\,(1 - u_c)$ $j = 1, \ldots n$ are the after-tax variable factor prices; Q is an m-dimensional vector of after-tax capital input purchase prices,

$$Q_{is} = q_{is} \left[1 - v_{is} - \sum_{\tau=0}^{\infty} \alpha\,(t,\, s + \tau)\, \alpha\,(t,\, s)^{-1} \, u_{cs+\tau}\,(1 - \varphi_{is}\, v_{is})\, d_{i\tau} \right]$$

and M is an m-dimensional vector of tax reductions at time t, due to CCAs arising from past investment expenditure,

$$M_{is} = u_{cs} \sum_{\tau=s}^{\infty} q_{is-\tau}\, I_{is-\tau} \left(1 - \varphi_{is-\tau}\, v_{is-\tau} \right) d_{i\tau} \, .$$

At any time period, M does not affect output supply and input demand decisions because from the vantage point of the present the vector is predetermined. A significant feature of a dynamic model is that current and future tax rates, credits, and allowances are explicitly accounted for in the analysis. Indeed, the future tax purchase prices of the capital stocks show the array of current and future tax policy instruments that affect the analysis.[5]

A firm maximizes the expected present value of the flow of funds (in other words, the right side of equation 14-10) by selecting output supply, variable input, and investment demand subject to the production function (equation 14-1), capital accumulation equations (equation 14-2), the inverse product demand function (equation 14-8), the exogenous current and future after-tax factor prices, and discount rates. This program can be solved in two stages. The first stage relates to the short-run decisions, and the second stage concerns the intertemporal production choices. Determination of the output supply and variable factor demands are conditional on the capital stocks. With this solution, a firm then proceeds to determine the demand for the capital inputs. In breaking the problem into two subsets, the first-stage solution, or short-run equilibrium, is found by maximizing after-tax variable profit at each point in time. Thus,

$$(14\text{-}11) \qquad \max_{y_s, v_s} \ P_s y_s - W_s^T v_s$$

subject to equations 14-1 and 14-8, and given the capital stocks. If we substitute equation 14-8 into 14-11, the first-order conditions are

$$(14\text{-}12a) \qquad H(\Upsilon_s^e, e_s)\left[1 + \xi_s^e\, \theta_s^e\right](1 - u_{cs}) - \lambda_s^e = 0$$

$$(14\text{-}12b) \qquad -W_s + \lambda_s^{eT}\nabla f_v = 0$$

where $\xi = \Upsilon(\partial H/\partial \Upsilon)/p$ is the inverse price elasticity of product demand, $\theta = (\partial \Upsilon/\partial y)\, y/\Upsilon$ is the conjectural elasticity, λ is the Lagrangian multiplier, and the superscript e denotes equilibrium values.[6]

From equation 14-12a, in short-run equilibrium a firm equates after-tax marginal revenue to marginal cost. The Lagrangian multiplier equals marginal cost. Equation 14-12b implies that relative after-tax variable factor prices equal relative marginal products of the respective variable factors. Equation set 14-12 holds for all time periods and, of course, for all firms in the industry. Equation set 14-12 shows how tax policy affects the short-run equilibrium. The CIT rate does not directly affect the short-run equilibrium. From equation set 14-12 it is relative variable factor and product prices that determine the short-run equilibrium, but these prices are independent of the CIT rate. The reason is that the CIT is a tax on variable profit in the short run, and as a consequence, it is based on the residual of the short-run income stream.

The CIT rate, ITC, and CCA rates indirectly affect the short-run equilibrium through their influence on the demand for the capital inputs. Changes in these rates affect the after-tax purchase price of the capital inputs and thereby alter the demand for the quasi-fixed factors. These changes in the capital input levels then influence the short-run supply of output and demand for the variable factors of production.

The short-run equilibrium conditions are consistent with many product market structures. The conjectural elasticity, θ, shows the nature of firm interdependence in the product market. If $\theta = 0$, then the product market is purely competitive because firms are price takers. If $\theta = 1$, then the product market is purely monopolistic because there is only a single producer. If $\theta = y/\Upsilon$, then the product market is oligopolistic, and the firms are characterized as Cournot-Nash oligopolists. In the last case, if firms have the same marginal cost in short-run equilibrium, then from equation 14-12a, firms have the same conjectural elasticity in short-run equilibrium.

An alternative way to characterize the short-run equilibrium conditions emphasizes both product market imperfections and the dual relation between price and quantity effects on variable profit. Consider a first-order approximation to the revenue of a firm in equilibrium,

$$(14\text{-}13) \quad H(\Upsilon_s, e_s)\, y_s = H(\Upsilon_s^e, e_s)\, y_s^e + H(\Upsilon_s^e, e_s)\left(1 + \xi_s^e\, \theta_s^e\right)(y_s - y_s^e).$$

Collecting terms yields

$$(14\text{-}14) \quad p_s\, y_s = p_s^e\left(1 + \xi_s^e\, \theta_s^e\right) y_s - p_s^e\, y_s^e\, \xi_s^e\, \theta_s^e .$$

From equation 14-14, total revenue equals revenue earned in a purely competitive product market plus the additional revenue earned in equilibrium because of oligopoly power.[7] If we define the purely competitive or shadow product price as $p_s^\sigma = p_s^e(1 + \xi_s^e\, \theta_s^e)$ and the after-tax shadow product price as $P_s^\sigma = p_s^\sigma(1 - u_{cs})$, then the short-run equilibrium conditions (equation set 14-12) can be obtained by

$$(14\text{-}15) \qquad \max_{y_s,\, v_s} P_s^\sigma\, y_s - W_s^T\, v_s$$

subject to the production function and the levels of the capital inputs. Thus firms act as if they maximize after-tax shadow variable profit, which is defined as after-tax shadow revenue minus after-tax variable input cost.[8] The reason is that the degree of product market imperfection is captured in the definition of shadow product price.

The short-run equilibrium conditions can be substituted into 14-15 to obtain the after-tax shadow variable profit function.

$$(14\text{-}16) \qquad \pi_s^\sigma = \Pi^\sigma \left(P_s^\sigma, W_s, K_{s-1}, \Delta K_s, A_s \right)$$

where π^σ is after-tax shadow variable profit, and Π^σ is the after-tax shadow variable profit function that is defined for nonnegative after-tax prices and capital inputs and is increasing in the after-tax shadow product price and capital inputs, decreasing in the after-tax variable factor prices and net investment levels.[9]

The dual relation between price and quantity effects in equilibrium can be seen by differentiating the after-tax shadow variable profit function by the after-tax shadow product price and the after-tax variable factor prices. This yields

$$(14\text{-}17a) \qquad\qquad y_s^e = \Pi_p^\sigma$$

$$(14\text{-}17b) \qquad\qquad v_s^e = -\nabla \Pi_w^\sigma.$$

The short-run equilibrium output supply and variable factor demands can be obtained from the after-tax shadow variable profit function. It implies that short-run equilibrium can be characterized by equations 14-17a and 14-17b. The attractive feature of this approach is that reduced form equations of output supply and variable factor demand are readily obtainable from the after-tax shadow variable profit function.

The second stage of the program involves the determination of demand for the capital inputs. This stage relates to the intertemporal aspects of production decisions. Capital input demand can be obtained by considering the expected present value of the after-tax shadow flow of funds. The objective is to

$$(14\text{-}18) \quad \max_{\{K_s\}_{s=t}^\infty} E_t \sum_{t=s}^\infty \alpha\,(t,s) \left(\Pi^\sigma \left(P_s^\sigma, W_s, K_{s-1}, \Delta K_s, A_s \right) - Q_s^T I_s \right)$$

subject to the capital accumulation equations (denoted by equation set 14-2). The first-order conditions for this problem at any time period, after equation set 14-2 is substituted into equation 14-18, are

$$(14\text{-}19) \quad \nabla\,(\partial \pi_s^\sigma / \partial \Delta K_s) - Q_s + E_s \alpha\,(s, s+1) \Big[\nabla\,(\partial \pi_{s+1}^\sigma / \partial K_s)$$

$$- \nabla\,(\partial \pi_{s+1}^\sigma / \partial \Delta K_{s+1}) + (I_m - \delta)\,Q_{s+1} \Big] = 0_m.$$

Equation set 14-19 implies that the marginal cost of a capital input is equated to the expected marginal benefit of that capital input.[10] The marginal cost consists of two components: the after-tax marginal adjustment cost and the after-tax purchase price. The expected marginal benefit consists of three components: the expected after-tax marginal profit, the expected after-tax adjustment cost saving, and the after-tax purchase price saving from installing and purchasing (or renting) the respective capital input in the previous period. Equation set 14-19 shows the intertemporal tradeoff between greater expected future after-tax profit due to increases in the capital inputs and smaller current after-tax profit resulting from increases in the capital inputs.

The complete set of equilibrium conditions is given by equation sets 14-17 and 14-19. Equation set 14-17 defines a short-run equilibrium; equation sets 14-17 and 14-19 define a temporary equilibrium of producer behavior. In the temporary equilibrium output supply, variable factor and capital input demands are determined.

Estimation Model and Tax Elasticities

This section parameterizes the dynamic model of production presented earlier. The dynamic nature of the model offers many advantages in determining the effect of tax policy on output supply and input demands. First, the model treats capital inputs differently from other factors of production because producers must incur adjustment costs to invest in capital. Second, the model allows differences in short-run, intermediate-run, and long-run effects of tax policy initiatives. These effects differ according to the extent of capital adjustment.

In the empirical specification of the model, it is assumed that there is one output, two variable factors (labor and intermediate inputs), and one quasi-fixed factor. In order to estimate the dynamic model of production, we need to parameterize the normalized shadow variable profit function (equation 14-16). This function is assumed to be a normalized quadratic and is written as

$$(14\text{-}20) \quad \pi_s^\sigma = \beta_0 + \beta_p\, P_s^\sigma + \beta_l\, W_{ls} + \beta_k\, K_{s-1} + \beta_a\, A_s$$
$$+ 0.5 \left(\beta_{pp} P_s^{\sigma 2} + \beta_{ll}\, W_{ls}^2 + \beta_{kk}\, K_{s-1}^2 + \beta_{aa}\, A_s^2 \right)$$
$$+ \beta_{pl}\, W_{ls}\, P_s^\sigma + \beta_{pk}\, P_s^\sigma\, K_{s-1} + \beta_{pa}\, P_s^\sigma\, A_s$$
$$+ \beta_{lk}\, W_{ls}\, K_{s-1} + \beta_{la}\, W_{ls}\, A_s + \beta_{ka}\, K_{s-1}\, A_s + 0.5\, \beta_{ii}\, \Delta K_s^2$$

where π_s^σ is the normalized shadow variable profit after taxes (normalization is by the after-tax price of intermediate inputs), P_s^σ is the normalized shadow price of output after taxes (see equations 14-13 through 14-15), W_{ls} is the normalized labor input price or normalized wage rate after taxes, K_s is the capital input, A_s is the indicator of technology, and ΔK_s represents net investment. All variables are indexed by the time period s.

From equation 14-20, we find the equilibrium conditions for output supply and variable factor demands by differentiating with respect to the relevant prices. Thus we obtain the following specific output supply and input demand functions (the general forms are given as equations 14-17a and 14-17b):

$$(14\text{-}21) \qquad y_s = \beta_p + \beta_{pp}\, P_s^\sigma + \beta_{pl}\, W_{ls} + \beta_{pk}\, K_{s-1} + \beta_{pa}\, A_s$$

$$(14\text{-}22) \qquad -v_{ls} = \beta_l + \beta_{ll}\, W_{ls} + \beta_{pl}\, P_s^\sigma + \beta_{lk}\, K_{s-1} + \beta_{la}\, A_s\,.$$

Because $-v_m = \pi^\sigma - P^\sigma y + W_l\, v_l$, the intermediate input demand equation is

$$(14\text{-}23) \qquad -v_{ms} = \beta_0 + \beta_k\, K_{s-1} + \beta_a\, A_s - 0.5\,\beta_{pp}\, P_s^{\sigma 2} - 0.5\,\beta_{ll}\, W_{ls}^2$$
$$+ 0.5\,\beta_{kk}\, K_{s-1}^2 + 0.5\,\beta_{aa}\, A_s^2 - \beta_{pl}\, P_s^\sigma\, W_{ls} + \beta_{ka}\, K_{s-1}\, A_s$$
$$+ 0.5\,\beta_{ii}\, \Delta K_s^2\,.$$

Thus equations 14-21, 14-22, and 14-23 define the short-run equilibrium conditions based on the normalized quadratic after-tax shadow variable profit function. These equations show how after-tax output and variable input prices affect output supply and variable input demands, given the levels of the capital inputs.

The equilibrium condition for the capital input is given by equation 14-19. Based on equation 14-20, the equilibrium condition for capital can be written as

$$(14\text{-}24)\ \beta_{ii}\, \Delta K_s - Q_s + (1+\rho)^{-1} \Big[E_s \Big(\beta_k + \beta_{kk}\, K_s + \beta_{pk}\, P_{s+1}^\sigma + \beta_{lk}\, W_{ls+1}$$
$$+ \beta_{ka}\, A_{s+1} - \beta_{ii}\, \Delta K_{s+1} + Q_{s+1}\, (1-\delta)\Big)\Big] = 0$$

where Q_s is the normalized after-tax purchase price of capital, δ is the depreciation rate, and ρ is the discount rate.

If we assume that after-tax relative prices, the discount rate, and the technology indicator are expected to remain constant, then we obtain the following:

$$(14\text{-}25) \qquad -\beta_{ii}\, \Delta K_{s+1} + (1+\rho)\,\beta_{ii}\, \Delta K_s + \beta_{kk}\, K_s + \beta_k + \beta_{pk}\, P_s^\sigma + \beta_{lk}\, W_{ls}$$
$$+ \beta_{ka}\, A_s - Q_s\, (1+\rho) + Q_s(1-\delta) = 0.$$

Rearranging, we get

(14-26) $-\beta_{ii} K_{s+1} + \left(\beta_{kk} + (2 + \rho) \beta_{ii}\right) K_s - (1 + \rho) \beta_{ii} K_{s-1}$

$$= W_{ks} - \left(\beta_k + \beta_{pk} P_s^\sigma + \beta_{lk} W_{ls} + \beta_{ka} A_s \right)$$

where the normalized after-tax rental rate is $W_{ks} = Q_s (\rho + \delta)$.

Equation 14-26 defines a second-order difference equation with respect to the capital stock. The solution to this equation is a flexible accelerator:

(14-27) $$K_s - K_{s-1} = m (K_s^l - K_{s-1})$$

where $m = -0.5 \left(\rho + \beta_{kk} / \beta_{ii} - [(\rho + \beta_{kk} / \beta_{ii})^2 + 4 \beta_{kk} / \beta_{ii}]^{0.5}\right)$ is the speed of adjustment of the capital stock and the long-run capital stock is $K_s^l = (-1 / \beta_{kk}) (\beta_k + \beta_{pk} P_s^\sigma + \beta_{lk} W_{ls} + \beta_{ka} A_s - W_{ks})$.

Therefore, by combining equations 14-7 and 14-8, we get

(14-28) $K_s = (0.5 / \beta_{kk}) \left(\rho + \beta_{kk} / \beta_{ii} - [(\rho + \beta_{kk} / \beta_{ii})^2 \right.$

$$+ 4 \beta_{kk} / \beta_{ii}]^{0.5} \left) \left(\beta_k + \beta_{pk} P_s^\sigma + \beta_{lk} W_{ls} + \beta_{ka} A_s - W_{ks} \right)$$

$$+ \left[1 + 0.5 \left(\rho + \beta_{kk} / \beta_{ii} - [(\rho + \beta_{kk} / \beta_{ii})^2 \right. \right.$$

$$+ 4 \beta_{kk} / \beta_{ii}]^{0.5} \left) \right] K_{s-1}.$$

Equation 14-28 shows the demand for the capital input. It is a function of the relative after-tax output prices, variable input prices, and rental rate, along with the discount rate and lagged quantity of the capital input.

The estimation model consists of the system of equations made up of equations 14-21, 14-22, 14-23, and 14-28. These equations describe a temporary equilibrium. There are four endogenous variables: output supply, y_s; labor and material input demands, v_{ls} and v_{ms}; and capital input demand, K_s. In addition, in the model the exogenous variables are the normalized after-tax prices, P_s^σ, W_{ls}, W_{ks}; the discount rate, ρ; lagged capital, K_{s-1}; and the technology indicator, A_s. The model is linear in the endogenous variables and nonlinear in the parameters.

The model estimates are obtained by jointly estimating equations 14-21, 14-22, 14-23, and 14-28, using the maximum likelihood estimator. The estimated profit function must be convex in prices. Thus the parameters must satisfy $\beta_{pp} > 0$, $\beta_{ll} > 0$, and $\beta_{pp} \beta_{ll} - \beta_{pl}^2 > 0$. In addition, the profit function must be concave in capital and net investment so that $\beta_{kk} < 0$ and $\beta_{ii} < 0$.

An important feature of this model is that there are adjustment costs associated with capital accumulation. These costs prevent producers from immediately adopting their long-run levels of capital, and thereby also labor, materials, and output. Producers adjust toward the long run. The speed of adjustment is given by *m* in equation 14-27. The dynamic adjustment process has implications for the effectiveness of tax policy changes. For example, in the short run, output supply depends on existing capital but not on the rental rate. This means that changes in the CCA rate that alter the rental rate of capital do not have an effect on the supply of output. As capital adjustment occurs and the capital input changes in response to the new CCA rate, however, output supply is affected by the new rate. Thus in a dynamic context it is important to distinguish between the short-, intermediate-, and long-run effects of tax policy. In the short run, no capital adjustment has occurred; in the intermediate run, capital adjustment has occurred for one period; and in the long run, the capital adjustment process has been completed.

Short-Run Equilibrium

The short-run equilibrium conditions are based on equations 14-21, 14-22, 14-23, and 14-28. The short-run equilibrium condition for output supply is

$$(14\text{-}29\text{a}) \quad y_s^s = \beta_p + \beta_{pp}\, P_s^\sigma + \beta_{pl}\, W_{ls} + \beta_{pk}\, K_{s-1} + \beta_{pa}\, A_s .$$

The labor and material input short-run demand functions are

$$(14\text{-}29\text{b}) \quad -v_{ls}^s = \beta_l + \beta_{ll}\, W_{ls} + \beta_{pl}\, P_s^\sigma + \beta_{lk}\, K_{s-1} + \beta_{la}\, A_s$$

$$(14\text{-}29\text{c}) \quad -v_{ms}^s = \beta_0 + \beta_k\, K_{s-1} + \beta_a\, A_s - 0.5\, \beta_{pp}\, P_s^{\sigma\,2} - 0.5\, \beta_{ll}\, W_{ls}^2$$
$$+ 0.5\, \beta_{kk}\, K_{s-1}^2 + 0.5\, \beta_{aa}\, A_s^2 - \beta_{pl}\, P_s^\sigma\, W_{ls} + \beta_{ka}\, K_{s-1}\, A_s$$
$$+ 0.5\, \beta_{ii}\, (K_s^s - K_{s-1})^2 .$$

The equation for the short-run demand for the capital input is

$$(14\text{-}29\text{d})\ K_s^s = (0.5\,/\,\beta_{kk}) \left(\rho + \beta_{kk}\,/\,\beta_{ii} - [(\rho + \beta_{kk}\,/\,\beta_{ii})^2 + 4\,\beta_{kk}\,/\,\beta_{ii}]^{0.5} \right)$$
$$\cdot \left(\beta_k + \beta_{pk}\, P_s^\sigma + \beta_{lk}\, W_{ls} + \beta_{ka}\, A_s - W_{ks} \right)$$
$$+ \left(1 + 0.5 \left(\rho + \beta_{kk}\,/\,\beta_{ii} - [(\rho + \beta_{kk}\,/\,\beta_{ii})^2 + 4\beta_{kk}\,/\,\beta_{ii}]^{0.5} \right) \right) K_{s-1}$$

where the superscript s on the endogenous variables signifies the short-run equilibrium of the demand functions.

The short-run equilibrium magnitudes of output supply and input demands are determined in the following manner: The short-run demand for capital depends on predetermined variables. These variables are relative after-tax prices, the indicator of technology, the discount rate, and lagged capital input. Next, the output supply and variable input demands are simultaneously determined. Output supply and labor demand depend on the after-tax relative prices of output and labor, the technology indicator, and lagged capital input. The intermediate input demand also depends on the short-run capital demand.

Intermediate-Run Equilibrium

The equations for the intermediate run are derived from the short-run equations. The intermediate run is defined with respect to the capital adjustment process after one period (that is, one year). The intermediate-run equilibrium condition for output supply is

$$(14\text{-}30\text{a}) \qquad y_{s+1}^{i} = \beta_{p} + \beta_{pp}\, P_{s}^{\sigma} + \beta_{pl}\, W_{ls} + \beta_{pk}\, K_{s}^{s} + \beta_{pa}\, A_{s}.$$

The labor and material input demand functions for the intermediate run are described as

$$(14\text{-}30\text{b}) \qquad -v_{ls+1}^{i} = \beta_{l} + \beta_{ll}\, W_{ls} + \beta_{pl}\, P_{s}^{\sigma} + \beta_{lk}\, K_{s}^{s} + \beta_{la}\, A_{s}$$

$$(14\text{-}30\text{c}) \quad -v_{ms+1}^{i} = \beta_{0} + \beta_{k}\, K_{s}^{s} + \beta_{a}\, A_{s} - 0.5\, \beta_{pp}\, P_{s}^{\sigma 2} - 0.5\, \beta_{ll}\, W_{ls}^{2}$$

$$+ \; 0.5\, \beta_{kk}\, K_{s}^{s2} + 0.5\, \beta_{aa}\, A_{s}^{2} - \beta_{pl}\, P_{s}^{\sigma}\, W_{ls} + \beta_{ka}\, K_{s}^{s}\, A_{s}$$

$$+ \; 0.5\, \beta_{ii}\, (K_{s+1}^{i} - K_{s}^{s})^{2}.$$

The equation for capital input intermediate-run demand is

$$(14\text{-}30\text{d}) \quad K_{s+1}^{i} = (\,0.5\,/\,\beta_{kk})\left(\rho + \beta_{kk}\,/\,\beta_{ii} - [(\,\rho + \beta_{kk}\,/\,\beta_{ii})^{2} \right.$$

$$+ \; 4\,\beta_{kk}\,/\,\beta_{ii}]^{0.5}\Big) \Big(\beta_{k} + \beta_{pk}\, P_{s}^{\sigma} + \beta_{lk}\, W_{ls} + \beta_{ka}\, A_{s} - W_{ks}\Big)$$

$$+ \; \Big\{ 1 + 0.5\, (\rho + \beta_{kk}\,/\,\beta_{ii} - [(\,\rho + \beta_{kk}\,/\,\beta_{ii})^{2} $$

$$+ \; 4\,\beta_{kk}\,/\,\beta_{ii}]^{0.5}\Big)\Big\}\, K_{s}^{s}.$$

Given the technology indicator and relative prices, these equations show the equilibrium after one year. The superscript i indicates the intermediate run. The intermediate-run equilibrium magnitudes of output supply and input demands are determined in the following manner: The intermediate-run demand for capital depends on predetermined variables. These variables are relative after-tax prices, the indicator of technology, the discount rate, and the short-run capital input. Next, output supply and variable input demands are simultaneously determined. These variables depend on the after-tax relative prices of output and labor, the technology indicator, and the short-run demand for capital.

Long-Run Equilibrium

In the long run, $\Delta K_s = 0$. Thus investment in the long run occurs only for replacement purposes. The long-run output supply equation is

$$(14\text{-}31a) \qquad y_s^l = \beta_p + \beta_{pp}\, P_s^\sigma + \beta_{pl}\, W_{ls} + \beta_{pk}\, K_s^l + \beta_{pa}\, A_s \,.$$

The labor and intermediate input demand equations for the long run are

$$(14\text{-}31b) \qquad -v_{ls}^l = \beta_l + \beta_{ll}\, W_{ls} + \beta_{pl}\, P_s^\sigma + \beta_{lk}\, K_s^l + \beta_{la}\, A_s$$

$$(14\text{-}31c) \qquad -v_{ms}^l = \beta_0 + \beta_k\, K_s^l + \beta_a\, A_s - 0.5\, \beta_{pp}\, P_s^{\sigma 2} - 0.5\, \beta_{ll}\, W_{ls}^2$$
$$+\ 0.5\, \beta_{kk}\, K_s^{l2} + 0.5\, \beta_{aa}\, A_s^2 - \beta_{pl}\, P_s^\sigma\, W_{ls}$$
$$+\ \beta_{ka}\, K_s^l\, A_s \,.$$

Capital input demand is given by the following equation:

$$(14\text{-}31d) \qquad K_s^l = (-1\,/\,\beta_{kk})\left(\beta_k + \beta_{pk}\, P_s^\sigma + \beta_{lk}\, W_{ls} + \beta_{ka}\, A_s - W_{ks}\right).$$

In the long run the demand for capital depends on exogenous variables (including the rental rate). Once this demand is obtained, then output supply and labor and intermediate input demands can be determined. Because the long-run demand for capital affects output supply and the demand for labor and intermediate inputs, then the rental rate affects these variables. Indeed, in the long run all inputs are variable factors.

The Effect of Tax Policy on Investment and Government Revenue

In order to determine the effect of tax policy in stimulating investment, it is necessary to determine the tax instrument elasticities of capital demand in each of the production runs. The tax instrument elasticities consist of two components. The first element is the effect of the tax instrument on the after-tax relative rental rate of capital (because this is the only relative price directly affected by the tax policy). The second component is the elasticity of the rental rate on the demand for capital in each of the production runs.

We now consider the effects of the tax instruments on the after-tax relative rental rate. The elasticity of the after-tax rental rate with respect to the ITC rate is

$$(14\text{-}32) \quad e_{itc,\,s} = -\,q_s\,(\rho + \delta)\,[1 + u_{cs}\,(\partial z_s / \partial v_s)]\,v_s / W_{ks}\,(1 - u_{cs}) < 0$$

where q is the normalized (using the before-tax price of the intermediate input) purchase price of capital before taxes. Increases in the ITC rate lower the relative price of the capital input. In cases in which an ITA exists, the elasticity of the rental rate of capital with respect to the allowance rate (ψ) is

$$(14\text{-}33) \quad e_{ita,\,s} = -\,q_s\,(\rho + \delta)\,[u_{cs} + u_{cs}\,(\partial z_s / \partial \psi_s)]\,\psi_s / W_{ks}\,(1 - u_{cs}) < 0.$$

Next, the effects of changes in the CCA rate also operate through the rental rate. This elasticity is

$$(14\text{-}34) \quad e_{cca,s} = -\,q_s\,(\rho + \delta)\,u_{cs}\,(\partial z_s / \partial d_s)\,d_s / W_{ks}\,(1 - u_{cs}) < 0.$$

Increases in the CCA rate lower the relative price of the capital input.

The CIT rate affects the normalized or relative after-tax rental rate. The CIT elasticity on the rental rate is

$$(14\text{-}35) \quad e_{cit,s} = q\,(\rho + \delta)\,(1 - v_s - u_{cs}\,z_s)\,u_{cs} / W_{ks}\,(1 - u_{cs}) > 0.$$

Clearly, decreases in the CIT rate cause the relative price of the capital input to fall.

The effect of tax policy on capital demand in the short, intermediate, and long runs is obtained by calculating the tax effect on the rental rate and then multiplying this effect by the rental rate elasticity of capital demand.

Next we want to determine the effect on government revenue from changes in the tax instruments. First, for an ITC, the change in government revenue is

$$(14\text{-}36) \qquad \Delta GR_s^e = q_s\left[K_s^e - (1 - \delta)\,K_{s-1}^e\right]v_s .$$

The superscript e denotes the particular equilibrium, $e = s,i,l,$ for short, intermediate, and long run. For an allowance with a rate of ψ_s then in the formula, υ_s is replaced by $\psi_s u_{cs}$. For a 1 percent change in a rate, the formula is multiplied by 0.01.

Next, if depreciation for tax purposes is declining balance, and tax credits do not affect depreciation for tax purposes, then the change in government revenue is

$$(14\text{-}37) \qquad \Delta GR_s^e = q_s \left[K_s^e - (1-\delta) \, K_{s-1}^e \right] u_{cs} \frac{\rho}{\rho + \upsilon_s}.$$

If depreciation for tax purposes is straight-line, and tax credits do not affect it, then the change in government revenue is

$$(14\text{-}38) \qquad \Delta GR_s^e = q_s \left[K_s^e - (1-\delta) \, K_{s-1}^e \right] u_{cs}.$$

Last, we consider the CIT. The base for the income tax rate is revenue, net of variable cost; interest payments; and allowances (all allowances— for example, capital cost and investment). Define the base in year s as

$$(14\text{-}39) \qquad E_s^e = P_s \, y_s^e - W_s^T \, v_s^e - r_{bs} \, B_{s-1} - CCA_s^e - ITA_s^e$$

where the CCA is (with one type of capital, see equation 14-5)

$$(14\text{-}40) \qquad CCA_s^e = \sum_{\tau=0}^{\infty} q_{s-\tau} \, I_{s-\tau}^e \, d_s$$

where $I_{s-\tau}^e = [K_{s-\tau}^e - (1-\delta) \, K_{s-\tau-1}^e]$. Also, the investment tax allowance is

$$ITA_s^e = \psi_s \, q_s \left[K_s^e - (1-\delta) K_{s-1}^e \right].$$

Now, the change in government revenue in this case is

$$\Delta GR_s = E_s^e \, u_{cs}.$$

We are in a position to calculate the ratio of additional capital expenditure in relation to the loss in government revenue associated with the various stimulus packages. The measure of capital expenditure per unit loss of government revenue associated with the tax instruments is referred to as the benefit-cost ratio. It is defined as

$$(14\text{-}41) \qquad B_{js}^e = \frac{q_s \, K_s^e \, e_{kjs}^e}{\Delta GR_{js}^e}$$

where the numerator is the nominal value of capital in the appropriate equilibrium, multiplied by the elasticity of capital with respect to the *j*th tax instrument (ITC, CCA, CIT). The numerator is the additional capital generated by a specific tax instrument. The denominator is the cost to the government of generating the additional capital.

Mexico

The structure of corporate income taxation in Mexico has undergone major changes in recent years. During the 1980s the Mexican corporate tax system allowed indexation of CCA only. Full indexation of the CIT base is now permitted. With indexation, corporations are no longer allowed to deduct the inflationary component of interest expenditure, nor would they have to accumulate the inflationary component of interest income (see Gil-Diaz 1990: 79). Taxable profits (defined as gross receipts minus purchases and business expenses, and net losses carried forward from other periods) are subject to tax at a rate of 35 percent (a rate of 42 percent prevailed before 1987). Depreciation deductions are indexed, or, as an alternative, the present value of depreciation calculated at a discount rate of 7.5 percent may be deducted fully in all regions except major metropolitan areas and in all sectors except the automobile sector. In major metropolitan areas only 60 percent of such value can be deducted in the first year; the remaining 40 percent is subject to CCAs.

It is instructive to compare the Mexican system of taxation of business income with that of a few of its capital exporting partners, namely, the United States and Canada. As shown in table 14-2, Mexico has moved some distance toward a cash flow type of taxation by allowing a deduction for the present value of the scheduled depreciation allowances for the life of each type of asset, calculated at a 7.5 percent annual rate of interest (see Gil-Diaz 1990). The tax incentive regime in Mexico has also undergone significant changes over time. During the past two decades, tax policy has been seen as a major vehicle for regional and sectoral development, whereas the revenue implications of these policies have been overlooked. A brief review of historical changes in the tax incentive regime in Mexico follows:

- *1955–1972.* Between 20 percent (for secondary industries) and 40 percent (for basic industries) of the corporate income of Mexican majority-owned enterprises was exempted from corporate taxation for various periods between five and ten years. The same industries also could receive, on application, exemption from certain indirect taxes and import duties on capital goods imports.
- *1972–1979.* Industries that were seen to promote decentralization and regional development were granted relief from import duties of 50 to 100 percent and a reduction in corporate tax liability ranging from 10 to 40 percent, depending on their location and type of activity.

Table 14-2. Taxation of Business Income, Mexico, United States, and Canada, 1991
(percent)

Tax	Mexico	United States	Canada
Corporate income[a]	35 + 3.9 = 38.9	34 + 6 = 40	28 + 15 = 43
Withholding			
Interest	35	30	28
Dividends	0–40	30	25
Technology transfer fees	21	30	25
Royalties	40	30	25
Indexation of deductions	Full	No	No
Loss carryforward	5	15	7
Loss carrybackward	0	3	3
Minimum/alternative minimum	2 percent on assets	20 percent on taxable income including tax preferences	0.175 percent on capital in excess of $10 million, creditable against 3 percent surtax on corporate profits
Capital gains			
Coverage	Full	Full	Two-thirds
Indexation	Full	No	No
Rate	35	34	28
Dividends deduction	No	Yes	Yes
Full expensing of investment	No; present value of CCAs immediately deductible	No	No
Investment tax credits	Regional, priority sectors	Energy investment, rehabilitation of real estate, targeted job credit	Regional, research and development

a. The profit-sharing rate in Mexico and the average provincial or state tax rates in the United States and Canada are added to the basic federal rate.
Source: Gil-Diaz (1990); IBFD (1988a); Price Waterhouse (1992); Ugarte (1988).

- *1979–1986.* The practice of import duty exemption was continued. In addition, tax incentive certificates (CEPROFIs) that provided tax credit in the range of 10 to 25 percent for investment in physical assets, depending on location and on type and size of the industry, were introduced. These certificates were negotiable and could be used against any federal tax liability. CEPROFIs proved quite popular and in 1983 amounted to 0.83 percent of the gross domestic product in revenue losses. The manufacturing sector was a major beneficiary of this scheme, but the mining, agriculture, and transportation industries also received a significant amount of resources. Among the manufacturing industries, paper and publishing, chemicals, and food and beverages received most of the assistance.

    Although CEPROFIs were the most important fiscal incentive, other special incentives offered by the Mexican government were export promotion incentives (CEDIs), development of duty-free zones, and special tax preferences to the automobile, cement, publishing, and mining industries.

- *1987–1990.* The CEPROFI scheme was significantly tightened and targeted to priority industries and preferred zones. The top tax credit rate for CEPROFIs was raised to 40 percent of total physical investment in 1986. In addition, Mexican-owned enterprises are eligible for employment tax credit up to 30 percent of three times the annual minimum wage in the area, multiplied by the number of new jobs created.

    Starting in 1989, full expensing of the present value of CCAs at a 7.5 percent discount rate was offered as an alternative option to standard CCAs in nonmetropolitan areas. In the metropolitan industrial areas of Mexico City, Monterrey, and Guadalajara, only 60 percent of the present value of depreciation allowances could be deducted in the first year. Also permissible were research and development ITCs at 15 percent for the purchase of technological research (20 percent for small enterprises), and 20 percent for capital purchases by technological enterprises (30 percent for small enterprises).

- *1991–present.* As of 1991 all CEPROFI-related incentives were eliminated. The immediate deduction of present value of investment expenditure, discounted at 7.5 percent per annum, still remains, however.

The Effects of Tax Policy on the Rental Rate and Capital

The model was applied to two Mexican industries: detergents (Standard Industrial Classification, SIC 390) and other chemicals (SIC 404). The data for these two Mexican industries for the period 1970 to 1983 were collected from a variety of Mexican government sources. These two industries are among the three largest industries in the industrial sector (Division V) composed of chemicals, petroleum derivatives, rubber, and plastic products. Together, these two industries accounted for 5.2 percent of total manufacturing output and 2.9 percent of total employment. The data on industry capital stock were developed by using the perpetual inventory method with an assumed depreciation rate of 8 percent, representing a weighted average of assumed depreciation rates of 10 percent for machinery and equipment and 2.5 percent for structures, respectively.[11] The quantity of labor was measured as the average number of employees during the year. The price of labor was derived by dividing the total employment cost during the year by the average number of employees. The quantity of intermediate input was obtained by dividing the cost of intermediate inputs by the input price index.

We will now examine the effects of corporate tax policy initiatives in stimulating capital expenditure in the short, intermediate, and long runs for the case of Mexico. The three tax instruments that we consider for Mexico are the CIT rate, the ITC rate, and the CCA rate. As discussed earlier in relation to the theoretical and empirical models, only the relative price of the capital input is directly affected by tax policy initiatives (see equations 14-32 through 14-35). Thus the relative after-tax rental rate is a crucial variable in the determination of the effects of tax policy initiatives on capital expenditure. In table 14-3 we present the elasticities of the tax instruments on the rental rate. Because the normalized after-tax rental rate on capital is the same for both industries, the results found for the elasticities of rental rate of capital with respect to the three instruments are also the same. These elasticities remain relatively constant over the sample period. As seen in table 14-3, a 1 percent increase in the CCA rate results in a 0.63 percent decrease in the normalized after-tax rental rate, whereas a 1 percent rise in the ITC rate leads to a 0.41 percent decline in the relative rental rate. In fact, a 1 percent increase in the CIT rate leads to about a 1.00 percent increase in the after-tax relative rental rate. The results for the short-, intermediate-, and long-run tax elasticities for capital demand appear in table 14-4.

Tax Incentives, Investment Effects, and Forgone Revenues

Focusing on investment expenditure provides only a partial view of the effects of tax policy, in this section we calculate the effect of investment

Table 14-3. Elasticity of Rental Rate of Capital with Respect to Tax Measures

Year	e_{itc}	e_{cca}	e_{cit}
1979	−0.405	−0.621	0.895
1980	−0.409	−0.635	0.918
1981	−0.409	−0.635	0.962
1982	−0.409	−0.635	1.021
1983	−0.409	−0.635	1.021

Source: Model results.

Table 14-4. Capital Demand Elasticity, Detergents and Other Chemicals, 1979 and 1983

Elasticity	Detergents		Other chemicals	
	1979	1983	1979	1983
Short run				
e_{kitc}	0.015	0.012	0.008	0.006
e_{kcca}	0.024	0.019	0.013	0.009
e_{kcit}	−0.034	−0.031	−0.018	−0.014
Intermediate run				
e_{kitc}	0.020	0.016	0.011	0.007
e_{kcca}	0.031	0.024	0.016	0.012
e_{kcit}	−0.045	−0.039	−0.023	−0.019
Long run				
e_{kitc}	0.022	0.017	0.012	0.008
e_{kcca}	0.034	0.027	0.018	0.013
e_{kcit}	−0.049	−0.043	−0.026	−0.021

Source: Model results.

per unit value of forgone government revenue. These measures are referred to as the investment effect per unit value of lost tax revenue in table 14-5. These calculations are presented for the most recent year (1983) in the data as well as an earlier year (1979), together with the mean and standard deviation for 1979 through 1983. The data in the table suggest that the effectiveness of the ITC for both Mexican industries has deteriorated in recent years and that the measure is not cost-effective in any of the runs. Accelerated CCAs have also proved not to be cost-effective tax incentive instruments, the cost-benefit ratio for this measure being less than one in all runs for the two industries. Finally, although corporate tax rate reductions have had fairly large stimulative effects on additional capital expenditure in the detergent and other chemicals industries, revenues forgone from such reductions far exceed the positive investment effects, thereby yielding a low benefit-cost ratio. Thus, it is apparent that all three tax incentives proved to be cost-ineffective in all runs for the two industries examined here.

Pakistan

Pakistan has followed a stable corporate tax rate regime since the early 1960s. The CIT at 30 percent and a supertax at 20 to 25 percent have been maintained consistently during the last two decades. Only in fiscal 1989–90 was the supertax rate reduced to 15 percent. Foreign direct investment receives tax treatment equivalent to domestic investment.

Table 14-5. Investment Effects per Unit Value of Lost Tax Revenue, Detergents and Other Chemicals, 1979 and 1983
(pesos)

			Effect		
Tax instrument	Industry	Year	Short run	Interme- diate run	Long run
Investment tax credit	Detergents	1979	0.55	0.69	0.74
	Other chemicals		0.28	0.36	0.40
	Detergents	1983	0.44	0.51	0.54
	Other chemicals		0.26	0.32	0.34
	Detergents	Mean[a]	0.57	0.71	0.77
		SD [b]	0.08	0.13	0.16
	Other chemicals	Mean	0.26	0.35	0.40
		SD	0.02	0.02	0.03
Accelerated capital consumption allowance	Detergents	1979	0.40	0.50	0.54
	Other chemicals		0.20	0.27	0.29
	Detergents	1983	0.32	0.38	0.40
	Other chemicals		0.19	0.24	0.25
	Detergents	Mean	0.42	0.52	0.57
		SD	0.06	0.09	0.12
	Other chemicals	Mean	0.19	0.26	0.29
		SD	0.01	0.02	0.03
Corporate income tax rate reductions	Detergents	1979	0.05	0.06	0.07
	Other chemicals		0.01	0.02	0.02
	Detergents	1983	0.03	0.04	0.05
	Other chemicals		0.01	0.01	0.01
	Detergents	Mean	0.04	0.06	0.06
		SD	0.01	0.01	0.01
	Other chemicals	Mean	0.01	0.01	0.02
		SD	0.00	0.00	0.00

a. 1970 through 1983.
b. SD = sample standard deviation.
Source: Model results.

Losses are permitted to be carried forward six years, but such losses are not permitted to be carried back. A sales tax at 12.5 percent is payable on all domestically manufactured goods by the producer and on imported goods by the importer. In fiscal 1989–90, import duties at different rates were imposed on imported machinery and equipment. These rates varied from 20 percent to 50 percent if similar machinery was not manufactured in Pakistan. A higher rate of 80 percent applied to imported machinery with domestic substitutes.

Pakistan has made significant changes in the regime of fiscal incentives through the CIT over time, relying on a variety of fiscal incentives to stimulate investment. These include accelerated CCAs for certain physical assets, full expensing for research and development investments, tax rebates, regional and industry-specific tax holidays, and ITCs. These incentives are briefly discussed below. Further details of the current tax regime are given in table 14-6.

Tax holidays for two years for specific industries (for example, engineering goods) and specific regions (most of the country except major metropolitan areas) were introduced in 1959–60. The holiday period was subsequently raised to four years in 1960–61. These tax holidays were eliminated in 1972–73 but reinstated again in 1974–75. Presently, tax holidays for five years are permitted to the following industries: engineering goods, poultry farming and processing, dairy farming, cattle or sheep breeding, fish farming, data processing, and agricultural machinery. Tax holidays are also available to all industries in designated areas of the country.

Industries are eligible for varying tax credits according to location. A general tax credit for balancing, modernization, and replacement of plant and equipment was introduced at a rate of 15 percent, but its application was restricted to designated areas. Since 1976–77, the credit was made available regardless of location and type of industry. This credit was withdrawn in 1989–90 but reintroduced in 1990–91.

CCAs follow accelerated schedules for machinery and equipment, transport vehicles, and housing for workers (25 percent), oil exploration equipment (100 percent), shipbuilding (20 to 30 percent), and structures (10 percent) on a declining-balance method. Expenditures relating to research and development, transfer and adaptation of technologies, and royalties are eligible for full expensing.

The Effects of Tax Policy on the Rental Rate and Capital

The model was applied to the wearing apparel (SIC 322) and the leather and leather products industries (SIC 323) of Pakistan for 1966 to 1984. The data on these two manufacturing industries were collected primarily from the various issues of the two annual publications of the government of Pakistan: the *Census of Manufacturing Industries* and the *Economic Survey*. In 1984 the wearing apparel industry contributed 0.63 percent of the total manufacturing output and employed roughly 1 percent of the total manufacturing labor force. In that same year, the leather and leather products industry accounted for 1.80 percent of the total value of output and employed 1 percent of the manufacturing labor force. Together,

Table 14-6. Corporate Income Tax System, Pakistan, 1990–91

Tax	Percent
CIT rates applied to all income except dividends and bonus shares	
Income tax rate	30
CIT rates applied to intercorporate dividends and bonus shares	
Income tax	0
Supertax rate	
Banking companies	25
Nonbanking companies	20
Supertax on dividends received by	
Domestic public companies	5
Foreign companies	15
Domestic private companies	20
Supertax on bonus shares issued by	
Public companies	10
Private companies	15
Surcharge[a]	10
Tax rebates on	
Supertax for nonbanking public companies	10
Supertax for small companies[b]	5
Supertax for companies engaged in specific economic activities[b]	10–15
Income and supertaxes for exports	25–75
Tax credits on investment in	
Shares and debentures of Equity Participation Fund	50
Debentures and negotiable bonds	5
Shares of industrial companies set up in undeveloped areas	10–30
Plant and machinery for balancing modernization, replacement, or extension	15
Depreciation allowances	
Normal (annual) depreciation allowances	5–30
Extra shift working allowance on plant[c]	50–100
Initial depreciation allowance	25–100

Tax holidays

Full tax holiday of 4–10 years available for companies engaged in manufacturing garments; key industries; manufacturing electrical equipment and components; fishing, cattle or sheep breeding, and dairy farming; exploration of specific minerals; industrial undertaking in export processing zone; production of defense equipment or armaments in specific areas; and industrial undertakings in specific backward regions. Partial tax holidays (25–50 percent of the capital), for 5–10 years, for companies in specific regions engaged in manufacturing goods, ship building and navigation, or generation and supply of electrical energy or hydraulic power.

a. Surcharges are levied on total income and supertaxes if the company's taxable income, including dividends, exceeds Rs100,000.
b. For nonbanking public companies, this is an additional tax rebate on supertax.
c. As percentage of normal depreciation allowance.
Source: Ehdaie (1991).

these two industries accounted for 2.40 percent of the manufacturing output in 1984.

The quantity of labor is measured as total number of days worked during the year, and a labor price index was developed by dividing total employment cost during the year by the number of days worked. The value of intermediate inputs includes the cost of electricity, petroleum fuel, natural gas, and imported and domestically produced miscellaneous materials. The quantity of materials was constructed by dividing the total value of intermediate inputs by an industry-level materials price deflator. The quantity of output was constructed by dividing the total value of output by an industry output deflator. The series on capital stock was developed by employing the perpetual inventory method to investment series and assuming a depreciation rate of 8 percent. This represents a weighted average of assumed depreciation rates of 10 percent for machinery and equipment and 2.5 percent for structures, respectively.[12]

We now consider the effects of the three tax instruments—the ITC rate, the CCA rate, and the CIT rate—on the rental rate of capital. The empirical results we obtained for the elasticities of rental rate of capital with respect to various tax measures for Pakistan's wearing apparel and leather products industries are shown in table 14-7. The magnitude of the ITC elasticity increased from 1977 to 1984. In 1984, a 1 percent rise in the ITC rate led to a fall of 0.39 percent in the normalized after-tax factor price of the capital input. During the same period of time, the CCA elasticity of the relative rental rate of capital decreased. The CIT elasticities differ slightly across the leather products and wearing apparel industries, but over time the elasticities differ dramatically. In the leather products industry a 1 percent change in the CIT rate led to a 0.42 percent rise in 1977 in the normalized after-tax rental rate of capital. In 1984, however, increases in the CIT rate resulted in a rise of only 0.04 percent in the relative rental rate. In 1977, a 1 percent increase in the CIT rate resulted in a 0.36 percent increase in the relative rental rate in the apparel industry. By 1984, a rise in the CIT rate led to a rise in the price of capital input of about 0.03 percent in the same industry. The ITC elasticities were

Table 14-7. Elasticity of Rental Rate of Capital with Respect to Tax Measures, Apparel and Leather, 1977 and 1984

Industry	Year	e_{ita}	e_{cca}	e_{cit}
Apparel	1977	−0.338	−0.285	0.359
	1984	−0.386	−0.225	0.034
Leather	1977	−0.326	−0.287	0.425
	1984	−0.386	−0.225	0.037

Source: Model results.

Table 14-8. *Capital Demand Elasticity, Apparel and Leather,*
1977 and 1984

Elasticity	Apparel		Leather	
	1977	*1984*	*1977*	*1984*
Short run				
e_{kitc}	0.011	0.004	0.003	0.002
e_{kcca}	0.009	0.002	0.003	0.001
e_{kcit}	−0.012	−0.004	−0.004	−0.0002
Intermediate run				
e_{kitc}	0.019	0.008	0.006	0.003
e_{kcca}	0.016	0.005	0.006	0.002
e_{kcit}	−0.021	−0.007	−0.008	−0.0003
Long run				
e_{kitc}	0.046	0.029	0.016	0.006
e_{kcca}	0.038	0.017	0.014	0.004
e_{kcit}	−0.048	−0.003	−0.021	−0.0006

Source: Model results.

larger in absolute value than the CCA and CIT elasticities in 1984, although in 1977 the CIT elasticities were larger than comparable elasticities for the ITC and CCA rates. The results for the short-, intermediate-, and long-run tax elasticities for capital demand appear in table 14-8.

Tax Incentives, Investment Effects, and Forgone Revenues

The benefit-cost ratios for each of the tax incentives in Pakistan are presented in table 14-9 for the most recent year (1984) of the data as well as for an earlier year (1977), together with the mean and standard deviation for the 1977–84 period. In carrying out these calculations, we note that investment is most responsive to changes in ITC. The losses in government revenues are quite similar for the ITC and CCAs, and therefore the ITC yields a slightly higher benefit-cost ratio than changes in the CCA. Reductions in the corporate tax rate result in losses to government revenues that far exceed the effect on investments. The effects of all measures on investment were smaller in recent years than in earlier years for the short and intermediate runs because of the observed decline in own-price elasticity of capital in recent years. Thus the data in table 14-9 suggest that the ITC became a cost-effective measure for both industries in recent years based on its effect only in the long run. A similar pattern of cost-effectiveness emerges for accelerated CCAs. Such allowances were not cost-effective in the short and intermediate runs and became cost-

*Table 14-9.   Investment Effects per Unit Value of Lost Tax Revenue,
Apparel and Leather, 1977 and 1984*
(rupees)

Tax instrument	Industry	Year	Effect		
			Short run	Interme- diate run	Long run
Investment tax credit	Apparel	1977	0.72	0.88	1.11
	Leather		0.26	0.25	0.24
	Apparel	1984	0.28	0.71	2.50
	Leather		0.11	0.28	2.54
	Apparel	Mean[a]	0.40	0.76	0.70
		SD [b]	0.18	0.34	2.13
	Leather	Mean	0.24	0.36	0.37
		SD	0.22	0.32	1.44
Accelerated capital consumption allowances	Apparel	1977	0.52	0.64	0.81
	Leather		0.18	0.18	0.17
	Apparel	1984	0.23	0.59	2.10
	Leather		0.09	0.23	2.13
	Apparel	Mean	0.31	0.60	0.51
		SD	0.13	0.27	1.70
	Leather	Mean	0.19	0.28	0.25
		SD	0.18	0.26	1.14
Corporate income tax rate reductions	Apparel	1977	0.05	0.13	0.21
	Leather		0.01	0.01	0.02
	Apparel	1984	0.00	0.00	0.00
	Leather		0.00	0.00	0.00
	Apparel	Mean	0.00	0.04	0.08
		SD	0.00	0.04	0.07
	Leather	Mean	0.00	0.00	0.01
		SD	0.00	0.00	0.01

a. 1966 through 1984.
b. SD = sample standard deviation.
Source: Model results.

effective in recent years only in the long run. Finally, reductions in the corporate tax rate greatly stimulated investment in both the apparel or leather products industries, but this stimulation was outweighed by major revenue losses to the national treasury. Thus for Pakistani industries, the three tax incentives considered were ineffective in stimulating investment in recent years. Still, in light of a better record of accelerated depreciation allowances and ITCs in earlier years, perhaps a redesign of such incentives with some consideration for refundability provisions and elimination of regulatory bottlenecks would help restore their effectiveness in stimulating investments.

Turkey

The CIT in Turkey provides a significant source of government revenues (accounting for 10 percent of total tax revenues) as well as serving as a major tool of industrial policy. The government has changed both the tax rate and the tax base many times during the past three decades. The statutory corporate tax rate hovered around 10 percent during the 1950s, rose to 20 percent in the 1960s, and grew to 25 percent in the 1970s. In 1980 it was raised to 50 percent, lowered to 40 percent in 1981, and then raised again to 46 percent (plus a defense surcharge of 3 percent) in 1985. It has stayed at that level since then. During these years there also have been significant changes in the tax base (see Bulutoglu and Thirsk 1991). Preferential treatment of public enterprises was eliminated in 1980 and has not been reinstated. Intercompany distribution of dividends has been made exempt from taxation, and corporate reorganizations are no longer subject to capital gains taxation. Inflationary adjustment of assets but not of liabilities has also been allowed.

In the following, we briefly summarize the current provisions of the corporate taxation and investment incentives regimes that appear in table 14-10. Taxable income of corporate entities (defined as book profits before taxes plus increases in pension reserves and general provision for bad debt minus investment and export allowances and depreciation deductions, and so forth) is currently taxed at a flat rate of 46 percent. A 3 percent defense surcharge is payable on this basic rate. In addition, a 1 percent tax is payable to the Social Assistance and Security Fund, and an additional 1 percent tax is levied for the Apprenticeship, Vocational, and Training Encouragement Fund, for a combined corporate tax rate of 49.38 percent. Corporate tax is withheld at source at varying rates, including 0 percent rates for dividend distributions, 5 percent for income from crude oil exploration, 10 percent on interest and movable property income, 20 percent for income from immovable property, and 25 percent for salaries and wages and patents and royalties.

Depreciation allowances are based on historical costs adjusted by the wholesale price index minus 10 percent. They take the form of ten-year interest-bearing bonds. Either the straight-line or the declining-balance method of depreciation may be chosen for any asset, but no switch is allowed from the straight-line to the declining-balance method during the life of the asset. Depreciation on movable fixed assets acquired on or after January 1, 1983, may be taken under a straight-line method at any

Table 14-10.   Corporate Income Tax System, Turkey, 1990–91

Tax	Percent
Corporate income, general	46
Withholding on payments by domestic corporation to foreign corporation	
Rental from fixed assets	20
Leasing	0.5
Royalties on patents	25
Professional services	15
Petroleum services	5
Interest on trade receivables	10
Other interest (loans and deposits)	10
Withholding on payments to nonresident individuals	
Rentals from immovable assets	20
Royalties on patents	25
Professional services	15
Interest on receivables and deposits	10
Value added tax	
Standard rate	12
Agricultural products	1
Basic foods, books, natural gas	6
Luxury goods	20
Petroleum products	13
Banking and insurance transactions	5
Investment tax allowance	30–100 of cost of specified assets
Export allowance	
Export earnings of manufacturers	12
Export earnings of traders	3
Export of fresh fruit and vegetables	12
International transport	12
Tourist establishments	20
Depreciation allowance	
Straight line	25
Declining balance	50

Source: Price Waterhouse (1992).

rate chosen by the taxpayer, up to an annual maximum of 25 percent. If the declining-balance method is used, the maximum allowable depreciation rate is 50 percent. Assets having values of less than TL 5,000 can be deducted. For structures and movable fixed assets acquired before January 1, 1983, the Ministry of Finance publishes maximum depreciation rates (on a straight-line basis) permissible for tax purposes. These rates typically are 4.0 percent for factory buildings, 15.0 to 20.0 percent for transport equipment, and 12.5 percent for machinery and equipment.

A value added tax is levied at a general rate of 12 percent. Banking and insurance transactions are subject to a 3 percent tax. An ITA in Turkey is a deduction from the taxable income for corporate tax purposes. The deduction is claimed in the year of investment on that portion of investment not subsidized by the government. Unused ITAs can be carried forward indefinitely. The ITA rate varies by region and type of investment.

Corporations can also set aside up to 25 percent of taxable income for future investments. The amount set aside at the discretion of the corporation is deducted from its taxable income and deposited in an interest-bearing account (earning the same interest as government bonds, usually about 20 percent per year) with the central bank. It can be withdrawn at any time with authorization from the State Planning Office and used for investment.

For tax purposes, capital is depreciated at a rate of up to 50 percent for machinery and equipment. Further assets can be revalued at the end of every calendar year.

A large number of nontax incentives are available to eligible investments. These include low-interest credit, funds for working capital, allocation of foreign exchange, and allowance for the importation of used equipment.

The Effects of Tax Policy on the Rental Rate and Capital

The model is applied to three Turkish industries: nonelectrical machinery (SIC 382), electrical machinery (SIC 383), and transport equipment (SIC 384) industries in the private sector only. It covers the period 1973 through 1985. These industries accounted for 20 percent of total manufacturing output and employment and 24 percent of manufacturing wages in 1985. The data on output, employment, intermediate input, and investment were obtained from a variety of Turkish government sources. The quantity of labor was measured as the average number of employees during the year. The price index was constructed by dividing the total employment cost during the year by the average number of employees. Intermediate inputs or materials include raw materials, components, containers, fuel, and electricity. The quantity of materials was constructed by dividing total value of materials by an industry materials deflator. The quantity of output was constructed by dividing the total value of output by the relevant industry output price deflator. The same deflator was used for the electrical machinery and transport equipment industries. The capital stock series was developed by applying the perpetual inventory method to investment series and by assuming a depreciation rate equal to 8 percent, representing a weighted average of assumed depreciation rates of 10 percent for machinery and equipment and 2.5 percent for structure [13]

The effects of the three tax instruments on the rental rate of capital are given in table 14-11. Because the normalized after-tax rental rate on capital is the same for the three industries, the results found for the tax elasticities are also the same. From table 14-11 we observe that the ITA elasticity increases during the sample period, whereas the CCA and CIT elasticities remain relatively constant. During the first half of the sample period, a 1 percent increase in the ITA rate decreases the after-tax rental rate by 0.20 percent. During the second half of the period, the elasticity ranges from −0.24 to −0.35. For most of the period the elasticity associated with the CIT rate ranges from 0.21 to 0.28 and then decreases in the last few years. Generally, the elasticity of the CCA rate ranges from 0.70 to 0.10 for most of the period. The results for the short-, intermediate-, and long-run tax elasticities for capital demand appear in table 14-12.

Tax Incentives, Investment Effects, and Forgone Revenues

Table 14-13 presents the benefit-cost ratios for the three Turkish industries for two years, 1975 and 1985, and the mean and standard deviation

Table 14-11. Elasticity of Rental Rate of Capital with Respect to Tax Measures, 1973–85

Year	e_{ita}	e_{cca}	e_{cit}
1973	−0.199	−0.065	0.210
1974	−0.195	−0.086	0.242
1975	−0.196	−0.084	0.238
1976	−0.199	−0.067	0.212
1977	−0.197	−0.078	0.229
1978	−0.193	−0.098	0.260
1979	−0.193	−0.096	0.259
1980	−0.242	−0.129	0.386
1981	−0.348	−0.147	0.259
1982	−0.345	−0.155	0.276
1983	−0.258	−0.064	0.057
1984	−0.258	−0.063	0.055
1985	−0.341	−0.099	0.101

Source: Model results.

Table 14-12. Capital Demand Elasticity, Machinery and Transport Equipment, 1974 and 1985

Elasticity	Electrical machinery		Nonelectrical machinery		Transport equipment	
	1974	*1985*	*1974*	*1985*	*1974*	*1988*
Short run						
e_{kita}	0.014	0.013	0.024	0.021	0.024	0.020
e_{kcca}	0.006	0.004	0.010	0.006	0.010	0.006
e_{kcit}	−0.017	−0.004	−0.029	−0.006	−0.029	−0.006
Intermediate run						
e_{kita}	0.021	0.021	0.037	0.033	0.037	0.032
e_{kcca}	0.009	0.006	0.016	0.009	0.016	0.009
e_{kcit}	−0.027	−0.006	−0.046	−0.009	−0.046	−0.009
Long run						
e_{kita}	0.034	0.034	0.059	0.052	0.055	0.051
e_{kcca}	0.015	0.009	0.026	0.015	0.026	0.015
e_{kcit}	−0.042	−0.009	−0.074	−0.015	−0.074	−0.015

Source: Model results.

for the sample period 1975 through 1985. A 1 percent increase in ITA had the largest effect on capital, although a similar change in CCA and CIT rate reduction had a relatively smaller effect. This is because the elasticity of the rental rate of capital with respect to the ITA is much higher than it is with respect to CCA and CIT rate reduction. The loss in tax revenue associated with reductions in the CIT rate is quite large and thus such a policy change yields a low benefit-cost ratio. The revenue losses are larger for the ITA than for changes in the CCA, and because investment effects are higher for the former measure, the net effect is to yield similar benefit-cost ratios for the two instruments. The benefit-cost ratio was smaller for almost all measures in 1985 than in 1975. This resulted from a decline in the elasticity of capital stock to a change in its own rental rate. Note that the capital stock increased over time, which implies that if the own-price elasticity of capital were to be constant, investment response to changes in rental rate would have to increase at the same rate as the increases in capital stock. It is unlikely that investment response would increase at the same rate because that would imply an unrealistic increase in the marginal product of capital. Thus it is reasonable to expect own-price elasticity of capital to decline over time. In conclusion, the data in the table suggest that ITA and CCA provisions proved to be effective instruments of public policy for investment promotion, especially in view of their intermediate- and long-run effects. The same could not, however, be said about CIT

Table 14-13. Investment Effects per Unit Value of Lost Tax Revenue, Machinery and Transport Equipment, 1975 and 1985
(Turkish lira)

			Effect		
Tax instrument	Industry	Year	Short run	Interme- diate run	Long run
Investment allowance	Electrical machinery	1975	0.63	0.97	1.50
	Nonelectrical machinery		1.00	1.59	2.62
	Transport equipment		1.14	1.71	2.56
	Electrical machinery	1985	0.40	0.72	1.54
	Nonelectrical machinery		0.86	1.42	2.49
	Transport equipment		1.00	1.54	2.40
	Electrical machinery	Mean[a]	0.53	0.84	1.37
		SD [b]	0.01	0.17	0.29
	Nonelectrical machinery	Mean	0.81	1.29	2.12
		SD	0.17	0.28	0.51
	Transport equipment	Mean	0.85	1.34	2.19
		SD	0.23	0.35	0.60
Accelerated capital consumption allowance	Electrical machinery	1975	0.56	0.86	1.33
	Nonelectrical machinery		0.89	1.42	2.34
	Transport equipment		1.01	1.53	2.28
	Electrical machinery	1985	0.38	0.68	1.45
	Nonelectrical machinery		0.81	1.33	2.34
	Transport equipment		0.94	1.44	2.25
	Electrical machinery	Mean	0.47	0.75	1.22
		SD	0.10	0.14	0.24
	Nonelectrical machinery	Mean	0.72	1.15	1.89
		SD	0.14	0.23	0.43
	Transport equipment	Mean	0.76	1.20	1.94
		SD	0.20	0.31	0.51
Corporate income tax rate reductions	Electrical machinery	1975	0.32	0.56	0.84
	Nonelectrical machinery		0.16	0.27	0.45
	Transport equipment		0.20	0.31	0.50
	Electrical machinery	1985	0.20	0.21	0.28
	Nonelectrical machinery		0.07	0.11	0.19
	Transport equipment		0.03	0.06	0.10
	Electrical machinery	Mean	0.06	0.01	0.00
		SD	0.36	0.28	0.45
	Nonelectrical machinery	Mean	0.05	0.03	0.07
		SD	0.37	0.51	0.88
	Transport equipment	Mean	0.08	0.02	0.12
		SD	0.71	0.28	0.96

a. 1973 through 1985.
b. SD = sample standard deviation.
Source: Model results.

rate tax rate reductions, which clearly resulted in windfall gains to existing capital without encouraging new investment.

Summary and Conclusions

This chapter provides an empirical framework for the assessment of the effects of tax policy on the array of producer decisions concerning output supplies and input demands in Mexico, Pakistan, and Turkey. We have specified and estimated a dynamic production structure model for this purpose for selected industries in each of the countries.

On the Elasticity of the Rental Rate of Capital with respect to Tax Instruments

The tax sensitivity of the rental rate of capital is quite inelastic with the single exception of its elasticity with respect to the corporate tax rate in Mexico, which is unitary (see table 14-14). In Mexico the rental rate of capital is most sensitive to corporate tax changes and relatively less to accelerated depreciations and investment credits. In Pakistan the sensitivity ranking of the three instruments is completely reversed, and changes in investment credits have the greatest influence on the rental rate of capital. In Turkey the rental rate is more responsive to changes in investment allowances than to accelerated capital cost allowances or corporate tax rate reductions.

On the Tax Sensitivity of the Capital Stock

The capital stock exhibits sensitivity to tax changes, but this sensitivity varies by tax measure, by industry, and by the adjustment period. Table 14-15 provides comparative evidence on the tax sensitivity of the capital stock by industry, by tax measure, and by adjustment period. For Mexico, elasticity estimates range from −0.014 to −0.043 for corporate tax changes; from 0.009 to 0.027 for CCAs; and from 0.006 to 0.017 for changes in ITCs. For Pakistani industries the responsiveness of capital

Table 14-14. Elasticity of Rental Rate of Capital with Respect to Tax Measures, Mexico, Pakistan, and Turkey

Country	Year	e_{itc}	e_{ita}	e_{cca}	e_{cit}
Mexico	1983	−0.409	n.a.	−0.635	1.021
Pakistan	1984	−0.386	n.a.	−0.225	0.035
Turkey	1985	n.a.	−0.341	−0.099	0.101

n.a. Not applicable.
Source: Model results.

Table 14-15. *Tax Sensitivity of Capital Stock, Selected Industries, Mexico, Pakistan, and Turkey*

Industry	e_{kitc}			e_{kita}			e_{kcca}			e_{kcit}		
	SR	IR	LR	SR	IR	LR	SR	IR	LR	SR	IR	LR
Mexico (1983)												
Detergents	0.012	0.016	0.017	n.a.	n.a.	n.a.	0.019	0.024	0.027	−0.031	−0.039	−0.043
Other chemicals	0.006	0.007	0.008	n.a.	n.a.	n.a.	0.009	0.012	0.013	−0.014	−0.019	−0.021
Pakistan (1984)												
Apparel	0.004	0.008	0.029	n.a.	n.a.	n.a.	0.002	0.005	0.017	−0.0004	−0.0007	−0.003
Leather	0.002	0.003	0.006	n.a.	n.a.	n.a.	0.001	0.002	0.004	−0.0002	−0.0003	−0.006
Turkey (1985)												
Electrical machinery	n.a.	n.a.	n.a.	0.013	0.040	0.034	0.004	0.006	0.009	−0.004	−0.006	−0.009
Nonelectrical machinery	n.a.	n.a.	n.a.	0.021	0.033	0.052	0.006	0.009	0.015	−0.006	−0.009	−0.015
Transport equipment	n.a.	n.a.	n.a.	0.020	0.032	0.051	0.006	0.009	0.015	−0.006	−0.009	−0.015

n.a. Not applicable.
SR = short run; IR = intermediate run; LR = long run.
Source: Model results.

stock to changes in CIT is quite small—elasticity estimates range from 0.0002 to –0.006; estimates of ITC elasticity range from 0.002 to 0.029; and finally for CCAs between 0.001 and 0.017. The last two sets of elasticities are compatible with the ones obtained for the Mexican industries. For Turkish industries, changes in investment allowances matter more for the effects on capital formation than alternative tax measures. Specifically, estimates of elasticity range from 0.013 to 0.052 with respect to changes in the ITA; from 0.004 to 0.015 with respect to changes in the CCAs; and from –0.004 to –0.015 with respect to changes in the CIT.

On Benefit-Cost Ratios

The model results suggest that tax policy affected production and investment and that some tax incentives were more effective than others (see table 14-16). Among the incentive measures examined, investment allowances proved to be a cost-effective instrument for investment promotion only to Turkish industries; and ITCs and accelerated depreciation provisions had mixed success, whereas corporate tax reductions met with dismal failure in promoting investment in a cost-effective manner in all cases for all countries. In regard to their effect in the long run, ITCs were cost-effective in two of the four industries studied. Accelerated CCAs also registered a similar performance and had an incremental benefit-cost ratio exceeding one in the long run for five out of seven industries studied. Corporate tax rate reductions stimulated investments but resulted in revenue losses exceeding this stimulative effect in all cases and in all runs considered in this study. Note that reductions in the corporate tax rate apply to a larger base of pretax profits than the smaller base of current investments relevant for ITCs. The cost-effectiveness of these incentives in the long run, except for reductions in corporate tax rates, which proved cost-ineffective in all cases, varies by country. In Turkey, investment allowances and CCAs were cost-effective. In Mexico, neither ITCs nor accelerated CCAs were cost-effective. In contrast, in Pakistan, both ITCs and accelerated CCAs were cost-effective. In the intermediate run, defined as the effect on tax policy after one year, only the investment allowances and accelerated CCAs available to Turkish industries proved cost-effective.

In sum, selective tax incentives such as ITCs, investment allowances, and accelerated CCAs are more cost-effective in promoting investment than more general tax incentives such as corporate tax rate reductions. In order to make selective tax incentives more effective, ITCs must be refundable and investment and depreciation allowances be permitted to be carried forward. If stimulation of investment expenditure is the sole objective of tax policy, reduction of the corporate tax rate is not a cost-effective instrument.

Table 14-16. Investment Expenditure per Unit Value of Lost Tax Revenue, Selected Industries, Mexico, Pakistan, and Turkey

	Effect		
	---	---	---
		Intermediate	
Tax instrument	Short run	run	Long run
Investment tax credit			
Mexico: detergents[a]	0.44	0.51	0.54
Mexico: other chemicals[a]	0.26	0.32	0.34
Pakistan: apparel[b]	0.28	0.71	2.50
Pakistan: leather[b]	0.11	0.28	2.54
Accelerated capital consumption allowance			
Mexico: detergents[a]	0.32	0.38	0.40
Mexico: other chemicals[a]	0.19	0.24	0.25
Pakistan: apparel[b]	0.23	0.59	2.10
Pakistan: leather[b]	0.09	0.23	2.13
Turkey: electrical machinery[c]	0.38	0.68	1.45
Turkey: nonelectrical machinery[c]	0.81	1.33	2.34
Turkey: transport[c]	0.94	1.44	2.25
Corporate income tax rate reductions			
Mexico: detergents[a]	0.03	0.04	0.05
Mexico: other chemicals[a]	0.01	0.01	0.01
Pakistan: apparel[b]	0.001	0.0002	0.007
Pakistan: leather[b]	0.00	0.00	0.00
Turkey: electrical machinery[c]	0.20	0.21	0.28
Turkey: nonelectrical machinery[c]	0.07	0.11	0.19
Turkey: transport[c]	0.03	0.06	0.10
Investment allowance			
Turkey: electrical machinery[c]	0.40	0.72	1.54
Turkey: nonelectrical machinery[c]	0.86	1.42	2.49
Turkey: transport equipment[c]	1.00	1.54	2.40

a. Pesos.
b. Rupees.
c. Turkish lira.
Source: Model results.

Notes

1. The model can be readily generalized to include multiple outputs. The production function is also assumed to be twice continuously differentiable, and quasi-concave in the inputs and net investments.

2. The issue of capital utilization is not addressed in this model. The problem of costly capital utilization implies that depreciation rates depend on prices,

technology, and market structure. Hence, the use of existing measures of capital stocks would be inappropriate because service lives are assumed to be independent of prices and technology. Costly capital utilization implies that capital stock measurement and technology determination must be modeled simultaneously. This is an interesting, complex, but secondary problem to determining the effects of tax policy on output supply and input demand.

3. The model can be readily modified to include ITAs.

4. This assumption is the Mortigliani-Miller hypothesis. It is also possible that with market imperfections firms can influence the rate of return on their financial capital (see Steigum 1983 and Bernstein and Nadiri 1986 for dynamic models in this context).

5. The formula for the after-tax purchase prices of the capital stocks can be simplified. If the discount rates are not expected to change, then

$$Q_{is} = q_{is}\left[1 - \upsilon_{is} - \left(\sum_{\tau=0}^{\infty} u_{cs+\tau}(1 - \varphi_{is}\upsilon_{is})\, d_{i\tau}\right)/(1+\rho)^{\tau}\right].$$

If, in addition, the tax rates and credits are not expected to change, then

$$Q_{is} = q_{is}\left[1 - \upsilon_i - u_c(1 - \varphi_i\upsilon_i)\left(\sum_{\tau=0}^{\infty} d_{i\tau}/(1+\rho)^{\tau}\right)\right].$$

The latter is the more standard formula and is a special case of the after-tax purchase price formula developed in the model (see Arrow and Kurz 1970; Hall and Jorgenson 1967, 1969).

6. The inverse price elasticity and the conjectural elasticity are not assumed to be constant. Equation 14-12a contains their equilibrium magnitudes. The production function is also part of the first-order conditions. The second-order conditions are assumed to be satisfied. The symbol ∇ represents the gradient vector.

7. Recall that $\xi < 0$ and $\theta > 0$, so the last set of terms on the right side of equation 14-14, including the minus sign, is positive.

8. The additional revenue and thereby profit arising from oligopoly power does not vary when it is evaluated at the equilibrium point. Thus the term affects the calculation of variable profit but does not affect the first-order conditions characterizing an equilibrium. As a consequence the expression can be ignored when defining shadow variable profit.

9. The function is also twice continuously differentiable, homogeneous of degree one and convex in after-tax prices, and concave in the capital inputs and net investment levels.

10. It is also assumed that the transversality conditions are satisfied. The symbol 0_m signifies an m-dimensional vector of zeros.

11. Because depreciation rates for the sample industries are not available, the estimates by Jorgenson and Yun (1991) for U.S. industries were used. The depreciation rate for nonresidential structures (0.025) was calculated as an average of the depreciation rates on various types of industrial structures. Inclusion of other types of buildings and structures did not alter the above depreciation rate significantly. The depreciation rate for producer durable equipment (0.10) was calculated as an average of the depreciation rates on a large number of electrical, nonelectrical, and transportation machinery and equipment categories.

The notes are similar to the ones used in Epstein and Yatchew (1985) and Epstein and Denny (1983).

12. See note 11.

13. See note 11.

References

Arrow, K. J., and M. Kurz. 1970. *Public Investment, the Rate of Return, and Optimal Social Policy.* Baltimore, Md.: Johns Hopkins University Press.

Bernstein, J. I., and P. Mohnen. 1991. "Price Cost Margins, Exports, and Productivity Growth, with an Application to Canadian Industries." *Canadian Journal of Economics* 24 (3): 638–59.

Bernstein, J. I., and M. I. Nadiri. 1986. "Financing and Investment in Plant and Equipment." In M. H. Peston and R. E. Quandt, eds., *Prices, Competition, and Equilibrium.* Oxford, U.K.: Philip Allan/Barnes & Noble.

———. 1988. "Corporate Taxes and the Structure of Production: A Selected Survey." In Jack M. Mintz and Douglas Purvis, eds., *The Impact of Taxation on Business Activity.* Kingston, Ont., Can.: John Deutsch Institute, Queen's University.

Bulutoglu, Kenan, and Wayne Thirsk. 1991. "Tax Reform in Turkey." World Bank, Public Economics Division, Washington, D.C.

Ehdaie, J. 1991. "Revenue Generating and Investment Aspects of the Corporate Income Tax System in Pakistan: An Agenda for Reform." World Bank, Country Economics Department, Washington, D.C.

Epstein, L. G. 1981. "Duality Theory and Functional Forms for Dynamic Factor Demands." *Review of Economic Studies* 48 (1): 81–95.

Epstein, L. G., and M. G. S. Denny. 1983. "The Multivariate Flexible Accelerator Model: Its Empirical Restrictions and an Application to U.S. Manufacturing." *Econometrica* 51 (3): 647–74.

Epstein, L. G., and A. J. Yatchew. 1985. "The Empirical Determination of Technology and Expectations: A Simplified Procedure." *Journal of Econometrics* 27 (2): 235–58.

Gil-Diaz, Francisco. 1990. "Reforming Taxes in Developing Countries: Mexico's Protracted Tax Reform." World Bank, Country Economics Department, Washington, D.C.

Guisinger, Stephen, and Associates. 1985. *Investment Incentives and Performance Requirements.* New York: Praeger.

Hall, Robert E., and Dale W. Jorgenson. 1967. "Tax Policy and Investment Behavior." *American Economic Review* 57 (June): 391–414.

———. 1969. "Tax Policy and Investment Behavior, Reply and Further Results." *American Economic Review* 59 (June): 388–401.

IBFD (International Bureau of Fiscal Documentation). 1988a. "Taxation in Latin America: Mexico." Amsterdam, the Netherlands.

———. 1988b. "Taxes and Investment in Asia and the Pacific: Pakistan." Amsterdam, the Netherlands.

———. 1988c. "The Taxation of Companies in Europe: Turkey." Amsterdam, the Netherlands.

Jorgenson, D. W., and K. Y. Yun. 1991. *Tax Reform and the Cost of Capital.* New York: Oxford University Press.

Mortensen, Dale T. 1973. "Generalized Costs of Adjustment and Dynamic Factor Demand Theory." *Econometrica* 41 (4): 657–66.

Price Waterhouse. 1992. *Corporate Taxes: A Worldwide Summary.* New York.

Steigum, E. 1983. "A Financial Theory of Investment Behavior." *Econometrica* 51 (3): 637–45.

Treadway, A. B. 1971. "On the Rational Multivariate Flexible Accelerator." *Econometrica* 39 (5): 845–55.

————. 1974. "The Globally Optimal Flexible Accelerator." *Journal of Economic Theory* 7(1): 17–39.

Ugarte, Fernando Sanchez. 1988. "Taxation of Foreign Investment in Mexico: The North American Perspective." Working Paper DP88-7. International Economics Program, University of Toronto, Canada.

15

TAX INCENTIVES, MARKET POWER, AND CORPORATE INVESTMENT

Dagmar Rajagopal and Anwar Shah

AN AREA OF only recent interest with respect to empirical research is the evaluation of tax and industrial policy for developing countries through the use of a production structure framework involving rental prices of capital services (see, for example, Bernstein and Shah, chapter 14 of the present volume; Feltenstein and Shah, 1993 and forthcoming; and Shah and Baffes, chapter 16 of this volume). These studies represent pioneering work for developing countries.

One of the main objectives of this chapter is to examine the effect of tax incentives on investment. By *investment* we mean not only changes in the stock of physical capital but also expenditure on research and development (R&D), which represents changes in the stock of knowledge capital. We calculate the effect of tax incentives on the rental prices of the services of physical and knowledge capital, and, in turn, the effect of these rental prices on both types of investment, in order to determine the effect of tax incentives on physical and R&D investment.

As Pindyck and Rotemberg (1983: 1072 n17) pointed out, the rental price of capital services calculated in the tradition of Christensen and Jorgenson (1969) is inconsistent with a rational expectations model because it implicitly assumes static expectations on the part of economic agents. Here we derive expressions for the rental prices of the services from physical and knowledge capital that incorporate the assumption of rational expectations. By this we mean that decisionmakers use all the information available to them at a given point in time in order to make unbiased forecasts of the values of economic variables that will prevail at a future point in time.

We do not assume a priori that the corporate income tax (CIT) and, hence, tax incentives affect the rental prices of capital services. Instead, we test for the absence or presence of the parameters of the CIT in the expressions for the rental prices of capital services. In empirical work on input demand functions, the assumption of perfect competition is usually maintained, so the possibility of short-run shifting of the CIT is ruled out (see, for example, Shah and Baffes, chapter 16 of this volume). Rather than maintaining this assumption, we test it against the alternative assumption that firms may be able to shift the CIT forward in the short run. In the latter case the expressions for the rental prices of capital services may be free of the parameters of the CIT, as we discuss below. The most likely scenario may well be that firms are only partially successful in shifting the CIT on to consumers. Instead of ruling out the possibility of full short-run forward shifting of the CIT a priori, however, we test the rental prices with and without tax parameters against each other. The rental prices of capital services are two of the most important channels through which tax incentives may or may not influence the production and investment decisions of firms. Therefore it is essential for policy-makers to be quite certain that tax incentives do indeed have an effect on these rental prices of capital services. This is the reason for the non-nested hypothesis tests whose results we report below. (On non-nested hypothesis tests see MacKinnon 1983 and 1992.)

Our data were taken from Pakistan's textile, chemical, and pharmaceutical industries and from Turkey's chemical and petroleum derivatives industries. For all these industries the models that used the rental prices of capital services without tax parameters were rejected by the alternative models, which used the rental prices with tax parameters. The rental prices with tax parameters could not be rejected, however, by the competing expressions that were free of the parameters of the CIT. For our samples we were thus able to show that the parameters of the CIT do enter the expressions for the rental prices of capital services. Having established this, we went on to calculate the effect of current tax incentives on investment in physical and knowledge capital and to find the ratios of investment gained to tax revenue lost for all our samples. Then we explored the effect of a change in tax incentives expected for the following year. We were able to do this because of our assumption of rational expectations for the parameters of the CIT as well as for the other variables of the model.

A large number of empirical studies have not produced any consensus among economists about the incidence of the CIT. Authors who try to assess the effect of taxes on the distribution of incomes usually make several different shifting assumptions for the CIT and then proceed to do their calculations for each of these shifting assumptions. (See, for example, Pechman 1985 for the United States; Ruggeri, van Wart, and Howard 1993 for Canada; and Gillespie and Vermaeten 1993 also for Canada.) Most of the earlier empirical studies regressed either the price of output or before-tax profits on changes in the CIT and other explanatory variables, trying to determine the effect of tax changes on either of these dependent variables. (See, for example, Davis 1972; Gordon 1967;

and Moffat 1970.) Harberger (1962) pointed out long ago, however, that a positive association between changes in the CIT and changes in either the price of corporate outputs or before-tax corporate profits does not prove the presence of short-run forward shifting of the CIT. Such a positive association can equally well be explained by the movement of capital from the corporate to the noncorporate sector (Harberger 1962). Nevertheless, empirical studies of the incidence of the CIT along the lines described above continued long after the publication of Harberger's seminal paper. In contrast, Hall (1964) took a completely different approach, which provided the inspiration for the work reported here. Hall estimated two production functions for the U.S. economy, one under the assumption that there was short-run forward-shifting of the CIT, another one for the hypothesis that such shifting was absent. Then he compared his estimation results to see which equation provided the better fit. His criterion for a "better" fit was the coefficient of determination R^2. We used non-nested hypothesis tests, instead, to test the alternative econometric models against each other.

It is the short-run effect of the CIT that determines whether the tax does or does not affect the rental prices of capital services. This is a question for partial equilibrium analysis. The long-run general equilibrium effects of the tax are quite similar, whether it is shifted in the short run or not. A tax that is fully shifted forward in the short run results in increased prices of corporate outputs, and therefore smaller quantities are demanded and produced. The output effect of a fully shifted CIT thus causes inputs to move from the corporate to the noncorporate sector, which is also the output effect of a CIT that was not shifted in the short run (Harberger 1962). Only the substitution effect of the tax differs, depending on whether it is shifted in the short run. As we explain below, it is the CIT's substitution effect that determines whether the tax influences the rental prices of capital services.

Our complete econometric model consists of one equation each for the variable inputs labor and materials, an equation for investment in physical capital, an equation for R&D expenditure (investment in knowledge capital), and an output equation. These five equations could be estimated for Pakistan's chemical and pharmaceutical industries and for Turkey's chemical and petroleum derivatives industries. The sample consisting of the Pakistani textile industry alone was too small for the estimation of the full model, however. We could not justify combining the textile industry with the chemical and pharmaceutical industries because the production methods of the textile industry are not likely to be similar to the technological structure of the chemical and pharmaceutical industries. Given the small sample size for the textile industry alone, we had to omit R&D investment and knowledge capital from the model for this industry, leaving us with only four equations and fewer parameters to be estimated.

We specified a quadratic approximation to an arbitrary normalized variable cost function. Instead of maintaining the hypothesis of zero marginal adjustment costs (MACs) at the origin, we tested this hypothesis and found that we had to reject it for Pakistan's textile industry and for Turkey's chemical and petroleum derivatives industries, whereas for Pakistan's chemical and pharmaceutical industries we were not able to reject the null hypothesis of zero MACs at the origin. Assuming zero MACs when there is no investment forces the researcher to treat the two variable inputs in an asymmetric way, as we show later. Therefore we did not make this assumption for any of our industries, even though we were not able to reject it for Pakistan's chemical and pharmaceutical industries. Because of our assumption of nonzero MACs at the origin, we were able to calculate the effect of tax incentives not only on investment but also on the demand for both of the variable factors of production.

We have organized the remainder of this chapter as follows: In the next section, we describe the intertemporal optimization model we used, outline the derivation of the rental prices of capital services, and provide the theoretical foundation for the estimating equations, which we then derive in the following section. We go on to explain how the effect of selected tax incentives is transmitted to the endogenous variables of the model, present our empirical results, and discuss their policy implications. In the last section we give a brief summary. The appendix to this chapter includes the sources for the data, an outline of how the variables were constructed from the raw data, the details for some of the derivations, the elasticity formulas, and information about the CIT in the two countries.

The Theoretical Model

Our theoretical model is presented here under three different sets of assumptions. We tested these three versions of the model against each other, using the non-nested hypothesis tests outlined later in the chapter.

The Theoretical Model under the Assumption of Perfect Competition, Hence No Short-Run Forward Shifting of the CIT

The assumption of rational rather than static expectations implies that managers expect economic variables to change over time and that they regard future prices and quantities as realizations of stochastic variables. Based on the information available to them at the present time s, they form expectations about prices and quantities at the times t, with t running from s to ∞. For example, the notation $\varepsilon_s(K_{pt})$ refers to the mathematical expectation of K_{pt}, conditional on Ω_s, the set of information available at time s. (K_{pt} stands for the stock of physical capital at time t.) The subjective expectations of economic agents are assumed to be equal to this mathematical expectation $\varepsilon_s(K_{pt})$.

We assume that the firm maximizes the expected value of the stream of its discounted future dividends in excess of the opportunity cost of equity capital—that is, its expected net present value. Therefore the firm's objective function is given by

$$(15\text{-}1) \quad V = \varepsilon_s \sum_{t=s}^{\infty} D_{s,t} \Big[(P_{yt})\,(Y_t) - \sum_{j=1}^{2} (W_{jt})\,(v_{jt}) - (i_{t,t+a})\,(A_t) - (u_{pt})\,(K_{pt}^{\&})$$

$$- (P_{pt})\,(I_{pt}) - (P_{kt})\,(I_{kt}) + DA_{t+1} - \text{CITP}_t \Big].$$

Because we use discrete rather than continuous time in this model, the net present value of the firm is a sum rather than an integral, and the discount factor is $D_{s,t} =$

$$\frac{1}{(1 + r_{s,t})\,(1 + \pi_{s,t})} = \frac{1}{1 + r_{s,t} + \pi_{s,t} + (r_{s,t})\,(\pi_{s,t})} \doteq \frac{1}{(1 + i_{s,t})}$$

rather than $e^{-(r+\pi)t} = e^{-it}$. Here $r_{s,t}$, $i_{s,t}$, and $\pi_{s,t}$ denote the real interest rate, nominal interest rate, and rate of inflation that between the current time period s and the future time period t. The other variables in the equation for the expected net present value of the firm are defined as follows, where the time subscript has been omitted from some of the variables for ease of notation:

P_{yt} = $(p_{yt})\,(1 + \pi_{0,t})$ = price of output in nominal terms.

p_{yt} = real price of output.

Y = quantity of output.

W_{jt} = $(w_{jt})\,(1 + \pi_{0,t})$ = nominal price of variable input j, $j = L, M$.

w_{jt} = real price of variable input j.

v_j = quantity of variable input j.

A = firm's debt + equity.

a = average time period for which A is outstanding at time t.

u_p = property tax rate.

$K_p^{\&}$ = assessed value of those of the firm's physical assets that are subject to the property tax. It is assumed here that assessment of properties takes place at infrequent intervals, so that the assessed value $K_p^{\&}$ is independent of the firm's true stock of physical capital K_p, and of its physical capital stock K_p^{*} for the purposes of the CIT.

P_{pt} = $(p_{pt})\,(1 + \pi_{0,t})$ = nominal price of physical investment goods.

p_{pt} = real price of physical investment goods.

P_{kt} = $(p_{kt})\,(1 + \pi_{0,t})$ = nominal price of expenditure on R&D.

p_{kt} = real price of expenditure on R&D.

I_p = amount of gross investment in physical capital.

I_k = amount of gross investment in knowledge capital, that is, amount of R&D.

DA_{t+1} $= A_{t+1} - A_t =$ new debt and equity issued during period t.
CITP_t = corporate income tax payments at time t, defined by

$$\text{CITP}_t = (u_{ct})\left[(P_{yt})\,(Y_t) - \sum_{j=1}^{2}(W_{jt})\,(v_{jt}) - (b_t)\,(i_{t,t+a})\,(A_t) - (u_{pt})\,(K_{pt}^{\&})\right.$$

$$- (\alpha_{kt})\,(P_{kt})\,(K_{kt}^{*}) - (\alpha_{pt})\,(P_{pt})\,(K_{pt}^{*}) - (q_{kt})\,(P_{kt})\,(I_{kt})$$

$$\left. - (q_{pt})\,(P_{pt})\,(I_{pt})\right] - (m_{pt})\,(P_{pt})\,(I_{pt})$$

where

u_c = statutory rate of the CIT.
b = ratio of debt to the sum of debt and equity A.
a_k = rate of depreciation of knowledge capital allowed by the CIT in Turkey.
a_p = rate of depreciation of physical capital allowed by the CIT in Pakistan as well as in Turkey.
K_k^{*} = stock of knowledge capital for the purposes of the CIT, relevant only for Turkey.
K_p^{*} = physical capital stock for the purposes of the CIT, relevant for both countries.
q_k = proportion of R&D expenditure that firms are allowed to expense—that is, to deduct from revenue in the year in which they have been incurred, in both countries.
q_p = proportion of investment in physical capital that firms are allowed to expense, only in Turkey.
m_p = rate of tax credit granted by the CIT for investment in physical capital, only in Pakistan.

The samples we estimated are three special cases of the above general model. We shall continue to point out the differences between the samples whenever it is required.

The firm's production function is given by

$$(15\text{-}2) \qquad Y_t = Y_t\,(v_{jt},\,K_{pt},\,K_{kt},\,I_{pt},\,I_{kt},\,t)$$

where Y_t is the quantity of output; v_{jt} is a (1 x 2)-vector of variable inputs; K_{pt} is the true stock of physical capital at the beginning of period t; and, as usual, time t acts as a proxy for technological change. The production function indicates that output Y is a function of the variable inputs v_j, the quasi-fixed inputs K_p and K_k, technological change, and gross investment in physical and knowledge capital. The fact that both kinds of investment appear in the production function implies the assumption that the firm experiences internal, nonseparable adjustment costs caused by both types of investment. (Treadway 1970, 1974 deals with the desirability of specifying adjustment costs as internal and non-separable.)

As Boadway and Bruce (1979) explain, lenders usually do not allow firms to borrow in order to distribute dividends or repurchase stock. This can be modeled as the constraint that dividends over and above the cost of equity capital are not permitted to exceed after-tax economic profits, as described by the following inequality:

$$(15\text{-}3)\ (P_{yt})\,(Y_t) - \sum_{j=1}^{2} (W_{jt})\,(v_{jt}) - (i_{t,t+a})\,(A_t) - (u_{pt})\,(K_{pt}^{\&}) - (P_{pt})\,(I_{pt})$$

$$-\,(P_{kt})\,(I_{kt}) + DA_{t+1} - \mathrm{CITP}_t \le (P_{yt})\,(Y_t) - \sum_{j=1}^{2} (W_{jt})\,(v_{jt}) - (i_{t,t+a})\,(A_t)$$

$$-\,(u_{pt})\,(K_{pt}^{\&}) - \delta_p\,(P_{pt})\,(K_{pt}) - \delta_k\,(P_{kt})\,(K_{kt}) - \mathrm{CITP}_t$$

where δ_p is the economic rate of depreciation of physical capital, and δ_k is the economic rate of depreciation of knowledge capital.

As Boadway and Bruce (1979) show, optimality requires inequality 15-3 to be strictly binding. After some simplifications (see the appendix to this chapter) we obtain the following borrowing constraint:

$$(15\text{-}4)\ DA_{t+1} = (P_{pt+1})\,(K_{pt+1}) - (P_{pt})\,(K_{pt}) + (P_{kt+1})\,(K_{kt+1}) - (P_{kt})\,(K_{kt}).$$

In the appendix to this chapter, we derive the following equation, which expresses physical investment as a function of K_p^* and α_p, the stock of physical capital and rate of depreciation for purposes of the CIT:

$$(15\text{-}5)\ (P_{pt})\,(I_{pt}) = (\alpha_{pt})\,(P_{pt})\,(K_{pt}^*) + (P_{pt+1})\,(K_{pt+1}^*) - (P_{pt})\,(K_{pt}^*).$$

The following investment constraint for physical capital is obtained from equation 15-5 by substituting the sum of replacement investment and net investment for gross investment on the left-hand side:

$$(15\text{-}6)\quad \delta_p\,(P_{pt})\,(K_{pt}) + (P_{pt+1})(K_{pt+1}) - (P_{pt})\,(K_{pt}) = (\alpha_{pt})\,(P_{pt})\,(K_{pt}^*)$$

$$+\,(P_{pt+1})\,(K_{pt+1}^*) - (P_{pt})\,(K_{pt}^*).$$

The analogous investment constraint for knowledge capital is given by

$$(15\text{-}7)\ \delta_k\,(P_{kt})\,(K_{kt}) + (P_{kt+1})\,(K_{kt+1}) - (P_{kt})\,(K_{kt}) = (\alpha_{kt})\,(P_{kt})\,(K_{kt}^*)$$

$$+\,(P_{kt+1})\,(K_{kt+1}^*) - (P_{kt})\,(K_{kt}^*).$$

Substituting for gross investment in physical and knowledge capital in the objective function of equation 15-1 and augmenting it by the production function of equation 15-2, the borrowing constraint of equation 15-4, and the investment constraints of equations 15-6 and 15-7, we obtain the following Lagrangian:

(15-8)

$$
\begin{aligned}
L = \varepsilon_s \sum_{t=s}^{\infty} D_{s,t} &\Big\{ (P_{yt})\,(\Upsilon_t) - \sum_{j=1}^{2} (W_{jt})\,(v_{jt}) - (i_{t,t+a})\,(A_t) - (u_{pt})\,(K_{pt}^{\&}) \\
&- \delta_p\,(P_{pt})\,(K_{pt}) - (P_{pt+1})\,(K_{pt+1}) + (P_{pt})\,(K_{pt}) \\
&- \delta_k\,(P_{kt})\,(K_{kt}) - (P_{kt+1})\,(K_{kt+1}) + (P_{kt})\,(K_{kt}) + DA_{t+1} - \text{CITP}_t \\
&- k_3 \big[\Upsilon_t - \Upsilon_t\,(v_{jt},\,K_{pt},\,K_{kt},\,I_{pt},\,I_{kt},t) \big] \\
&- k_2 \big[DA_{t+1} - (P_{pt+1})\,(K_{pt+1}) + (P_{pt})\,(K_{pt}) - (P_{kt+1})\,(K_{kt+1}) + (P_{kt})\,(K_{kt}) \big] \\
&- k_1 \big[\delta_p\,(P_{pt})\,(K_{pt}) + (P_{pt+1})\,(K_{pt+1}) - (P_{pt})\,(K_{pt}) - (\alpha_{pt})\,(P_{pt})\,(K_{pt}^{*}) \\
&\quad - (P_{pt+1})\,(K_{pt+1}^{*}) + (P_{pt})\,(K_{pt}^{*}) \big] \\
&- k_4 \big[\delta_k\,(P_{kt})\,(K_{kt}) + (P_{kt+1})\,(K_{kt+1}) - (P_{kt})\,(K_{kt}) - (\alpha_{kt})\,(P_{kt})\,(K_{kt}^{*}) \\
&\quad - (P_{kt+1})\,(K_{kt+1}^{*}) + (P_{kt})\,(K_{kt}^{*}) \big] \Big\}
\end{aligned}
$$

where k_1 to k_4 are Lagrangian multipliers.

We describe the firm's decisionmaking process as if it takes place in three stages, although in practice all these decisions may well be taken at the same time. At the first stage, managers choose the least-cost combination of inputs, given a particular quantity of output and given the present stocks of physical and knowledge capital. At the next stage, executives determine the optimal amount of output, still assuming the capital stocks to remain constant. The third step of the decisionmaking process is to choose the optimal rates of change of the firm's stocks of physical and knowledge capital.

The least-cost input quantities $v_j^{\#}$ are found as follows: at time t the Lagrangian (equation 15-8) is differentiated partially with respect to inputs v_{1t} and v_{2t}, the derivatives are set equal to zero, and the first equation is divided by the second one. The expectations operator is unnecessary, because at time t the variables of the same period are known with certainty. Furthermore, the discount factor vanishes because $D_{t,t} = 1$. Therefore we get the well-known result $w_{1t}/w_{2t} = \text{MPP}_1/\text{MPP}_2$, where MPP stands for marginal physical product. This equation implicitly defines the least-cost input quantities as functions of the following variables:

(15-9) $v_{jt}^{\#} = v_{jt}^{\#}\,(w_{jt},\,\Upsilon_t,\,K_{pt},\,K_{kt},\,I_{pt},\,I_{kt},\,t), \qquad j = 1, 2.$

Accordingly, the minimum variable cost functions in real and in nominal terms are given by the following two equations:

$$(15\text{-}10) \qquad \sum_{j=1}^{2} (v_{jt}^{\#})\,(w_{jt}) = g_t^{\#}\,(w_{jt},\, \Upsilon_t,\, K_{pt},\, K_{kt},\, I_{pt},\, I_{kt},\, t)$$

and

$$(15\text{-}11) \qquad \sum_{j=1}^{2} (v_{jt}^{\#})\,(W_{jt}) = G_t^{\#}\,(\pi_{0,t},\, w_{jt},\, \Upsilon_t,\, K_{pt},\, K_{kt},\, I_{pt},\, I_{kt},\, t)$$

$$= (1 + \pi_{0,t})\,(g_t^{\#}).$$

For Pakistan's textile industry, knowledge capital K_{kt} and R&D investment I_{kt} do not appear in the minimum variable cost functions (equations 15-10 and 15-11). We approximate the minimum variable cost function of equation 15-10 by a quadratic normalized cost function, which in turn is the basis for the estimating equations for labor and materials derived in a later section. These equations for labor and materials are the same for all three versions of the model, regardless of the assumptions we make about market structure and short-run forward shifting of the CIT. For Pakistan's textile industry the factor demand equations contain neither knowledge capital nor R&D investment.

The above cost functions are increasing, continuous, concave, and linearly homogeneous in the two input prices, increasing in output, and decreasing in investment in physical and knowledge capital. We know from duality theory that the cost function incorporates all the information about a firm's production structure that its production function contains. In particular, the presence of physical investment I_{pt} and R&D investment I_{kt} in equations 15-10 and 15-11 indicates that the firm experiences internal, nonseparable adjustment costs.

The next step of the decisionmaking process is to choose the optimal amount of output $\Upsilon_t^{\#}$. We incorporate the minimum variable cost function (equation 15-11) into the Lagrangian (equation 15-8), after which the production function is no longer necessary as a separate constraint. Differentiating equation 15-8 partially with respect to Υ_t and setting the derivative equal to zero, we obtain the following equilibrium condition:

$$(15\text{-}12) \qquad (T_{ct})\,(P_{yt}) - T_{ct}\,\frac{\partial G_t^{\#}}{\partial \Upsilon_t^{\#}} = 0$$

where

$$T_{ct} = 1 - u_{ct}.$$

When we divide both sides of equation 15-12 by T_{ct} we obtain the well-known first-order condition that price has to be equal to marginal cost, or $P = MC$.

Equation 15-12 implicitly defines profit-maximizing output $Y_t^{\#}$ as a function of the price of output and of the variables that are arguments in the minimum variable cost function:

$$(15\text{-}13) \qquad Y_t^{\#} = Y_t^{\#} (P_{yt}, W_{jt}, K_{pt}, K_{kt}, I_{pt}, I_{kt}, t).$$

We used a linear approximation of equation 15-13 as the output equation for the version of our model in which perfect competition is assumed, but only for the two larger samples. For the small sample, Pakistan's textile industry, knowledge capital and R&D expenditure had to be omitted from output equation 15-13.

The final step is to determine the firm's optimal stocks of physical capital $K_p^{\#}$ and of knowledge capital $K_k^{\#}$ for the time period $(t + 1)$. After we incorporate the optimal level of output Y_t into the Lagrangian (equation 15-8) and combine terms, the latter becomes

(15-14)

$$
\begin{aligned}
L = \varepsilon_s \sum_{t=s}^{\infty} D_{s,t} \Big\{ & T_{ct} \Big[(P_{yt})\, [Y_t^{\#}(\cdot)] - G_t^{\#}(\cdot) - (b_t)\,(i_{t,t+a})\,(A_t) - (u_{pt})\,(K_{pt}^{\&}) \Big] \\
& - (1 - b_t)\,(i_{t,t+a})\,(A_t) + DA_{t+1} + (u_{ct})\,(\alpha_{kt})\,(P_{kt})\,(K_{kt}^{*}) \\
& + (u_{ct})\,(\alpha_{pt})\,(P_{pt})\,(K_{pt}^{*}) \\
& - \Big[1 - (u_{ct})\,(q_{kt}) \Big]\Big[(\delta_k)\,(P_{kt})\,(K_{kt}) + (P_{kt+1})\,(K_{kt+1}) - (P_{kt})\,(K_{kt}) \Big] \\
& - \Big[1 - (u_{ct})\,(q_{pt}) - (m_{pt}) \Big]\Big[(\delta_p)\,(P_{pt})\,(K_{pt}) + (P_{pt+1})\,(K_{pt+1}) - (P_{pt})\,(K_{pt}) \Big] \\
& - k_2 \Big[DA_{t+1} - (P_{pt+1})\,(K_{pt+1}) + (P_{pt})\,(K_{pt}) - (P_{kt+1})\,(K_{kt+1}) + (P_{kt})\,(K_{kt}) \Big] \\
& - k_1 \Big[\delta_p\,(P_{pt})\,(K_{pt}) + (P_{pt+1})\,(K_{pt+1}) - (P_{pt})\,(K_{pt}) - (\alpha_{pt})\,(P_{pt})\,(K_{pt}^{*}) \\
& \quad - (P_{pt+1})\,(K_{pt+1}^{*}) + (P_{pt})\,(K_{pt}^{*}) \Big] \\
& - k_4 \Big[\delta_k\,(P_{kt})\,(K_{kt}) + (P_{kt+1})\,(K_{kt+1}) - (P_{kt})\,(K_{kt}) - (\alpha_{kt})\,(P_{kt})\,(K_{kt}^{*}) \\
& \quad - (P_{kt+1})\,(K_{kt+1}^{*}) + (P_{kt})\,(K_{kt}^{*}) \Big] \Big\}.
\end{aligned}
$$

Differentiating equation 15-14 partially with respect to the control variables A_{t+1}, K_{pt+1}^{*}, K_{kt+1}^{*}, K_{pt+1}, and K_{kt+1}, setting the partial derivatives equal to zero, and solving the resulting system of equations, we obtain the following two optimality conditions (for details of these calculations see the appendix to this chapter):

(15-15)

$$-\frac{1}{(1+r_{t,t+1})}\,\varepsilon_t\!\left(\frac{\partial g_{t+1}^{\#}}{\partial K_{pt+1}^{\#}}\right) - \frac{T_{ct}}{\varepsilon_t\,(T_{ct+1})}\,\frac{\partial g_t^{\#}}{\partial I_{pt}^{\#}} + \frac{(1-\delta_p)}{(1+r_{t,t+1})}\,\varepsilon_t\!\left(\frac{\partial g_{t+1}^{\#}}{\partial I_{pt+1}^{\#}}\right)$$

$$= \frac{1}{(1+r_{t,t+1})}\,\frac{\varepsilon_t\,(p_{pt+1})}{\varepsilon_t\,(T_{ct+1})}\left\{\varepsilon_t\,(i_{t+1,\,t+1+a})\,[1-\varepsilon_t\,(b_{t+1})\,\varepsilon_t\,(u_{ct+1})] + \delta_p\right\}$$

$$-(1+\pi_{p,t+1})\,\frac{\varepsilon_t\,(p_{pt+1})}{\varepsilon_t\,(T_{ct+1})}\,(m_{pt}) + \frac{(1-\delta_p)}{(1+r_{t,t+1})}\,\frac{\varepsilon_t\,(p_{pt+1})}{\varepsilon_t\,(T_{ct+1})}\,\varepsilon_t\,(m_{pt+1})$$

$$-(1+\pi_{t,t+1})\,\frac{\varepsilon_t\,(p_{pt+1})}{\varepsilon_t\,(T_{ct+1})}\,(q_{pt})\,(u_{ct}) + \frac{(1-\delta_p)}{(1+r_{t,t+1})}\,\frac{\varepsilon_t\,(p_{pt+1})}{\varepsilon_t\,(T_{ct+1})}\,\varepsilon_t\,(q_{pt+1})\,\varepsilon_t\,(u_{ct+1})$$

$$-\frac{\varepsilon_t\,(p_{pt+1})\,(i_{t,t+1} + \delta_p)\,\varepsilon_t\,(\alpha_{pt+1})\,\varepsilon_t\,(u_{ct+1})}{\varepsilon_t\,(T_{ct+1})\,(1+r_{t,t+1})\,[i_{t,t+1} + \varepsilon_t\,(\alpha_{pt+1})]}$$

(15-16)

$$-\frac{1}{(1+r_{t,\,t+1})}\,\varepsilon_t\!\left(\frac{\partial g_{t+1}^{\#}}{\partial K_{kt+1}^{\#}}\right) - \frac{T_{ct}}{\varepsilon_t\,(T_{ct+1})}\,\frac{\partial g_t^{\#}}{\partial I_{kt}^{\#}} + \frac{(1-\delta_k)}{(1+r_{t,\,t+1})}\,\varepsilon_t\!\left(\frac{\partial g_{t+1}^{\#}}{\partial I_{kt+1}^{\#}}\right)$$

$$= \frac{1}{1+r_{t,t+1}}\,\frac{\varepsilon_t\,(p_{kt+1})}{\varepsilon_t\,(T_{ct+1})}\left\{\varepsilon_t\,(i_{t+1,t+1+a})\,[1-\varepsilon_t\,(b_{t+1})\,\varepsilon_t\,(u_{ct+1})] + \delta_k\right\}$$

$$-(1+\pi_{t,\,t+1})\,\frac{\varepsilon_t\,(p_{kt+1})}{\varepsilon_t\,(T_{ct+1})}\,(q_{kt})\,(u_{ct}) + \frac{(1-\delta_k)}{(1+r_{t,\,t+1})}\,\frac{\varepsilon_t\,(p_{kt+1})}{\varepsilon_t\,(T_{ct+1})}\,\varepsilon_t\,(q_{kt+1})\,\varepsilon_t\,(u_{ct+1})$$

$$-\frac{\varepsilon_t\,(p_{kt+1})\,(i_{t,\,t+1} + \delta_k)\,\varepsilon_t\,(\alpha_{kt+1})\,\varepsilon_t\,(u_{ct+1})}{\varepsilon_t\,(T_{ct+1})\,(1+r_{t,\,t+1})\,[i_{t,\,t+1} + \varepsilon_t\,(\alpha_{kt+1})]}\,.$$

The left-hand side of equation 15-15 represents the expected discounted marginal benefit from increasing the stock of physical capital, reduced by adjustment costs incurred during the current year but increased by the adjustment costs saved during the next year by investing this year instead. In short, the left-hand side of equation 15-15 represents the expected discounted after-tax *net* marginal benefit from increasing the stock of physical capital. The right-hand side of equation 15-15 represents the rental price of the services from physical capital in the absence of full shifting of the CIT. We are going to denote this rental price rp_{pt}(tax) because it contains tax parameters. Under the assumption of perfect competition K_{pt+1}, next year's stock of physical capital, is chosen optimally if the expected discounted after-tax net marginal benefit from investment in physical capital is equal to $rp_{pt}(tax)$, the rental price of the services from physical capital.

The Turkish CIT does not give an investment credit for physical investment. Therefore the terms involving m_{pt} and m_{pt+1} on the right-hand side of equation 15-15 are equal to zero for our Turkish sample. In Pakistan, in contrast, the CIT does not allow any part of investment expenditure to be expensed, so for the three industries of Pakistan the terms containing q_{pt} and q_{pt+1} vanish.

Equation 15-15 provides the theoretical foundation for the estimating equation for physical investment, which we derive in a later section for the version of the model in which perfect competition is assumed.

The left-hand side of equation 15-16 represents the expected discounted after-tax net marginal benefit from increasing the stock of knowledge capital. The right-hand side of equation 15-16 represents the rental price of the services from knowledge capital in the absence of full shifting of the CIT. Because it contains tax parameters, it is denoted $rp_{kt}(tax)$. Next year's capital stock K_{kt+1} is chosen optimally if the expected discounted after-tax net marginal benefit from investment in knowledge capital is equal to this rental price of the services from knowledge capital $rp_{kt}(tax)$.

In Pakistan the CIT does not allow accelerated depreciation for knowledge capital, α_{kt+1} is equal to zero, and the last term on the right-hand side of equation 15-16 vanishes for Pakistan's chemical and pharmaceutical industries.

The optimality condition shown in equation 15-16 is the theoretical basis for the estimating equation for R&D investment that we derive later for the version of the model in which perfect competition is assumed. Needless to say, equation 15-16 does not apply to Pakistan's textile industry, for which we had to omit both the stock of knowledge capital and the rate of R&D investment.

The rental prices of capital services defined by the first-order conditions of equations 15-15 and 15-16 are consistent with rational expectations on the part of the firm's decisionmakers. These rental prices incorporate not only the current year's parameters of the CIT but those for the next year as well. The optimality conditions of equations 15-15 and 15-16 also take into account the effect of next year's investment, which in turn is partly determined by the tax parameters for the next year and the one after that. In this way equations 15-15 and 15-16 link the present investment decision to all future years.

It is worth pointing out that the expected average cost of debt and equity capital $\varepsilon_t (i_{t+1,\ t+1+a})$ appears in both rental prices of capital services. Although the current rate of inflation does not influence the rental prices of capital services, the rate of inflation and, hence, the nominal interest rate, which at time $(t + 1)$ is expected to prevail over the average lifetime of the firm's debt and equity capital, do affect the rental prices of capital services. By increasing these rental prices, expected future inflation and expected nominal interest rates reduce the firm's optimal stocks of physical and knowledge capital.

From equation 15-15 it can be seen that, other things being equal, an increase in m_{pt} (this year's tax credit for physical investment) reduces the rental price of the services from physical capital, thereby increasing the desired stock of physical capital and thus physical investment. This is, of course, the effect intended by public policymakers. An expected increase in m_{pt+1} (next year's tax credit for physical investment), however, increases the rental price of the services from physical capital and thus reduces physical investment. It agrees with intuition that firms will invest less during the current year if they expect more favorable tax treatment during the next year. Similarly, an increase in q_{pt} (this period's tax allowance for physical investment) has the effect of reducing the rental price of the services from physical capital, thus increasing the optimal stock of physical capital and rate of physical investment. Increased tax allowances for physical investment expected for the following year, however, raise the rental price of the services from physical capital, other things being equal, thereby reducing investment in physical capital.

From equation 15-16 we see that a small increase in q_{kt} (this year's tax allowance for R&D expenditure) reduces the rental price of the services from knowledge capital, thereby increasing the desired stock of knowledge capital and rate of R&D investment, as intended by policymakers. An expected increase in q_{kt+1} (next year's tax allowance for R&D investment), however, increases the rental price of the services from knowledge capital, thus reducing R&D expenditure, which makes intuitive sense. In Pakistan, firms are allowed to expense the full amount of R&D in the year in which it is undertaken—that is, $q_{kt} = 1$ and cannot be increased beyond 1. To study the effect of full expensing of R&D expenditure, we need to examine what would happen if q_{kt} were reduced by a small amount. As equation 15-16 shows, this would increase the rental price of the services from knowledge capital and, hence, reduce R&D investment. In other words, the tax allowance q_{kt} and R&D investment I_{kt} move in the same direction. If, however, the expected tax allowance q_{kt+1} were reduced, the rental price of the services from knowledge capital would fall and R&D expenditure would increase. So q_{kt+1} (next year's tax allowance for R&D investment) and this year's R&D expenditure I_{kt} move in opposite directions.

It can easily be shown—by differentiating the right-hand side of equation 15-15 partially with respect to $\varepsilon_t(\alpha_{pt+1})$ and the right-hand side of equation 15-16 with respect to $\varepsilon_t(\alpha_{kt+1})$—that an increase in the expected rate of accelerated depreciation reduces the rental prices of the services from physical and knowledge capital, which will increase investment in both types of capital. This agrees with intuition and is the effect intended by public policy.

In this section we made the assumption of perfect competition, which implies that firms are not able to pass the CIT on to consumers by increasing the prices of their outputs. Under this assumption the parameters of the CIT are present in the expressions for the rental prices of capital services. In the next section we shall make the assumption that full short-run forward shifting of the CIT takes place. In that case the expressions for the rental prices of capital services would be free of tax parameters, as we demonstrate below. Some readers may think it obvious that a fully shifted CIT that leaves after-tax profits at the level of profits in the absence of the tax change, will not influence the rental prices of capital services. What is intuitively obvious to some, however, others may find hard to believe. Besides, if the connection between full short-run forward shifting of the CIT and the expressions for the rental prices of capital services were completely obvious, one would expect it to have been mentioned somewhere in the literature. To the best of our knowledge no reference to this connection has ever been made. We are not claiming that a situation of full shifting of the CIT is very likely to occur in any given industry. All we are arguing is that the possibility of full shifting ought to be ruled out by the results of hypothesis tests, not by the researcher's prior beliefs. Because it is so important for policymakers to be certain that tax parameters are indeed present in the rental prices of capital services, it is not desirable to assume away the possibility of full short-run forward shifting of the CIT by making the conventional assumption of perfect competition.

In the following subsection we provide the theoretical basis for the estimating equations under the joint assumptions of market power and full short-run forward shifting of the CIT. In addition, we derive the expressions for the rental prices of capital services for that situation.

The Theoretical Model under the Assumptions of Market Power and Full Short-Run Forward Shifting of the CIT

Short-run forward shifting of the CIT is possible only in an industry in which firms have market power, and only if they do not fully exercise this market power before a change in the CIT. There are many possible reasons for firms to have unexerted market power—for example, fear of antitrust prosecution, or limit pricing used in order to deter the growth of rival firms. We are assuming limit pricing in this section, simply because it can be most easily incorporated into an intertemporal optimization framework. The effect of full short-run forward shifting of the CIT on the rental prices of capital services is the same, however, regardless of the conditions that make such shifting possible.

We first study a limit-pricing firm in the absence of the CIT. The purpose of this discussion is to show that the optimal output of a limit-pricing firm is larger than the optimal output of a firm that does not practice limit pricing. A limit-pricing firm, therefore, is able to reduce its output in response to a change in the CIT. Because the change in the CIT applies to its rivals as well, the limit-pricing firm need not worry that its reduction in output might change the conditions of entry or expansion for the rival firms. In the second part of this section we present our theoretical model for the joint assumptions of market power and full shifting of the CIT.

In the absence of the CIT, we obtain the firm's net present value by setting $CITP_t = 0$ in equation 15-1. We number this objective function without CIT-payments equation 15-1' (not reproduced here). We assume that industry demand Y_t^I depends on income X and the price P_{ys} of substitute goods. Industry demand Y_t^I consists of the demand Y_t for the output of the dominant firm (or group of firms) and of the demand R_t for the output of rival firms:

$$(15\text{-}17) \qquad Y_t^I (X, P_{ys}) = Y_t + R_t$$

If R_t is zero, the dominant firm uses limit pricing in order to prevent the entry of potential rivals. If R_t is positive, the firm practices limit pricing in order to prevent the output of the industry's competitive fringe from growing too fast. We assume that the dominant firm is subject to the following entry constraint:

$$(15\text{-}18) \qquad DR_{t+1} (= R_{t+1} - R_t) = c_t (Y_t^{\&} - Y_t)$$

where $Y_t^{\&}$ is the output of the dominant firm at which there is no change in the output R_t of rival firms, and $c_t \geq 0$ is a reaction coefficient. (See Gaskins 1971 for a similar constraint; Gaskins, however, used continuous rather than discrete time and a nonentry price rather than a nonentry output.) The entry constraint of equation 15-18 implies that the output of rival firms increases if the dominant firm reduces its own output Y_t below the nonentry output $Y_t^{\&}$.

The borrowing constraint of equation 15-4 and the minimum variable cost function of equation 15-11 are the same as in the previous subsection. We incorporate equation 15-11 into the objective function of equation 15-1', augment it by the borrowing constraint of equation 15-4 and the entry constraint of equation 15-18, and obtain the following Lagrangian:

$(15\text{-}19)$

$$L = \varepsilon_s \sum_{t=s}^{\infty} D_{s,t} \left\{ (P_{yt}) (Y_t) - G_t^o (\cdot) - (i_{t,t+a}) (A_t) - (u_{pt}) (K_{pt}^{\&}) \right.$$

$$- (P_{pt}) (I_{kt}) - (P_{kt}) (I_{kt}) + DA_{t+1}$$

$$- k_2 \left[DA_{t+1} - (P_{pt+1}) (K_{pt+1}) + (P_{pt}) (K_{pt}) - (P_{kt+1}) (K_{kt+1}) + (P_{kt}) (K_{kt}) \right]$$

$$- k_4 \left[DR_{t+1} - c_t (\Upsilon_t^\& - \Upsilon_t) \right] \Big\} .$$

In the Lagrangian of equation 15-19 the superscript o denotes optimality for the case without the CIT.

We differentiate equation 15-19 with respect to output, set the derivative equal to zero, denote the optimal output by Υ_t^o, and obtain the following optimality condition:

$$(15\text{-}20) \quad \left[\Upsilon_t^o \frac{(dP_{yt})}{d\Upsilon_t^I} \underbrace{\left(\frac{d\Upsilon_t^I (X_t, P_{yst})}{d\Upsilon_t^o} \right)}_{= 1 \text{ by } 15\text{-}17} + P_{yt} - \frac{\partial G_t^o}{\partial \Upsilon_t^o} \right] - k_4 c_t = 0 .$$

P_{yt} is not a constant in equation 15-20 because we do not assume perfect competition here. The first-order condition of equation 15-20 states in effect that in equilibrium marginal revenue equals marginal cost plus the term $k_4 c_t$. We want to know the sign of $k_4 c_t$. Because the reaction coefficient c_t is a positive constant by assumption, we only need to determine the sign of k_4: the Lagrangian multiplier k_4 represents the contribution of DR_{t+1} to the objective function. The net present value of the firm will fall, other things being equal, as the result of an increase in the output of rival firms, so k_4 is negative. Therefore the term $k_4 c_t$ is negative and has the same influence on the firm's optimal output that a reduction in marginal cost would have: it raises output above the level that would be optimal if the firm did not engage in limit pricing. We have thus shown that there is scope for a limit-pricing firm to reduce its output in response to a change in the CIT.

Next, we assume that the CIT exists and then ask the question: what would be the firm's first-order conditions if it were completely successful in shifting the CIT on to consumers in the short run?

The entry constraint is analogous to equation 15-18 above, except that we denote the nonentry output for the case of full short-run shifting as Υ_t^+. The least-cost combination of inputs is independent of whether full tax shifting does or does not take place. Therefore the derivation of the firm's minimum variable cost function $G_t^{\#}(\text{fs})$ ("fs" stands for full shifting) is the same as the derivation of $G_t^{\#}$ above, and $G_t^{\#}(\text{fs})$ can be incorporated into the objective function immediately. For the sake of the argument we assume that the dominant firm is able to choose its output in such a way as to make its after-tax profit equal to its profit prior to the tax change, the definition of full tax shifting. This assumption is captured in the following equation:

(15-21) $(P_{yt})\,(\Upsilon_t) - G_t^{\#}\,(\text{fs})\,(\cdot) - (i_{t,t+a})\,(b_t)\,(A_t) - (u_{pt})\,(K_{pt}^{\&})$

$\qquad - \delta_p\,(P_{pt})\,(K_{pt}) - \delta_k(P_{kt})\,(K_{kt}) - \text{CITP}_t$

$\qquad = (P_{yt})\,(\Upsilon_t^o\,) - G_t^o\,(\cdot) - (i_{t,t+a})\,(b_t)\,(A_t) - (u_{pt})\,(K_{pt}^{\&})$

$\qquad - \delta_p(P_{pt})\,(K_{pt}) - \delta_k(P_{kt})\,(K_{kt})$

where Υ_t^o and G_t^o are the firm's optimal output and minimum variable cost function prior to the change in the CIT. The left-hand side of equation 15-21 represents the firm's after-tax profit, whereas the right-hand side stands for its profit prior to the change in the CIT.

We augment the objective function of equation 15-1 by the borrowing constraint of equation 15-4, the modified entry constraint of equation 15-18, and the shifting assumption of equation 15-21 to obtain the following Lagrangian:

(15-22)

$$L = \varepsilon_s \sum_{t=s}^{\infty} D_{s,t} \Big\{ (P_{yt})\,(\Upsilon_t) - G_t^{\#}(\text{fs})\,(\cdot) - (i_{t,t+a})\,(A_t) - (u_{pt})\,(K_{pt}^{\&})$$

$$- (P_{pt})\,(I_{pt}) - (P_{kt})\,(I_{kt}) + DA_{t+1} - \text{CITP}_t$$

$$- k_2 \Big[DA_{t+1} - (P_{pt+1})\,(K_{pt+1}) + (P_{pt})\,(K_{pt}) - (P_{kt+1})\,(K_{kt+1}) + (P_{kt})\,(K_{kt}) \Big]$$

$$- k_6 \Big[DR_{t+1} - c_t(\Upsilon_t^+ - \Upsilon_t) \Big]$$

$$- k_5 \Big[(P_{yt})\,(\Upsilon_t) - G_t^{\#}(\text{fs})\,(\cdot) - (i_{t,t+a})\,(b_t)\,(A_t) - (u_{pt})\,(K_{pt}^{\&})$$

$$- \delta_p\,(P_{pt})\,(K_{pt}) - \delta_k\,(P_{kt})\,(K_{kt}) - \text{CITP}_t$$

$$- (P_{yt})\,(\Upsilon_t^o) + G_t^o\,(\cdot) + (i_{t,t+a})\,(b_t)\,(A_t) + (u_{pt})\,(K_{pt}^{\&})$$

$$+ \delta_p\,(P_{pt})\,(K_{pt}) + \delta_k\,(P_{kt})\ (K_{kt}) \Big] \Big\}.$$

We differentiate equation 15-22 with respect to Υ_t, set the derivative equal to zero, and obtain the following optimality condition:

(15-23)

$$T_{ct} \Bigg[\Upsilon_t^{\#}(\text{fs}) \underbrace{\frac{dP_{yt}}{d\Upsilon_t^I} \frac{d\Upsilon_t^I(X_t, P_{yst})}{d\Upsilon_t^{\#}(\text{fs})}}_{= 1 \text{ by } 15\text{-}17} + P_{yt} - \frac{\partial G_t^{\#}(\text{fs})}{\partial \Upsilon_t^{\#}(\text{fs})} \Bigg] (1 - k_5) - k_4\,c_t = 0.$$

In the absence of the CIT, k_5 would vanish, and T_{ct} would be equal to 1. If the dominant firm did not use limit pricing to deter entry, k_4 would be equal to zero as well. In that case equation 15-23 would reduce to the well-known equilibrium condition that marginal revenue has to equal marginal cost, or $MR = MC$.

A cutback in output by the dominant firm in response to the change in the CIT may prompt rival firms to increase their own output R. In that case industry output Y^I and therefore the price of output P_y may not change, and the dominant firm may be prevented from shifting the CIT forward. In this context, however, it does not matter how likely or unlikely it is for a dominant firm to be able to succeed completely in shifting the CIT forward in the short run. We only want to find out what the firm's rental prices of capital services would be if it did succeed in shifting the CIT completely. Therefore we assume that entry conditions remain unchanged for the dominant firm. In particular, we assume that the difference between the firm's nonentry output and its actual output is the same before and after the change in the CIT:

$$(15\text{-}24) \qquad Y_t^{\&} - Y_t^o = Y_t^+ - Y_t^{\#}(\text{fs}).$$

The first-order condition shown in equation 15-23 implies that optimal output $Y_t^{\#}(\text{fs})$ depends on the following variables:

$$(15\text{-}25) \quad Y_t^{\#}(\text{fs}) = Y_t^{\#}(\text{fs}) \, (X_t, P_{yst}, W_{jt}, K_{pt}, I_{pt}, K_{kt}, I_{kt}, t, T_{ct}, k_4, k_5).$$

For all our samples equation 15-25 provides the theoretical foundation for the output equation that we derive in the following section for the joint assumptions of market power and full short-run forward shifting of the CIT. (For Pakistan's textile industry, knowledge capital and R&D investment were omitted from equation 15-25.)

Next, we derive the first-order conditions that have to be satisfied for the two capital stocks K_{pt+1} and K_{kt+1} to be chosen in an optimal way, given the joint assumptions of market power and full short-run shifting of the CIT. We substitute the sums of replacement investment and net investment for gross investment in both types of capital in the Lagrangian of equation 15-22, use equations 15-21 and 15-24, and obtain

$$(15\text{-}26)$$

$$L = \varepsilon_s \sum_{t=s}^{\infty} D_{s,t} \left\{ (P_{yt}) \, (Y_t^o) - G_t^o \, (\cdot) - (i_{t,t+a}) \, (A_t) - (u_{pt}) \, (K_{pt}^{\&}) \right.$$

$$- \delta_p (P_{pt}) \, (K_{pt}) - (P_{pt+1}) \, (K_{pt+1}) + (P_{pt}) \, (K_{pt})$$

$$- \delta_k \, (P_{kt}) \, (K_{kt}) - (P_{kt+1}) \, (K_{kt+1}) + (P_{kt}) \, (K_{kt}) + DA_{t+1}$$

$$- k_2 \left[DA_{t+1} - (P_{pt+1})(K_{pt+1}) + (P_{pt})(K_{pt}) - (P_{kt+1})(K_{kt+1}) + (P_{kt})(K_{kt}) \right]$$

$$- k_6 \left[DR_{t+1} - c_t (Y_t^+ - Y_t^\#(\text{fs})) \right] \Big\}.$$

The Lagrangian of equation 15-26 does not contain any of the parameters of the CIT. It is therefore not surprising that under the assumptions made here the optimality conditions for the stocks of physical and knowledge capital are also free of tax parameters. The derivation of these first-order conditions can be found in appendix 15. The equilibrium conditions are given by

$$(15\text{-}27) \quad - \frac{1}{1 + r_{t,\,t+1}} \, \varepsilon_t \left(\frac{\partial g_{t+1}^o}{\partial K_{pt+1}^o} \right) - \frac{\partial g_t^o}{\partial I_{pt}^o} + \frac{(1 - \delta_p)}{1 + r_{t,\,t+1}} \, \varepsilon_t \left(\frac{\partial g_{t+1}^o}{\partial I_{pt+1}^o} \right)$$

$$= \frac{1}{1 + r_{t,\,t+1}} \, \varepsilon_t \left(\hat{p}_{pt+1} \right) \left[\delta_p + \varepsilon_t \left(i_{t+1,\,t+1+a} \right) \right]$$

$$(15\text{-}28) \quad - \frac{1}{1 + r_{t,\,t+1}} \, \varepsilon_t \left(\frac{\partial g_{t+1}^o}{\partial K_{kt+1}^o} \right) - \frac{\partial g_t^o}{\partial I_{kt}^o} + \frac{(1 - \delta_k)}{1 + r_{t,\,t+1}} \, \varepsilon_t \left(\frac{\partial g_{t+1}^o}{\partial I_{kt+1}^o} \right)$$

$$= \frac{1}{1 + r_{t,\,t+1}} \, \varepsilon_t \left(\hat{p}_{kt+1} \right) \left[\delta_k + \varepsilon_t \left(i_{t+1,\,t+1+a} \right) \right]$$

The left-hand sides of the first-order conditions of equations 15-27 and 15-28 represent the expected net marginal benefits from increasing the two capital stocks, whereas their right-hand sides are the rental prices of the services from physical and knowledge capital, respectively. Hereafter we shall denote the right-hand side of equation 15-27 as $rp_{pt}(\text{fs})$, that is, the rental price of the services from physical capital in a situation of full shifting of the CIT. Similarly, the right-hand side of equation 15-28 will be denoted as $rp_{kt}(\text{fs})$ for the rental price of the services from knowledge capital.

In the next section we shall derive estimating equations for physical and R&D investment from equations 15-27 and 15-28. These are the investment equations that are relevant under the assumptions of market power and full short-run forward shifting of the CIT. (For Pakistan's textile industry, equation 15-28 does not apply.)

The first-order conditions of equations 15-27 and 15-15 both correspond to equations 7 and 16 of Pindyck and Rotemberg (1983). The difference is that our model incorporates nonseparable internal adjustment costs resulting from gross investment in physical and knowledge capital.

At the time of the change in the CIT the dominant firm's capital stocks are still the same as they would be in the absence of the tax. But over time the firm's optimal capital stocks in the presence of full tax shifting evolve differently from its optimal capital stocks prior to the change in the CIT. The reason for this difference is that the firm's optimal output in the case of full tax shifting is less than its equilibrium output prior to the change in the CIT, and a lower output causes lower equilibrium capital stocks.

Once again, we have dealt in this section with the question of what the optimality conditions for the capital stocks would be if a firm with unexerted market power succeeded completely in shifting the CIT forward. Full shifting may not occur very often; it may never happen at all. We are simply suggesting that one should let the data, rather than one's prior beliefs, decide whether or not full tax shifting occurred in a particular industry during the period being studied.

Up to now we have considered only the two extreme pairs of joint assumptions: "perfect competition, no short-run forward shifting of the CIT" and "market power, full tax shifting." There is a third possibility, however: firms may have some unexerted market power and therefore *try* to shift the CIT forward, but they may not succeed completely. This possibility is briefly discussed in the following subsection.

The Theoretical Model under the Assumptions of Market Power and Partial or No Short-Run Forward Shifting of the CIT

If the firms in an industry have some unexerted market power and try to pass the CIT on to their customers in the form of higher output prices, equation 15-25 is the relevant output equation. But if the firms do not succeed completely in shifting the CIT forward, the assumption of full tax shifting (equation 15-21) does not apply. Therefore the parameters of the CIT occur in the rental prices of capital services, and the latter are defined by the optimality conditions shown in equations 15-15 and 15-16. This case is perhaps the one that is most likely a priori, although most empirical studies are based on the assumption of perfect competition.

The three versions of our model are summarized in figure 15-1. In the following section we derive the estimating equations for these three versions. We then outline the non-nested hypothesis tests by which we tested these versions against each other.

Derivation of the Estimating Equations from the Theoretical Models, Non-Nested Hypothesis Tests

The variable cost function g_t of equation 15-10 was approximated by a quadratic function, a flexible functional form that provides a second-

Figure 15-1. Versions of the Model

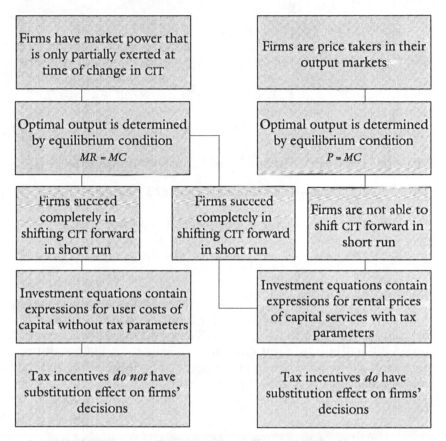

Source: Authors.

order approximation to an arbitrary normalized variable cost function. Using the quadratic functional form enabled us to solve the first-order conditions explicitly for the optimal rate of investment. The quadratic functional form has the disadvantage, however, that it is not invariant to the choice of numéraire input. Therefore we estimated the model twice, using labor and materials as the numéraire input in turn.

Equation 15-29 gives the quadratic normalized variable cost function for the complete model, where W_{1t} is the price of the numéraire input, $w_{2t} = W_{2t}/W_{1t}$, and the a_{ij} are coefficients to be estimated. For the smaller sample of the Pakistani textile industry, all the terms containing R&D investment I_{kt} and the stock of knowledge capital K_{kt} vanish in equation 15-29 as well as in all subsequent equations.

(15-29)

$$G_t / W_{1t} = v_{1t} + (w_{2t})(v_{2t}) = g_t(w_{2t}, K_{pt}, K_{kt}, I_{pt}, I_{kt}, \Upsilon_t, t)$$

$$= a_0 + a_2(w_{2t}) + a_P(K_{pt}) + a_K(K_{kt}) + a_{IP}(I_{pt}) + a_{IK}(I_{kt}) + a_\Upsilon(\Upsilon_t) + a_t(t)$$

$$+ 0.5\left[a_{22}(w_{2t})^2 + a_{PP}(K_{pt})^2 + a_{KK}(K_{kt})^2 + a_{IPIP}(I_{pt})^2 + a_{IKIK}(I_{kt})^2\right.$$

$$+ a_{\Upsilon\Upsilon}(\Upsilon_t)^2 + a_{tt}(t)^2\Big] + a_{2P}(w_{2t})(K_{pt}) + a_{2K}(w_{2t})(K_{kt}) + a_{2IP}(w_{2t})(I_{pt})$$

$$+ a_{2IK}(w_{2t})(I_{kt}) + a_{2\Upsilon}(w_{2t})(\Upsilon_t) + a_{2t}(w_{2t})(t) + a_{PK}(K_{pt})(K_{kt})$$

$$+ a_{PIP}(K_{pt})(I_{pt}) + a_{PIK}(K_{pt})(I_{kt}) + a_{P\Upsilon}(K_{pt})(\Upsilon_t) + a_{Pt}(K_{pt})(t)$$

$$+ a_{KIP}(K_{kt})(I_{pt}) + a_{KIK}(K_{kt})(I_{kt}) + a_{K\Upsilon}(K_{kt})(\Upsilon_t) + a_{Kt}(K_{kt})(t)$$

$$+ a_{IPIK}(I_{pt})(I_{kt}) + a_{IP\Upsilon}(I_{pt})(\Upsilon_t) + a_{IPt}(I_{pt})(t) + a_{IK\Upsilon}(I_{kt})(\Upsilon_t)$$

$$+ a_{IKt}(I_{kt})(t) + a_{\Upsilon t}(\Upsilon_t)(t) \, .$$

Equation 15-30 gives the demand for input v_{2t}, which according to Shephard's lemma is equal to $\partial g_t / \partial w_{2t}$ (Shephard 1953, 1970). In equation 15-30 and in subsequent estimating equations, an additive disturbance term allows for errors in optimization and measurement and for omitted variables:

(15-30)

$$v_{2t} = a_2 + a_{22}(w_{2t}) + a_{2P}(K_{pt}) + a_{2K}(K_{kt}) + a_{2IP}(I_{pt}) + a_{2IK}(I_{kt})$$

$$+ a_{2\Upsilon}(\Upsilon_t) + a_{2t}(t) + u_{2t} \, .$$

The demand for input v_{1t} can be obtained from equation 15-29 as follows:

(15-31)

$$v_{1t} = (G_t / W_{1t}) - (w_{2t})(v_{2t})$$

$$= a_0 + a_P(K_{pt}) + a_K(K_{kt}) + a_{IP}(I_{pt}) + a_{IK}(I_{kt}) + a_\Upsilon(\Upsilon_t) + a_t(t)$$

$$+ 0.5\left[-a_{22}(w_{2t})^2 + a_{PP}(K_{pt})^2 + a_{KK}(K_{kt})^2 + a_{IPIP}(I_{pt})^2 + a_{IKIK}(I_{kt})^2\right.$$

$$+ a_{\Upsilon\Upsilon}(\Upsilon_t)^2 + a_{tt}(t)^2\Big] + a_{PK}(K_{pt})(K_{kt}) + a_{PIP}(K_{pt})(I_{pt}) + a_{PIK}(K_{pt})(I_{kt})$$

$$+ a_{PY}(K_{pt})(Y_t) + a_{Pt}(K_{pt})(t) + a_{KIP}(K_{kt})(I_{pt}) + a_{KIK}(K_{kt})(I_{kt})$$

$$+ a_{KY}(K_{kt})(Y_t) + a_{Kt}(K_{kt})(t) + a_{IPIK}(I_{pt})(I_{kt}) + a_{IPY}(I_{pt})(Y_t)$$

$$+ a_{IPt}(I_{pt})(t) + a_{IKY}(I_{kt})(Y_t) + a_{IKt}(I_{kt})(t) + a_{Yt}(Y_t)(t) + u_{1t}.$$

Equations 15-30 and 15-31 are the estimating equations for the demand for labor and for materials. They are the same for all the versions of our model because the variable cost function is independent of our assumption about the absence or presence of market power, and does not depend on whether or not there is short-run forward shifting of the CIT.

Using equation 15-29 as the specification for our normalized variable cost function implies the assumption that the firm's MACs are different from zero when investment is zero. Of course, it is obvious that adjustment costs themselves have to be zero in the absence of any investment. But the change in adjustment costs resulting from the first small unit of investment need not be zero when investment begins to take place. Although it is reasonable to assume that MACs start out small and increase as the firm invests more and more, there is no a priori reason why they have to begin at exactly zero.

To appreciate better what is involved in assuming that MACs are zero at the origin, it helps to examine the expressions for MACs. The MACs caused by physical investment can be found by differentiating equation 15-29 partially with respect to I_{pt}; they are given by equation 15-32. Similarly, the MACs due to changes in the stock of knowledge capital (equation 15-33) are obtained by differentiating equation 15-29 partially with respect to I_{kt}:

(15-32)

$$\text{MAC}_P = \frac{\partial g_t}{\partial I_{pt}} = a_{IP} + a_{IPIP}(I_{pt}) + (a_{2IP})(w_{2t}) + (a_{PIP})(K_{pt})$$

$$+ (a_{KIP})(K_{kt}) + (a_{IPIK})(I_{kt}) + (a_{IPY})(Y_t) + (a_{IPt})(t)$$

(15-33)

$$\text{MAC}_K = \frac{\partial g_t}{\partial I_{kt}} = a_{IK} + a_{IKIK}(I_{kt}) + (a_{2IK})(w_{2t}) + (a_{PIK})(K_{pt})$$

$$+ (a_{KIK})(K_{kt}) + (a_{IPIK})(I_{pt}) + (a_{IKY})(Y_t) + (a_{IKt})(t).$$

From equation 15-32 we see that the marginal adjustment costs for physical investment are equal to zero in the absence of physical investment only if the following conditions hold:

(15-34) $a_{IP} = a_{2IP} = a_{PIP} = a_{KIP} = a_{IPIK} = a_{IPY} = a_{IPt} = 0.$

Similarly, from equation 15-33 it is clear that the MACs for R&D investment are zero at the origin only if the following constraints are satisfied:

$$(15\text{-}35) \quad a_{IK} = a_{2IK} = a_{PIK} = a_{KIK} = a_{IPIK} = a_{IKY} = a_{IKt} = 0.$$

If physical and knowledge investment are both equal to zero, the term containing a_{IPIK} is equal to zero automatically. Therefore the null hypothesis of zero MACs at the origin imposes twelve constraints for the two larger samples—Pakistan's chemical and pharmaceutical industries and Turkey's chemical and petroleum derivatives industries. Because we had to omit R&D investment and knowledge capital for the smaller sample of Pakistan's textile industry, equation 15-35 is irrelevant for it. In addition, equation 15-34 has to be modified by omitting a_{KIP} and a_{IPIK} because neither of these parameters occurs in the cost function for the smaller sample to begin with. The assumption of zero MACs at the origin therefore imposes only five constraints for the sample of Pakistan's textile industry.

When the conditions of equations 15-34 and 15-35 are imposed, the number of parameters to be estimated is reduced; hence, the number of degrees of freedom is increased for any hypothesis tests the researcher might want to conduct. (Berndt, Fuss, and Waverman 1980 and Bernstein and Shah, chapter 14 in this book, are two of many papers in which zero MACs at the origin are imposed.) This reduction in the number of parameters is useful, especially for relatively small samples. The increase in the number of degrees of freedom is not without cost, however. Equations 15-30 and 15-31 show that under the assumption of zero MACs at the origin investment would occur in equation 15-31 for the numéraire input v_1 but not in equation 15-30 for the other variable input v_2. The terms $a_{IPIP}(I_{pt})^2$ and $a_{IKIK}(I_{kt})^2$ occur in equation 15-31 but not in equation 15-30, and all the other terms involving investment are zero in equations 15-30 and 15-31 if MACs are constrained to be zero in the absence of investment. Because the choice of numéraire input is quite arbitrary, the asymmetric treatment of the two variable inputs cannot be justified by economic arguments. In order to test the hypothesis of zero MACs, we implemented quasi-likelihood ratio tests (Gallant and Jorgenson 1979) for our three samples. These tests compare Q_1 (the value of the minimum distance criterion for the maintained hypothesis of nonzero MACs) to Q_0 (the value of the objective function under the null hypothesis of zero MACs). The test statistic $(n)(Q_0 - Q_1)$ has a χ^2-distribution with degrees of freedom equal to the number of constraints imposed by the null hypothesis. We report the results from these tests in table 15-1.

As we explained above, for Pakistan's textile industry the null hypothesis of zero MACs in the absence of physical investment imposes five constraints. The critical value of χ^2 for a level of significance of $\alpha = 0.05$ and for five degrees of freedom is 11.0705. This critical value is smaller than

Table 15-1. Results from the Quasi-Likelihood Ratio Tests for the Hypothesis of Zero MACs

Sample	Test statistic
Pakistan's textile industry	14.0674
Pakistan's chemical and pharmaceutical industries	16.4988
Turkey's chemical and petroleum derivatives industries	26.4010

Source: Authors.

our test statistic for this sample, so we had to reject the null hypothesis of zero MACs for Pakistan's textile industry. For the other two samples the null hypothesis of zero MACs in the absence of either physical or R&D investment imposes twelve constraints, which implies a critical χ^2-value of 21.0261 for twelve degrees of freedom and $\alpha = 0.05$. For Pakistan's chemical and pharmaceutical industries this critical value exceeded the test statistic, so we failed to reject the null hypothesis. In the case of Turkey's chemical and petroleum derivatives industries, however, the test statistic was greater than 21.0261, so we had to reject the null hypothesis. For two of our samples, both economic arguments and the quasi-likelihood ratio tests thus suggested that we not impose the constraints implied by assuming zero MACs in the absence of investment. In the case of Pakistan's chemical and pharmaceutical industries, however, only the economic argument against treating the two variable inputs differently prevented us from assuming zero MACs at the origin. Therefore we did not impose the constraints of equations 15-34 and 15-35 for any of our three samples. Instead, we specified the factor demand equations derived from the normalized variable cost function with nonzero marginal adjustment costs in the absence of investment. As a result we were able to study the effect of tax incentives on both variable inputs because, according to our specification of the two factor demand equations, investment occurs in both of them. (See, for example, table 15-6 below.)

The estimating equations for output depend on the assumption about the absence or presence of market power in the industries of our samples. Under the assumption of perfect competition the output equation is a linear approximation of equation 15-13. Only the observable variables are used as explanatory variables, and the F_{ij} are coefficients to be estimated:

$$(15\text{-}36) \quad Y_t = F_0 + F_{PY}(P_{yt}/W_{1t}) + F_2(w_{2t}) + F_P(K_{pt}) + F_K(K_{kt})$$

$$+ F_{IP}(I_{pt}) + F_{IK}(I_{kt}) + F_t(t) + u_{yt}.$$

As a result of internal, nonseparable adjustment costs, firms experience a temporary reduction in output. We therefore expect the coefficients F_{IP} and F_{IK} to be negative.

Under the assumption that the dominant firm (or group of firms) has market power and lowers its output after an increase in the CIT, the output equation is a linear approximation of equation 15-25, where again only the observable variables are used as explanatory variables:

$$(15\text{-}37) \quad Y_t = F_0 + F_X (X_t / W_{1t}) + F_{PYS} (P_{yst} / W_{1t}) + F_2 (w_{2t}) + F_P (K_{pt})$$

$$+ F_K (K_{kt}) + F_{IP} (I_{pt}) + F_{IK} (I_{kt}) + F_c (T_{ct}) + F_t(t) + u_{yt}.$$

Following the example of Pindyck and Rotemberg (1983), the optimality conditions of equations 15-15 and 15-16 or of equations 15-27 and 15-28 can be used as alternative estimating equations for gross investment in physical capital (I_{pt}) and in knowledge capital (I_{kt}), depending on the assumption about the absence or presence of full short-run forward shifting of the CIT.

Under the assumption that there is no full short-run forward shifting of the CIT, we obtain the following estimating equation for physical investment from the optimality condition of equation 15-15 (see the appendix to this chapter for the details of the derivation):

$(15\text{-}38)$

$$I_{pt} = \left\{ 1 / \left[a_{PP} + \left[T_{ct} / \varepsilon_t (T_{ct+1}) \right] (1 + r_{t,t+1}) \, a_{IPIP} - a_{PIP} (1 - \delta_p) \right] \right\}$$

$$\left\{ (1 - \delta_p) a_{IP} - a_P - \left[T_{ct} / \varepsilon_t (T_{ct+1}) \right] (1 + r_{t,t+1}) \, a_{IP} \right.$$

$$- \left[T_{ct} / \varepsilon_t (T_{ct+1}) \right] (1 + r_{t,t+1}) \, a_{IP2} \, (w_{2t}) + \left[(1 - \delta_p) \, a_{IP2} - a_{P2} \right] \varepsilon_t \, (w_{2t+1})$$

$$+ \left[a_{PIP} (1 - \delta_p)^2 - a_{PP} (1 - \delta_p) - \left[T_{ct} / \varepsilon_t (T_{ct+1}) \right] (1 + r_{t,t+1}) \, a_{PIP} \right] (K_{pt})$$

$$+ \left[a_{KIP} (1 - \delta_p)(1 - \delta_k) - a_{PK} (1 - \delta_k) \left[T_{ct} / \varepsilon_t (T_{ct+1}) \right] (1 + r_{t,t+1}) \, a_{KIP} \right] (K_{kt})$$

$$+ \left[a_{KIP} (1 - \delta_p) - a_{PK} - \left[T_{ct} / \varepsilon_t (T_{ct+1}) \right] (1 + r_{t,t+1}) \, a_{IPIK} \right] (I_{kt})$$

$$- \left[T_{ct} / \varepsilon_t (T_{ct+1}) \right] (1 + r_{t,t+1}) \, a_{IPY} (Y_t) + \left[(1 - \delta_p) \, a_{IPY} - a_{PY} \right] \varepsilon_t (Y_{t+1})$$

$$- \left[T_{ct} / \varepsilon_t (T_{ct+1}) \right] (1 + r_{t,t+1}) \, a_{IPt} (t) + \left[(1 - \delta_p) \, a_{IPt} - a_{Pt} \right] (t + 1)$$

$$+ \left[(1 - \delta_p) \, a_{IPIP} - a_{PIP} \right] \varepsilon_t (I_{pt+1}) + \left[(1 - \delta_p) \, a_{IPIK} - a_{PIK} \right] \varepsilon_t (I_{kt+1})$$

$$- \left. (1 + r_{t,t+1}) \, rp_{pt} \, (\text{tax}) \right\} + u_{Ipt}.$$

Similarly, we use the first-order condition of equation 15-16 to obtain the estimating equation for R&D expenditure, that is, investment in knowledge capital I_{kt}:

(15-39)

$$I_{kt} = \left\{ 1 / \left[a_{KK} + \left[T_{ct} / \varepsilon_t (T_{ct+1}) \right] (1 + r_{t,t+1}) \, a_{IKIK} - a_{KIK} (1 - \delta_k) \right] \right\}$$

$$\left\{ (1 - \delta_k) \, a_{IK} - a_K - \left[T_{ct} / \varepsilon_t (T_{ct+1}) \right] (1 + r_{t,t+1}) \, a_{IK} \right.$$

$$- \left[T_{ct} / \varepsilon_t (T_{ct+1}) \right] (1 + r_{t,t+1}) \, a_{IK2} \, (w_{2t}) + \left[(1 - \delta_k) \, a_{IK2} - a_{K2} \right] \varepsilon_t (w_{2t+1})$$

$$+ \left[a_{KIK} (1 - \delta_k)^2 - a_{KK} (1 - \delta_k) - \left[T_{ct} / \varepsilon_t (T_{ct+1}) \right] (1 + r_{t,t+1}) \, a_{KIK} \right] (K_{kt})$$

$$+ \left[a_{PIK} (1 - \delta_k) (1 - \delta_p) - a_{PK} (1 - \delta_p) - \left[T_{ct} / \varepsilon_t (T_{ct+1}) \right] (1 + r_{t,t+1}) \, a_{PIK} \right] (K_{pt})$$

$$+ \left[a_{PIK} (1 - \delta_k) - a_{PK} - \left[T_{ct} / \varepsilon_t (T_{ct+1}) \right] (1 + r_{t,t+1}) \, a_{IPIK} \right] (I_{pt})$$

$$- \left[T_{ct} / \varepsilon_t (T_{ct+1}) \right] (1 + r_{t,t+1}) \, a_{IKY} \, (Y_t) + \left[(1 - \delta_k) \, a_{IKY} - a_{KY} \right] \varepsilon_t (Y_{t+1})$$

$$- \left[T_{ct} / \varepsilon_t (T_{ct+1}) \right] (1 + r_{t,t+1}) \, a_{IKt} \, (t) + \left[(1 - \delta_k) \, a_{IKt} - a_{Kt} \right] (t + 1)$$

$$+ \left[(1 - \delta_k) \, a_{IKIK} - a_{KIK} \right] \varepsilon_t (I_{kt+1}) + \left[(1 - \delta_k) \, a_{IPIK} - a_{KIP} \right] \varepsilon_t (I_{pt+1})$$

$$\left. - (1 + r_{t,t+1}) \, rp_{kt} \, (\text{tax}) \right\} + u_{Ikt} \, .$$

Equations 15-38 and 15-39 show that investment in physical capital I_{pt} depends not only on the stock of physical capital K_{pt} and on the following period's expected physical investment $\varepsilon_t(I_{pt+1})$ but also on the stock of knowledge capital K_{kt}, on R&D investment I_{kt} for the current period, and on $\varepsilon_t(I_{kt+1})$, the amount of R&D expenditure expected for the next period. Similarly, R&D expenditure I_{kt} depends on physical investment for the current and next periods, on the stocks of both types of capital, and on R&D investment expected for the next period. For Pakistan's textile industry, equation 15-39 is irrelevant, and all terms involving the stock of knowledge capital or R&D investment vanish in equation 15-38.

If there were full short-run forward shifting of the CIT in an industry, the relevant equilibrium conditions would be equations 15-27 and 15-28, which can be solved for investment in physical and knowledge capital. Alternatively, the estimating equations for I_{pt} and I_{kt} for this version of our model can be obtained from equations 15-38 and 15-39 by setting T_{ct} and $\varepsilon_t(T_{ct+1})$ equal to 1, and by replacing $rp_{pt}(\text{tax})$ with $rp_{pt}(\text{fs})$ and $rp_{kt}(\text{tax})$ with $rp_{kt}(\text{fs})$:

(15-40)

$$I_{pt} = \left\{ 1 / \left[a_{PP} + (1 + r_{t,t+1}) \, a_{IPIP} - a_{PIP} (1 - \delta_p) \right] \right\} \left\{ - a_P - (\delta_p + r_{t,t+1}) \, a_{IP} \right.$$

$$- (1 + r_{t,t+1}) \, a_{IP2} \, (w_{2t}) + \left[(1 - \delta_p) \, a_{IP2} - a_{P2} \right] \varepsilon_t (w_{2t+1})$$

$$+\left[a_{PIP}(1-\delta_p)^2 - a_{PP}(1-\delta_p) - (1+r_{t,t+1})\,a_{PIP}\right](K_{pt})$$

$$+\left[a_{KIP}(1-\delta_p)(1-\delta_k) - a_{PK}(1-\delta_k) - (1+r_{t,t+1})\,a_{KIP}\right](K_{kt})$$

$$+\left[a_{KIP}(1-\delta_p) - a_{PK} - (1+r_{t,t+1})\,a_{IPIK}\right](I_{kt})$$

$$-(1+r_{t,t+1})\,a_{IPY}(Y_t) + \left[(1-\delta_p)\,a_{IPY} - a_{PY}\right]\varepsilon_t(Y_{t+1})$$

$$-(1+r_{t,t+1})\,a_{IPt}(t) + \left[(1-\delta_p)\,a_{IPt} - a_{Pt}\right](t+1)$$

$$+\left[(1-\delta_p)\,a_{IPIP} - a_{PIP}\right]\varepsilon_t(I_{pt+1}) + \left[(1-\delta_p)\,a_{IPIK} - a_{PIK}\right]\varepsilon_t(I_{kt+1})$$

$$\left.-\ (1+r_{t,t+1})\,rp_{pt}(\text{fs})\right\} + u_{Ipt}$$

(15-41)

$$I_{kt} = \left\{1/\left[a_{KK} + (1+r_{t,t+1})\,a_{IKIK} - a_{KIK}(1-\delta_k)\right]\right\}\left\{-a_K - (\delta_k + r_{t,t+1})\,a_{IK}\right.$$

$$-(1+r_{t,t+1})\,a_{IK2}(w_{2t}) + \left[(1-\delta_k)\,a_{IK2} - a_{K2}\right]\varepsilon_t(w_{2t+1})$$

$$+\left[a_{KIK}(1-\delta_k)^2 - a_{KK}(1-\delta_k) - (1+r_{t,t+1})\,a_{KIK}\right](K_{kt})$$

$$+\left[a_{PIK}(1-\delta_k)(1-\delta_p) - a_{PK}(1-\delta_p) - (1+r_{t,t+1})\,a_{PIK}\right](K_{pt})$$

$$+\left[a_{PIK}(1-\delta_k) - a_{PK} - (1+r_{t,t+1})\,a_{IPIK}\right](I_{pt})$$

$$-(1+r_{t,t+1})\,a_{IKY}(Y_t) + \left[(1-\delta_k)\,a_{IKY} - a_{KY}\right]\varepsilon_t(Y_{t+1})$$

$$-(1+r_{t,t+1})\,a_{IKt}(t) + \left[(1-\delta_k)\,a_{IKt} - a_{Kt}\right](t+1)$$

$$+\left[(1-\delta_k)\,a_{IKIK} - a_{KIK}\right]\varepsilon_t(I_{kt+1}) + \left[(1-\delta_k)\,a_{IPIK} - a_{KIP}\right]\varepsilon_t(I_{pt+1})$$

$$\left.-(1+r_{t,t+1})\,rp_{kt}(\text{fs})\right\} + u_{Ikt}.$$

Equation 15-41 does not apply to Pakistan's textile industry, and in equation 15-40 all terms involving K_{kt} or I_{kt} are zero for this industry. The following is a summary of the estimating equations for the three different versions of our model.

- Joint assumptions of perfect competition and zero short-run forward shifting of the CIT: estimating equations 15-30, 15-31, 15-36, 15-38, and 15-39.
- Joint assumptions of market power and zero or partial short-run forward shifting of the CIT: estimating equations 15-30, 15-31, 15-37, 15-38, and 15-39.

- Joint assumptions of market power and full short-run forward shifting of the CIT: estimating equations 15-30, 15-31, 15-37, 15-40, and 15-41.

The endogenous variables output and investment occur as explanatory variables in the other equations. Therefore we estimated the system with nonlinear three-stage least squares in order to avoid simultaneous equations bias, using the predetermined variables as the instruments. The question arose as to how to obtain the expected values of future exogenous variables. In this chapter we are making the assumption of rational rather than static expectations. This implies that economic agents are assumed to use all the relevant information available to them at time s in order to make unbiased forecasts of the values of certain stochastic variables at a future time t. This does not mean that we assume perfect foresight on the part of business executives. Any individual forecast may turn out to be wrong. All we are assuming is that on average the forecasts are equal to the subsequently realized actual values of the variables concerned—that is, that the bias of the forecasts is zero. Therefore we use the subsequent realizations of these stochastic variables as "backcasts" of the unobservable expectations and replace expected values by their subsequently realized actual values (compare, for example, Kennan 1979: 1444, 1447, 1453).

After we replace the expected values of the exogenous variables by their subsequent realizations, we still have to deal with the expected values of the three endogenous variables Y_{t+1}, I_{pt+1}, and I_{kt+1} in the estimating equations for gross investment. We handle these endogenous variables by using the definition of rational expectations of Muth (1961: 316): "Expectations, since they are informed predictions of future events, are essentially the same as the predictions of the relevant economic theory." The estimating equations for output and investment, each shifted forward by one time period, would be the relevant economic theory for obtaining $\varepsilon_t(Y_{t+1})$, $\varepsilon_t(I_{pt+1})$, and $\varepsilon_t(I_{kt+1})$. The expected values $\varepsilon_t(Y_{t+2})$, $\varepsilon_t(I_{pt+2})$, and $\varepsilon_t(I_{kt+2})$, however, occur as explanatory variables in the equations for investment at time $t+1$, so we would be back where we started. Instead, we replace the three expected endogenous variables $\varepsilon_t(Y_{t+1})$, $\varepsilon_t(I_{pt+1})$, and $\varepsilon_t(I_{kt+1})$ by instruments. We obtain these instruments by using ordinary least squares to regress Y_{t+1}, I_{pt+1}, and I_{kt+1} on the exogenous variables of the next time period.

In the last part of this section, we sketch the non-nested hypothesis tests (see MacKinnon 1983 and 1992) that we implemented in order to test the three versions of our models against each other. The intuitive idea behind such tests is as follows: If model I were correct, adding the fitted values of the endogenous variables obtained from model II would not make any significant contribution to the estimation of model I. Similarly, the estimated values of the endogenous variables obtained by estimating model I would not help in the estimation of model II if II were the correct model. For example, we add the fitted value for labor obtained from model I, denoted *LFIT*(I), as an explanatory variable in the labor equation in model II. If *LFIT*(I) does not help in estimating labor in model II—that is, if model I cannot reject model II—our trust in model II is increased. This trust would be even greater if model II in turn were able to reject model I. In what follows we apply this idea to two of the three versions of our model.

Assuming market power and full short-run forward shifting of the CIT, we can write the system of equations as follows:

$$(15\text{-}42) \quad (I_{pt}, I_{kt}, L_t, M_t, \Upsilon_t)' = f_{jt}\big[\beta, rp_{pt}\,(\text{fs}),\, rp_{kt}\,(\text{fs}),\, p_{yst},\, x_t\big] + u_{jt}^{\text{fs}},$$

$$u_{jt}^{\text{fs}} \sim N(0, \Omega_{\text{fs}})$$

where β is the vector of regression coefficients to be estimated by the system of equations 15-42; Ω denotes the variance-covariance matrix of the system of equations; and for Pakistan's textile industry the equation for R&D investment I_{kt} has to be omitted from the system of equations 15-42, as well as from the systems of equations 15-43 through 15-45.

Under the joint assumptions of perfect competition and no short-run forward shifting of the CIT, the system of equations can be written as:

$$(15\text{-}43) \quad (I_{pt}, I_{kt}, L_t, M_t, \Upsilon_t)' = F_{jt}\big[\tau, rp_{pt}\,(\text{tax}),\, rp_{kt}\,(\text{tax}),\, p_{yt}\big] + u_{jt}^{\text{tax}},$$

$$u_{jt}^{\text{tax}} \sim N(0, \Omega_{\text{tax}})$$

where τ is the vector of regression coefficients to be estimated by the system of equations 15-43.

Each non-nested hypothesis "test" is actually a pair of tests. We try to use model I to reject model II, then we see whether model I in turn can be rejected by model II. Testing the pair of joint hypotheses "market power, full short-run forward shifting of the CIT" against the alternative pair of hypotheses "perfect competition, no tax shifting" involves estimating the following composite model:

$$(15\text{-}44) \quad (I_{pt}, I_{kt}, L_t, M_t, \Upsilon_t)' = (1-S)\big\{f_{jt}\big[\beta, rp_{pt}\,(\text{fs}),\, rp_{kt}\,(\text{fs}),\, p_{yst},\, x_t\big]\big\}$$

$$+ (S)\,(\hat{F}_{jt}) + u_{jt}^c \qquad u_{jt}^c \sim N(0, \Omega_{\text{fs}})$$

where $\hat{F}_{jt} = F_{jt}(\hat{\tau}, rp_{pt}\,(\text{tax}),\, rp_{kt}\,(\text{tax}),\, p_{yt})$ are the fitted values of the exogenous variables obtained by estimating the system of equations 15-43, and S is a coefficient to be estimated. As we mentioned before, the null hypothesis of the system of equations 15-42 cannot be rejected by the alternative hypothesis of the system of equations 15-43 if the fitted values from the system of equations 15-43 do not contribute significantly to the estimation of the system of equations 15-42, that is, if the estimated coefficient S is not statistically significant. Therefore the t value of the coefficient S is the test statistic for this half of the pair of non-nested hypothesis tests.

Testing the pair of joint hypotheses "perfect competition, no short-run forward shifting of the CIT" against the alternative pair of hypotheses "market power, full tax shifting" involves estimating the following composite model:

$$(15\text{-}45) \quad (I_{pt}, I_{kt}, L_t, M_t, Y_t)' = (1 - S)\left\{ F_{jt}\left[\tau, rp_{pt}(\text{tax}), rp_{kt}(\text{tax}), p_{yt}\right]\right\}$$
$$+ (S)\,(\hat{f}_{jt}) + u^c_{jt} \qquad u^c_{jt} \sim N(0, \Omega_{\text{tax}})$$

where $\hat{f}_{jt} = f_{jt}(\hat{\beta}, rp_{pt}(\text{fs}), rp_{kt}(\text{fs}), p_{yst}, x_t)$ are the estimated values of the exogenous variables obtained by estimating the system of equations 15-42. The test statistic is again the value of t for the estimated coefficient S.

In total we performed three such pairs of non-nested hypothesis tests in order to test the three versions of our model against each other. We used the software package TSP for all our computations.

In this section we derived the estimating equations from the three versions of our model that had been explained in the previous section. We also outlined the non-nested hypothesis tests that we implemented in order to test the three versions of our model against each other. Our empirical results are presented in the following section.

The Empirical Results and Their Policy Implications

Before turning to the non-nested hypothesis tests, we present in table 15-2 the elasticities of the demand for labor and for materials with respect to small changes in the input prices. The formulas from which these and all subsequent elasticities were computed can be found in appendix 15.

The results in table 15-2 show that for all three samples the two own-price elasticities have the correct negative signs. Moreover, for Pakistan's chemical and pharmaceutical industries, e_{LWL} (the own-price elasticity of labor) and e_{LWM} (the elasticity of labor with respect to a small change in the price of materials) are both significantly different from zero.

For Pakistan's textile industry, the elasticities of labor and materials with respect to a small change in the rental price of the services from R&D capital are not available, because that sample was too small to include R&D expenditure and the stock and rental price of knowledge capital in the model.

Tables 15-3 through 15-5 contain the results from the three pairs of non-nested hypothesis tests that we implemented for each of our samples.

We first tested the two pairs of joint hypotheses "perfect competition, no short-run forward shifting of the CIT" and "market power, full tax shifting" against each other, as reported in table 15-3.

For Pakistan's chemical and pharmaceutical industries we had to reject the pair of assumptions that these industries have market power and that there is complete short-run forward shifting of the CIT. For Pakistan's textile industry, by contrast, we had to reject the joint hypotheses of perfect competition and no short-run forward shifting of the CIT. Finally, for Turkey's chemical and petroleum derivatives industries, neither pair of

Table 15-2. Short-Run Elasticity of Demand for Labor and for Materials with Respect to Input Prices

Elasticity	Pakistan's textile industry	Pakistan's chemical and pharmaceutical industries	Turkey's chemical and petroleum derivatives industries
e_{LWL}	−0.19357 (0.17765)	−0.65946 (0.12897)	−0.55852 (1.1155)
e_{LWM}	0.18171 (0.18624)	0.66601 (0.13436)	0.54899 (1.0980)
e_{LRPK}	n.a.	−0.000009 (0.000016)	0.00243 (0.00280)
e_{LRPP}	0.01187 (0.01990)	−0.00654 (0.00800)	0.00710 (0.02657)
e_{MWL}	0.54117 (1.2996)	0.16471 (0.17406)	0.63971 (0.37986)
e_{MWM}	−0.55771 (1.3425)	−0.16710 (0.17672)	−0.78010 (0.44216)
e_{MRPK}	n.a.	0.00056 (0.00091)	0.00167 (0.00119)
e_{MRPP}	0.01654 (0.07174)	0.00183 (0.00480)	0.13872 (0.07711)

n.a. Not applicable.

Note: Midpoint of samples. Estimated standard errors in parentheses.

L = labor; M = materials; RPK = rental price of services from knowledge capital; RPP = rental price of services from physical capital; WL = price of labor, WM = price of materials.

Source: Authors.

Table 15-3. First Pair of Non-nested Hypothesis Tests

Industry	Null hypothesis: Market power, full short-run forward shifting of CIT			Null hypothesis: Perfect competition, no short-run forward shifting of CIT		
	$\hat{S}$	t	Outcome	$\hat{S}$	t	Outcome
Pakistan's chemical and phar- maceutical industries	0.66631	2.4135	Null hypothesis rejected	0.33256	0.88986	Null hypothesis not rejected
Pakistan's textile industry	0.00004	0.44626	Null hypothesis not rejected	0.79750	6.7864	Null hypothesis rejected
Turkey's chemical and petroleum derivatives industries	−0.11882	−0.52409	Null hypothesis not rejected	0.15954	1.2535	Null hypothesis not rejected

$\hat{S}$ = estimate of the coefficient S; t = t-value for the coefficient S.
Source: Authors.

joint hypotheses was able to reject the alternative set of hypotheses; that is, the two non-nested hypothesis tests were inconclusive. The safest conclusion from all these ambiguous results may well be that both these polar cases (either no shifting or full shifting) ought to be rejected in favor of the third version of our model. In this intermediate case we assume market power on the part of firms but allow for the possibility that they may not be completely successful in their attempt at shifting the CIT forward in the short run.

Next, we tested the two pairs of joint hypotheses "market power, full short-run forward shifting of the CIT" and "market power, partial or no tax shifting" against each other. These results are reported in table 15-4.

For Pakistan's textile industry (the smallest sample) the tests were inconclusive; in other words, neither pair of joint hypotheses was able to reject the competing pair of joint assumptions. For the two larger samples, however, the joint assumptions of market power and full short-run forward shifting of the CIT had to be rejected quite decisively, whereas the competing pair of assumptions (market power, partial or no tax shifting) could not be rejected. Because the assumption of market power was part of both of these alternative pairs of joint hypotheses, this set of tests in effect rejects the assumption of full tax shifting, rather than that of market power. By rejecting the assumption of full short-run forward

Table 15-4. Second Pair of Non-nested Hypothesis Tests

	Null hypothesis: Market power, full short-run forward shifting of CIT			Null hypothesis: Market power, partial or no short-run tax shifting		
Industry	$\hat{S}$	t	Outcome	$\hat{S}$	t	Outcome
Pakistan's chemical and pharmaceutical industries	0.94279	17.349	Null hypothesis rejected	0.054236	0.089889	Null hypothesis not rejected
Pakistan's textile industry	−2.8632	−0.92865	Null hypothesis not rejected	0.16138	0.44813	Null hypothesis not rejected
Turkey's chemical and petroleum derivatives industries	0.99939	26.835	Null hypothesis rejected	0.44761	1.5679	Null hypothesis not rejected

$\hat{S}$ = estimate of the coefficient S; t = t-value for the coefficient S.
Source: Authors.

Table 15-5. Third Pair of Non-nested Hypothesis Tests

	Null hypothesis: Market power, partial or no tax shifting			Null hypothesis: Perfect competition, no short-run forward shifting of CIT		
Industry	$\hat{S}$	t	Outcome	$\hat{S}$	t	Outcome
Pakistan's chemical and pharmaceutical industries	−0.084358	−0.88697	Null hypothesis not rejected	0.81649	6.8073	Null hypothesis rejected
Pakistan's textile industry	0.021923	0.56634	Null hypothesis not rejected	0.97375	18.525	Null hypothesis rejected
Turkey's chemical and petroleum derivatives industries	0.33998	1.5080	Null hypothesis not rejected	0.88055	4.7627	Null hypothesis rejected

$\hat{S}$ = estimate of the coefficient S; t = t-value for the coefficient S.
Source: Authors.

shifting of the CIT, we have in effect ruled out the possibility that the rental prices of capital services may be free of the parameters of the CIT. Needless to say, this is good news for policymakers because the rental prices of capital services are two of the most important channels through which tax incentives are assumed to influence the production and investment decisions of firms.

In the final set of non-nested hypothesis tests we tested the pairs of joint assumptions "perfect competition, no tax shifting" and "market power, partial or no tax shifting" against each other. Both these pairs of joint hypotheses imply rental prices of capital services that contain the parameters of the CIT, but they differ in assuming either perfect competition or market power. Although this last pair of tests may not appear to be very interesting from the point of view of public policy, its results are nevertheless important. They tell us which of the two alternative output equations (15-36 or 15-37) to use for further analysis because equation 15-36 is based on the assumption of perfect competition, whereas market power is assumed in equation 15-37. It is important to ensure that we have a correctly specified regression model before computing possible effects of tax incentives. We report the results from this last set of non-nested hypothesis tests in table 15-5.

It can be seen in table 15-5 that for all three samples the hypothesis of market power could not be rejected by the competing hypothesis of perfect competition, whereas the assumption of perfect competition was rejected by that of market power quite unambiguously. These results are contrary to the conventional assumption of perfect competition, which is made in most empirical studies of individual industries or of the manufacturing sector as a whole. The results of table 15-5 thus show that for our three samples it would have been a mistake to assume perfect competition. It would have been a misspecification of the econometric model to use equation 15-36 as the output equation rather than equation 15-37, which is based on the assumption of market power on the part of firms. Given the large values of the test statistic t, we have reasonable confidence in these results, in spite of the comparatively small sizes of all our samples.

Having convinced ourselves that the parameters of the CIT do enter the expression(s) for the rental price(s) of capital services, we proceeded to examine the effect of selected tax incentives on the endogenous variables of our model. In keeping with our test results, we made the joint assumptions that there was market power in the industries of our three samples and that the firms were not able to shift the CIT forward completely, which is why their rental prices of capital services were influenced by the CIT.

First, we examined the effect of the current tax credit for physical investment not only on physical investment but also on R&D investment (where relevant), output, and the demands for the variable inputs, labor and materials. These results apply only to Pakistan because Turkey uses a tax allowance rather than a tax credit for physical investment.

Equation 15-46 shows that the elasticity of physical investment with respect to small changes in the current tax credit for physical investment (denoted e_{IPMPT}) is composed of the effect of the tax credit m_{pt} on the rental price of the services from physical capital $rp_{pt}(\text{tax})$ and of the effect of the latter on physical investment I_{pt}. Theory predicts each term of this expression to be negative, making their product positive:

$$(15\text{-}46) \qquad e_{IPMPT} = \frac{\partial I_{pt}}{\partial rp_{pt}(\text{tax})} \frac{\partial rp_{pt}(\text{tax})}{\partial m_{pt}} \frac{m_{pt}}{I_{pt}} > 0 .$$

Equation 15-47 shows that the current tax credit for physical investment influences R&D investment by affecting not only physical investment but also output:

$$(15\text{-}47) \; e_{IKMPT} = \left(\frac{\partial I_{kt}}{\partial I_{pt}} + \frac{\partial I_{kt}}{\partial Y_t} \frac{\partial Y_t}{\partial I_{pt}}\right) \frac{\partial I_{pt}}{\partial rp_{pt}(\text{tax})} \frac{\partial rp_{pt}(\text{tax})}{\partial m_{pt}} \frac{m_{pt}}{I_{pt}} .$$

As we explained earlier, when the firm undertakes physical or R&D investment, it experiences adjustment costs in the form of a temporary reduction in output. The increase in both types of investment induced by the tax credit is therefore predicted to reduce output temporarily. Therefore we expect e_{YMPT}, the elasticity of output Y_t with respect to changes in the tax credit for physical investment m_{pt}, to be negative. (See Treadway 1970 and 1974 on the desirability of specifying adjustment costs as internal and nonseparable, as we did in our model.) Equation 15-48 shows the effect of the tax credit m_{pt} on the rental price of the services from physical capital $rp_{pt}(\text{tax})$, on both kinds of investment, and finally on output Y_t:

$$(15\text{-}48) \; e_{YMPT} = \left(\frac{\partial Y_t}{\partial I_{pt}} + \frac{\partial Y_t}{\partial I_{kt}} \frac{\partial I_{kt}}{\partial I_{pt}}\right) \frac{\partial I_{pt}}{\partial rp_{pt}(\text{tax})} \frac{\partial rp_{pt}(\text{tax})}{\partial m_{pt}} \frac{m_{pt}}{Y_t} < 0.$$

The elasticities of the demands for the variable inputs v_j, $j = L, M$, with respect to small changes in the tax credit for physical investment, are composed of several effects that are described in equation 15-49. The temporary reduction in output (because of the adjustment costs caused by both types of investment) is responsible for a reduction in the demand for input v_j. The increases in physical and R&D investment cause an increase or a reduction in the demand for the jth variable input, depending on whether v_j is a complement of or a substitute for both kinds of capital. These elasticities, denoted e_{JMPT}, may thus be either positive or negative if v_j and the two capital inputs are complements, but they have to be negative if the variable input and the two types of capital are substitutes.

$$(15\text{-}49) \quad e_{JMPT} = \left(\frac{\partial v_{jt}}{\partial I_{pt}} + \frac{\partial v_{jt}}{\partial Y_t} \frac{\partial Y_t}{\partial I_{pt}} + \frac{\partial v_{jt}}{\partial I_{kt}} \frac{\partial I_{kt}}{\partial I_{pt}} + \frac{\partial v_{jt}}{\partial Y_t} \frac{\partial Y_t}{\partial I_{kt}} \frac{\partial I_{kt}}{\partial I_{pt}} \right)$$
$$\frac{\partial I_{pt}}{\partial rp_{pt} \,(\text{tax})} \frac{\partial rp_{pt} \,(\text{tax})}{\partial m_{pt}} \frac{m_{pt}}{v_{jt}} .$$

Elasticity formulas 15-46 through 15-49 are valid for any functional form. In appendix 15 we evaluate these expressions for the quadratic normalized variable cost function and the estimating equations derived from it in the previous section. In table 15-6 we report the numerical values for the above elasticities for the midpoint of the time period within our sample period for which the investment tax credit was in effect (1977 through 1983).

The positive sign of e_{IPMPT} for all three industries confirms that an increase in the tax credit for physical investment would cause the firms to undertake more physical investment, no doubt the effect intended by policymakers. It remains to be seen, however, how the amount of additional investment would compare with the loss in tax revenue as the result of a more generous tax credit for physical investment. The fact that e_{IKMPT} (the elasticity of R&D investment with respect to small changes in the tax credit for physical investment) is positive as well implies that the tax credit for physical investment stimulated investment in knowledge as well as in physical capital.

In table 15-7 we compare the benefits and costs of an increase in the current tax credit. The following is an example of how these results were

Table 15-6. Elasticity of Endogenous Variables with Respect to Small Changes in Current Tax Credit for Physical Investment in Pakistan, 1980

Elasticity	Textile industry	Chemical industry	Pharmaceutical industry
e_{IPMPT}	0.00251	0.34202	0.59796
e_{IKMPT}	n.a.	0.10893	0.23844
e_{YMPT}	−0.00091	−0.00062	−0.00093
e_{LMPT}	−0.00136	−0.24853	−0.17691
e_{MMPT}	−0.01303	−0.00461	−0.00151

n.a. Not applicable.

e_{IPMPT} = percentage change in physical investment, I_{pt}, caused by a 1 percent change in the current tax credit for physical investment, m_{pt}; IK = R&D expenditure, I_{kt}; Y = output, Y_t; L = labor, L_t; M = materials, M_t.

Source: Authors.

Table 15-7. Benefit and Cost of a 10 Percent Change in Tax Credit for Physical Investment in Pakistan
(rupees)

Industry	Benefit	Cost	Benefit-cost ratio
Textiles	276,053	16,497,204	0.017
Chemicals	8,917,552	3,910,979	2.280
Pharmaceuticals	3,582,797	898,755	3.986

Note: Benefit is defined as increase in physical investment. Cost is defined as reduction in tax revenue.
Source: Authors.

calculated: We know from table 15-6 that e_{IPMPT} (the percentage change in physical investment divided by the percentage change in the current tax credit for physical investment) for Pakistan's textile industry was 0.00251 for the year 1980. This implies that a 10 percent change in m_{pt} would cause a 0.0251 percent change in physical investment. This works out to 276,053 rupees because physical investment in Pakistan's textile industry was Rs1,099,813,550 for the year 1980. The same 10 percent increase in the tax credit m_{pt} above its 1980 level of 15 percent would have caused a reduction in tax revenue of Rs$(0.015)(1,099,813,550) =$ 16,497,204 for the government. We divided the benefits by the costs to obtain the ratio 0.017.

Given the small sizes of our samples, we have to be careful when drawing policy conclusions from the results of table 15-7. The benefit-cost ratio for Pakistan's textile industry is so much smaller than one, however, that it would appear to be a reasonable conclusion that the tax credit for physical investment was an ineffective instrument of economic policy for this industry during the sample period. For Pakistan's chemical and pharmaceutical industries, in contrast, the calculated increase in physical investment is so much greater than the loss in tax revenue that it appears to be safe to conclude that the tax credit for physical investment was an effective instrument of government policy for these two industries.

In Turkey the tax incentive for physical investment is a tax allowance rather than a tax credit. (Whereas a tax credit reduces the firm's tax liability by the fraction m_p of physical investment, a tax allowance reduces the firm's tax base by the fraction q_p of physical investment.) To see how a tax allowance influences investment in physical and R&D capital, output, and the demand for labor and materials, the general elasticity formulas 15-46 through 15-49 can be adapted easily by substituting q_{pt} for m_{pt} in all of them. Appendix 15 gives the elasticity formulas for our particular specification of the normalized variable cost function and for the estimat-

Table 15-8. Elasticity of Endogenous Variables with Respect to Small Changes in the Current Tax Allowance for Physical Investment in Turkey, 1978

Elasticity	Industrial chemicals	Other chemicals	Petroleum derivatives
e_{IKQPT}	0.11461	0.07560	0.27484
e_{IPQPT}	0.03280	0.05045	0.12302
e_{YQPT}	−0.10513	−0.06934	−0.20235
e_{LQPT}	−0.00903	−0.00489	−0.03881
e_{MQPT}	−0.37515	−0.19530	−0.55530

e_{IKQPT} = percentage change in R&D expenditure, I_{kt}, in response to a 1 percent change in the current tax allowance, q_{pt}; IP = physical investment, I_{pt}; Y = output, Y_t; L = labor, L_t; M = materials, M_t.

Source: Authors.

ing equations derived from it. Table 15-8 reports the effects of a small change in q_{pt}, the current tax allowance for physical investment, on the endogenous variables of the model for the midpoint of the sample period. Our sample for Turkey consists of the industrial chemical, other chemical, and petroleum derivatives industries.

As with a tax credit, an increase in the current investment allowance for physical capital reduces the rental price of the services from physical capital, which in turn results in more investment in physical capital. This is confirmed by the positive sign of e_{IPQPT} in table 15-8. For the three Turkish industries, increased investment in physical capital also led to more R&D investment, as the positive sign of e_{IKQPT} shows. The increase in physical and knowledge investment caused adjustment costs, which manifested themselves as temporary reductions in output, hence the negative sign of e_{YQPT}.

It is not enough that the current tax allowance promotes an increase in investment. We also need to find out how this increase compares with the government's loss in tax revenue. Table 15-9 is a report on these calculations.

In table 15-9 we show that for Turkey's industrial and other chemical industries the revenue loss due to an increase in q_{pt}, the current investment allowance for physical capital, far exceeded the increase in physical investment caused by this change in q_{pt}. For Turkey's petroleum derivatives industries, however, the benefit-cost ratio was only a little lower than one. These results demonstrate the importance of studying the effects of tax incentives for individual industries, rather than for the manufacturing sector as a whole: the same policy instrument may well be cost-effective for some industries while at the same time being quite ineffective in others.

Table 15-9. Benefit and Cost of a 10 Percent Change in Current Tax Allowance for Investment in Physical Capital in Turkey
(Turkish lira)

Industry	Benefit	Cost	Benefit-cost ratio
Industrial chemicals	3,017,351	11,867,020	0.254
Other chemicals	2,949,615	7,542,127	0.391
Petroleum derivatives	3,147,639	3,300,646	0.954

Note: Benefit is defined as increase in physical investment. Cost is defined as reduction in tax revenue.
Source: Authors.

Next, we turn to tax incentives for R&D investment, or investment in knowledge capital. These took the form of tax allowances in Pakistan as well as in Turkey. We concentrate on the effect of these tax allowances on R&D investment. The general expression for the elasticity of R&D investment I_{kt} with respect to a small change in the current tax allowance q_{kt} can be obtained from equation 15-46 by substituting q_{kt} for m_{pt} and I_{kt} for I_{pt}. Appendix 15 contains the elasticity formula for the specific estimating equations that were derived in the preceding section from the quadratic normalized variable cost function.

In table 15-10 we report the elasticities of R&D expenditure I_{kt} with respect to a small change in the current tax allowance q_{kt} (the fraction of R&D that firms are allowed to expense), for the midpoint of the sample period. In the case of Pakistan's chemical and pharmaceutical industries, 1974 was the midpoint of the sample period. (Because we did not model R&D investment for Pakistan's textile industry, we were not able to examine the effect of the R&D allowance on this industry.) The year 1978 was the midpoint of the sample period for Turkey's industrial chemicals, other chemicals, and petroleum derivatives.

The tax allowance was 100 percent during the sample period, so it is reasonable to study the effect of a small reduction in q_{kt}, rather than the

Table 15-10. Elasticity of R&D Investment with Respect to Small Changes in Current Tax Allowance for R&D Investment

Industry	Elasticity
Pakistan's chemicals	0.51857
Pakistan's pharmaceuticals	0.09110
Turkey's industrial chemicals	0.05484
Turkey's other chemicals	0.03920
Turkey's petroleum derivatives	0.11356

Source: Authors.

effect of a small increase in this tax allowance. For example, reducing the tax allowance from 100 percent to 90 percent would have increased the rental price of the services from knowledge capital and therefore reduced R&D investment. In other words, the tax allowance and R&D investment both move in the same direction—they are positively related. This is confirmed by the positive sign of the elasticities for all five industries in table 15-10.

The fact that the elasticity of R&D expenditure with respect to small changes in the R&D allowance is positive for five industries in two countries is evidence that this tax incentive influences R&D investment in the desired direction. It does not indicate, however, whether the amount of R&D expenditure stimulated by R&D allowances is large enough in comparison with the tax revenue lost by governments because of it. This question is addressed by the benefit-cost calculations reported in table 15-11.

The data in table 15-11 show that the tax allowance for R&D investment was a relatively more cost-effective policy instrument in Pakistan than in Turkey, in the sense that its benefit-cost ratios were on the average higher for Pakistan than for Turkey. Within the same country, however, the R&D allowance affected the individual industries in remarkably different ways. For example, for Pakistan's chemical industry the benefit-cost ratio was greater than one, whereas it was less than one-quarter for the same country's pharmaceutical industry. These results show that the tax allowance for R&D investment may well be a rather effective instrument of public policy for specific industries in some countries. It ought to be studied further and in detail, that is, for individual industries rather than for a country's manufacturing sector as a whole.

Our model incorporates rational expectations about the tax parameters as well as about all the other variables. This means that our expressions

Table 15-11. Benefit and Cost of a 10 Percent Change in Current Tax Allowance for R&D Investment

Industry	Benefit	Cost	Benefit-cost ratio
Pakistan's chemicals	21,676 R.	15,675 R.	1.383
Pakistan's pharmaceuticals	18,657 R.	76,800 R.	0.243
Turkey's industrial chemicals	1,646,171 T.L.	12,907,611 T.L.	0.128
Turkey's other chemicals	1,743,816 T.L.	19,128,593 T.L.	0.091
Turkey's petroleum derivatives	1,482,901T.L.	5,615,069 T.L.	0.264

R&D = research and development.

Note: Benefit is defined as change in R&D investment. Cost is defined as change in tax revenue.

Source: Authors.

for the rental prices of capital services are also influenced by tax incentives expected for the next year, not only by those in effect for the current year. (See equations 15-15 and 15-16.) Therefore we were able to analyze not only the effect of tax credits and tax allowances in force during the current year but also the effect of these tax incentives expected for the following year.

In table 15-12 we report the elasticities of physical and R&D investment with respect to small changes in Pakistan's expected tax credit for the next period, $\varepsilon_t(m_{pt+1})$. These elasticities were computed for the year 1980, the midpoint of the period during which the tax credit was in effect. The general expressions for these two elasticities can be obtained from the formulas 15-46 and 15-47 by substituting m_{pt+1} for m_{pt}. In appendix 15 we present the corresponding elasticity formulas for the estimating equations that were derived in the previous section. Equation 15-15 predicts that the elasticities of physical and R&D investment with respect to next year's tax credit have the opposite sign from the elasticities with respect to the current tax credit. It is intuitively reasonable that if firms expect an increase in the investment tax credit for the following year, they are likely to reduce their investment during the current year. As can be seen from table 15-12, $e_{IPMPT+1}$ and $e_{IKMPT+1}$ in fact have the predicted negative signs.

Comparing table 15-12 with table 15-6, we see that the elasticities with respect to next year's tax credit for physical investment are smaller in absolute value than the corresponding elasticities with respect to the current investment tax credit. Because the current tax credit is known with certainty, whereas the investment credit for the next time period can only be anticipated, it is reasonable that the effects of the former should be numerically larger than the effects of the latter.

In table 15-13 we report the elasticities of physical and R&D investment with respect to small changes in Turkey's tax allowance for physical capital expected for the next period, $\varepsilon_t(q_{pt+1})$. These elasticities were

Table 15-12. Elasticity of Physical and R&D Investment with Respect to Small Changes in Tax Credit for Physical Investment Expected for Following Year, Pakistan, 1980

Elasticity	Textile industry	Chemical industry	Pharmaceutical industry
$e_{IPMPT+1}$	−0.00202	−0.27483	−0.48051
$e_{IKMPT+1}$	n.a.	−0.08753	−0.19160

n.a. Not applicable.

$e_{IPMPT+1}$ = percentage change in physical investment, I_{pt}, in response to a 1 percent change in m_{pt+1}, the tax credit for physical investment expected for the following year; IK = R&D investment, I_{kt}.

Source: Authors.

Table 15-13. Elasticity of R&D and Physical Investment with Respect to Small Changes in Tax Allowance for Physical Investment Expected for Following Year, Turkey, 1978

Elasticity	Industrial chemicals	Other chemicals	Petroleum derivatives
$e_{IKQPT+1}$	−0.08698	−0.05737	−0.20857
$e_{IPQPT+1}$	−0.02489	−0.03828	−0.09335

$e_{IKQPT+1}$ = percentage change in R&D expenditure, I_{kt}, caused by a 1 percent change in q_{pt+1}, the tax allowance for physical investment expected for the following year; IP = physical investment, I_{pt}.

Source: Authors.

computed for 1978, the midpoint of the sample period. Formulas 15-46 and 15-47 can be used to obtain the general expressions for these two elasticities by simply substituting q_{pt+1} for m_{pt}. The specific elasticity formulas for the estimating equations derived in the preceding section can be found in appendix 15. According to equation 15-15 the elasticities of physical and R&D investment with respect to next year's tax allowance have the opposite sign from the elasticities with respect to the current tax allowance. It agrees with intuition that firms that expect an increase in the tax allowance for physical investment for the following year will probably reduce physical investment during the current year. That $e_{IPQPT+1}$ and $e_{IKQPT+1}$ do indeed have the predicted negative signs can be seen in table 15-13.

As with Pakistan's tax credit for physical investment, we see that for Turkey's tax allowance for physical investment the elasticities with respect to the tax incentive expected for the following year are numerically smaller than the corresponding elasticities with respect to the current tax incentive. (Compare tables 15-8 and 15-13.)

Finally, in table 15-14, we report the elasticities of R&D investment with respect to small changes in the expected R&D allowance for the next period, $\varepsilon_t(q_{kt+1})$. These elasticities were calculated for the midpoint of the sample period (1974 for Pakistan and 1978 for Turkey). The general expression for the elasticity of R&D investment I_{kt} with respect to a small change in the tax allowance expected for time $t + 1$ can be obtained from formula 15-46 by substituting q_{kt+1} for m_{pt} and I_{kt} for I_{pt}. Appendix 15 contains the specific elasticity formula for the estimating equations that we derived in the preceding section. Again, equation 15-16 predicts that the elasticity of R&D investment with respect to the R&D allowance expected for next year has the opposite sign from the elasticity with respect to the current tax allowance. Whereas the current R&D allowance is positively related to R&D investment, the tax allowance expected for next year is inversely related to R&D expenditure. If firms expect a reduction in this

Table 15-14. Elasticity of R&D Investment with Respect to Small Changes in R&D Allowance Expected for Following Year

Industry	Elasticity
Pakistan's chemical industry	−0.42390
Pakistan's pharmaceutical industry	−0.07447
Turkey's industrial chemicals	−0.04162
Turkey's other chemicals	−0.02975
Turkey's petroleum derivatives	−0.08617

Source: Authors.

tax allowance for the following year, they have an incentive to increase their R&D expenditure during the current year, while the tax climate is still favorable. This is the economic reason why R&D investment I_{kt} and the R&D allowance q_{kt+1} expected for the following year move in opposite directions. As table 15-14 shows, the elasticities indeed have the predicted negative sign for the five industries.

Comparing tables 15-10 and 15-14, we see that the elasticities with respect to next year's tax allowance for R&D investment are numerically smaller than the corresponding elasticities with respect to the current R&D allowance, and that they are of opposite sign. As we discussed earlier, this agrees with intuition; we expect firms to postpone R&D and therefore reduce their current R&D expenditure if they anticipate more favorable tax treatment of R&D during the coming year, or vice versa.

The results of tables 15-13 and 15-14 suggest that governments may be well advised not to announce improved tax incentives too far in advance. Such an early announcement would reduce both physical and R&D investment during the current year. Governments can obtain the same increase in next year's investment without the loss in current investment if they do not announce improvements in next year's tax incentives during the current year.

In this section we have presented our empirical results and discussed their policy implications. The next section concludes the chapter.

Summary

We have used an intertemporal model of a firm optimizing its expected net present value to provide the theoretical basis for our estimating equations and, at the same time, to derive expressions for the rental prices of capital services that are consistent with rational rather than static expectations on the part of economic agents. We have presented three different versions of our theoretical model, depending on the assumptions about the absence or presence of market power and full short-run forward shifting of the CIT. In version 1, because we assume perfect competition, short-run forward shifting of the CIT is impossible, and the rental prices of capital services contain tax parameters. In version 2, firms may have some unexerted market power, and they may succeed completely in shifting the CIT on to consumers in the short run. We demonstrated that in that case the expressions for the rental prices of capital services would be free of the parameters of the CIT. In version 3, firms in an intermediate situation may again have some unexerted market power, but they may be unsuccessful in shifting the CIT forward completely. In this third case the parameters of the CIT also enter the expressions for the rental prices of capital services. We specified a quadratic normalized variable cost function and derived estimating equations from it for the three versions of our model. We tested the three versions of the model against each other by using non-nested hypothesis tests.

These tests showed that for our samples the hypothesis of market power was able to reject that of perfect competition. This result contradicts the conventional assumption of perfect competition that is frequently made in empirical work. For the industries we studied and for the time periods involved, incorrectly assuming perfect competition would have involved using the wrong output equation, a misspecification of the model. (Output equation 15-36 is based on the assumption of perfect competition, whereas the assumption in output equation 15-37 is that firms have market power that they do not exert fully at the time of the change in the CIT.)

Even though the firms in the industries we studied had market power during the sample period, our hypothesis tests showed that they were not able to shift the CIT forward completely in the short run. This result agrees with our prior expectation that although firms with unexerted market power are quite likely to make an attempt at passing the CIT on to their customers in the form of higher output prices, it is very unlikely that such attempts will be completely successful. Only in the case of complete short-run forward shifting of the CIT are the rental prices of capital services free of the parameters of the CIT. If the firms have to bear even part of the burden of the CIT in the short run, their after-tax profits differ from their profits prior to the tax change, and the expressions for the rental prices of capital services contain tax parameters.

With our non-nested hypothesis tests we are able to determine only whether full short-run forward shifting of the CIT is absent or present. If full tax shifting is absent, our tests are not able to distinguish between different degrees of tax shifting. (As we mentioned before, tax parameters affect the rental prices of capital services in situations of partial tax shifting as well as in the case of no shifting, and we test the rental prices of capital services with and without tax parameters against each other.) This limitation of our model does not matter from the point of view of tax policy, however. Our non-nested hypothesis tests are able to answer the question whether tax incentives do or do not influence the rental prices of capital services. It is well known that the rental prices of capital services are two of the main channels through which tax incentives may influence investment. Therefore it is important to test for the presence or absence of tax parameters in the rental prices of capital services, instead of assuming a priori that they are present.

The precondition for full tax shifting—that is, unexerted market power—may well be met for some industries, but not for others. Therefore it is important to conduct these hypothesis tests for individual industries, rather than for the whole manufacturing sector. Collecting the required data and doing the necessary computations is a time-consuming task but one that is well worth the effort, given the important policy implications of the results.

Because our tests showed that tax incentives did have an effect on the production and investment decisions of the firms in our samples, we computed estimates of the effect of several tax incentives on the endogenous variables of the model. Table 15-15 presents a summary of the results we obtained on the effectiveness of tax incentives.

These results are quite mixed and vary by industry. For example, in Pakistan the investment tax credit had a highly stimulative effect on investment in the chemical and pharmaceutical industries but little effect on the textile industry. R&D expensing proved to be a cost-effective measure only for Pakistan's chemical industry. In contrast, Turkish tax

Table 15-15. Effectiveness of Current Investment Incentives

Tax instrument	Incremental benefit-cost ratio
Tax credit for physical investment	
Pakistan's textile industry	0.017
Pakistan's chemical industry	2.280
Pakistan's pharmaceutical industry	3.986
Tax allowance for physical investment	
Turkey's industrial chemicals	0.254
Turkey's other chemicals	0.391
Turkey's petroleum derivatives	0.954
Tax allowance for R&D investment	
Pakistan's chemical industry	1.383
Pakistan's pharmaceutical industry	0.243
Turkey's industrial chemicals	0.128
Turkey's other chemicals	0.091
Turkey's petroleum derivatives	0.264

Note: Data from tables 15-7, 15-9, and 15-11.
Source: Authors.

incentive measures (tax allowances for both physical and R&D investment) resulted in higher revenue losses as compared with their effect on investment. Only the tax allowance for physical investment came close to being cost-effective for Turkey's petroleum derivatives industry, which has a benefit-cost ratio almost equal to one.

Finally, we also analyzed what effect changes in tax incentives expected for the following year have on both types of investment during the current year. We found that improved tax credits or tax allowances anticipated for the following year will prompt firms to invest less during the current year, in effect causing them to postpone part of their investment expenditure. The effect of next year's tax incentives is, however, numerically smaller than that of this year's tax credits and allowances.

Appendix. Details of Derivations, Elasticity Formulas, Sources for the Data, and Corporate Income Taxes in Pakistan and Turkey

In this appendix we provide the derivations for some of the equations in the text, present the formulas for the elasticities we used, give the sources for our data, and describe the tax structures and investment incentives of Pakistan and Turkey.

Derivation of the Borrowing Constraint of Equation 15-4

Equation 15-3 is repeated here for convenience as equation 15A-1:

(15A-1)

$$
(P_{yt})\,(Y_t) - \sum_{j=1}^{2}(W_{jt})\,(v_{jt}) - (i_{t,t+a})\,(A_t) - (u_{pt})\,(K_{pt}^{\&}) - (P_{pt})\,(I_{pt})
$$
$$
- (P_{kt})\,(I_{kt}) + DA_{t+1} - \mathrm{CITP}_t \le (P_{yt})\,(Y_t) - \sum_{j=1}^{2}(W_{jt})\,(v_{jt})
$$
$$
- (i_{t,t+a})\,(A_t) - (u_{pt})\,(K_{pt}^{\&}) - \delta_p\,(P_{pt})\,(K_{pt}) - \delta_k\,(P_{kt})\,(K_{kt}) - \mathrm{CITP}_t .
$$

Equation 15A-2 simplifies 15A-1:

(15A-2)

$$
-(P_{pt})\,(I_{pt}) - (P_{kt})\,(I_{kt}) + DA_{t+1} \le -\delta_p\,(P_{pt})\,(K_{pt}) - \delta_k\,(P_{kt})\,(K_{kt}) .
$$

Gross investment in physical capital $(P_{pt})(I_{pt})$ is the sum of replacement investment $\delta_p(P_{pt})(K_{pt})$ and of net investment $(P_{pt+1})(K_{pt+1}) - (P_{pt})(K_{pt})$. Similarly, R&D expenditure $(P_{kt})(I_{kt})$ is the sum of replacement investment in knowledge capital $\delta_k(P_{kt})(K_{kt})$ and of net investment in knowledge capital $(P_{kt+1})(K_{kt+1}) - (P_{kt})(K_{kt})$. Therefore equation 15A-2 can be simplified further:

(15A-3)

$$- (P_{pt+1})(K_{pt+1}) + (P_{pt})(K_{pt}) - (P_{kt+1})(K_{kt+1}) + (P_{kt})(K_{kt}) + DA_{t+1} \leq 0 .$$

Because optimality requires this inequality to be strictly binding (see Boadway and Bruce 1979), it can be rewritten as the following equation:

(15A-4)

$$DA_{t+1} = (P_{pt+1}) \, (K_{pt+1}) - (P_{pt}) \, (K_{pt}) + (P_{kt+1}) \, (K_{kt+1}) - (P_{kt}) \, (K_{kt}) .$$

Equation 15A-4 is the same as equation 15-4 in the text.

Derivation of Investment Equation 15-5

Equation 15A-5 defines K_p^*, the value of the stock of physical capital for tax purposes, at the beginning of period 1:

(15A-5) $(P_{p1}) \, (K_{p1}^*) = (1 - \alpha_{p0}) \, (P_{p0}) \, (K_{p0}^*) + (P_{p0}) \, (I_{p0}) .$

Similarly, the value of K_p^* at the beginning of periods 2, 3, and 4 is defined by equations 15A-6 through 15A-8. Subtracting equation 15A-7 from equation 15A-8, we obtain equation 15A-9:

(15A-6)

$$P_{p2} K_{p2}^* = (1 - \alpha_{p1}) \, (1 - \alpha_{p0}) \, P_{p0} K_{p0}^* + (1 - \alpha_{p1}) \, P_{p0} I_{p0} + P_{p1} I_{p1}$$

(15A-7)

$$P_{p3} \, K_{p3}^* = (1 - \alpha_{p2}) \, (1 - \alpha_{p1}) \, (1 - \alpha_{p0}) \, P_{p0} \, K_{p0}^* + (1 - \alpha_{p2}) \, (1 - \alpha_{p1}) \, P_{p0} \, I_{p0}$$

$$+ (1 - \alpha_{p2}) \, P_{p1} \, I_{p1} + P_{p2} \, I_{p2}$$

(15A-8)

$$P_{p4} \, K_{p4}^* = (1 - \alpha_{p3}) \, (1 - \alpha_{p2}) \, (1 - \alpha_{p1}) \, (1 - \alpha_{p0}) \, P_{p0} \, K_{p0}^*$$

$$+ (1 - \alpha_{p3}) \, (1 - \alpha_{p2}) \, (1 - \alpha_{p1}) \, P_{p0} \, I_{p0} + (1 - \alpha_{p3}) \, (1 - \alpha_{p2}) \, P_{p1} \, I_{p1}$$

$$+ (1 - \alpha_{p3}) \, P_{p2} \, I_{p2} + P_{p3} \, I_{p3}$$

Subtracting equation 15A-7 from equation 15A-8, we obtain equation 15A-9:

(15A-9)

$$P_{p4} \, K_{p4}^* - P_{p3} \, K_{p3}^*$$

$$= \left[(1 - \alpha_{p3}) - 1\right](1 - \alpha_{p2})\,(1 - \alpha_{p1})\,(1 - \alpha_{p0})\,P_{p0}\,K_{p0}^*$$

$$- (\alpha_{p3})\,(1 - \alpha_{p2})\,(1 - \alpha_{p1})\,P_{p0}\,I_{p0} - (\alpha_{p3})\,(1 - \alpha_{p2})\,P_{p1}\,I_{p1}$$

$$- (\alpha_{p3})\,P_{p2}\,I_{p2} + P_{p3}\,I_{p3} = (-\alpha_{p3})\,(P_{p3}\,K_{p3}^{*}) + P_{p3}\,I_{p3}.$$

By analogy:

(15A-10) $\ (P_{pt+1})\,(K_{pt+1}^*) - (P_{pt})\,(K_{pt}^*) = (-\,\alpha_{pt})\,(P_{pt})\,(K_{pt}^*) + (P_{pt})\,(I_{pt})\ .$

Solving equation 15A-10 for $(P_{pt})(I_{pt})$, we obtain

(15A-11) $\ (P_{pt})\,(I_{pt}) = (P_{pt+1})\,(K_{pt+1}^*) - (P_{pt})\,(K_{pt}^*) + (\alpha_{pt})\,(P_{pt})\,(K_{pt}^*)\ .$

Equation 15A–11 is equal to equation 15-5 in the text. It is analogous to the following equation in regard to the true stock of physical capital and its economic rate of depreciation:

(15A-12) $\quad (P_{pt})\,(I_{pt}) = (P_{pt+1})\,(K_{pt+1}) - (P_{pt})\,(K_{pt}) + (\delta_p)\,(P_{pt})\,(K_{pt})\ .$

Equation 15A-12 states the well-known fact that gross investment in physical capital is equal to net investment plus replacement investment.

Derivation of equations 15-15 and 15-16

For convenience, equation 15-14 is repeated here as equation 15A-13:

(15A-13)

$$L = \varepsilon_s \sum_{t=s}^{\infty} D_{s,t} \left\{ T_{ct} \left[(P_{yt}) \left[Y_t^{\#}(\cdot) \right] - G_t^{\#}(\cdot) - (b_t)\,(i_{t,t+a})\,(A_t) - (u_{pt})\,(K_{pt}^{\&}) \right] \right.$$

$$- (1 - b_t)\,(i_{t,t+a})\,(A_t) + DA_{t+1} + (u_{ct})\,(\alpha_{kt})\,(P_{kt})\,(K_{kt}^*)$$

$$+ (u_{ct})\,(\alpha_{pt})\,(P_{pt})\,(K_{pt}^*)$$

$$- \left[1 - (u_{ct})\,(q_{kt})\right]\left[(\delta_k)\,(P_{kt})\,(K_{kt}) + (P_{kt+1})\,(K_{kt+1}) - (P_{kt})\,(K_{kt})\right]$$

$$-[1 - (u_{ct})\,(q_{pt}) - (m_{pt})][(\delta_p)\,(P_{pt})\,(K_{pt}) + (P_{pt+1})\,(K_{pt+1}) - (P_{pt})\,(K_{pt})]$$

$$- k_2[DA_{t+1} - (P_{pt+1})\,(K_{pt+1}) + (P_{pt})\,(K_{pt}) - (P_{kt+1})\,(K_{kt+1}) + (P_{kt})\,(K_{kt})]$$

$$- k_1[\delta_p\,(P_{pt})\,(K_{pt}) + (P_{pt+1})\,(K_{pt+1}) - (P_{pt})\,(K_{pt}) - (\alpha_{pt})\,(P_{pt})\,(K_{pt}^*)$$

$$- (P_{pt+1})\,(K_{pt+1}^*) + (P_{pt})\,(K_{pt}^*)]$$

$$- k_4[\delta_k\,(P_{kt})\,(K_{kt}) + (P_{kt+1})\,(K_{kt+1}) - (P_{kt})\,(K_{kt}) - (\alpha_{kt})\,(P_{kt})\,(K_{kt}^*)$$

$$- (P_{kt+1})\,(K_{kt+1}^*) + (P_{kt})\,(K_{kt}^*)]\Big\}.$$

Differentiating equation 15A-13 with respect to A_{t+1}, setting the derivative equal to zero, noting that at time t the variables of the same period are known with certainty, that $D_{t,t} = 1$ and that $D_{t,t+1} = 1/(1 + i_{t,t+1})$, we obtain

(15A-14)

$$0 = (1 - k_2) + \varepsilon_t\,\Big\{[1/(1 + i_{t,t+1})]\,[-(T_{ct+1})\,(b_{t+1})\,(i_{t+1,t+1+a})$$

$$- (1 - b_{t+1})\,(i_{t+1,t+1+a}) - 1 + k_2]\Big\}.$$

After combining terms and simplifying, we can rewrite equation 15A-14 as:

(15A-15) $- (k_2)\,(i_{t,t+1}) = -i_{t,t+1} + \varepsilon_t\,(i_{t+1,t+1+a})\,[1 - \varepsilon_t\,(b_{t+1})\,\varepsilon_t\,(u_{ct+1})].$

Implicit in equation 15A-15 and in subsequent equations is the assumption that the expected value of a product is equal to the product of the expected values.

Differentiating equation 15A-13 with respect to $K_p^*\,(t+1)$ and setting the derivative equal to zero, we arrive at

(15A-16) $0 = (k_1)\,\varepsilon_t\,(P_{pt+1}) + \varepsilon_t\,\Big\{[1/(1 + i_{t,t+1})][(\alpha_{pt+1})\,(u_{ct+1})\,(P_{pt+1})$

$$+ (k_1)\,(\alpha_{pt+1})\,(P_{pt+1}) - (k_1)\,(P_{pt+1})]\Big\}.$$

Multiplying equation 15A-16 by $(1 + i_{t,t+1})/\varepsilon_t(P_{pt+1})$ and solving for k_1, we obtain

(15A-17) $$k_1 = \frac{-\varepsilon_t\,(\alpha_{pt+1})\,\varepsilon_t\,(u_{ct+1})}{i_{t,t+1} + \varepsilon_t\,(\alpha_{pt+1})}.$$

Differentiating equation 15A-13 with respect to K_{pt+1}, setting the derivative equal to zero, and noting that some terms vanish because of equation 15-12, we arrive at

(15A-18)

$$0 = - T_{ct} \frac{\partial G_t^{\#}}{\partial I_{pt}^{\#}} \frac{\partial I_{pt}^{\#}}{\partial K_{pt+1}^{\#}} + \varepsilon_t (P_{pt+1}) \left[(m_{pt}) + (u_{ct})(q_{pt}) - 1 - k_1 + k_2 \right]$$

$$+ \varepsilon_t \Bigg\{ D_{t,t+1} \left[(k_1)(1 - \delta_p)(P_{pt+1}) - T_{ct+1} \frac{\partial G_{t+1}^{\#}}{\partial K_{pt+1}^{\#}} - T_{ct+1} \frac{\partial G_{t+1}^{\#}}{\partial I_{pt+1}^{\#}} \frac{\partial I_{pt+1}^{\#}}{\partial K_{pt+1}^{\#}} \right.$$

$$\left. - (1 - \delta_p)(P_{pt+1}) \left[(m_{pt+1}) + (u_{ct+1})(q_{pt+1}) - 1 \right] - (k_2)(P_{pt+1}) \right] \Bigg\}$$

where $\partial I_{pt}^{\#} / \partial K_{pt+1}^{\#} = 1$, and $\partial I_{pt+1}^{\#} / \partial K_{pt+1}^{\#} = (\delta_p - 1)$.

Rearranging terms in equation 15A-18, we obtain

(15A-19)

$$- \frac{\varepsilon_t (T_{ct+1})}{1 + i_{t,t+1}} \varepsilon_t \left(\frac{\partial G_{t+1}^{\#}}{\partial K_{pt+1}^{\#}} \right) - T_{ct} \frac{\partial G_t^{\#}}{\partial I_{pt}^{\#}} + \frac{\varepsilon_t (T_{ct+1})}{1 + i_{t,t+1}} \varepsilon_t \left(\frac{\partial G_{t+1}^{\#}}{\partial I_{pt+1}^{\#}} \right) (1 - \delta_p)$$

$$= \frac{\varepsilon_t (P_{pt+1})}{1 + i_{t,t+1}} \left[(k_1) + (k_1)(i_{t,t+1}) - (k_1) + (k_1)(\delta_p) \right]$$

$$+ \frac{\varepsilon_t (P_{pt+1})}{1 + i_{t,t+1}} \left[- (k_2) - (k_2)(i_{t,t+1}) + (k_2) \right]$$

$$- \frac{\varepsilon_t (P_{pt+1})}{1 + i_{t,t+1}} (1 - \delta_p) \left[1 - \varepsilon_t (m_{pt+1}) - \varepsilon_t (u_{ct+1}) \varepsilon_t (q_{pt+1}) \right]$$

$$+ \varepsilon_t (P_{pt+1}) \left[1 - (m_{pt}) - (u_{ct})(q_{pt}) \right].$$

Substituting equations 15A-15 and 15A-17 into equation 15A-19 and denoting the left-hand side of the equation by LHS, we arrive at

(15A-20)

$$\text{LHS} = \frac{\varepsilon_t (P_{pt+1})}{1 + i_{t,t+1}} (\delta_p - 1) + \varepsilon_t (P_{pt+1})$$

$$- \varepsilon_t (P_{pt+1}) \left[(u_{ct}) (q_{pt}) - \frac{(1 - \delta_p) \varepsilon_t (u_{ct+1}) \varepsilon_t (q_{pt+1})}{1 + i_{t,t+1}} \right]$$

$$- \varepsilon_t (P_{pt+1}) \left[(m_{pt}) - \frac{(1 - \delta_p) \varepsilon_t (m_{pt+1})}{1 + i_{t,t+1}} \right]$$

$$- \frac{(i_{t,t+1}) \varepsilon_t (P_{pt+1})}{1 + i_{t,t+1}} + \frac{\varepsilon_t (P_{pt+1})}{1 + i_{t,t+1}} \left\{ \varepsilon_t (i_{t+1,t+1+a}) \left[1 - \varepsilon_t (b_{t+1}) \varepsilon_t (u_{ct+1}) \right] \right\}$$

$$- \frac{\varepsilon_t (P_{pt+1}) (i_{t,t+1} + \delta_p) \varepsilon_t (\alpha_{pt+1}) \varepsilon_t (u_{ct+1})}{(1 + i_{t,t+1}) \left[i_{t,t+1} + \varepsilon_t (\alpha_{pt+1}) \right]}.$$

Combining terms in equation 15A-20, we get

$$(15A\text{-}21) \quad \text{LHS} = \frac{\varepsilon_t (P_{pt+1})}{1 + i_{t,t+1}} \left\{ \delta_p + \varepsilon_t (i_{t+1,t+1+a}) \left[1 - \varepsilon_t (b_{t+1}) \varepsilon_t (u_{ct+1}) \right] \right\}$$

$$- \varepsilon_t (P_{pt+1}) \left[(m_{pt}) - \frac{(1 - \delta_p) \varepsilon_t (m_{pt+1})}{1 + i_{t,t+1}} \right]$$

$$- \varepsilon_t (P_{pt+1}) \left[(u_{ct}) (q_{pt}) - \frac{(1 - \delta_p) \varepsilon_t (u_{ct+1}) \varepsilon_t (q_{pt+1})}{1 + i_{t,t+1}} \right]$$

$$- \frac{\varepsilon_t (P_{pt+1}) (i_{t,t+1} + \delta_p) \varepsilon_t (\alpha_{pt+1}) \varepsilon_t (u_{ct+1})}{(1 + i_{t,t+1}) \left[i_{t,t+1} + \varepsilon_t (\alpha_{pt+1}) \right]}.$$

We replace the nominal variables of equation 15A-21 by their real counterparts, which are given by

$$G_{t+1} = (1 + \pi_{0, t}) (1 + \pi_{t, t+1}) (g_{t+1})$$

$$G_t = (1 + \pi_{0,t}) (g_t)$$

$$P_{pt+1} = (1 + \pi_{0,t}) (1 + \pi_{t,t+1}) (p_{pt+1})$$

$$(1 + i_{t,t+1}) = (1 + r_{t,t+1}) (1 + \pi_{t,t+1}).$$

The result of this substitution is the following equation:

$$(15A\text{-}22)$$

$$- \frac{(1 + \pi_{0,t}) (1 + \pi_{t,t+1}) \varepsilon_t (T_{ct+1})}{(1 + r_{t,t+1}) (1 + \pi_{t,t+1})} \varepsilon_t \left(\frac{\partial g_{t+1}^{\#}}{\partial K_{pt+1}^{\#}} \right) - (1 + \pi_{0,t}) \, T_{ct} \frac{\partial g_t^{\#}}{\partial I_{pt}^{\#}}$$

$$+ \frac{(1 + \pi_{0,t}) (1 + \pi_{t,t+1}) \varepsilon_t (T_{ct+1})}{(1 + r_{t,t+1}) (1 + \pi_{t,t+1})} \varepsilon_t \left(\frac{\partial g_{t+1}^{\#}}{\partial I_{pt+1}^{\#}} \right) (1 - \delta_p)$$

$$= \frac{(1 + \pi_{0,t})\,(1 + \pi_{t,t+1})\,\varepsilon_t(p_{pt+1})}{(1 + r_{t,t+1})\,(1 + \pi_{t,t+1})} \left\{ \delta_p + \varepsilon_t(i_{t+1,\,t+1+a})\left[1 - \varepsilon_t(b_{t+1})\,\varepsilon_t(u_{ct+1})\right] \right\}$$

$$- \varepsilon_t(p_{pt+1})\left[(1 + \pi_{0,t})\,(1 + \pi_{t,t+1})\,(u_{ct})\,(q_{pt})\right.$$

$$\left. - \frac{(1 - \delta_p)\,(1 + \pi_{0,t})\,(1 + \pi_{t,t+1})\,\varepsilon_t(u_{ct+1})\,\varepsilon_t(q_{pt+1})}{(1 + r_{t,t+1})\,(1 + \pi_{t,t+1})} \right]$$

$$- \varepsilon_t(p_{pt+1})$$

$$\left[(1 + \pi_{0,t})\,(1 + \pi_{t,t+1})\,(m_{pt}) - \frac{(1 - \delta_p)\,(1 + \pi_{0,t})\,(1 + \pi_{t,t+1})\,\varepsilon_t(m_{pt+1})}{(1 + r_{t,t+1})\,(1 + \pi_{t,t+1})}\right]$$

$$- \frac{(1 + \pi_{0,t})\,(1 + \pi_{t,t+1})\,\varepsilon_t(p_{pt+1})\,(i_{t,t+1} + \delta_p)\,\varepsilon_t(\alpha_{pt+1})\,\varepsilon_t(u_{ct+1})}{(1 + r_{t,t+1})\,(1 + \pi_{t,t+1})\left[i_{t,t+1} + \varepsilon_t(\alpha_{pt+1})\right]}$$

Dividing both sides of equation 15A-22 by $(1 + \pi_{0,t})$, $\varepsilon_t(T_{ct+1})$, we obtain

(15A-23)

$$-\frac{1}{1 + r_{t,t+1}}\,\varepsilon_t\left(\frac{\partial g_{t+1}^{\#}}{\partial K_{pt+1}^{\#}}\right) - \frac{T_{ct}}{\varepsilon_t(T_{ct+1})}\frac{\partial g_t^{\#}}{\partial I_{pt}^{\#}} + \frac{(1 - \delta_p)}{1 + r_{t,t+1}}\,\varepsilon_t\left(\frac{\partial g_{t+1}^{\#}}{\partial I_{pt+1}^{\#}}\right)$$

$$= \frac{1}{1 + r_{t,t+1}}\frac{\varepsilon_t(p_{pt+1})}{\varepsilon_t(T_{ct+1})}\left\{ \varepsilon_t(i_{t+1,t+1+a})\left[1 - \varepsilon_t(b_{t+1})\,\varepsilon_t(u_{ct+1})\right] + \delta_p\right\}$$

$$- (1 + \pi_{t,t+1})\frac{\varepsilon_t(p_{pt+1})}{\varepsilon_t(T_{ct+1})}\,(u_{ct})\,(q_{pt}) + \frac{(1 - \delta_p)}{(1 + r_{t,t+1})}\frac{\varepsilon_t(p_{pt+1})}{\varepsilon_t(T_{ct+1})}\,\varepsilon_t(u_{ct+1})\,\varepsilon_t(q_{pt+1})$$

$$- (1 + \pi_{t,t+1})\frac{\varepsilon_t(p_{pt+1})}{\varepsilon_t(T_{ct+1})}\,(m_{pt}) + \frac{(1 - \delta_p)\varepsilon_t(p_{pt+1})}{(1 + r_{t,t+1})\varepsilon_t(T_{ct+1})}\,\varepsilon_t(m_{pt+1})$$

$$- \frac{\varepsilon_t(p_{pt+1})\,(i_{t,t+1} + \delta_p)\,\varepsilon_t(\alpha_{pt+1})\,\varepsilon_t(u_{ct+1})}{\varepsilon_t(T_{ct+1})\,(1 + r_{t,t+1})\left[i_{t,t+1} + \varepsilon_t(\alpha_{pt+1})\right]}.$$

Equation 15A-23 is equal to equation 15-15 in the text. Equation 15-16 of the text is analogous to equation 15-15, except that the subscript p for physical capital has to be replaced by the subscript k for knowledge capital, and m_{kt} as well as $\varepsilon_t(m_{kt+1})$ are equal to zero because in both countries there is a tax allowance rather than a tax credit for R&D expenditure. The interested reader can verify this by differentiating equation 15A-13 with respect to A_{t+1}, K_{kt+1}, and K^*_{kt+1}, and eliminating the Lagrangian multipliers k_1 and k_2 by substitution, as was done above.

Derivation of Equations 15-27 and 15-28

For convenience, the Lagrangian of equation 15-26 of the text is repeated here as 15A-24:

(15A-24)

$$L = \varepsilon_s \sum_{t=s}^{\infty} D_{s,t} \bigg((P_{yt}) \, (\Upsilon^o_t) - G^o_t \, (\cdot) - (i_{t,t+a}) \, (A_t) - (u_{pt}) \, (K^{\&}_{pt})$$

$$- \delta_p (P_{pt}) \, (K_{pt}) - (P_{pt+1}) \, (K_{pt+1}) + (P_{pt}) \, (K_{pt})$$

$$- \delta_k \, (P_{kt}) \, (K_{kt}) - (P_{kt+1}) \, (K_{kt+1}) + (P_{kt}) \, (K_{kt}) + DA_{t+1}$$

$$- k_2 \Big[DA_{t+1} - (P_{pt+1}) \, (K_{pt+1}) + (P_{pt}) \, (K_{pt}) - (P_{kt+1}) \, (K_{kt+1}) + (P_{kt}) \, (K_{kt}) \Big]$$

$$- k_6 \Big\{ DR_{t+1} - c_t [\Upsilon^+_t - \Upsilon^\#_t (\text{fs})] \Big\} \bigg).$$

Differentiating (15A-24) with respect to A_{t+1}, setting the derivative equal to zero, noting that current period variables are known with certainty and that $D_{t,t+1} = 1/(1 + i_{t,t+1})$, we obtain

(15A-25) $$0 = 1 - k_2 + \frac{1}{1 + i_{t,t+1}} \Big[k_2 - 1 - \varepsilon_t \, (i_{t+1,t+1+a}) \Big].$$

Multiplying both sides of 15A-25 by $(1 + i_{t,t+1})$ and simplifying, we get

(15A-26) $$(i_{t,t+1}) \, (1 - k_2) = \varepsilon_t \, (i_{t+1,t+1+a}).$$

Differentiating 15A-24 with respect to K_{pt+1}, setting the derivative equal to zero, and noting that several terms vanish because of the first-order condition of equation 15-23 in the text, we arrive at

(15A-27)

$$0 = - \frac{\partial G^o_t}{\partial I^o_{pt}} \frac{\partial I^o_{pt}}{\partial K^o_{pt+1}} - \varepsilon_t \, (P_{pt+1}) \, (1 - k_2)$$

$$+ \frac{1}{1 + i_{t,t+1}} \Bigg[-\varepsilon_t \bigg(\frac{\partial G^o_{t+1}}{\partial K^o_{pt+1}} \bigg) + \varepsilon_t \, (P_{pt+1}) \, (1 - \delta_p - k_2) - \varepsilon_t \bigg(\frac{\partial G^o_{t+1}}{\partial I^o_{pt+1}} \frac{\partial I^o_{pt+1}}{\partial K^o_{pt+1}} \bigg) \Bigg]$$

where $\partial I^o_{pt} / \partial K^o_{pt+1} = 1$, and $\partial I^o_{pt+1} / \partial K^o_{pt+1} = (\delta_p - 1)$.

Rearranging terms in 15A-27, we obtain

$$(15A\text{-}28) \quad -\frac{1}{1+i_{t,t+1}} \varepsilon_t \left(\frac{\partial G^o_{t+1}}{\partial K^o_{pt+1}}\right) - \frac{\partial G^o_t}{\partial I^o_{pt}} + \frac{(1-\delta_p)}{1+i_{t,t+1}} \varepsilon_t \left(\frac{\partial G^o_{t+1}}{\partial I^o_{pt+1}}\right)$$

$$= \frac{\varepsilon_t (P_{pt+1})}{1+i_{t,t+1}} \left[(i_{t,t+1})(1-k_2) + \delta_p \right].$$

Substituting equation 15A-26 into 15A-28, we get

$$(15A\text{-}29) \quad \text{LHS} = \frac{\varepsilon_t (P_{pt+1})}{1+i_{t,t+1}} \left[\delta_p + \varepsilon_t (i_{t+1,t+1+a})\right].$$

In order to obtain real rather than nominal variables, we can rewrite equation 15A-29 as follows:

$$(15A\text{-}30) \quad -\frac{(1+\pi_{0,t})(1+\pi_{t,t+1})}{(1+r_{t,t+1})(1+\pi_{t,t+1})} \varepsilon_t \left(\frac{\partial \mathcal{g}^o_{t+1}}{\partial K^o_{pt+1}}\right) - (1+\pi_{0,t}) \frac{\partial \mathcal{g}^o_t}{\partial I^o_{pt}}$$

$$+\frac{(1+\pi_{0,t})(1+\pi_{t,t+1})}{(1+r_{t,t+1})(1+\pi_{t,t+1})} \varepsilon_t \left(\frac{\partial \mathcal{g}^o_{t+1}}{\partial I^o_{pt+1}}\right)(1-\delta_p)$$

$$= \frac{(1+\pi_{0,t})(1+\pi_{t,t+1})}{(1+r_{t,t+1})(1+\pi_{t,t+1})} \varepsilon_t (p_{pt+1}) \left[\delta_p + \varepsilon_t (i_{t+1,t+1+a})\right].$$

Dividing both sides of equation 15A-30 by $(1 + \pi_{0,t})$ yields

$$(15A\text{-}31) \quad -\frac{1}{1+r_{t,t+1}} \varepsilon_t \left(\frac{\partial \mathcal{g}^o_{t+1}}{\partial K^o_{pt+1}}\right) - \frac{\partial \mathcal{g}^o_t}{\partial I^o_{pt}} + \frac{(1-\delta_p)}{1+r_{t,t+1}} \varepsilon_t \left(\frac{\partial \mathcal{g}^o_{t+1}}{\partial I^o_{pt+1}}\right)$$

$$= \frac{\varepsilon_t (p_{pt+1})}{1+r_{t,t+1}} \left[\delta_p + \varepsilon_t (i_{t+1,t+1+a})\right].$$

Equation 15A-31 is equal to equation 15-27 of the text. Furthermore, if in equation 15A-23 we set $m_{pt} = \varepsilon_t(m_{pt+1}) = q_{pt} = \varepsilon_t(q_{pt+1}) = \varepsilon_t(u_{ct+1}) = 0$, therefore $T_{ct} = \varepsilon_t(T_{ct+1}) = 1$, then equation 15A-23 reduces to 15A-31.

Equation 15-28 of the text can be derived in an analogous way: equation 15A-24 is differentiated with respect to K_{kt+1}, and the derivative is set equal to zero. After substituting for k_2 from equation 15A-26, we obtain the optimality condition of equation 15-28 of the text.

Derivation of the Estimating Equations for Physical and R&D Investment

Estimating equations for gross investment I_{pt} and I_{kt} can be obtained from the equilibrium conditions of equations 15-15 and 15-16 or 15-27 and 15-28, according to which the expected net marginal benefits from physical and knowledge capital have to be equal to the rental prices of capital services. K_{pt} and K_{kt}, the capital stocks at the beginning of period t, are given to the firm, but the next period's capital stocks are determined by the optimality conditions of 15-15 and 15-16 or 15-27 and 15-28. Therefore I_{pt} and I_{kt} are endogenous variables. We note for future reference that gross investment can be written as the sum of replacement investment and new investment: $I_{pt} = \delta_p K_{pt} + (K_{pt+1} - K_{pt})$, and $I_{kt} = \delta_k K_{kt} + (K_{kt+1} - K_{kt})$. From these two identities we can obtain the expressions for K_{pt+1} and K_{kt+1} used later. In order to solve 15-15 and 15-16 or 15-27 and 15-28 for the optimal rates of investment, the following derivatives are required:

(15A-32)

$$\partial g_{t+1} / \partial K_{pt+1} = a_P + a_{PP}(K_{pt+1}) + a_{PK}(K_{kt+1}) + a_{P2}(w_{2t+1})$$

$$+ a_{PY}(Y_{t+1}) + a_{PIP}(I_{pt+1}) + a_{PIK}(I_{kt+1}) + a_{Pt}(t+1)$$

(15A-33)

$$\partial g_t / \partial I_{pt} = a_{IP} + a_{IPIP}(I_{pt}) + a_{IPIK}(I_{kt}) + a_{IP2}(w_{2t})$$

$$+ a_{PIP}(K_{pt}) + a_{KIP}(K_{kt}) + a_{IPY}(Y_t) + a_{IPt}(t)$$

(15A-34)

$$\partial g_{t+1} / \partial I_{pt+1} = a_{IP} + a_{IPIP}(I_{pt+1}) + a_{IPIK}(I_{kt+1}) + a_{IP2}(w_{2t+1})$$

$$+ a_{PIP}(K_{pt+1}) + a_{KIP}(K_{kt+1}) + a_{IPY}(Y_{t+1}) + a_{IPt}(t+1)$$

(15A-35)

$$\partial g_{t+1} / \partial K_{kt+1} = a_K + a_{KK}(K_{kt+1}) + a_{PK}(K_{pt+1}) + a_{K2}(w_{2t+1})$$

$$+ a_{KY}(Y_{t+1}) + a_{KIP}(I_{pt+1}) + a_{KIK}(I_{kt+1}) + a_{Kt}(t+1)$$

(15A-36)

$$\partial g_t / \partial I_{kt} = a_{IK} + a_{IKIK} (I_{kt}) + a_{IPIK} (I_{pt}) + a_{IK2} (w_{2t})$$

$$+ a_{PIK} (K_{pt}) + a_{KIK} (K_{kt}) + a_{IKY} (Y_t) + a_{IKt} (t)$$

(15A-37)

$$\partial g_{t+1} / \partial I_{kt+1} = a_{IK} + a_{IKIK} (I_{kt+1}) + a_{IPIK} (I_{pt+1}) + a_{IK2} (w_{2t+1})$$

$$+ a_{PIK} (K_{pt+1}) + a_{KIK} (K_{kt+1}) + a_{IKY} (Y_{t+1}) + a_{IKt} (t+1).$$

First, we make the assumption that there is partial or no short-run forward shifting of the CIT. In order to obtain the equation for gross investment in physical capital I_{pt}, we substitute equations 15A-32 through 15A-34 into the optimality condition of equation 15-15, replace K_{pt+1} by $(I_{pt} + K_{pt} - \delta_p K_{pt})$ and K_{kt+1} by $(I_{kt} + K_{kt} - \delta_k K_{kt})$, solve for I_{pt}, and add an error term:

(15A-38)

$$I_{pt} = \left(1 \, / \, \{ a_{PP} + [T_{ct} / \, \varepsilon_t (T_{ct+1})] (1 + r_{t,t+1}) \, a_{IPIP} - a_{PIP} (1 - \delta_p) \} \right)$$

$$\left((1 - \delta_p) \, a_{IP} - a_P - [T_{ct} / \, \varepsilon_t (T_{ct+1})] (1 + r_{t,t+1}) \, a_{IP} \right.$$

$$- [T_{ct} / \varepsilon_t (T_{ct+1})] (1 + r_{t,t+1}) \, a_{IP2} (w_{2t}) + [(1 - \delta_p) \, a_{IP2} - a_{P2}] \, \varepsilon_t (w_{2t+1})$$

$$+ \{ a_{PIP} (1 - \delta_p)^2 - a_{PP} (1 - \delta_p) - [T_{ct} / \varepsilon_t (T_{ct+1})] (1 + r_{t,t+1}) \, a_{PIP} \} (K_{pt})$$

$$+ \{ a_{KIP} (1 - \delta_p)(1 - \delta_k) - a_{PK} (1 - \delta_k) - [T_{ct} / \varepsilon_t (T_{ct+1})](1 + r_{t,t+1}) a_{KIP} \} (K_{kt})$$

$$+ \{ a_{KIP} (1 - \delta_p) - a_{PK} - [T_{ct} / \varepsilon_t (T_{ct+1})] (1 + r_{t,t+1}) \, a_{IPIK} \} (I_{kt})$$

$$- [T_{ct} / \varepsilon_t (T_{ct+1})] (1 + r_{t,t+1}) \, a_{IPY} (Y_t) + [(1 - \delta_p) \, a_{IPY} - a_{PY}] \, \varepsilon_t (Y_{t+1})$$

$$- [T_{ct} / \varepsilon_t (T_{ct+1})] (1 + r_{t,t+1}) \, a_{IPt} (t) + [(1 - \delta_p) \, a_{IPt} - a_{Pt}] (t+1)$$

$$+ [(1 - \delta_p) \, a_{IPIP} - a_{PIP}] \, \varepsilon_t (I_{pt+1}) + [(1 - \delta_p) \, a_{IPIK} - a_{PIK}] \, \varepsilon_t (I_{kt+1})$$

$$- (1 + r_{t,t+1}) \, rp_{pt} (\text{tax}) \bigg) + u_{Ipt}.$$

Equation 15A-38 is equal to equation 15-38 in the text.

In order to obtain the equation for R&D investment I_{kt}, we substitute equations 15A-35 through 15A-37 into the optimality condition of equation 15-16, again replacing K_{pt+1} by $(I_{pt} + K_{pt} - \delta_p K_{pt})$ and K_{kt+1} by $(I_{kt} + K_{kt} - \delta_k K_{kt})$. Then we solve for I_{kt} and add an error term:

(15A-39)

$$I_{kt} = \left(1/\left\{a_{KK} + [T_{ct}/\varepsilon_t(T_{ct+1})](1 + r_{t,t+1})\, a_{IKIK} - a_{KIK}(1 - \delta_k)\right\}\right)$$

$$\left((1 - \delta_k)\, a_{IK} - a_K - [T_{ct}/\varepsilon_t(T_{ct+1})](1 + r_{t,t+1})\, a_{IK}\right.$$

$$- [T_{ct}/\varepsilon_t(T_{ct+1})](1 + r_{t,t+1})\, a_{IK2}\,(w_{2t}) + [(1 - \delta_k)\, a_{IK2} - a_{K2}]\,\varepsilon_t\,(w_{2t+1})$$

$$+ \left\{a_{KIK}(1 - \delta_k)^2 - a_{KK}(1 - \delta_k) - [T_{ct}/\varepsilon_t(T_{ct+1})](1 + r_{t,t+1})\, a_{KIK}\right\}(K_{kt})$$

$$+ \left\{a_{PIK}(1 - \delta_k)(1 - \delta_p) - a_{PK}(1 - \delta_p) - [T_{ct}/\varepsilon_t(T_{ct+1})](1 + r_{t,t+1})\, a_{PIK}\right\}(K_{pt})$$

$$+ \left\{a_{PIK}(1 - \delta_k) - a_{PK} - [T_{ct}/\varepsilon_t(T_{ct+1})](1 + r_{t,t+1})\, a_{IPIK}\right\}(I_{pt})$$

$$- [T_{ct}/\varepsilon_t(T_{ct+1})](1 + r_{t,t+1})\, a_{IKY}(Y_t) + [(1 - \delta_k)\, a_{IKY} - a_{KY}]\,\varepsilon_t\,(Y_{t+1})$$

$$- [T_{ct}/\varepsilon_t(T_{ct+1})](1 + r_{t,t+1})\, a_{IKt}\,(t) + [(1 - \delta_k)\, a_{IKt} - a_{Kt}]\,(t + 1)$$

$$+ [(1 - \delta_k)\, a_{IKIK} - a_{KIK}]\,\varepsilon_t\,(I_{kt+1}) + [(1 - \delta_k)\, a_{IPIK} - a_{KIP}]\,\varepsilon_t\,(I_{pt+1})$$

$$\left. - (1 + r_{t,t+1})\, rp_{kt}\,(\text{tax})\right) + u_{Ikt}\,.$$

Equation 15A-39 is equal to equation 15-39 in the text.

Next, we show what the two estimating equations for investment in physical and knowledge capital would be in an industry with unexerted market power, if the firms succeeded in shifting the CIT forward completely. To this end we substitute equations 15A-32 through 15A-34 into the first-order condition of equation 15-27 and solve for I_{pt}. Then we substitute equations 15A-35 through 15A-37 into the optimality condition of equation 15-28 and solve for I_{kt}. The first-order conditions of equations 15-27 and 15-28 differ from the conditions of equations 15-15 and 15-16 in only two respects: the factor $T_{ct}/\varepsilon_t(T_{ct+1})$ is missing from the second term on the left-hand sides of equations 15-27 and 15-28, and the right-hand sides of equations 15-27 and 15-28 represent the rental prices of capital services under the assumption of full shifting, whereas the right-hand sides of equations 15-15 and 15-16 represent the rental prices of capital services in the absence of full short-run shifting of the CIT. Therefore the two alternative estimating equations for investment in physical capital I_{pt} and for R&D expenditure I_{kt} can also be obtained from equations 15A-38 and 15A-39 by setting $T_{ct} = \varepsilon_t(T_{ct+1}) = 1$ and by replacing $rp_{pt}(\text{tax})$ with $rp_{pt}(\text{fs})$ and $rp_{kt}(\text{tax})$ with $rp_{kt}(\text{fs})$:

(15A-40)

$$
I_{pt} = \left\{ 1 / \left[a_{PP} + (1 + r_{t,t+1})\, a_{IPIP} - a_{PIP}(1 - \delta_p) \right] \right\} \left\{ - a_P - (\delta_p + r_{t,t+1})\, a_{IP} \right.
$$

$$
- (1 + r_{t,t+1})\, a_{IP2}\,(w_{2t}) + \left[(1 - \delta_p)\, a_{IP2} - a_{P2} \right] \varepsilon_t\,(w_{2t+1})
$$

$$
+ \left[a_{PIP}(1 - \delta_p)^2 - a_{PP}(1 - \delta_p) - (1 + r_{t,t+1})\, a_{PIP} \right] (K_{pt})
$$

$$
+ \left[a_{KIP}(1 - \delta_p)(1 - \delta_k) - a_{PK}(1 - \delta_k) - (1 + r_{t,t+1})\, a_{KIP} \right] (K_{kt})
$$

$$
+ \left[a_{KIP}(1 - \delta_p) - a_{PK} - (1 + r_{t,t+1})\, a_{IPIK} \right] (I_{kt})
$$

$$
- (1 + r_{t,t+1})\, a_{IPY}\,(Y_t) + \left[(1 - \delta_p)\, a_{IPY} - a_{PY} \right] \varepsilon_t\,(Y_{t+1})
$$

$$
- (1 + r_{t,t+1})\, a_{IPt}\,(t) + \left[(1 - \delta_p)\, a_{IPt} - a_{Pt} \right] (t + 1)
$$

$$
+ \left[(1 - \delta_p)\, a_{IPIP} - a_{PIP} \right] \varepsilon_t\,(I_{pt+1}) + \left[(1 - \delta_p)\, a_{IPIK} - a_{PIK} \right] \varepsilon_t\,(I_{kt+1})
$$

$$
\left. - (1 + r_{t,t+1})\, rp_{pt}\,(\text{fs}) \right\} + u_{Ipt}.
$$

Equation 15A-40 is equal to equation 15-40 in the text.

(15A-41)

$$
I_{kt} = \left\{ 1 / \left[a_{KK} + (1 + r_{t,t+1})\, a_{IKIK} - a_{KIK}(1 - \delta_k) \right] \right\} \left\{ - a_K - (\delta_k + r_{t,t+1})\, a_{IK} \right.
$$

$$
- (1 + r_{t,t+1})\, a_{IK2}\,(w_{2t}) + \left[(1 - \delta_k)\, a_{IK2} - a_{K2} \right] \varepsilon_t\,(w_{2t+1})
$$

$$
+ \left[a_{KIK}(1 - \delta_k)^2 - a_{KK}(1 - \delta_k) - (1 + r_{t,t+1})\, a_{KIK} \right] (K_{kt})
$$

$$
+ \left[a_{PIK}(1 - \delta_k)(1 - \delta_p) - a_{PK}(1 - \delta_p) - (1 + r_{t,t+1})\, a_{PIK} \right] (K_{pt})
$$

$$
+ \left[a_{PIK}(1 - \delta_k) - a_{PK} - (1 + r_{t,t+1})\, a_{IPIK} \right] (I_{pt})
$$

$$
- (1 + r_{t,t+1})\, a_{IKY}\,(Y_t) + \left[(1 - \delta_k)\, a_{IKY} - a_{KY} \right] \varepsilon_t\,(Y_{t+1})
$$

$$
- (1 + r_{t,t+1})\, a_{IKt}\,(t) + \left[(1 - \delta_k)\, a_{IKt} - a_{Kt} \right] (t + 1)
$$

$$
+ \left[(1 - \delta_k)\, a_{IKIK} - a_{KIK} \right] \varepsilon_t\,(I_{kt+1}) + \left[(1 - \delta_k)\, a_{IPIK} - a_{KIP} \right] \varepsilon_t\,(I_{pt+1})
$$

$$
\left. - (1 + r_{t,t+1})\, rp_{kt}\,(\text{fs}) \right\} + u_{Ikt}.
$$

Equation 15A-41 is equal to equation 15-41 in the text.

Elasticity Formulas, Assuming Partial or No Shifting of the CIT

We define $DENPt = \{a_{PP} + [T_{ct}/\varepsilon_t(T_{ct+1})](1 + r_{t,t+1})a_{IPIP} - a_{PIP}(1 - \delta_p)\}$, and $DENKt = \{a_{KK} + [T_{ct}/\varepsilon_t(T_{ct+1})](1 + r_{t,t+1})a_{IKIK} - a_{KIK}(1 - \delta_k)\}$, where $DENPt$ stands for the denominator of equation 15-38 for I_{pt}, and $DENKt$ similarly denotes the denominator of equation 15-39 for I_{kt}. I_{pt} and I_{kt}, in turn, are physical and R&D investment, respectively. (The reader may want to compare the first rows of equations 15-38 and 15-39 to the definitions given above.)

FORMULAS FOR TABLE 15-2

$$e_{11} = \frac{\partial v_{1t}}{\partial w_{1t}}\frac{w_{1t}}{v_{1t}} = \Big\{a_{22}\,(w_{2t})$$

$$- \left[a_Y + a_{YY}\,(Y_t) + a_{PY}\,(K_{pt}) + a_{KY}\,(K_{kt}) + a_{YT}\,(t) + a_{IPY}\,(I_{pt}) + a_{IKY}\,(I_{kt})\right](F_2)$$

$$+ \left[a_{IP} + a_{IPIP}\,(I_{pt}) + a_{PIP}\,(K_{pt}) + a_{KIP}\,(K_{kt}) + a_{IPIK}\,(I_{kt}) + a_{IPY}\,(Y_t) + a_{IPT}\,(t)\right]$$

$$(1 + r_{t,t+1})\left[T_{ct}/\varepsilon_t\,(T_{ct+1})\right]a_{IP2}/DENP_t$$

$$+ \left[a_{IK} + a_{PIK}\,(K_{pt}) + a_{IKIK}\,(I_{kt}) + a_{KIK}\,(K_{kt}) + a_{IPIK}\,(I_{pt}) + a_{IKY}\,(Y_t) + a_{IKT}\,(t)\right]$$

$$(1 + r_{t,t+1})\left[T_{ct}/\varepsilon_t\,(T_{ct+1})\right]a_{IK2}/DENK_t\Big\}\,(w_{2t}/v_{1t})$$

$$+ \Big\{\left[a_{IK} + a_{IKIK}(I_{kt}) + a_{PIK}(K_{pt}) + a_{KIK}(K_{kt}) + a_{IPIK}(I_{pt}) + a_{IKY}\,(Y_t) + a_{IKT}\,(t)\right]$$

$$(1 + r_{t,t+1})\left[rp_{kt}\,(\text{tax})\right]/DENK_t\Big\}\,(1/v_{1t})$$

$$+ \Big\{\left[a_Y + a_{YY}\,(Y_t) + a_{PY}\,(K_{pt}) + a_{KY}\,(K_{kt}) + a_{YT}\,(t) + a_{IPY}\,(I_{pt}) + a_{IKY}\,(I_{kt})\right]$$

$$(F_{IK})\,(1 + r_{t,t+1})\left[rp_{kt}\,(\text{tax})\right]/DENK_t\Big\}\,(1/v_{1t})$$

$$+ \Big\{\left[a_{IP} + a_{IPIP}\,(I_{pt}) + a_{PIP}\,(K_{pt}) + a_{KIP}\,(K_{kt}) + a_{IPIK}\,(I_{kt}) + a_{IPY}\,(Y_t) + a_{IPT}\,(t)\right]$$

$$(1 + r_{t,t+1})\left[rp_{pt}\,(\text{tax})\right]/DENP_t\Big\}\,(1/v_{1t})$$

$$+ \Big\{\left[a_Y + a_{YY}\,(Y_t) + a_{PY}\,(K_{pt}) + a_{KY}\,(K_{kt}) + a_{YT}\,(t) + a_{IPY}\,(I_{pt}) + a_{IKY}\,(I_{kt})\right]$$

$$(F_{IP})\,(1 + r_{t,t+1})\left[rp_{pt}\,(\text{tax})\right]/DENP_t\Big\}\,(1/v_{1t}) = -\,(e_{12} + e_{1P} + e_{1K})\,.$$

$$e_{12} = \frac{\partial v_{1t}}{\partial w_{2t}}\frac{w_{2t}}{v_{1t}} = \Big\{-\,(a_{22})\,(w_{2t})$$

$$+ \left[a_Y + a_{YY}\,(Y_t) + a_{PY}\,(K_{pt}) + a_{KY}\,(K_{kt}) + a_{YT}\,(t) + a_{IPY}\,(I_{pt}) + a_{IKY}\,(I_{kt})\right](F_2)$$

$$-\left[a_{IP} + a_{IPIP}\,(I_{pt}) + a_{PIP}\,(K_{pt}) + a_{KIP}\,(K_{kt}) + a_{IPIK}\,(I_{kt}) + a_{IPY}\,(Y_t) + a_{IPT}\,(t)\right]$$

$$(1 + r_{t,t+1})\left[T_{ct}/\varepsilon_t\,(T_{ct+1})\right]a_{IP2}/DENP_t$$

$$-\left[a_{IK} + a_{PIK}\,(K_{pt}) + a_{IKIK}\,(I_{kt}) + a_{KIK}\,(K_{kt}) + a_{IPIK}\,(I_{pt}) + a_{IKY}\,(Y_t) + a_{IKT}\,(t)\right]$$

$$\left.(1 + r_{t,t+1})\left[T_{ct}/\varepsilon_t\,(T_{ct+1})\right]a_{IK2}/DENK_t\right\}(w_{2t}/v_{1t})$$

$$e_{1K} = \frac{\partial v_{1t}}{\partial rp_{kt}\,(\text{tax})}\frac{rp_{kt}\,(\text{tax})}{v_{1t}}$$

$$= \left\{-\left[a_{IK} + a_{IKIK}(I_{kt}) + a_{PIK}(K_{pt}) + a_{KIK}(K_{kt}) + a_{IPIK}\,(I_{pt}) + a_{IKY}\,(Y_t) + a_{IKT}\,(t)\right]\right.$$

$$\left.(1 + r_{t,t+1})\left[rp_{kt}\,(\text{tax})\right]/DENK_t\right\}(1/v_{1t})$$

$$-\left\{\left[a_Y + a_{YY}\,(Y_t) + a_{PY}\,(K_{pt}) + a_{KY}\,(K_{kt}) + a_{YT}\,(t) + a_{IPY}\,(I_{pt}) + a_{IKY}\,(I_{kt})\right]\right.$$

$$\left.(F_{IK})\,(1 + r_{t,t+1})\left[rp_{kt}\,(\text{tax})\right]/DENK_t\right\}(1/v_{1t})$$

$$e_{1P} = \frac{\partial v_{1t}}{\partial rp_{pt}\,(\text{tax})}\frac{rp_{pt}\,(\text{tax})}{v_{1t}}$$

$$= \left\{-\left[a_{IP} + a_{IPIP}\,(I_{pt}) + a_{PIP}\,(K_{pt}) + a_{KIP}\,(K_{kt}) + a_{IPIK}\,(I_{kt}) + a_{IPY}\,(Y_t) + a_{IPT}\,(t)\right]\right.$$

$$\left.(1 + r_{t,t+1})\left[rp_{pt}\,(\text{tax})\right]/DENP_t\right\}(1/v_{1t})$$

$$-\left\{\left[a_Y + a_{YY}\,(Y_t) + a_{PY}\,(K_{pt}) + a_{KY}\,(K_{kt}) + a_{YT}\,(t) + a_{IPY}\,(I_{pt}) + a_{IKY}\,(I_{kt})\right]\right.$$

$$\left.(F_{IP})\,(1 + r_{t,t+1})\left[rp_{pt}\,(\text{tax})\right]/DENP_t\right\}(1/v_{1t})$$

$$e_{21} = \frac{\partial v_{2t}}{\partial w_{1t}}\frac{w_{1t}}{v_{2t}}$$

$$= \left\{-a_{22} - (a_{Y2})\,(F_2) + (a_{IP2})^2\left[T_{ct}/\varepsilon_t\,(T_{ct+1})\right](1 + r_{t,t+1})/DENP_t\right.$$

$$\left.+ (a_{IK2})^2\left[T_{ct}/\varepsilon_t\,(T_{ct+1})\right](1 + r_{t,t+1})/DENK_t\right\}(w_{2t}/v_{2t})$$

$$+ \left\{\left[a_{IK2} + (a_{Y2})\,(F_{IK})\right](1 + r_{t,t+1})/DENK_t\right\}\left[rp_{kt}\,(\text{tax})/v_{2t}\right]$$

$$+ \left\{\left[a_{IP2} + (a_{Y2})\,(F_{IP})\right](1 + r_{t,t+1})/DENP_t\right\}\left[rp_{pt}\,(\text{tax})/v_{2t}\right]$$

$$= -(e_{22} + e_{2P} + e_{2K})$$

$$e_{22} = \frac{\partial v_{2t}}{\partial w_{2t}} \frac{w_{2t}}{v_{2t}}$$

$$= \left\{ a_{22} + (a_{Y2})\,(F_2) - (a_{IP2})^2 \left[T_{ct}/\varepsilon_t\,(T_{ct+1}) \right] (1 + r_{t,t+1})\,/\,DENP_t \right.$$

$$\left. - (a_{IK2})^2 \left[T_{ct}/\varepsilon_t\,(T_{ct+1}) \right] (1 + r_{t,t+1})/DENK_t \right\} (w_{2t}/v_{2t})$$

$$e_{2K} = \frac{\partial v_{2t}}{\partial rp_{kt}\,(\text{tax})} \frac{rp_{kt}\,(\text{tax})}{v_{2t}}$$

$$= -\left\{ \left[a_{IK2} + (a_{Y2})\,(F_{IK}) \right] (1 + r_{t,t+1})\,/\,DENK_t \right\} \left[rp_{kt}\,(\text{tax})\,/\,v_{2t} \right]$$

$$e_{2P} = \frac{\partial v_{2t}}{\partial rp_{pt}\,(\text{tax})} \frac{rp_{pt}\,(\text{tax})}{v_{2t}}$$

$$= -\left\{ \left[a_{IP2} + (a_{Y2})\,(F_{IP}) \right] (1 + r_{t,t+1})\,/\,DENP_t \right\} \left[rp_{pt}\,(\text{tax})\,/\,v_{2t} \right].$$

For the Pakistani textile industry, $I_{kt} = K_{kt} = rp_{kt}(\text{tax}) = rp_{kt}(\text{fs}) = 0$ because data limitations prevented us from including R&D and knowledge capital in the model for that industry.

FORMULAS FOR TABLE 15-6

$$e_{1MP} = \frac{\partial v_{1t}}{\partial m_{pt}} \frac{m_{pt}}{v_{1t}}$$

$$= \left(\left[a_{IP} + a_{IPIP}\,(I_{pt}) + a_{PIP}\,(K_{pt}) + a_{KIP}\,(K_{kt}) + a_{IPIK}\,(I_{kt}) + a_{IPY}\,(Y_t) + a_{IPT}\,(t) \right] \right.$$

$$+ \left[a_Y + a_{YY}\,(Y_t) + a_{PY}\,(K_{pt}) + a_{KY}\,(K_{kt}) + a_{IPY}\,(I_{pt}) + a_{IKY}\,(I_{kt}) + a_{YT}\,(t) \right] (F_{IP})$$

$$+ \left[a_{IK} + a_{PIK}\,(K_{pt}) + a_{IKIK}\,(I_{kt}) + a_{KIK}\,(K_{kt}) + a_{IPIK}\,(I_{pt}) + a_{IKY}\,(Y_t) + a_{IKT}\,(t) \right]$$

$$\left\{ a_{PIK}\,(1 - \delta_k) - a_{PK} - \left[T_{ct}/\varepsilon_t\,(T_{ct+1}) \right] (1 + r_{t,t+1})\,a_{IPIK} \right\} / DENK_t \right)$$

$$\left[(1 + i_{t,t+1})\,\varepsilon_t\,(p_{pt+1})\,(m_{pt}) \right] / \left\{ (DENP_t) \left[\varepsilon_t\,(T_{ct+1}) \right] (v_{1t}) \right\}$$

$$e_{2MP} = \frac{\partial v_{2t}}{\partial m_{pt}} \frac{m_{pt}}{v_{2t}} = \left(a_{IP2} - (a_{Y2})\,(F_{IP}) \right.$$

$$+ (a_{IK2}) \left\{ a_{PIK}\,(1 - \delta_k) - a_{PK} - \left[T_{ct}/\varepsilon_t\,(T_{ct+1}) \right] (1 + r_{t,t+1})\,a_{IPIK} \right\} / DENK_t \right)$$

$$\left[(1 + i_{t,t+1})\,\varepsilon_t\,(p_{pt+1})\,(m_{pt}) \right] / \left\{ (DENP_t) \left[\varepsilon_t\,(T_{ct+1}) \right] (v_{2t}) \right\}$$

$$e_{IKMP} = \frac{\partial I_{kt}}{\partial m_{pt}} \frac{m_{pt}}{I_{kt}} = \left\{ a_{PIK}(1-\delta_k) - a_{PK} - \left[T_{ct}/\varepsilon_t(T_{ct+1}) \right](1 + r_{t,t+1})\, a_{IPIK} \right.$$

$$\left. - \left[T_{ct}/\varepsilon_t(T_{ct+1}) \right](1 + r_{t,t+1})\,(a_{IKY})\,(F_{IP}) \right\}$$

$$\left[(1 + i_{t,t+1})\,\varepsilon_t(p_{pt+1})\,(m_{pt}) \right] / \left\{ (DENK_t)\,(DENP_t)\left[\varepsilon_t(T_{ct+1}) \right](I_{kt}) \right\}$$

$$e_{IPMP} = \frac{\partial I_{pt}}{\partial m_{pt}} \frac{m_{pt}}{I_{pt}}$$

$$= \left[(1 + i_{t,t+1})\,\varepsilon_t(p_{pt+1})\,(m_{pt}) \right] / \left\{ (DENP_t)\left[\varepsilon_t(T_{ct+1}) \right](I_{pt}) \right\}$$

$$e_{IMP} = \frac{\partial Y_t}{\partial m_{pt}} \frac{m_{pt}}{Y_t}$$

$$= \left(F_{IP} + (F_{IK})\left\{ a_{PIK}(1-\delta_k) - a_{PK} - \left[T_{ct}/\varepsilon_t(T_{ct+1}) \right](1 + r_{t,t+1})\, a_{IPIK} \right\} / DENK_t \right)$$

$$\left[(1 + i_{t,t+1})\,\varepsilon_t(p_{pt+1})\,(m_{pt}) \right] / \left\{ (DENP_t)\left[\varepsilon_t(T_{ct+1}) \right](Y_t) \right\}.$$

The formula for e_{IKMP} is not relevant for Pakistan's textile industry, and all the terms involving I_{kt} and K_{kt} are equal to zero in the remaining formulas above.

FORMULAS FOR TABLE 15-8

$$e_{1QP} = \frac{\partial v_{1t}}{\partial q_{pt}} \frac{q_{pt}}{v_{1t}}$$

$$= \left(\left[a_{IP} + a_{IPIP}(I_{pt}) + a_{PIP}(K_{pt}) + a_{KIP}(K_{kt}) + a_{IPIK}(I_{kt}) + a_{IPY}(Y_t) + a_{IPT}(t) \right] \right.$$

$$+ \left[a_Y + a_{YY}(Y_t) + a_{PY}(K_{pt}) + a_{KY}(K_{kt}) + a_{IPY}(I_{pt}) + a_{IKY}(I_{kt}) + a_{Yt}(t) \right](F_{IP})$$

$$+ \left[a_{IK} + a_{PIK}(K_{pt}) + a_{IKIK}(I_{kt}) + a_{KIK}(K_{kt}) + a_{IPIK}(I_{pt}) + a_{IKY}(Y_t) + a_{IKT}(t) \right]$$

$$\left\{ a_{PIK}(1-\delta_k) - a_{PK} - \left[T_{ct}/\varepsilon_t(T_{ct+1}) \right](1 + r_{t,t+1})\, a_{IPIK} \right\} / DENK_t \right)$$

$$\left[(1 + i_{t,t+1})\,\varepsilon_t(p_{pt+1})\,(u_{ct})\,(q_{pt}) \right] / \left\{ (DENP_t)\left[\varepsilon_t(T_{ct+1}) \right](v_{1t}) \right\}$$

$$e_{2QP} = \frac{\partial v_{2t}}{\partial q_{pt}} \frac{q_{pt}}{v_{2t}} = \left(a_{IP2} + (a_{Y2})(F_{IP}) \right.$$

$$+ (a_{IK2})\left\{ a_{PIK}(1-\delta_k) - a_{PK} - \left[T_{ct}/\varepsilon_t(T_{ct+1}) \right](1 + r_{t,t+1})\, a_{IPIK} \right\} / DENK_t \right)$$

$$\left[(1 + i_{t,t+1})\,\varepsilon_t(p_{pt+1})\,(u_{ct})\,(q_{pt}) \right] / \left\{ (DENP_t)\left[\varepsilon_t(T_{ct+1}) \right](v_{2t}) \right\}$$

$$e_{IKQP} = \frac{\partial I_{kt}}{\partial q_{pt}} \frac{q_{pt}}{I_{kt}}$$

$$= \left\{ a_{PIK} (1 - \delta_k) - a_{PK} - \left[T_{ct} / \varepsilon_t (T_{ct+1}) \right] (1 + r_{t,t+1}) (a_{IPIK}) \right.$$

$$\left. - \left[T_{ct} / \varepsilon_t (T_{ct+1}) \right] (1 + r_{t,t+1}) (a_{IKY}) (F_{IP}) \right\}$$

$$\left[(1 + i_{t,t+1}) \varepsilon_t (p_{pt+1}) (u_{ct}) (q_{pt}) \right] / \left\{ (DENK_t) (DENP_t) \left[\varepsilon_t (T_{ct+1}) \right] (I_{kt}) \right\}$$

$$e_{IPQP} = \frac{\partial I_{pt}}{\partial q_{pt}} \frac{q_{pt}}{I_{pt}}$$

$$= \left[(1 + i_{t,t+1}) \varepsilon_t (p_{pt+1}) (u_{ct}) (q_{pt}) \right] / \left\{ (DENP_t) \left[\varepsilon_t (T_{ct+1}) \right] (I_{pt}) \right\}$$

$$e_{YQP} = \frac{\partial Y_t}{\partial q_{pt}} \frac{q_{pt}}{Y_t}$$

$$= \left(F_{IP} + (F_{IK}) \left\{ a_{PIK} (1 - \delta_k) - a_{PK} - \left[T_{ct} / \varepsilon_t (T_{ct+1}) \right] (1 + r_{t,t+1}) a_{IPIK} \right\} / DENK_t \right)$$

$$\left[(1 + i_{t,t+1}) \varepsilon_t (p_{pt+1}) (u_{ct}) (q_{pt}) \right] / \left\{ (DENP_t) [\varepsilon_t (T_{ct+1})] (Y_t) \right\}$$

FORMULA FOR TABLE 15-10

$$e_{IKQK} = \frac{\partial I_{kt}}{\partial q_{kt}} \frac{q_{kt}}{I_{kt}}$$

$$= \left[(1 + i_{t,t+1}) \varepsilon_t (p_{kt+1}) (u_{ct}) (q_{kt}) \right] / \left\{ (DENK_t) \left[\varepsilon_t (T_{ct+1}) \right] (I_{kt}) \right\}$$

FORMULAS FOR TABLE 15-12

$$e_{IKMPT+1} = \frac{\partial I_{kt}}{\partial m_{pt+1}} \frac{m_{pt+1}}{I_{kt}}$$

$$= \left\{ a_{PIK} (1 - \delta_k) - a_{PK} - \left[T_{ct} / \varepsilon_t (T_{ct+1}) \right] (1 + r_{t,t+1}) a_{IPIK} \right.$$

$$\left. - \left[T_{ct} / \varepsilon_t (T_{ct+1}) \right] (1 + r_{t,t+1}) (a_{IKY}) (F_{IP}) \right\}$$

$$+ \left[(\delta_p - 1) \varepsilon_t (p_{pt+1}) \varepsilon_t (m_{pt+1}) \right] / \left\{ (DENK_t) (DENP_t) \left[\varepsilon_t (T_{ct+1}) \right] (I_{kt}) \right\}$$

$$e_{IPMPT+1} = \frac{\partial I_{pt}}{\partial m_{pt+1}} \frac{m_{pt+1}}{I_{pt}}$$

$$= \left[(\delta_p - 1)\ \varepsilon_t\,(p_{pt+1})\ \varepsilon_t\,(m_{pt+1}) \right] / \left\{ (DENP_t)\left[\varepsilon_t\,(T_{ct+1}) \right](I_{pt}) \right\}$$

FORMULAS FOR TABLE 15-13

$$e_{IKQPT+1} = \frac{\partial I_{kt}}{\partial q_{pt+1}} \frac{q_{pt+1}}{I_{kt}}$$

$$= \left\{ a_{PIK}\,(1 - \delta_k) - a_{PK} - \left[T_{ct} / \varepsilon_t\,(T_{ct+1}) \right](1 + r_{t,t+1})\ a_{IPIK} \right.$$

$$\left. - \left[T_{ct} / \varepsilon_t\,(T_{ct+1}) \right](1 + r_{t,t+1})\,(a_{IKY})\,(F_{IP}) \right\}$$

$$\left[(\delta_p - 1)\ \varepsilon_t\,(p_{pt+1})\ \varepsilon_t\,(u_{ct+1})\ \varepsilon_t\,(q_{pt+1}) \right] / \left\{ (DENK_t)\,(DENP_t)\left[\varepsilon_t\,(T_{ct+1}) \right](I_{kt}) \right\}$$

$$e_{IPQPT+1} = \frac{\partial I_{pt}}{\partial q_{pt+1}} \frac{q_{pt+1}}{I_{pt}}$$

$$= \left[(\delta_p - 1)\ \varepsilon_t\,(p_{pt+1})\ \varepsilon_t\,(u_{ct+1})\ \varepsilon_t\,(q_{pt+1}) \right] / \left\{ (DENP_t)\left[\varepsilon_t(T_{ct+1}) \right](I_{pt}) \right\}$$

FORMULA FOR TABLE 15-14

$$e_{IKQKT+1} = \frac{\partial I_{kt}}{\partial q_{kt+1}} \frac{q_{kt+1}}{I_{kt}}$$

$$= \left[(\delta_k - 1)\ \varepsilon_t\,(p_{kt+1})\ \varepsilon_t\,(u_{ct+1})\ \varepsilon_t\,(q_{kt+1}) \right] / \left\{ (DENK_t)\left[\varepsilon_t\,(T_{ct+1}) \right](I_{kt}) \right\}.$$

Data Description and Construction of the Variables

Most of the data for Pakistan used in this study were obtained from various issues of the *Census of Manufacturing Industries* (Pakistan 1966–85) and the *Economic Survey Statistical Supplement: 1987–88* (Pakistan 1988). Most of the data for Turkey came from the *Statistical Yearbook of Turkey* (Turkey, various years) and from unpublished tax data (Turkey, various years). They cover the period from 1973 through 1986. The variables were constructed as follows:

- *Land and Buildings.* The quantities of land and buildings were constructed by dividing the stocks by the investment deflator. The stocks were constructed by employing the perpetual inventory method, with the depreciation rate set equal to 0.05. As starting values for the stocks, we used the 1956 end-of-year book values of land and buildings.

- *Machinery and Equipment.* The quantities of machinery and equipment were constructed in the same way as those of the land-and-buildings variable, except that a depreciation rate of 0.10 was used.
- *Rental Prices of the Services from Physical and Knowledge Capital.* The right-hand sides of equations 15-15, 15-16, 15-27, and 15-28 were used to calculate the user costs of capital.
- *Labor.* The quantity of labor was measured as the total number of days worked during the year for Pakistan, and as the average number of employees during the year for Turkey. The price index was constructed by dividing total employment cost during the year by the number of days worked (Pakistan) or the number of employees (Turkey).
- *Intermediate Inputs.* Intermediate inputs for Pakistan include electricity, petroleum fuel, natural gas, and imported and domestically produced miscellaneous materials. Intermediate inputs for Turkey include raw materials, components, containers, fuel, and electricity. Aggregate price and quantity indexes were constructed from these components by using the Tornqvist approximation of the Divisia index.
- *Output.* The quantity of output was constructed by dividing the total value of output by the manufacturing output deflator.

The Structure of Corporate Taxation and Investment Incentives

We describe the structure of the CIT, including its investment incentives, first for Pakistan and then for Turkey.

PAKISTAN. Pakistan has followed a stable corporate tax rate regime since the early 1960s. The corporate income tax at 30 percent and a supertax at 25 percent have been maintained consistently during the last two decades. Only in fiscal 1989–90 was the supertax rate brought down to 15 percent. Foreign direct investment receives tax treatment equivalent to domestic investment. Losses are allowed to be carried forward six years but are not permitted to be carried back. A sales tax at 12.5 percent is payable on all domestically manufactured goods by the producer and on imported goods by the importer. In fiscal 1989–90, import duties at differential rates were imposed on imported machinery and equipment. These rates varied from 20 percent to 50 percent if similar machinery was not manufactured in Pakistan, and a higher rate of 80 percent applied to imported machinery with domestic substitutes. Businesses were further subject to a large number of miscellaneous licensing fees and charges.

The regime of fiscal incentives through the corporate income tax has experienced significant changes over time. From time to time, Pakistan has relied on a variety of fiscal incentives to stimulate investment. These include accelerated capital consumption allowances for certain physical assets, full expensing for R&D investments, tax rebates, regional and industry-specific tax holidays, and investment tax credits. These are briefly discussed below.

Tax holidays. Tax holidays for two years for specific industries (for example, for those manufacturing engineering goods) and specific regions (most of the country except major metropolitan areas) were introduced in 1959–60. The holiday period was subsequently raised to four years in 1960–61. These tax holidays were eliminated in 1972–73 but reinstated again in 1974–75. Presently, tax holidays for five years are permitted to engineering goods, poultry farming and processing, dairy farming, cattle or sheep breeding, fish farming, data processing, agricultural machinery, and also to all industries in designated areas of the country.

Investment tax credits. Industries are eligible for varying tax credits according to location. A general tax credit for balancing, modernization, and replacement of plant and equipment was introduced at a rate of 15 percent, but its application was restricted to designated areas. From 1976–77 to the time it was withdrawn in 1989–90, the credit was made available regardless of location and type of industry.

Tax rebates. Companies exporting goods manufactured in Pakistan are entitled to a rebate of 55 percent of taxes attributable to such sales.

Accelerated capital consumption allowances. Capital consumption allowances follow accelerated schedules for machinery and equipment, transport vehicles, and housing for workers (25 percent), oil exploration equipment (100 percent), ship building (20 to 30 percent), and structures (10 percent) on a declining-balance method. Expenditure relating to research and development, transfer and adaptation of technologies, and royalties is eligible for full expensing.

All the pertinent provisions of the tax code, including the general tax incentives available to the chemical and pharmaceutical industries, are embodied in the rental prices of capital services discussed in this chapter.

TURKEY. What follows is a description of Turkey's tax structure and investment incentives.

Corporate tax base and rate. Taxable income of corporate entities (defined as book profits before taxes plus increases in pension reserves and general provision for bad debt minus investment and export allowances and depreciation deductions, and so on) is currently taxed at a flat rate of 46 percent. A 3 percent defense surcharge is payable on this basic rate. In addition, a 1 percent tax is payable to the Social Assistance and Security

Fund, and an additional 1 percent tax is levied for the Apprenticeship, Vocational, and Training Encouragement Fund, for a combined corporate tax rate of 49.38 percent. Corporate tax is withheld at source at varying rates with 0 percent rates for dividend distributions, 5 percent for income from crude oil exploration, 10 percent on interest and movable property income, 20 percent for income from immovable property, and 25 percent for salaries and wages and patents and royalties.

Inventory valuation. Inventories must be valued for tax purposes at their actual historical costs with no adjustment for inflation. If cost cannot be determined on an individual basis, a moving average determination is acceptable.

Capital gains. Capital gains and losses are included in the determination of taxable income.

Dividend distributions. Dividend distributions and intercompany dividends are not taxed.

Depreciation deductions. Depreciation allowances are based on historical costs adjusted by the wholesale price index minus 10 percent and take the form of ten-year interest-bearing bonds. Either the straight-line or declining-balance method of depreciation may be chosen for any asset, but no switch is allowed from the straight-line to the declining-balance method during the life of the asset. Depreciation on movable fixed assets acquired on or after January 1, 1983, may be taken under a straight-line method at any rate chosen by the taxpayer, up to an annual maximum of 25 percent. If the declining-balance method is used, the maximum allowable depreciation rate is 50 percent. Assets having values less than 5,000 Turkish lira can be deducted. For structures and movable fixed assets acquired before January 1, 1983, the Ministry of Finance publishes maximum depreciation rates (on a straight-line basis) permissible for tax purposes. These rates typically are 4.0 percent for factory buildings, 15.0 to 20.0 percent for transport equipment, and 12.5 percent for machinery and equipment.

Other taxes. A value added tax is levied at a general rate of 10 percent. Banking and insurance transactions are subject to a 3 percent tax.

Investment incentives. Several incentives for investment are available through the tax code. These are discussed below:

- *Investment incentive allowance.* The investment incentive allowance is a deduction from the taxable income for corporate tax purposes. The deduction is claimed in the year of investment on that portion of investment not subsidized by the government. Unused investment allowances can be carried forward indefinitely. The rate of investment allowance varies by region and type of investment (table 15A-1).
- *Special incentives for scientific R&D.* In addition to the 100 percent investment allowance, the following incentives for R&D are also available:

Table 15A-1. Rate of Investment Allowance, by Region and Type of Investment
(percent)

Region, industry, or activity	Rate
Region	
Developed regions	30
Normal regions	40
Second priority regions	60
First priority regions	100
Priority industries[a]	100
Scientific research and development	100

a. Includes energy; electronics and communications; medical equipment; health, agriculture, and animal husbandry; tourism and education; and marine products.
Source: Treasury Department, personal communication with authors.

Tax postponement. Twenty percent of the amount of corporate tax may be spread in nine equal installments without interest to three years following the year in which the R&D expenditure is made, provided that the tax so postponed not exceed the amount of such expenditure made in the corresponding year.

Tax exempt status for corporations carrying out scientific research and development. Effective January 1, 1986, corporations carrying out scientific R&D could apply for tax exempt status.

- *Investment finance fund.* Corporations can set aside up to 25 percent of taxable income for future investments. The amount set aside at the discretion of the corporation is deducted from its taxable income and deposited in an interest-bearing account (earning the same interest as government bonds, usually about 20 percent per year) with the central bank. It can be withdrawn any time with authorization from the State Planning Office and used for investment.

- *Real estate tax exemption.* For investments qualifying for investment allowances, real estate taxes are waived for several years.

- *Accelerated capital consumption allowances.* As discussed earlier, accelerated depreciations up to a limit of 50 percent can be claimed for machinery and equipment. Further assets can be revalued at the end of every calendar year.

- *Customs exemption.* Machinery that embodies new technology and improves the international competitiveness of Turkish industries can be imported free of customs duties.

- *Export allowance.* If a company exports industrial goods for more than US$250,000 per year, it can take a 20 percent deduction of its profits realized on the exports. If the exporter is not the manufacturer of the goods, only a 5 percent exemption applies.

- *Nontax incentives.* A large number of nontax incentives are available to eligible investments. These include low-interest credit, funds for working capital, allocation of foreign exchange, and allowance for import of used equipment.

All the pertinent provisions of the tax code are embodied in the rental prices of capital services discussed in this chapter.

Note

An earlier version of this chapter can be found in Rajagopal and Shah (1992).

References

Berndt, Ernst R., Melwyn Fuss, and Leonard Waverman. 1980. "Dynamic Adjustment Models of Industrial Energy Demand: Empirical Analysis for U.S. Manufacturing, 1947–1974." Paper prepared for Electric Power Research Institute, Palo Alto, Calif.

Boadway, Robin W., and Neil Bruce. 1979. "Depreciation and Interest Deductions and the Effect of the Corporation Income Tax on Investment." *Journal of Public Economics* 11 (1): 93–105.

Christensen, L. R., and D. W. Jorgenson. 1969. "The Measurement of U.S. Real Capital Input, 1929–1967." *Review of Income and Wealth* 15 (4): 293–320.

Davis, J. M. 1972. "An Aggregate Time Series Analysis of the Short-Run Shifting of Company Taxation in the United Kingdom." *Oxford Economic Papers, n.s.* 24 (2): 259–86.

Feltenstein, A., and A. Shah. 1993. "General Equilibrium Effects of Taxation on Investment in a Developing Country: The Case of Pakistan." *Public Finance* 48 (3): 366–86.

———. Forthcoming. "General Equilibrium Effects of Investment Incentives in Mexico." *Journal of Development Economics.*

Gallant, A. R., and D. W. Jorgenson. 1979. "Statistical Inference for a System of Simultaneous, Non-linear, Implicit Equations in the Context of Instrumental Variable Estimation." *Journal of Econometrics* 11 (2/3): 275–302.

Gaskins, D. W., Jr. 1971. "Dynamic Limit Pricing: Optimal Pricing under Threat of Entry." *Journal of Economic Theory* 3 (3): 306–22.

Gillespie, W. I., and F. Vermaeten. 1993. "Tax Incidence in Canada." Paper presented at the meeting of the Canadian Economics Association, Ottawa, Can., June 4–6.

Gordon, R. J. 1967. "The Incidence of the Corporation Income Tax in U.S. Manufacturing, 1925–62." *American Economic Review* 57 (4): 731–58.

Hall, Challis A. Jr. 1964. "Direct Shifting of the Corporate Income Tax in Manufacturing." *American Economic Review* 54 (3): 258–71.

Harberger, A. C. 1962. "The Incidence of the Corporation Income Tax." *Journal of Political Economy* 70 (3): 215–40.

Jorgenson, D. W., and Z. Griliches. 1967. "The Explanation of Productivity Change." *Review of Economic Studies* 34:249–83.

Kennan, J. 1979. "The Estimation of Partial Adjustment Models with Rational Expectations." *Econometrica* 47 (6): 1441–55.

MacKinnon, J. G. 1983. "Model Specification Tests against Non-Nested Alternatives." *Econometric Reviews* 2 (1): 85–110.

———. 1992. "Model Specification Tests and Artificial Regressions." *Journal of Economic Literature* 30 (1): 102–46.

Moffat, W. R. 1970. "Taxes in the Price Equation: Textiles and Rubber." *Review of Economics and Statistics* 52 (3): 253–61.

Muth, J. F. 1961. "Rational Expectations and the Theory of Price Movements." *Econometrica* 29 (3): 315–35.

Pakistan, Federal Bureau of Statistics. 1966–85. *Census of Manufacturing Industries*. Karachi.

Pakistan, Finance Division. 1988. *Economic Survey Statistical Supplement: 1987–88*. Islamabad.

Pechman, J. A. 1985. *Who Paid the Taxes, 1966–85*. Washington, D.C.: Brookings Institution.

Pindyck, R. S., and J. J. Rotemberg. 1983. "Dynamic Factor Demands and the Effects of Energy Price Shocks." *American Economic Review* 73 (5): 1066–79.

Rajagopal, Dagmar, and Anwar Shah. 1992. "Tax Incentives, Market Power, and Corporate Investment: A Rational Expectations Model Applied to Pakistani and Turkish Industries." Policy Research Working Paper WPS 908. World Bank, Washington, D.C.

Ruggeri, G. C., D. van Wart, and R. Howard. 1993. "The Redistributional Impact of Government Spending and Taxation in Canada." Paper presented at the meeting of the Canadian Economics Association, Ottawa, Can., June 4–6.

Shephard, R. W. 1953. *Cost and Production Functions*. Princeton, N.J.: Princeton University Press.

———. 1970. *Theory of Cost and Production Functions*. Princeton, N.J.: Princeton University Press.

Treadway, A. B. 1970. "Adjustment Costs and Variable Inputs in the Theory of the Competitive Firm." *Journal of Economic Theory* 2 (4): 329–47.

———. 1974. "The Globally Flexible Accelerator." *Journal of Economic Theory* 7 (1): 17–39.

Turkey, State Institute of Statistics. Various years. *Statistical Yearbook of Turkey*. Publication 1250. Ankara.

DO TAX POLICIES STIMULATE INVESTMENT IN PHYSICAL AND R&D CAPITAL?

16

Anwar Shah and John Baffes

TAX POLICY INSTRUMENTS are frequently used to stimulate private investments in both industrial and developing countries. The effect of such policies in meeting stated policy objectives, especially in developing countries, remains an unexplored area of research. In this chapter we specify an empirical framework to evaluate the cost-effectiveness of incentives for industrial and technological development offered through the tax code. We take a first step in quantifying the stimulative effect of investment incentives on additional investment and also draw implications of such measures for government revenues. Our most important point of departure from previous studies on this subject for developing countries is that we model a dynamic production structure with endogenous capacity utilization. Taxes and incentives enter into the user cost of capital and thereby affect producer decisions regarding the choice of technology. Empirical estimation of this model allows one to infer the effect of investment incentives as well as the implications on revenue forgone of such tax expenditure within the framework of cost-benefit analysis.

We have chosen Pakistan as a case study for an empirical examination of the effectiveness of investment incentives in view of the policy emphasis placed on those instruments by policymakers. First, we describe the corporate tax structure in Pakistan. We then develop the theoretical model as well as the empirical specification. After discussing the data, estimation procedure, and the empirical results, we carry out policy simulations and draw overall policy implications from the analyses presented.

We conclude that the investment tax credit has not been an effective instrument for stimulation of investment in Pakistan and that the private investment stimulation offered by this measure falls short of the revenues forgone by the government. In contrast, full expensing allowed for research and development (R&D) expenditure has been found to be a cost-effective instrument of tax policy.

Corporate Tax Incentives in Pakistan

Pakistan has followed a stable corporate tax rate regime since the early 1960s. A corporate income tax rate at 30 percent and a supertax rate at 25 percent have been maintained consistently during the last two decades. Only in fiscal 1989–90 was the supertax rate brought down to 15 percent. Foreign direct investment receives tax treatment equivalent to domestic investment. Losses are allowed to be carried forward six years, but no carryback of such losses is permitted. A sales tax at 12.5 percent is payable on all domestically manufactured goods by the producer and on imported goods by the importer. During 1989–90, import duties at differential rates were imposed on imported machinery and equipment. These rates vary from 20 to 50 percent if similar machinery is not manufactured in Pakistan, and a higher rate of 80 percent applies to imported machinery with domestic substitutes. Businesses are further subject to a large number of miscellaneous licensing fees and charges.

The regime of fiscal incentives through the corporate income tax has undergone significant changes in the past twenty years. From time to time, Pakistan has relied on a variety of fiscal incentives to stimulate investment. These include accelerated capital consumption allowances for certain physical assets, full expensing for R&D investments, tax rebates, regional and industry-specific tax holidays, and investment tax credits. These are briefly discussed below.

- *Tax holidays.* A two-year tax holiday for specific industries (for example, engineering goods) and specific regions (most of the country except major metropolitan areas) was introduced in 1959–60. The holiday period was subsequently raised to four years in 1960–61. These tax holidays were eliminated in 1972–73 but reinstated in 1974–75. Presently, five-year tax holidays are permitted to the engineering goods and data processing industries, to manufacturers of agricultural machinery, to the poultry farming and processing, dairy farming, cattle or sheep breeding, and fish farming industries, and to all industries in designated nonmetropolitan areas of the country.
- *Investment tax credits.* Industries are eligible for varying tax credits according to location. A general tax credit for balancing, modernization, and replacement of plant and equipment was introduced at a rate of 15 percent in 1975–76, but its application was restricted to designated areas. Since 1976–77, the credit was made available regardless of location and type of industry. This credit was withdrawn in 1989–90 and reinstated in 1990–91.
- *Tax rebates.* Companies exporting goods manufactured in Pakistan are entitled to a rebate of 55 percent of taxes attributable to such sales.

- *Accelerated capital consumption allowances.* Capital consumption allowances follow accelerated schedules for machinery and equipment, transport vehicles, and housing for workers (25 percent), oil exploration equipment (100 percent), shipbuilding (20–30 percent), and structures (10 percent) on a declining-balance method. Expenditure relating to R&D, transfer and adaptation of technologies, and royalties are eligible for full expensing.

Of the incentives enumerated earlier, two general ones—namely, investment tax credit for physical investment and full expensing of R&D expenditure—are the subjects of investigation in this chapter. Because these two types of incentives are widely used in both the industrial and the developing countries, an evaluation of their effect is expected to yield some lessons of general interest to policymakers in Pakistan and elsewhere. In the following sections we present an empirical examination of this issue.

The Model

A flexible accelerator dynamic factor demand model is an eminently suitable tool with which to examine the effect of tax policies on investment in a developing economy (Epstein and Denny 1983). The model allows for a flexible and nonrestrictive technology while capturing and quantifying short-run divergence of fixed factors from their equilibrium values.[1] We include the theoretical underpinnings and empirical form of this model in the discussion that follows.

Consider that a typical firm in a manufacturing industry faces the following short-run cost function:

$$(16\text{-}1) \qquad C(K, I, W, \Upsilon) = \text{Min}_Z \left[W'Z : \Upsilon = F(Z, K, I) \right]$$

where Z denotes the vector of perfectly adjustable factors, K denotes the vector of quasi-fixed stocks, I denotes gross investment in those stocks, Υ is the level of output, and W is the price vector associated with the perfectly adjustable inputs. $F(Z, K, I)$ describes the technology and satisfies all classical properties: twice continuously differentiable, increasing in (Z, K) and decreasing in I. The fact that it is decreasing in I reflects the assumption that the quasi-fixed factors are subject to increasing internal costs of adjustment (Mortensen 1973; Treadway 1970, 1974). $C(K, I, W, \Upsilon)$ is the instantaneous cost function, which satisfies $C \geq 0$; C is increasing in (Υ, I) and decreasing in K; C is convex in I and concave in W.

At any point in time the representative firm takes input prices, output, and state of technology as given and minimizes the discounted sum of future costs over an infinite horizon. Specifically, the firm selects the investment path I_t ($t = 0, ..., \infty$), which solves

(16-2)

$$V(K, \Upsilon, P) = \text{Min} \left(\int_0^\infty e^{-rt} \left(C(K, I, W, \Upsilon) + P'K \right) dt;\ \dot{K} = I - \delta K;\ K \big|_{t=0} = K_0 \right)$$

where δ is a diagonal matrix composed of the depreciation rates; δ_i is the depreciation rate of the ith stock; P is the user cost (rental rate) vector corresponding to K; r is the real rate of discount, which is assumed to be constant. We assume static expectations with respect to level of output and prices; that is, we assume that the current level of output and prices will prevail forever. The remaining notation is defined as follows: ($'$) denotes transposition: ($^{-1}$) denotes inversion; a dot over a function denotes differentiation with respect to time. Finally, subscripts of functions denote differentiation (for example, V_P denotes differentiation of V with respect to vector P).

The user cost of capital embodies the provisions in the tax codes and is defined as follows (chapter 2, this volume): $P = q(\lambda + \delta)(1 - \gamma - \tau\pi)\,[(1 - \tau)\theta]^{-1}$, where q = purchase price of capital; λ = weighted average of the real cost of debt and equity finance; δ = economic depreciation rate; γ = investment tax credit rate; τ = corporate tax rate; π = present value of depreciation allowances; θ = profitability parameter (appendix 16B offers a compete discussion of these parameters).

$V(K, \Upsilon, P)$ is the value function and is characterized by the following set of properties (for notational convenience we suppress its arguments): $V \geq 0$; V is concave in P; $(r + \delta)V_K' - P - V_{KK}K^* < 0$; $V_K' < 0$; $rV_\Upsilon' - V_{\Upsilon K}K^* > 0$.

After defining the value function we apply the following analog of Shephard's lemma for the quasi-fixed inputs (McLaren and Cooper 1980):

(16-3a) $\dot{K}^*(K, \Upsilon, P) = V_{PK}^{-1} (rV_P' - K)$.

Furthermore, for the perfectly adjustable inputs, we apply

(16-3b) $Z^*(K, \Upsilon, P) = -rV_W' + V_{WK}\dot{K}^*$.

Equations 16-3a and 16-3b define the policy functions or the optimal stock profiles for both quasi-fixed (equation 16-3a) and perfectly adjustable (equation 16-3b) factors.

In order to implement the model empirically, we have to approximate equation 16-2 by a functional form. We specify the following quadratic value function (Epstein and Denny 1983):

$$(16\text{-}4) \quad V(K, Y, P) = (1/2) [P' \ W'] \begin{bmatrix} B_{PP} & B_{PW} \\ B'_{PW} & B_{WW} \end{bmatrix} \begin{bmatrix} P \\ W \end{bmatrix} Y + [P' \ W'] \begin{bmatrix} A_{PK}^{-1} \\ A_{WK} \end{bmatrix} K$$

$$+ [P' \ W'] \begin{bmatrix} r^{-1} A_{PK}^{-1} & 0 \\ 0 & r^{-1} \end{bmatrix} \begin{bmatrix} H_P \\ F_W \end{bmatrix}.$$

B_{PP}, A_{PK}, A_{WK}, B_{WW}, B_{PW}, H_P, and F_W denote appropriately dimensional matrix parameters; B_{PP}, B_{WW}, and B_{PW} are symmetric matrices.

Applying Shephard's lemma analog (equation 16-3a) to the value function (equation 16-4) results in

$$(16\text{-}5a) \quad \dot{K}^* = (r - A_{PK}) \, K + r A_{PK} \Big(B_{PP} P + B_{PW} W \Big) Y + H_P.$$

$K^* = K^*(K_0, K, Y, P)$ denotes the levels of net investment, or the dynamic factor demands. Further, applying equation 16-3b to equation 16-4 will yield the demands for the perfectly adjustable inputs:

$$(16\text{-}5b) \quad Z^*(K, Y, P) = -r \Big(B_{WW} W + B_{PW} P \Big) Y - r A_{WK} (K - r^{-1} \dot{K}^*) - F_W.$$

Equations 16-5a and 16-5b form the basis for estimation. Appendix 16A offers a detailed description of the steps involved to arrive at these equations.

Data, Estimation, and Results

Data in the current study cover 1956 through 1985 for total private sector manufacturing industries in Pakistan and were obtained from various Pakistan government publications (Pakistan 1956–85, 1989). A total of five inputs were included in the study: three quasi-fixed (land and buildings, machinery and equipment, and R&D) and two perfectly adjustable (labor and intermediate inputs). Descriptive statistics regarding growth rates of inputs as well as input shares in total costs are given in table 16-1. A detailed description of the data and the derivation of the rental rates of capital are offered in appendix 16B.

Because the model of the previous section was developed in a framework of continuous time, some modifications had to be made to render it estimable. First, $\dot{K}$ was replaced by the discrete approximation ($K_t - K_{t-1}$) and the system of equations 16-5a and 16-5b was modified accordingly

Table 16-1. Growth of Inputs and Input Shares in Pakistan's Manufacturing Industry
(percent)

Period	Land and buildings	Machinery and equipment	Research and development	Labor	Interme-diate inputs
Average annual growth rates of inputs					
1956–65	12.7	11.2	11.5	6.2	8.4
1966–75	0.1	3.6	4.2	4.2	8.0
1976–85	3.2	1.2	15.8	–0.2	13.4
Average input shares in total cost					
1956–65	14.4	32.6	0.4	39.2	13.4
1966–75	13.7	38.0	0.4	35.1	12.8
1976–85	8.5	34.2	0.5	38.7	18.1

Source: Authors' calculations from data described in appendix 16B.

(appendix 16A). Second, the time trend, which is a measure of output augmenting technical change, enters the equations as a discrete approximation of the exponential function $e^{-\beta t}$. Finally, a disturbance error term is additively appended to each equation. These disturbance terms reflect random errors in optimization and are assumed to possess classical statistical properties. Although the introduction of such an error structure is an ad hoc procedure, it shares the merit of keeping estimation straightforward while focusing on economic characteristics of the model.

Because of the nonlinear nature of the model as well as the large number of parameters to be estimated, some simplifications were made. First, the model was estimated in reduced form (equations 16A-11 and 16A-12) as described in appendix 16A. Second, the two blocks of equations were estimated separately. Because equation 16-5a is a closed-form solution for endogenous variables, seemingly unrelated regressions were used to estimate this set of equations. In particular, the nonlinear iterated seemingly unrelated regressions (ITSUR) procedure available in SAS (1988) was used to estimate the parameters of each equation simultaneously. After obtaining the predicted K^* we estimated the two equations corresponding to the perfectly adjustable factors, again by using ITSUR. Because the covariance matrices were iterated to convergence, the estimated parameters are asymptotically equivalent to full information likelihood estimates (under the assumptions of the error and model structure). Finally, in order to account for heteroskedasticity, we divided the inputs by the output, so the system was expressed in the form of input-output ratios.

Price elasticities are calculated as $\varepsilon_{ij} = (\partial K_i / \partial P_j)(P_j / K_i)$, where K_i refers to quantity use of input i, and P_j refers to the rental rate of input j. Those expressions pertain to short-run elasticities. To obtain the long-run elasticities we calculate the steady-state level of stocks, K^*. This results in the substitution of the matrix A_{PK} by the matrix $(A_{PK} - r)^{-1} A_{PK}$ in equation 16-5a. Long-run elasticities are then derived in a straightforward fashion. Output and tax elasticities are obtained in a similar manner.

In table 16-2 we report parameter estimates regarding the quasi-fixed factors as well as the perfectly adjustable factors.[3] Of all these parameter estimates, adjustment coefficients are of special interest. These coefficients give the speed of adjustment of the capital inputs to their respective long-run equilibrium levels. Specifically, the land and buildings coefficient (M_{11}) is –0.19, which indicates that about 19 percent of the adjustment process takes place within a year, or, alternatively, it takes more than five years for the full adjustment to occur. On the contrary, the coefficient associated with machinery and equipment (M_{22}) indicates that the full adjustment will occur in slightly less than two years. Finally, the R&D adjustment coefficient (M_{33}) indicates that 26 percent of the adjustment process will occur within a year. The relatively slow adjustment of R&D as opposed to machinery and equipment is consistent with studies of Canadian manufacturing (Bernstein 1986), the electrical industries of the United States and Japan (Nadiri and Prucha 1989), and the U.S. Bell system (Nadiri and Prucha, 1990). Another result of interest is the cross-adjustment coefficients of land and buildings and of machinery and equipment with R&D. Contrary to the findings by Bernstein as well as Nadiri and Prucha (1989), here we find that a deficient stock of R&D induces substantial decrease in physical capital.[4]

In table 16-3 we report short- and long-run price and output elasticities. The short-run response of capital use to own-rental rate changes is negative as expected and very small in magnitude. Long-run responses, in contrast, are substantially larger and exceed unity for land and buildings. Increases in output have a positive long-run effect on all inputs with the elasticity exceeding unity for physical assets and R&D capital. Note that with the exception of machinery and equipment all other inputs satisfied the Le Chatelier principle (that is, the long-run own-price response is greater than its short-run counterpart).

In table 16-4 we report the corporate tax rate and investment tax credit elasticities. As expected, increases in the corporate income tax rate adversely affect factor utilization in both the short and the long run, whereas increases in the investment tax credit have the opposite effect (with the exception of one case). The effect, as indicated by elasticity values, is uniformly small.

The Effect of Tax Policies on Investment

The estimated model can be used to evaluate the effect on investment of alternative tax policy instruments per unit of forgone revenues. This criterion can then be used to rank instruments as to their relative efficacy. For

Table 16-2. *Reduced Form Parameter Estimates*

Parameter	Estimate	Parameter	Estimate	Parameter	Estimate	Parameter	Estimate
Quasi-fixed factors							
M_{11}	−0.190 (−0.77)	M_{12}	−0.048 (−0.44)	M_{13}	10.21 (0.70)	G_{11}	−0.276 (0.87)
M_{21}	−0.101 (−0.23)	M_{22}	−0.556 (−2.74)	M_{23}	60.14 (2.29)	G_{12}	0.345 (0.87)
M_{31}	0.006 (2.37)	M_{32}	−0.001 (−0.29)	M_{33}	−0.263 (−1.77)	G_{21}	−1.448 (−2.42)
E_{11}	−0.090 (−0.24)	E_{12}	−0.141 (−0.24)	E_{13}	0.199 (0.27)	G_{22}	1.396 (1.95)
E_{21}	0.531 (0.79)	E_{22}	−0.812 (−0.77)	E_{23}	1.695 (0.53)	G_{31}	0.006 (1.76)
E_{31}	−0.001 (−0.08)	E_{32}	−0.003 (−0.47)	E_{33}	−0.005 (−0.67)	G_{32}	−0.001 (−0.28)
β	0.038 (2.30)	H_1	−40.55 (−1.01)	H_2	−219.3 (−2.71)	H_3	−0.323 (−0.79)
Perfectly adjustable factors							
R_{11}	−0.136 (−0.75)	R_{12}	0.348 (1.83)	S_{11}	0.140 (0.45)	S_{21}	0.119 (3.09)
R_{21}	0.436 (2.87)	R_{22}	−0.571 (−2.43)	S_{12}	0.087 (1.58)	S_{22}	0.077 (2.78)
Q_{11}	0.156 (0.34)	Q_{21}	−0.197 (−0.86)	S_{13}	4.392 (0.95)	S_{23}	0.225 (0.10)
Q_{12}	−1.223 (−0.27)	Q_{22}	0.251 (0.60)	F_1	1527.4 (16.17)	F_2	380.4 (7.99)
Q_{13}	0.241 (0.28)	Q_{23}	0.331 (0.76)				

Note: Numbers in parentheses denote *t* ratios. For definitions of the coefficients, see appendix.

Source: Authors' estimates.

this purpose, we used model parameters to simulate the effect of three policy changes: (a) increase in investment tax credit; (b) reduction in the corporate tax rate; (c) full-expensing option for R&D, summary results of which are presented in table 16-5.

Table 16-3. Short- and Long-Run Price and Output Elasticities

Elasticity	Short run	Long run
ε_{11}	−0.083	−1.703
ε_{12}	−0.141	−0.214
ε_{13}	0.232	0.700
ε_{14}	−0.410	−0.657
ε_{15}	0.429	3.010
ε_{21}	0.148	−0.819
ε_{22}	−0.244	−0.214
ε_{23}	0.245	0.169
ε_{24}	−0.699	−0.422
ε_{25}	0.532	2.390
ε_{31}	−0.007	−0.851
ε_{32}	−0.064	0.150
ε_{33}	−0.133	−0.163
ε_{34}	0.207	0.511
ε_{35}	−0.033	1.268
ε_{41}	0.049	0.110
ε_{42}	−0.075	−0.074
ε_{43}	0.095	0.096
ε_{44}	−0.075	−0.180
ε_{45}	0.146	0.130
ε_{51}	−0.125	−0.165
ε_{52}	0.168	0.135
ε_{53}	0.258	−0.050
ε_{54}	0.423	0.828
ε_{55}	−0.514	−0.811
η_{1Q}	−0.049	1.693
η_{2Q}	−0.206	1.614
η_{3Q}	−0.011	1.287
η_{4Q}	0.140	0.082
η_{5Q}	0.210	0.218

Note: Elasticities are calculated at sample means. The subscripts denote: 1 = land and buildings; 2 = machinery and equipment; 3 = research and development; 4 = labor; 5 = intermediate inputs; Q = output; ε_{ij} denotes the percentage change in input use i attributable to a 1 percent change in the rental rate of input j, whereas η_{iQ} denotes the percentage in input use i attributable to a 1 percent output change.

Source: Authors' estimates.

Table 16-4. Short- and Long-Run Tax Elasticities

Elasticity	Short run	Long run	Elasticity	
$\zeta_{1\tau}$	−0.031	−0.237	$\phi_{1\tau}$	0.100
$\zeta_{2\tau}$	−0.017	−0.142	$\phi_{2\tau}$	0.094
$\zeta_{3\tau}$	−0.006	−0.058	$\psi_{1\gamma}$	−0.044
$\zeta_{4\tau}$	−0.002	−0.003	$\psi_{2\gamma}$	−0.041
$\zeta_{5\tau}$	−0.003	−0.011		
$\zeta_{1\gamma}$	0.018	0.151		
$\zeta_{2\gamma}$	0.007	0.081		
$\zeta_{3\gamma}$	0.005	0.054		
$\zeta_{4\gamma}$	−0.001	0.002		
$\zeta_{5\gamma}$	0.002	0.008		

Note: Calculated at sample means. The subscripts denote: 1 = land and buildings; 2 = machinery and equipment; 3 = research and development; 4 = labor; 5 = intermediate inputs; τ = corporate tax rate; γ = investment tax credit. $\zeta_{i\tau}$ denotes the percentage change in input use i attributable to a 1 percent change in τ. $\zeta_{i\gamma}$ denotes the percentage change in input use i attributable to a 1 percent change in γ. $\phi_{i\tau}$ denotes the percentage change in the rental rate of input i attributable to a 1 percent change in τ. $\psi_{i\gamma}$ denotes the percentage change in the rental rate of input i attributable to a 1 percent change in γ. Because γ was introduced in 1976–77, the elasticities represent the average of nine observations only.
Source: Authors' estimates.

Increase in Investment Tax Credit

Currently the investment tax credit in Pakistan is 15 percent. The first policy simulation assumes an increase in the credit from 15 percent to 30 percent for 1983, 1984, and 1985. As can be seen from the investment equation (equation 16A-11) as well as the rental rate formula, a change in the investment tax credit has two effects on investment: (a) the price effect and (b) the feedback effect. A high investment tax credit reduces the effective cost of capital for all three quasi-fixed inputs (table 16-4). This in turn induces more investment, given downward sloping factor demands (own-price effect). Depending on the complementarity and substitutability conditions among the three types of investment, however, the cross-price effect may be either positive or negative; this is consistent with the sign of cross-price elasticities. For example, a price increase of machinery and equipment positively affects investment in land and buildings and negatively affects investment in R&D (table 16-3). Moreover, in the second and third periods of the simulation experiment (1984 and 1985), the change in investment depends not only on the rental rates of capital but also on the lagged level of capital stocks (feedback effect determined by the signs of own- and cross-adjustment coefficients).

Table 16-5. Impact of Tax Policy on Investment at Existing Output Levels

	Change in investment (percent)	Cumulative for 1983–85 (million rupees)
Increase in investment tax credit from 15 to 30 percent		
Effect on factor demands		
Land and buildings	8.8	4,484
Machinery and equipment	15.7	25,201
Research and development	4.9	241
Total change in investment		29,926
Forgone revenues		31,416
Incremental benefit-cost ratio[a]	0.95	
Reduction in corporate income tax rate from 55 to 30 percent		
Effect on factor demands		
Land and buildings	3.2	1,763
Machinery and equipment	13.6	21,671
Research and development	4.0	192
Total change in investment		23,626
Forgone revenues		33,511
Incremental benefit-cost ratio[a]	0.71	
Full-expensing option for investment in research and development		
Investment gains		443
Loss in government revenues		298
Benefit-cost ratio[b]	1.49	

Note: The simulations assume changes in the tax regime for 1983, 1984, and 1985.
a. Total change in investment divided by forgone revenues.
b. Investment gains divided by loss in government revenues.
Source: Authors' calculations.

In the first section of table 16-5 we show the average annual change in investment from simulation consistent with those two effects: 8.8 percent for land and buildings, 15.7 percent for machinery and equipment, and 4.9 percent for R&D. The high percentage change in machinery and equipment may be attributed to the high coefficient of adjustment as well as the high own-price elasticity. The three-year total cumulative change in investment is estimated to have been 29,926 million rupees.[5]

Still, an increase in the investment tax credit implies forgone revenues for the government.[6] These forgone revenues are estimated to have been 31,416 million rupees (cumulative from 1983 through 1985 for all three factors). Although this policy change results in an increase in aggregate investment, forgone revenues exceed the investment stimulus by a small margin. The incremental benefit-cost ratio is estimated to equal 0.95 with such a policy initiative.

Reduction in the Corporate Income Tax Rate

As mentioned earlier, the corporate tax rate is currently set at 55 percent. A second simulation assumes a reduction in the corporate rate from 55 percent to 30 percent. The two types of effects on investment (price and feedback) described above apply here too. In the second section of table 16-5 we give the results of this simulation. Looking at the individual types of investment, we see that machinery and equipment presents a substantial increase (13.6 percent), followed by R&D (4.0 percent) and land and buildings (3.2 percent). Such difference in investment change is expected because of the high coefficient of adjustment exhibited by machinery and equipment as opposed to the other two types of investment. The three-year aggregate change in investment is estimated to have been 23,626 million rupees.

Forgone revenues associated with such a change in the corporate tax rate, however, are estimated to exceed changes in aggregate investment by a significant margin (33,511 million rupees). That gives an incremental benefit-cost ratio substantially less than unity, 0.71.[7]

Full-Expensing Option for R&D

Pakistan offers a full-expensing option for R&D investment. This measure, according to the calculations presented in the third section of table 16-5, is seen to be a cost-effective instrument for R&D investment stimulation. The R&D investment gains were calculated to be 443 million rupees, whereas the losses in government revenues are 298 million rupees. That gives an incremental benefit-cost ratio greater than unity (1.49).

Before we conclude this chapter, some comments concerning the limitations of the model are in order. The model used here is a partial equilibrium one; as such, it does not capture several indirect effects that might take place. Furthermore, it is assumed that forgone revenues are adequate reflections of the costs of the hypothesized reform, at least within the partial equilibrium framework employed here. In turn, there is an implicit assumption that a unit increase in investment has the same social value, that is, that investments are equally productive. That may not necessarily be the case, especially when one considers investment in R&D, which enhances growth more than investment in physical capital. Therefore the assumption of no indirect effects or, alternatively, of equality between the shadow and the observed costs and benefits of the reform (as discussed in Dréze and Stern 1987) can be viewed as an implicit acceptance of the neutrality-of-tax approach as described in Kay and King (1983).[8]

Summary and Policy Implications

We have employed a flexible accelerator type of model for Pakistani manufacturing by using data covering 1956 through 1985. Three quasi-fixed (land and buildings, machinery and equipment, and R&D) and two perfectly adjustable (labor and intermediate materials) inputs entered the cost function. Machinery and equipment exhibited higher adjustment rates and higher short-run own-price elasticity than land and buildings and R&D. The tax elasticities were very low.

The simulation showed that the incremental cost-benefit ratio associated with changes in investment tax credit and corporate tax rate was smaller than one. A full-expensing option for R&D investment was found to be cost-effective. Pakistan currently follows a regime of high taxes and low incentives in major metropolitan areas and one of high taxes and high incentives in selected less developed areas. The simulation analysis conducted above suggests that fiscal incentives for investment were generally not cost-effective. Perhaps public policy emphasis should be placed on creating and maintaining a low tax regime. With regard to short-run investment stimulation, however, an increase in the investment tax credit was found to be more efficient than a reduction in the corporate tax rate.

Appendix 16A. Derivation of Input Demands

Rewrite the value function defined in equation 16-4 as

$$(16A\text{-}1) \quad V(K, \Upsilon, P) = (1/2)\left(P' B_{PP}P + W' B'_{PW}P + P' B_{PW}W + W' B_{WW}W\right)\Upsilon$$

$$+ P' A_{PK}^{-1} K + W' A_{WK}K + P' r^{-1} A_{PK}^{-1} H_P + W' r^{-1} F_W,$$

and consider again the Shephard's lemma analog regarding the quasi-fixed inputs,

$$(16A\text{-}2) \qquad \dot{K}^*(K,\Upsilon,P) = V_{PK}^{-1}\left(rV_P' - K\right).$$

Differentiating equation 16A-1 with respect to P and transposing the resulting expression gives

$$(16A\text{-}3) \quad V_P' = \left(B_{PP}P + B_{PW}W\right)\Upsilon + A_{PK}^{-1}K + r^{-1}A_{PK}^{-1}H_P.$$

Differentiating V_P' with respect to K and inverting yields

(16A-4) $$V_{PK}^{-1} = A_{PK}.$$

Substituting equations 16A-3 and 16A-4 into equation 16A-2 results in

(16A-5) $$\dot{K}^*(K, \Upsilon, P) = A_{PK}\left\{r\left[\left(B_{PP}P + B_{PW}W\right)\Upsilon + A_{PK}^{-1}K + r^{-1}A_{PK}^{-1}H_P\right] - K\right\}.$$

Rearranging terms in equation 16A-5 yields the dynamic factor demands

(16A-6) $$\dot{K}^* = \left(r - A_{PK}\right)K + rA_{PK}\left(B_{PP}P + B_{PW}W\right)\Upsilon + H_P.$$

The Shephard's lemma analog regarding the perfectly adjustable inputs is given by

(16A-7) $$Z^*(K, \Upsilon, P) = -rV_W' + V_{WK}\dot{K}^*.$$

Differentiating equation 16A-1 with respect to W and transposing the resulting expression gives

(16A-8) $$V_W' = \left(B_{WW}W + B_{PW}P\right)\Upsilon + A_{WK}K + r^{-1}F_W.$$

Differentiating V_W with respect to K yields

(16A-9) $$V_{WK} = A_{WK}.$$

Substituting equations 16A-8 and 16A-9 into equation 16A-7 and rearranging terms results in the input demands for the perfectly adjustable factors:

(16A-10) $$Z^*(K, \Upsilon, P) = -r\left(B_{WW}W + B_{PW}P\right)\Upsilon - rA_{WK}(K - r^{-1}\dot{K}^*) - F_W.$$

To eliminate nonlinearities in the estimation, we expressed equations 16A-6 and 16A-10 in reduced form; the discrete time approximation is

(16A-11) $$K_t = (I + M)K_{t-1} + (EP + GW)\Upsilon(1 + \beta)^{-t} + H_P \text{ and}$$

(16A-12) $$Z_t = (RW + QP)\Upsilon + S(K - r^{-1}\dot{K}^*) - F_W.$$

where $M = (r - A_{PK})$, $E = rA_{PK}B_{PP}$, $G = rA_{PK}B_{PW}$, $Q = -rB_{WW}$, $R = -rB_{WW}$, and $S = -rA_{WK}$ are the estimated matrix parameters in reduced form; I denotes a (3 x 3) identity matrix; and t is the time subscript.

A descriptive exposition of the reduced-form matrix parameters has as follows:

$$M = \begin{bmatrix} M_{11} & M_{12} & M_{13} \\ M_{21} & M_{22} & M_{23} \\ M_{31} & M_{32} & M_{33} \end{bmatrix}, \quad E = \begin{bmatrix} E_{11} & E_{12} & E_{13} \\ E_{21} & E_{22} & E_{23} \\ E_{31} & E_{32} & E_{33} \end{bmatrix}, \quad G = \begin{bmatrix} G_{11} & G_{12} \\ G_{21} & G_{22} \\ G_{31} & G_{32} \end{bmatrix}, \quad H_P = \begin{bmatrix} H_1 \\ H_2 \\ H_3 \end{bmatrix},$$

$$R = \begin{bmatrix} R_{11} & R_{12} \\ R_{21} & R_{22} \end{bmatrix}, \quad Q = \begin{bmatrix} Q_{11} & Q_{12} & Q_{13} \\ Q_{21} & Q_{22} & Q_{23} \end{bmatrix}, \quad S = \begin{bmatrix} S_{11} & S_{12} & S_{13} \\ S_{21} & S_{22} & S_{23} \end{bmatrix}, \quad F_W = \begin{bmatrix} F_1 \\ F_2 \end{bmatrix}.$$

The structural form parameters of equation 16A-11 and equation 16A-12 are then recovered from the reduced form as follows: $A_{PK} = (I + r - M)$, $B_{PP} = (r - M)^{-1} r^{-1} E$, $B_{PW} = (r - M)^{-1} r^{-1} G$, $B_{WW} = -r^{-1} Q$, $B_{PW} = -r^{-1} R$, and $A_{WK} = -r^{-1} S$.

Finally, the vectors representing prices are defined as

$$P' = \begin{bmatrix} P_1 & P_2 & P_3 \end{bmatrix}, \text{ and } W' = \begin{bmatrix} W_1 & W_2 \end{bmatrix}.$$

where P_1, P_2, and P_3 denote the rental rates of land and buildings, machinery and equipment, and R&D, respectively; and W_1 and W_2 denote labor and intermediate inputs prices, respectively.

Appendix 16B. Data Description and Construction of Variables

Most of the data used in this study were obtained from various issues of *Census of Manufacturing Industries* and *the Economic Survey Statistical Supplement: 1987–88* and cover the years from 1956 through 1985 (Pakistan 1956–1985; Pakistan 1989). The construction of variables was done as follows:

- *Land and buildings.* Quantity of land and buildings was constructed by dividing stocks by the investment deflator. Stocks were constructed by employing the perpetual inventory method, with depreciation rate set equal to 0.05. As a starting value of stocks we used the 1956 end-of-year book value of land and buildings. The rental rate of land and buildings was calculated by invoking the following formula (chapter 2, this volume): $P_t = q_t(\lambda + \delta)(1 - \gamma - \tau\pi)[(1 - \tau)\theta]^{-1}$, where $P_t =$ user cost (rental rate) of land and buildings; $q_t =$ investment deflator; $\lambda =$ weighted average of the real cost of debt and equity finance, where the weight is given by the ratio of shareholders' equity to total capital employed (constructed from data reported in various published and unpublished sources; it ranges between 0.047 and 0.110);

δ = depreciation rate (set to 0.05); γ = investment tax credit (introduced in 1977, 0.15); τ = corporate tax rate including supertax rate (equal to 0.55 as reported in budget speeches); π = present value of investment allowances received by the firm; θ = profitability parameter (set to 0.90).

- *Machinery and equipment.* Quantity and rental rate of machinery and equipment were constructed analogously to that of land and buildings variables except that the depreciation rate used was set to 0.10.
- *R&D.* Quantity of R&D was constructed by dividing R&D stocks by the gross domestic product deflator. R&D stocks were constructed using the perpetual inventory method with the depreciation rate set equal to 0.10. R&D expenses were obtained from the *Industrial Statistics Yearbook* (United Nations, various years) and various government of Pakistan data sources (Pakistan 1956–85, 1989). When data on R&D investment were not available we used the expenses of royalties and other fees. Rental rate of R&D was calculated by invoking the formula for rental rate described earlier and setting π = 1.0 and δ = 0.10.
- *Labor.* Quantity of labor was measured as the total number of days worked during the year. The price index was constructed by dividing total employment cost during the year by number of days worked.
- *Intermediate inputs.* Intermediate inputs include electricity, petroleum fuel, natural gas, and imported and domestically produced miscellaneous materials. Aggregate price and quantity indexes were constructed from these components by using the Tornquist approximation of the Divisia index.
- *Output.* Quantity of output was constructed by dividing total value of output by the manufacturing output deflator.

Notes

1. Recent advances in dynamic duality (for example, see Epstein and Denny 1983) have facilitated empirical applications of such models, so the underlying economic relationships characterizing the industry can be examined without imposing severe restrictions on the technology.

2. A complete characterization of the properties of the value function as well as the cost function can be found in Epstein and Denny 1983; the profit function can be found in Epstein 1981.

3. The results reported in table 16-2 (which were used in all subsequent calculations) are based on static expectations. In addition we run the model by using first- and second-order autoregressive expectation schemes regarding rental rates and output. Results for land and buildings and for machinery and equipment were fairly insensitive in regard to adjustment rates and elasticities. On the contrary, R&D showed a high degree of sensitivity.

4. A note regarding the significance levels of the estimated coefficients is in order. Out of a total of forty-six parameters estimated, slightly more than one-third (sixteen parameters) have absolute values exceeding 1.70. Admittedly,

based on this fact one would conclude that the model did not perform in a satisfactory manner. There are, however, several other characteristics that one might consider in judging the performance of such models. Two such characteristics are adjustment coefficients falling within the [−1, 0] interval, and the Le Chatelier principle (short-run own-price elasticities less than their long-run counterparts).

5. All rupee amounts have been calculated at 1976 constant terms.

6. Forgone revenues associated with an increase in the investment tax credit were calculated as $(0.15-0.30)*I$, where I denotes the value of net investment in all three types of capital (cumulative 1983–85). In particular, the revenue losses for 1983, 1984, and 1985 were calculated to be 9,363, 11,225, and 12,893 million rupees, respectively.

7. Forgone revenues associated with reduction in the corporate tax rate were calculated as $(0.55-0.30)*\pi$, where π denotes the cumulative profits of the manufacturing industry for 1983–85.

8. In particular, Kay and King (1983) write regarding the neutrality-of-tax approach, "A neutral tax system is one which seeks to raise revenue in ways that avoid distortionary effects. . . . [I]t is designed to minimize as far as possible the impact of the tax structure on the economic behaviour of agents in the economy" (18).

References

Bernstein, J. I. 1986. *Research and Development, Tax Incentives, and the Structure of Production and Financing.* Toronto, Can.: University of Toronto Press

Drèze, J., and N. Stern. 1987. "The Theory of Cost-Benefit Analysis." In A. J. Auerbach and M. Feldstein, eds., *Handbook of Public Economics.* Vol. 2. New York: North-Holland.

Epstein, L. G. 1981. "Duality Theory and Functional Forms for Dynamic Factor Demands." *Review of Economic Studies* 48 (1): 81–95.

Epstein, L. G., and M. G. S. Denny. 1983. "The Multivariate Flexible Accelerator Model: Its Empirical Restrictions and an Application to U.S. Manufacturing." *Econometrica* 51 (3): 647–74.

Kay, J. A., and M. A. King. 1983. *The British Tax System.* New York: Oxford University Press.

McLaren, K., and R. Cooper. 1980. "Intertemporal Duality: Application to the Theory of the Firm." *Econometrica* 48: 1755–62.

Mortensen, D. T. 1973. "Generalized Costs of Adjustment and Dynamic Factor Demand Theory." *Econometrica* 41: 657–65.

Nadiri, M. I., and I. R. Prucha. 1989. "Comparison and Analysis of Productivity Growth and R&D Investment in the Electrical Machinery Industries of the United States and Japan." New York University and University of Maryland, New York and College Park.

———. 1990. "Dynamic Factor Demand Models, Productivity Measurement, and Rates of Return: Theory and Empirical Application to the Bell System." *Structural Change and Economic Dynamics* 1 (2): 263–89.

Pakistan, Federal Bureau of Statistics. 1956–1985. *Census of Manufacturing Industries.* Karachi.

Pakistan, Finance Division. 1989. *Economic Survey Statistical Supplement: 1987–88.* Islamabad.

SAS (Statistical Analysis System) Institute. 1988. *User's Guide.* Cary, N.C.

Treadway, A. B. 1970. "Adjustment Costs and Variable Inputs in the Theory of Competitive Firm." *Journal of Economic Theory* 2: 329–47.

——. 1974. "The Globally Optimal Flexible Accelerator." *Journal of Economic Theory* 7 (1): 17–39.

United Nations. Various years. *Industrial Statistics Yearbook.* New York.

MACROECONOMIC IMPLICATIONS OF INVESTMENT INCENTIVES IN MEXICO

17

Andrew Feltenstein and Anwar Shah

DURING THE PAST several decades, public policy officials in Mexico have experimented with many tax instruments designed to promote private capital formation. Among such initiatives were general and industry-specific tax credits, employment tax credits, and corporate rate reductions. In this chapter we examine the relative efficacy of such tax instruments using a dynamic computable general equilibrium framework.

The chapter is organized as follows. First, we present an outline of the tax policy environment for the corporate sector in Mexico. We then present the details of the model and highlight alternative tax incentive regimes and model simulation results. Finally, we provide a summary of the results.

Tax Incentives for Investment in Mexico

Tax incentive regimes in Mexico have undergone significant changes over time. These are briefly discussed below:

- *1955–72.* Between 20 percent (for secondary industries) and 40 percent (for basic industries) of the corporate income of Mexican majority-owned enterprises was exempted from corporate taxation for periods of five to ten years. The same industries also could receive, on application, exemption from certain indirect taxes and import duties on capital goods imports.
- *1972–79.* Industries that were seen to promote decentralization and regional development were granted import duty relief of 50 to 100 percent and reduction in corporate tax liability ranging from 10 to 40 percent, depending on their location and type of activity.
- *1979–86.* The practice of import duty exemption was continued. In addition, tax incentive certificates (CEPROFIs) provided tax credit in

the range of 10 to 25 percent for investment in physical assets, depending on location and on type and size of the industry. These certificates were negotiable and could be used against any federal tax liability by the holder.

* *1986–present.* The tax incentive certificate scheme was significantly tightened and targeted to priority industries and preferred zones (see table 17A-1, in the appendix). The top tax credit rate for CEPROFIs was raised to 40 percent of total physical investment in 1986. In addition, Mexican-owned enterprises are eligible for employment tax credits of up to 30 percent of three times the annual minimum wage in the area multiplied by the number of new jobs created. In addition, full expensing of the present value of capital consumption allowances, calculated using a 7.5 percent discount rate, was allowed in nonmetropolitan areas. In the metropolitan industrial areas of Mexico City, Monterrey, and Guadalajara, only 60 percent of the present value of depreciation allowances could be deducted in the first year. Currently permissible is a research and development (R&D) investment tax credit at 15 percent for the purchase of technological research (20 percent for small and microeconomic enterprises) and 20 percent for capital purchases by technological enterprises (30 percent for small enterprises).

Further details regarding the corporate income taxation and forgone revenues due to tax incentives in Mexico are given in the appendix.

Model Specification

In this section we develop the model we use to analyze a variety of fiscal issues in Mexico. In particular, the model is designed to look at the implications for revenues, sectoral investment, and the balance of payments of several different tax programs. We consider investment tax credits and employment tax credits. The model can easily be extended to incorporate accelerated depreciation allowances, tax holidays, and immediate full expensing. Our model also permits experimentation with changes in the structure of indirect taxation as well as the personal income tax. The model is intended to be a microeconomic optimizing structure that generates macroeconomic outputs. Because our aim is empirical implementation, much of the structure we incorporate is chosen because of the availability of data.

We use a two-period general equilibrium system in which all agents have perfect foresight and, hence, correctly anticipate in period 1 the prices of period 2. We need to specify the behavior of production and consumption and of government output, taxation, and deficit financing. We need also to specify the exchange rate regime and the characteristics of the trade system. A solution is found for both periods simultaneously, so we will be determining outcomes for both years and, hence, the corresponding rates of change.

Production

There are eight factors of production and three types of financial assets. These are:

1–5 Capital types
6 Urban labor
7 Money
8 Domestic bonds
9 Foreign bonds
10 Rural labor
11 Land

The five types of capital correspond to the five productive sectors, which do not include agriculture, that we will describe shortly. Each of these factors and financial assets is replicated in each period, so we have, for example, period 1 capital and period 2 capital. Period 1 money will be the numéraire. Thus the model has twenty-two dimensions, or prices.

An input-output matrix is used to determine intermediate and final production. This matrix is replicated in each of two years. Corresponding to each sector in the input-output matrix, value added is produced that uses capital and urban labor for the nonagricultural sectors, and land and rural labor in agriculture. The technology that produces this value added is sector-specific.[1] Our data source for the input-output matrix is *Matriz de Insumo-Producto Anno 1978* (NIS 1983). Here, a matrix of seventy-two sectors is derived that represents Mexico's technology for 1980. We have not attempted to update the matrix for the years that we will be analyzing. Because it is not our intention to work at this level of sectoral disaggregation, we have aggregated the technology to seven sectors by adding corresponding rows and columns. The resulting sectors and the corresponding sectors in the initial matrix are shown in table 17-1. We denote the resulting input-output matrix by A.[2]

The specific formulation of the firm's problem is as follows: Let y_{Ki}^j, y_{Li}^j be the inputs of capital and urban labor to the jth nonagricultural sector in period i. Let Υ_{Gi} be the outstanding stock of government infrastructure in period i. The production of value added is then given by

$$(17\text{-}1) \qquad va_{ji} = va_{ji}\left(\Upsilon_{Ki}^j, \Upsilon_{Li}^j, \Upsilon_{Gi}\right).$$

Recall that capital is sector-specific and there are two types of labor. In the case of agriculture, equation 17-1 takes the same form, except that land is substituted for capital, and rural labor is substituted for urban labor. We are supposing that there is a single type of infrastructure,

Table 17-1. Aggregate Input-Output Sectors

Aggregate sector	Corresponding disaggregated sectors
Agriculture	1–4
Manufacturing	5, 7–61
Petroleum	6
Commerce	62, 63
Transportation	64
Communications and services	65–72
Imports	

Source: NIS (1983).

although extensions to sector-specific infrastructure would present no problem. Infrastructure may be thought of as, for example, roads, communications, and education and enters private production as an increase in productivity.

It is assumed that sector j minimizes cost with respect to capital and urban labor in the case of a nonagricultural sector and with respect to land and rural labor in the case of agriculture. Sector j pays value added taxes on inputs of capital and labor, given by t_{Ki}^j, t_{Li}^j, respectively, in period i. We assume that no taxes are paid on the use of land by agriculture, although agriculture is taxed on its use of labor.[3] We will also suppose that the sector may be given an employment tax credit. This credit is given by a percentage rebate on the value of the firm's wage bill. Hence the effective price for labor paid by sector j is

$$\tilde{P}_{Lij} = (1 + t_{Lij} - a_{ij}) P_{Li}$$

where a_{ij} is the employment tax credit given to sector j. Similarly, the effective price of capital for sector j is

$$\tilde{P}_{Kij} = (1 + t_{Kij}) P_{Kij}.$$

Thus if $\tilde{P}_{Kij}$ and $\tilde{P}_{Lij}$ are the prices of capital and labor in period i, then the prices charged by enterprises, P_i, are given by

(17-2) $$\{P_i\} = va\,(P, \Upsilon_{Gi})\,(1 + t)\,(I - A)^{-1}$$

where $va(P, \Upsilon_{Gi})$ is the vector of cost-minimizing value added per unit of output, subject to $P = (\tilde{P}_{Kij}, \tilde{P}_{Lij})$ and Υ_{Gi}, and $t = (t_{Ki}, t_{Li})$.

Here, we treat imports as a single product that is distinct from domestic production.[4] Thus there is no value added by factors in imports.

Rather, imports require foreign exchange, which is, in turn, produced by exports.

We suppose that each type of sectoral capital is produced via a sector-specific investment technology that uses inputs of capital and labor to produce new capital. Investment is carried out by the private sector, and because the capital that is produced in one period becomes available only in the next period, investors must pay for the input cost of its production in the current period but will receive the revenue from that capital in the next period. We will assume that investment is entirely financed by domestic borrowing and that investors sell domestic bonds to pay their factors of production.[5] Accordingly, investors equate the cost of borrowing, given by the interest rate, with the anticipated future returns on capital.

Investors are affected by several fiscal parameters in making their decision. They receive an investment tax credit as well as a depreciation allowance. They also pay a capital, or profit tax, on the returns to their investment. Let us define the following notation:

k_i = the investment tax credit in period i (percent)
d_i = the depreciation allowance in period i (percent)[6]
t_{ki} = the profit (capital) tax rate (percent)
C_{Hi} = the cost of producing the quantity H_i of capital in period i
r_i = the interest rate in period i
p_{Ki} = the return to capital in period i
P_{Mi} = the price of money in period i

Suppose, then, that the rental price of capital in period $i + 1$ is P_{Ki+1}. If C_{Hi} is the cost-minimizing cost of producing the quantity of capital, H_i, then future debt obligations must be equal to the return on new capital. Hence

$$(17\text{-}3) \qquad C_{Hi}(1 - k_i - d_i) = \frac{1 - t_{k2}\, P_{K2}\, H_1}{1 + r_i}$$

where r_i is the interest rate in period i, given by

$$(17\text{-}4) \qquad r_i = 1/P_{Bi}$$

where P_{Bi} is the price of a bond in period i.[7]

Thus all sectors in the economy pay both income and profit taxes to the government, although certain sectors (in particular, agriculture) may receive subsidies. These taxes are collected by the central government, which uses them to finance its own expenditure activities.

The government produces public goods, using capital and labor as inputs to production. These goods are divided between those used for development, represented by capital expenditure, and those that are represented by current expenditure and have no direct effect on private output.[8] The government's target for the output of public goods is determined exogenously in each time period as a fraction of gross domestic product (GDP). No attempt is made, therefore, to model an optimizing government.

Consumption

There are two types of consumers, representing rural and urban labor. We suppose that both consumer classes have the same demand patterns for goods and that their demands for the seven different types of goods are given by constant fractions of their incomes.[9] Thus urban and rural consumers differ only in regard to their initial wealth.

Consumers maximize intertemporal utility functions, which have as arguments the levels of consumption and leisure in each of the two periods. We permit rural-urban migration in that rural workers can choose to become urban labor if the relative wage is favorable. Consumers maximize these utility functions subject to intertemporal budget constraints. They save by holding money, domestic bonds, and possibly foreign currency. They require money for transactions, but their demand for money is sensitive to changes in the interest rate. Consumers receive income from their labor, from the rental on any capital or land that they own, and from the interest payments on bonds that they have purchased. They may also receive direct transfer payments from the government. They pay sales taxes on the goods they consume and tariffs on imported goods. Their bond holdings are also subject to a capital loss if the domestic interest rate falls. The maximization problem for consumers is thus

$$(17\text{-}5) \qquad \max U(x) \; x = \left(x_1 , x_{L1} , x_2 , x_{L2} \right)$$

such that

$$(17\text{-}5a) \quad (1 + t_i) \, P_i x_i + P_{Lui} x_{Lui} + P_{Lri} x_{Lri} + P_{Mi} x_{Mi} + P_{Bi} x_{Bi} + e_i P_{BFi} x_{BFi}$$

$$= P_{Ki} (1 - \delta) \, i_K + P_{Ai} A_0 + P_{Lui} L_{ui} + P_{Lri} L_{ri} + P_{Mi} M (i - 1)$$

$$+ r_{(i-1)} x_{B(i-1)} + P_{Bi} x_B (i-1) + e_i P_{BFi} x_{BF} (i-1) + TR_i$$

$$(17\text{-}5b) \quad \log P_{Mi} x_{Mi} = a + b \log (1 + t_i) \, P_i x_i - c \log r_i$$

$$(17\text{-}5c) \quad \log P_{Bi} x_{Bi} - \log e_i P_{BFi} x_{BFi} = \alpha + \beta \, (\log r_i - \log e_i r_{Fi})$$

$$(17\text{-}5d) \quad \log (L_{ui} / L_{ri}) = a_1 + a_2 \log(P_{Lui} - P_{Lri}) / (P_{Lui} + P_{Lri})$$

if $P_{Lui} \geq P_{Lri}$; otherwise, $\log(L_{ui}/L_{ri}) = 0$

(if the representative household is rural; otherwise, labor holdings are constant)

$$(17\text{-}5e) \qquad P_{B2}\, x_{B2} = s\,(1 + t_2)\, P_2 x_2$$

where

P_i	= the price vector of consumption goods in period i
x_i	= the vector of consumption in period i
t_i	= the vector of sales tax rates in period i
P_{Lui}	= the price of urban labor in period i
L_{ui}	= holdings of urban labor in period i
P_{Lri}	= the price of rural labor in period i
L_{ri}	= holdings of rural labor in period i
a_2	= the elasticity of rural-urban migration
P_{Ki}	= the price of capital in period i
K	= the initial holding of capital
δ	= the rate of depreciation of capital
x_{Li}	= the consumption of leisure in period i
P_{Mi}	= the price of money in period i (money in period 1 is the numéraire and, hence, has a price of 1; a decline in the relative price of money from one period to the next represents inflation)
x_{Mi}	= holdings of money in period i
P_{Bi}	= the discount price of a domestic bond in period i
r_i	= the domestic interest rate in period i
x_{Bi}	= the quantity of domestic bonds purchased in period i
e_i	= the exchange rate in terms of units of domestic currency per unit of foreign currency in period i
P_{BFi}	= the foreign currency discount price of foreign bonds in period i
x_{BFi}	= the quantity of foreign bonds purchased in period i
TR_i	= transfer payments from the government in period i

and where a, b, c, α, β are estimated constants.

Thus the left-hand side of equation 17-5a represents the value of consumption of goods and leisure and of financial assets. In particular, it incorporates the sales and value added tax rates that consumers may face. The right-hand side contains the value of consumers' holdings of capital and labor and the principal values and interest that they receive from the domestic and foreign financial assets that they held at the end of the previous period. Thus their budget constraint is affected by both interest and exchange rates. Equation 17-5b is a standard money demand equation in which the demand for cash balances depends on the domestic interest rate and the value of intended consumption. Equation 17-5b thus represents an interest-sensitive transactions-demand-for-money function. Accordingly, money is not in the consumers' utility function, and they are required to hold money in the final period in order to pay for their consumption in that period. Equation 17-5c says that the proportion of savings made up of domestic and foreign interest-bearing assets depends on relative domestic and foreign interest rates, deflated by the exchange rate. If no holding of foreign assets is permitted, then savings is made up entirely of domestic bonds. Finally, equation 17-5d is a migration equation that says that the change in consumers' relative holdings of urban and rural labor depends on the relative wage rates. We chose the particular form shown for the dependent variable so that the term in parentheses ( ) would have a maximum value of 1 and a minimum value of 0. Thus a_2 is the elasticity of substitution between urban and rural labor. Some interpretation is necessary here. The specification says that the representative rural household starts off in period 1 holding only rural labor. If the urban wage is higher than the rural wage, then a portion of the rural labor becomes urban labor, depending on the elasticity a_2 and the wage differential. Labor does not move in the other direction, however; if the period 2 rural wage is higher than the urban wage, there is no immigration back to the country. The representative urban consumer never moves any of his or her labor to the country. Thus the utility function of rural consumers stays constant when they move to the city.

Consumers save by purchasing domestic and foreign bonds, in addition to holding money. They receive the interest payments on these bonds as well as possible capital gains. As indicated in equation 17-5c, we allow for the possibility of consumers' holding foreign assets by formulating a portfolio balance model. In this model, consumers divide their savings between domestic and foreign assets on the basis of relative interest rates that are deflated by the expected rate of change of the domestic currency in relation to the foreign currency. There is an elasticity of substitution between domestic and foreign assets, so we do not necessarily obtain factor-price equalization.

Consumers pay market prices plus sales taxes for all goods except agriculture, which may, for some consumers, be subsidized. Personal income taxes are not paid directly by consumers but are withheld at the enterprise level, where profit taxes are also collected. The total value of consumption by consumers in each period must be equal to their corresponding income, so we do not permit personal borrowing. In the final period of the model we impose an exogenous savings rate on consumers, as in equation 17-5e.[10] Thus savings rates are endogenously determined by intertemporal maximization in period 1 and are exogenously determined in the last period.

In order to generate the necessary parameters in the maximization problem of Mexican consumers, we have derived consumption weights from the aggregation of the original input-output matrix.[11] We did not directly estimate an elasticity of demand for leisure but experimented with various values. Foreign consumers are represented by an export equation that determines the total U.S. dollar amount that they will spend on Mexican exports. This total is then divided into consumption of Mexican output of agriculture, manufacturing, and petroleum with shares of 0.075, 0.531, and 0.394, respectively.[12] The aggregate export equation was estimated by ordinary least squares, using annual data for nonoil exports during the period 1950–85 with the results shown in equation 17-6. The estimation in equation 17-6 has been carried out in nominal terms so as to correspond to the specification of the general equilibrium model, which incorporates prices.

(17-6)

$$\log E = -0.88 - 0.12 \log RP + 0.12 \log RP_{-1} - 0.22 \log RP_{-2}$$
$$ (0.69) \quad (-0.04) \qquad\qquad (0.31) \qquad\qquad (-0.64)$$

$$+ 1.75 \log U - 0.77 \log U_{-1} - 0.88 \log U_{-2}$$
$$ (2.13) \qquad\qquad (-0.65) \qquad\qquad (-1.18)$$

$$+ 0.95 \log E_{-1}$$
$$ (14.05)$$

$$R^2 = 0.99 \qquad H\text{–statistic} = 1.48.$$

We give the following definitions:

E = Mexican nonoil exports in US\$
RP = Price of Mexican exports in US\$ relative to the U.S. price index
U = U.S. nominal gross national product (GNP)

The figures in parentheses are t-statistics. We notice that U.S. GNP and the lagged dependent variable are significant and that the long-run elasticities all have the correct signs. The long-run relative price elasticity is 4.4, whereas that of U.S. GNP is 2.0.[13] Finally, we did not attempt to estimate an oil export equation, and oil exports were taken to be exogenous.

Two other equation estimations are needed to close the determination of consumption. A money demand equation was estimated from annual data for 1950 through 1985. We wish to estimate an equation of the form

$$(17\text{-}7) \qquad\qquad \log M_0^d = a_1 + a \log C_2 + ar$$

where

$$\log M - \log M = \beta \, (\log M^d - \log M).$$

Here, we give the following definitions:

M^d = the desired stock of money
M = the money supply
C = nominal consumption
r = the domestic interest rate
b = an adjustment parameter representing the speed of adjustment of actual to desired stocks

In order to maintain homogeneity in consumption, as required in the general equilibrium model,[14] we set $a_1 = 1$ and obtain

$$(17\text{-}8) \qquad \log M / C = \beta a_0 + \beta a_2 r + (1 - \beta) \log M_{-1} / C.$$

We estimated equation 17-8 for the period 1950–85, using $M1$ for money and replacing r with π, the inflation rate in the wholesale price index.[15] The results are

$$(17\text{-}9) \quad \log M / C = -0.37 - 0.23r + 0.83 \log M_{-1} / C.$$
$$\qquad\qquad\quad (-0.41) \quad (-3.71) \quad (7.21)$$

$$R^2 = 0.65 \quad \text{D.W.} = 1.88$$

We may then identify the underlying parameters as

$$(17\text{-}10) \qquad a_0 = -2.18, \; a_1 = 1, \; a_2 = -1.35, \; \beta = 0.17$$

so the demand-for-money function given in equation 17-7 is

$$(17\text{-}11) \qquad\qquad M = 0.113 \; r^{-1.35} C.$$

We must also estimate the portfolio balance equation given in equation 17-5c.

$$(17\text{-}12) \quad \log (x_d / x_f) = b_0 + b_1 (e - e_{-1}) + b_2 \log (x_d / x_{f_{-1}})$$

where x_d and x_f represent the peso value of domestic and foreign asset holdings by Mexican consumers, respectively, and e is the exchange rate of pesos and U.S. dollars. This was estimated for 1970 through 1985, annual data being taken from Zedillo 1986, because there is no information on capital flight prior to 1970.

$$(17\text{-}13) \quad \log{(x_d / x_f)} = \underset{(2.79)}{0.28} - \underset{(-3.00)}{0.72} \; (e - e_{-1}) + 0.45 \, (x_d / x_{f_{-1}})$$

$$R^2 = 0.74 \quad \text{D.W.} = 2.48 \, .$$

We thus note that all parameters are significant and have the correct sign. We tried a number of different specifications of the portfolio balance equation, attempting to determine the effect of relative interest rates. In none of the tests did we find interest rates to be significant, however, probably because of the controls that were in place on Mexican interest rates for much of the sample period.

For our current application we also require some estimate of the elasticity of rural-urban migration. We have therefore used data from the period 1970–82 to estimate equation 17-5d. The resulting parameters are

$$(17\text{-}14)$$

$$\log{(L_{ui} / L_{ri})} = \underset{(5.26)}{2.43} + \underset{(3.45)}{5.00} \; \log{(P_{Lui} - P_{Lri}) / (P_{Lui} + P_{Lri})}$$

$$R^2 = 0.54 \quad \text{D.W.} = 1.21.$$

Thus we see that the elasticity of substitution of urban and rural labor with respect to the wage rate is 5.0, a relatively high figure. This probably reflects the period of the sample, when urban wages were rising rapidly in response to increases in oil prices, and there were large movements of labor from the country to the city.

Transfer Payments and Government Financing

The government collects income, profit, and sales taxes, as well as import duties, and it pays subsidies and, implicitly, investment tax credits, depreciation allowances, and employment tax credits. In addition, the government must cover both domestic and foreign interest obligations on public debt. The deficit of the central government in period 1, D_1, is then given by

$$(17\text{-}15) \qquad D_1 = G_1 + S_1 + r_1 B_0 + e_1 r_{F1} B_{F0} - T_1$$

where S_1 represents subsidies, including tax credits, given in period 1; G_1 is spending on goods and services; T_1 represents period 1 taxes; and B_0 and B_{F0} reflect domestic and foreign interest obligations of the government, respectively, based on its initial stocks of debt. Thus for example, policies that cause the exchange rate to depreciate will increase foreign interest payments. T_1 represents total revenues of the government.

There are several types of subsidies that the government may use to support consumption or production. The first of these is a support to value added of the sector in question, given by

$$(17\text{-}16) \qquad t_{ai} \left(P_{Ki} y_{aKi} + P_{Li} y_{aLi} \right)$$

where t_{ai} is the support rate given to the sector's value added in period i and the term in parentheses is the nominal cost of the sector's value added. The second type of subsidy is a guaranteed price to sectoral output. Here, the government announces a support price for the sector's output. If the market price falls below this support, then some fraction of the difference is made up by the government as a direct subsidy to producers. Hence the support payments are given by

$$(17\text{-}17) \qquad (P_{ai}^{*} - P_{ai})\, y_{ai}$$

where P_{ai}^{*} is the target price of output. If the term in equation 17-17 is negative, then no subsidy is paid.

A third possible subsidy is a support paid to consumption of the sector's products. Here, we suppose that the government announces a maximum price, P_{ci}, for consumption. If the market price of sectoral output rises above this in period i, then some fraction of the difference, f_i, is paid by the government, thereby reducing the effective price to consumers. Accordingly, the payment made for this is given by

$$(17\text{-}18) \qquad \sum f_i (P_{ai}^{*} - P_{ci})\, x_{ai}$$

where x_{ai} is the total private consumption of sectoral output in period i.

The resulting deficit is financed by a combination of monetization and domestic and foreign borrowing. Thus if y_{BG1} represents the face value of domestic bonds sold by the government in period 1, and C_{F1} represents the dollar value of its foreign borrowing, then its budget deficit in period 2 is given by

$$(17\text{-}19) \quad D_2 = G_2 + S_2 + r_2\,(y_{BG1} + B_0) + e_2 r_{F2}\,(C_{F1} + B_{F0}) - T_1$$

where $r_2\,(y_{BG1} + B_0)$ represents the interest obligations on its initial domestic debt plus borrowing from period 1, and $e_2 r_{F2}(C_{F1} + B_0)$ is the interest payment on the initial stock of foreign debt plus foreign borrowing in period 1.

The Foreign Sector and Exchange Rate Determination

The foreign sector is represented by a simple export equation in which aggregate demand for nonoil exports is determined by domestic and foreign price indexes and world income. Hence the foreign currency value of nonoil exports is sensitive to changes in the exchange rate as well as to domestic price changes. We take the dollar value of oil exports to be exogenous. The specific form of the nonoil export equation is

$$(17\text{-}20) \qquad \Delta X_{no} = \sigma_1 \left[\pi_i / (\Delta e_i \pi_{Fi}) \right] + \sigma_2 \Delta y_{wi}$$

where the left-hand side of the equation represents the change in the dollar value of Mexican nonoil exports in period i, π_i is inflation in the domestic price index, Δe_i is the percentage change in the exchange rate, and π_{Fi} is the foreign rate of inflation. Also, Δy_{wi} represents the percentage change in world income, denominated in dollars. Finally, σ_1 and σ_2 are corresponding elasticities. It is then assumed that the rest of the world spends constant shares on each Mexican nonoil export. Thus equation 17-20 determines total spending on nonoil exports, and Mexican prices determine the volume of each export. The parameter values used to determine equation 17-20 are derived from the long-run values of the parameter estimates in equation 17-6.

The combination of the export equation and domestic supply responses then determines aggregate exports. Demand for imports is endogenous and is derived from the domestic consumers' maximization problems, which also determine their demand for foreign assets. Foreign lending has not been modeled, but has been taken to be exogenous. Thus gross capital inflows are exogenous, but the overall change in reserves is endogenous, depending on the savings behavior and demand for imports of consumers.

Apart from producing infrastructure, collecting taxes, and financing the budget deficit, the government also attempts to adjust the exchange rate. The supply of foreign reserves y_{FGi} available to the government in period i is given by

$$(17\text{-}21) \qquad y_{FGi} = y_{FG(i-1)} + X_i - M_i + x_{F(i-1)} - x_{Fi} + C_{Fi}.$$

Here, x_{Fi} represents the demand for foreign assets by citizens of the home country, so $x_{F(i-1)} - x_{Fi}$ represents private capital flows. C_{Fi} represents exogenous foreign borrowing by the home government.

All terms on the right-hand side of equation 17-21 are solved from the maximization problems of the domestic and foreign consumers. The government also has a demand for assets that, we suppose, is determined by an exchange rate rule. Consider figure 17-1, which represents the government's exchange rate rule in period i. The horizontal axis represents the market exchange rate in period i, e_i, and the vertical axis represents the government's demand for foreign assets. In addition, let x_{Fi} represent whatever the government feels to be the critical level of foreign reserves in period i. This critical level is determined exogenously.

Let us suppose that the exchange rate in period i depreciates from the previous period. Hence $e_i > e_{i-1}$. Then, as in figure 17-1, we derive a unique government demand for reserves, x_{FGi} in the figure. Equivalently, if there is a slight decrease in the equilibrium supply of foreign reserves of the government below its critical level, then there is a sharp depreciation in the exchange rate. We may then construct excess demand by the government for foreign reserves, D_{Fi}, as

$$D_{Fi} = x_{FGi} - y_{FGi}.$$

Figure 17-1.   *Government Demand for Foreign Reserves*

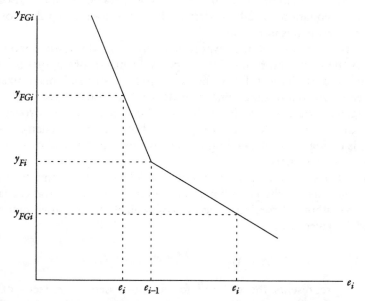

Note: y_{FGi} = actual demand for foreign reserves in period i; y_{Fi} = target level of foreign reserves in period i; e_i = exchange rate in period i.

Source: Authors' calculations.

Thus the government creates a correspondence between changes in the exchange rate and movements away from the critical level of reserves. If, as an extreme case, the graph in figure 17-1 becomes horizontal at x_{Fi}, then this corresponds to a pure float when reserves fall to their critical level. This is the scenario of much of the literature on the balance-of-payments crisis.[16] A graph that is close to horizontal below x_{Fi} may be taken as representing the policy of a nervous government, whereas a graph that is closer to vertical reflects a relatively unconcerned policy.

Simulation Results

In this section we will use our model to carry out a series of numerical exercises using Mexican data.

Calibration

The primary goal of our study is to be able to make certain quantitative judgments concerning the effect of changes in fiscal parameters on domestic real and financial variables. We wish first to simulate the model for 1987 and 1988, the most recent years for which we have comparable data. In order to simulate the estimated form of our model, we have taken initial allocations to be the stocks at the end of 1986. Thus a unit of urban or rural labor, for example, is taken to be that quantity that earned 1 peso in 1986. A unit of capital is that amount that earned a rent of 1 peso in 1986, as is a unit of land. Stocks of money, bonds, and foreign bonds are taken to have their actual values at the end of 1986. The model is solved through use of a computer program written by A. Feltenstein, which computes a fixed point of the intertemporal model.

As a first experiment we wish to see how well our model replicates reality. We thus carry out a simulation for 1987 and 1988 in which all exogenous parameters take on their actual historical values for those years. In particular, we take oil exports to have their actual values. We have attempted to estimate effective rates for all taxes and tariffs and have taken the real values of government spending to be the actual values in each year.[17] In particular, investment tax credits are uniformly set at 10 percent, as are employment tax credits. We have set the desired level of foreign reserves of the government at zero and we have set the slope of devaluation at four when reserves fall below the desired level, that is, if the government has negative net reserves. If reserves rise above zero, then the slope of revaluation is set at two. Clearly, these numbers are arbitrary and in reality would be subject to constant change. Nonetheless, the figures chosen serve as the basis for comparison. Finally, we will also suppose that no supports are paid for either production or consumption. We will experiment in later simulations with tax credits. The resulting outcome is given in table 17-2.

Table 17-2. Benchmark Simulation

Parameter	1987 Simulated	1987 Historical	1988 Simulated	1988 Historical
Nominal GDP (1,000 billion pesos)	192.9	(192.9)	366.0	(397.6)
Real GDP (1,000 billion 1980 pesos)	48.0	(48.0)	49.9	(48.5)
Government spending (1,000 billion pesos)	45.9	(55.1)	102.4	(94.7)
Revenue (1,000 billion pesos)	28.1	(28.8)	57.6	(56.4)
Government budget deficit	–17.8	(–26.3)	–44.8	(–38.3)
Exports (1,000 billion pesos)	20.8	(–28.9)	–47.4	(–47.2)
Imports (1,000 billion pesos)	12.4	(18.0)	25.4	(42.1)
Trade balance (1,000 billion pesos)	8.4	(10.9)	22.0	(5.1)
Inflation rate[a]	135.6	(135.6)	82.4	(107.8)
Interest rate (percent)	103.1	(103.1)	81.6	(62.0)
Exchange rate (pesos/U.S. dollars)	1,025.7	(1,025.7)	2,111.7	(2,249.4)
Real exchange rate[b]	100.0	(100.0)	88.4	(94.8)
Change in reserves (billions of U.S. dollars)	–1.1	(5.8)	–3.3	(–7.0)
Net real capital formation, 1986–88[c]				
Manufacturing	n.a.	n.a.	100.0	n.a.
Petroleum	n.a.	n.a.	100.0	n.a.
Commerce	n.a.	n.a.	100.0	n.a.
Transportation	n.a.	n.a.	100.0	n.a.
Communication and services	n.a.	n.a.	100.0	n.a.

n.a. Not applicable.

Note: Numbers in parentheses are historical values. Sources for historical values are *Cuentas Nacionales de Mexico, International Financial Statistics,* and various accounts made available by the Mexico division of the World Bank.

a. Rate of inflation in wholesale price index.

b. Wholesale price index divided by nominal exchange rate.

c. These are index numbers used to make comparisons for effects of introducing investment and employment tax credits.

Source: Historical figures come from Sistema de Cuentas Consolidades de la Nación (1985). Simulated figures are the outputs of the computer program.

Let us make some observations concerning the calibration of our model.

- Nominal GDP is calculated as $C + I + G + X - M$. To calculate real GDP, we use the GDP deflator, calculated as the price index of value added (this is very close to the wholesale price index). Thus nominal GDP in 1988 is seen to be below its actual values because we underestimate the rate of inflation in that year. We overestimate the growth rate in 1988 real GDP by about 3.0 percentage points.
- Tax revenues are the sum of value added, sales, and excise taxes; profit and income taxes; and tariffs. These correspond to the revenues of the federal government and thus do not represent as broad a coverage as given in the accounts of the consolidated public sector. In particular, we do not include nontax revenue or sales of public enterprises. Direct taxes are the corporate and personal income taxes, whereas indirect taxes are the value added, sales, and excise taxes. We thus see that the simulated aggregate tax collections are good approximations of the actual Mexican numbers.
- Expenditure represents expenditure of the federal government and therefore does not include public enterprises. In particular, the figures we have used for actual expenditure are derived as the sum of (a) federal wages; (b) federal purchases of goods and services; (c) current transfers from the federal government, not including transfer payments to state enterprises; (d) federal capital expenditure; and (e) total interest payments.[18] We have treated public enterprises in our consolidation as taxpaying private firms. We note that in 1987 we slightly underestimate expenditure, possibly because we are not attributing the full debt obligations that the government actually had as an initial stock. In 1988, in contrast, expenditure has risen above its actual value. This is largely because the simulated 1988 interest rate is higher than its actual value, causing the simulated government debt service to be higher than in reality. Accordingly, we overestimate the size of the government's budget deficit in 1988.
- The actual amount of the aggregate value of exports, in domestic currency, is underpredicted for 1987 and becomes more accurate in 1988. Recall that we generate exports from an export equation in which oil exports are exogenous in dollar terms and nonoil exports are endogenous, depending on endogenous relative domestic and foreign prices and exogenous foreign income. Simulated imports are underestimated in both years and more severely underestimated in 1988. As a

result, the domestic currency value of the simulated trade balance is overestimated in 1988. This is primarily the result of the more rapid depreciation of the simulated real exchange rate in the simulated outcome than in reality.

- The inflation and nominal interest rate movements have the correct direction of change, although the decline in inflation is overestimated. For actual values we have taken annual averages of the corresponding indexes. For inflation we use the wholesale price index, whereas for interest rates we use the treasury bill rate given in *International Financial Statistics* (various years). The simulated figures for 1987 are calibrated to the actual rates because no rate of change can be calculated in the first year. In 1988 we see that our model generates a slightly positive real interest rate, as compared with the actual negative real interest rate of 45 percent.

- The nominal exchange rate depreciates slightly less rapidly in the simulation than in reality.[19] Recall, however, that our choices for the critical level of foreign reserves as well as for the depreciation rules shown in figure 17-1 are essentially arbitrary. Actually, the Mexican government does not follow a single exchange rate rule for two years and may oppose devaluation more strongly than our rule indicates. We also show a somewhat more rapid real devaluation between the two periods than actually occurred. This is mainly a result of the simulated rate of inflation, which is higher than the actual rate.

We thus note that our model seems to generate a reasonably accurate replication of actual Mexican outcomes for 1987–88. It does not seem unreasonable, therefore, to use the behavioral structure of the model to carry out counterfactual simulations. We should note that our model may not be the most satisfactory means of predicting dynamic changes over time. Ideally, we should have a framework in which agents live for more than two periods and in which adjustment costs are explicitly modeled.

Counterfactual Simulations

In this section we will consider certain hypothetical policies.

AN INCREASE IN THE INVESTMENT TAX CREDIT. First, we simulate the effects of introducing a uniform increase in the investment tax credit for all the sectors that use capital as an input to production. Recall that agriculture uses land and rural labor as inputs, whereas imports do not use physical inputs. Accordingly, we will suppose that sectors 2–6, given in table 17-1, are each now given a 20 percent investment tax credit. All other parameters in the simulation remain unchanged from the exercise reported in table 17-2. The outcomes are given in table 17-3.

Table 17-3. Effect of 20 Percent Investment Tax Credit

Parameter	1987	1988
Nominal GDP (1,000 billion pesos)	211.1	432.6
Real GDP (1,000 billion 1980 pesos)	47.6	49.0
Government spending (1,000 billion pesos)	50.8	121.7
Revenue (1,000 billion pesos)	30.8	67.8
Government budget deficit	−20.0	−53.9
Exports (1,000 billion pesos)	22.0	57.5
Imports (1,000 billion pesos)	13.5	29.9
Trade balance (1,000 billion pesos)	8.5	27.6
Inflation rate[a]	159.8	99.3
Interest rate (percent)	148.4	114.4
Exchange rate (pesos/U.S. dollars)	1,084.9	2,531.4
Real exchange rate[b]	95.9	81.9
Change in reserves (billions of U.S. dollars)	−1.3	−4.4
Net real capital formation, 1986–88 [c]		
Manufacturing	n.a.	102.5
Petroleum	n.a.	105.0
Commerce	n.a.	101.4
Transportation	n.a.	100.1
Communications and services	n.a.	103.0

n.a. Not applicable.
GDP = Gross domestic product.
a. Rate of inflation in wholesale price index.
b. Wholesale price index divided by nominal exchange rate.
c. Index numbers based on corresponding levels of investment in table 17-2.
Source: Simulated outputs of the computer program.

We thus notice that the 20 percent investment tax credit has brought about a rise in the rate of inflation in both periods, as compared with the benchmark rates in table 17-2. This increase has been caused largely by the rise in the government budget deficit, both in nominal terms and as a percentage of GDP. Accordingly, the aggregate loss of reserves by the central bank is greater in this case than in the initial simulation. We see that the real interest rate has risen significantly in both periods in response to the increased budget deficits. Thus the effect on the real interest of increased availability of capital is more than outweighed by higher budget deficits. In addition, the real exchange rate has depreciated, leading consumers to decrease their holdings of domestic debt, as compared with the real exchange rate in table 17-2. Accordingly, the price of domestic debt falls, leading to a further increase in the real interest rate. Thus we see that there have been uniform increases in the rates of net real capital formations across sectors. These increases are somewhat less than might be expected, as the increased real interest rates tend to mitigate the positive effects of the investment incentives. Because factors are transferred from current to capital production, and our model's time horizon is not long enough to incorporate fully the effects of the increased sectoral capital, real GDP has slightly declined in both periods.

A REDUCTION IN THE CORPORATE INCOME TAX RATE. Because a 20 percent investment tax credit seems to offer some stimulus to capital formation but also seems to have certain adverse macroeconomic effects, let us now suppose that the government attempts to generate an investment increase by reducing the tax rate on capital income. We will thus suppose that the statutory tax rate on capital income is lowered from 42 percent to 35 percent. The resulting outcomes are given in table 17-4.

Table 17-4. Effect of Reduction in Capital Income Tax Rate

Parameter	1987	1988
Nominal GDP (1,000 billion pesos)	196.5	374.1
Real GDP (1,000 billion 1980 pesos)	48.0	49.7
Government spending (1,000 billion pesos)	46.7	103.8
Revenue (1,000 billion pesos)	27.3	58.6
Government budget deficit	–19.4	–45.2
Exports (1,000 billion pesos)	19.5	49.4
Imports (1,000 billion pesos)	12.5	25.9
Trade balance (1,000 billion pesos)	7.0	23.5
Inflation rate[a]	140.0	84.0
Interest rate (percent)	93.2	79.9
Exchange rate(pesos/U.S. dollars)	960.0	2,143.5
Real exchange rate[b]	108.7	96.0
Change in reserves (billions of U.S. dollars)	–1.1	–3.3
Net real capital formation, 1986–88 [c]		
Manufacturing	n.a.	104.9
Petroleum	n.a.	109.3
Commerce	n.a.	105.3
Transportation	n.a.	105.6
Communications and services	n.a.	104.4

n.a. Not applicable.
GDP = Gross domestic product.
a. Rate of inflation in wholesale price index.
b. Wholesale price index divided by nominal exchange rate.
c. Index numbers based on corresponding levels of investment in table 17-2.
Source: Simulated outputs of the computer program.

We observe that this change has had rather unexpected outcomes. In particular, we see that the rate of capital formation has increased significantly, as compared with that in table 17-3. The reasons for this outcome are straightforward. The budget deficit of the central government was 9.47 percent of GDP in 1987 and 12.46 percent of GDP in 1988 in the simulation reported in table 17-3. In table 17-4 the corresponding figures are 9.87 and 12.08 percent. Thus over the two years of the simulation, the reduction in the capital income tax rate has had approximately the same aggregate effect on the real budget deficit as did raising the investment tax credit. The reduction in the capital tax rate, in contrast, has had the effect of sharply lowering the real interest rate, unlike the situation in the previous example, when real interest rates rose. The reason for this change comes from the behavior of the real exchange rate. Here, as compared with table 17-3, there is an appreciation in the real exchange rate because the relative value of domestic capital rises in response to the capital income tax reduction, which affects the entire capital stock. Accordingly, the public increases its holdings of domestic debt, causing the price of domestic bonds to rise and the real interest rate to fall. Moreover, the incentive offered by the capital income tax cut lowers the cost of capital but does not increase the cost of borrowing, as did the investment tax credits. In addition, the tax cut brings about lower inflation rates and lower losses in foreign reserves than do the investment tax credits. Under such circumstances, tax cuts seem to be superior to investment tax credits in stimulating investment.

A CHANGE IN THE EMPLOYMENT TAX CREDIT. Finally, let us suppose that the government attempts to use employment tax credits rather than investment tax credits as a policy instrument. In particular, we will look at a program in which the 10 percent investment tax credit from the base case is maintained. The employment tax credit is raised so that the overall deficit implications are the same as in the simulation in which the investment tax credits were increased. Capital tax rates are maintained at their level of the base simulation of table 17-2. We cannot solve analytically for an employment tax credit that gives precisely the same budgetary outcome as in table 17-3. Rather, we search for employment tax credit rates that result in approximately that outcome. It turns out that a 3 percent increase in the employment tax credit—that is, an employment tax credit of 13 percent—yields the following budget-neutral outcome, given in table 17-5.

We thus observe that the new regime leads to budget deficits that are almost identical, both in nominal and in real terms, to those of table 17-3. The real outcomes of this scenario are different, however. In particular, we see that, with the exception of the transportation sector, all sectors have lower rates of capital formation in this case than in

Table 17-5. Effect of 10 Percent Investment Tax Credit and 13 Percent Employment Tax Credit

Parameter	1987	1988
Nominal GDP (1,000 billion pesos)	213.0	431.1
Real GDP (1,000 billion 1980 pesos)	48.0	48.8
Government spending (1,000 billion pesos)	51.0	121.4
Revenue (1,000 billion pesos)	30.9	67.7
Government budget deficit	−20.2	−53.7
Exports (1,000 billion pesos)	22.1	57.6
Imports (1,000 billion pesos)	13.6	29.7
Trade balance (1,000 billion pesos)	8.5	27.9
Inflation rate[a]	149.8	99.1
Interest rate (percent)	115.5	90.5
Exchange rate (pesos/U.S. dollars)	1,086.7	2,529.2
Real exchange rate[b]	104.3	89.2
Change in reserves (billions of U.S. dollars)	−1.3	−4.4
Net real capital formation, 1986–88[c]		
Manufacturing	n.a.	102.2
Petroleum	n.a.	101.0
Commerce	n.a.	100.9
Transportation	n.a.	100.5
Communications and services	n.a.	101.1

n.a. Not applicable.
GDP = Gross domestic product.
a. Rate of inflation in wholesale price index.
b. Wholesale price index divided by nominal exchange rate.
c. Index numbers based on corresponding levels of investment in table 17-2.
Source: Simulated outputs of the computer program.

table 17-3. They thus also have considerably lower rates of capital formation than in table 17-4, the simulation that incorporates reduced capital tax rates. Therefore we again conclude that a reduction in the capital income tax rate is superior in promoting investment to either employment or investment tax credits.

Summary and Conclusions

We have constructed an intertemporal general equilibrium model designed to examine certain fiscal policies that directly affect investment and employment. In particular, we have considered sectoral investment tax credits as well as uniform employment credits. The model also permits the consideration of price and consumption subsidies and can easily be extended to other policies affecting investment. Among these are accelerated depreciation allowances and immediate full expensing.

We have developed a methodology for solving the model numerically and have applied the model to Mexico. After attempting to replicate the actual outcomes of 1987 and 1988, we turned to a series of counterfactual simulations. We compared the effects of doubling the investment tax credit with the effects of an equal yield 16.7 percent decrease in the capital income tax rate. That is, the cost to the government of both policies is the same. We observed that the overall budgetary implications of the two policies are approximately equivalent. The capital income tax reduction, however, directly lowers the cost of capital, thereby reducing the real interest rate and, hence, increasing the rate of capital formation, in relation to investment tax credit increases. Accordingly, it appears in this case that capital income tax reductions are more effective in stimulating investment than are investment tax credits. This example also indicates that simply examining the budgetary implications of different investment policies is not sufficient to predict their outcomes.

Finally, we looked at the effects of a budget-neutral reduction in the employment tax credit. We found that this policy is inferior to either of the other two in promoting capital formation. We conclude that, at least in the Mexican case, a policy of reducing the capital income tax seems to be rather effective. We also noted the importance of using an intertemporal model because investment decisions are, of course, forward-looking. We observed that investment policies affect different sectors in a nonuniform way, indicating the importance of using sector-specific capital in our model.

Appendix. Corporate Structure and Investment Incentives in Mexico

The structure of corporate income taxation in Mexico has undergone major changes since early 1987. Here, we describe current tax structure, occasionally referring to the tax system in effect before 1987.

- *Corporate income tax base and rate.* The corporate income tax base is now completely indexed. Taxable profits (defined as gross receipts minus costs, business expenses, dividends corresponding to the previous period of earnings, and net losses carried forward from other periods) are subject to tax at a rate of 35 percent (a rate of 42 percent prevailed before 1987). Depreciation deductions are indexed; as an alternative, the present value of depreciation, calculated at a discount rate of 7.5 percent, may be deducted fully in all regions except major metropolitan areas and in all sectors except the automobile sector. In major metropolitan areas only 60 percent of such value can be deducted in the first year, and the remaining 40 percent is subject to capital consumption allowances.

- *Assets tax.* An assets tax at a rate of 2 percent of the average value of assets of business enterprises and creditable against their income tax liability in Mexico was levied in 1989.
- *Dividend income.* Starting in 1989, dividends were no longer deductible by the corporation distributing them, nor could they be included in the gross income of the recipient. The withholding tax on dividend distributions varies with the source (whether or not paid from accumulated earnings already taxed—the net tax profit account—or paid from untaxed other sources) and with the tax regime faced by the recipient, as shown in table 17A-1.
- *Interest income and royalties.* Beginning in 1991 the withholding tax rate on interest income became 35 percent, and the rate on payments for technical assistance, know-how, and the transfer of technology and on fees paid to nonresidents (including royalties for patents when licensed in connection with the rendering of technical assistance) became 21 percent. Payments for the use of other privileges, such as for the licensing of trademarks or trade names, or patents without the rendering of technical assistance, were taxed at 40 percent.
- *Goods in bonded warehouses.* These goods are subject to a 3 percent tax either on the value on which import duties are assessed or on the declared value, whichever is greater.
- *Profit sharing.* All businesses in Mexico are obliged to share 10 percent of their profits with employees.
- *Social security and payroll taxes.* Employers are obliged to contribute to social security coverage for workers (11 percent of workers' weekly

Table 17A-1. Tax Credits for Investment in Mexico, 1988
(percent)

Beneficiary	Zone 1: Highest national priority	Zone 2: Highest state priority	Zone 3A: Area of controlled growth	Zone 3B: Area of consolidation	Remaining zones
Priority industry					
Category 1	30	20	none	none	15
Category 2	20	15	none	none	10
Small industry	30	30	none	20	20
Micro industry	40	40	none	30	30

Source: IBFD (1988).

wages), children's nurseries (1 percent of wages), and an occupational risk fund (from 5 to 167 percent of wages). In addition, employers contribute 5 percent of wages to the National Housing Fund and 1 percent of wages in support of education.

- *Value added tax.* The general 15 percent rate of the value added tax is applicable to all transactions concluded in the border and free zones.
- *Assets tax.* An assets tax at a rate of 2 percent of the average value of total assets of business enterprises and creditable against their income tax liability in Mexico was levied in 1989.

As discussed earlier in this chapter, the tax incentive regime in Mexico has undergone significant changes over time. A summary view of the taxation of business income is given in table 17A-2 and details regarding forgone revenues due to fiscal incentives are repeated in table 17A-3 through 17A-11.

Table 17A-2.   Taxation of Business Income, Mexico, United States, and Canada, 1990–91
(percent)

Tax	Mexico (1991)	United States (1990)	Canada (1990)
Corporate income tax rate[a]	35 + 3.9 = 38.9	34 + 6 = 40	28 + 15 = 43
Withholding tax rates			
Interest	35	30	28
Dividends	0–40	30	25
Technology transfer fees	21	30	25
Royalties	40	30	25
Indexation of deductions	Full	No	No
Loss carryforward	5	15	7
Loss carrybackward	0	3	3
Minimum or alternative minimum tax	2 percent on assets	20 percent on taxable income inclusive of tax preferences	0.175 percent on capital in excess of $10 million creditable against 3 percent surtax on corporate profits
Capital gains tax			
Coverage	Full	Full	Two-thirds
Indexation	Full	No	No
Rate	35	34	28
Dividends deduction	No	Yes	Yes
Full expensing of investment	No	No	No
Investment tax credits	Regional and priority sectors	Energy investment, rehabilitation of real estate, targeted job credit	Regional, research and development

a. The profit-sharing rate in Mexico and the average provincial or state tax rates in the United States and Canada are added to the basic federal rate.

Source: Gil-Diaz (1989); IBFD (1988); Mancera Hermanos (1989); Price Waterhouse (1988, 1989); and Ugarte (1988).

Table 17A-3.   *Fiscal Incentives in Mexico, 1980–1988*
(millions of pesos)

		Fiscal incentives[a]	
Year	*Implied GDP deflator*	*Current prices*	*1980 Constant prices*
1980	100.0	22,046	22,046
1981	126.0	38,006	30,163
1982	202.8	53,753	26,505
1983	386.1	34,952	9,053
1984	614.4	37,192	6,053
1985	963.1	48,900	5,077
1986	1,679.5	109,152	6,499
1987	4,082.2	202,324	4,957
1988	6,192.7	96,257	1,554

a. Includes CEPROFIs, agreement of annual validity, and incentives for export promotion.

Source: Instituto Nacional de Estadistica, Geografía e Informatica, Secretaría de Programación y Presupuesto, Dirección General de Política de Ingresos, Secretaría de Hacienda y Crédito Público.

Table 17A-4. *Forgone Revenue Because of Fiscal Incentives, 1983–1988*
(millions of pesos)

Instrument	1983		1984		1985		1986		1987		1988	
	Pesos	*Percent*	*Pesos*	*Percent*	*Pesos*	*Percent*	*Pesos*	*Percent*	*Pesos*	*Percent*	*Pesos*	*Percent*
CEPROFIS	17,021	48.2	24,749	55.9	26,173	42.2	80,559	55.7	159,151	54.5	82,230	42.8
Agreements of annual validity	2,298	6.5	5,273	11.9	7,687	12.4	25,926	18.6	43,687	15.0	13,969	7.3
Border areas and duty free zones	4,780	13.5	6,030	13.6	17,187	27.7	25,143	18.0	75,687	26.0	50,222[a]	26.1
CEDIS	2,614	7.4	5,615	12.4	4,329	7.0	4,227	3.0	7,395	2.5	35,450	18.5
Other	8,584	24.3	2,575	5.8	6,699	10.8	3,784[b]	2.7	6,030[b]	2.0	10,257[b]	5.3
Total	35,297	100.0	44,242	100.0	62,075	100.0	139,639	100.0	291,650	100.0	192,128	100.0

a. January–June 1988.

b. Includes import tax returns to exporters (drawbacks): 2,227 million pesos in 1986, 5,689 million pesos in 1987, and 10,257 million pesos in 1988.

Source: Unpublished data from Secretaría de Hacienda y Crédito Público.

Table 17A-5. Forgone Revenues Because of Investment Tax Credits (CEPROFIs), 1986–88
(millions of pesos)

Industry	1986		1987		1988	
	Pesos	Percent	Pesos	Percent	Pesos	Percent
Investment and employment	44,618	55.8	99,397	62.8	14,391	17.5
Priority industries	35,662	44.6	81,564	51.5	9,611	11.7
Small industries	1,520	1.9	4,348	2.8	1,870	2.3
Microindustries	157	0.2	440	0.3	168	0.2
National machinery and equipment	6,715	8.4	12,246	7.7	2,665	3.2
Employment generation	604	0.7	799	0.5	77	0.1
Mining and metallurgy	8,353	10.5	22,999	14.5	4,340	5.3
Basic products (milk)	3,133	3.9	6,440	4.1	9,938	12.1
Industrial development	94	0.1	1,510	1.0	80	0.1
Technology development	368	0.5	258	0.1	..	..
Merchant fleet	17,437	21.8	13,547	8.6	1,492	1.8
Other	5,917	7.4	14,163	8.9	51,989	63.2
Total	79,920	100.0	158,284	100.0	82,250	100.0

.. Negligible.
Source: Secretaría de Hacienda y Crédito Público.

Table 17A-6. Forgone Revenue Because of Investment Tax Credits by Sector Activity, Mexico, 1979–88
(millions of pesos)

Industry	1979	1980	1981	1982	1983	1984	1985	1986	1987	1988
Agriculture and forestry	1	8	18	776	1,736	676	1,705	4,273	10,028	31,468
Minerals	3	24	591	2,504	1,104	845	1,264	9,790	26,587	4,781
Manufacturing industries	23	3,368	10,401	13,454	10,845	18,266	21,485	47,702	96,958	20,344
Construction	2	22	548	82	124	34	34	1,845	10,546	20,716
Electricity	..	..	33	106	36	147	404	158	2,711	12
Commerce and hotels	n.r.	3	159	1,243	1,006	1,015	19	16	344	2,101
Transport and communications	66	174	829	1,634	619	2,781	2,056	16,225	9,596	855
Finance and real estate	n.r.	n.r.	34	183	21	3	3	5	212	279
Community services	6	223	324	1,656	1,263	981	129	520	1,111	813
Total	101	3,822	12,937	21,638	16,754	24,748	27,099	80,534	158,093	81,369

.. Negligible.
Source: Dirección General de Política de Ingresos; Secretaría de Hacienda y Crédito Público.

Table 17A-7. *Forgone Revenues by Investment Tax Credits by Manufacturing Industry, Mexico, 1979–88*

	1979	1980	1981	1982	1983	1984	1985	1986	1987	1988
Food, drinks, and tobacco	1	402	583	1,597	1,124	1,448	1,337	2,673	6,830	3,043
Textiles	5	218	445	700	366	450	285	1,156	4,280	765
Wood and wood products	1	64	203	262	105	99	234	321	565	736
Paper and paper products	..	123	215	560	345	547	809	1,598	3,439	7,151
Chemicals and petroleum derivatives	5	165	1,521	2,365	1,235	1,768	2,270	3,627	11,025	4,669
Production of nonmetallic minerals	6	1,804	2,666	2,169	1,250	1,557	3,449	5,895	11,254	1,182
Basic metals	1	308	3,556	3,203	4,103	8,055	9,298	24,441	47,572	785
Metallic products, machinery and equipment	4	278	1,198	2,565	2,269	4,286	3,759	7,933	11,793	1,587
Other industries	..	6	14	33	48	56	44	58	200	426
Total	23	3,368	10,401	13,454	10,845	18,266	21,485	47,702	96,958	20,344

.. Negligible.
Source: Dirección General de Política de Ingresos; Secretaría de Hacienda y Crédito Público, May 16, 1989.

Table 17A-8. *Forgone Revenue Because of Fiscal Incentives to Border Areas and Duty-Free Zones, 1983–1988*
(millions of pesos)

Instrument	1983		1984		1985		1986		1987		1988	
	Pesos	Percent	Pesos	Percent	Pesos	Percent	Pesos	Percent	Pesos	Percent	Pesos	Percent
Tax exemption for importation of basic and semi-basic products[a]	4,337	90.7	5,582	92.5	15,986	93.1	23,829	96.5	72,289	99.8	50,222[b]	99.9
Commercial centers	131	2.7	167	2.8	267	1.6	—	—	161	0.2	58	0.1
Industrial promotion	169	3.3	285	4.7	925	5.4	872	3.5	—	—	—	—
Other	153	3.2	—	—	—	—	—	—	—	—	—	—
Total	4,780	100.0	6,034	100.0	17,178	100.0	24,701	100.0	72,450	100.0	150,280	100.0

— Not available.

a. Main goods are chicken, cheese, butter, used tires and furniture, lard, domestic appliances, canned fruit and vegetables, auto parts, flour products, and clothing.

b. January–June 1988.

Source: Unpublished data from Secretaría de Hacienda y Crédito Público.

Table 17A-9. *Forgone Revenue Because of Agreements of Annual Validity, 1983–88*
(millions of pesos)

	1983		1984		1985		1986		1987		1988	
Instrument	Pesos	Percent	Pesos	Percent	Pesos	Percent	Pesos	Percent	Pesos	Percent	Pesos	Percent
Production of cars and components	46	2.0	1,310	24.8	1,420	18.5	n.a.	n.a.	n.a.	n.a.	n.a.	n.a.
Components	n.a.	n.a.	369	7.0	0	0.0	n.a.	n.a.	n.a.	n.a.	n.a.	n.a.
Final imports	n.a.	n.a.	0	0.0	0	0.0	n.a.	n.a.	n.a.	n.a.	n.a.	n.a.
Final assembly	n.a.	n.a.	941	17.8	1,420	18.5	n.a.	n.a.	n.a.	n.a.	n.a.	n.a.
Imports of primary materials, parts and semimanufactured goods	839	36.5	1,781	33.8	4,146	53.9	13,604	62.8	37,027	92.9	924	12.0
Other	1,413	61.5	2,182	41.4	2,121	27.6	8,048	37.2	2,846	7.1	6,804	88.0
Bottled soft drinks	0	0.0	0	0.0	0	0.0	8,000	37.0	2,739	6.8	6,804	88.0
Flowers for export	0	0.0	0	0.0	0	0.0	48	0.2	107	0.3	n.a.	n.a.
Total	2,298	100.0	5,273	100.0	7,687	100.0	21,652	100.0	39,873	100.0	7,728	100.0

n.a. Not applicable.
Source: Secretaría de Hacienda y Crédito Público.

Table 17A-10. *Forgone Revenue Because of Fiscal Incentives to Support Export Sector, 1983–88*
(millions of pesos)

Instrument	1983 Pesos	1983 Percent	1984 Pesos	1984 Percent	1985 Pesos	1985 Percent	1986 Pesos	1986 Percent	1987 Pesos	1987 Percent	1988 Pesos	1988 Percent
Manufacturing	1,090	41.7	449	8.0	943	15.4	n.a.	n.a.	n.a.	n.a.	n.a.	n.a.
Trading companies	1,323	50.6	4,888	87.1	3,386	55.3	3,154	48.9	158	1.2	n.a.	n.a.
Technology and services[a]	201	7.7	278	4.9	1,122	18.3	1,073	16.6	7,237	55.3	35,450	77.6
Import tax return to exporters (drawbacks)	0	0.0	0	0.0	671	11.0	2,227	34.5	5,689	43.5	10,257	22.4
Total	2,614	100.0	5,615	100.0	6,122	100.0	6,454	100.0	13,084	100.0	45,707	100.0

n.a. Not applicable.

a. Mainly construction materials and services.

Source: Secretaría de Hacienda y Crédito Público.

Table 17A-11. Distribution of Fiscal Incentives by Economic Zone, 1986–88
(millions of current pesos)

	1986		1987		1988	
Economic zone	Pesos	Percent	Pesos	Percent	Pesos	Percent
Priority areas	37,987	48.5	93,664	63.6	11,412	74.4
Controlled areas	26,590	33.9	27,083	18.4	919	6.0
Rest of country	13,818	17.6	26,490	18.0	2,993	19.6
Total	78,395	100.0	147,237	100.0	15,314	100.0

Source: Secretaría de Hacienda y Crédito Público.

Notes

1. The use of neoclassical value added functions "sitting above" an input-output matrix is common. The reader may wish to see Shoven and Whalley (1984) for articles in which this approach is used. An application and detailed description of functional forms are given in Feltenstein (1986).

2. A computer program that permits the user to aggregate particular rows and columns arbitrarily is available on request from A. Feltenstein.

3. The interpretation of these taxes is thus as a profit tax and a personal income tax that is withheld at the source.

4. This assumption permits us to avoid problems of corner solutions, that is, solutions in which a good is either entirely domestically produced or entirely imported.

5. We assume that all foreign borrowing for investment is carried out by the government; implicitly, then, the government is borrowing for the private investor, but the debt thereby incurred is publicly guaranteed. In regard to Mexico, this may be viewed as the situation existing after the financial collapse.

6. This may be interpreted as an accelerated depreciation allowance because the firm is permitted to take the allowance in the current period, although the capital does not come on line until the next period.

7. This formulation of the investment tax credit is adapted from Auerbach and Hines (1988).

8. Current spending may, by its effect on wages, the availability of capital, and the interest rate, indirectly have considerable effect on private output. Feltenstein and Morris (1990) and Shah (1992) examine the effect on private output of spending on public infrastructure.

9. The assumption of equal relative spending on different goods by both urban and rural consumers is probably inaccurate. There is, however, insufficient data for us to estimate individual demand functions.

10. The exogenous savings rate is imposed so that there will be a demand by consumers for bonds in the final period. Otherwise, all outstanding debt would have to be paid off and, in particular, the entire stock of public debt would have to be liquidated.

11. Consumption weights for domestic goods are derived from NIS (1983, table 1); the weights for imports came from NIS (1983, table 5).

12. These shares are derived from Sistema de Cuentas Consolidades de la Nación (1985), table 69, where we have used 1982 shares in exports.

13. Thus in estimation we treat the relative price index as being exogenous, although in the general equilibrium model it is an endogenous variable.

14. A uniform increase in the price level cannot have an effect on excess demand (as would be the case if $a = 1$) if we are to demonstrate the existence of an equilibrium.

15. This substitution was made because interest rates were controlled for much of our sample period and, hence, do not reflect true opportunity costs. Our general equilibrium model, however, uses r.

16. See, for example, Obstefeld (1984) or Krugman (1979).

17. The estimations of the tax and tariff rates are derived from recent work carried out by the World Bank in Mexico.

18. We do not include transfer payments to state enterprises because in our simulations we treat state enterprises as part of the private sector. They are thus profit-maximizing enterprises and do not receive transfers.

19. We are using the average exchange rates for $Q1$ 1987 and $Q1$ 1988 to represent actual nominal exchange rates.

References

Auerbach, Alan J., and James R. Hines. 1988. "Investment Tax Incentives and Frequent Tax Reforms." *American Economic Review* 78, papers and proceedings (May): 211–17.

Feltenstein, Andrew. 1986. "An Intertemporal General Equilibrium Analysis of Financial Crowding Out: A Policy Model and An Application to Australia." *Journal of Public Economics* 31:79–104.

Feltenstein, Andrew, and Stephen Morris. 1990. "Fiscal Stabilization and Exchange Rate Instability." *Journal of Public Economics* 42:329–56.

Gil-Diaz, Francisco. 1989. "Mexico's Protracted Tax Reform." World Bank, Country Economics Department, Washington, D.C.

IBFD (International Bureau of Fiscal Documentation). 1988. Supplement 71 (June). Washington, D.C.

Krugman, P. 1979. "A Model of Balance-of-Payments Crisis." *Journal of Money, Credit, and Banking* 11:311–25.

Mancera Hermanos y Cia., S.C. 1989. Circular a Clientes. (Tax Brief.) Mexico, D.F.

NIS (National Institute of Statistics). 1983. *Matriz de Insumo-Producto Anno 1978*. Mexico.

Obstefeld, Maurice. 1984. "Balance-of-Payments Crises and Devaluation." *Journal of Money, Credit, and Banking* 16:208–17.

Price Waterhouse. 1988. *Corporate Taxes: A Worldwide Summary*. New York.

Shah, Anwar. 1992. "Dynamics of Public Infrastructure and Private Sector Productivity and Profitability." *Review of Economics and Statistics* (February): 28–36.

Shoven, J. B., and J. Whalley. 1984. "Applied General Equilibrium Models of Taxation and Intentional Trade." *Journal of Economic Literature* (September).

Sistema de Cuentas Consolidades de la Nacion. 1985. Mexico City.

Ugarte, Fernando Sanchez. 1988. "Taxation of Foreign Investment in Mexico: The North American Perspective." International Economics Program Working Paper DP88-7. University of Toronto, Canada.

Zedillo, Ernesto. 1986. "Capital Flight: Some Observations on the Mexican Case." Paper presented at the Conference on Capital Flight and Third World Debt, Institute for International Economics, Washington, D.C.

18

MODELING THE GENERAL EQUILIBRIUM EFFECTS OF INVESTMENT INCENTIVES: THE PHILIPPINE CASE

Ramon L. Clarete

INVESTMENT INCENTIVES PLAY an important role in the industrialization strategies of developing countries. These incentives typically consist of duty and tax exemptions on imported capital equipment, tax holidays, depreciation and investment allowances, and similar measures. Although they are not part of the regular budgetary outlays of the government, nevertheless the duties and taxes forgone in granting such incentives have opportunity costs. It is interesting to find out from a policy perspective if such costs outweigh the marginal benefits of the additional capital employed as a result of these fiscal incentives.

A related policy issue concerns the rationing of such investment incentives through such schemes as prioritizing the various sectors in the economy with respect to their strategic importance in the country's overall industrialization goal. Such discriminatory schemes for allocating these tax incentives are significant in explaining the way different countries allocate investment resources and thus the direction of their economic development.

In this chapter, I analyze these policy issues using an applied dynamic general equilibrium model of the Philippine economy. I focus on the duty drawbacks and tax rebates on imported capital equipment.

None of the existing empirical work on Philippine investment incentives has included analyses of their effects in a general equilibrium setting. Gregorio (1979) computed the effects of these incentives on the protection enjoyed by Philippine industries. Using a partial equilibrium model, Manasan (1986) calculated their effects on the rates of return of industry and on factor prices and use. Sicat (1967, 1968) and Hooley and Sicat (1967) argued that the country's investment incentives were inadequate to absorb the growing labor force because of savings constraints, complicated administrative procedures, and fairly regulated investment policy in the country. Authors of other studies on incentives in the Philippines did not attempt to analyze these measures quantitatively (for example, de Leon 1981; Manasan 1988).

Using 1989 as a benchmark, I designed a dynamic applied general equilibrium model of the Philippines consisting of twelve sectors. Developing a new model was necessary because existing applied general equilibrium models of the Philippine economy are mostly static in nature (Bautista 1987; Clarete 1991; Clarete and Roumasset 1987; and Habito 1984). The existing multiperiod general equilibrium models of the Philippine economy (Gaspay and Gotsch 1992; Go 1988) are designed to analyze policy measures other than fiscal investment incentives.

In the next section, I give an overview of the general equilibrium model used in the study. Then I discuss how investments and savings are incorporated into the general equilibrium model. I follow this discussion with a review of the current investment incentives in the Philippines. After describing the empirical data that were used to calibrate the Philippine model and the data on fiscal investment measures, I present the empirical results of the study. The last section consists of a summary of the main findings.

Overview of the Basic Model

The general equilibrium model used in this study is for a small open economy. It consists of twelve production sectors, each of which produces an import substitute (O) and an exported good (E). The respective production technologies in these sectors are each represented with a constant elasticity transformation (CET) function between the import substitute and the exported good (see figure 18-1).

Three primary factors are used in every production sector: labor (L), capital (K), and a sector-specific factor (F). Labor and capital are perfectly mobile in the model. The sector-specific factor consists largely of fixed capital inputs in production. The three factors are combined through use of a constant elasticity-of-substitution (CES) function to generate the value added of the sector (V).

Intermediate inputs (C_i) are used in fixed proportion to total production of the sector. The individual commodities used as intermediate inputs are first aggregated through use of a Leontief function to produce a composite intermediate input (A). This composite intermediate input is then combined with the value added (V) in that sector to produce the joint output of the sector. A Leontief function is used in aggregating the value added and the composite intermediate input.

The individual intermediate input used in production is an Armington-aggregated good. From a modeling point of view, it is convenient to form twelve additional production sectors. Each of these Armington

Figure 18-1. Production Technology Structure

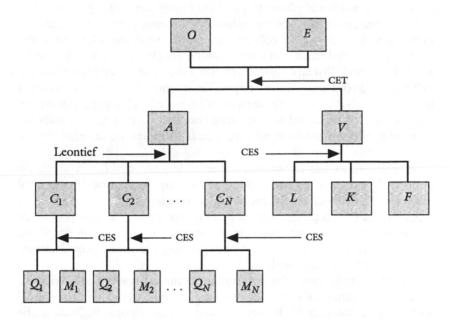

Source: Author's calculations.

sectors generates a composite product made up of an imported good (*M*) and its local substitute (*Q*). These Armington goods are in turn purchased for intermediate and final uses. Given this structure of production activities, locally produced goods are thus used only as inputs in the Armington sectors and for exports. All the other product demands in the model are satisfied with Armington composite goods.

The country is a price-taking economy in both imports and exports. The modeling problem associated with small open-economy models, wherein those relatively inefficient sectors in excess of the number of primary factors are shut down in a counterfactual equilibrium, does not arise in the model for two reasons.

One reason is the inclusion of sector-specific factors in the model, which then ensure that there are at least as many nontradable factors as there are sectors in the model. Another reason is that it is assumed that local and imported goods are less than perfectly substitutable.

There is only one aggregate consumer in the model where income is generated from the endowment of primary factors used in production. The income is allocated between current and future consumption.

Current consumption in turn consists of the twelve Armington-composite goods, whereas future consumption is made up of the various investment goods the consumer is willing to purchase in any given time period.

The government imposes the following domestic indirect tax measures in the model: an excise tax collected at the manufacturer's level or at the border on selected items and a value added tax (VAT) that is collected by a credit method. Primary agriculture and exports are exempted from the VAT system. From a modeling perspective, it would have been convenient to treat the VAT as a simple tax on value added. This paper, however, retains the credit method of collecting the VAT, consisting of a sales tax and tax credits on the intermediate inputs. Imports are covered by the VAT.

In addition to the excise and value added taxes, there is a tax on imports, based on the border price of the imported good in the local currency. The model also includes the corporate income tax. This tax is featured as a tax on profits in each production sector. Because profits are the imputed earnings on fixed or sector-specific factors, the corporate income tax is therefore important in explaining the investment decisions made by agents in the model.

Out of its tax income, the government demands goods and services to produce government services. These demands are embodied in the model with a utility function of the government, whose arguments include the consumption and investment demands of the government sector. Investment demands of the government are assumed to be applied only in the services sector of the model. Corporations that are owned and operated by the government but operate in the other sectors of the model are not central and are excluded in the model.

The model is calibrated to Philippine economic data for the year 1989. The substitution elasticities that underlie the calibration process are all assumed to be equal to one. The applied general equilibrium model of the Philippine economy is solved using the mathematical programming system for general equilibrium analysis (MPS/GE), developed by Rutherford (1990).

Capital Formation and Savings in the Model

The standard analysis of the effects of investment incentives applies the concept of the *user cost of capital* (Auerbach 1983; Jorgenson 1963), defined as the shadow price of capital to which investors will equate the value of the marginal product of capital. This incorporates the cost of credit and the economic depreciation rate, net of the present value of investment incentives.

The amount of investment a firm wants to make (or equivalently the level of incremental capital stock a firm wants to employ in production in period s) is obtained from solving the following optimization problem:

(18-1) $\displaystyle \max_{K_s} V_s = \sum_{t=s}^{L} \left\{ \frac{(1-\tau_s)\,\pi_t}{(1+i)^t} - p_s^K(1-\Gamma_s)\,K_s \left[1 + \frac{\delta}{(1+i)^t} \right] \right\}$

where V_s is the net present value of the gross investments in time period s; K_s is equal to capital investments made in period s; δK_s is the depreciation cost per period; π_t is the payment for services rendered by the capital stock in production in period t; τ_s is the corporate income tax rate; Γ_s is the value in period s of fiscal investment incentives; i is the opportunity cost of money used to discount future to present value terms; and p_s^K is the price of the capital asset in period s.

If the firm is in short-run equilibrium in period s and expects π_t, which incorporates the optimal mix of the variable factors of production, to persist to perpetuity at its level in period s, then the optimization problem can be expressed as

(18-2) $\displaystyle \max_{K_s} V_s = \frac{(1-\tau_s)\,\pi_s}{i} - p_s^K(1-\Gamma_s)\,K_s \left(1 + \frac{\delta}{i} \right)$

as L, the life of the capital asset, in equation 18-1 goes to infinity. The first-order condition of the optimization problem (after dropping the subscript s, denoting the contemporaneous period when the investment decision is made) is given by

(18-3) $\displaystyle (1-\tau)\frac{\partial \pi}{\partial K} = p_s^K(1-\Gamma)(i+\delta).$

This can be expressed in a form that portrays the concept of the user cost of capital:

(18-4) $\displaystyle \frac{\partial Q(K;M)}{\partial K} = \frac{(i+\delta)\,p^K(1-\Gamma)}{p^Q(1-\tau)}.$

$Q(K;M)$ is the production function of the firm in which all variable inputs represented by the vector, M, are optimally combined; p^Q is the producer price of Q. The right-hand side of equation 18-4 is the user cost of capital, which consists of the marginal cost of producing the capital good, p^K; the corporate income tax rate, τ; the investment incentives, Γ; and the cost of funds, i.

The present value of the fiscal investment incentives, Γ, lowers the user cost of capital, c, and accordingly increases the desired level of capital stock. Because the rate of depreciation and the capital stock in the preceding period are known, the desired level of capital stock obtained from this optimization problem also tells how much investment the firm is willing to make in period s.[1]

Corporate income tax rates and fiscal incentives are, in general, sector-specific, and accordingly the user cost of capital to sector j is

$$(18\text{-}5) \qquad c_j = (i+\delta) p^K \left[1 + \frac{(\tau_j - \Gamma_j)}{(1-\tau_j)} \right]$$

where

$$\frac{\partial c_j}{\partial i} > 0; \quad \frac{\partial c_j}{\partial \delta} > 0; \quad \frac{\partial c_j}{\partial \Gamma_j} < 0; \quad \frac{\partial c_j}{\partial p^K} > 0; \quad \text{and} \quad \frac{\partial c_j}{\partial \tau_j} > 0.$$

It is interesting to note that the user cost of capital is positively related to the difference between the corporate tax rate and the value of the investment incentives. One can therefore reduce the cost of capital by reducing the rate of the corporate tax rather than by increasing the investment incentives rate.

If Γ consists of a duty drawback on imported capital equipment, then the user cost of capital is lower, the higher the tariff protection is on imported capital:

$$(18\text{-}6) \qquad c_j = (i+\delta) p^K \left[1 + \frac{\left(\tau_j - \frac{t_j}{(1+t_j)} \right)}{(1-\tau_j)} \right].$$

Production of Capital Good

There is one homogeneous supply of a capital good that is produced locally using the following production function:

$$(18\text{-}7) \qquad I = \underset{i=1}{\overset{S}{\underset{N}{\text{Min}}}} \left[\left(\sum_{s=1}^{2} \alpha_{Is} A_{siI}^{\rho_I} \right)^{\frac{1}{\rho_I}} \right]$$

which transforms producer goods into the homogeneous capital good in fixed proportions. The producer goods are either locally produced ($s = 1$) or imported ($s = 2$). The two are combined in a production function of the constant elasticity of substitution to produce a composite producer good that then becomes an input into the Leontief production function for the capital good.

Allocation of New Capital Goods

The total supply of variable and fixed (sector-specific) capital in the economy is updated at the end of every time period with the new capital good produced in that time period. But this additional supply of capital becomes productive only in the next time period. Hansen and Koopmans (1972) modeled the economy as consisting of sectors that use old vintage capital, both of which produce the identical producer good. Those sectors with the old vintage capital are stuck with the amount of fixed capital that they have until their sector-specific capital is completely depreciated. The sectors with new vintage capital update their supply of capital in every time period with the new capital goods that are produced in that period. Also, the new vintage capital is mobile between sectors.

Therefore the new capital that is produced in every time period is used either as sector-specific or as variable capital. But rather than introducing old and new vintage capital production sectors, which increases the dimension of the model considerably,[2] we use the following way of allocating the supply of new capital goods (see also figure 18-2):

$$(18-8) \qquad T_K \, (F_i^S, K^S, -K) = 0 \qquad\qquad i = 1, 2, \ldots, N.$$

The rationale is that a part of the total supply of the capital goods produced in a given time period is truly variable. Structures (buildings, office spaces), for example, can be used by any production sector in the economy. Other capital goods become part of the economy's fixed capital formation that is specific to the sector.

Figure 18-2. Allocation of New Capital Good Production

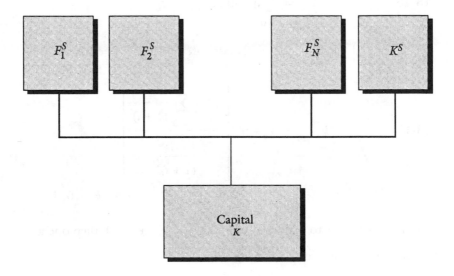

Source: Author's calculations.

Savings

The aggregate consumer in the model is assumed to maximize the following intertemporal utility function:

$$(18\text{-}9) \qquad \qquad \text{Max } U(\bar{C}_t, \bar{C}_{t+1})$$

subject to

$$\sum_i \bar{p}_{it}^C \, \bar{C}_{hit} + \left(\frac{\bar{p}_{i(t+1)}^{*C} \, \bar{C}_{h(t+1)}}{1+i} \right) = \Upsilon_{ht}^d$$

where $\bar{C}$ denotes the vector of current or future consumption; p^{*C} is the vector of expected future prices of these goods; and Υ^d is the household's disposable income.

We can break this utility maximization problem down into two problems: one of allocating disposable income between savings and current consumption, and one of allocating savings and current consumption into their component consumption and investment demands.

Suppose the utility function of the consumer can be represented by a Stone-Geary utility function for the consumer. Let η^k be the marginal propensity to consume out of period $t + k$ and let ε_k be the subsistence consumption.

$$(18\text{-}10) \qquad \qquad U_h = \sum_{k=0}^{1} \eta_k \ln(\bar{C}_{t+k} - \varepsilon_k).$$

The demand functions for goods associated with this function are:

$$(18\text{-}11) \qquad \bar{C}_{(t+k)} = \varepsilon_k + \eta_k \left[\frac{\Upsilon_t^d - \sum_{s=0}^{1} \dfrac{\bar{P}_{t+s}\, \varepsilon_s}{(1+i)^s}}{\dfrac{\bar{P}_{t+k}}{(1+i)^k}} \right]$$

$$k = 0, 1$$

If we restrict the η's to add up to one and $\sum_{s=0}^{1} p_{t+s}\, \varepsilon_s = 0$, then one gets the familiar consumption and savings functions:

(18-12)
$$C_t = \bar{P}_t \varepsilon + \eta \Upsilon_t^d$$
$$S_t = -\bar{P}_t \varepsilon + (1 - \eta) \Upsilon_t^d.$$

The price expectation assumption implied in this derivation is myopic.

Fiscal Investment Incentives and Model Calibration

The structure of Philippine investment incentives has undergone several revisions, the latest being the issuance of executive order 226, also known as the Omnibus Investments Code of 1987. Before this, several pieces of legislation were promulgated, modifying these fiscal measures, which originated with the Investments Incentives Act in 1967. The incentives provided for in this code are administered by the Board of Investments (BOI) and the Export Processing Zone Authority.

The 1987 Investments Code is a consolidation of the various incentives and privileges already in place and provides new measures, including incentives to enterprises located in less-developed areas, privileges granted to holders of the Special Investor Resident Visa, and incentives granted to regional headquarters and regional warehouses located in the Philippines and to firms located in the export processing zone. Two of the important additions are the income tax holiday for enterprises engaged in a preferred area of investments and the provision of a labor expenses allowance for tax deduction purposes. The tax holiday measure was introduced to make the structure of the country's investment incentives comparable with those in other countries of the Association of Southeast Asian Nations (ASEAN).

Following Manasan (1988), the country's prevailing incentives may be broken down into three categories: tax exemptions, deductions, and credits. The *tax exemptions* include the income tax holiday, tax and duty exemptions on imported capital equipment and spare parts, and tax and duty exemptions on imported raw materials used to produce export products. The *tax deduction* measures include an investment allowance equal to 100 percent of the infrastructure investments undertaken by eligible firms in preferred areas and where the infrastructure service system is inadequate, and a wage expense allowance equal to 50 percent of the expense. In order to avail itself of the latter, the registered firm has to meet the prescribed capital labor ratio. If the firm is located in less- developed areas, the wage expense allowance can go up to 100 percent of the labor cost. The *tax credits* are for tax and duties on raw materials and domestic capital equipment and spare parts, had these items been imported. The raw materials are limited to those used for producing export products.

The firms that are eligible to receive the above incentive measures are classified into pioneer and nonpioneer industries. Additional special treatment is provided to the former because these firms are in sectors declared by the government to be critical in promoting the country's industrialization and export enhancement programs. Thus nonpioneer firms receive income tax holiday privileges for a period of four years from commercial operation in contrast to six years for pioneer firms. In several cases this period may be extended up to eight years, but the pioneer firm must have met the local content provision and the prescribed capital-to-labor ratio and have earned a net foreign exchange income amounting to at least $500,000 annually in the first three years of operation.

Machinery and capital equipment that are imported by eligible firms are exempted from customs duties and applicable internal taxes. This privilege is available within five years from the time the code becomes effective. A similar benefit applies to the stock and genetic materials imported by agricultural producers within ten years from the start of commercial operation and to raw materials and intermediate inputs used in producing export products.

Investment allowances for tax deductions are provided for up to 100 percent of the cost of major infrastructure and public utility investments needed by the firm in areas where such infrastructure facilities and public utilities are not available. If the total cost of the investments is not deducted in the year that they are undertaken, the remaining balance can be deducted in subsequent tax periods. This incentive is intended to help disperse industries to less-developed areas of the country. Firms that locate in these areas are also accorded pioneer status.

Unlike other countries, the Philippines grants no additional investment allowances for purposes of tax deduction. The government also does not provide depreciation allowances.

Eligible firms can deduct up to 50 percent of their direct labor expenses if they meet the prescribed ratio of capital equipment to the number of workers. The benefit is available within five years from registration of eligible firms. The purpose of this incentive is to offset in part the capital-intensive bias of previous investment measures and to increase the labor absorption of eligible firms.

Tax credits of up to 100 percent of the expenses for purchasing domestic capital equipment and accompanying spare parts are provided within five years from the effective date of the code. Agricultural producers are provided a similar benefit for a period of ten years in their purchases of domestic breeding stock and genetic materials.

Because taxes and duties are also waived for imported capital equipment, spare parts, breeding stock, and genetic materials, these inputs are practically exempted from all applicable indirect taxes within five years from the effective date of the code. There are, of course, five extra years of benefit accruing to agricultural producers for breeding stock and genetic materials.

Credits are also provided for taxes and duties paid on imported raw materials and intermediate inputs used in the manufacture of export products. As in the case of capital equipment, spare parts, breeding stock, and genetic materials, raw materials and intermediate inputs used in the manufacture of export products are practically exempted from applicable indirect taxes.

Other privileges include access to bonded manufacturing and trading warehouse systems and exemption from wharfage duties and any export tax, duty, impost and fees, and contractor taxes. These privileges are available to exporters, who are also entitled to tax- and duty-free importation of spare parts. Nonexporting eligible firms are allowed tax and duty exemptions on imported spare parts accompanying imported capital equipment. Exporting firms are also exempted from local taxes and licenses and from real taxes on production equipment and machinery not attached to the real estate.

Nonfiscal incentives are also provided to investors. These measures include the simplification of custom procedures; unrestricted use of consigned equipment; employment of foreign nationals in supervisory, technical, and advisory positions within a period of five years from the date of registration; and preferential rates for publicly provided water and electricity.

The current investment incentive code does not offer any depreciation allowances, investment allowances other than for infrastructure investments, or interest cost allowances for tax deduction purposes. Accelerated depreciation allowances used to be a major feature in the country's code of investment incentives, but in 1981 they were withdrawn from the list of incentives available to investors.

Previous Investment Incentives

Before the current legislation on incentives, four related laws were passed by the Philippine government to encourage investments. The first investment incentives legislation, known as the Investment Incentives Act (RA 5186), was passed in 1967. This was followed by RA 6135, or the Export Incentives Act, which was enacted in 1970 to encourage investments in export-producing sectors. Presidential decree (PD) 1789, also known as the Omnibus Investments Code of 1981, was issued by President Ferdinand Marcos in that year to consolidate the provisions contained in the two previous pieces of investment legislation. Batas Pambansa (BP) 391 was passed into law in 1983 to simplify the existing Omnibus Investments Code of 1981.[3] Executive order 226 is the 1987 Omnibus Investments Code.

The country's list of incentive measures had been changed through time to one with fewer fiscal measures. Although this list has been simplified, the latest modification in 1987 introduced a new measure—the income tax holiday. This recent measure was intended to make the country's list as competitive as those in the other ASEAN countries.

There are important differences in treatment between pioneer and nonpioneer firms and between export and nonexporting firms. For example, under the tax exemption or deferment measures, PD 1789 granted full exemption to pioneer firms and only half to nonpioneer firms. BP 391 granted full exemption to exporting firms, both pioneer and nonpioneer, full deferment to exporting pioneer firms, and half deferment to nonexporting nonpioneer firms. In the case of the measure providing tax and duty credits on imported capital equipment and spare parts, BP 391 granted full credit to exporting firms, full credit but repayable to nonexporting pioneer firms, and half credit but repayable to nonexporting nonpioneer firms. This is in contrast to exporting firms, which received nonrepayable full tax credit under the same law. In the case of tax credit on net value earned, BP 391 granted 10 percent tax credit on net value earned to pioneer firms and 5 percent to nonpioneer firms, regardless of whether they were exporting or not.

Tariff-Related Incentives

Trade-related incentives are important measures in the current set of investment incentives. These measures are in the form of duty exemptions and tax rebates. The government agencies in charge of supervising and granting these measures vary by the kind of incentive measures. They include the BOI, the Export Processing Zone Authority, and the Philippine Veterans Investment Development Corporation. In order to avail themselves of these incentives, the firms must register with the government agency concerned. For duty exemptions, they then have to show their certificate of eligibility to the Bureau of Customs; for duty drawbacks, they have to supply additional documents and other papers that show how much tax credit they are going to get from the government.

Assessment Studies

Early studies (1960s, 1970s) on the country's investment incentive measures are placed in the context of the then-going debate between the economic nationalists and those who recognize the importance of foreign investments to spur economic growth and employment in the country. Sicat (1967) regards the country's pioneering investment incentives law passed in 1967 as a workable compromise between economic nationalism and the recognition that foreign enterprises add to economic progress.

One gets the impression from reading the study that the country's incentive measures are mainly offered to foreign investors. In the same study, Sicat explains that the flow of foreign investments into the country would depend on the government's definition of "pioneer areas." He stresses the need to widen the scope of this definition to enlarge the participation of foreign investors. He refers to the rules on foreign investments as too restrictive, making the investment climate less attractive to them and resulting in a slower rate of economic growth and labor force absorption. Sicat also criticizes the complicated procedure of monitoring and supervising the granting of such incentives.

In 1968 Sicat again picked up the debate on the merits of offering investment incentives to foreigners (Sicat 1968). In this paper, he outlines a few arguments in favor not only of offering the existing set of measures to foreigners but also of liberalizing such measures. He encapsulates the arguments in propositions on the following issues: how to fill the gap in domestic savings and investments and how to complement technology transfers, employment generation, competition enhancement that increases efficiency, and economic interlinkages among various sectors. Sicat notes that foreign investments (mostly American) are engaged in mining, public utilities, trade, agriculture, and import-substituting manufacturing, which have enjoyed high rates of profit as a result of trade protection. He further notes that the amount of foreign investments that responded to the 1967 legislation was not sufficient to absorb the growing labor force of the economy. He suggests that the law must be modified further to attract more foreign investments.

Hooley and Sicat (1967) argue that the investment incentives will not necessarily alter the aggregate level of investments if there is a binding constraint on the level of domestic savings. What these measures will accomplish is the reallocation of existing savings into areas with higher rates of return, which these incentives induce.[4]

The quantitative links between the package of investment incentive measures and the rates of return were estimated by Gregorio (1979). In this study, she computed the internal rates of return and the user cost of capital in the presence of the investment incentive measures. She found that the rate of return was increased by 2 percentage points as a result of accelerated depreciation, 2 percentage points as a result of tax exemption on imported capital equipment, 3 percentage points as a result of the expansion of reinvestment allowance, and 4 percentage points as a result of additional deduction of direct labor and the cost of local raw materials. The user cost of capital was reduced by 14 percentage points because of accelerated depreciation, 15 percentage points because of tax exemption on imported capital equipment, 10 percentage points because of tax credit for withholding tax on interest on foreign loans, 19.7 percentage points for reinvestment allowances, and 3.5 percentage points for labor training allowances, and 18.4 percentage points because of labor expense allowance.

The above quantitative effects indicate that the incentives, if firms avail themselves of them, will indeed affect the level or allocation of investment resources in the Philippines. Whether investments have increased or been significantly reallocated because of these measures depends on the actual use of the privileges. De Leon (1981) claims that only 11 percent of total annual investments enjoyed the investment incentives. Even if the respective proportions of savings and gross domestic capital formation to gross national product have increased, there was no strong reason to believe that this was the result of the government's incentive measures.

Manasan (1986) updated her earlier study (Gregorio 1979), focusing on the changes in investment laws embodied in the Omnibus Investments Code of 1981 and the BP 391 in 1983. The 1981 changes consolidated the incentive measures on investments and exports previously contained in two separate pieces of legislation and did away with some of the measures such as accelerated depreciation allowances. BP 391 modified several areas of the provisions of the investment incentives in the investment code. Manasan used the internal rate of return and user cost of capital to measure the effects of these two laws for a representative industry.

Official Assessment

There is hardly any attempt on the part of the BOI, which supervised the granting of these incentives, to measure the cost of the effect of the incentives. This agency seems to monitor only the aggregate increase in investments and exports and to attribute whatever gains the country has made to the investment incentives that it provides and whatever insufficient investment performance to exogenous factors such as the peace and order situation prevailing in the country. Hardly any pronouncement is made by the agency regarding the opportunity cost of these investment incentives.

The 1989 Investment Priorities Plan (IPP) contains a few paragraphs assessing the 1988 IPP. The following are the highlights of the official evaluation. There were a total of 288 investment areas in the 1988 plan. Sixty-two percent of these were in the manufacturing sector and 24 percent were in agriculture. The 1,337 investment projects that the BOI supported yielded a total investment of 30.97 billion pesos, "the highest investments so far recorded," according to the 1989 IPP. This amount was 47.5 percent over the 1988 investment target of 20 billion pesos and 160 percent over the target of the 1987 IPP of 11.9 billion pesos. These new investments would provide about 128,052 jobs when the projects were fully operational. This number is 56 percent over the 82,101 jobs created by the 1987 investment projects.

The actual distribution of investments made in 1988 differed significantly from the 1988 IPP projection. Seventy-four percent of the actual investments in 1988 were in manufacturing, and only 10 percent were in agriculture. The remaining share went to public utilities and to projects related to energy or aimed at promoting tourism. In manufacturing the largest investor was the chemical sector, followed by the electrical and electronic product industry and the textile and garment groups. With respect to the number of projects, the largest investor was the garment industry, followed by prawns, textiles, wood products, and electrical and electronic products.

The regional dispersal of enterprises, which was one of the objectives of the 1988 IPP, appeared to be given a boost. In 1988 the share of the National Capital Region in the total investment projects (at least those supported by the BOI) declined to 47.4 percent from 59.3 percent in 1987. The BOI attributes this change to its locational policy.

Static and Dynamic Economic Effects of Fiscal Incentives

In this section, I discuss the results of the analysis of investment incentives using a static general equilibrium model. As mentioned at the beginning of the chapter, the focus of the study is on the duty drawbacks and tax rebates on imported capital equipment. But before discussing this subject, I would like to examine the salient features of the data on fiscal incentives and indirect taxes and how they are used in the model.

Data on Indirect Taxes and Fiscal Incentives

The estimated average indirect and corporate tax rates in the Philippine economy in 1989 are shown in table 18-1. The statutory rates are adjusted to take into account the inefficient administration of these taxes and the duties and taxes forgone as a result of the fiscal incentives. I describe these adjustments briefly.

Let t, τ, s, τ^*, and l be the book rate, the effective tax revenue rate, the implicit subsidy rate due to tax incentives, the duty forgone, and the leakage rate resulting from imperfect enforcement of the tax or import duty (for example, tax evasion) on an ad valorem basis, respectively. Then $t - l = -\tau^* + s + \tau$. If there are no fiscal incentives, then the effective tax rate τ is consistent with the observed tax revenues that the government collects. Otherwise, the rate also includes the tax or duty forgone by the government as a result of the tax.

Because we are modeling fiscal incentives as well, we have to treat the government as receiving the actual and forgone revenue of the tax. Thus the average tax rate that is used in the model is equal to τ, inclusive of the taxes and duties forgone.

Table 18-1. *Average Indirect Tax Rates*
(percent)

CGE code	Sectors	Tariff rates	Excise tax rates	VAT rates
01	Crops	28.351	0.000	0.000
02	Livestock	26.908	0.000	0.000
03	Fishery	23.314	0.000	0.000
04	Natural resources	11.757	0.927	1.102
05	Agricultural processing	31.530	6.178	1.341
06	Textiles	34.526	0.000	1.543
07	Wood, paper, rubber	29.909	0.000	1.414
08	Chemicals	19.630	0.000	1.200
09	Petroleum	13.287	4.118	0.000
10	Machinery	21.249	8.580	1.543
11	Other industries	23.428	3.432	1.543
12	Services	0.000	0.000	1.234

Note: CGE stands for computable general equilibrium model.
Source: Basic data, Philippines (1990).

The duty or tax drawback incentive, s_j, is equal to $-(t_j - l_j)$ if the incentive applies to the entire volume of imported goods. Because only a portion (say, α) of the total imported good j is covered, s_j is equal to $-\alpha(t_j - l_j)$. In the model these tax and duty drawbacks are applied only on the importation of machinery.

I estimated α using the proportion of the data on tax and duty forgone by the government as estimated by the Tariff Commission. In 1989 the amount of import duties forgone amounted to 1.35 billion pesos, and the amount of tax revenue forgone (for both the excise and the value added taxes) was 0.94 billion pesos. The proportions of excise and value added tax rebates are obtained from the actual proportions of the two tax revenues to their total.

To obtain the data on indirect tax rates in table 18-1, I adjusted the book rates for the tax and duty forgone and the inefficiencies in tax enforcement. This was done in the following way:

$$\tau_j = \left[\frac{\sum_j (R_j + D_j)}{\sum_j (t_j + s_j) M_j} \right] t_j$$

where M, R, and D are, respectively, the base of the tax, the actual revenue, and the duties and taxes forgone. This adjustment implies that

Table 18-2. Equity Investments in Projects Approved by the BOI, 1989

Sector	Amount (millions of pesos)	Share (percent)
Agriculture	1,604.94	4.04
Commerce	817.46	2.06
Construction	19.10	0.05
Energy-related projects	82.56	0.21
Export traders	54.27	0.14
Financial institutions	2.50	0.01
Fishery	838.92	2.11
Manufacturing	26,909.77	67.81
Mining	3,140.08	7.91
Public utilities	260.19	0.66
Real estate	1,651.38	4.16
Regional headquarters	19.67	0.05
Service exporters	19.23	0.05
Services	1,369.24	3.45
Tourism-oriented projects	2,895.02	7.30
Total	39,684.33	100.00

Source: National Statistical Coordination Board (1991).

the inefficiency in tax enforcement is equally as bad in all sectors in the economy.[5]

The government then uses the duties and taxes forgone on imported machinery to subsidize investments. The value of fiscal investment incentives, Γ_j, discussed previously, is estimated from the data provided in table 18-2. Table 18-2 is about the equity investments in BOI-approved projects that are eligible to receive the fiscal incentives.

The proportions in table 18-2 are used to allocate the total amount of taxes and duties forgone to the various sectors in the model. These proportions are further adjusted to take into account the importance of capital equipment to the sector. I assumed in this study that because of their relatively lower capital intensity the primary agricultural sectors (sectors 1, 2, and 3) do not receive any of the incentives in the form of tax and duty drawbacks on imported capital equipment. If this assumption is an incorrect statement about the Philippine economy, the error that it causes is likely to be small.

Table 18-3 is used to allocate the aggregate investments reported in the country's national income accounts to the various sectors of the model. In table 18-4 I show the way fiscal incentives are allocated to the various sectors of the model, using the information described in the preceding two tables.

Table 18-3.   Capital Investments of Newly Registered Domestic Stock Corporation and Partnerships by Sector, 1989

Sector	Amount (millions of pesos)	Share (percent)
Agriculture, fishery, and forestry	258.30	3.19
Construction	276.16	3.41
Electricity, gas, water	0.63	0.01
Financial sector	3,871.85	47.81
Manufacturing	1,902.30	23.49
Mining and quarrying	211.02	2.61
Services	288.27	3.56
Trade	1,015.58	12.54
Transport	274.81	3.39
Total	8,098.91	100.00

Source: Data from Securities and Exchange Commission.

Policy Experiments

Three counterfactual simulations were conducted in this study. One simulation involves withdrawing the duty drawback and tax rebates applied on imported machinery while continuing the subsidies on investments. In the second policy experiment the tax and duty drawback scheme on imported machinery is retained, but the subsidies are provided on an equal rate basis. In doing this experiment, the computation of an endogenous uniform subsidy rate on investments assumed a constant level of real government spending. The third simulation withdraws the entire package of tax and duty rebates on imported capital equipment as well as discontinues the granting of investment subsidies.

These simulations are chosen to address the two policy issues mentioned earlier—the opportunity cost of fiscal incentives and the effect of a discriminatory scheme of allocating such incentives.

The User Cost of Capital

The changes in the user cost of capital are shown by sector in table 18-5. The components of this cost include the marginal cost of producing the capital good and the sector-specific investment subsidy rate and the corporate income tax rate.

The withdrawal of the duty drawback package of incentives (case A) increases the user cost of capital. This is because the policy change increases the cost of producing capital goods in the economy. With the

Table 18-4. *Computation of Incentive Rates for the Twelve Sectors of the Model*

Sector	Sectoral shares (percent)		Amount (billions of pesos)		
	Invest-ment	Incen-tives	Invest-ment	Incen-tives	Incentive rate
1 Crops	1.67	..	1.67	..	..
2 Livestock and poultry	0.81	..	0.82	..	..
3 Fishery	0.71	..	0.71	..	..
4 Resource industries	2.61	8.12	2.62	0.22	8.39
5 Agricultural processing	11.35	32.77	11.43	0.88	7.70
6 Textile, apparel, footwear, leather	3.17	9.14	3.19	0.24	7.53
7 Wood, paper, rubber	2.30	6.65	2.32	0.18	7.77
8 Chemicals	1.39	4.02	1.40	0.11	7.85
9 Petroleum refineries	1.47	4.23	1.48	0.11	7.45
10 Machinery	1.58	10.73	1.59	0.29	18.19
11 Other industries	2.23	6.43	2.24	0.17	7.58
12 Services	70.72	17.91	71.19	0.47	0.66
Total	100.00	100.00	100.67	2.67	n.a.

n.a. Not applicable.
.. Negligible.
Source: Tables 18-2 and 18-3 and simulation runs using this study's twelve-sector CGE model of the Philippines.

duty drawback scheme removed, the cost of producing imported machinery rises and with that, the cost of producing capital goods. Except for services, all the sectors display an almost uniform rate of increase in the cost of capital goods. The cost of capital for the majority of the sectors increases by close to 0.77 percent, and that for services rises by about 1 percent.

Making the investment subsidy rate uniform (case B) also increases the user cost of capital, except for the services sector. The primary agricultural sectors experience no change in their respective user costs of capital. It is also interesting to note that compared with case A, the percentage increases of user costs of capital in case B are substantially larger. The reason for this is that the revenue-neutral uniform incentive rate for investments is significantly lower than the existing investment incentives rates in the former case. Thus these effects in case B also show those of reducing the average investment incentive rate. These changes are relatively more evident in the case of the machinery and transport equipment sector, in which the user cost of capital rises by 18.44 percent. This result

Table 18-5. *Percentage Change in User Cost of Capital, by Sector*

Sector		Case A	Case B	Case C
1	Crops	0.7692	0.0001	0.7742
2	Livestock and poultry	0.7692	0.0001	0.7742
3	Fishery	0.7692	0.0001	0.7742
4	Resource industries	0.7691	5.7711	6.5901
5	Agricultural processing	0.7691	4.9846	5.7975
6	Textile, apparel, footwear, leather	0.7691	4.7926	5.6040
7	Wood, paper, and rubber	0.7691	5.0603	5.8737
8	Chemicals	0.7691	5.1578	5.9720
9	Petroleum refineries	0.7691	4.7000	5.5107
10	Machinery	0.7691	18.4413	7.0406
11	Other industries	0.7690	4.8444	5.6562
12	Services	1.0060	−2.4560	−1.4875

Note: In case A, duty drawbacks and tax credits are withdrawn. In case B, the discriminatory manner of providing investment incentives is replaced with a uniform subsidy rate on investment purchases. In case C, both case A and B conditions apply.

Source: Simulation runs using this study's twelve-sector CGE model of the Philippines.

is consistent with the drastic reduction in the investment incentives rate from 18.19 percent to the uniform 3.1 percent.

It is interesting to note that the decline in the user cost of capital for services is significant and results from the increase in its investment incentives rate from 0.6 percent to the uniform rate of 3.1 percent. In the other sectors, however, the average rate fell from 8.12 percent. These changes imply that the user cost of capital has to fall for services and rise for the other covered sectors.

Removing both the duty and tax rebates on imported machinery and making the investment subsidies uniform (case C) also increase the user cost of capital except for services. This percentage increase is higher than that in case A because investment subsidies fell as a result of a lower uniform investment incentives rate. These increases are also higher than those in case B (except for machinery) because the cost of imported machinery increases with the removal of the duty drawback, which causes the cost of producing the capital goods to rise.

Again, it is interesting to note that the increase in the cost of capital in the machinery and transport equipment sector is lower compared with that in case B (18.441 percent versus 7.041 percent), apparently because of the removal of the duty drawback scheme, which, ironically, would tend to increase the cost of producing capital goods.

The decline in the services sector's user cost of capital also fell, but by a lower percentage than in case B.

Changes in Investments

In table 18-6, I show the effects of these experiments on the volume of investments. Because of a higher cost of capital as reported in table 18-5, private investments decline by roughly 557 million pesos when the duty drawback scheme is withdrawn (case A). The majority of the downward adjustment in private investments occurs in the services sector, which experienced the highest increase in cost of capital. This sector consists of construction, public utilities, trade, and financial and personal services, and accordingly its output is fairly large. Of the 100.67 billion pesos in investments in 1989, the sector accounted for about 70 billion pesos in investments.

Agricultural processing is a far second in regard to reduction in investments. Consisting mostly of food, beverages, and tobacco, this sector is at least a third of the country's entire manufacturing sector. About 70.18 million pesos in investments are expected to disappear if the fiscal incentives are withdrawn. This figure is an insignificant percentage of the 11.43 billion pesos of investments made in this sector in 1989.

Natural resources, textiles, wood, and other industries also experience lower investments in the range of 14 million to about 20 million pesos.

Table 18-6. Changes in Investments, by Sector
(millions of pesos)

Sector		Case A	Case B	Case C
1	Crops	–11.12	–10.86	–10.88
2	Livestock and poultry	–5.44	–5.31	–5.31
3	Fishery	–4.75	–4.64	–4.64
4	Resource industries	–15.97	122.81	122.80
5	Agricultural processing	–70.18	456.18	456.11
6	Textile, apparel, footwear, leather	–19.59	121.81	121.79
7	Wood, paper, and rubber	–14.20	94.08	94.06
8	Chemicals	–8.58	58.06	58.06
9	Petroleum refineries	–9.08	55.24	55.22
10	Machinery	–8.67	231.62	72.48
11	Other industries	–13.78	86.80	86.77
12	Services	–375.11	–1,750.55	–1,751.06
13	Government investments	1,531.72	1,193.60	1,508.25
	Total	975.22	648.85	803.66

Note: In case A, duty drawbacks and tax credits are withdrawn. In case B, the discriminatory manner of providing investment incentives is replaced with a uniform subsidy rate on investment purchases. In case C, both case A and B conditions apply.

Source: Simulation runs using this study's twelve-sector CGE model of the Philippines.

Investments in the remaining sectors of the economy also decline but at a lower rate of, at most, 11 million pesos.

These numbers on changes in investments appear to be consistent with what is observed in existing studies that the fiscal incentives hardly change the investment behavior of businesses in the country (for example, see Gregorio 1979). It should be mentioned here that the package of investment incentives offered by the government consists also of depreciation and investment allowances, tax holidays, and related measures, and these are not considered in this study. This is a plausible reason why the model is turning out relatively small changes in investments when the tax and duty drawbacks are withdrawn.

In case B, investments generally increase, with the exception of the primary sectors and services, despite the larger rise in the user cost of capital. This is clearly evident with the investments in the machinery and transport equipment sector. This result may be explained by the policy of applying a uniform investment incentives rate to the nonagricultural sectors of the economy.

In the case of services, investments went down by about 1.8 billion pesos, despite the decrease in the user cost of capital, as a result of a reallocation of investment resources to other sectors in the economy. The results in case C are similar to those in case B.

The decline in losses from private investments is more than offset by an increase in government investments, which rises as a result of higher income from the previously forgone duties on imported machinery (as in cases A and C) and the decline in the average investment incentives rate to the uniform rate of 3.1 percent (cases B and C).

One-Period Welfare Effects

The data in table 18-7 show the one-period welfare implications of the policy experiments. In the benchmark case, the real income of the government amounts to 110.798 billion pesos, whereas that of the private sector is 780.424 billion pesos. The total gross domestic product of the economy is 891.222 billion pesos. In case A, the government's real income rises by about 2.146 percent because of the elimination of the tax rebate and duty drawback incentives applied on imported machinery. That of the private sector falls—but by an insignificant 0.016 percent. The economy is therefore made better off with the elimination of the duty drawback scheme for investments.

The policy experiment conducted in case B involves retaining the tax rebate and duty drawback incentives but making the investment subsidy rate uniform in all the sectors in the model, subject to holding the real government spending constant. Thus the real income of the government in table 18-7 for case B is the same as in the benchmark case. The real income of the private sector has not changed in this experiment.

Table 18-7. One-Period Welfare Effects of Investment Incentives

Scenario	Government	Private	Total
Real income (billions of pesos)			
Base case	110.798	780.424	891.222
Case A	113.176	780.299	893.475
Case B	110.798	780.423	891.222
Case C	113.012	780.256	893.269
Change (percent)			
Case A	2.146	−0.016	0.253
Case B	−0.000	0.000	−0.000
Case C	1.998	−0.021	0.230

Note: In case A, duty drawbacks and tax credits are withdrawn. In case B, the discriminatory manner of providing investment incentives is replaced with a uniform subsidy rate on investment purchases. In case C, both case A and B conditions apply.

Source: Simulation runs using this study's twelve-sector CGE model of the Philippines.

In case C, the real income of the government increases by close to 2 percent, but that of the private sector falls, again by an insignificant amount (0.02 percent), suggesting an increase in the overall real income by about 0.23 percent.

On the basis of these numbers, it appears that the current package of investment incentives is Pareto-inferior to the alternative policy environments conducted in this study. In case B, investments rise without any decline in government incomes. In cases A and C, the economy comes out even better: investments rise with the total real income, albeit by less than 1 percent.

Dynamic Effects

The numbers, however, report only the static welfare effects of investment incentives. A correct evaluation of the welfare implications of the policy experiment would have to involve computing the present value of the stream of real incomes accruing to the government and the private sectors of the economy that are induced by the policy environment and comparing this with the benchmark aggregate income. Thus we do not have any basis on which to decide whether the economy is made better or worse off by the fiscal incentive measures analyzed in this chapter.

A multiperiod analysis was done and its results are reported in table 18-8 and figures 18-3 and 18-4. The numbers reported in the table suggest that the economy is worse off if the package of investment incentives is withdrawn. I should make clear that this package includes the granting of tax rebates and duty drawbacks to prospective investors. The

Table 18-8. Present Values of Real Consumption, Investment, and Income

	Base case	Case A	Case B	Case C
Consumption				
Value (millions of pesos)	61,638.63	60,997.11	61,637.43	61,439.22
Change (percent)		−1.041	−0.002	−0.324
Investment				
Value (millions of pesos)	8,337.92	8,233.58	8,337.99	8,310.12
Change (percent)		−1.251	0.001	−0.333
Income				
Value (millions of pesos)	69,976.56	69,230.68	69,975.41	69,749.34
Change (percent)		−1.066	−0.002	−0.325

Note: In case A, duty drawbacks and tax credits are withdrawn. In case B, the discriminatory manner of providing investment incentives is replaced with a uniform subsidy rate on investment purchases. In case C, both case A and B conditions apply.

Source: Simulation runs using this study's twelve-sector CGE model of the Philippines.

present value of real income in the economy goes down by about 1.000 percent in case A, 0.002 percent in case B, and 0.324 percent in case C.

These results can be explained by the essence of the duty drawback scheme. This undermines the distortive effect of taxing imported machinery to protect the local producers of their substitutes. In a price-taking economy such as the Philippines, this protection entails a deadweight loss. To the extent that there are many investors who avail themselves of these duty drawbacks on imported machinery, the distortive effect of the protection is partly offset, which then confers some benefits to the economy. Thus withdrawing the package clearly removes those benefits, although it increases the real income of the government sector, as table 18-8 confirms.

These numbers, however, are not clearly supportive of the current investment incentives package; a simple elimination or reduction in the tariff rate on imported machinery can surpass the beneficial effects of a duty drawback because those benefits can be made available to all users of imported machinery. It is recognized, nonetheless, that reducing the tariff may reduce the tax income of the government sector. But these losses can be more than offset by the efficiency gains in the private sector of the economy.

It is not at all clear that investments actually increased because of these incentives. The numbers in table 18-8 are indicative of the withdrawal of the package of incentives or its modifications. Thus, in case A, getting rid of the duty drawback scheme appears to reduce investments by about 1.25 percent. But this effect can clearly be explained by the fact that the

Figure 18-3. Effects of Investment Incentives on Real Investments

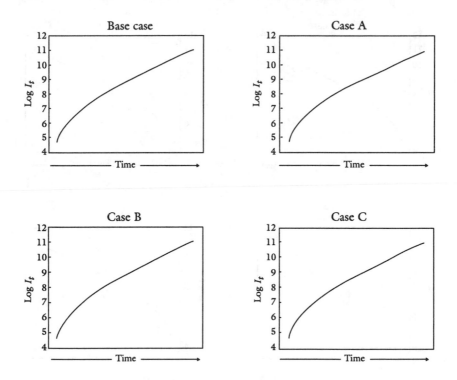

action actually increases the price of machinery in the country, which in turn causes a rise in the price of investment goods. Reducing the tariff rates on imported machinery can augment investments more than the duty drawback scheme.

In case C, the decline in investments is smaller, resulting from the withdrawal of the duty drawback scheme plus making uniform the investment subsidy rate. As explained in table 18-6, the uniform incentive rate of 3.1 percent is actually lower than the average incentive rate of about 8.0 percent in the benchmark policy regime, thereby increasing the user cost of capital. There is no change in investments in case B.

Conclusion

In this chapter, I have developed a general equilibrium analytical framework for analyzing some investment incentives currently used by the Philippine government. I have applied it to analyze the static and multiperiod economic effects of such incentives on the user cost of capital, investments, and economic welfare. The current package of incentive

Figure 18-4. Effects of Investment Incentives on Real Consumption

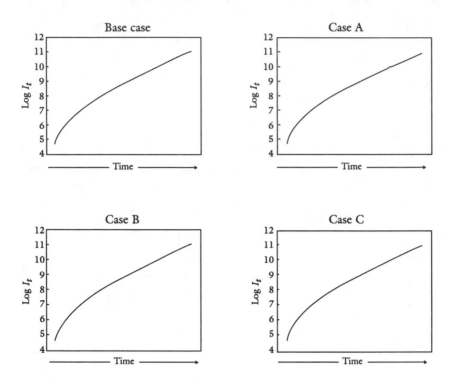

measures consists of tax rebates and duty drawbacks on imported machinery, apportioned to the various producers of the economy on a priority-nonpriority rationing scheme. The package may be described as inducing two sets of policy distortion.

First, it makes imported machinery cheaper than other imported products in the economy. And second, the package discriminates among the various industries or firms in allocating such subsidies. I examine both issues in a static framework.

The withdrawal of the duty drawback package of incentives (case A) increases the user cost of capital because by withdrawing the tax rebate and duty drawback incentives on imported machinery, an important input in producing capital goods, the government increases the cost of producing capital goods in the economy. If the investment subsidy rate is made uniform and the duty drawback scheme is retained (case B), the user cost of capital also rises, and at a higher rate than it does if the duty and tax rebate package of incentives is removed. These effects also hold in case C when both changes A and B are applied. Thus one can conclude that the current package of incentives examined in this study has the effect of lowering the user cost of capital.

Investments generally decline as a result of these changes in the user cost of capital. In both cases A and C, (private) investments fall substantially because of the withdrawal of the tax and duty drawbacks on imported machinery, although these losses are more than offset by the increase in government investments resulting from higher incomes.

In all three policy experiments (A, B, and C), the economy is better off in a static sense. But caution is suggested in using these results because they are one-period welfare effects. A better evaluation of the welfare implications of the policy experiment would involve computing the present value of the stream of real incomes accruing to the government and private sectors of the economy that are induced by the policy environment and comparing this figure with the benchmark aggregate income.

This multiperiod analysis was done, and the present values of total income under the various policy regimes seem to suggest that the Philippines is better off with the present package of investment incentives. The explanation for this is that the duty drawback scheme included in the package of investment incentives actually undermines the distortive effect of the protection on machinery and transport equipment. These numbers in fact suggest that a better scheme of promoting investments may include the elimination of or reduction in the tariff imposed on imported machinery and transport equipment. This point could have been made more clearly if one additional simulation was done in which the tariff rate on imported machinery was withdrawn and the package of investment subsidies eliminated or made moderately low and uniform.

The effects, however, are small in relation to the benchmark figures and suggest that the fiscal incentives hardly matter at all. Gregorio (1979) has argued that indeed this is so. On this issue, one should distinguish between the levels of distortion from the incentive structure. The size of the changes is affected by the level of investment subsidy. This number is 2.67 billion pesos, barely 1 percent of the Philippine's gross domestic product. If we calibrated the model to 1988, we would have been working with over 6 billion pesos of taxes and duties forgone as a result of investment incentives, and clearly the equivalent income variation would have increased significantly.

It is the incentive structure induced by the fiscal incentive measure that is worrisome. This structure tends to accord more investment resources to a portion of the economy that is deemed important in the government's industrialization strategy. Our figures on investments, although small, indicate that the fiscal incentives have a significant effect on investment allocation.

Notes

The author is grateful to Mary Ann Pabiloa and Prudence Orani for research assistance and to Rayna Roxas for formatting the chapter.

1. A related concept is that of the effective tax rate, which is the effective wedge "between the rate of return on investment and the rate of return on the savings used to finance the investment" (King and Fullerton 1984). Auerbach (chapter 2, this volume) decomposes this rate as consisting of, first, the wedge between the "required rate of return, r, and the corporation's return before tax" and, second, the wedge between r and the return to the firm after all taxes.

2. This is what Rutherford (1988) calls "the curse of dimensionality."

3. "Batas Pambansa" is a Filipino term that is synonymous to "(Philippine) Republic Act." The former refers to a Philippine law promulgated by the country's unicameral legislature under a parliamentary form of government during the Martial Law regime (early 1970s to early 1980s), and the latter refers to a Philippine law passed by both houses of the country's bicameral legislature under a democratic form of government before and after Martial Law rule.

4. This point is not necessarily unique to the Philippines. See Shah and Toye 1978.

5. The ideal approach would have been to get sector-specific leakage rates, but this kind of information is not available.

References

Auerbach, Alan. 1983. "Corporate Taxation in the United States." Brookings Paper on Economic Activity 2. Brookings Institution, Washington, D.C.

Ballard, Charles, Don Fullerton, John Shoven, and John Whalley. 1985. *A General Equilibrium Model for Tax Policy Evaluation*. Chicago, Ill.: University of Chicago Press.

Bautista, Carlos C. 1987. "Macroeconomic Adjustment: An Applied Non-Walrasian General Equilibrium Approach." Ph.D. diss., University of the Philippines, School of Economics, Quezon City.

Clarete, Ramon L. 1991. "Tax Burden and Institutional Distortions in a Developing Country: A General Equilibrium Analysis of Selected Philippine Taxes." In Javad Khalilzadeh-Shirazi and Anwar Shah, eds., *Tax Policy in Developing Countries*. Washington, D.C.: World Bank.

Clarete, Ramon L., and James Roumasset. 1987. "A Shoven-Whalley Model of a Small Economy: An Illustration with Philippine Tariffs." *Journal of Public Economics* 32 (2): 247–61.

de Leon, Terresita. 1981. "The Effectivity of the Investment Incentives Laws in Influencing the Flow of Investments." Undergraduate thesis, University of the Philippines, School of Economics, Quezon City.

Gaspay, Manuel S., and Carl H. Gotsch. 1992. "Sector Policies and Economic Performance in the ASEAN Region," A Final Report to the Agricultural Policy Assistance Program II, USAID. Stanford University, Food Research Institute, Palo Alto, Calif.

Go, Delfin. 1988. "Growth and Adjustment in the Philippines—A Dynamic General Equilibrium Analysis." Ph.D. diss. Harvard University, John F. Kennedy School of Government, Cambridge, Mass.

Gregorio, Rosario. 1979. "An Economic Analysis of the Effects of Philippine Fiscal Incentives for Industrial Promotion." Ph.D. diss., University of the Philippines, School of Economics, Quezon City.

Habito, Cielito F. 1984. "Equity and Efficiency Trade-offs in Philippine Tax Policy Analysis: A General Equilibrium Approach." Ph.D. diss., Harvard University, John F. Kennedy School of Government, Cambridge, Mass.

Hansen, Terje, and Tjalling C. Koopmans. 1972. "On the Definition and Computation of a Capital Stock Invariant under Optimization." *Journal of Economic Theory* 8 (6): 487–523.

Hooley, R. W., and G. P. Sicat. 1967. "Investment Demand in Philippine Manufacturing." Discussion Paper 67-2. University of the Philippines, School of Economics, Quezon City.

Jorgenson, D. W. 1963. "Capital Theory and Investment Behavior." *American Economic Review* 53 (May): 247–59.

King, Mervyn A., and Don Fullerton, eds. 1984. *The Taxation of Income from Capital: A Comparative Study of the United States, the United Kingdom, Sweden, and West Germany.* Chicago, Ill.: University of Chicago Press.

Manasan, Rosario G. 1986. "Impact of BOI Incentives on Rate of Return, Factor Prices, and Relative Factor Use: A Comparative Analysis of Incentives under PD 1789 and BP 391." Staff Paper Series 86-01. Philippine Institute for Development Studies, Makati.

———. 1988. "A Review of Investment Incentives in ASEAN Countries." Working Paper Series 88-27. Philippine Institute for Development Studies, Makati.

National Statistical Coordination Board. 1991. *Philippines Statistical Yearbook 1990.* Makati, Philippines.

Philippines, Bureau of Internal Revenue. 1990. *1989 Annual Report of Tax Collections.* Quezon City.

Rutherford, Thomas. 1988. "General Equilibrium Modeling with MPS/GE." University of Western Ontario, London, Ontario.

———. 1990. "MPS/GE: A Mathematical Program for Solving General Equilibrium Models."

Shah, S. M. S., and J. F. J. Toye. 1978. "Fiscal Incentives for Firms in Some Developing Countries: Survey and Critique." In J. F. J. Toye, ed., *Taxation and Economic Development.* London: Billing and Sons.

Sicat, Geraldo. 1967. "An Analysis of the Investment Incentives Act of 1967." Discussion Paper 67-10. University of the Philippines, Institute of Economic Development and Research, School of Economics, Quezon City.

———. 1968. "Economic Incentives and Foreign Investments." Discussion Paper 68-15. University of the Philippines, Institute of Economic Development and Research, School of Economics, Quezon City.

 NDEX

Ad hoc model, 260

Adjustment costs: market power econometric model and marginal, 548, 567–69; in measuring METRs, 66–67, 149–50, 162 nn6–9; in production structure models, 505, 512, 514–15, 623; for R&D, 232–33, 274; in tax holiday models, 192 n8. *See also* Production structure models

Adjustment speeds, 233, 623

Adverse selection models, 48–49, 50

Africa, 437, 439, 445, 452

Aleem, Irfan, 213–14, 226 n12

Alpalhoa, R., 339 n6

Amazon Development Authority (SUDAM), 322, 325, 327, 333

Amazon Investment Fund (FINAM), 322, 325

Anderson, Krister, 144

Aoki, Reiko, 250

Appropriability. *See* Spillovers

Aramaki, Kenji, 144

Arbitrage assumptions, 70–72

Armington-aggregated good, 674–75

Asia-Pacific region. *See* Association of Southeast Asian Nations

Association of Southeast Asian Nations (ASEAN): effectiveness of tax incentives in, 19; and Philippine incentives, 681, 684; tax competition and use of incentives by, 437, 438–39, 445–51, 452

Asymmetric information. *See* Information asymmetries

Auerbach, Alan, 7–8, 9, 66, 73, 78, 130 n34, 138, 149, 150, 153, 201, 202, 226 n6, 700 n1

Average effective tax rate, 59, 97, 310; in models for foreign investment, 483, 486, 487, 491. *See also* Marginal effective tax rate

Baffes, John, 24, 97, 99

Baily, Martin, 238

Banco de Mexico, 489

Bangladesh, 35, 167–71, 185–88

Bankruptcy, 204–5. *See also* Debt

Banks, and information asymmetries, 218, 219

Barro, R. J., 45